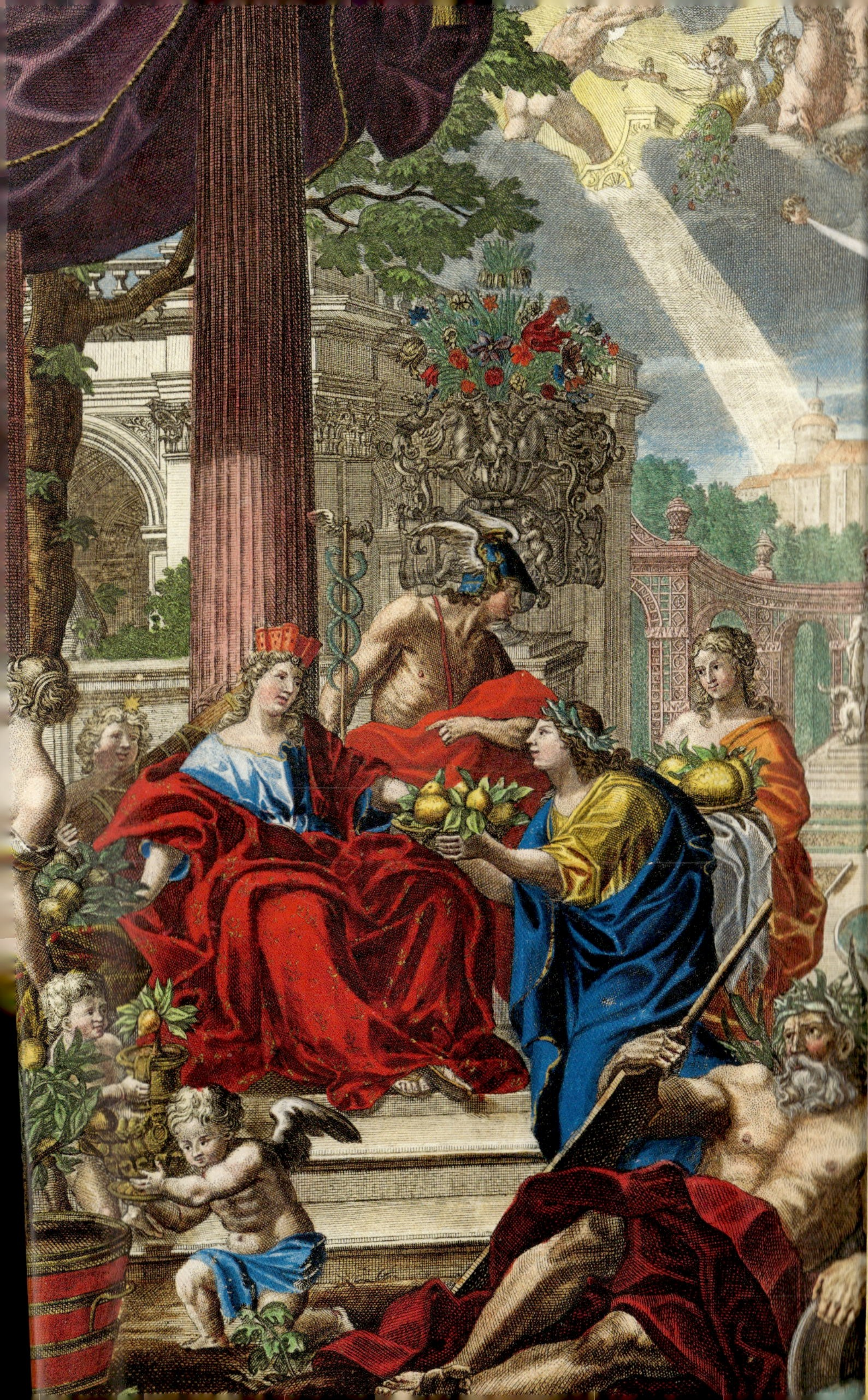

I0823240

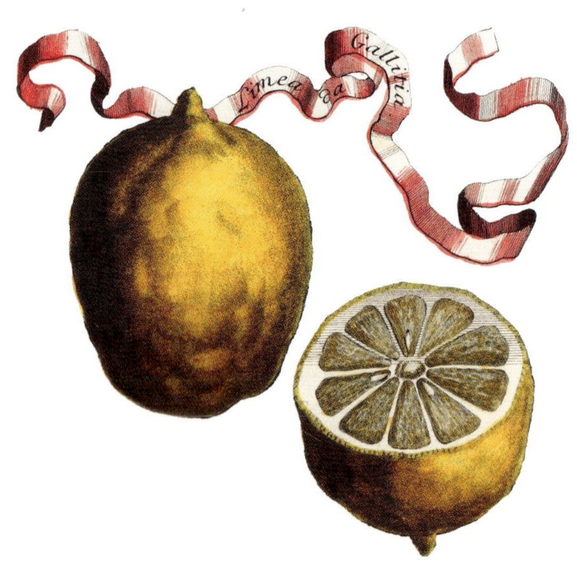
Limea da Gallitia

Johann Christoph Volkamer

The Book of CITRUS FRUITS

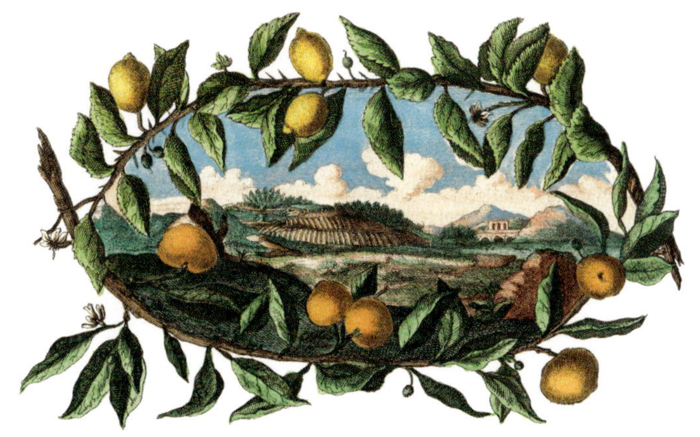

The Complete Plates 1708—1714

The copies used for printing belong to the
STADTARCHIV FÜRTH & UNIVERSITÄTSBIBLIOTHEK ERLANGEN-NÜRNBERG

TASCHEN

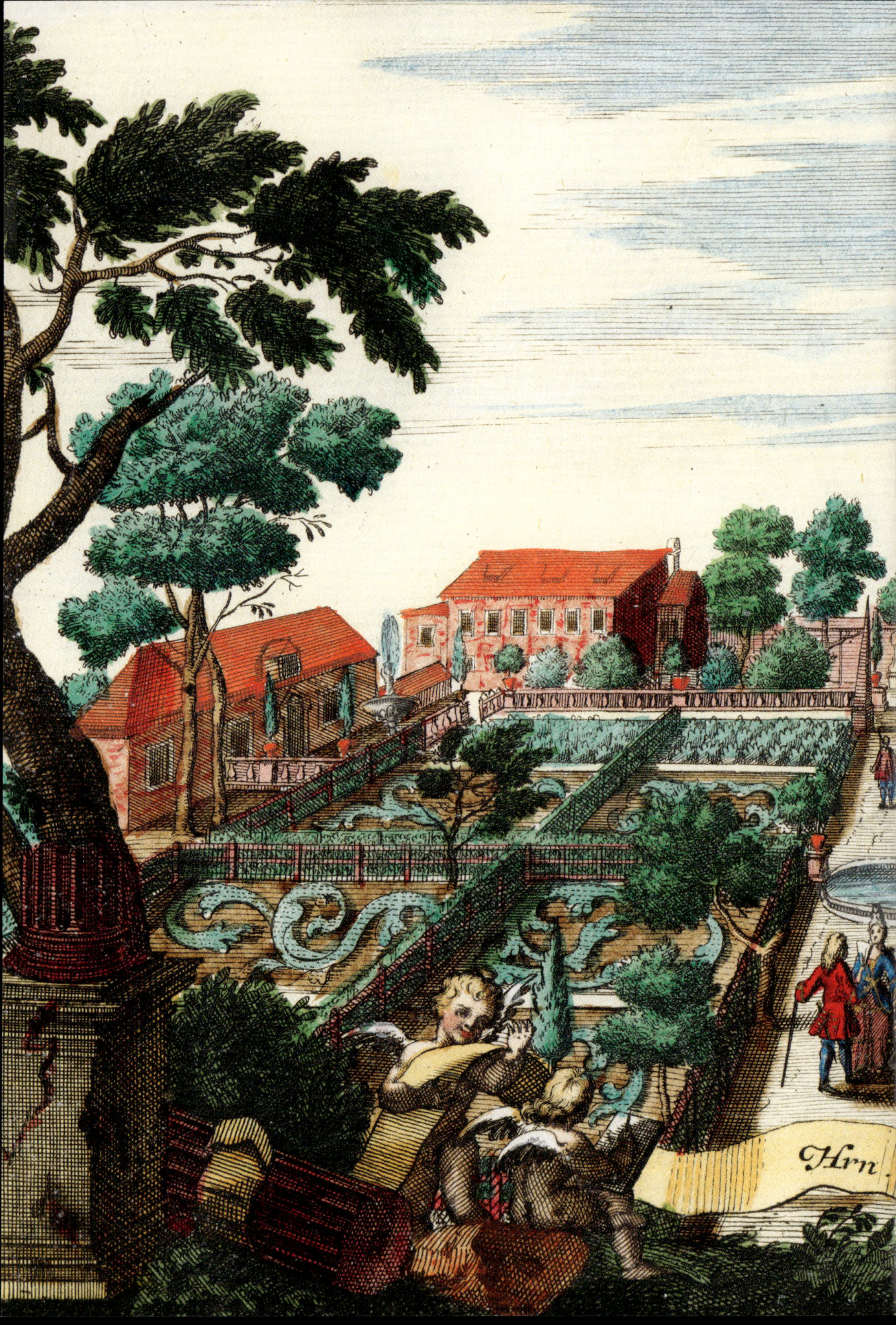
Hrn

IRIS LAUTERBACH

Nürnbergische
HESPERIDES,

Oder

Gründliche Beschreibung

Der Edlen

Citronat/ Citronen/

und

Pomerantzen-Früchte/

Wie solche / in selbiger und benachbarten Gegend/
recht mögen eingesetzt/gewartet/erhalten und fortgebracht werden/
Samt einer ausführlichen Erzehlung der meisten Sorten/welche theils zu Nürnberg würcklich gewachsen/theils von verschiedenen fremden Orten dahin gebracht worden/
Auf das accurateste in Kupffer gestochen/
in
Vier Theile
eingetheilet
und mit nützlichen Anmerckungen erkläret.

Beneben der

FLORA,

Oder
Curiosen Vorstellung

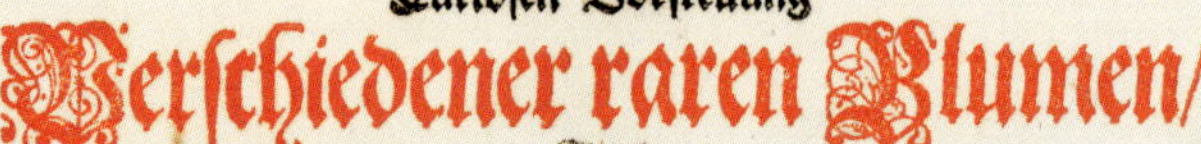

Samt
Einer Zugabe etlicher anderer Gewächse / und ausführlichem Bericht/
wie eine richtig-zutreffende Sonnen-Uhr im Garten-Feld von Bux anzulegen/
und die Gärten nach der Perspectiv leichtlich aufzureissen/
Wie auch einem Bericht von denen in des Authoris Garten stehenden
COLUMNIS MILLIARIBUS,
Mit Röm. Käyserl. Maj. allergnädigst-verliehenem PRIVILEGIO,
Herausgegeben
von

J. C. V.

Nürnberg/
Zu finden bey Johann Andreä Endters seel. Sohn und Erben.
M DCC VIII.

"Heavenly Fruits" Johann Christoph Volkamer's *Hesperides*

IRIS LAUTERBACH

"The orange or pomerance tree is undisputedly the most beautiful of all flowering trees. Its straight trunk, its uniform and even wood, its large and glossy leaves, its beautiful flowers, its exquisite fruits, its well-shaped crown and very lovely greenness are throughout so constituted that one must admire them. Several types of orange trees are distinguished, such as lemons, limes, bergamot oranges, pomaceous fruits, Chinese pomeroys etc., but the differences between them are negligible, merely that some of them are trees having trunks and others are dwarfs or shrubs, or because the fruits of some are sweet and those of others rather bitter; all of them retain their beautiful foliage in all seasons."

The French horticultural theorist Antoine-Joseph Dezallier d'Argenville (1680–1765) captured in these words the fascination citrus trees exerted in the Baroque era as well as the significance of orangery cultivation in classic French horticulture (*La théorie et la pratique du jardinage*; translation from the French edition of 1713, p. 214). In 1713 he added two chapters on citrus culture to the second edition of his influential book on the theory and practice of horticulture, which had first been published in Paris in 1709.

Citrus trees are a feast for the eye with their slender form, magnificent evergreen foliage and fruits in glowing colours; the fruits and candied peel are an aromatic treat for the palate, whilst the scent of the volatile oils obtained from the fruits and flowers is intoxicating. As many horticultural writers of the 17th and 18th centuries noted, the evergreen trees that bloom and fruit at the same time in orangeries evoke the idea of a timeless paradise of blissful happiness: "For, when in winter everything has died down from frost and

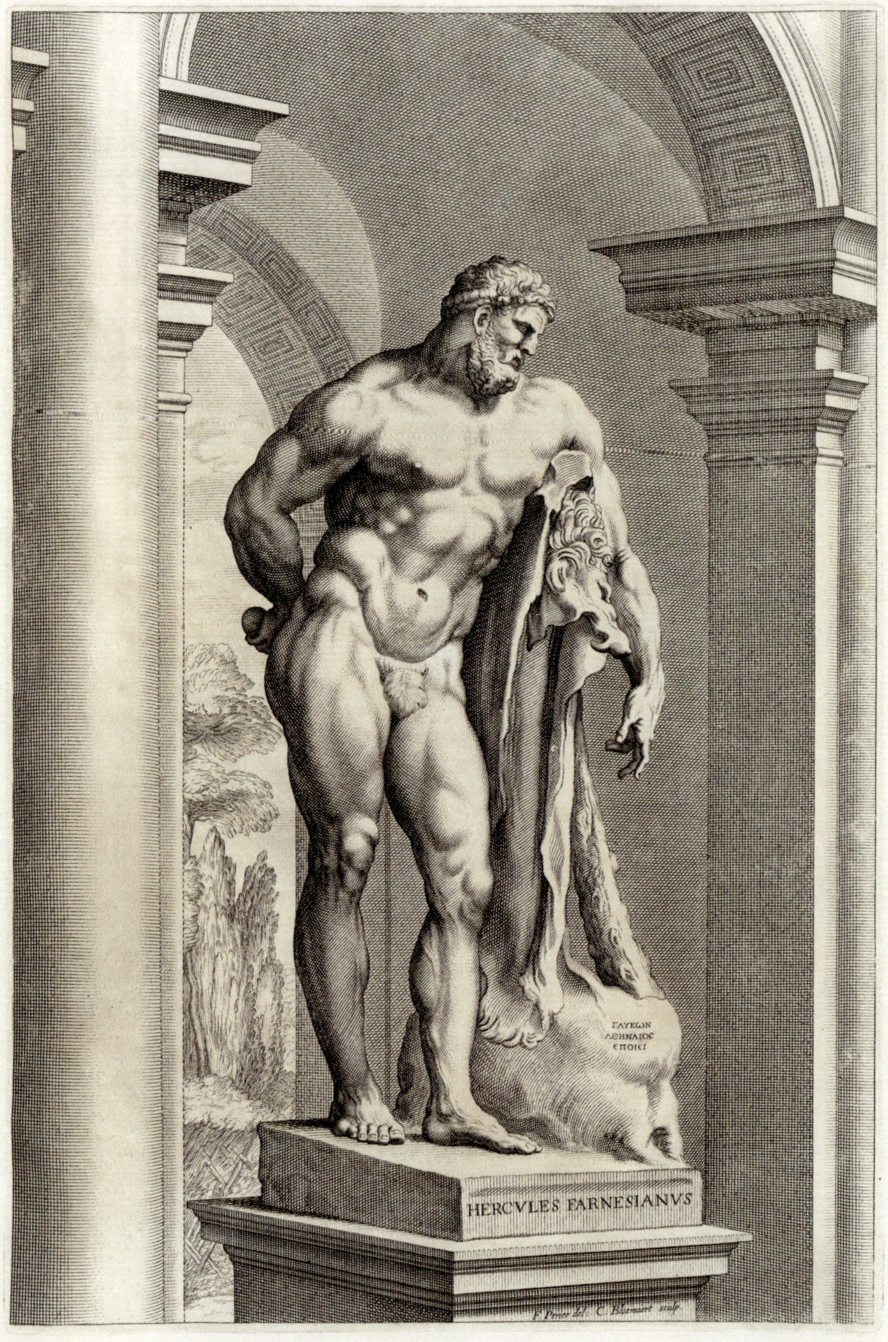
ΓΛΥΚΩΝ
ΑΘΗΝΑΙΟΣ
ΕΠΟΙΕΙ
HERCVLES FARNESIANVS
F. Perier del. C. Bloemaert sculp.

great cold, indeed everything is covered with deep snow and the cruel north wind rages so that nothing else can be, as if it would storm over all of Nature and cast it down, one sees in these glorious Paradise gardens with the utmost amazement how the loveliest and rarest of little trees of several types stay green and bloom; one has white, lovely fragrant flowers, another yellow, a third red, a fourth lavender and the like; one has ripe, another unripe fruits, all suffused with the most splendid, aromatic scent, and that must indeed refresh a man as in an eternal Spring." (Hesse 1706, p. 35f.) The Golden Apples of the Hesperides, called *poma aurantia* in Latin and from which the old German word *'Pomeranze'* for 'bitter orange' derives, are in fact citrus fruits. The ancient myth emphasises how precious the fruits are, which make even earthly gardens resemble Paradise. In this mythical garden of the Greek gods there stood a fabulous tree laden with golden fruits, guarded by the dragon Ladon and tended by three Nymphs – Aegle, Arethusa and Hesperia – the daughters of Atlas and Night. The name Hesperides derives from Hesperos, the Greek name for the Evening Star or Venus. The virtuous hero Hercules overcame the dragon and thus won the precious fruits, which were presented to him by the Hesperides. It is clear already in this myth how highly prized the genus *Citrus* was, both the trees and their fruits, as too the special care needed for its cultivation, the growing and the tending.

The genus *Citrus*, which belongs to the Rutaceae, the rue family, originated in various parts of Asia and comprises some of the earliest plants to have been cultivated. In southern China, the sweet orange (*Citrus sinensis* L.) is referred to over 4,000 years ago. Genoese and Portuguese merchants introduced advanced cultivars of it into Italy in the 15th or early 16th century. The bitter orange (*Citrus aurantium* L.), the lemon (*Citrus limon* L.) and the lime (*Citrus aurantiifolia* (Christm.) Swingle) arrived in the Middle and Near East from eastern Asia and from there were likely introduced into Italy by the Crusaders. The citron (*Citrus medica* L., *Citrus limonimedica* L.), on the other hand, must have been native to Italy by the first century BC at the latest. Known already in Arabic and Moorish settlements by the Middle Ages, bitter oranges and lemons began to be cultivated in Tuscany in the 14th century. Thousands of years of cultivating *Citrus* had given rise to a large number of varieties and forms.

Page 6
Title-page / Titelseite / Page de titre
From: *Nürnbergische Hesperides*, 1708, vol. I

Cornelis Bloemaert, after François Perrier, **The Farnese Hercules / Herkules Farnese / Hercule Farnèse**
Engraving. From: Giovanni Battista Ferrari, *Hesperides, sive de malorum aureorum cultura et usu*, Rome, 1646, p. 29
Göttingen, Niedersächsische Staats- und Universitätsbibliothek

Citrus plants at court: heraldic motif and collectors' item

It was Hercules, alongside Apollo, who above all became established in the iconography of European courts in the Renaissance and the Baroque era as a brave and virtuous hero, and thereby a figure with whom nobles might seek to identify. Copies of the celebrated monumental sculpture of Hercules from the Farnese collection, which depict him with the three apples of the Hesperides in his hand (p. 8), adorn numerous Baroque gardens, evoking associations with the mythical garden of the gods tended by the Hesperides. Over the course of the 16th and 17th centuries, cultivating *Citrus* came to be viewed as a welcome challenge. The Medici, originally merchants who had risen to the status of grand dukes as the reigning house of the Grand Duchy of Tuscany, associated the old Latin name for the citron, *malus medica* ('medicinal apple'), with their armorial bearings. They viewed citrus fruits as heraldic motifs that resembled the orange-coloured spheres on the Medici coat of arms. Still today, the Boboli Gardens in Florence and the Villa Medici gardens in Castello boast two of the oldest, largest and most diverse *Citrus* collections to be found in Europe. Since the 16th century, citrus trees featured in gardens as treasures from the vegetable kingdom; their fruits – reproduced with great skill in wax, pottery and later porcelain or depicted in paintings (p. 11) – became prized collectors' items in cabinets of curiosities and exhibits in the collections amassed by princes (p. 57). Moreover, the heraldic relevance of citrus fruits for the ruling House of Orange in the Netherlands in the 17th century also ensured that the botanical gardens in Leiden and Amsterdam in particular became centres of *Citrus* cultivation.

Citrus north of the Alps: craving, trade and science

It wasn't just a question of appealing to visiting princes though – Italian Renaissance gardens, adorned with works of sculpture, some of it on a monumental scale, together with fountains and flora such as citrus trees that intoxicated the senses, met with an overwhelmingly enthusiastic response from scholars, poets and merchants. Johann Schwind, mayor of Frankfurt, had "received a bright spark of inspiration during a journey in Italy undertaken a few years ago" (Merian 1641) that ignited his passion for horticulture (p. 12). Johann Christoph Volkamer (1644–1720) also often recalled his own trip to Italy and remembered "with the greatest of pleasure the very fine palaces there" (vol. II, Preamble). The famous yearning ballad sung by the young Mignon in Goethe's *Wilhelm Meister's Apprenticeship* (1795/96) expresses the universal fascination with Italy as a land of lush gardens: "Do you know that land? where the lemon trees bloom, / in dark foliage the golden oranges glow, / a caressing breeze wafts from blue skies, / myrtle stands still and laurel grows tall, / Do you know it?"

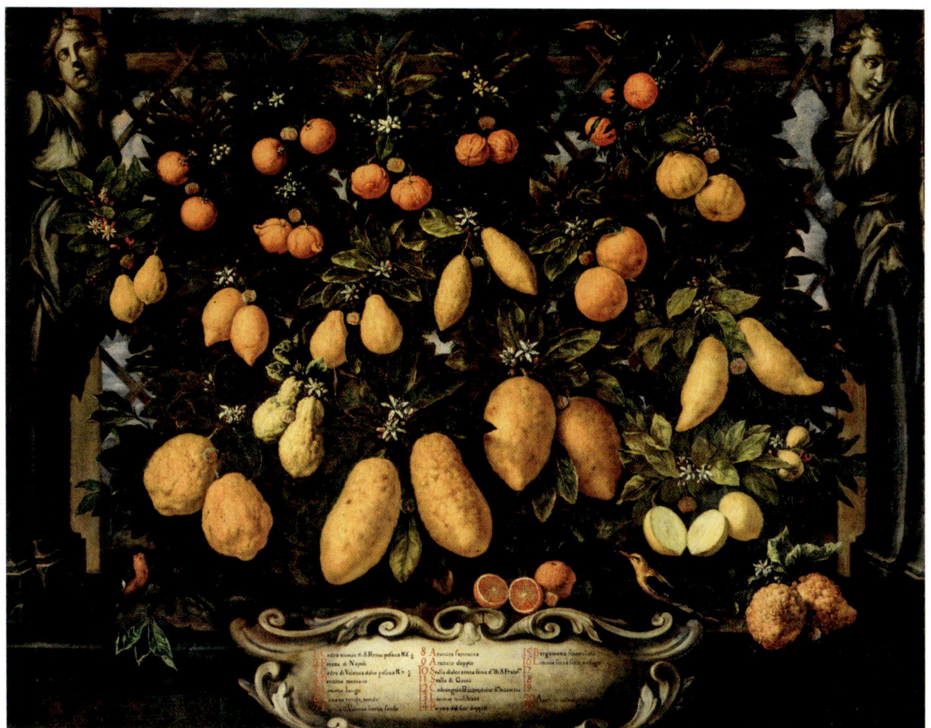

Citrus fruits were known north of the Alps as early as the Middle Ages, while their use in folkloric and devotional practices has a long tradition, for instance in funerary rites. In Judaism, the fruit known as *etrog*, a variety of citron, is used in celebrating Sukkot, the Feast of Tabernacles. Volkamer called the *etrog* "Cedro col Pigolo" or "Jewish citron apple" (vol. 1, p. 121).

The manifold medicinal properties of citrus fruits were described already in the writings of Antiquity, and since early modern times the fruits have been used as a remedy for scurvy, a vitamin C deficiency that plagued mariners on the long sea voyages undertaken in the Age of Discovery. The physicians and apothecaries who studied citrus plants with an interest in their therapeutic properties were often excellent botanists. Business contacts and communication among scholars undertaking their research at prestigious Italian universities were crucial to the cultural transference between Italy and Germany

Bartolomeo Bimbi, ***Cedri, limoni e aranci***, 1715
Citrons, lemons and oranges / Zitronatzitronen, Zitronen und Orangen / Cédrats, citrons et oranges
Oil on canvas, 174 × 233 cm (68 ½ × 91 ¾ in.)
Poggio a Caiano, Villa Medicea, Museo della Natura Morta

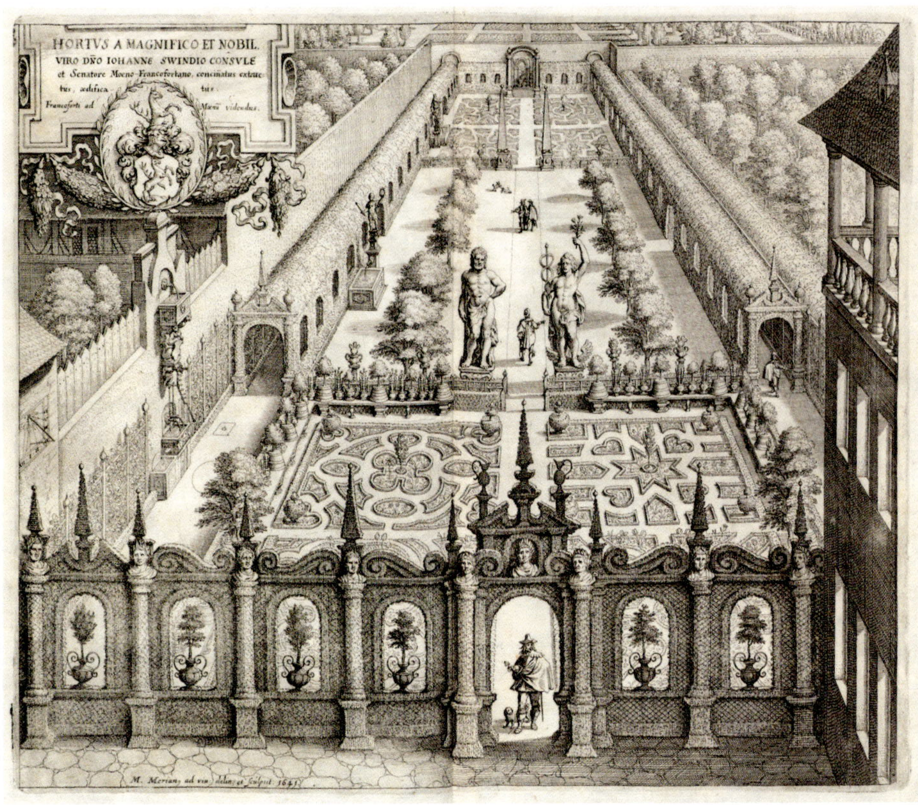

that took place from the 16th century onwards in the fields of horticulture and botany. Horticulture as practised in the Free Cities of the Holy Roman Empire, and not just at the courts in Vienna, Prague, Munich, Stuttgart and Dresden, was of pivotal importance for the introduction of citrus plants into Central Europe. Foremost in this respect were Augsburg, which maintained close trade links with Italy in the 16th century through the Fugger family of merchants and bankers, and Nuremberg, whose patrician and affluent residents maintained their own close contact with northern Italy.

Extensive botanical and horticultural knowledge was required to make the cultivation of citrus fruits possible in northern regions, where the plants must be sheltered over

Matthäus Merian, **Mayor Johann Schwind's garden in Frankfurt am Main**
Garten des Bürgermeisters Johann Schwind in Frankfurt am Main
Le jardin de Johann Schwind, maire de Francfort-sur-le-Main
Engraving and etching. From: Matthäus Merian, *Florilegium renovatum et auctum*, Frankfurt am Main, 1641
Munich, Bayerische Staatsbibliothek, Res/2 Oecon. 40,1

the winter, and imparting this arcane knowledge has, since the 16th century, been among the most difficult challenges and greatest technological achievements in horticulture. From the second third of the 16th century onwards, citrus trees in Central Europe were cultivated all year round either in the ground or in pots in gardens (p. 103) and were thus maintained not only by the courts of princes but also by the prosperous burghers of Nuremberg as well as the Fugger family in Augsburg.

The Nuremberg merchant Johann Christoph Volkamer published his *Nürnbergische Hesperides* in 1708, with a second volume, *Continuation der Nürnbergischen Hesperidum*, appearing in 1714. Publication of these works saw their author, with his avowed passion for *Citrus* as the "finest adornment to any garden", firmly established in a long tradition. Based as it was on the state of knowledge at the time, Volkamer's work on the Hesperides provides an extraordinarily comprehensive classification and description of citrus trees and shrubs in a lavishly illustrated text. Moreover, this is the first systematic description in German of the genus *Citrus*. In a series of remarkable juxtapositions, the copperplates show each fruit life-size at the top hovering above a number of *vedute* showing gardens, country houses, villas and landscapes on an entirely different scale. The volumes of Volkamer's *Hesperides* can be approached from various angles – botany, landscape and garden architecture as well as topography. However, any cursory perusal is out of the question because the work comprises some 750 pages and more than 250 plates. Volkamer had begun working on it by 1695 at the latest and had intended there to be a third volume to complete it.

The Volkamer family

The author's family is the key to understanding and appreciating the scientific ambition and international scope of his work on the Hesperides. Johann Christoph Volkamer came from a family who "gave to the world many scholars, courtiers and soldiers" (Will 1758), while the understandably frequent confusion with the Volckamers, a patrician family from Nuremberg, has been noted and corrected since the 18th century. Johann Volkamer (1576–1661), the grandfather of the author here in question, became prosperous because of the silk factory he established at Rovereto in northern Italy and by applying himself to trade, as the result of which in 1614 he acquired a property in Gostenhof, a suburb of Nuremberg, with a view to laying out a garden, which his grandson, Johann Christoph Volkamer, later enlarged.

Johann Georg Volkamer (1616–1693), Johann Christoph's father, was a scientific scholar of international renown. After studying medicine at Jena and Altdorf Universities and in Padua from 1638 to 1641, he spent nearly two years travelling in Italy to further his studies. His itinerary took him via Venice, Ferrara, Bologna, Florence, Pisa, Livorno and Lucca to Rome and Naples, and from there to Nice, Marseilles and Montpellier,

Toulouse, Bordeaux, Orléans and Paris. In 1643 he finally took his doctorate in Altdorf. During another trip to Italy in 1658, he was invited to become a member of the Academia Recuperatorum in Padua. His extraordinary erudition in so many fields – natural history, astronomy, physics and botany – made him famous, and in 1676 he was appointed a member of the Leopoldina, the Imperial Academy of Natural History, eventually becoming its president in 1686. For his membership of both this academy and the Pegnitz Flower Society (from 1646), he chose the pseudonym Helianthus, 'Sunflower', and in fact his keen interest in sundials led him to build some himself, a further demonstration of how his curiosity kept up with the times.

The author of the *Hesperides*, Johann Christoph Volkamer, was the eldest son of Johann Georg. A very much younger brother (1662–1744), who was named Johann Georg after his father and who followed in his footsteps professionally, made a name for himself as a "famous medicus who was regarded as Germany's greatest botanist" (Will 1758). Johann Christoph, on the other hand, took over the silk factory established by his grandfather in Rovereto, making the business still more successful. In addition, he also managed a brass foundry at Laufamholz near Nuremberg (p. 246). Respected as a "distinguished and reputable merchant" who held several high posts in his native city, Johann Christoph acquired "a vast knowledge of growing and cultivating citrus trees, flowers and garden plants" (Will 1758). He lived in Rovereto from 1660 until at least 1668. His years there also provided him with an opportunity for visiting gardens in northern Italy and throughout his later life he retained all his original enthusiasm for them even though it is highly likely that he never crossed the Alps again after those early formative years in northern Italy. Volkamer spent the rest of his life in Nuremberg, where he devoted himself to his garden and growing citrus, whilst keeping up a lively correspondence with like-minded enthusiasts around the world.

The publishing history of the *Hesperides* – a survey

Volkamer had initially planned his *Nürnbergische Hesperides* to be a one-volume work. In March 1706 he was granted the imperial patent permitting publication but the work did not appear in print until two years later, in 1708, when it was published by Endter in Nuremberg (p. 6). The author seems to have intervened constantly in the printing process and the composition of the book because copies of the first edition differ from one another in various details: the *vedute* of some plates were altered, signatures of

Franz Ertinger, after Charles Emmanuel Biset, **Citrus cultivation and harvest** (detail)
Zitruspflege und Ernte / Culture et récolte des agrumes
Engraving. Frontispiece from: Frans van Sterbeeck, *Citricultura,* Antwerp, 1682
Geneva, Bibliothèque du Conservatoire et Jardin Botaniques

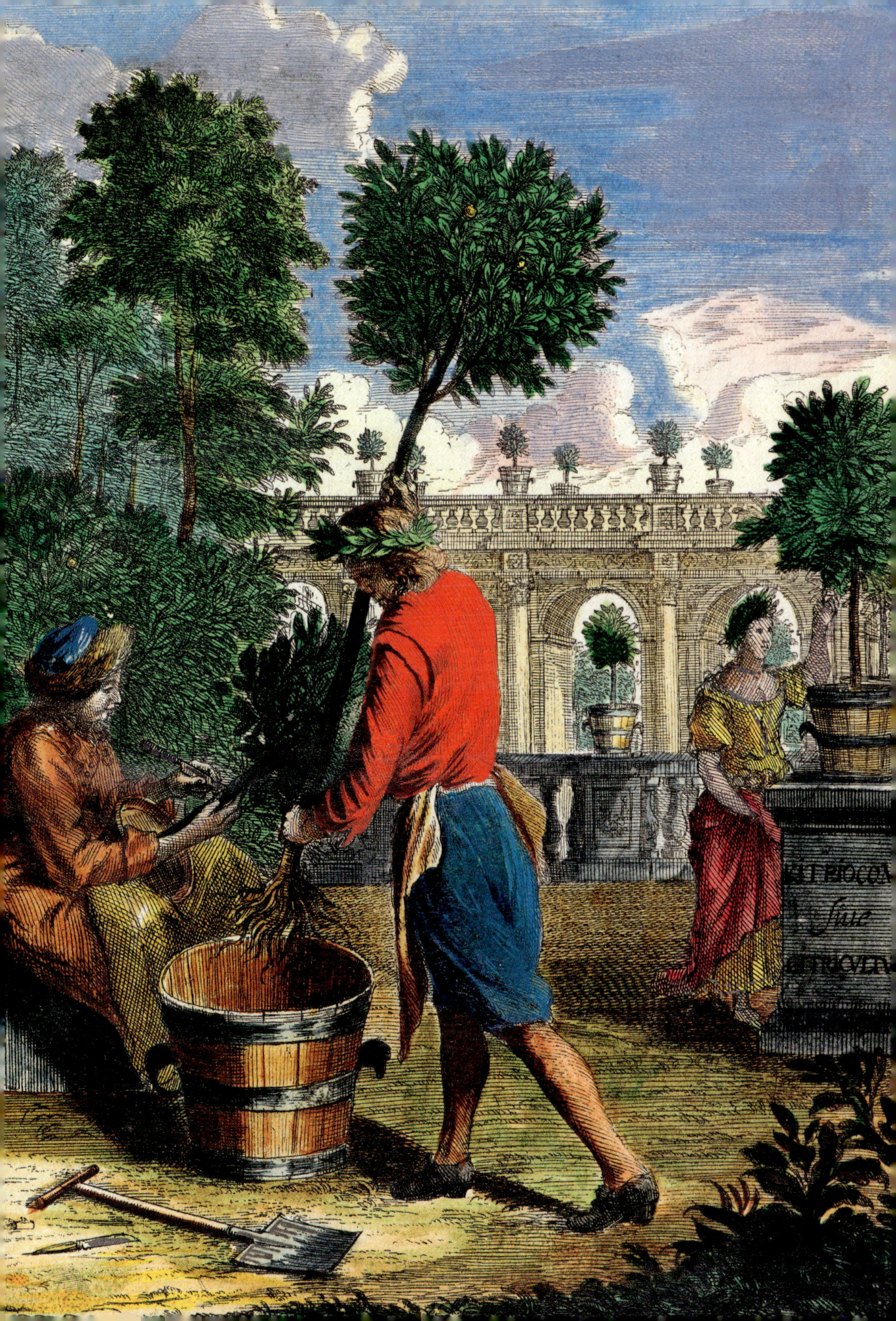

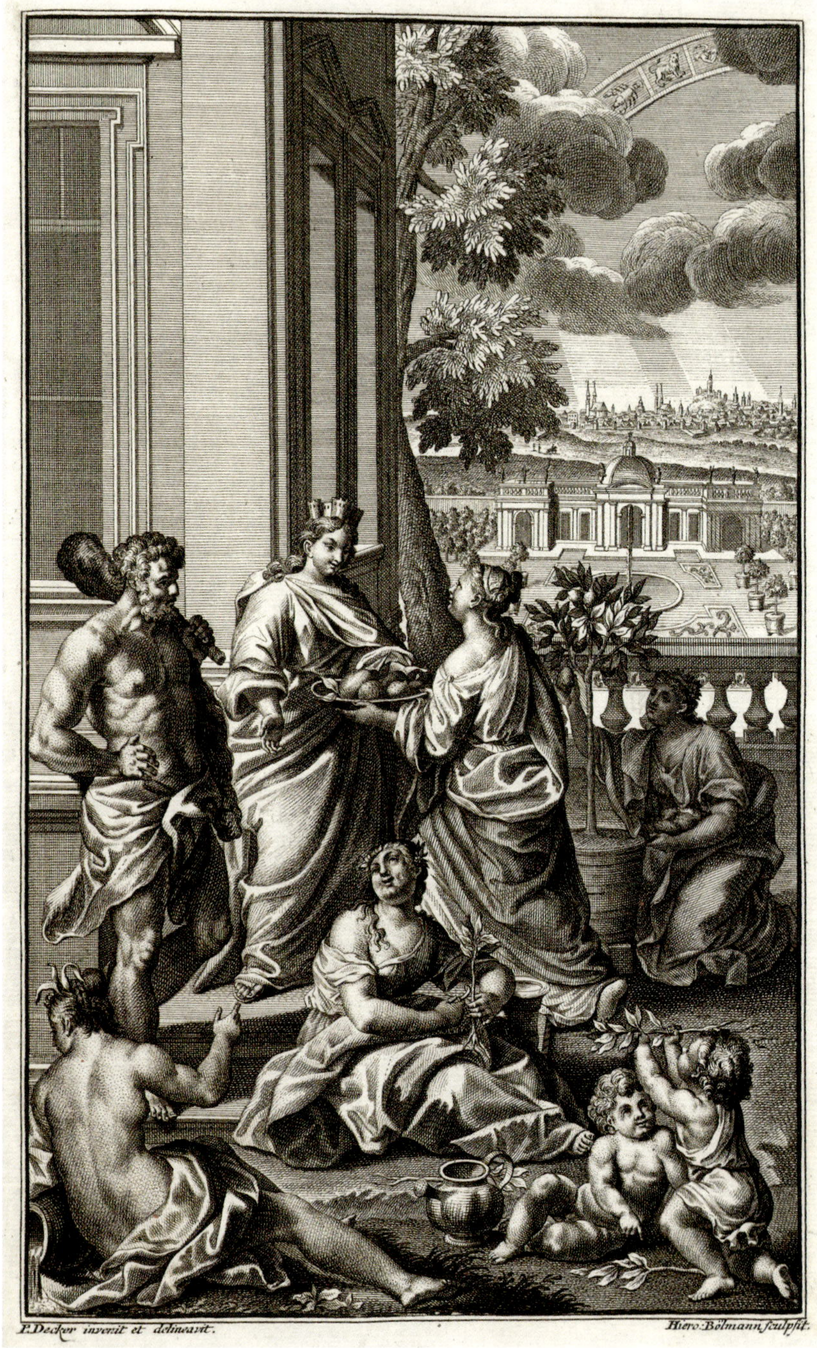
P. Decker invenit et delineavit.
Hiero: Bölmann sculpsit.

the copperplate engravers were added subsequently and later proofs of some of the copperplates were even bound into a number of copies. The final page features a list of typographical errors from this 1708 edition.

A second edition was also published in that same year, with a different title-page and frontispiece. The author's name now appears in full and the names of the publisher and agent have been changed. The new frontispiece reprints the original, albeit in mirror-image, and differs from it in certain details. The frontispiece copperplate from the first edition (p. 2) had, therefore, evidently been used elsewhere and perhaps because no one expected it would be needed for further editions. The square fields framing the initials in the first edition have been replaced by rectangular ones of the kind that also appear in the second volume. Since the errors noted in the first edition had been acted upon, the list of "Corrigenda" was omitted from the second edition.

At the urging of foreign scholars, Volkamer had Erhard Reusch (1678–1740), a philologist and lawyer, make a Latin translation of the first volume. This was published in 1713 with a frontispiece re-employed from the second (1708) edition. Volkamer was clearly quite willing then to lavish money on enhancing his international reputation since the Latin edition of the first volume was no less elaborately produced than the German original. The Latin text and the plates match the German edition and the ordering and numbering of the pages are identical to those of the original. The translator, however, added an account of the state of current research into citrus cultivation.

The patent for printing the second volume, which is a considerably thicker book, is dated 21 August 1714. It was published more quickly than the first volume, within the same year in fact, and as *Continuation der Nürnbergischen Hesperidum* in Frankfurt and Leipzig.

The *Hesperides* is not dedicated, in the usual way, to any specific dignitary, such as someone on the Council of the Free City of Nuremberg or even to a respected patrician, a practice that would have been used to target a market in such circles. Volkamer seems to have been so rich that he did not need the financial backing usually associated with a dedication. Indeed, he wrote repeatedly that he had spared neither expense nor effort and made a point of emphasising how proud he was "that no one has hitherto described so extensively and so numerously / these supreme adornments of garden architecture / or produced it with fitting copperplates" (vol. II, Preamble). An overview of the publishing history makes it apparent that both the author and publishers were astonished at the

The Hesperides presenting Noris with gifts of citrus fruits /
Die Hesperiden bieten Noris Zitrusfrüchte dar / Les Hespérides offrent des agrumes à Noris
Frontispiece for the unpublished third volume of *Nürnbergische Hesperides*, 1714–1720
Universitätsbibliothek Erlangen-Nürnberg, H61/2 RAR.A 35[2, p. 1

success of the 1708 first edition. When the first volume met with a positive reception, Volkamer published a second edition, followed by the Latin translation and, finally, his *Continuation* in German. A planned Latin translation of the second volume, to which an extensive description of the Hesperides myth in ancient sculpture and on carved gems was to be added, never came to fruition.

After the *Continuation* was published, Volkamer, who was now over 70, continued to devote himself to growing citrus in his garden at Gostenhof whilst also continuing to correspond with colleagues abroad to gather further material for his magnum opus. No subsequent volume was printed before he died in 1720 although the material collected in preparation for it is now in the Germanisches Nationalmuseum in Nuremberg (p. 19). The contents of this projected later volume can be inferred from a new find, a book with 62 plates which came to light in the Universitätsbibliothek Erlangen-Nürnberg: the plates are final proofs for the third volume of the *Nürnbergische Hesperides*. Besides copperplates featuring the usual combination of fruits and *vedute*, the Erlangen volume also includes the frontispiece (p. 16), three vignettes (pp. 19, 50, 94), a plan of the orangery laid out by Count Neithardt in Breslau (p. 78) and a "View of the Royal Gardens and Palace in Berlin" (p. 20). The latter view documents plans to enlarge the Royal Palace in Berlin; the draughtsman, Paul Decker the Younger (1685–1742), had probably been informed of these plans by his elder brother, who had worked on construction of the Palace up until 1706 under Andreas Schlüter. A drawing by the same artist, *Prospect des Königlichen Schlosses und Garten zu Charlot(t)enburg eine Stundt von Berlin* [View of the Royal Palace and Garden at Charlottenburg, an hour from Berlin], has also survived (p. 32), and an engraving of this view, too, was probably intended for the third volume of the *Hesperides*. The *terminus ante quem* for the copperplates produced and signed by the engraver Joseph a Montalegre for the third volume is the year when he died: 1718.

Volkamer's Nuremberg garden – *quasi centrum Europae*

Several plates in the *Hesperides* depict Volkamer's garden at Gostenhof, a suburb of Nuremberg: the first volume includes a bird's-eye view (pp. 46/47) amongst various other depictions and the second shows it on the frontispiece (p. 48). The latter volume also contains a bird's-eye view on a larger scale of the garden which by then had been redesigned (pp. 272/273). The plates reveal that Volkamer's citrus trees were planted in the ground as well as in pots. To protect them during the winter, a temporary wooden shelter, which could be dismantled in the spring, was erected between the house and the 'orangery' (pp. 26/27, 90/91). Temporary orangeries such as this one are still frequently found on the shores of Lake Garda, and Volkamer even devoted a separate copperplate to an earlier design for one (p. 134/135). The carved figures of the three Hesperides on the entablature

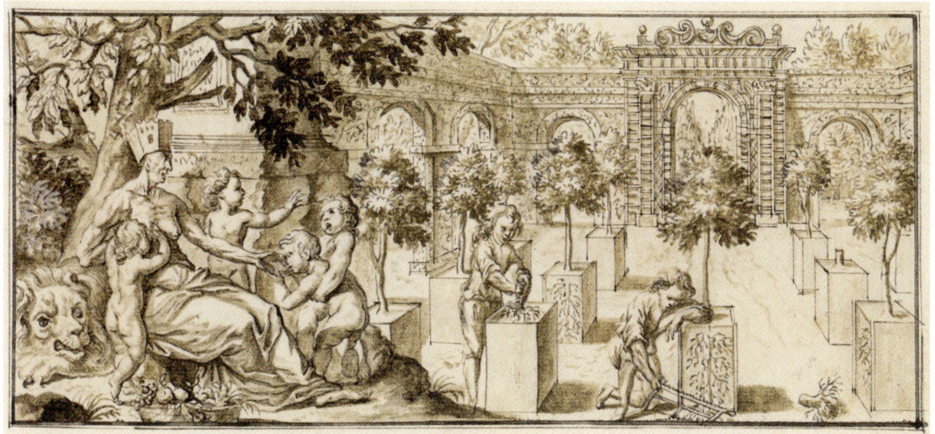

of Volkamer's orangery seem to be watching over the citrus trees and other exotic plants to ensure that they will thrive (pp. 90/91).

The bird's-eye view of the garden, most of which served as a kitchen garden, has a caption in Latin in the second volume of the *Hesperides*: *Viridarium Suburbaneum Johan Cristoffori Volckameri in Norimberga* [Johann Christoph Vol[c]kamer's suburban house garden in Nuremberg]. In using such a label, on the ancient Roman model, Volkamer was laying claim to his international reputation. With his copperplates of ancient reliefs and free-standing sculpture based on the Hercules myth, also in this second volume, he was placing himself firmly in the Roman tradition (pp. 97, 98), a fashionable practice in Nuremberg art and cultural life in the 17th century and an association between cultures which the painter, copperplate engraver and biographer of artists, Joachim von Sandrart (1606–1688), amongst others, consistently promoted, particularly with his *Teutsche Academie*.

Ties with Rome and Florence had been maintained since the days of Johann Georg Volkamer the Elder, and Johann Christoph's brother had also visited these two Italian cities in 1685. Johann Christoph may have been seeking to play on affinities he saw between his own family, silk manufacturers but who also included a number of distinguished physicians (in Italian, *medici*), and the House of Medici, whose wealth, after all, came from the textile trade. He may even have taken the heraldic significance of citrus for the Medici

Allegorical representation of citrus cultivation
Allegorische Darstellung zur Zitruskultur / Allégorie de la culture des agrumes
Vignette for the unpublished third volume of *Hesperides*, 1714–1720
Pen and grey wash, 14.9 × 20.5 cm (5 7/8 × 8 1/8 in.)
Nuremberg, Germanisches Nationalmuseum, Graphische Sammlung, ZR 3196 Kaps 726

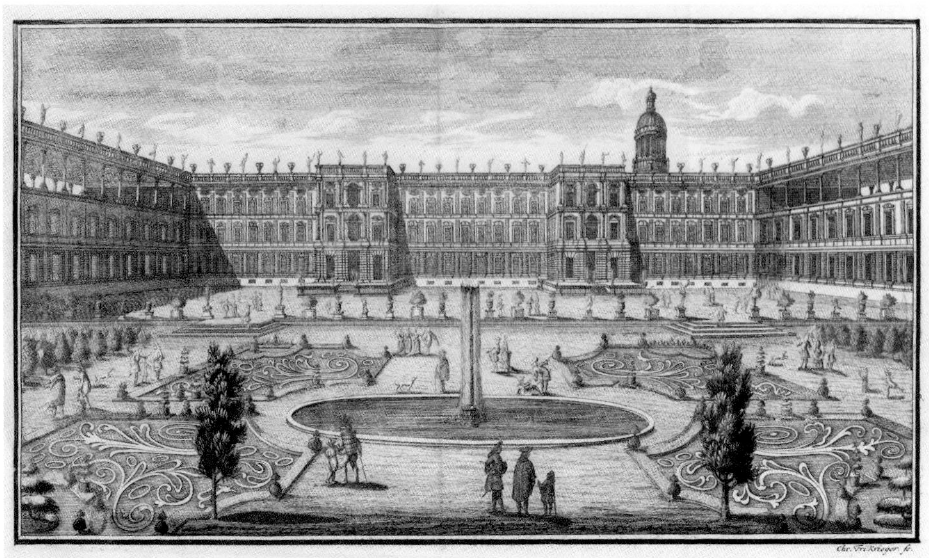

and applied it to his own family, while throughout his work he refers to the garden owned by his brother, Johann Georg, as a herb garden, notably abbreviating *'in Horto Medico Volckameri'* to *'H. M. V.'* in the Latinate manner.

Volkamer is bound to have been familiar with the series of copperplates by Giovanni Battista Falda (1643–1678) depicting Roman gardens, *Li Giardini di Roma* (1683), which was reprinted by the Sandrart press in Nuremberg in 1695. The Roman Hesperides on the frontispiece, "Gli Esperidi Romani", are the guardians of the gardens and citrus plantations of the Roman capital (p. 28). Falda showed the garden of the Villa Medici (p. 31), featuring an obelisk and several works of mostly ancient sculpture. In July 1709 Johann Christoph Volkamer had an equestrian statue in the labyrinth of his garden (p. 38) at Gostenhof replaced by a one-third-scale replica of the 'Obeliscus Constantinopolitanus', which Theodosius I had had set up in Constantinople in 390 AD. For his interpretation of the Egyptian hieroglyphs on the obelisk Volkamer used the work of several scholars, including Athanasius Kircher, a Jesuit based in Rome who had published writings on the *Obeliscus Pamphilius* in 1650 and the *Obeliscus Aegyptiacus* in 1666.

Christoph Friedrich Krieger, after Paul Decker the Younger, **View of the Royal Garden and Palace in Berlin**
Prospect des Königlichen Gartens und Schlosses zu Berlin / Vue du jardin et du château royal de Berlin
Engraving and etching. Plate for the unpublished third volume of *Nürnbergische Hesperides*, 1714–1720
Universitätsbibliothek Erlangen-Nürnberg, H61/2 RAR.A 35[2, p. 6

Volkamer's description of his own obelisk, which is just under seven metres (23 feet) high (p. 37) and now stands in the Hammer Industrial Estate in Laufamholz, a suburb of Nuremberg, was published in 1713. This essay was either bound in to the second volume of the *Hesperides* or added later to the first volume. The description appears in the first volume of the copy kept in Fürth presented here, and with its Latin title it follows the style of other works on ancient obelisks published in the latter half of the 17th century. Volkamer closed his description of the monument, which is surmounted by a dove, with a heartfelt wish for "a sure and lasting peace that has hitherto been so longed for and wished for by all of Europe" (bound with vol. 1, p. 16). These hopes were fulfilled by the Treaty of Utrecht, which ended the War of the Spanish Succession in 1713.

Volkamer devoted an equally lengthy description to the construction of the boxwood sundial installed in his garden at Gostenhof in 1696 (pp. 41; vol. 1, pp. 245–248) and to a *Columna Milliaria* (p. 45; vol. 1, pp. 253–255) added in 1697. This milestone was modelled on the ancient *Milliarium aureum* in the Forum Romanum, which marked the point from which distances to various important cities in the Roman Empire were once measured (they were perhaps also listed on the stone). In the Gostenhof garden, maps were mounted halfway up the four columns which supported a baldachin roof and also on a fifth, free-standing column in the middle. Resembling a cartographic anamorphosis, this unusual garden feature subjected European topography from Lemberg, Jylland (Jutland) and Salisbury via Perpignan to Bari to a perspective that related the importance of those European cities to that of Nuremberg. A commonplace in the rhetoric employed to praise cities from the late 15th century, Nuremberg was known as the commercial hub of the continent – *quasi centrum Europae*. This attribute is expressed with great originality in the columnar monument that adorned Volkamer's garden there.

Citrus and local patriotism

The folio format, the substantial quantity of text and the numerous plates justified the high price of 12 Taler for the two volumes of the *Hesperides* although it was certainly far more expensive than the many other, less compendious horticultural publications of its day. Volkamer's publishers also produced the several volumes of *Garten-Wissenschafft* [Horticultural Science] by Wolf Albrecht Stromer von Reichenbach, a Nuremberg patrician, which cost only 1 Taler and 8 Groschen. A great many garden books were published in both Nuremberg and Augsburg in the last decades of the 17th century, testament to the economic upturn after the end of the Thirty Years' War and the keen interest in horticulture that prevailed in the Free Cities of the Holy Roman Empire. Volkamer was familiar with many of these books and quoted some of their authors, including Agostino Mandirola, Wolfgang Jakob Dümler and Stromer von Reichenbach.

Johann Christoph Volkamer was lavish with the superlatives when he laid his own work on citrus at the feet of his native Nuremberg, "this Queen of German cities":

"Natives and foreigners alike will readily concede / to my Fatherland / noble Nuremberg / the reputation / of being the best-situated / most beautifully built city in the German Empire / and not just provided with all necessities / but also with all delights. Among these last are accounted / most justifiably / gardens for art and pleasure / which reveal themselves to be as exquisitely beautiful and lovely / as they are large and numerous / within and without the city walls."

Volkamer intended his work on citrus as a tribute to his native city. That this was indeed so is made absolutely clear down to the last detail in the frontispiece, created by Paul Decker the Elder (1677–1713) and his younger brother of the same name (p. 2). In the first volume, the Hesperides – assisted by Mercury, the god of merchants, and by Hercules in the other volumes – offer fruit to Noris, the proud personification of Nuremberg. The topographical setting in the background is the city of Nuremberg in the first volume and, in the second, Volkamer's garden at Gostenhof (p. 48). In the frontispiece of the first volume, a Crown Imperial *(Fritillaria imperialis)* looms large in the bunch of flowers behind Mercury, undoubtedly a pointed allusion to the historical role played by the city as the place where the Imperial Regalia, and, therefore, the Imperial Crown of the Holy Roman Empire were kept.

In the 17th and 18th centuries, the gardens owned by German patricians and the middle-classes were often depicted against the backdrop of a *veduta*. Descriptions of horticulture and the cultivation of plants, vegetation and flora were highly suited to effusions of local patriotism, and since gardens show how residents identified with their prosperous cities (p. 54), they were interpreted in several of the city records from this time as communal achievements. Hence the first plate in the second part of the *Hesperides*, featuring a lofty *"Cedro grosso Bondolotto"* towering above a *veduta* of the Free City of Nuremberg (p. 150), should be viewed as a statement of local patriotism. This is equally true of the Breslau citrus catalogue compiled by Caspar Wilhelm Scultetus (s. l. 1731), which was influenced by Volkamer's *Hesperides*, and the publications dealing with Caspar Bose's garden in Leipzig (p. 34). Volkamer corresponded with Bose (1645–1700), who was renowned far and wide for the rare and exotic plants he grew, including a valuable and cherished citrus collection mentioned in 1686 as the "Hesperides Bosianae".

Joseph a Montalegre
View of the Schwöbber Palace and Gardens of Otto von Münchhausen near Hamelin
Ansicht der Schloss- und Gartenanlage Schwöbber von Otto von Münchhausen bei Hameln
Vue du château et du jardin Schwöbber d'Otto von Münchhausen près de Hamelin
From: *Continuation der Nürnbergischen Hesperidum*, 1714, vol. II, plate VIII

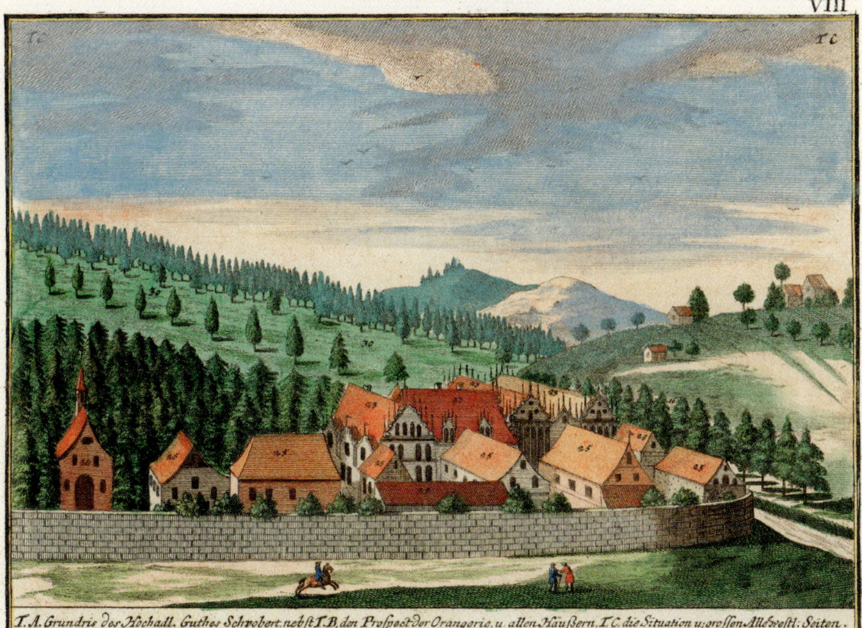

T. A. Grundris des Hochadl. Guthes Schrobert. nebst T. B, den Prospect der Orangerie. u. allen Häußern. T. C. die Situation u; grossen Allee westl: Seiten.

N. 1. Thier Garten.
N. 2. Thier Hauß.
N. 3. Neue Orangen. } jeder von 10 Fenstern
N. 4. alte Orangen }
N. 5. Garten Cabinet.
N. 6. die Orangerie bestehend in 20 vollkomenen Alleen. jede 30 der schönsten bäumen hat. der Orange Platz ist gros 40° und breit 8° die° zu 16 gerechnet.
N. 7. 3 spring Fontaine mit ihren passens.
N. 8. Winter Ananas treib=Hauß.

N. 9. Sommer Ananas treib=Hauß
N. 10. Sommer treib Hauß.
N. 11. der Nelcken=Platz.
N. 12. Melonen bette Platz.
N. 13 Zwey Fasahnen Garten
N. 14 Lorie=und kleiner Orangen Platz
N. 15 das Garten Hauß.
N. 16. ein schöner Dannen Waldt worinen sie allemal Alleen weis stehen.
N. 17. Allee von ansehnlicher höhe. 100° lang.

N. 18 Blumen Garten.
N. 19. die Forellen bäch. N. 20. Teiche
N. 21. Küchen Garten. N. 22. Baum Garten.
N. 23. die Wohn=Gebäude. N. 24. die Kirche.
N. 25. die Vorwercker=brau häußer u. übrigen Gebäude zur Haußhaltung. N. 26. der Feigen Wald.
N. 27. der Kirschen Wald. N. 28. Reit Platz.
N. 29. Reben Platz. N. 30. die grosse Allee ist 2ng. breit 5° lg.
N. 31 trockner grabe an dessen mauren Pfirschen Birn. u. viel fruchtbahre Bäume stehen. N. 32. die Korn u. Segen Mühle.

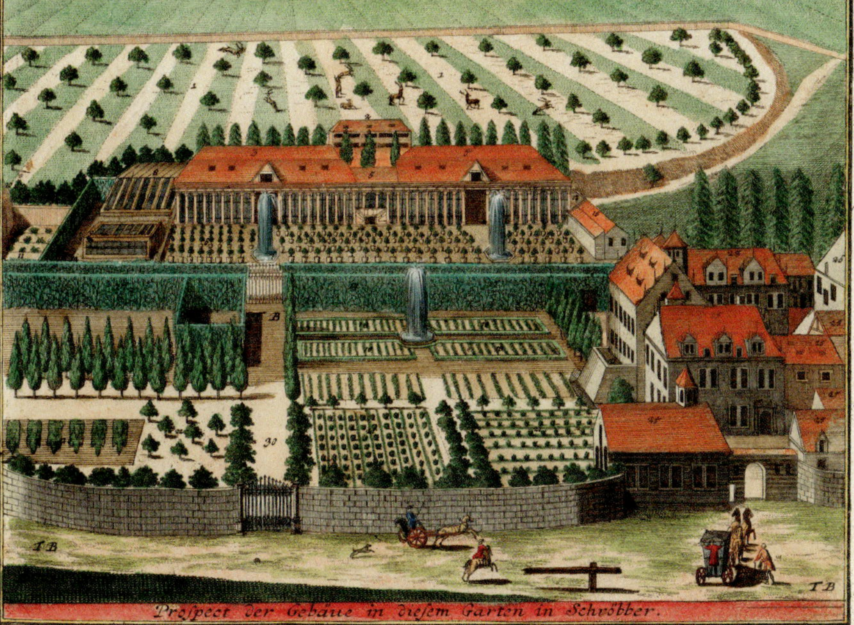

Prospect der Gebäue in diesem Garten in Schwöbber.

Ios: à Montalegre sc.

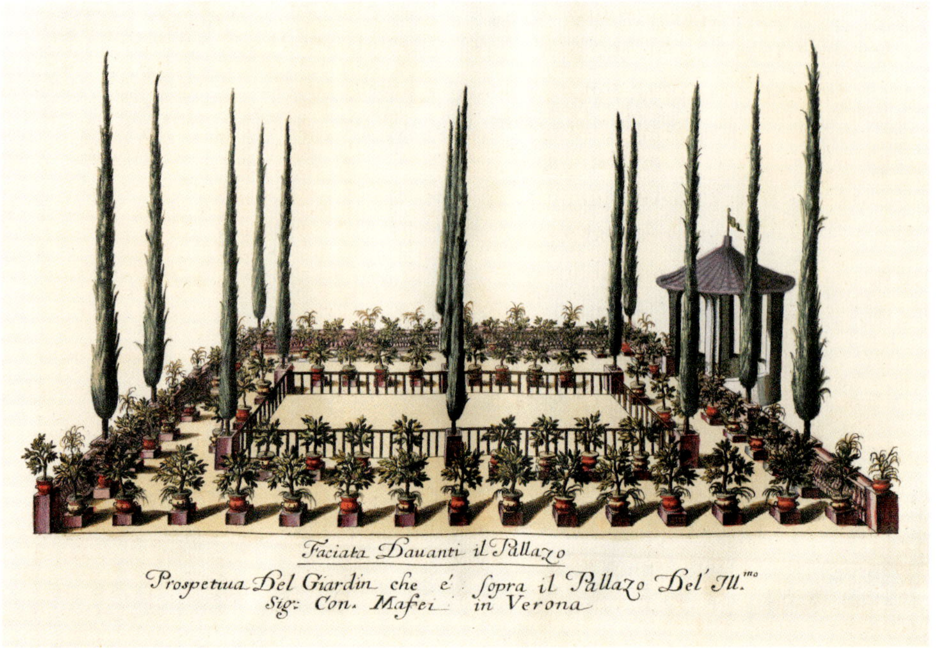

Merchant and naturalist

The Volkamer family, who had lived in Nuremberg since the late 16th century, were not only prosperous merchants but also internationally renowned scholars. Although they were not patricians they were so firmly rooted in the social life of the Free City and the administrative councils that governed it that they were accorded a high level of respect. Nuremberg's reputation at this time became established to a notable degree through the achievements of its local artists and the scholars working in the city and at Altdorf University.

In many respects the *Hesperides* mirrors the interests, personal relations and knowledge in various fields not only of the author himself but also his family – including his grandfather, with his broad range of interests, his father, a scholar and polymath, and his younger brother, a well-known scientist, to all of whom Johann Christoph owed a great deal. His brother, Johann Georg, had earned an international reputation in 1700 on the strength of his botanical work, *Flora Noribergensis sive Catalogus Plantarum in Agro*

Garden of the Palazzo Maffei in Verona
Garten des Palazzo Maffei in Verona / Jardin du Palazzo Maffei à Vérone
From: *Continuation der NürnbergischenHesperidum*, 1714, vol. II, plate after p. 8
Vienna, Österreichische Nationalbibliothek

Noribergensi Tam sponte nascentium, quam exoticarum (Nuremberg, second edition, 1718). Only two of its more than 400 pages (p. 276 f.), however, were given over to oranges, citrons and lemons. It does not include many plates and most of them depict exotic plants Johann Georg cultivated in his garden, although no citrus appears among the illustrations. The reason for what might have caused his brother Johann Christoph, some 20 years his senior, to have committed himself to the tireless production of a series of volumes of such an original and sophisticated work on citrus, covering all the expenses incurred in the writing and publishing it himself, might be that the *Nürnbergische Hesperiden* is the scholarly life's work of a "distinguished and respected merchant" who was also a dedicated amateur with a burning desire to make a contribution of his own in respectful competition, a case of familial *aemulatio*. Early in 1720, and just six months before he died, Johann Christoph was finally given the satisfaction, at the age of 76, of being admitted to the Imperial Academy of Natural History, as his father and brother had been before him.

While his father and brother had written their scientific works in Latin, Johann Christoph wrote in German for people like himself – amateur horticulturalists – although he still quoted Latin sources and was as fluent in it as he was in Italian. Viewed in this context, the *Hesperides* represents a remarkable achievement in terms of development. The work is a hybrid: on the one hand it is distinguished by its author's efforts to apply the scientific method consistently, and, on the other, by his insistence on writing it in German so that it might be understood by everyone. Basilius Besler's (1561–1629) magnificently monumental *Hortus Eystettensis* (s. l. 1613), written in Latin, was presumably a model for Volkamer (p. 59), owing to its precise and almost life-sized reproductions, but if not then at the very least he would have been aware of its existence.

The *Hesperides*, by contrast, grew out of attempts first made in the mid-17th century to develop German as a language of science. In its promotion of language and literature, the Pegnitz Flower Society, founded in 1644, played a leading role in Nuremberg in this objective. Johann Georg Volkamer the Elder was a member. Although Giovanni Battista Ferrari's book on citrus (1646) was written in Latin, most European works on the subject published in the latter half of the 17th century were written in their authors' native languages: this is true of Commelin (1676), Sterbeeck (1682), French horticultural works and those written by Germans. Basing his description and classification of lemons on long years of empirical observation and precise analysis, Volkamer produced a genuinely original contribution to the "noble science of botany and herbalism" (vol. 1, p. 4f.), and even though he was a merchant by profession rather than a naturalist, his work more than meets the high standards achieved by botanical publications of his day.

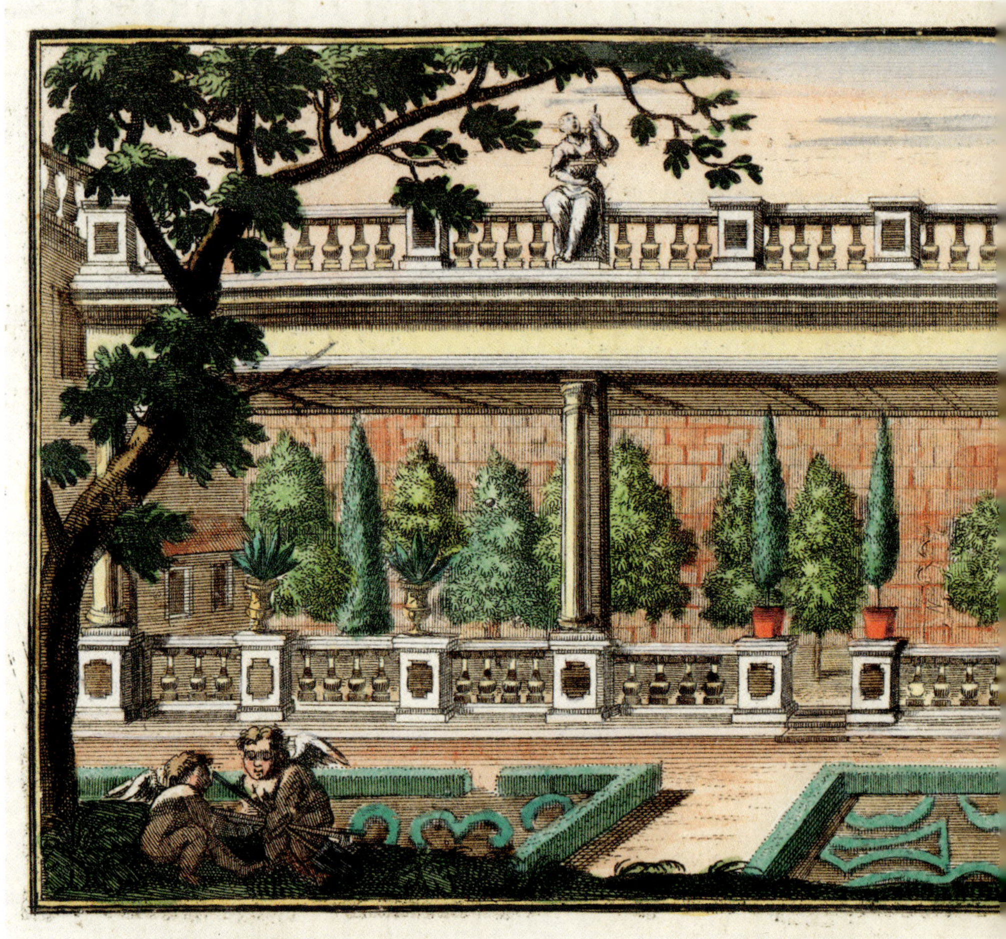

Volkamer's book is still listed today as a standard reference work on the classification of plants belonging to the genus *Citrus*. To give one example of his enduring importance, in their *Histoire naturelle des Orangers* (Paris, 1818/19), the botanists Joseph-Antoine Risso and Alexandre Poiteau named one variety of orange a "Bigaradier de Volcamer / Melangolo de Volcamerio" (p. 60).

Antecedents: works on citrus

The earliest book to classify citrus plants was published in Rome in 1646 as *Hesperides, sive de malorum aureorum cultura et usu* by the Jesuit father Giovanni Battista Ferrari (1584–1655). Its numerous plates show fruits, branches and blossoms (p. 71) as well

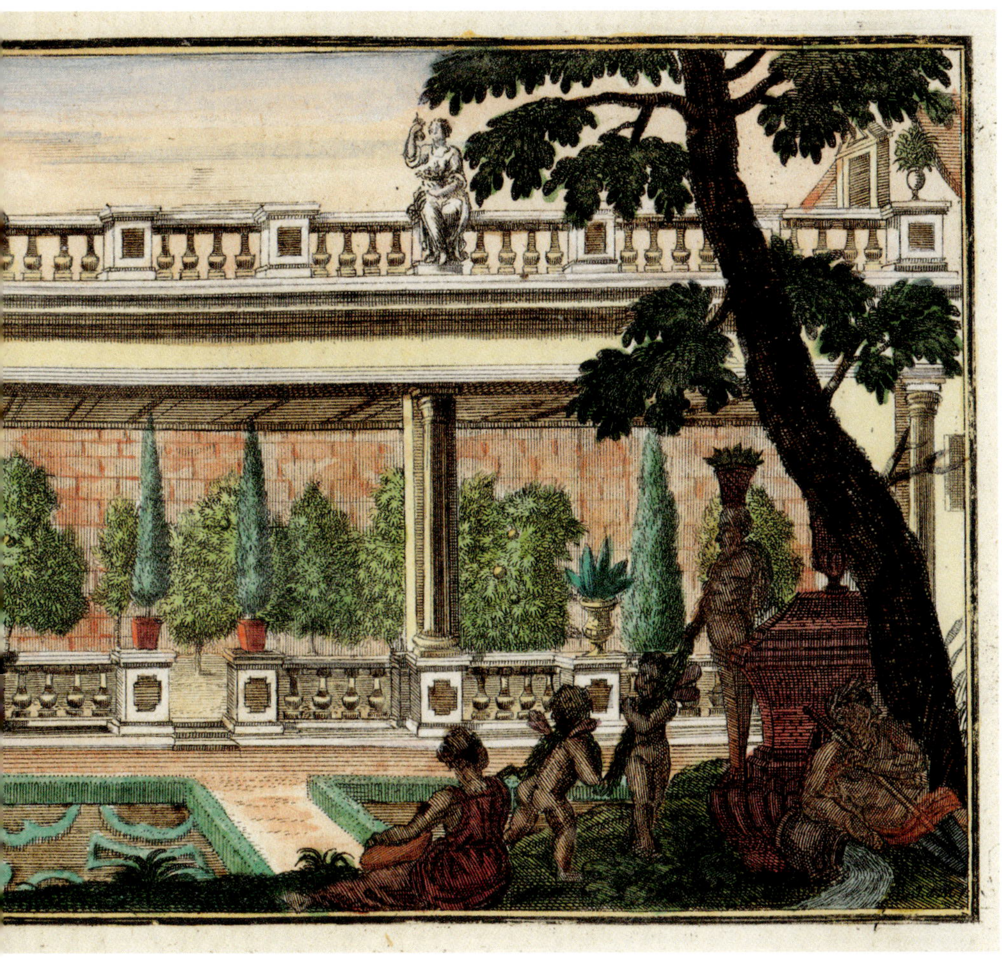

as entire orangeries. The book also features several fine illustrations of the Hesperides myth, designed by leading artists of the day in Rome, including Pietro da Cortona (p. 68), Francesco Albani and Nicolas Poussin. As head gardener and botanist to the Barberini in Rome, Ferrari had access to the botanical illustrations in what is known as the 'Museo Cartaceo' [Paper Museum], a collection of engravings and drawings amassed by Cassiano dal Pozzo (1588–1657), a patron of the arts with a scholarly eye (p. 75). Ferrari had

Volkamer's orangery at Gostenhof, view from the garden
Volkamers Pomeranzenhaus in Gostenhof, Ansicht vom Garten
L'orangerie de Volkamer à Gostenhof, vue depuis le jardin
From: *Nürnbergische Hesperides*, 1708, vol. 1, vignette p. 9

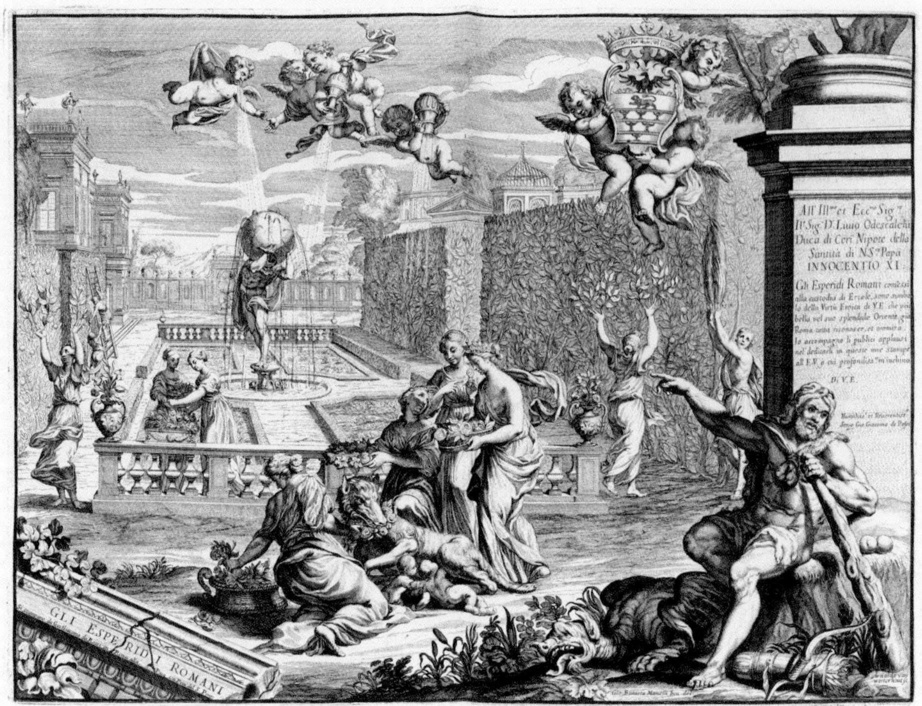

already earned a reputation in Italy and abroad with his book *Flora overo cultura dei fiori* (Latin: Rome, 1632, Italian: Rome, 1638). The Volkamer family owned copies of both this work and the Ferrari book on citrus, which were quoted by both Johann Georg the Younger and Johann Christoph. The latter's frontispiece and vignettes dealing with the Hesperides myth paraphrase the copperplates in Ferrari's book. Another authority frequently referred to by Johann Christoph is Jan Commelin (1629–1692), "the peerless botanist in Amsterdam" (vol. 1, p. 17) and the author of the *Nederlantze Hesperides* (Amsterdam, 1676; p. 77). Johann Christoph's brother, Johann Georg, had met Commelin in person in Amsterdam.

Erhard Reusch, the translator of the first volume of the *Hesperides* into Latin, added a review of earlier and more recent publications dealing with the genus *Citrus* to the text

Arnold van Westerhout, after Giovanni Battista Manelli, **Hercules, Atlas and the Hesperides**
Herkules, Atlas und die Hesperiden / Hercule, Atlas et les Hespérides
Copperplate engraving and etching
Frontispiece of: Giovanni Battista Falda, *Li Giardini di Roma*, Rome, 1683
Munich, Bayerische Staatsbibliothek, Res/2 Ital. 61

of that volume: running to 24 folio pages, Reusch's *Dissertatio Epistolica de Praecipuis Hesperidum Scriptoribus, iisque tam Antiquis quam Recentioribus* lends the *Hesperides* the academic weight that was lacking in Volkamer's approach to his subject matter and his idiosyncratic vernacular prose style. Right at the beginning, Reusch mentions Giovanni Pontano (1429–1503), Ferrari and Commelin before proceeding to discuss what writers from Greco-Roman Antiquity said about citrus since the time of Theophrastus. Reusch touched on mythology, etymology and even the writings of Arab scholars, and working through his sources chronologically he arrived at the early modern era, presenting a number of authorities from right across Europe who wrote about citrus in Latin, Italian, French, Dutch, English and German. Apart from Pontano, Ferrari and Commelin, the writers Reusch mentioned by country and language include the following: the Italian physicians, poets and scholars Battista Fiera, Celio Calcagnini, Pietro Nato and Giuseppe Lanzoni; Ulisse Aldrovandi (1522–1605), the naturalist who founded the botanical gardens in Bologna in 1568, and Ovidio Montalbano (1601–1672), a scholar in Bologna who published Aldrovandi's research on trees (1668); Agostino Mandirola, the author of *Italiänische Blumen- und Pomerantzen-Garten* (Nuremberg, 1679); the garden books of the French scholars René Rapin and Pierre Morin, as well as the *Nouveau traité des orangers et citronniers* (1692) and the *Traité de la culture des orangers, citronniers, grenadiers et oliviers* (Paris, 1676). Reusch duly acknowledged at great length the writings on citrus by the renowned gardener to the French court Jean-Baptiste de la Quintinie (1626–1688) as well as those by English and Dutch experts in the field. Apart from Commelin, the latter group includes Frans van Sterbeeck (1631–1693), whose *Citricultura* (Antwerp, 1682) is highly likely to have been a source of inspiration for Volkamer (pp. 15, 81, 89), and Henrik van Oosten, the author of *De Nederlandsen Hof, beplant met Bloemen, Ooft en Orangerijen* (Leiden, 1703). The Germans reviewed by Reusch include not only the writers of works on citrus but also scholars he named because Volkamer had corresponded with them and exchanged seeds and plants with them; a prime example is Otto von Münchhausen (1643–1717), whose Schwöbber Palace and garden near Hamelin features in several illustrations to the *Hesperides* as a model for the cultivation of exotic plants (pp. 23, 274).

Reusch reviewed far more specialist publications than Volkamer mentioned in his own published text, though it is safe to assume that Volkamer was also familiar with the writers and works Reusch listed. Quite how exceptional Volkamer's *Hesperides* is, however, becomes particularly apparent when it is compared to the works named above: in their case, the text is the predominant feature. There are not so many copperplate illustrations in the works of Commelin and Sterbeeck but the engravings that do appear demonstrate a desire for both accuracy of reproduction and decorative layout. Ferrari's book is the only one listed by Reusch to place scientific pictorial representation on an equal footing with the text, so that copperplates depicting branches and foliage, flowers and whole or dissected fruits are decoratively entwined with banderoles containing nomenclature and classification (p. 71). Like Ferrari, Volkamer aimed at precision of reproduction but presented many more varieties of citrus in his work.

Volkamer's intended readers: "For the delectation of curious devotees and gardeners desirous of learning"

Volkamer wrote his work for affluent garden-owners who had sufficient spare time and income to be able to devote themselves to their gardens and the study of botany. The author noted that he had invested "numerous leisure hours in studying citrus fruits / for my own pleasure" (vol. II, Preamble). In both volumes of the *Hesperides* and drawing on years of direct experience, Volkamer presented a wide-ranging survey on the cultivation of citrus, namely: constructing temporary orangeries and glasshouses; tending and fertilising plants and bringing them through the winter; propagation and pruning; treating diseases; and protecting plants from pests such as scale insects, which Volkamer examined under a microscope and reproduced greatly enlarged for the benefit of his readers (p. 115).

Volkamer devoted several chapters, written from a garden-owner's point of view, to the personal qualities required (p. 85): "Accordingly, no stupid or idle person is suited to being a gardener / because he must have good scientific knowledge and a good eye [...] A gardener must also be intelligent and thoughtful [...] Further, a gardener should be industrious and untiring" (vol. I, p. 71 f.). He seems, however, to have had rather bad luck with his own gardeners if we are to believe the number of complaints about "malicious pranks [played] by such dishonourable and ungodly gardeners" (vol. I, p. 75), or else theft and neglect of the plants in their charge. Volkamer's vernacular abounds with idiomatic expressions such as the warning he gave about boastful gardeners who do not know their work: "Who does not see from this / that not all are cooks / who brandish long knives" (vol. I, p. 73). He also translated into verse a fable told by Ferrari in his book on *Flora*. Two boys bent on mischief have neglected the garden left in their care and are punished by the goddess Flora who transforms them into a snail and a caterpillar – the twin scourge of all garden-owners. Volkamer wittily made near-anagrams out of this metamorphosis by playing on the boys' names "Schenck" (becoming *'Schnecke'*, meaning 'snail') and "Paur" (turned into *'Raupe'*, meaning 'caterpillar'). He also depicted the metamorphosis (p. 92) much more dramatically than Ferrari did: 'Paur's' transformation into a caterpillar is suggested by the hair growing on his hands – not mentioned in the Italian original – while 'Schenck', already changing into a snail, is crawling along on the ground.

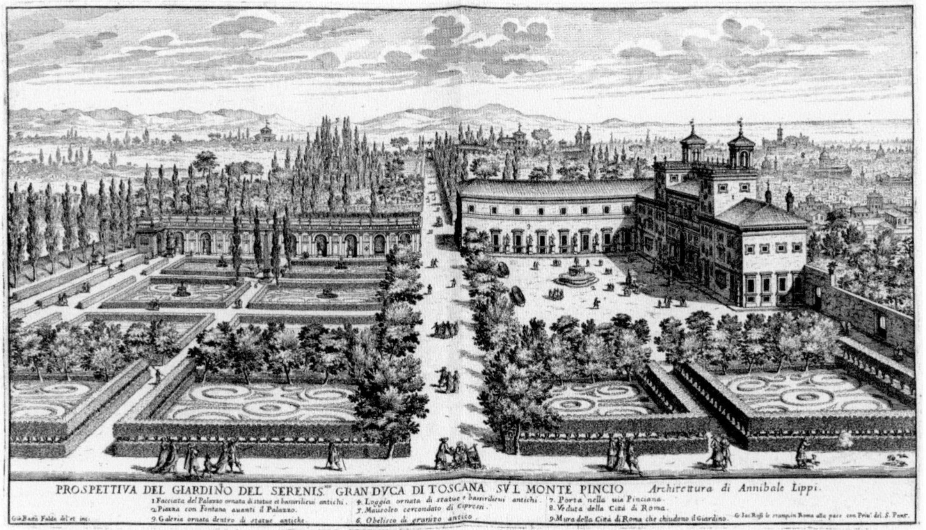

Heavenly fruits

The fruits and flowers, no matter whether large or small, are reproduced life-size in the plates illustrating both volumes of Volkamer's *Hesperides*, from blossoming auricula to coconuts, pineapples and pummelos. Some of the copperplates are clearly divided into representing a fruit at the top with a trompe-l'œil *veduta* beneath (e. g. pp. 211, 360). This arrangement, however, could not be used consistently throughout because the fruits vary so much in size, and it is this which led to the collage-like pictorial layout for which Volkamer's work is known, even if there are, of course, precedents in books on flowers published in Nuremberg around 1700 and in other botanical works (p. 82).

Readers of the first volume eager to see the reproductions of citrus fruits and flowers must be patient until Chapter 23 (p. 67). Along with detailed illustrations of the fruits, and the flowers which in this plate only are greatly magnified, Volkamer showed the famous Nuremberg observatory. Established on a rampart of the walled city in 1678 by Georg Christoph Eimmart, an astronomer and copperplate engraver, this public observatory was filled with visitors in May 1706, on the occasion of a total solar eclipse. This inclusion of a plate with citrus fruits depicted above the observatory expresses Volkamer's scientific drive and recalls the method by which he intended to present his findings, since

Giovanni Battista Falda, ***"Prospettiva del giardino del Serenis.mo Granduca di Toscana sul Monte Pincio"***
View of the Villa Medici in Rome / Ansicht der Villa Medici in Rom / Vue de la villa Médicis à Rome
Copperplate engraving and etching. From: Giovanni Battista Falda, *Li Giardini di Roma*, Rome, 1683
Munich, Bayerische Staatsbibliothek, Res/2 Ital. 61

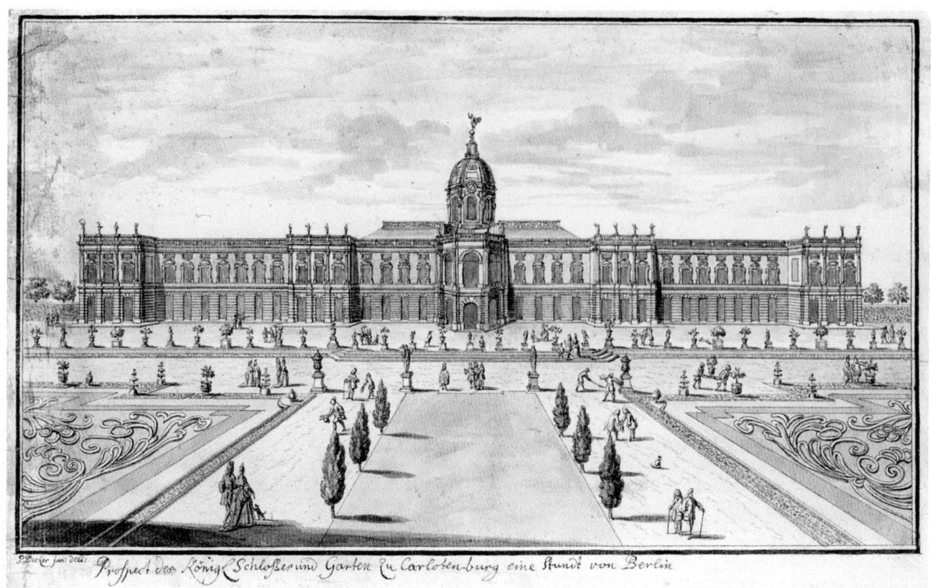

throughout the work he repeatedly notes that he used a "mycroscopium" or "magnifying glass". The explanation for the recurring layout used in the plates is that his aesthetic and scientific agenda is based on juxtaposing and contrasting close-up and distant, by means of a microscope as well as a telescope. Volkamer's distinctive bifocal collage technique presents the fruit life-size in close-up at the top and underneath a *veduta* viewed from a distance. The observatory plate also expresses Volkamer's interest in celestial bodies, a passion he shared with his father and many of his Nuremberg contemporaries. The combination of observatory and an enlargement of a microscopic view might even be interpreted as an allusion to the iconographic invention that unifies the copperplates in the *Hesperides*: after all, the precious fruits look like huge celestial bodies in the skies above each city, landscape and garden view.

In all three Volkamer volumes, the genus *Citrus* is subdivided into citrons (*Citrus medica* L., *Citrus limonimedica* L.), lemons and limes (*Citrus limon* L., *Citrus aurantiifolia* (Christm.) Swingle) and bitter oranges, sweet oranges and pummelos (*Citrus auran-*

Paul Decker the Younger
View of the Royal Palace and Gardens at Charlot[t]enburg, an hour from Berlin, *c.* 1706
Prospect des Königl[ichen] Schlosses und Garten zu Charlot[t]enburg eine Stundt von Berlin
Vue du château et du jardin royal de Charlot[t]enburg à une heure de Berlin
Pen and grey wash, 26.8 × 42.8 cm (10 ½ × 16 ⅞ in.)
Nuremberg, Germanisches Nationalmuseum, Graphische Sammlung, ZR 6562 Kaps 1077

tium L., *Citrus sinensis* L., *Citrus maxima* L.). Following the myth as related by Ferrari and other botanical writers, Volkamer assigned different fruits and their cultivation in various parts of Italy to each of the three Hesperides: Aegle is thus credited with cultivating citrons on the shores of Lake Garda, Arethusa is said to have brought lemons to the Ligurian coast and Hesperia was said to have introduced oranges to Calabria. The corresponding three parts of the first volume begin with allegorical representations of the Hesperides in turn in front of a garden, or with a lake or the sea in the background. The second volume presents the name of each sister within a decorative wreath on the three introductory pages, but no corresponding figurative representation has survived for the projected third volume.

In his commentaries on each variety of citrus, Volkamer has done his best to ensure accurate statements on the size, shape, colour and scent of the tree or shrub, its leaves, blossoms and fruits, when the fruits ripen and where they originally came from, as well as how the tree or shrub is to be cultivated. He is particularly interested in propagation, whether from seed, seedlings, leaves or even a thorn ("spine"). The overarching principle informing Volkamer's work is empirical observation, and the knowledge he imparted was gained from cultivating his own garden, often, in the course of invoking Ferrari or Commelin, deploring the controversies of classification and the lack of standardised botanical nomenclature. The commentary on each variety of citrus begins with a general description and an enumeration of the "usefulness and uses" of its fruits. The author makes frequent reference to the *Vollständiges Nürnbergisches Koch-Buch* (Nuremberg, 1691), a local cookery-book that contained a wealth of recipes for sweet and savoury dishes made with lemons, citrons and oranges. Citrus fruits, fresh or candied, were invariably a must at princely or patrician tables, whilst they were also indispensable to the making of the eau de cologne that was so popular in the Baroque era. Volkamer included an image of his 'scent room' in the orangery at Gostenhof as the fragrance of orange blossoms wafted through its windows into the room (pp. 243, 258/259).

Since citrus varieties tend to mutate spontaneously and because they were intensively cultivated in the Baroque era, in the 17th century huge variation developed in the forms of citrus trees and shrubs, blossoms, foliage and fruits. This was assiduously noted and described by gardeners and botanists and the mutations were – whenever possible – cultivated as new varieties. Volkamer listed numerous fruits that do not feature in Ferrari's work, and in fact, Volkamer's body of work reveals a diversity unknown in earlier works on citrus. Like Ferrari, he shows monstrous "grotesques" or "freaks", as he called unusual fruits he assumed had resulted from spontaneous mutation or from grafting. In Ferrari's work, there are certain extravagant or oddly furrowed fruit forms which look particularly bizarre (p. 71). Volkamer also showed several unusual varieties, including "fruit-bearing",

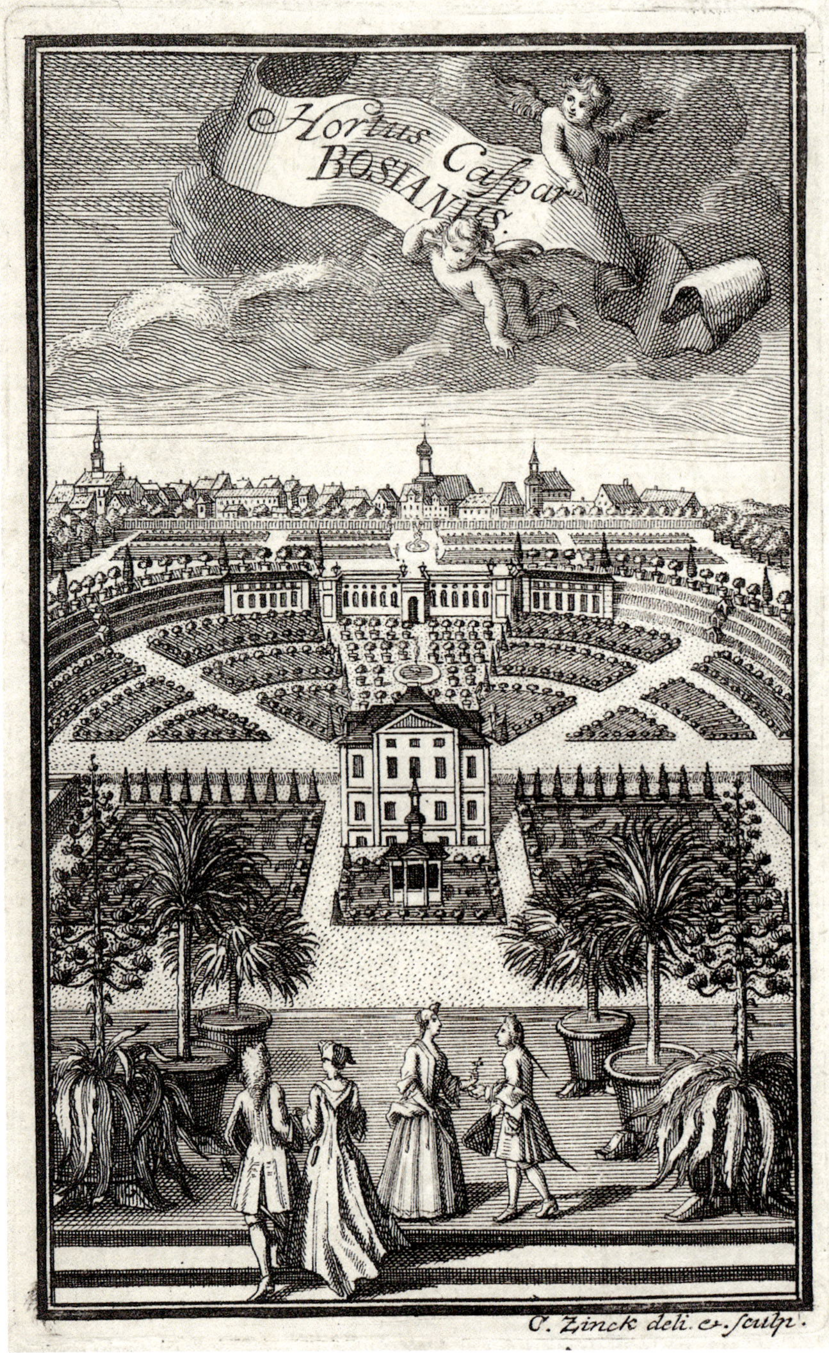
Hortus Caspar
BOSIANUS.
C. Zinck deli. & sculp.

i.e. "pregnant" *(fetifero)* fruits, such as an unusual "Cedro con frutto in frutto" [citron with a fruit inside the fruit] in the third volume, or other fruits he called "hermaphrodites" because of spurs on their peel. He does not seem to have known blood oranges, whilst the Mandarin orange *(Citrus reticulata Blanco)* was not introduced into Europe until the 19th century.

"Sulphurous yellow' and 'lemon-coloured": botany and visual representation

In his descriptive commentaries, Volkamer conveys subtly nuanced colour values for what were often iridescent, striped, patterned, chequered or mottled fruits, flowers, leaves and branches: for example, the "very dark and greenish-black colour" of the Pomo d'Adamo, which is also called a "black lemon" (vol. 1, p. 167); the "sulphurous yellow and green striped", "orange-yellow or deep saffron yellow", "light sulphurous yellow or lemon colour" of the Aranzo fiamato (vol. 1, p. 196); and the "many subtle greenish stripes" of fruits called "grotesques" (vol. 1, p. 172). Volkamer's original drawings of fruits, none of which seem to have survived unfortunately, are certain to have been coloured. The copperplates of the fruits reveal an attempt to extract from the graphic medium a subtle impression of the colour and veining of both fruits and leaves. Since the plates in the third volume were not coloured, however, readers must picture for themselves the differences in colour effects and representation made by these copperplates in comparison with the coloured plates in the first two volumes.

Several hand-coloured copies and a number of individual copperplates of the *Hesperides* have survived although with noticeably different colouring. The copy reproduced here was owned by the patrician Holzschuher family in Nuremberg and was coloured in the 18th century while still in their possession. Frequently blurring the patterns and colour variations of both fruits and leaves, its handling of colour does not allow the veining of these parts of the plant to stand out so clearly. Specific groupings of fruit are shown in uniform yellow, orange or light yellow, their foliage and branches in turquoise green. Even so, a few striped or otherwise patterned fruits are picked out attractively by the way in which they have been tinted. Unlike later colouration schemes, which on the whole avoid vibrant colours and tend to produce modest transitions, the copy here is notable for the way in which colour structures each picture. It is colour that emphasises close-up (fruit) and distance (the *veduta*), top and bottom. In most cases, the sky and clouds have

C. Zinck, **Orangery in Caspar Bose's Leipzig garden**
Orangerie im Garten des Caspar Bose in Leipzig / Orangerie du jardin de Caspar Bose à Leipzig
Engraving and etching. Title-page from Achatz Friedrich Wehmann, *Hortus Caspar Bosianus*, Leipzig, 1723
Universitätsbibliothek Erlangen-Nürnberg, H61/TREW.Ex 650

been added crisply in blue and white to 'divide the plates in half'. The bold colour tones used to depict the façades of villas in the Veneto, for instance – turquoise, pink, purple and even lemon yellow! – are, of course, not realistic. These vibrant colours do, however, appeal immediately to the noblest of the five senses, the visual, and achieve an attractive, highly decorative overall effect in these copperplates and vignettes, hence in the *Hesperides* as a whole. Essentially, careful colouration has transformed Volkamer's scholarly botanical work on citrus into a showcase of illustrated science.

Volkamer distinguished between citrus plants he knew only from fruits and leaves which had been sent to him and those he cultivated in his own garden to flower and bear fruit. He expressed his pride in having "industriously drawn" all the fruits in his book "from nature" (vol. I, p. 7). By the 17th century, Nuremberg had an established tradition of middle-class and patrician amateurs painting and drawing from nature. Volkamer therefore fitted in with local practice in taking up pen and pencil himself. The sole exception – according to his own statement – is a grapefruit picked in the Bose Gardens in Leipzig in 1705. It only bore the one fruit, as Volkamer tells it, so he had to have a drawing of it sent to him (vol. I, p. 173 and 189).

Far fewer varieties of citrus were available in Germany than south of the Alps, and so the usual practice was to procure them directly from Italy or to buy them at the Frankfurt and Leipzig trade fairs. In the first volume Volkamer gives a list of varieties that could be acquired around Lake Garda (vol. I, p. 107 f.). He recommends the way in which citrus is cultivated there, providing in one copperplate an example of a "limonaia" from one of the temporary orangeries of the kind still in use today on the shores of the lake (pp. 134/135). Volkamer also mentioned Genoa, which he knew from Joseph Furttenbach's account from 1627 of his travels in Italy, *Newes Itinerarium Italiae* (vol. II, fol. 78r), and featured the villa landscape and sea views around Genoa as well as nearby Nervi in large copperplates, although it is unlikely that he travelled there himself.

Primula, pistachio and pineapple

Apart from citrus, Volkamer grew and described other exotic, southern plants (p. 133), giving space to these at the end of each of his three volumes, as with the coffee tree, for example, in the third volume (p. 463). A work entitled *Flora Noribergensis, Oder Nürnbergische Flora* forms a fifth section of the first volume, but although it ultimately derives from the work of his brother, Johann Georg, it is not identical with the latter's more substantial work of the same name. In this fifth section can be found 66 representations of

Obeliscus Constantinopolitanus
From: *Nürnbergische Hesperides*, 1708, vol. I, appendix *Obeliscus*, plate IV

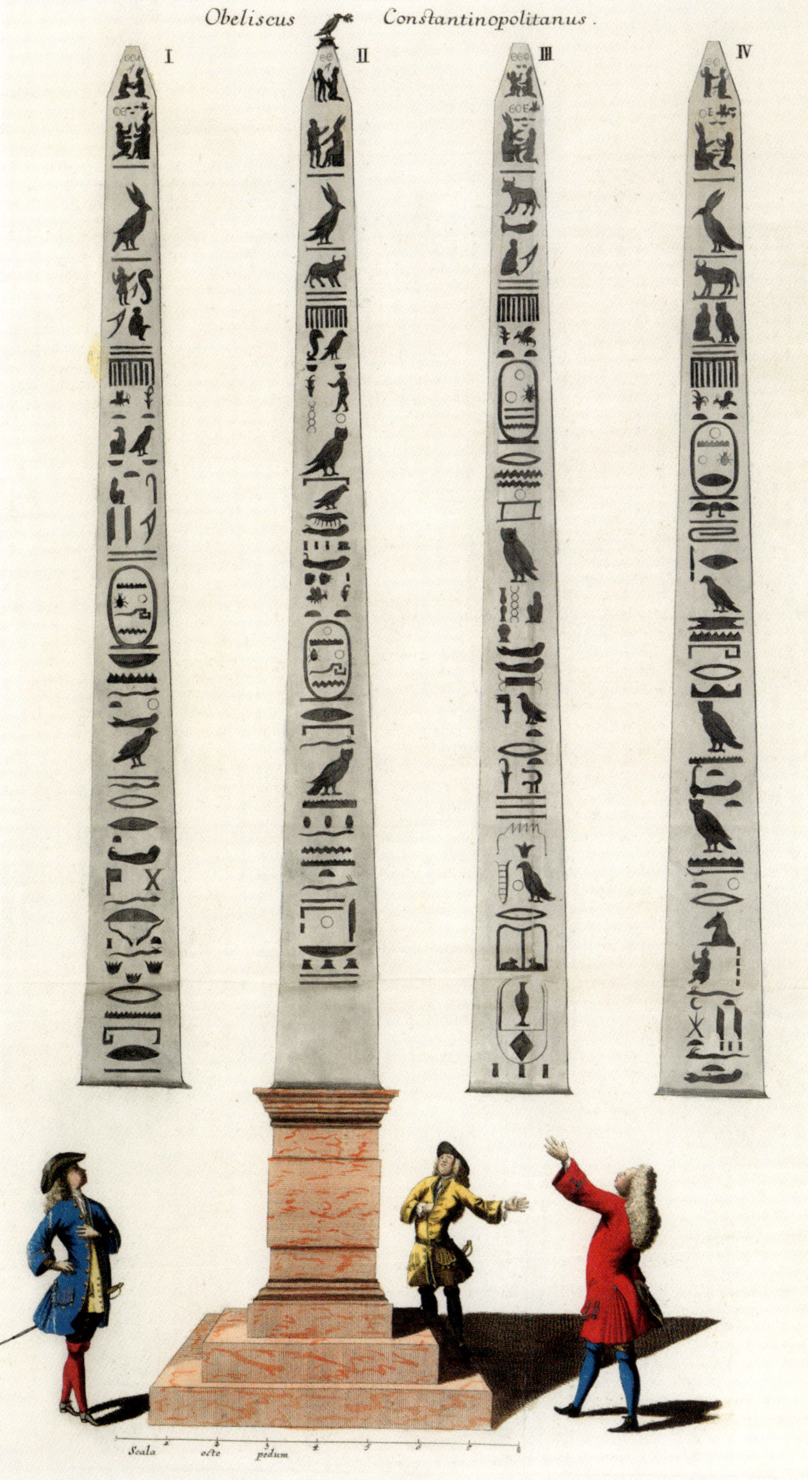
Obeliscus Constantinopolitanus.
I
II
III
IV
Scala octo pedum

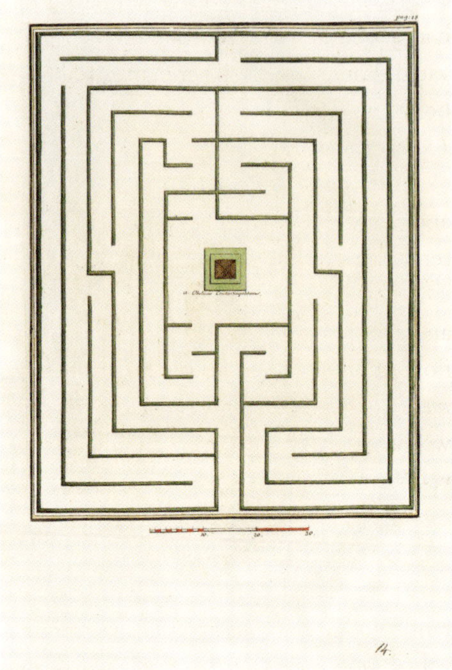

"Bear's Ear" (*Primula auricula* L.), an especially popular garden flower at the time, followed by 49 depictions of cowslips (*Primula veris* L.), in turn followed by representations of certain interesting, even spectacular flowers from Johann Georg's garden. From his own garden at Gostenhof, Johann Christoph described, among other exotics, the olive tree, bay tree and strawberry tree, the pistachio and aubergine. This last was regarded as unwholesome food because it "made people stupid or drove them mad" (vol. I, p. 243). The second volume of the *Hesperides* ends with descriptions of various palms, the dragon tree (genus *Dracaena*) and cotton plant, with special attention being given to the pineapple, the "Queen of Fruits", which had been cultivated in European greenhouses since the late 17th century. Michael Friedrich Lochner (1662–1720), a Nuremberg physician

Labyrinth in the Papafava garden in Padua
Labyrinth im Papafava-Garten in Padua / Labyrinthe dans le jardin Papafava à Padoue
From: *Continuation der Nürnbergischen Hesperidum*, 1714, vol. II, plate p. 17

Labyrinth in Volkamer's garden at Gostenhof
Labyrinth in Volkamers Garten in Gostenhof / Labyrinthe dans le jardin de Volkamer à Gostenhof
From: *Continuation der Nürnbergischen Hesperidum*, 1714, vol. II, plate p. 18

and naturalist who had studied with Johann Georg Volkamer in Italy in 1684–1685 and had acquired the Hummelstein manor near Nuremberg in 1691 where he then cultivated exotic and southern plants, published a work on the pineapple in 1716. It was later bound in with some copies of the *Hesperides (Commentatio de Ananasa sive nuce pinea Indica, vulgo Pinhas).*

In his descriptions of fruits such as pineapples, but also humming-birds, cockroaches and tarantulas, Volkamer consulted the works of Maria Sibylla Merian (1647–1717), a contemporary of almost the same age who had lived in Nuremberg from 1670 until 1681. The famous naturalist knew the Volkamers through family and scholarly connections and exchanged ideas with Johann Georg the Younger on her research into the insects and flora of Suriname in South America. Her sensational *Metamorphosis Insectorum Surinamensium* (pp. 104, 105, 107) was published in 1705. Johann Christoph Volkamer was also well acquainted with Merian, and in 1706 he was even sent a pummelo from Suriname via Amsterdam, where she was then living.

Botanical networking

Johann Christoph Volkamer – like his brother and his father – exchanged ideas constantly with numerous garden-owners and gardeners in Germany and abroad. He received valuable information from Hamelin, Hamburg, Leipzig, Dresden, Breslau, Bohemia, Holland, Italy, Spain, South America (Suriname, Curaçao), the Cape of Good Hope at the southern tip of Africa and many other places near and far. Fruits, seedlings, seeds and even entire plants, with either naked roots or root balls, were sent to him. His Italian correspondents worked in places his father and brother had also visited while studying in Italy (including Padua, Bologna, Rome and Naples). Unfortunately, Johann Christoph's letters have not survived, and in the *Hesperides* he only mentions by name a handful of the people with whom he exchanged ideas and corresponded. More frequently he simply refers to them as "good friends".

Botanical research in the early modern age operated by means of extensive international networks. One of the largest collections of correspondence on medicine, botany and the natural sciences was amassed by Christoph Jakob Trew (1695–1769), a Nuremberg physician and botanist. He too came from a scholarly family and also knew the Volkamers. Both Johann Georg Volkamer senior and junior are represented in Trew's collection by a copious correspondence with like-minded scholars throughout the world. They exchanged ideas with gardeners and botanists, and their gardens and places of work are also mentioned in the *Hesperides.* Checking such references systematically against the extant correspondence of Johann Christoph's father and brother makes it possible to identify some of these "good friends" of the author without too much difficulty. The gardener of Schwöbber Palace, for instance, was Johann Friedrich Berner, whose correspondence from the years 1712 to 1717 has survived.

Plant inventories and citrus catalogues are also mentioned when they were included with letters written to the Volkamers, as, for example, a list of citrus varieties sent from Padua in 1717 by Giorgio Cornaro to the Volkamers in Nuremberg. Several letters written to Johann Georg mention his brother, Johann Christoph, when the sender wanted to do him the favour of sending him citrus trees or fruits. The Trew collection makes abundantly clear that Johann Christoph Volkamer in his research into citrus plants made use of contacts that existed between his family and the Nuremberg scientific community. For the historical study of networking for research purposes, therefore, the *Hesperides* represents both a boon and a challenge.

Mundus in litteris – the world in a book: Nuremberg, Padua, Bologna, Beijing, Cape Town, Curaçao

"For my first Nuremberg *Hesperidibus*, I / had, along with the fruits that were drawn, a great many views and gardens / in this area around Nuremberg / depicted from life and printed. However, because / while this work was in preparation / I kept thinking of Italy / and remembered with the greatest of pleasure the very fine palaces / which, to my great astonishment, the aristocracy in Venice own, both those that have stood for a long time and others that have recently been built / on the River Brenta / from Padua almost as far as Venice, / I took the decision / to have the very same / and other outstanding buildings that have been erected there / captured in copperplates / and to place / extravagantly magnificent Italian views and palaces / beneath the fruits reproduced. It cost me no little effort / until I ran into a good friend / who travelled through the same landscape / drawing most accurately from life right down to all the cracks in the stone; also adding some views of Verona and Bologna. Even so, I have finally succeeded in this respect / and my wish has, therefore, been granted / and so I have been able to adorn each of all the different types of fruit / with a splendid palace / or with another lovely Italian view" (vol. II, Preamble).

Volkamer's *Hesperides* is thus a compendium which is just as informative about topographical features as it is instructive on botany. Generally speaking, there is no specific link associating any particular fruit with the buildings or city view reproduced with it. Quite the contrary, in fact, since Volkamer evidently allocated his representations on the purely pragmatic basis of size. The *vedute* are grouped by region and thereby also convey a sense of local colour.

The author's close ties with his native city are the reason for the reproductions in the first volume of manor houses, castles and gardens in and around Nuremberg and, at

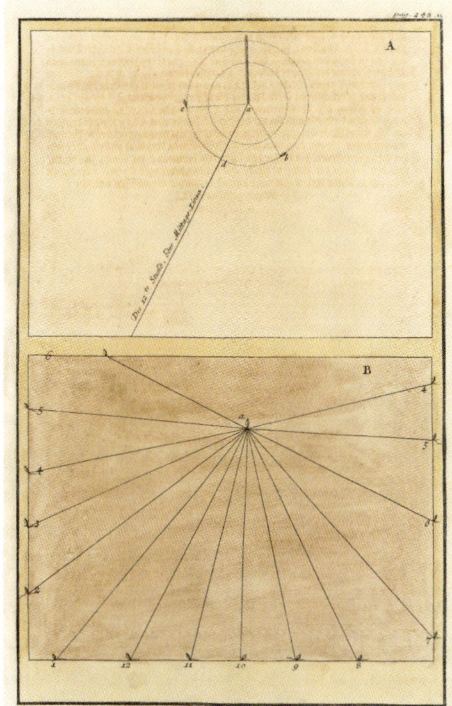

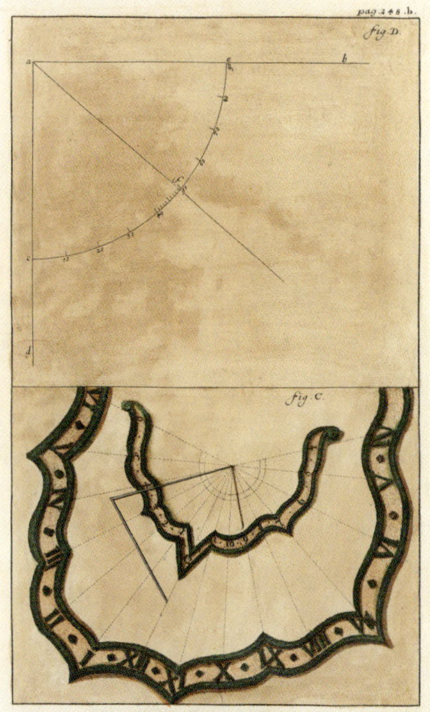

the end of the book, views of the surrounding landscape. Many of the Nuremberg views are taken from copperplates engraved by Johann Alexander Boener (1647–1720), who was an acquaintance of Volkamer's. The last decade of the 17th century and the first decade of the 18th were the most productive period of Boener's career (p. 111).

A number of well-known Nuremberg gardens are missing from the *Hesperides*, presumably because no Boener design existed that could be adapted for use as an illustration. It is also safe to assume that, rather than doing the work himself, Volkamer left the task of adapting Boener's *vedute* to the format required for the plates in the *Hesperides* to the copperplate engravers who would produce the plates. The proportions had to be changed, usually to make them narrower, while they were also embellished with a painterly foreground and often an equally fictitious landscape background. It is interesting to note that Volkamer himself gave instructions for adapting one garden layout plan to a view

Plan of the boxwood sundial at Gostenhof
Plan der Buchsbaum-Sonnenuhr in Gostenhof / Plan du cadran solaire en buis à Gostenhof
From: *Nürnbergische Hesperides*, 1708, vol. 1, plates pp. 248a and 248b

that needed to be corrected for linear perspective (pp. 108, 109; vol. 1, pp. 249–251). For the *vedute* – but not the fruit! – Volkamer undoubtedly allowed artistic licence, making concessions in the interests of promoting the aesthetic quality of the representation. The large-format Nuremberg views created by Johann Adam Delsenbach (1687–1765), a draughtsman and copper engraver, were not published until about 1715 and so were not available as models when the first volume of Volkamer's work went to press.

However, Delsenbach did contribute a plate showing St Georgen near Bayreuth (pp. 264/265) and a bird's-eye view of Schönbrunn Palace and its gardens (pp. 262/263) to the second volume of the *Hesperides*. Volkamer had large-scale *vedute* of the gardens in Erlangen (pp. 266–269), at Schwöbber Palace (pp. 23, 274) and in Passau (pp. 276, 277) engraved after earlier designs by the Decker brothers and other draughtsmen. Some of the copperplate engravers who worked on the *Hesperides* were also employed by Paul Decker the Elder for his great book on architecture, *Fürstlicher Baumeister* (Augsburg, 1711–1713). The second volume of the *Hesperides* ends with views of Villa Allegri in Cuzzano di Grezzana (pp. 270/271), other villas and gardens on the Brenta, in Padua (p. 63), Verona (pp. 24, 119) and the Euganean Hills, together with two *vedute* of Bologna. The Republic of Venice and the Free City of Nuremberg were on a comparable footing since they were both sovereign polities. The aristocracy of Venice and Padua spent their summers *(villeggiatura)* in the country, while the summer holidays taken by Nuremberg patricians similarly represented an aristocratic, urbane interpretation of a leisured culture of country living rather than a courtly lifestyle. The name of the man commissioned by Johann Christoph Volkamer to capture "from life" the Venetian villas where citrus plants were also cultivated is unknown. Volkamer's draughtsman must, however, have been close to Vincenzo Coronelli (1650–1718), a Venetian cartographer who was also a Franciscan friar. A collection of *vedute* by Coronelli was published in 1711; depicting the villas on the Brenta, these illustrations are surprisingly similar in structure to the plates in Volkamer's work (p. 116). The selections, however, are not identical, and since some of the buildings are only found in the *Hesperides*, Volkamer's work must also be viewed as a magisterial source for the architectural history of the Veneto villa culture.

The same holds for the villas owned by the aristocracy of Bologna depicted in the copperplates for the third projected volume which have only recently come to light. Both Johann Georg Volkamer the Elder and Johann Georg the Younger had spent time as students in the venerable university city of Bologna (p. 127), which had, since time immemorial, been called *"la dotta, la grassa"* ("the learned, the rich"). Since the 17th century, one of the city's chief industries had been the manufacture of silk. That may explain why Johann Christoph also maintained commercial links with Bologna, which at the time was part of the Papal States. The characteristic presentation of the city of Bologna (pp. 124, 411) corresponds to the way Nuremberg is showcased in the first volume: at the top is a "Cedro dolce", with a skyline of churches and towers beneath it. Volkamer borrowed this *veduta* of Bologna from the title-page (p. 124) of Giuseppe Maria Mitelli's *Le Arti per Via* (Bologna, 1660). In his *Dissertatio* (1713), as mentioned earlier, Erhard Reusch named two important naturalists from Bologna: Ulisse Aldrovandi in Bologna and Ovidio Montalbano, both of whom had had a scholarly interest in citrus (p. 72). Aldrovandi's collections were incorporated into the Istituto delle Scienze, one of the most prestigious scientific academies of its day (est. 1711). The botanists who worked there included Lelio Trionfetti (1647–1722) and his successor as director of the Botanical Gardens, Giuseppe Monti (1682–1760), both of whom corresponded with the Volkamers in Nuremberg. Monti even named Nuremberg as the only city in Germany – alongside several other significant botanical gardens elsewhere in Europe – with whose specialists he exchanged ideas, and regularly quoted from Johann Georg Volkamer's *Flora* as well as the *Hesperides*.

Since the late 16th century, the aristocracy had built country houses in the environs of Bologna, especially on the slopes and summits of the hills to the south and southwest of the city. This trend shows up on maps of Bologna dating from the late 17th century and from around 1700 (such as Agostino Mitelli's 1692 map of Bologna). While this flourishing villa culture figures prominently in literature and the theatre, it was seldom mentioned in travel accounts of the time or even in descriptions of cities. In the 17th and 18th centuries, most travellers to the area from abroad were on their Grand Tour – upper-class young men visiting the cultural highlights of Italy to finish off their education with a flourish. They tended to stay only briefly in Bologna before going on to Florence, Rome or Naples, the leading cultural and political centres. The tradition of travel guides and opulent copperplate series was upheld above all in Rome, the seat of the Papacy, where publishing houses made the most of it. While Bologna was part of the Papal States, unlike Rome it did not have any-thing like Rome's facilities for illustrating works on secular architecture. The earliest *vedute* of Bologna, which were copied over and over again for decades, come from a topographical work by the map engraver Jan Blaeu, who published a series of eight views of Bologna in 1663. The first extensive series of *vedute* was not published until 1732, when Johann Georg Merz, a printer in Augsburg, published a number of copperplates produced by Friedrich Bernhard Werner, a Silesian engraver. These were followed in the late 18th century by a series of copperplates by Pio Panfili, however, no villas or gardens feature in either of these series, nor do they appear in other *vedute* of

Editor's note regarding the plate captions: The botanical names and classifications follow Volkamer's data. The location details are listed in English using modern spelling. In some cases this has resulted in discrepancies compared with the original inscriptions on the plates. The index of places in the appendix also includes the German and French location details.

Bologna published in the late 18th and early 19th centuries. Viewed in this context, the copperplates in the third volume of the *Hesperides* deserve closer scrutiny. The palaces and gardens of the great aristocratic families of Bologna are reproduced here along with La Montagnola, which served as an urban promenade in Bologna (p. 409), and the well-known pilgrimage church of San Michele in Bosco (p. 424), whilst the Madonna di San Luca is featured in the second volume (p. 388). Cavernous country inns in spectacular rural settings (p. 413) look at first sight like stage sets for Verdi's *Rigoletto*. Individual motifs in certain plates have been taken from various earlier designs – such as copperplates by Agostino Mitelli or Georg Andreas Böckler – and arbitrarily recombined. Architectural motifs, such as the fortress-like *palazzi* bristling with crenellations, aqueducts and views of fountains, have been turned into *capricci*, whimsically eclectic views of Bologna or the surrounding Emilian countryside with an emphasis on local attractions. This approach is most obvious in a plate featuring the Giambologna statue of Neptune which has been spirited away from the centre of Bologna to adorn some fictitious garden (p. 435). Even though the handling of perspective in these *vedute* looks amateurish, they still richly deserve to be treated as important examples of pictorial documentation.

The captions to the preliminary drawings held in the Germanisches Nationalmuseum are also from the hand of an Italian who was familiar with the region (p. 123). Without them, there would be no information regarding the aspects of the buildings and facilities they describe. Unfortunately, however, the name of the man who "drew them from life" is unknown in this case as well. Might it have been Vincenzo Coronelli, who is said to have planned to write a travel guide to the city of Bologna in 1713? It is, on the other hand, highly unlikely to have been Johann Jakob Schübler, a Nuremberg architect whose name appears on the back of one of the preliminary drawings.

The last plates in the second and third volumes of the *Hesperides* feature *vedute* of Nazareth, Beijing, Cape of Good Hope (p. 128) and Brazil. Johann Christoph Volkamer's intellectual horizons were so broad that they encompassed far more than Europe alone. *Mundus in litteris* – the world of the intellect, of science, which Volkamer, merchant and citrus collector, inhabited – is mirrored in his *Hesperides*.

Wilhelm Pfann, after Johann Christoph Volkamer, **Columna Milliaria**
Milestone / Meilensäule / Colonne milliaire
From: *Nürnbergische Hesperides*, 1708, vol. 1, plate after p. 255

Pages 46/47
Paul Decker the Younger, **Volkamer's garden at Gostenhof near Nuremberg**
Volkamers Garten in Gostenhof bei Nürnberg / Le jardin de Volkamer à Gostenhof, près de Nuremberg
From: *Nürnbergische Hesperides*, 1708, vol. 1, plate after p. 8

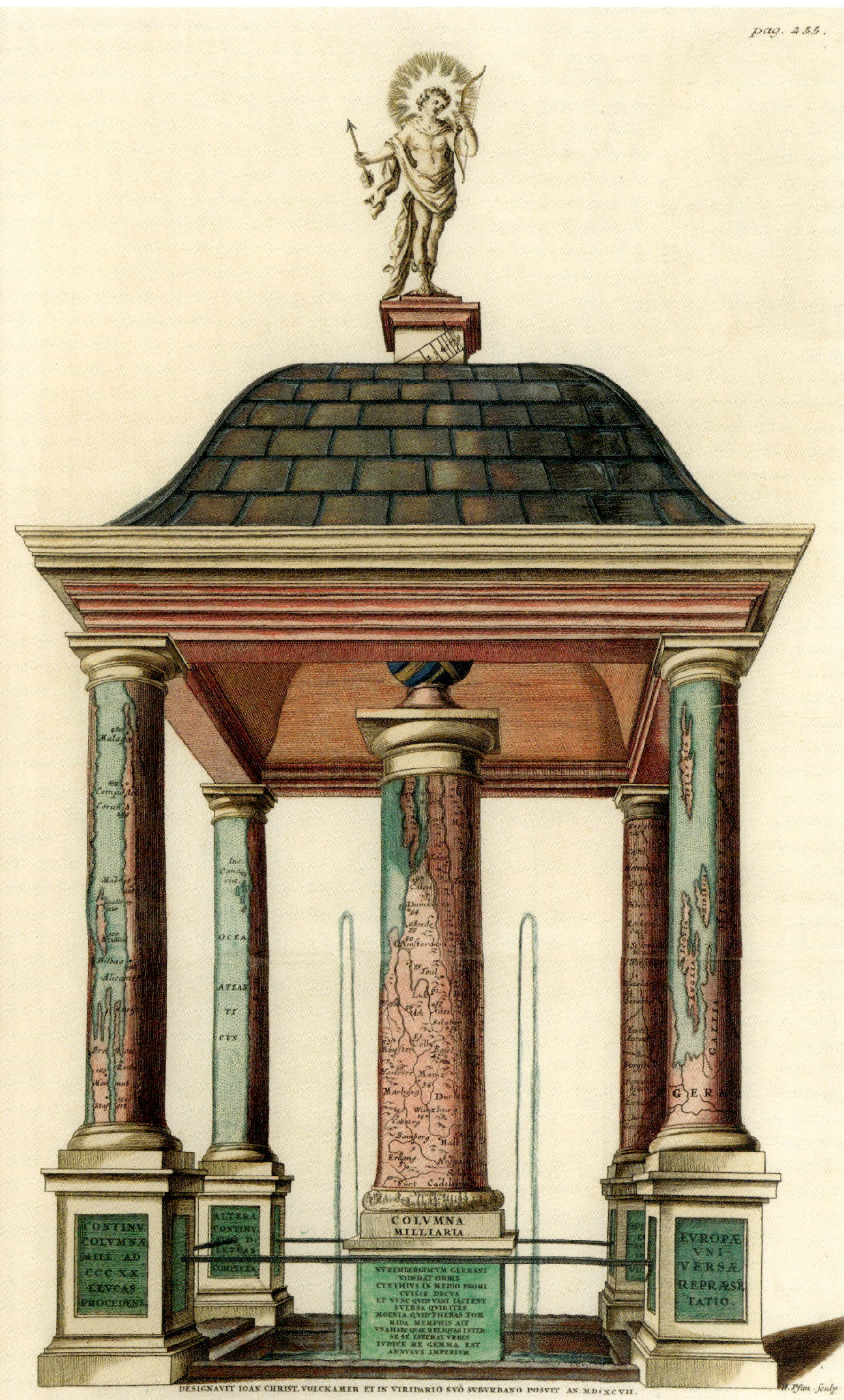
CONTINV. COLVMNÆ MILL. AD CCCXX LEVCAS PROCEDENS
ALTERA CONTINV. AD D. LEVCAS COMPLEXA
COLVMNA MILLIARIA
NVREMBERGIACVM GERMANI VIDERAT ORBIS CYNTHIVS IN MEDIO PROMI CVISSE DECVS ET NVNC QVID VANI IACTENT EVERSA QVIRITES MOENIA QVID THEBAS TOR RIDA MEMPHIS AIT VNA HAEC QVAE RELIQVAS INTER SE SE EFFERAT VRBES IVDICE ME GEMMA EST ANNVLVS IMPERIVM
EVROPÆ VNIVERSÆ REPRÆSETATIO.
DESIGNAVIT IOAN CHRIST. VOLCKAMER ET IN VIRIDARIO SVÒ SVBVRBANO POSVIT AN. MDCXCVII.
W. Pfan. sculp.

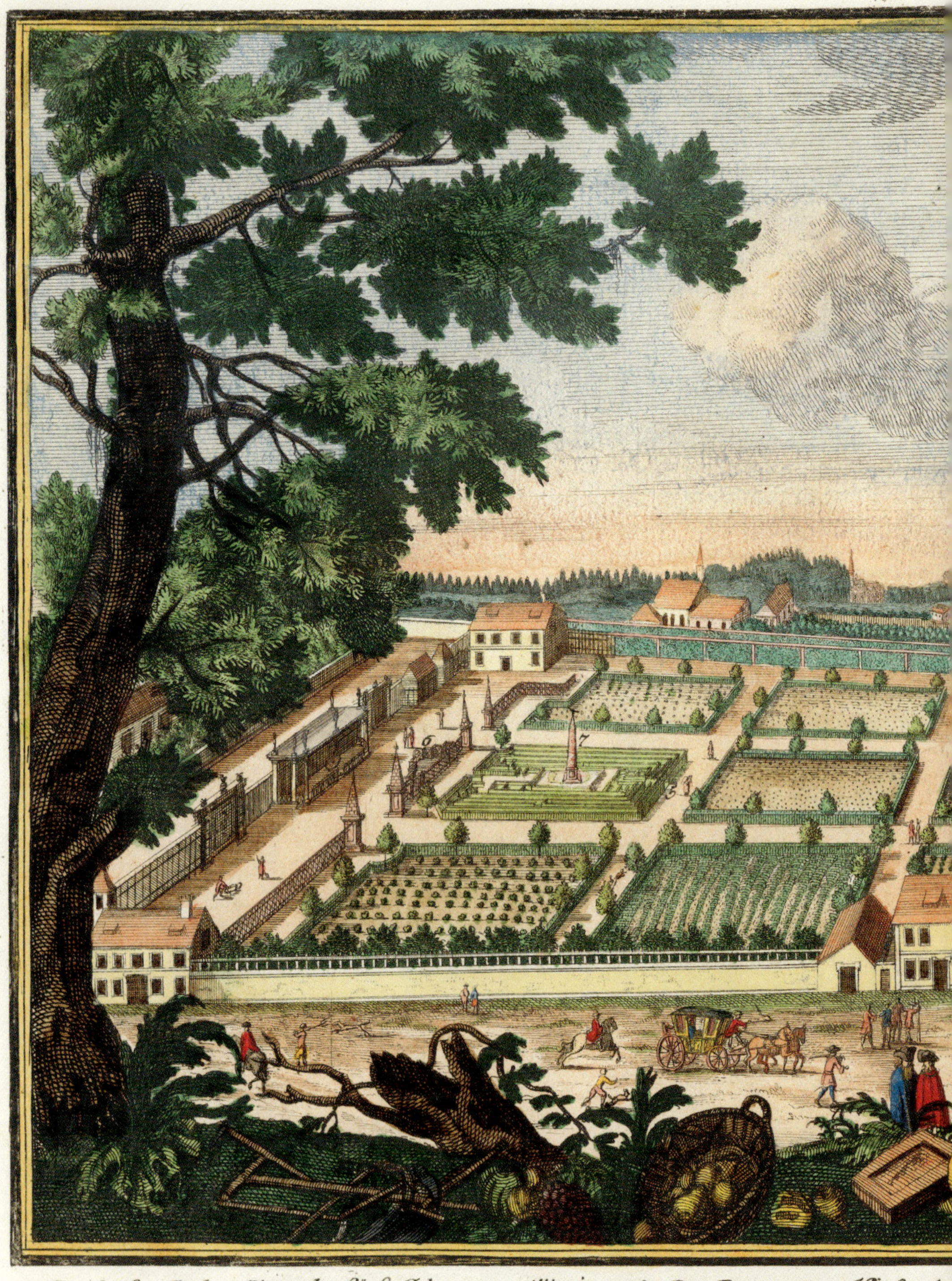

pag. 8

1. Das Waßer-Rad. 2 Platz der fünf Columnen milliarien. 3. Das Pomeranzen-Hauß. 4
7 Obeliscus Constantinopolitanus a

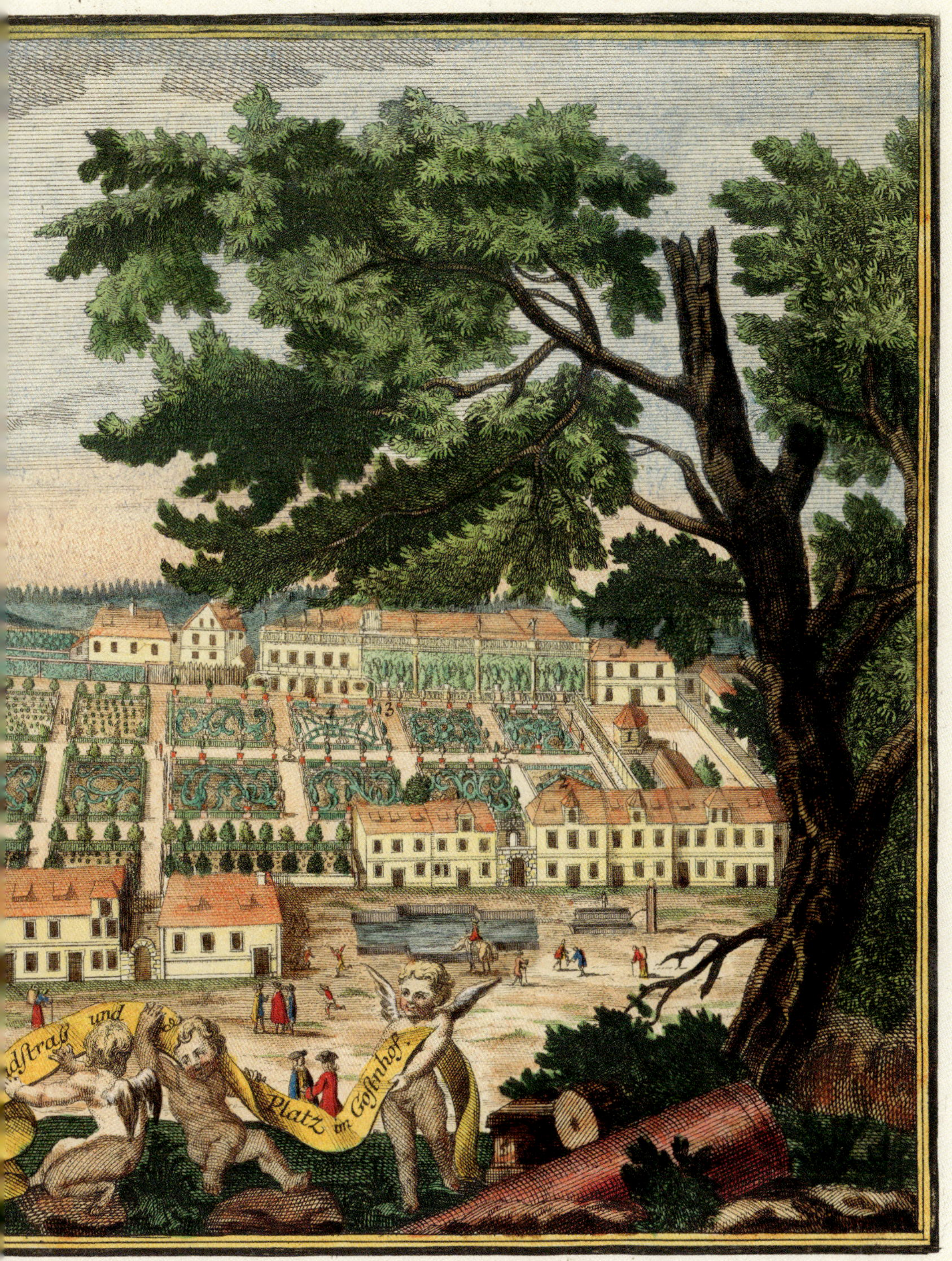

Sonnen-Uhr von Bux: . 5 . Der Irrgarten . 6 . Das Schild Crotten Weyerlein . P. Decker fec:
nem stück stein 20½ schuhlang .

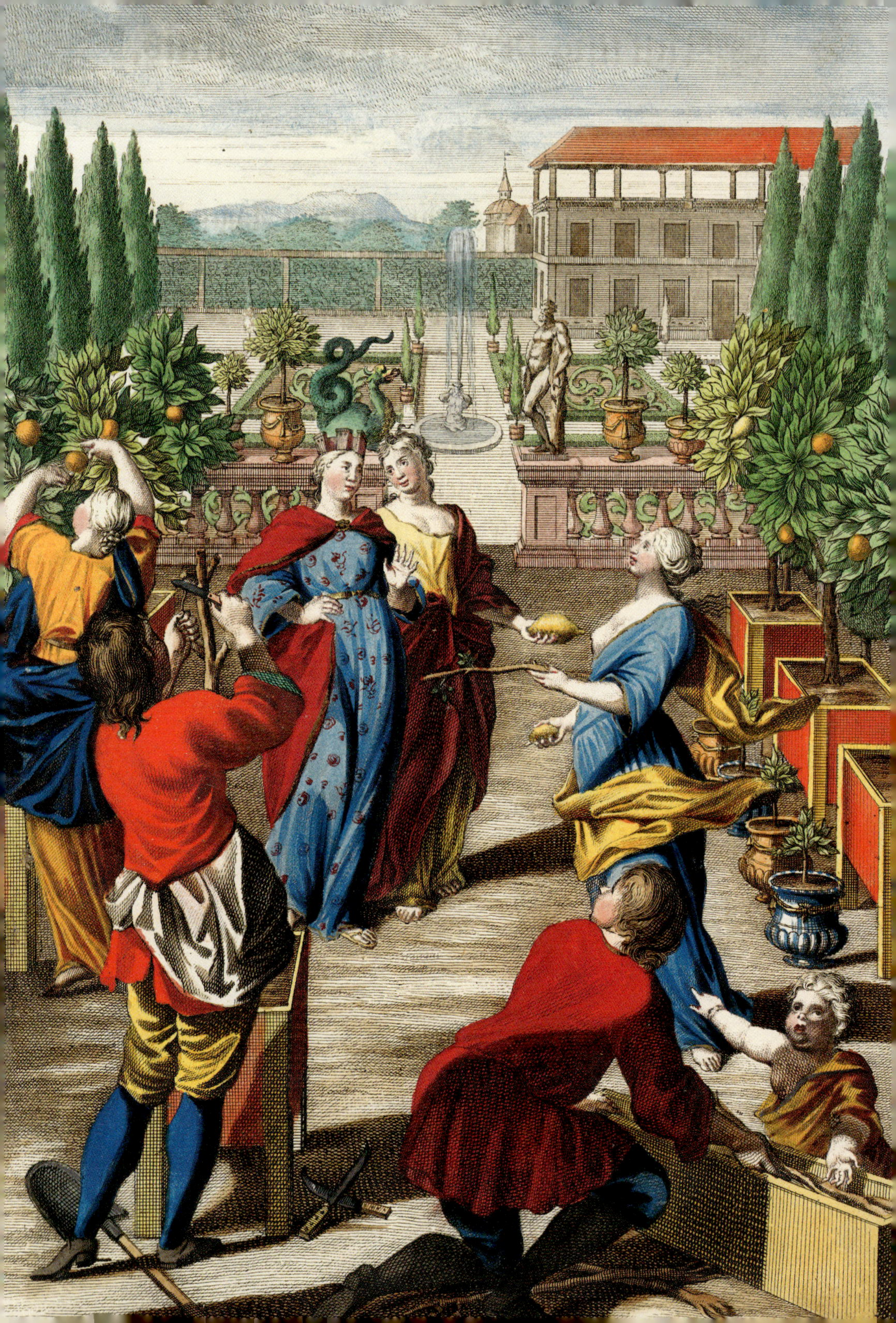

„Himmlische Früchte“ Johann Christoph Volkamers Hesperidenwerk

IRIS LAUTERBACH

„Der Orangen- oder Pommerantzen-Baum ist unwidersprechlich der schönste unter allen wegen ihrer Blüthe hochgeachteten Bäumen. Sein gerader Stamm, sein gleiches und ebenes Holtz, seine grosse und gläntzende Blätter, seine schöne Blüthen, seine vortreffliche Früchte, seine wohleingerichtete Crone und sehr schöne Grüne, sind durchgehends so beschaffen, daß man sie bewundern muß. Man theilet die Orangerien in vielerley Sorten, als Citronen, Limonen, Bergamoten, Adams-Aepffel, Chinesische Pommerantzen, etc. deren Unterschied darinnen bestehet, daß die einen hochstämmig, die andern aber niedrig, und daß bey den einen die Frucht süß, bey den andern aber herb ist. Sie behalten ihre schöne Blätter allezeit.“

Der französische Gartentheoretiker Antoine-Joseph Dezallier d'Argenville (1680–1765) fasst mit diesen Worten die Faszination, die im Barockzeitalter von der Zitrus ausging, sowie die Bedeutung der Orangeriekultur für den klassischen französischen Garten zusammen (*La théorie et la pratique du jardinage*; deutsche Übersetzung: *Die Gärtnerey, so wohl in ihrer Theorie oder Betrachtung, als Praxis oder Übung*, Augsburg 1731, S. 269). Seinem einflussreichen Buch zur Theorie und Praxis der Gartenkunst, das 1709 in Paris erschienen war, fügte er 1713 in der zweiten Auflage zwei Kapitel zur Zitruskultur hinzu.

Mit schlankem Wuchs, immergrüner Blätterpracht, mit Blüten und leuchtend farbigen Früchten erfreuen die Zitrusbäume das Auge; die Früchte und kandierten Schalen erfrischen mit ihrem aromatischen Geschmack die Zunge; der Duft ätherischer Öle aus Früchten und Blüten betört die Nase. Wie viele Gartenautoren des 17. und 18. Jahrhunderts festhielten, erweckten die immergrünen, gleichzeitig blühenden

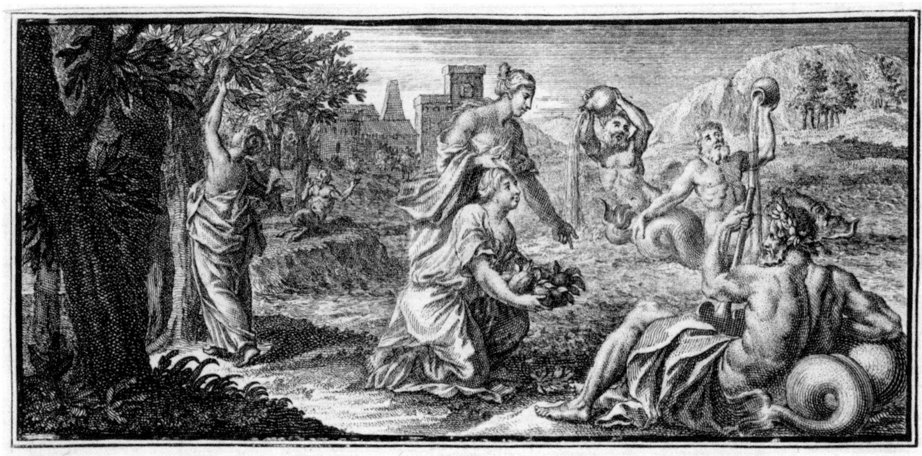

und fruchtenden Bäume in Orangerien die Vorstellung einer zeitlosen, paradiesischen Glückseligkeit: „Denn wenn im Winter vor Frost und grosser Kälte alles erstorben, ja alles mit tieffen Schnee bedecket ist, und der grausame Nordwind dermassen wütet, daß es nicht anders läst, als wenn er die gantze Natur bestürmen und über einen Hauffen werfen wolte, so siehet man in diesen herrlichen Paradieß-Garten, mit der allergrösten Verwunderung, wie die allerschönsten und raresten Bäumlein in so mancherley Gestalt, daher grünen und blühen, eines hat weisse liebliche wohlriechende Blumen ein anders gelbe, das dritte rothe, das vierdte Purpurfarben, und dergleichen, das eine hat zeitige, das andere unzeitige Früchte, alles mit dem allerschönsten durchdringenden Geruche, und muß ja einen Menschen als in einen steten Frühling eine neue Erquickung geben." (Hesse 1706, S. 35 f.).

Die goldenen Äpfel der Hesperiden, von deren lateinischer Bezeichnung als *poma aurantia* sich das Wort Pomeranze ableitet, sind Zitrusfrüchte. Der antike Mythos hebt

Page 48
Paul Decker the Younger, **Noris and the Hesperides in Volkamer's garden at Gostenhof**
Noris und die Hesperiden in Volkamers Garten in Gostenhof
Noris et les Hespérides dans le jardin de Volkamer à Gostenhof
Frontispiece from *Continuation der Nürnbergischen Hesperidum*, 1714, vol. II

The Hesperides presenting a river god with the gift of citrus fruits
Die Hesperiden bieten einem Flussgott Zitrusfrüchte dar
Les Hespérides offrent des agrumes à un dieu du fleuve
Engraving and etching. Vignette for the unpublished third volume of *Nürnbergische Hesperides*, 1714–1720
Universitätsbibliothek Erlangen-Nürnberg, H61/2 RAR.A 35[2, p. 3

die Kostbarkeit der Früchte hervor, die auch irdische Gärten dem Paradies gleichen lassen. Im mythischen Garten der Götter steht der sagenumwobene Baum mit den goldenen Früchten, bewacht von dem Drachen Ladon und gehegt von drei Nymphen – den Hesperiden Aegle, Arethusa und Hesperthusa –, den Töchtern des Atlas und der Nacht. Der Name der Hesperiden geht auf den Abendstern Hesperos, den Stern der Venus, zurück. Der Tugendheld Herkules überwindet den Drachen und erringt die wertvollen Früchte, die ihm von den Hesperiden dargeboten werden. Bereits im Mythos kommt die hohe Wertschätzung der Gattung Zitrus – des Baums ebenso wie der Früchte – zum Ausdruck wie auch die besondere Zuwendung, die für ihre Kultur – die Aufzucht und Pflege – erforderlich ist.

Der Ursprung der Zitrus, der Agrumen, die zu den ältesten Kulturpflanzen gehören, liegt in verschiedenen Regionen Asiens. In Südchina lässt sich bereits vor 4000 Jahren die Orange (*Citrus sinensis* L.) nachweisen. Im 15. oder frühen 16. Jahrhundert brachten Genueser und portugiesische Kaufleute hochkultivierte Sorten der süßen Orange nach Italien. Die ursprünglich ebenfalls aus Asien stammende Bitterorange oder Pomeranze (*Citrus aurantium* L.), die Zitrone (*Citrus limon* L.) und die Limone (*Citrus aurantiifolia* (Christm.) Swingle) gelangten aus Asien in den Vorderen Orient und wurden von dort vermutlich durch die Kreuzritter nach Italien eingeführt, während die Zedratzitrone (*Citrus medica* L., *Citrus limonimedica* L.) in Italien spätestens im ersten vorchristlichen Jahrhundert heimisch gewesen sein muss. Im arabischen und maurischen Kulturkreis bereits im Mittelalter bekannt, wurden Bitterorangen und Zitronen seit dem 14. Jahrhundert in der Toskana kultiviert. Der jahrtausendelange Züchtungsprozess der Zitrus hatte mit der Zeit eine große Anzahl an Varianten und Formen hervorgebracht.

Zitruspflanzen am Fürstenhof: Heraldisches Motiv und Sammlungsobjekt

In der Kultur der Fürstenhöfe der Frühen Neuzeit etablierte sich in der Herrscherikonografie neben Apoll vor allem Herkules als starker Tugendheld und damit Identifikationsfigur. Kopien der berühmten Monumentalskulptur des Herkules aus der Sammlung Farnese, der in seiner Hand die drei Äpfel der Hesperiden hält (S. 8), schmücken zahlreiche Gärten des Barock und ließen den von den Hesperiden gehüteten mythischen Garten der Götter assoziieren. Die Kultur der Zitrus wurde im Verlauf des 16. und 17. Jahrhunderts zu einer wichtigen Herausforderung. Die Familie Medici, ursprünglich Kaufleute, die zum Herrschergeschlecht des Herzogtums Toskana aufgestiegen waren, setzte die lateinische Bezeichnung *malus medica* für die Zitronat-Zitrone in Beziehung zu ihrem Familiennamen und sah in den Agrumen heraldische Früchte, die den Kugeln im Medici-Wappen ähneln. Im Boboli-Garten in Florenz und im Garten der Villa Medici in Castello findet sich noch heute eine der ältesten, größten und an Varietäten reichsten Agrumensammlungen Europas. Die Zitrusbäume wurden seit dem 16. Jahrhundert als vegetabile Kostbarkeiten in Gärten gezeigt; ihre Früchte wurden – künstlerisch nachgebildet aus Wachs, Keramik und später Porzellan oder wiedergegeben auf Gemälden (S. 11) – zu Kunstkammerobjekten und Exponaten fürstlicher Sammlungen (S. 57). Die heraldische Relevanz der Früchte für das niederländische Herrscherhaus Oranien ließ im 17. Jahrhundert auch Holland, besonders die botanischen Gärten in Leiden und Amsterdam, zu Zentren der Zitruskultur werden.

Zitrus nördlich der Alpen: Wunsch, Wirtschaft, Wissenschaft

Nicht nur bei fürstlichen Besuchern, auch in der Welt der Gelehrten, Dichter und Kaufleute stießen die mit Skulpturen, Monumenten, Brunnen und sinnlich betörenden Gewächsen wie den Agrumen ausgestatteten italienischen Gärten der Renaissance auf große Begeisterung. So hatte der Frankfurter Bürgermeister Johann Schwind seine Leidenschaft für die Gartenkunst (Merian 1641), „einen starcken Feuerfunken zur Entzündung dieses Geistes […] auf der vor wenigen Jahren getanen italienischen Reisen empfangen" (S. 12). Auch Johann Christoph Volkamer (1644–1720) dachte häufig an seinen Aufenthalt in Italien und erinnerte sich „der überaus schönen Palläste vergnüglichst" (Bd. II, Vor-Ansprach). Johann Wolfgang von Goethes berühmtes sehnsüchtiges Lied des Mädchens Mignon in *Wilhelm Meisters Lehrjahre[n]* (1795/96) bringt die Faszination Italiens als Land der üppigen Gärten zum Ausdruck: „Kennst du das Land? wo die Zitronen blühn, / Im dunklen Laub die Gold-Orangen glühn, / Ein sanfter Wind vom blauen Himmel weht, / die Myrte still und hoch der Lorbeer steht, / Kennst du es wohl?"

Bereits im Mittelalter waren Zitrusfrüchte nördlich der Alpen bekannt. Im religiösen und volkstümlichen Brauchtum hat ihre Verwendung eine lange Tradition, etwa im Begräbniskult. In der jüdischen Religion wird die sogenannte Etrog, eine bestimmte Zedratart, in der Liturgie des Laubhüttenfestes verwendet. Volkamer bezeichnet die Etrogfrucht als „Cedro col Pigolo" oder „Juden-Citronat-Apfel" (Bd. I, S. 121).

Die vielfältigen medizinischen Qualitäten der Zitrus wurden bereits durch antike Autoren hervorgehoben. Seit der Frühen Neuzeit nutzte man die Zitrus als Heilmittel gegen den Scharbock (Skorbut), eine auf den langen Seereisen der Entdecker häufige

Hans Simon Holtzbecker, **Orange branch with flowers and fruits**
Pomeranzenzweig mit Blüten und Früchten / Branche d'oranger portant fleurs et fruits
Body colour on parchment. From: Hans Simon Holtzbecker, *Florilegium für den Hamburger Bürgermeister Barthold Moller*, 1660/65, fol. 86
Hamburg, Staats- und Universitätsbibliothek Carl von Ossietzky, Cod. in scrin. 297

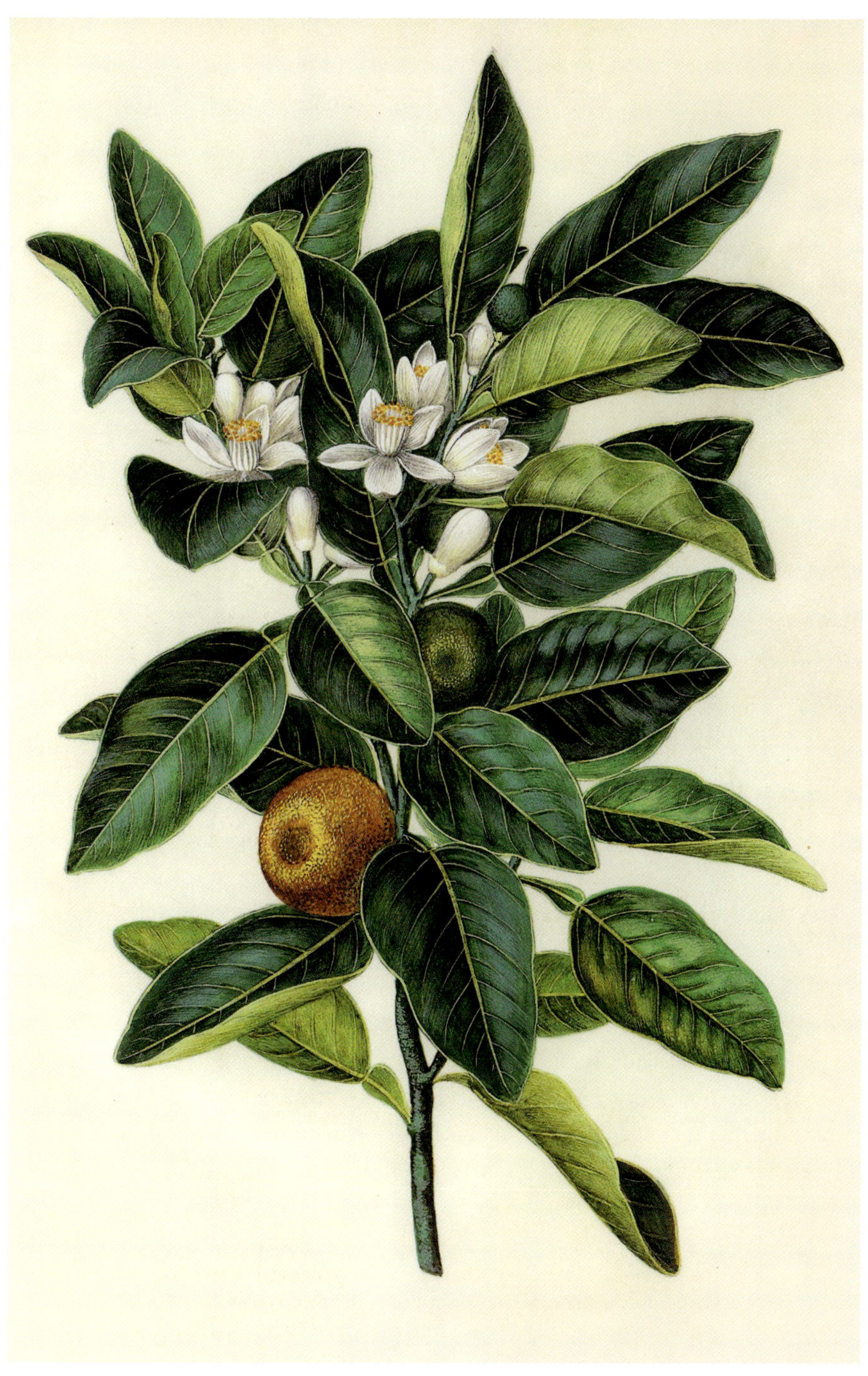

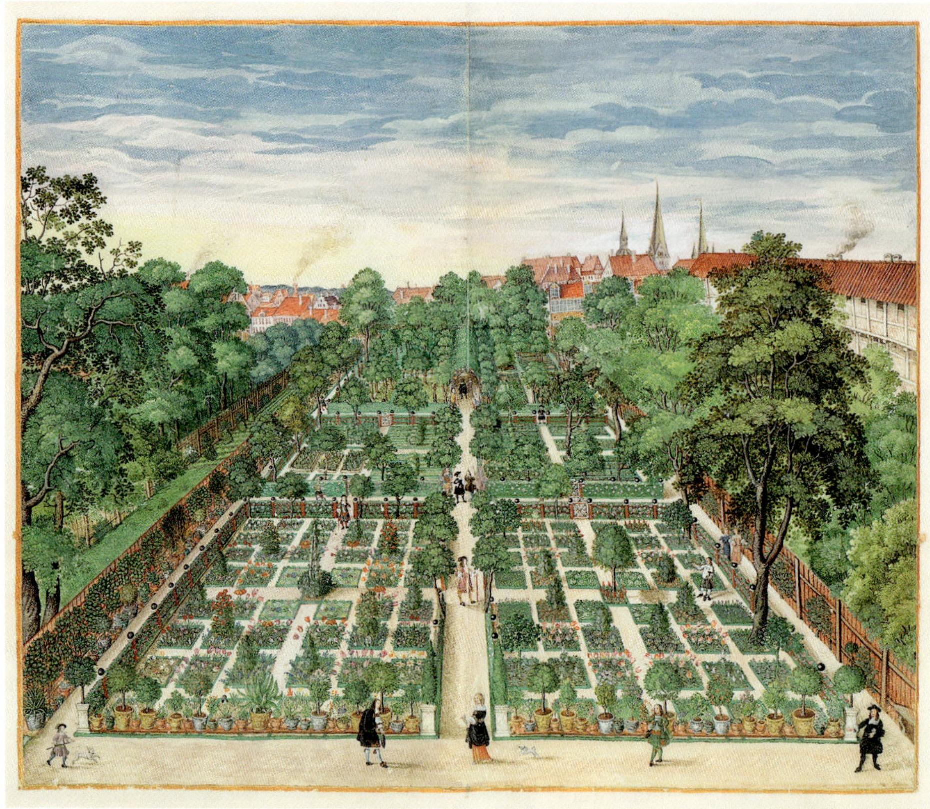

Erkrankung aufgrund eines Mangels an Vitamin C. Mit den Agrumen beschäftigten sich auch die Ärzte und Apotheker, die aufgrund ihres Interesses für die Heilwirkungen der Pflanzen gleichzeitig oft herausragende Botaniker waren. Geschäftliche Kontakte sowie Verbindungen unter den Gelehrten, die an den berühmten italienischen Universitäten studierten, waren seit dem 16. Jahrhundert wesentlich für den Kulturtransfer zwischen Italien und Deutschland im Bereich der Gartenkunst und der Botanik. Neben den Fürstenhöfen wie etwa Wien, Prag, München, Stuttgart oder Dresden war die Gartenkultur in den Freien Reichsstädten für die Einführung der Agrumen in Mitteleuropa von zentraler Bedeutung. Hervorzuheben sind Augsburg, das im 16. Jahrhundert über die Kaufleute und Bankiers aus der Familie Fugger enge Handelsbeziehungen nach

Hans Simon Holtzbecker, **Caspar Anckelmann's garden in Hamburg**, *c.* 1669
Der Garten von Caspar Anckelmann in Hamburg / Le jardin de Caspar Anckelmann à Hambourg
Body colour on parchment, 32.4 × 40.0 cm (12 ¾ × 15 ¾ in.). From: *Horti Anckelmanniani*, 1664–1671 vol. 1, fols. 2v/3r. Staatliche Museen Berlin, Kupferstichkabinett, 78 D 4, fol. 2r/3v

Italien pflegte, und Nürnberg, dessen Patriziat und Bürgerschaft ebenfalls intensive Verbindungen nach Norditalien unterhielten.

Die Kultivierung der Zitrus in den nördlichen Regionen, in denen die Pflanzen überwintert werden müssen, war und ist nur dank umfangreicher botanischer und gärtnerischer Kenntnisse möglich, deren Übermittlung seit dem 16. Jahrhundert zu den großen Herausforderungen und technischen Leistungen im Bereich der Gartenkunst gehörte. Vom zweiten Drittel des 16. Jahrhunderts an wurden in Mitteleuropa nicht nur in den fürstlichen Anlagen, sondern auch in den Gärten wohlhabender Nürnberger Bürger sowie in denen der Familie Fugger in Augsburg Zitrusbäume sowohl im Erdreich als auch in Pflanzenkübeln kultiviert (S. 103).

Als der Nürnberger Kaufmann Johann Christoph Volkamer im Jahr 1708 seine Publikation *Nürnbergische Hesperides* vorlegte, der er 1714 unter dem Titel *Continuation der Nürnbergischen Hesperidum* einen zweiten Band folgen ließ, reihte er sich mit seiner Passion für die Zitrus als die „schönste Zierde des Garten-Wesens“ in eine lange Tradition ein. Das Hesperidenwerk bietet auf der Basis des damaligen Kenntnisstandes eine außerordentlich umfangreiche Klassifikation und Beschreibung der Agrumen in Wort und Bild. Gleichzeitig handelt es sich um die erste systematische Beschreibung der Gattung Zitrus in deutscher Sprache. Die Kupferstiche zeigen in ungewöhnlicher Kombination oben in Originalgröße die Frucht, unten als Vedute Gärten, Landhäuser, Villen und Landschaften. Volkamers Hesperidenwerk kann man sich unter verschiedenen Fragestellungen – zur Botanik ebenso wie zur Garten- und Architekturgeschichte oder Topografie – annähern. Gegen eine schnelle Untersuchung jedoch sperrt sich das rund 750 Seiten und über 250 Tafeln umfassende Werk, an dem der Autor seit spätestens 1695 arbeitete und das um einen dritten Band ergänzt werden sollte.

Familie Volkamer

Der Schlüssel für das Verständnis und die Einschätzung des wissenschaftlichen Anspruches und des internationalen Horizontes des Hesperidenwerks liegt in der Familie des Autors. Johann Christoph Volkamer entstammte einer Familie, die „der Welt viele Gelehrte, Hofleute und Kriegsbediente gegeben hat“ (Will 1758). Die naheliegende, häufige Verwechslung mit der Nürnberger Patrizierfamilie Volckamer wird bereits seit dem 18. Jahrhundert thematisiert und berichtigt. Johann Volkamer (1576–1661), der Großvater unseres Autors, der mit seiner Seidenmanufaktur, die er im oberitalienischen Rovereto errichtete, und durch seine Handelstätigkeit gut verdiente, hatte 1614 in der Nürnberger Vorstadt Gostenhof ein Grundstück für einen Garten erworben, den sein Enkel Johann Christoph später weiter ausbaute.

Johann Georg Volkamer (1616–1693), der Vater Johann Christophs, war ein international anerkannter Gelehrter. Nach dem Studium der Medizin an den Universitäten Jena und Altdorf sowie – von 1638 bis 1641 – in Padua trat er eine knapp zweijährige Studienreise an, die ihn über Venedig, Ferrara, Bologna, Florenz, Pisa, Livorno und Lucca nach Rom und Neapel führte und von dort nach Nizza, Marseille, Montpellier, Toulouse, Bordeaux, Orléans und Paris, bevor er 1643 in Altdorf promoviert wurde. Während einer weiteren Italienreise im Jahr 1658 ernannte ihn die Academia Recuperatorum in Padua zum Mitglied. Seine außerordentliche Gelehrsamkeit als Naturforscher, Astronom, Physiker und Botaniker machte ihn berühmt. 1676 nahm ihn die Kaiserliche Akademie der Naturforscher, die Leopoldina, auf; seit 1686 stand er ihr sogar als Präsident vor. Als Mitglied sowohl der Leopoldina als auch des Pegnesischen Blumenordens (seit 1646) wählte er den Namen Helianthus, Sonnenblume, und mit dem Interesse für Sonnenuhren, die er auch selber konstruierte, war er auf der Höhe seiner Zeit.

Der älteste Sohn Johann Georg Volkamers, der 1644 geborene Johann Christoph, ist der Autor des Hesperidenwerks. Ein deutlich jüngerer Bruder, der wie der Vater Johann Georg hieß (1662–1744), trat als Arzt in dessen Fußstapfen und machte sich einen Namen als „berühmter Medicus, der für den größten Botanicus in Deutschland gehalten wurde" (Will 1758). Johann Christoph hingegen übernahm erfolgreich die großväterliche Seidenfabrik in Rovereto und setzte den Seidenhandel fort. Er betrieb außerdem bei Laufamholz einen Messinghammer (S. 246). Respektiert als „ein vornehmer und angesehener Kaufmann" mit mehreren renommierten Ämtern in seiner Heimatstadt, eignete er sich eine „ungemeine Wissenschaft von der Ziehung und Cultur der Agrumi, Blumen und Gartengewächse" (Will 1758) an. Von 1660 bis mindestens 1668 lebte er in Rovereto. Dieser Aufenthalt galt den Geschäften, gab ihm aber auch die Möglichkeit, oberitalienische Gärten zu besichtigen, die ihn fortan für den Rest seines Lebens begeistern sollten. Vieles spricht dafür, dass Johann Christoph Volkamer nach den prägenden Jugendjahren in Norditalien die Alpen nicht mehr überquerte. Den Rest seines Lebens verbrachte er in Nürnberg und widmete sich seinem Garten und der Zitruskultur – in intensiver Korrespondenz mit seinesgleichen im Rest der Welt.

Die Editionsgeschichte des Hesperidenwerks

Volkamer plante zunächst nur einen Band mit dem Titel *Nürnbergische Hesperides*. Dieser erhielt im März 1706 das kaiserliche Druckprivileg, erschien aber erst zwei Jahre

David von Cölln, **Orange tree in planter** (detail), *c.* 1733
Orangenbaum im Kübel / Oranger en pot
Oil on canvas, 140 × 91 cm (55 ⅛ × 35 ⅞ in.). Stockholm, Nationalmuseum

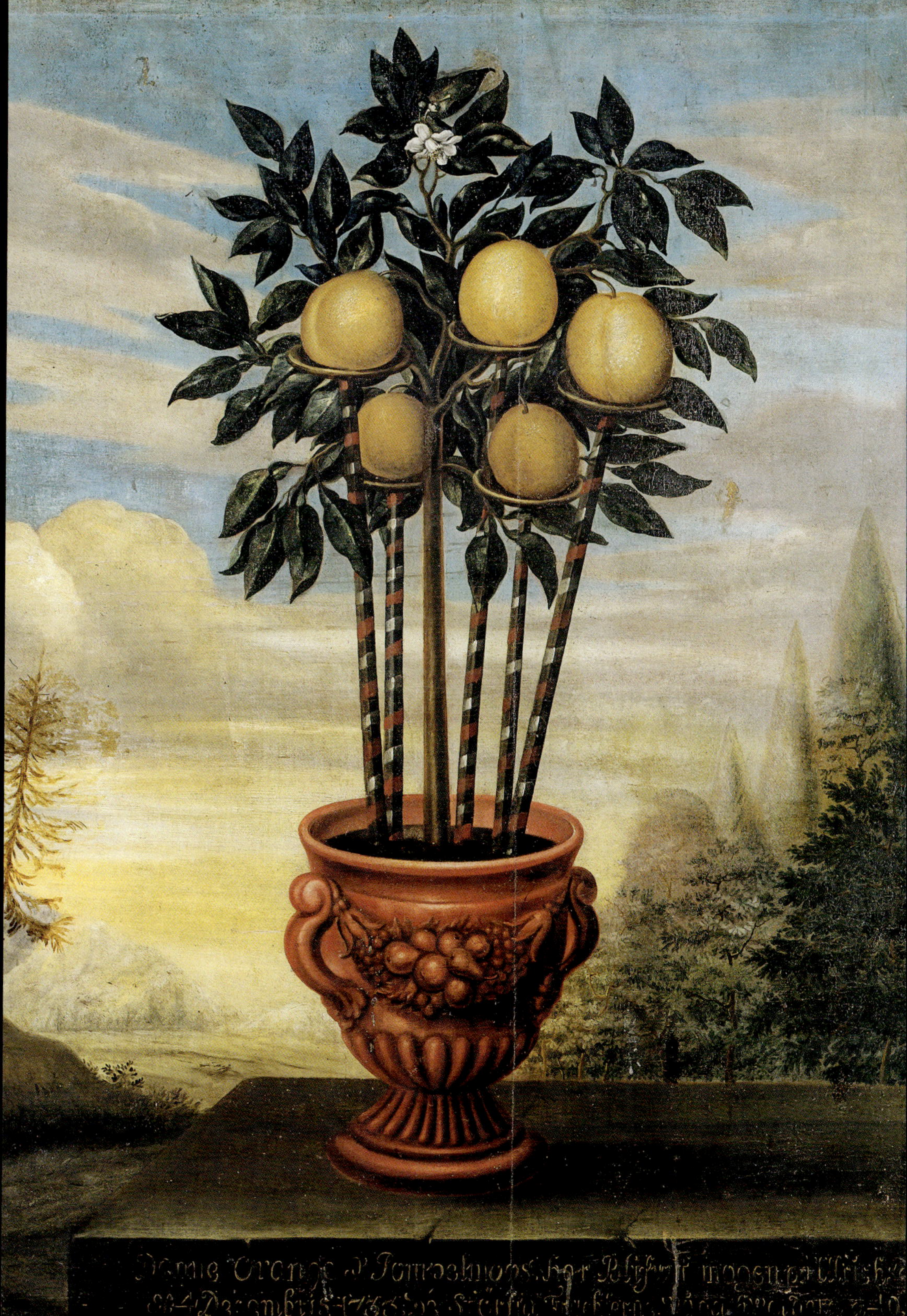

später, 1708, im Nürnberger Verlag Endter (S. 6). Der Autor nahm auf den Druck und die Zusammenstellung des Buchs kontinuierlich Einfluss, und dadurch sind die Exemplare der ersten Auflage nicht alle identisch: Die Vedutenmotive mancher Tafeln wurden verändert, nachträglich wurden Signaturen der Kupferstecher eingefügt und manche Kupferstichtafeln in späteren Zuständen eingebunden. Auf der letzten Seite der ersten Auflage von 1708 befindet sich eine Liste der Druckfehler.

Noch im selben Jahr erschien eine zweite Auflage des Werkes, die sich von der ersten unter anderem durch das Titelblatt und das Titelkupfer unterscheidet. Nun ist der Name des Autors ausgeschrieben und die Vertriebs- und Verlagsangabe verändert. Das neue Titelkupfer ist ein seitenverkehrter Nachstich des ersten und weicht in einigen Einzelheiten von diesem ab. Die Kupferplatte des ersten Frontispizes (S. 2) war also offenbar schon weiterverwendet worden, da man nicht damit gerechnet hatte, sie für weitere Auflagen zu benötigen. Die quadratischen Rahmenfelder der Initialen der ersten Auflage sind durch rechteckige ersetzt, wie sie auch im zweiten Band erscheinen. Die Liste der mittlerweile ausgeführten „Corrigenda" ist weggelassen.

Auf Drängen ausländischer Gelehrter hin ließ Volkamer durch den Philologen und Juristen Erhard Reusch (1678–1740) eine lateinische Übersetzung des ersten Bandes anfertigen, die 1713 erschien. Der Autor ließ sich seine internationale Bekanntheit also einiges kosten, zumal der lateinische Band dem ersten auch in der Ausstattung in keiner Weise nachsteht. Das Titelkupfer wurde von der zweiten Auflage von 1708 übernommen. Der lateinische Text und die Tafeln entsprechen, auch in der Seitenabfolge, der deutschen Ausgabe. Der Übersetzer fügte einen Forschungsbericht zur Zitruskultur an.

Auf den 21. August 1714 ist das Druckprivileg des nächsten, deutlich umfangreicheren Bandes datiert, der diesmal schneller, nämlich im selben Jahr, unter dem Titel *Continuation der Nürnbergischen Hesperidum* in Frankfurt und Leipzig erschien.

Das Hesperidenwerk wurde nicht, wie damals üblich, einem speziellen Würdenträger – etwa dem Rat der Reichsstadt Nürnberg oder einem bestimmten Patrizier – gewidmet, um so zu einer gezielten Verbreitung in den entsprechenden Kreisen beizutragen. Volkamer scheint vielmehr so wohlhabend gewesen zu sein, dass er die mit einer Widmung verbundene Gratifikation nicht benötigte. Immer wieder schreibt er, dass er weder Kosten noch Mühe gescheut habe, und formuliert seinen Stolz darauf, „daß keiner noch so ausführlich und so Zahlreich bis hieher / diese ungemeine Zierathen des Garten-Baues beschrieben / und mit den gehörigen Kupfern vor Augen gelegt habe" (Bd. II, Vor-Ansprach). Die Editionsgeschichte macht deutlich, dass Autor und Verlag vom großen Erfolg der ersten Auflage 1708 überrascht wurden. Als das Echo auf den ersten Band positiv ausfiel, publizierte Volkamer zunächst eine zweite Auflage, dann die lateinische Übersetzung und schließlich in deutscher Sprache die *Continuation*. Die

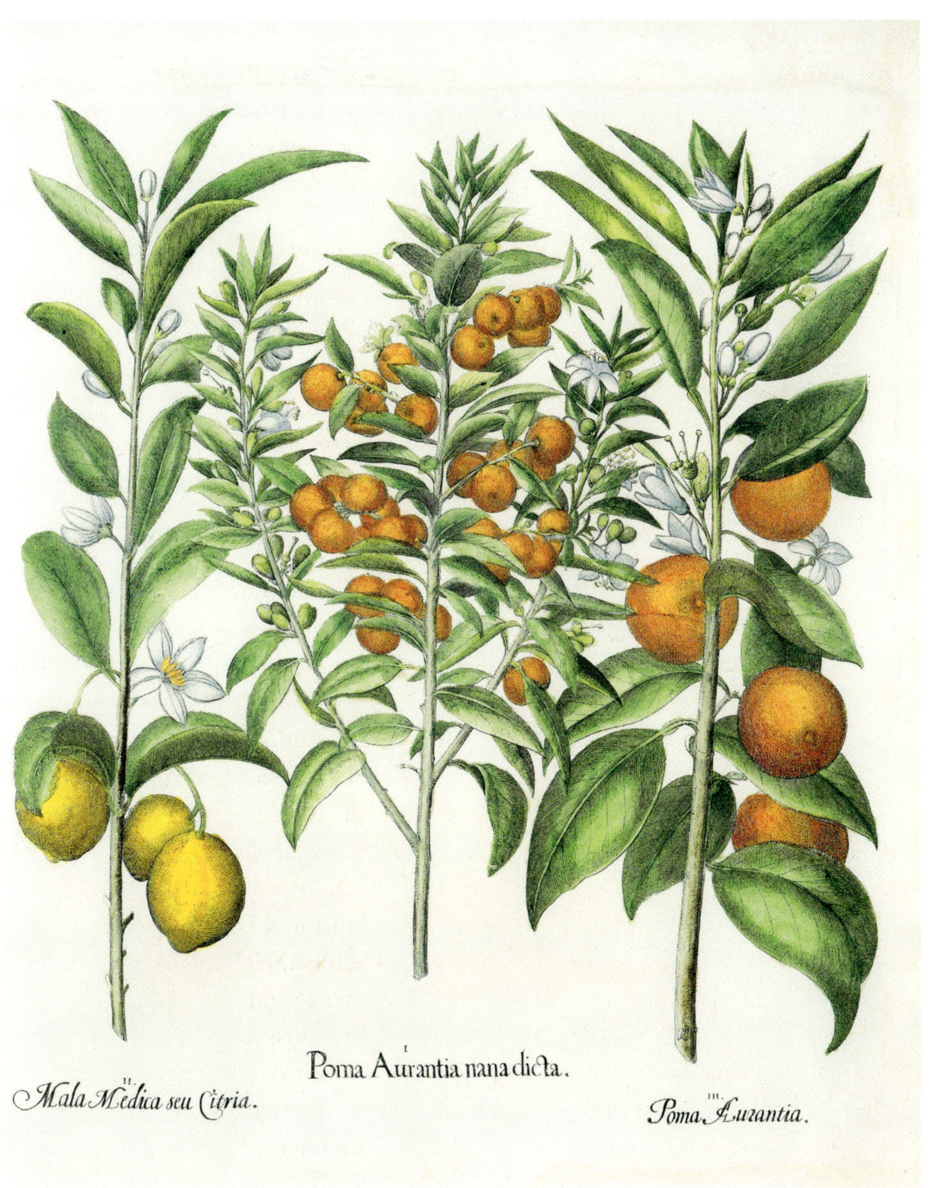

Basilius Besler, **Branches with lemons, dwarf oranges and bitter oranges**
Zweige von Zitrone, Zwergorange, Pomeranze
Branches de citronnier, oranger à fruits nains et oranger amer
From: Basilius Besler, *Hortus Eystettensis*, s.l., 1613, pl. 140
Eichstätt, Universitätsbibliothek, Bischöfliches Seminar

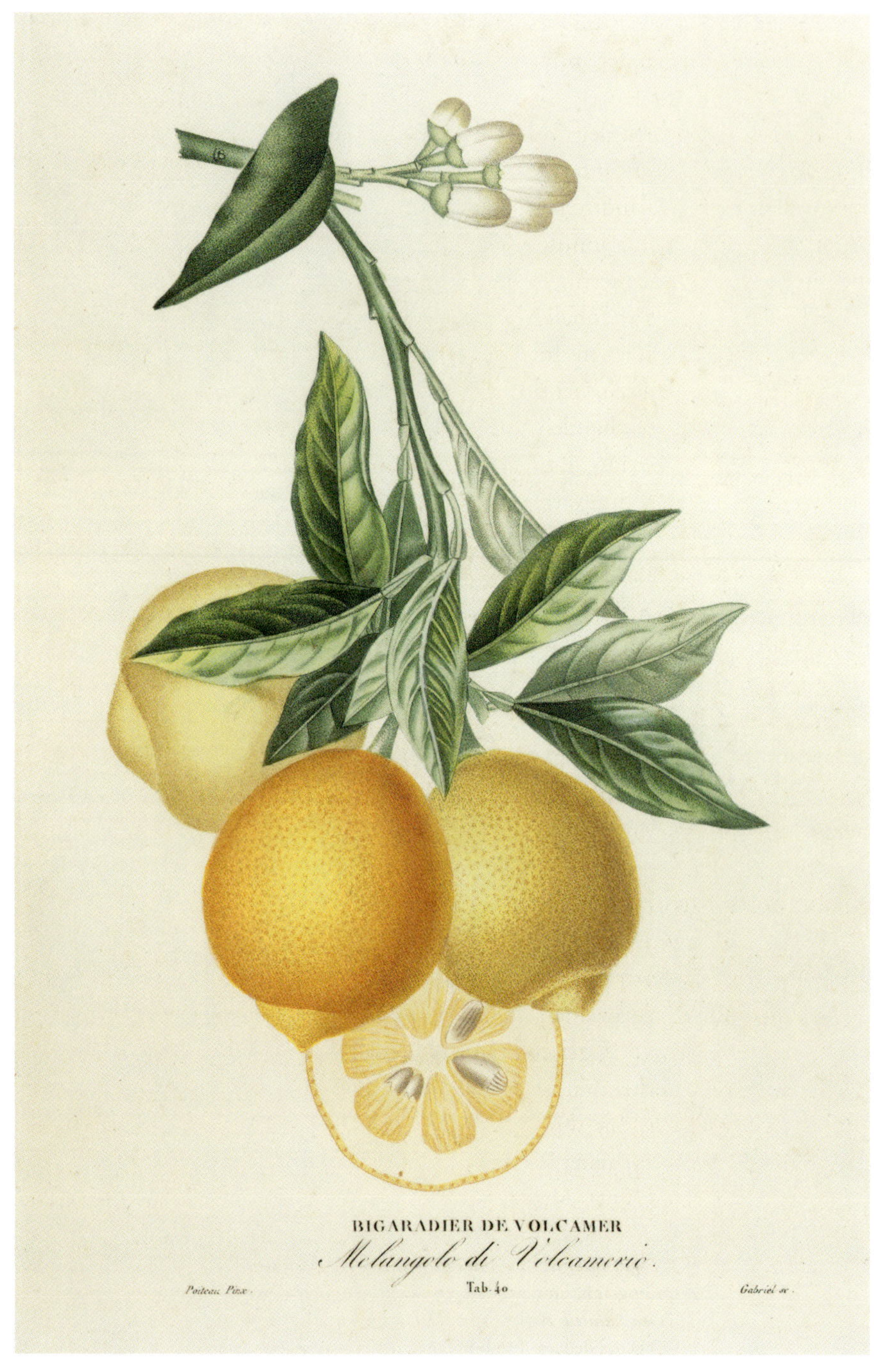
BIGARADIER DE VOLCAMER
Melangolo di Volcamerio.
Poiteau Pinx.
Tab. 40
Gabriel sc.

geplante lateinische Übersetzung des zweiten Bandes, der eine umfangreiche Darstellung des Hesperidenmythos in der antiken Skulptur und auf Gemmen angefügt werden sollte, unterblieb.

Auch nach Erscheinen der *Continuation* widmete sich der über 70-jährige Volkamer in seinem Garten in Gostenhof weiterhin der Zitruskultur, sammelte Material und korrespondierte mit ausländischen Kollegen, um sein großes Werk zu ergänzen. Einen weiteren Hesperiden-Band konnte er vor seinem Tod 1720 nicht mehr in Druck geben. Vorbereitendes Material hierfür ist im Germanischen Nationalmuseum in Nürnberg jedoch erhalten (S. 19). Der Inhalt des geplanten Fortsetzungsbandes lässt sich nun dank eines neuen Fundes erschließen. In der Universitätsbibliothek Erlangen-Nürnberg ist ein Band mit 62 Tafeln erhalten, bei denen es sich um Andrucke für den dritten Band der *Nürnbergischen Hesperiden* handelt. Der Erlanger Band umfasst außer Kupferstichen in der gewohnten Kombination von Frucht und Vedute noch das Titelkupfer (S. 16), drei Vignetten (S. 19, 50, 94), die Aufnahme der Orangerie des Grafen Neithardt in Breslau (S. 78) und einen Prospect des Königlichen Gartens und Schlosses zu Berlin“ (S. 20). Der „Prospect“ dokumentiert eine Erweiterungsplanung für das Berliner Schloss, über die der Zeichner Paul Decker der Jüngere (1685–1742) vermutlich durch seinen älteren Bruder informiert war. Dieser war bis 1706 bei Andreas Schlüters Berliner Schlossbau beschäftigt. Ein vom selben Künstler gezeichneter „Prospect des König[lichen] Schlosses und Garten zu Charlot[t]enburg eine Stundt von Berlin“ ist ebenfalls erhalten; auch diese Ansicht sollte wahrscheinlich für den dritten Band des Hesperidenwerks gestochen werden (S. 32). Terminus ante quem für die von dem Stecher Joseph a Montalegre signierten Kupferstiche für den dritten Band ist dessen Todesjahr 1718.

Volkamers Nürnberger Garten – *quasi centrum Europae*

Volkamers Garten in der Nürnberger Vorstadt Gostenhof ist auf mehreren Tafeln des Hesperidenwerks porträtiert: im ersten Band mit einer Ansicht aus der Vogelschau (S. 46/47) und weiteren einzelnen Tafeln sowie im zweiten Band mit dem Titelkupfer (S. 48) und einer größeren Vogelschau der mittlerweile veränderten Anlage (S. 272/273). Auf den Tafeln ist zu erkennen, dass Volkamers Zitrusbäume sowohl im Erdreich als auch in Kübeln wuchsen. Im Winter schützte sie ein zwischen dem Wohnhaus und der „Pomeranzenstube“ eingezogener Witterungsschutz aus Holz, der sich im Frühjahr wieder abbauen ließ (S. 26/27, 90/91). Abschlagbare Pomeranzenhäuser wie diese sind nach wie

Bigaradier de Volcamer / Melangolo de Volcamerio
Colour lithograph. From: Joseph-Antoine Risso and Alexandre Poiteau, *Histoire naturelle des Orangers*, Paris, 1818/19, vol. 5, p. 91, pl. XL
Göttingen, Niedersächsische Staats- und Universitätsbibliothek

vor am Gardasee üblich – Volkamer zeigt dieses Vorbild in einem eigenen Kupferstich (S. 134/135). Die geschnitzten Figuren der drei Hesperiden auf dem Gebälk scheinen über die Zitrusbäume und andere exotische Pflanzen zu wachen, um sicherzustellen, dass sie gedeihen (S. 90/91).

Die Vogelschau des Gartens, der zu einem großen Teil freilich für den Anbau von Gemüse genutzt wurde, ist im zweiten Band des Hesperidenwerks in lateinischer Sprache betitelt: *Viridarium Suburbaneum Johan Cristoffori Volckameri in Norimberga*. Mit dieser an antik-römischen Vorbildern orientierten Bezeichnung beanspruchte Volkamer internationale Aufmerksamkeit. Auch mit den Kupferstichen antiker Reliefs und Skulpturen zum Herkulesmythos im zweiten Band des Hesperidenwerks stellte er sich in eine römische Tradition (S. 97, 98), zu der die Nürnberger Kunst und Kultur gerade im 17. Jahrhundert in enger Verbindung standen – ein Kulturtransfer, den der Maler, Kupferstecher und Verleger Joachim von Sandrart (1606–1688) unter anderem mit seiner *Teutschen Academie* wesentlich beförderte.

Beziehungen nach Rom und Florenz bestanden seit der Zeit des älteren Johann Georg Volkamer, und auch der Bruder unseres Autors hatte 1685 diese Städte aufgesucht. Johann Christoph spielte demnach möglicherweise mit einer gewissen Affinität seiner eigenen, in der Seidenfabrikation tätigen Familie, deren international renommierteste Mitglieder Ärzte – ital. *medici* – waren, zu der aus dem Tuchhandel aufgestiegenen Familie Medici. Die heraldische Relevanz der Agrumen für die Medici mag Johann Christoph Volkamer auch auf seine eigene Familie bezogen haben. Den Garten seines Bruders Johann Georg bezeichnet er durchgehend als Heilkräutergarten und kürzt „in Horto Medico Volckameri" latinisierend zu „H. M. V." ab.

Volkamer kannte sicherlich den 1695 im Verlag Sandrart in Nürnberg verlegten Nachdruck der Kupferstichserie *Li Giardini di Roma* (Rom 1683) von Giovanni Battista Falda (1643–1678). Auf dem Frontispiz sind es „Gli Esperidi Romani", die römischen Hesperiden, in deren Obhut die Gärten und Agrumen der Urbs gedeihen (S. 28). Falda zeigt unter anderem den Garten der Villa Medici (S. 31) mit seinem Obelisken und seiner Vielfalt an antiken und neuzeitlichen Skulpturen. Auch der Nürnberger Kaufmann Johann Christoph Volkamer ließ im Juli 1709 im Labyrinth (S. 38) des Gostenhofer Gartens eine Reiterstatue durch eine auf ein Drittel verkleinerte Kopie des „Obeliscus Constantinopolitanus" ersetzen, den Theodosius I. im Jahr 390 in Konstantinopel hatte aufrichten lassen. In seiner Deutung der Hieroglyphen bezieht sich Volkamer unter anderem auf den in Rom wirkenden gelehrten Jesuiten Athanasius Kircher, der 1650 Schriften zum *Obeliscus Pamphilius* und 1666 zum *Obeliscus Aegyptiacus* publiziert hatte. 1713 erschien Volkamers Beschreibung des knapp sieben Meter hohen Obelisken (S. 37), der heute im Industriegut Hammer im Nürnberger Vorort Laufamholz steht. Diese

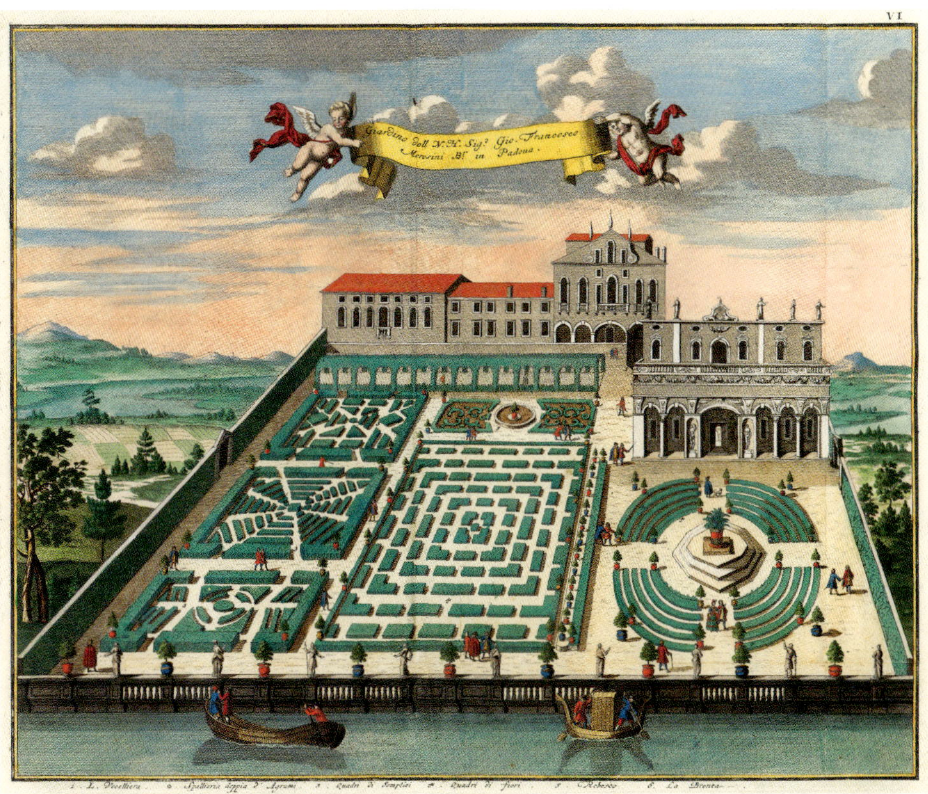

Abhandlung wurde dem zweiten Band des Hesperidenwerks angebunden oder nachträglich dem ersten Band hinzugefügt. Im hier vorgelegten Exemplar aus Fürth befindet sich die Beschreibung im ersten Band. Sie reiht sich mit ihrem lateinischen Titel in die zahlreichen Veröffentlichungen zu antiken Obelisken der zweiten Hälfte des 17. Jahrhunderts ein. Volkamer beschloss die Beschreibung dieses mit einer Friedenstaube bekrönten Monuments mit dem Wunsch nach einem „von gantz Europa bisher so sehr verlangten und gewünschten sichern und beständigen Friedens“ (angebunden an Bd. I, S. 16). Diese Hoffnung wurde mit dem Frieden von Utrecht erfüllt, der 1713 den Spanischen Erbfolgekrieg beendete.

Die Konstruktion der 1696 aus Buchs angelegten Sonnenuhr im Gostenhofer Garten beschreibt der Autor ebenso ausführlich (S. 41; Bd. I, S. 245–248) wie die 1697

Morosini's garden in Padua / Garten Morosini in Padua / Jardin Morosini à Padoue
From: *Continuation der Nürnbergischen Hesperidum*, 1714, vol. II, plate VI

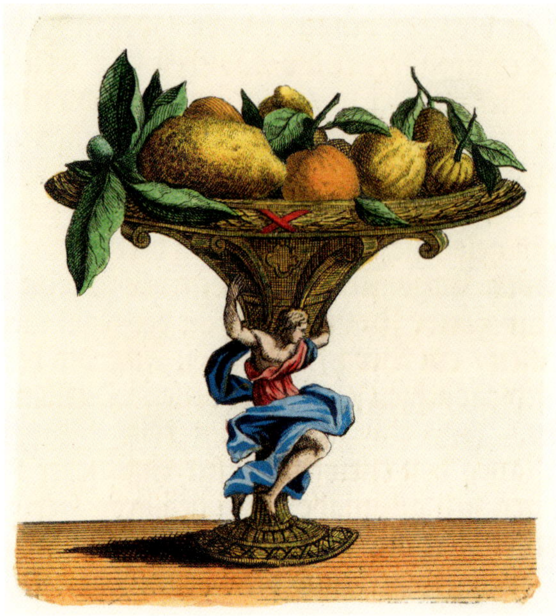

entstandene *Columna Milliaria* (S. 45; Bd. 1, S. 253–255). Vorbild dieser Meilensäule war das antike *Milliarium aureum* auf dem Forum Romanum, von dem aus die Entfernungen wichtiger Orte im römischen Imperium gemessen und angegeben wurden. In Gostenhof waren auf vier einen Baldachin tragenden Säulen sowie einer fünften, freistehenden Säule in der Mitte Landkarten aufmontiert, die gleich einer kartografischen Anamorphose die europäische Topografie von Lemberg, Gotland und Salisbury über Perpignan bis Bari einer auf Nürnberg bezogenen Bedeutungsperspektive unterwarfen. Die seit dem späten 15. Jahrhundert verwendete und zum Topos des Städtelobs gewordene Bezeichnung Nürnbergs als Handelszentrum des Kontinents – *quasi centrum Europae* – findet in diesem Säulenmonument des Kaufmanns Volkamer einen prägnanten Ausdruck.

Zitrus und Bürgerstolz

Das Folioformat, der große Textumfang und die vielen Tafeln rechtfertigten den hohen Preis von zwölf Talern für die beiden Bände des Hesperidenwerks, das sich auch hierin gegenüber den zahlreichen kleineren Gartenpublikationen seiner Zeit deutlich abhob. Die im selben Verlag erschienene mehrbändige *Garten-Wissenschafft* des Nürnberger Patriziers Wolf Albrecht Stromer von Reichenbach etwa kostete nur einen Taler acht Groschen. Bei Augsburger und Nürnberger Verlagen waren in den letzten Jahrzehnten des 17. Jahrhunderts zahlreiche Gartenbücher erschienen, die den wirtschaftlichen Aufschwung nach Ende des Dreißigjährigen Krieges und das lebhafte Interesse an der Gartenkultur in den Freien Reichsstädten belegen. Volkamer kannte viele dieser

Goblet bowl with citrus fruits / Fußschale mit Zitrusfrüchten / Bol à gobelets aux agrumes
From: *Nürnbergische Hesperides*, 1708, vol. 1, p. 87

Bücher und zitiert einige von ihnen, so Agostino Mandirola, Wolfgang Jakob Dümler und Stromer von Reichenbach.

Mit einer Akkumulation von Superlativen legte Johann Christoph Volkamer seine Publikation zur Zitrus seiner Heimatstadt Nürnberg, „diese[r] Königin der teutschen Städte“ zu Füßen: „Meinem Vatterland / dem edlen Nürnberg / geben In- und Ausländer / ungezwungen den Ruhm/ daß es die wolgelegenste / schönst-gebauteste / und nicht allein mit aller Bedürffniß / sondern auch mit allen Ergötzlichkeiten / best-versehenste Stadt im teutschn Reich seye. Zu diesen letztern rechnet man / mit dem besten Fug / die Kunst- und Lust-Gärten / welche so auserlesen schön und anmuthig sich darstellen / als groß und zahlreich die Menge derselbigen / in- und ausserhalb der Ring-Mauren ist.“

Volkamer verstand sein Zitrus-Werk als Hommage an seine Heimatstadt. Dies machen die von Paul Decker dem Älteren (1677–1713) und seinem gleichnamigen jüngeren Bruder gezeichneten Titelkupfer bis in Einzelheiten hinein deutlich (S. 2). Der Personifikation Nürnbergs, der stolzen Noris, bieten die Hesperiden ihre Früchte dar, im ersten Band assistiert von Merkur, dem Gott der Kaufleute, in den anderen Bänden von Herkules. Die topografische Kulisse im Hintergrund zeigt im ersten Band die Stadt Nürnberg und im zweiten Volkamers Garten in Gostenhof (S. 48). Im ersten Frontispiz ragt aus dem Blumenstrauß hinter Merkur eine Kaiserkrone, *Fritillaria imperialis*, hervor, zweifellos ein Hinweis auf die historische Rolle der Stadt als Aufbewahrungsort der Reichskleinodien und damit auch der Kaiserkrone.

Bürgerliche Gärten des 17. und 18. Jahrhunderts wurden häufig vor dem Hintergrund der Stadtkulisse gezeigt (S. 54). Pflanzenkultur und Gartenkunst, Vegetation und Flora eignen sich für lokalpatriotische Beschreibungen. Sie zeigen die Identifikation der Bürger mit ihrer blühenden Stadt und wurden im 17. und 18. Jahrhundert in zahlreichen Stadtchroniken als Errungenschaften des Gemeinwesens interpretiert. So ist die erste Tafel im zweiten Teil des Hesperidenwerks mit dem großen „Cedro grosso Bondolotto“ über der Ansicht der Freien Reichsstadt Nürnberg als lokalpatriotisches Statement zu verstehen (S. 150). Dies gilt auch für den vom Hesperidenwerk beeinflussten Breslauer Zitruskatalog von Caspar Wilhelm Scultetus (s. l. 1731) oder für die Publikationen zu Caspar Boses Garten in Leipzig (S. 34). Mit Bose (1645–1700), dessen Garten für seine seltenen exotischen Gewächse weithin berühmt war und dessen kostbare Zitrussammlung 1686 als „Hesperides Bosianae“ bezeichnet wurde, korrespondierte Volkamer.

Der Kaufmann als Wissenschaftler

Die seit dem späten 16. Jahrhundert in Nürnberg ansässige Familie Volkamer, finanziell erfolgreiche Kaufleute und international renommierte Gelehrte, gehörte zwar nicht dem Patriziat an, war in den sozialen und verwaltenden Gremien der Reichsstadt aber verankert und hoch angesehen. Generell erlangte die Freie Reichsstadt Nürnberg großes Renommee durch die Leistungen ihrer Künstler und der hier und an der Universität Altdorf tätigen Wissenschaftler.

Im Hesperidenwerk spiegeln sich in vielfacher Hinsicht die Interessen, persönlichen Bekanntschaften und Kenntnisse nicht nur des Autors selbst, sondern auch seiner Familie – des vielfach interessierten Großvaters, des umfassend gelehrten Vaters und des wissenschaftlich renommierten jüngeren Bruders, denen er viel verdankte. Der Bruder Johann Georg hatte sich im Jahr 1700 mit seinem 407 Seiten starken botanischen Traktat *Flora Noribergensis Sive Catalogus Plantarum in Agro Noribergensi Tam sponte nascentium, quam exoticarum* (Nürnberg, 2. Auflage 1718) international einen Namen gemacht. Auf nur zwei Seiten (S. 276 f.) widmet er sich den Pomeranzen, Zitronaten und Zitronen. Die wenigen Tafeln zeigen mehrheitlich exotische Pflanzen, die Johann Georg Volkamer in seinem Garten kultivierte, aber keine Zitrus. Fragt man, was seinen um knapp 20 Jahre älteren Bruder Johann Christoph dazu veranlasst haben mag, unermüdlich einen Band seines originellen und komplexen Werks über die Zitrus nach dem anderen in Angriff zu nehmen, zu finanzieren und zu publizieren, so lautet die Antwort: Die *Nürnbergischen Hesperiden* sind das wissenschaftliche Lebenswerk eines „vornehmen und angesehenen Kaufmanns" und zugleich passionierten Dilettanten, der hiermit seinen Beitrag zu einem edlen, gelehrten Wettstreit, einer innerfamiliären *aemulatio* leistete. Auch Johann Christoph wurde schließlich Anfang 1720, ein halbes Jahr vor seinem Tod, im Alter von 76 Jahren die Genugtuung zuteil, wie schon sein Vater und Bruder in die Kaiserliche Akademie der Naturforscher aufgenommen zu werden.

Der Vater und der Bruder schrieben ihre wissenschaftlichen Abhandlungen auf Lateinisch. Johann Christoph Volkamer hingegen schrieb für seinesgleichen – für gärtnerische Dilettanten – auf Deutsch, obwohl er lateinische Literatur zitierte und die Sprache ebenso beherrschte wie die italienische. In diesem Kontext stellt das Hesperidenwerk eine bemerkenswerte Transferleistung dar. Im Bemühen um wissenschaftliche Systematik einerseits und Allgemeinverständlichkeit in deutscher Sprache andererseits hat es eine Zwittergestalt. Basilius Beslers (1561–1629) prachtvolle Edition des *Hortus Eystettensis* (s. l. 1613), im Anspruch der exakten bildlichen Wiedergabe und genauen Beschreibung vermutlich eines der Vorbilder für Volkamer und ihm zweifellos bekannt (S. 59), ist in lateinischer Sprache verfasst.

Ludwig Christoph Glotsch, after Johann Christoph Volkamer
Citrus fruits and flowers above the Nuremberg observatory
Zitrusfrüchte und -blüten über der Nürnberger Sternwarte
Fleurs et fruits d'agrumes au-dessus de l'observatoire de Nuremberg
From: *Nürnbergische Hesperides*, 1708, vol. 1, plate p. 103

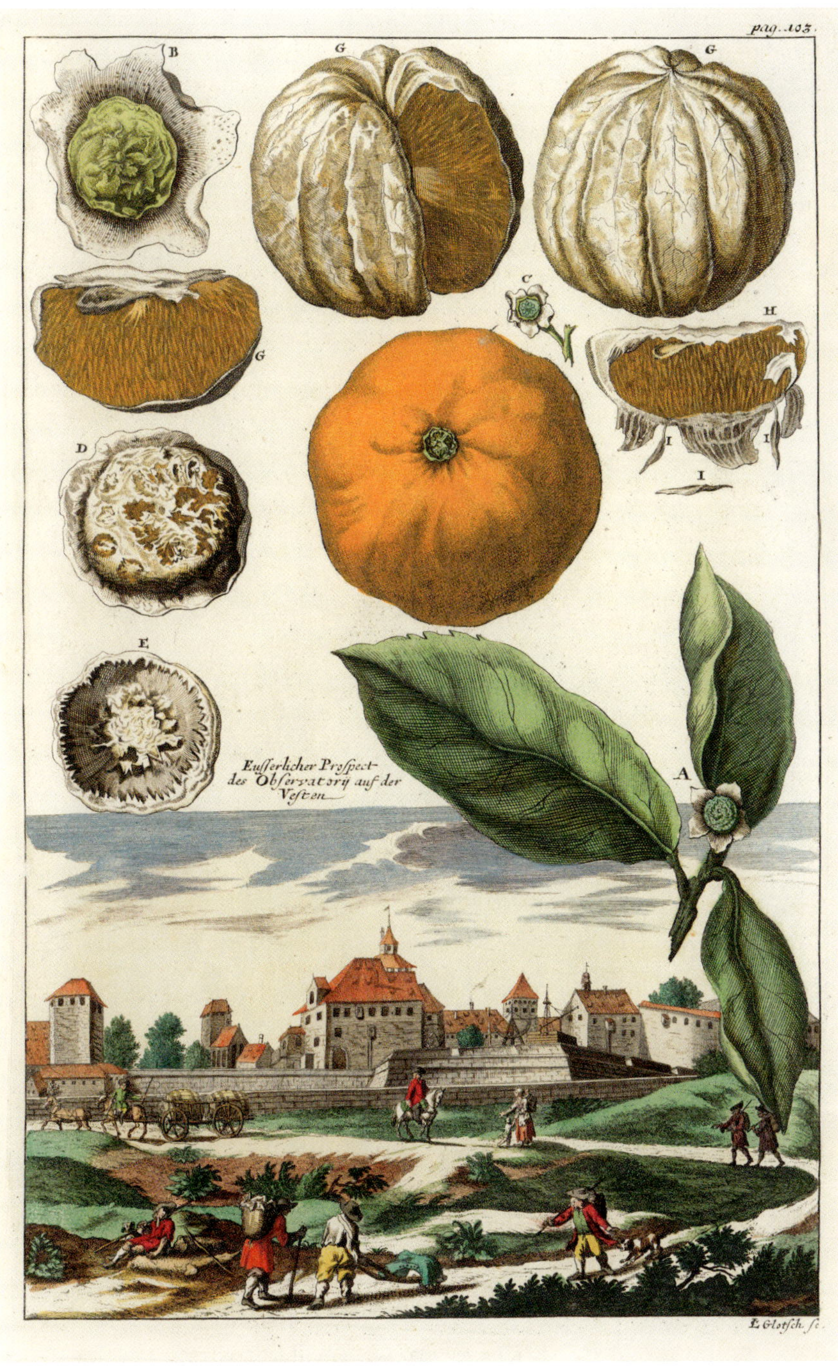
pag. 103.
B
G
G
C
G
H
D
I
I
I
E
Eusserlicher Prospect des Observatory auf der Vesten
A
L. Glotsch sc.

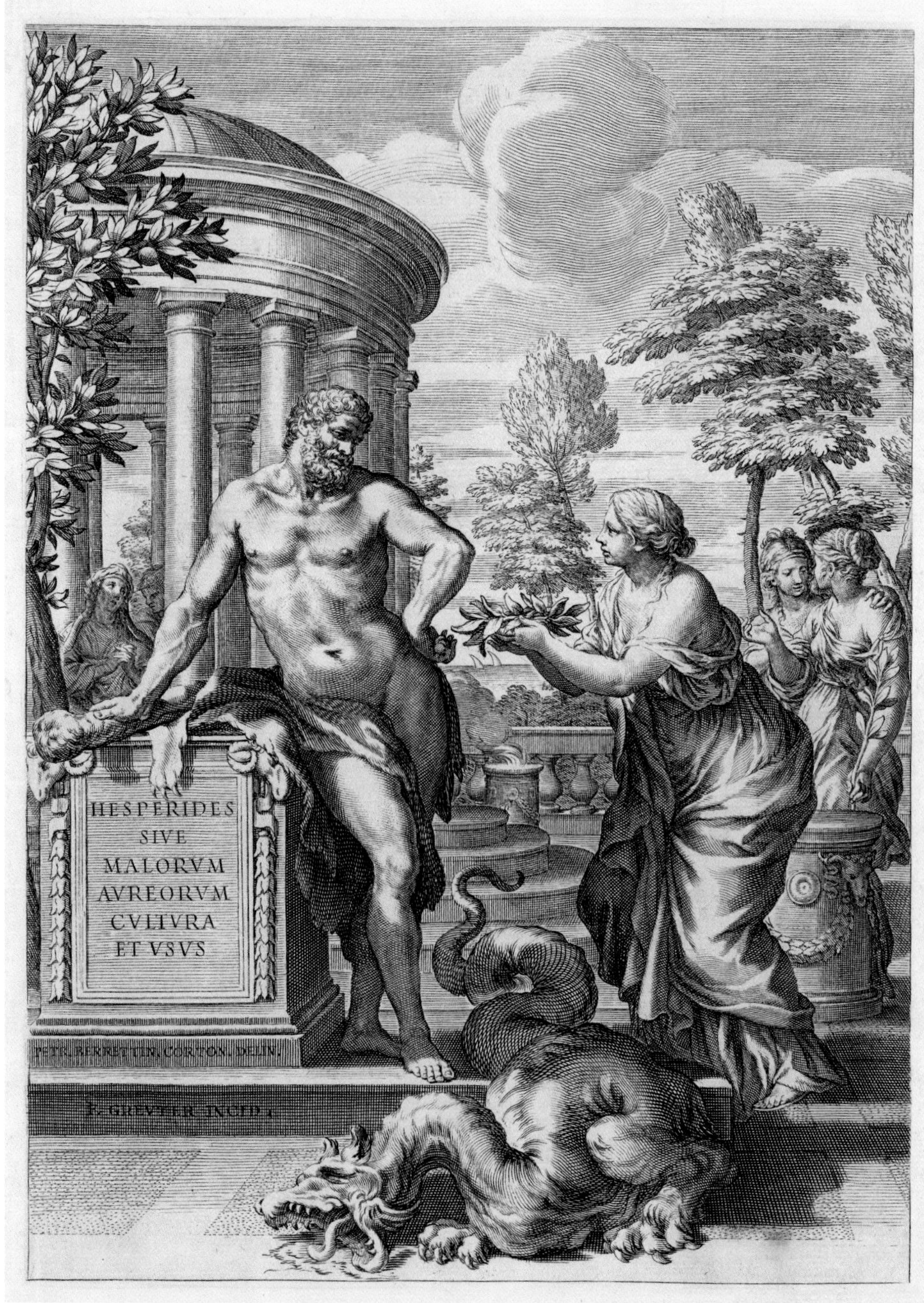
HESPERIDES
SIVE
MALORVM
AVREORVM
CVLTVRA
ET VSVS
PETR. BERRETTIN. CORTON. DELIN.
I. GREVTER INCID.

Das Hesperidenwerk hingegen steht im Zusammenhang der seit der Mitte des 17. Jahrhunderts unternommenen Bemühungen, die deutsche Sprache zur Wissenschaftssprache zu entwickeln. In Nürnberg nahm der 1644 gegründete Pegnesische Blumenorden, dem Johann Georg Volkamer senior beigetreten war, als Sprachgesellschaft eine führende Rolle ein. War Giovanni Battista Ferraris (1584–1655) Zitrusbuch von 1646 noch in lateinischer Sprache verfasst, so sind die meisten Zitruswerke der zweiten Hälfte des 17. Jahrhunderts in der jeweiligen Nationalsprache geschrieben; dies gilt etwa für Commelin (1676), Sterbeeck (1682), die französischen Traktate und die einschlägigen Werke deutscher Autoren. Aufgrund langer Erfahrung und Beobachtung sowie genauer Analyse liefert Volkamer mit seiner Beschreibung und Klassifizierung der Zitronen einen originellen Beitrag zur „Edle[n] Botanica und Kräutter-Wissenschaft“ (Bd. 1, S. 4 f.). Obwohl er ein Kaufmann, kein Wissenschaftler war, entspricht sein Werk dem hohen Niveau botanischer Publikationen seiner Zeit.

Bis heute wird sein Werk als eine der Referenzen für die Zitrusklassifikation aufgeführt. So nannten zum Beispiel die Botaniker Joseph-Antoine Risso und Alexandre Poiteau in ihrer *Histoire naturelle des Orangers* (Paris 1818/19) eine Pomeranze „Bigaradier de Volcamer / Melangolo de Volcamerio“ (S. 60).

Vorbilder: Publikationen zu den Agrumen

Das Buch des Jesuitenpaters Ferrari, das 1646 unter dem Titel *Hesperides, sive de malorum aureorum cultura et usu* in Rom erschien, ist die früheste Publikation mit einer klassifizierenden Darstellung der Zitrus. Das Werk gibt auf zahlreichen Kupfertafeln Früchte, Zweige und Blüten (S. 71) sowie Orangerien wieder und enthält darüber hinaus künstlerisch herausragende Darstellungen zum Hesperidenmythos, die von den besten römischen Künstlern der Zeit entworfen wurden, unter anderem von Pietro da Cortona (S. 68), Francesco Albani und Nicolas Poussin. Ferrari, der Gärtner und Botaniker der Barberini in Rom, hatte Zugriff auf die botanischen Darstellungen des sogenannten „Museo Cartaceo“, der Sammlung von Aufzeichnungen und Zeichnungen des gelehrten Kunstmäzens Cassiano dal Pozzo (1588–1657; S. 75). Ferrari hatte sich bereits durch sein Buch *Flora overo cultura dei fiori* (lateinische Ausg.: Rom 1632, italienische Ausg.: Rom 1638) international einen Namen gemacht. Sowohl dieses Werk als auch sein Zitrusbuch waren im Besitz der Familie Volkamer und werden von dem jüngeren Johann

After Pietro da Cortona, **Hercules and the Hesperides**
Herkules und die Hesperiden / Hercule et les Hespérides
Engraving and etching. Frontispiece of: Giovanni Battista Ferrari, *Hesperides, sive de malorum aureorum cultura et usu,* Rome, 1646
Göttingen, Niedersächsische Staats- und Universitätsbibliothek

Georg ebenso zitiert wie von Johann Christoph. Die Titelkupfer und Vignetten zum Hesperidenmythos paraphrasieren die Kupferstiche aus Ferraris Buch. Neben Ferrari ist auch Jan Commelin (1629–1692), „der unvergleichliche Botanicus zu Amsterdam" (Bd. 1, S. 17), Autor der *Nederlantze Hesperides* (Amsterdam 1676), eine oft genannte Autorität im Hesperidenwerk Volkamers (S. 77). Sein Bruder Johann Georg hatte Commelin in Amsterdam persönlich kennengelernt.

Erhard Reusch, der Übersetzer des ersten Hesperidenbandes, fügte Volkamers Text eine 24 Folioseiten lange Diskussion älterer und neuerer Literatur zur Gattung Zitrus an: *Dissertatio Epistolica de Praecipuis Hesperidum Scriptoribus, iisque tam Antiquis quam Recentioribus*. Die *Dissertatio* verleiht dem Hesperidenwerk den akademischen Habitus, der Volkamers Ausführungen und seiner eigenen, volkstümlichen Ausdrucksweise fehlt. Reusch nennt gleich zu Anfang Giovanni Pontano (1429–1503), Ferrari und Commelin und legt anschließend ausführlich dar, was Autoren der griechischen und der römischen Antike seit Theophrast zur Gattung Zitrus zu sagen hatten. Er äußert sich zur Mythologie, zur Etymologie und sogar zu den Schriften arabischer Gelehrter. Chronologisch fortschreitend nähert er sich der Frühen Neuzeit und bezieht sich auch hier auf eine Reihe von Autoritäten aus ganz Europa, die in lateinischer, italienischer, französischer, niederländischer, englischer und deutscher Sprache über Agrumen geschrieben haben. Außer Pontano, Ferrari und Commelin referiert Reusch, nach Nationen und Sprachen getrennt, unter anderen folgende Autoren: die italienischen Ärzte, Dichter und Gelehrten Battista Fiera, Celio Calcagnini, Pietro Nato und Giuseppe Lanzoni; den Naturforscher Ulisse Aldrovandi (1522–1605), der in Bologna 1568 den botanischen Garten gründete, und den Bologneser Gelehrten Ovidio Montalbano (1601–1672), der Aldrovandis Forschungen zur Baumkunde herausgab (1668); Agostino Mandirola, den Verfasser des *Italiänischen Blumen- und Pomerantzen-Garten* (Nürnberg 1679). Die Gartenbücher der Franzosen René Rapin und Pierre Morin werden vorgestellt; außerdem der *Nouveau traité des orangers et citronniers* (1692) und der *Traité de la culture des orangers, citronniers, grenadiers et oliviers* (Paris 1676). Die Schriften des renommierten französischen Hofgärtners Jean-Baptiste de la Quintinie (1626–1688) zur Zitrus werden ausführlich gewürdigt, sodann diejenigen englischer und holländischer Autoren. Außer Commelin sind dies Frans van Sterbeeck (1631–1693), dessen Buch *Citricultura* (Antwerpen 1682) für Volkamer sicher vorbildlich war (S. 15, 81, 89), und Henrik van Oostens *De Nederlandsen Hof, beplant met Bloemen, Ooft en Orangerijen* (Leiden 1703). Für Deutschland erwähnt Reusch außer Autoren auch Partner, die eher durch Korrespondenz und Tausch von Samen und Pflanzen als durch eigene Publikationen hervorgetreten sind, so Otto von Münchhausen (1643–1717), dessen Schloss und Garten Schwöbber bei Hameln auf mehreren

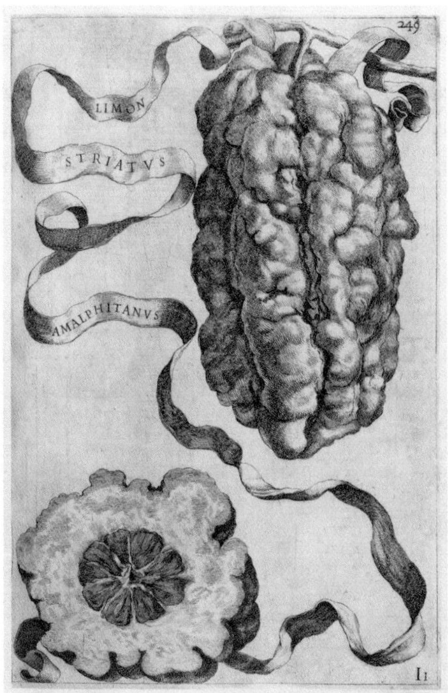

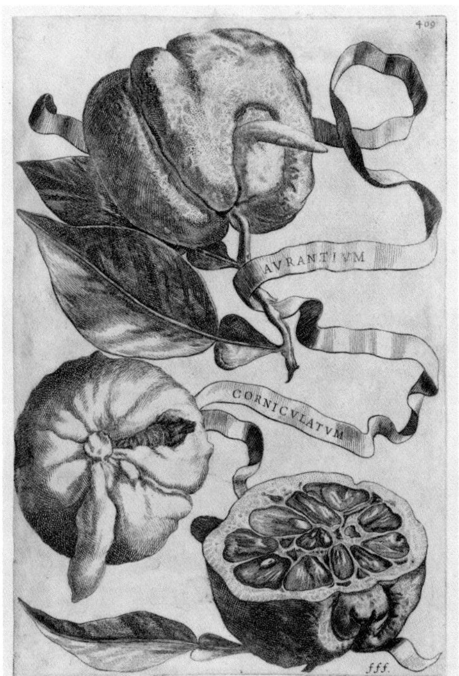

Abbildungen im Hesperidenwerk als Vorbild für die Kultur exotischer Gewächse dargestellt wird (S. 23, 274).

Reusch referiert weitaus mehr Literatur als Volkamer sie in seinem publizierten Text selbst erwähnt. Es ist jedoch davon auszugehen, dass die genannten Autoren und Werke auch ihm vertraut waren. Der hohe Rang von Volkamers Hesperidenwerk wird vor dem Hintergrund der zitierten Literatur besonders deutlich: In den meisten der genannten Werke dominiert der Text. Die nicht sehr zahlreichen Kupferstiche bei Commelin und Sterbeeck sind um eine gleichzeitig präzise und dekorative Wiedergabe bemüht. Lediglich Ferraris Buch stellt dem Text eine wissenschaftliche Bilddokumentation im Kupferstich zur Seite: Zweige und Blätter, Blüten sowie vollständige oder aufgeschnittene

Limon striatus Amalphitanus
Engraving and etching. From: Giovanni Battista Ferrari, *Hesperides, sive de malorum aureorum cultura et usu*, Rome, 1646, p. 249. Göttingen, Niedersächsische Staats- und Universitätsbibliothek

Aurantium corniculatum
Engraving and etching, From: Giovanni Battista Ferrari, *Hesperides, sive de malorum aureorum cultura et usu*, Rome, 1646, p. 409. Göttingen, Niedersächsische Staats- und Universitätsbibliothek

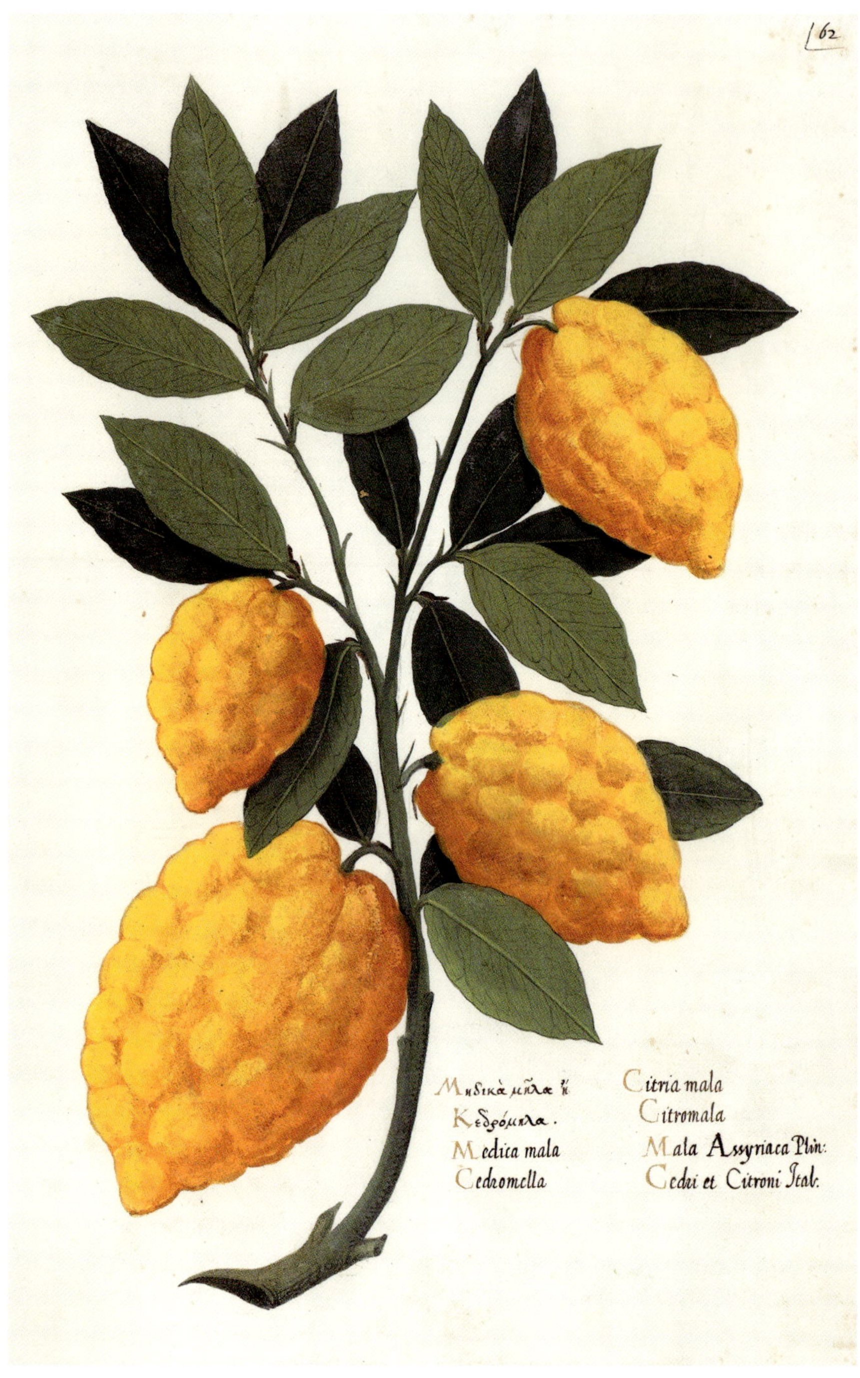

162
Μηδικὰ μῆλα ἢ
Κεδρόμηλα.
Medica mala
Cedromella
Citria mala
Citromala
Mala Assyriaca Plin:
Cedri et Citroni Ital:

Früchte werden von einem Schriftband mit dem Namen und Klassifikationshinweis dekorativ umschlungen (S. 71). Das Bemühen um Präzision der Wiedergabe teilt Volkamer mit Ferrari, er übertrifft ihn aber in der Anzahl der behandelten und gezeigten Zitrusvarietäten.

Volkamers Publikum: „Denen curiosen Liebhabern und Lehrbegierigen Gärtnern zu Gefallen“

Volkamer schrieb sein Werk für wohlhabende Gartenbesitzer, die Mittel und Zeit erübrigen konnten, sich intensiv mit ihren Gärten und der Botanik zu beschäftigen. Der Autor berichtet, für „die Erforschung der Agrumi etliche müssige Stunden / zu meiner Vergnügung“ investiert zu haben (Bd. II, Vor-Ansprach). In beiden Bänden seines Werks widmet er sich, ausgehend von eigenen langjährigen Erfahrungen, ausführlich der Zitruskultur: der Konstruktion von abschlagbaren Pomeranzenhäusern sowie von Glashäusern; der Pflege, Düngung und Überwinterung der Gewächse; ihrer Vermehrung und ihrem Schnitt; der Behandlung von Krankheiten; dem Schutz vor Ungeziefer wie der Schildlaus, die er mikroskopisch untersuchte und in starker Vergrößerung wiedergibt (S. 115).

In mehreren Kapiteln beschäftigt sich Volkamer – von der Warte eines Gartenbesitzers aus – mit den Anforderungen an den Gärtnerberuf (S. 85): „Solchem nach gehöret kein tummer Kopf und fauler Tropf zu einem Gärtner / dann Er muß eine gute Wissenschafft und Erkennung haben [...] Es muß auch ein Gärtner klug und nachdencklich seyn [...] Ferner soll ein Gärtner fleissig und unverdrossen seyn“ (Bd. I, S. 71 f.). Er scheint mit seinen eigenen Gärtnern keine guten Erfahrungen gemacht zu haben, denn es dominiert das Lamento über „boßhafftige Bubenstücke solcher Ehr- und Gottesvergessenen Gärtner“ (Bd. I, S. 75), über Diebstahl und Vernachlässigung der Pflanzen. Für Volkamers volkstümliche Sprache sind Redensarten charakteristisch, wie seine Warnung vor großtuerischen Gärtnern, die ihr Handwerk nicht verstünden: „Wer siehet hieraus nicht / daß nicht alle Köche sind / die lange Messer tragen“ (Bd. I, S. 73). In Verse überführt Volkamer eine Fabel, die bereits Ferrari in seinem Buch zur *Flora* erzählt. Zwei Spitzbuben vernachlässigen den ihrer Obhut anvertrauten Garten und werden zur Strafe von der Göttin Flora in eine Schnecke und eine Raupe verwandelt – die Geißeln eines jeden Gartenbesitzers. Die anagrammatische Metamorphose lässt bei Volkamer den Namen „Schenck“ zu „Schneck“ und „Paur“ zu „Raup“ werden. Die Darstellung auf der zugehörigen Tafel ist bei Volkamer (S. 92) drastischer als bei Ferrari, da „Paurs“

Ulisse Aldrovandi, ***Medica mala***, second half of 16th century
From: *L'Erbario di Ulisse Aldrovandi*, vol. VIII, pl. 62
Biblioteca Universitaria di Bologna, Museo Aldrovandi, Ms 124

Verwandlung in eine Raupe – anders als im italienischen Vorbild – an der beginnenden Behaarung der Hände sichtbar wird, während sich „Schenck“ schon molluskenartig verformt auf dem Boden windet.

Himmlische Früchte

Die Früchte und Blüten sind – ob groß, ob klein – auf den Tafeln der Hesperidenbände in natürlicher Größe wiedergegeben: die Aurikelblüten ebenso wie die Kokosnuss, die Ananas und die Pampelmusen. Einige der Kupferstiche weisen eine klare Aufteilung in die Fruchtdarstellung oben und das als Trompe-l'œil gestaltete Blatt mit der Vedute darunter auf (z. B. S. 211, 360). Dieses Schema ließ sich angesichts der unterschiedlichen Größe der Früchte jedoch nicht durchhalten und führte zu einem collageartigen Bildaufbau, für den Volkamers Werk bekannt ist, der aber auch Vorläufer in Nürnberger Blumenbüchern der Zeit um 1700 sowie in anderen botanischen Werken hat (S. 82).

Der Leser muss sich im ersten Band bis zum 23. Kapitel gedulden, um die erste Abbildung von Zitrusfrüchten und -blüten zu sehen (S. 67). Unter Detaildarstellungen der Früchte und der nur auf dieser Tafel vielfach vergrößerten Blüten zeigt Volkamer die berühmte Nürnberger Sternwarte, die 1678 durch den Astronom und Kupferstecher Georg Christoph Eimmart auf einer der Burgbasteien der Stadt gegründet worden war. Dieses öffentliche Observatorium fand im Mai 1706 anlässlich einer totalen Sonnenfinsternis großen Zulauf. Die Tafel mit den Zitrusfrüchten über der Sternwarte bringt den wissenschaftlichen Impetus des Autors zum Ausdruck und demonstriert die Methode, mit deren Hilfe er den Dingen auf den Grund gehen will: Im ganzen Werk betont er immer wieder, ein „Mycroscopium“ oder „Vergrößerungsglas“ zu benutzen. Mit der programmatischen Gegenüberstellung von nah und fern, von Mikroskop und Fernglas, erklärt sich zugleich die durchgehende Bildstrategie im Aufbau der Tafeln. Die charakteristische bifokale Collagetechnik präsentiert oben in Originalgröße und Nahsicht die Frucht und unten in Fernsicht die Vedute. Gleichzeitig bringt die Tafel Volkamers Interesse für die Gestirne des Himmels zum Ausdruck, das er mit seinem Vater und vielen seiner Nürnberger Landsleute teilte. Möglicherweise lässt sich die Kombination von Sternwarte und mikroskopischer Vergrößerung als ein Hinweis auf die Bilderfindung der Kupferstiche des Hesperidenwerks deuten: Schließlich erscheinen die kostbaren Früchte wie riesige Himmelsgestirne am Firmament über Stadt, Landschaft und Garten.

In allen drei Bänden Volkamers wird die Zitrus untergliedert in Zedrat-zitronen (*Citrus medica* L., *Citrus limonimedica* L.), Zitronen und Limonen (*Citrus limon* L., *Citrus aurantiifolia* (Christm.) Swingle) sowie die bitteren Pomeranzen, süßen Orangen und Pampelmusen (*Citrus aurantium* L., *Citrus sinensis* L., *Citrus grandis* L.). Dem von Ferrari und anderen Autoren referierten Mythos folgend, weist Volkamer den

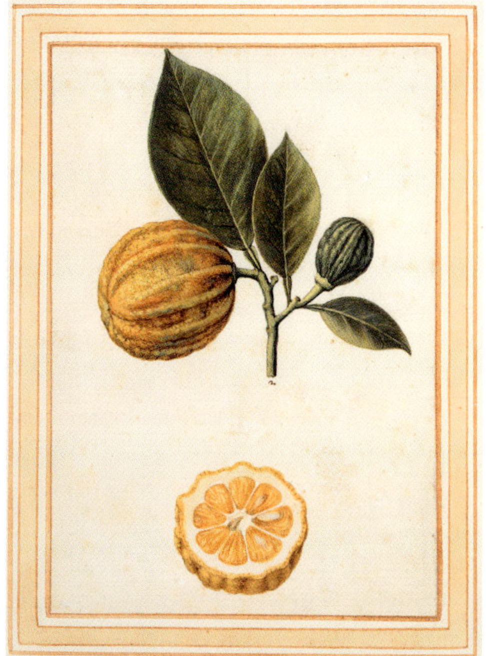

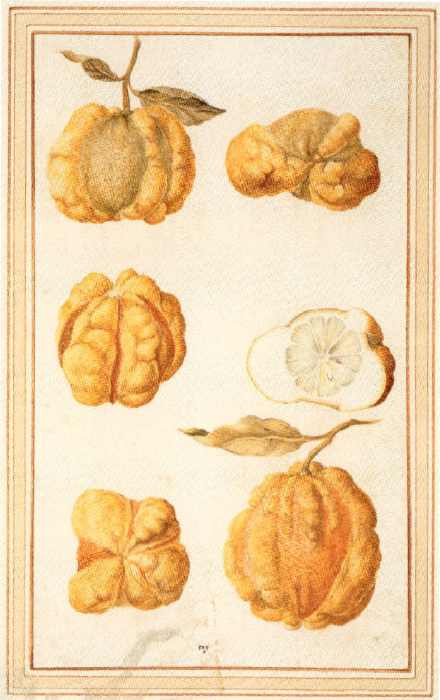

drei Hesperiden verschiedene Früchte und ihre Kultur in verschiedenen italienischen Regionen zu: Aegle habe sich am Gardasee um die Kultur der Zedratzitronen verdient gemacht, ihre Schwester Arethusa habe die Zitronen an die ligurische Küste gebracht und Hesperthusa die Pomeranzen nach Kalabrien. Die entsprechenden drei Teile des ersten Bandes werden von allegorischen Darstellungen der Hesperiden vor einem Garten und dem See beziehungsweise dem Meer im Hintergrund eröffnet. Im zweiten Band steht auf den drei Einleitungsseiten der Name der jeweiligen Hesperide in einem Blätterkranz; für den dritten Band ist keine entsprechende figürliche Darstellung überliefert.

Vincenzo Leonardi

Preliminary drawings for Ferrari's *Hesperides, sive de malorum aureorum cultura et usu*, 1646

London, The Royal Collection, Museo Cartaceo di Cassiano dal Pozzo

***Citrus sinensis* (L.) Osb.**

Ribbed sweet orange / Gestreifte süße Orange / Orange douce striée

pl. 401, "Aurantium striatum". Watercolour over black chalk, 21.1 × 14.8 cm (8 ¼ × 5 ⅞ in.). RL 19345

***Citrus medica* L. and *Citrus aurantium* L. (?)**

Citron and bitter orange / Zitrone und Pomeranze / Citron et orange amère

Watercolour over graphite, 36.7 × 22.2 cm (14 ½ × 8 ¾ in.). RL 19367

Volkamer bemüht sich in seinen Beschreibungen jeder einzelnen Zitruspflanze um exakte Aussagen zu Größe, Wuchsform, Farbe und Duft des Baumes, der Blätter, der Blüten und Früchte, dem Zeitpunkt der Reife, der Provenienz der Früchte, der Kultur des Baums. Die Vermehrung aus Samen, Stecklingen, Blättern und sogar einem Dorn („Stachel") interessiert ihn besonders. Das wissenschaftliche Grundprinzip der Autopsie ist die oberste Regel seines Werks. Volkamer teilt Erkenntnisse aus der Kultur im eigenen Garten mit und beklagt häufig, unter Berufung auf Ferrari oder Commelin, die umstrittene Klassifizierung und die uneinheitliche botanische Nomenklatur. Die Darstellung der verschiedenen Zitrusarten beginnt jeweils mit einer allgemeinen Beschreibung und einer Aufzählung zum „Nutzen und Gebrauch" der Früchte. Vielerorts beruft sich der Autor auf das *Vollständige Nürnbergische Koch-Buch* (Nürnberg 1691), das eine Fülle von Rezepten süßer und salziger Speisen mit Zitronen, *Cedri* und Pomeranzen zu bieten hat. Auf der fürstlichen und bürgerlichen Tafel durften Zitrusfrüchte, ob frische oder kandierte, nicht fehlen und ihre Verwendung für die Herstellung der im Zeitalter des Barock so beliebten Riechwässer war unabdingbar. Volkamer zeigt seine „Duftstube" im Pomeranzenhaus in Gostenhof, durch deren Fenster der Duft der Orangenblüten in den Raum drang (S. 243, 258/259).

Aufgrund der Neigung der Zitrusarten zu starken Veränderungen und aufgrund intensiver Kultur entstand im 17. Jahrhundert eine große Formenvielfalt der Bäume, Blüten, Blätter und Früchte, die von Gärtnern und Botanikern mit großem Interesse protokolliert, beschrieben und – sofern möglich – weitergezüchtet wurden. Volkamer führt zahlreiche Früchte auf, die bei Ferrari nicht vorkommen. Sein Corpus weist damit eine bis dahin in der Zitrusliteratur unbekannte Vielfalt auf. Monströse „Bizzarrie" oder „Mißgeburten", wie er ungewöhnliche, seiner Vermutung nach durch zufällige Mutationen oder als Ergebnis von Pfropfung entstandene Früchte nennt, zeigt er ebenso wie Ferrari, bei dem manche extravaganten oder kurios gefurchten Fruchtformen besonders bizarr wirken (S. 71). Ungewöhnliche Varietäten wie „fruchttragende" *(fetifero)*, „schwangere" Früchte zeigt Volkamer mehrfach, etwa den ausgefallenen „Cedro con frutto in frutto" im dritten Band oder die aufgrund der Sporne ihrer Schalen „hermaphroditisch" genannten Früchte. Blutorangen jedoch scheint er nicht gekannt zu haben, und auch die Mandarine *(Citrus reticulata Blanco)* wurde erst im 19. Jahrhundert aus Südostasien eingeführt.

„Schwefel-gelb" und „Citronenfarb": Botanik und Repräsentation

Anschaulich vermittelt Volkamer in seinen Beschreibungen differenzierte Farbwerte der häufig changierenden, gestreiften, geflammten, gescheckten oder gefleckten Früchte, Blüten, Blätter und Zweige: etwa die „gantz dunckele und schwartz-grüne Farbe" der auch

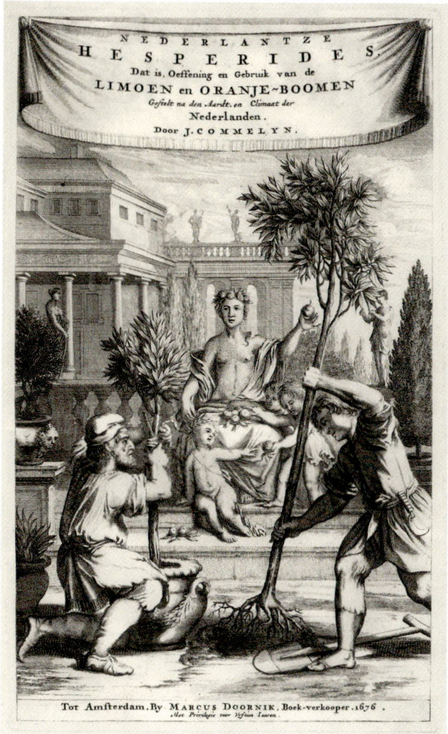

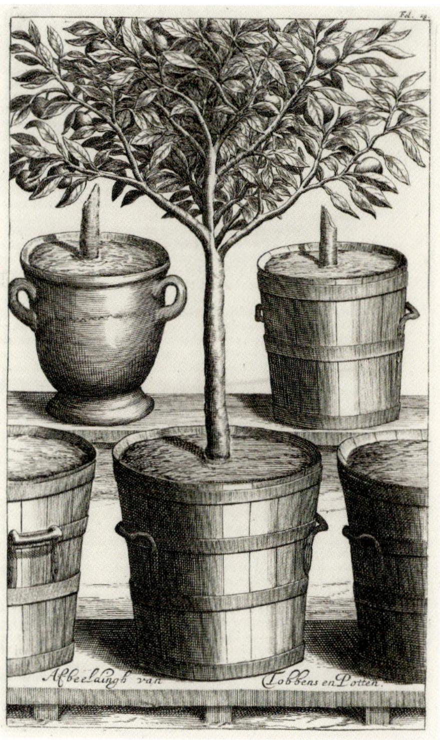

als „schwartze Citronen“ bezeichneten Pomi d'Adamo (Bd. 1, S. 167), „schwefel-gelbe und grüne Streiffe[n]“, „Pomerantzen- oder hoch Saffran-gelb“, „liecht Schwefel-gelbe aber Citronenfarb“ des Aranzo fiamato (Bd. 1, S. 196), „viele subtile grünliche Streiffe[n]“ der als „Bizzarrie“ bezeichneten Früchte (Bd. 1, S. 172). Volkamers Zeichnungen der Früchte, von denen leider keine einzige erhalten zu sein scheint, waren sicherlich koloriert. Die Kupferstiche der Früchte versuchen dem grafischen Medium einen differenzierten Eindruck der Farbigkeit und Musterung der Früchte und Blätter abzuringen. Da die Tafeln des dritten Bandes nicht koloriert wurden, kann der Leser dieses Nachdrucks sich die

Allegorical representation of citrus cultivation
Allegorische Darstellung zur Zitruskultur / Allégorie de la culture des agrumes
Engraving and etching. Frontispiece of: Jan Commelin, *Nederlantze Hesperides,* Amsterdam, 1676
Universitätsbibliothek Erlangen-Nürnberg, H61/2 TREW.D 206

Citrus planters / Zitruskübel / Pots et bacs à agrumes
Engraving and etching. From: Jan Commelin, *Nederlantze Hesperides,* Amsterdam, 1676, fol. 29
Universitätsbibliothek Erlangen-Nürnberg, H61/2 TREW.D 206

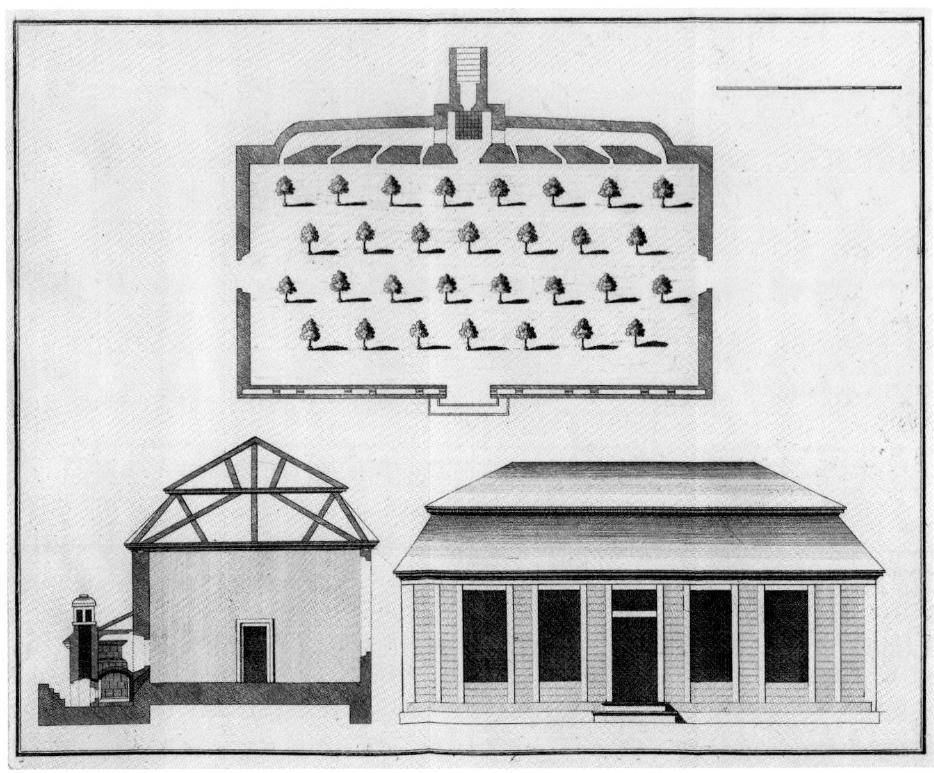

Unterschiede in der Wirkung und Aussage der Kupferstiche im Vergleich mit den farbigen Tafeln der beiden ersten Bände vor Augen führen.

Es haben sich mehrere kolorierte Exemplare und Einzeltafeln der Hesperiden-Bände erhalten, deren Farben sich jedoch unterscheiden. Das reproduzierte Exemplar stammt aus dem Besitz der Familie Holzschuher und wurde bereits im 18. Jahrhundert koloriert, als der Band noch dieser Nürnberger Patrizierfamilie gehörte. Die Kolorierung lässt die Unterschiede in der Zeichnung der Früchte und Blätter freilich weniger deutlich hervortreten und überspielt häufig deren Muster und Farbvariationen. Jeweils in einheitlichem Gelb, Orange oder Hellgelb sind bestimmte Fruchtgruppen gefasst, die Blätter und Zweige in Türkisgrün. Allerdings sind einige gestreifte oder geflammte Früchte ent-

Count Neithardt's orangery in Breslau (Wrocław)
Die Orangerie des Grafen Neithardt in Breslau (Wrocław) / L'orangerie du comte Neithardt à Wrocław
Engraving and etching. Plate for the unpublished third volume of *Nürnbergische Hesperides*, 1714–1720
Universitätsbibliothek Erlangen-Nürnberg, H61/2 RAR.A 35[2, p. 5

sprechend farblich attraktiv hervorgehoben. Anders als in späteren Kolorierungen, die im Allgemeinen keine starken Farben verwenden und eher dezente Übergänge zeigen, unterscheidet im vorliegenden Exemplar die Farbe über den Bildaufbau. Sie betont nah (Frucht) und fern (Vedute), oben und unten, indem in den meisten Fällen ganz entschieden Himmel und Wolken in Blau und Weiß angelegt sind und die Tafel „halbieren“. Die knalligen Töne etwa der venetischen Villenfassaden – Türkis, Rosa, Purpur oder Zitronengelb! – stimmen nicht mit der Realität überein. Die leuchtenden Farben sprechen jedoch den edelsten menschlichen Sinn, das Auge, unmittelbar an. Sie erzielen eine attraktive, höchst dekorative Gesamtwirkung der Kupferstiche und Vignetten und damit des gesamten Hesperidenwerks. Mit der aufwendigen Kolorierung vollzieht sich die entscheidende Verwandlung von Volkamers gelehrtem botanischen Zitrustraktat in ein Werk der Repräsentation der Wissenschaft.

Volkamer unterscheidet die Agrumen, von denen er lediglich Früchte und Blätter zugesandt bekam, von denjenigen, die er selbst in seinem Garten kultivierte und dort zur Blüte und Fruchtung brachte. Er rühmt sich, er habe die Früchte allesamt „mit eigner Hand nach dem Leben fleissig abgezeichnet“ (Bd. I, S. 7). Bereits im 17. Jahrhundert gab es in Nürnberg eine ausgeprägte Tradition der Naturmalerei und Zeichnung durch bürgerliche und patrizische Dilettanten. Dass Volkamer selbst zu Stift und Feder griff, hatte also durchaus eine lokale Tradition. Die einzige Ausnahme stellt – nach seiner Aussage – die 1705 im Bosischen Garten in Leipzig gepflückte Pampelmuse dar, von der es nur eine einzige Frucht gegeben habe, sodass er sich eine Zeichnung habe schicken lassen müssen (Bd. I, S. 173 und 189).

In Deutschland waren bei Weitem nicht so viele Zitrusarten erhältlich wie südlich der Alpen. Es war daher üblich, die Agrumen direkt aus Italien zu beziehen oder auf der Frankfurter und der Leipziger Messe zu kaufen. Volkamer führt im ersten Band eine Liste von Arten auf, die am Gardasee zu erwerben waren (Bd. I, S. 107 f.). Er empfiehlt die dortige Zitruskultur und führt in einem Kupferstich ein Beispiel für eine „limonaia“, eines der am Gardasee noch heute üblichen abschlagbaren Pomeranzenhäuser, vor Augen (S. 134/135). Zwar erwähnt er auch Genua, das er aus Joseph Furttenbachs italienischer Reisebeschreibung *Newes Itinerarium Italiae* von 1627 kannte (Bd. II, fol. 78r), und zeigt in großen Kupferstichen die aus dem Meer emporwachsende Villenlandschaft um die Stadt herum sowie das nahegelegene Nervi, aber es ist fraglich, ob er selbst jemals dort war.

Primel, Pistazie und Ananas

Volkamer kultivierte und beschrieb außer den Agrumen auch andere exotische und südländische Gewächse (S. 133), denen er sich jeweils am Ende seiner drei Bände widmet, so im dritten Band dem Kaffeebaum (S. 463). Im ersten Band schließt sich als fünfter Teil unter dem Titel *Flora Noribergensis, Oder Nürnbergische Flora* eine Abhandlung an, die auf den Bruder Johann Georg zurückgeht, aber nicht mit dessen umfangreicherem Buch gleichen Titels identisch ist. Nach 66 „Bären-Oehrlein" (*Primula auricula* L.), besonders beliebte Gartenblumen in dieser Zeit, und 49 Schlüsselblumen (*Primula veris* L.) folgen weitere besonders interessante und spektakuläre Blumen aus dem Garten des Bruders. Aus dem Bestand des Gostenhofer Gartens beschreibt Johann Christoph Volkamer unter anderem den Oliven-, Lorbeer- und Erdbeerbaum, die Pistazie und die Aubergine, die man für ungesund hielt, weil sie „thumm oder doll mache" (Bd. 1, S. 243). Im zweiten Band folgen Beschreibungen verschiedener Palmen, des Drachenbaums und der Baumwolle, vor allem aber der Ananas, der „Königin der Früchte", die seit dem späten 17. Jahrhundert in europäischen Gewächshäusern kultiviert wurde. Der Nürnberger Arzt und Naturforscher Michael Friedrich Lochner (1662–1720), der 1684/85 mit Johann Georg Volkamer in Italien studiert und 1691 das Landhaus Hummelstein bei Nürnberg erworben hatte, wo er exotische und südländische Gewächse kultivierte, publizierte 1716 einen Traktat über die Ananas, der manchen Exemplaren des Hesperidenwerks nachträglich angebunden wurde *(Commentatio de Ananasa sive nuce pinea Indica, vulgo Pinhas)*.

In der Darstellung von Früchten, etwa der Ananas, ebenso wie von Kolibri, Kakerlake und Vogelspinne ließ sich Volkamer von den Publikationen der etwa gleichaltrigen Maria Sibylla Merian (1647–1717) inspirieren, die von 1670 bis 1681 in Nürnberg lebte. Die berühmte Forscherin kannte die Familie Volkamer aufgrund familiärer und wissenschaftlicher Kontakte und tauschte sich mit Johann Georg dem Jüngeren über ihre Forschungen zu den Insekten und Pflanzen im südamerikanischen Land Surinam aus. 1705 erschien ihre aufsehenerregende Publikation *Metamorphosis Insectorum Surinamensium* (S. 104, 105, 107). Johann Christoph Volkamer erhielt 1706 aus Surinam via Amsterdam, wo Merian zu dieser Zeit lebte, eine Pampelmuse übersandt.

Botanische Netzwerke

Johann Christoph Volkamer stand – ebenso wie sein Bruder und sein Vater – in intensivem Austausch mit vielen Gartenbesitzern und Gärtnern im In- und Ausland. Aus Hameln, Hamburg, Leipzig, Dresden, Breslau, Böhmen, Holland, Italien, Spanien, Südamerika (Surinam, Curaçao) und vom Kap der Guten Hoffnung in Afrika sowie aus vielen anderen Orten erhielt er Informationen und es wurden ihm Früchte, Stecklinge,

Franz Ertinger, ***Limoniae Flores***
Lemon branch with flowers and fruit / Zitronenzweig mit Blüten und Frucht / Branche de citronnier portant fleurs et fruits
Engraving. From: Frans van Sterbeeck, *Citricultura*, Antwerp, 1682, pl. 5
Geneva, Bibliothèque du Conservatoire et Jardin Botaniques

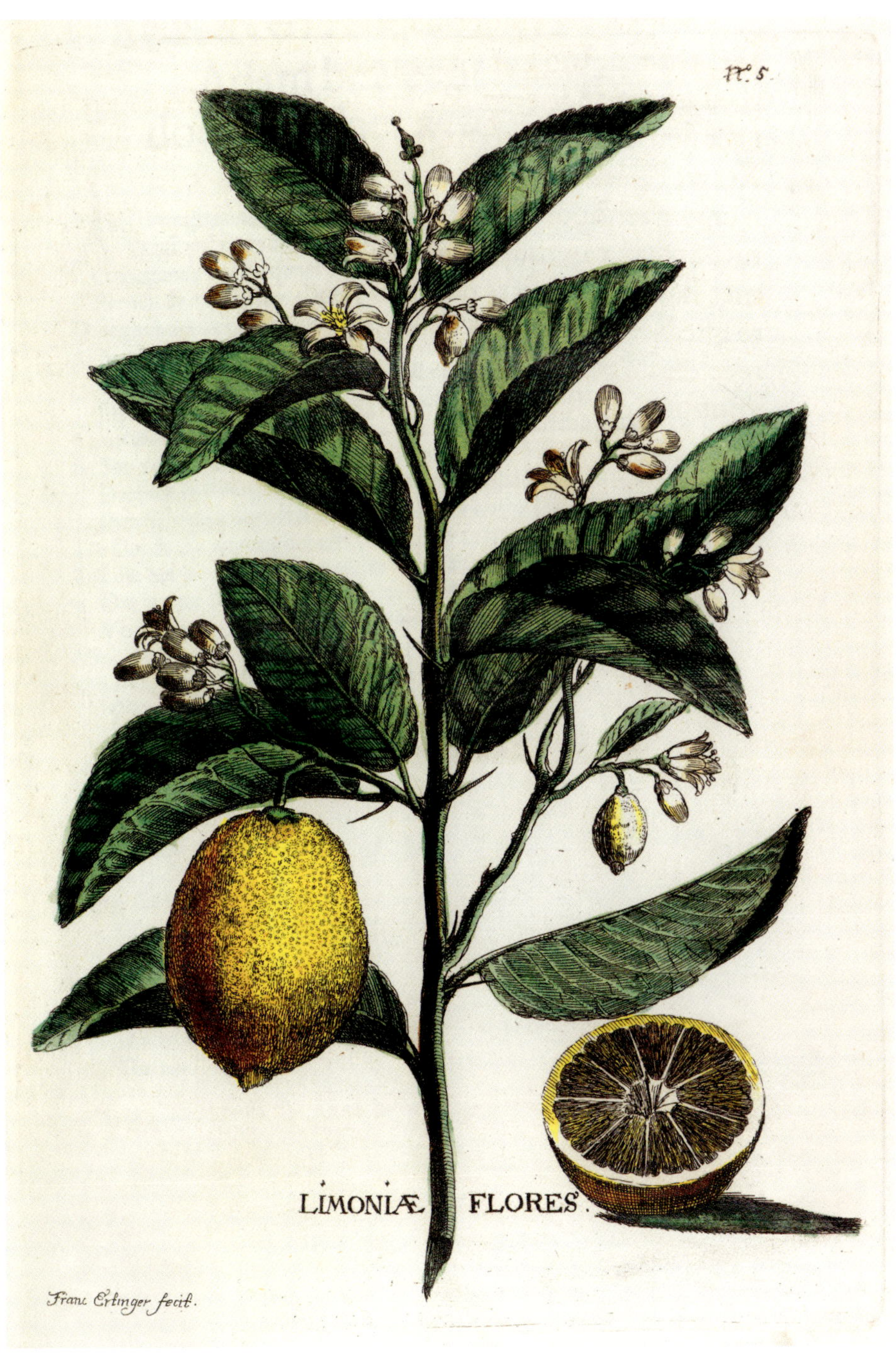
N.° 5.
LIMONIÆ FLORES.
Franc. Ertinger fecit.

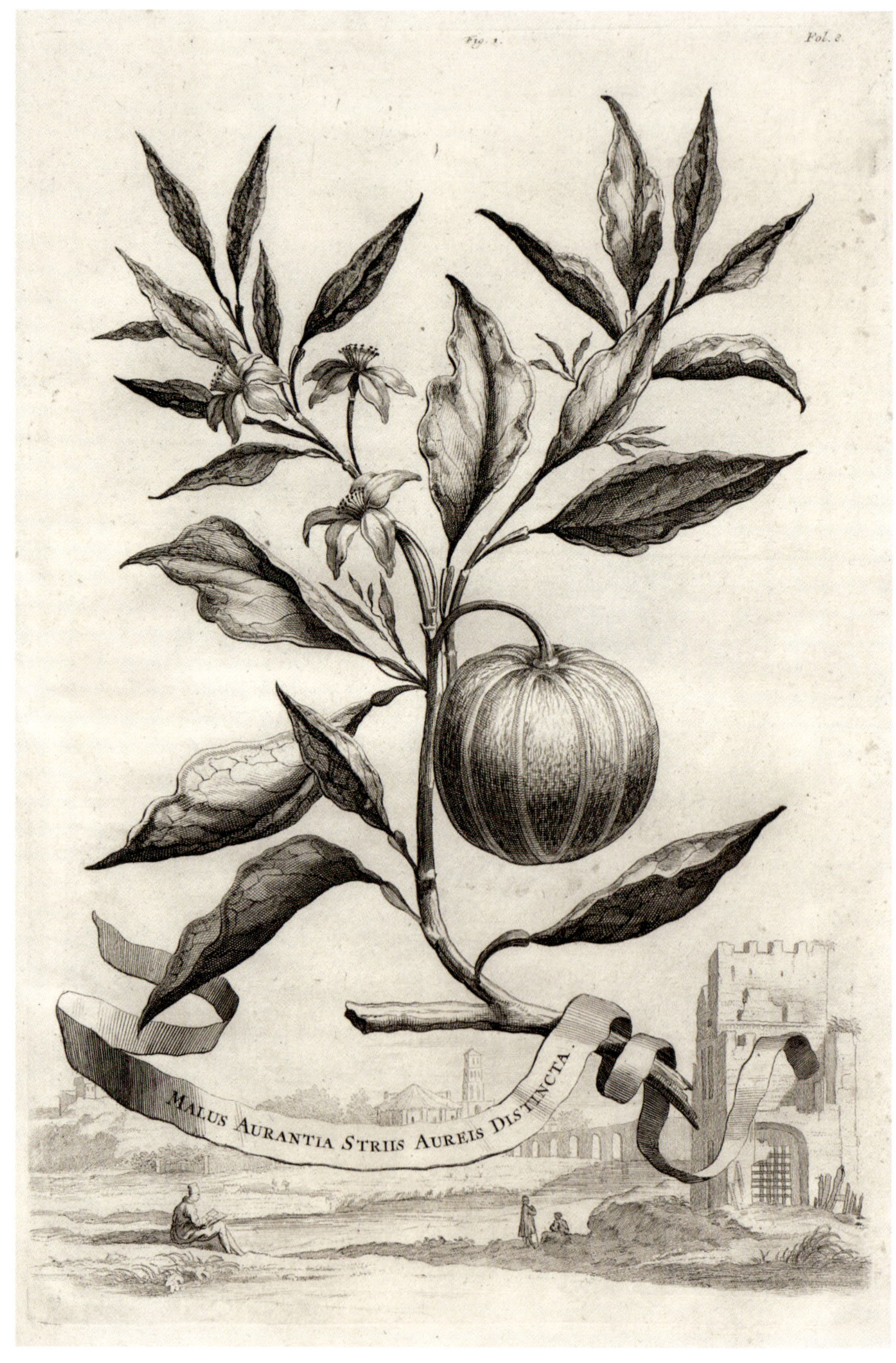
Fig. 1.
Fol. 2
Malus Aurantia Striis Aureis Distincta.

Samen oder ganze Gewächse zugesandt, ob wurzelnackt oder mit Wurzelballen. Seine italienischen Korrespondenten arbeiteten an Orten, die auch sein Vater und Bruder während ihres Studiums besucht hatten (Padua, Bologna, Rom, Neapel u. a.). Leider sind Johann Christoph Volkamers Briefe nicht erhalten, und im Hesperidenwerk erwähnt er nur wenige seiner Tausch- und Korrespondenzpartner namentlich. Häufiger bezeichnet er sie pauschal als „gute Freunde“.

Die botanische Forschung der Frühen Neuzeit funktionierte dank ausgedehnter internationaler Netzwerke. Eine der größten Sammlungen von Korrespondenzen zur Medizin, Botanik und den Naturwissenschaften trug der Nürnberger Arzt und Botaniker Christoph Jakob Trew (1695–1769) zusammen, Spross einer Gelehrtenfamilie auch er und mit Familie Volkamer bekannt. Die Wissenschaftler Johann Georg Volkamer senior und junior sind in Trews Sammlung mit umfangreichen internationalen Briefwechseln vertreten. Sie tauschten sich mit Gärtnern und Botanikern aus, deren Gärten und Wirkungsorte auch im Hesperidenwerk erwähnt werden. Vergleicht man diese Erwähnungen systematisch mit der Korrespondenz von Vater und Bruder, kann man so manchen der „guten Freunde“ Johann Christoph Volkamers ohne Weiteres identifizieren. Bei dem im Hesperidenwerk erwähnten Gärtner von Schloss Schwöbber handelt es sich zum Beispiel um Johann Friedrich Berner, dessen Korrespondenz aus den Jahren 1712 bis 1717 erhalten ist.

Auch Pflanzenverzeichnisse und Zitruskataloge werden als Beigaben von Briefen an die Familie Volkamer aufgeführt, so zum Beispiel eine 1717 von Giorgio Cornaro aus Padua nach Nürnberg geschickte Aufstellung von Agrumen. In zahlreichen Briefen an Johann Georg ist die Rede von seinem Bruder Johann Christoph, dem die Absender durch die Übersendung von Zitrusbäumen oder -früchten gefällig sein wollten. Die Sammlung Trew führt in aller Deutlichkeit vor Augen, dass Johann Christoph Volkamer sich für seine Forschungen über die Agrumen der Kontakte bediente, die innerhalb seiner Familie und der wissenschaftlichen Nürnberger Gemeinschaft existierten. Für die Netzwerkforschung ist das Hesperidenwerk daher eine Fundgrube und eine Herausforderung zugleich.

Malus aurantia striis aureis distincta
Orange twig with flowers and striped fruit / Pomeranzenzweig mit Blüten und gestreifter Frucht / Branche d’oranger portant fleurs et fruits cannelés
From: Abraham Munting, *Phytographia curiosa*, Amsterdam, 1711, fol. 8, fig. 1
Munich, Bayerische Staatsbibliothek, 2 Phyt. 219, 3

Mundus in litteris – die Welt im Buch: Nürnberg, Padua, Bologna, Peking, Kapstadt, Curaçao

„Bei meinen ersten Nürnbergischen *Hesperidibus*, habe ich / unter die abgezeichneten Früchte / lauter um hiesige Nürnbergische Gegend sich befindliche Prospecte und Gärten / nach dem Leben entwerffen und setzen lassen. Weil ich aber / bei Ausfertigung dieses Wercks / zum öfftern an Italien gedacht / und mich der überaus schönen Palläste vergnüglichst erinnert habe / welche die Edlen zu Venedig / mit grosser Verwunderung/ an dem Fluß Brenta / von Padua an bis gen Venedig hin / stehend und angelegt besitzen / so habe ich den Entschluß genommen / selbige / und auch andere daselbst aufgestellte vortreffliche Gebäude / ins Kupffer zu bringen / und unter die abcopirte Früchte / eitel prächtige Italianische Prospecten und Palläste zu setzen. Es hat mich nicht wenig Mühe gekostet / bis ich einen guten Freund angetroffen / der selbige Landschafft durchreiset/ und alle nachfolgende Risse / auf das accurateste / nach dem Leben gezeichnet; zu welchen zugleich sich einige Veronesische / und Bolognesische anfügen. Doch ist es endlich auch hierinnen mir gelungen / und bin ich meines Wunsches gewähret worden / und habe also eine jedwede Frucht / mit einem kostbaren Pallast / oder mit einem andern anmuthigen Italianischen Prospect / ausschmücken können." (Bd. II, Vor-Ansprach)

Volkamers Hesperidenwerk ist als topografische Sammlung ebenso aufschlussreich wie als botanisches Werk. Eine spezifische Zuordnung zwischen Frucht und wiedergegebener Anlage besteht generell nicht. Vielmehr hat Volkamer die Darstellungen ganz offensichtlich pragmatisch je nach Größe verteilt. Die Veduten sind regional gruppiert und vermitteln Lokalkolorit.

Dass im ersten Band Landhäuser, Schlösser und Gärten in und bei Nürnberg sowie am Schluss des Bandes Szenen der Nürnberger Landschaft wiedergegeben werden, erklärt sich aus der Verbundenheit des Autors mit seiner Heimatstadt. Viele der Nürnberger Ansichten folgen den Kupferstichen Johann Alexander Boeners (1647–1720), der mit Volkamer bekannt war und seine produktivste Schaffensphase im letzten Jahrzehnt des 17. und ersten Jahrzehnt des 18. Jahrhunderts erlebte (S. 111).

Die Tatsache, dass manche prominente Nürnberger Gärten im Hesperidenwerk nicht erscheinen, lässt sich vermutlich damit begründen, dass kein Vorbild von Boener vorlag, das für eine Hesperidentafel hätte adaptiert werden können. Boeners Veduten wurden wahrscheinlich nicht von ihm selbst, sondern vom jeweiligen Kupferstecher für das Format der Tafel im Hesperidenwerk adaptiert, insgesamt in den Proportionen verändert, meistens in der Breite gestaucht sowie mit einem malerischen Vordergrund und häufig einem ebenso fiktiven landschaftlichen Hintergrund versehen. Interessanterweise gibt Volkamer selbst eine Anweisung, wie man einen Gartenplan in eine perspektivische Ansicht überträgt (S. 108, 109; Bd. I, S. 249–251). Bei den Veduten duldete Volkamer

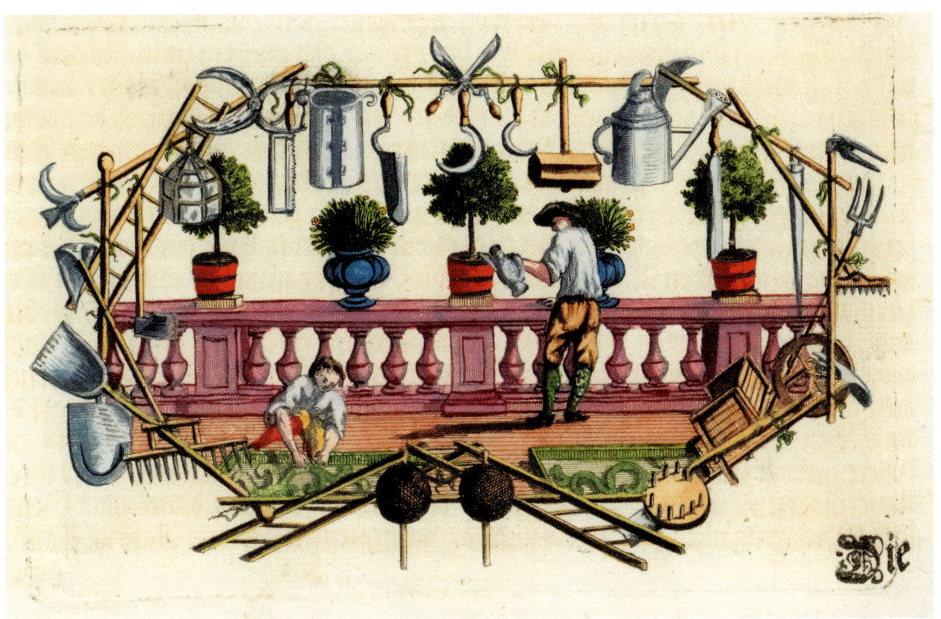

jedenfalls – anders als bei den Früchten! – einen gestalterischen Spielraum mit Zugeständnissen an die malerische Qualität der Darstellung. Die großformatigen Nürnberg-Ansichten des Zeichners und Kupferstechers Johann Adam Delsenbach (1687–1765) erschienen erst ab etwa 1715, lagen bei Drucklegung von Volkamers erstem Band also noch nicht vor.

Zum zweiten Band des Hesperidenwerks trug Delsenbach eine Tafel zu St. Georgen bei Bayreuth (S. 264/265) und eine Vogelschau von Schloss und Garten Schönbrunn (S. 262/263) bei. Großformatige Veduten der Gärten von Erlangen (S. 266–269), Schloss Schwöbber (S. 23, 274) und Passau (S. 276, 277) ließ Volkamer nach Vorlagen der Gebrüder Decker und anderer Zeichner stechen. Einige der Kupferstecher des Hesperidenwerks arbeiteten auch für die große Architekturpublikation Paul Deckers des Älteren, den *Fürstlichen Baumeister* (Augsburg 1711–1713). Ansichten der Villa Allegri in Cuzzano di Grezzana (S. 270/271) sowie weiterer Villen und Gärten an der Brenta, in Padua (S. 63), Verona (S. 24, 119) und den Euganeischen Hügeln sowie zwei bolognesische Veduten schließen sich im zweiten Band des Hesperidenwerks an. Als souveräne Gemeinwesen waren die Republik Venedig und die Freie Reichsstadt Nürnberg

Gardeners with their tools / Gärtner mit Gartenwerkzeug / Jardiniers et outils de jardinage
From: *Nürnbergische Hesperides*, vol. 1, vignette p. 76

vergleichbar. Bei der Villeggiatura, dem sommerlichen Aufenthalt des venezianischen und paduanischen Adels auf dem Land, und der Sommerfrische des Nürnberger Patriziats und Stadtbürgertums handelte es sich nicht um eine höfische, sondern um eine adlige und stadtbürgerliche Kultur des Landlebens. Wer die venetischen Villen, in denen auch Agrumen kultiviert wurden, im Auftrag des Nürnberger Kaufmanns „nach dem Leben" aufnahm, ist nicht bekannt. Volkamers Zeichner muss dem venezianischen Kartografen und Franziskanerminoriten Vincenzo Coronelli (1650–1718) nahegestanden haben. 1711 publizierte Coronelli eine Sammlung von Veduten der Brenta-Villen, die den Tafeln Volkamers im Bildaufbau verblüffend ähneln (S. 116). Die Auswahl ist jedoch nicht identisch. Da einige der Gebäude lediglich bei Volkamer überliefert sind, ist sein Werk als eine sehr wichtige architekturhistorische Quelle für die Villenkultur des Veneto anzusehen.

Ähnlich verhält es sich mit den Villen des bolognesischen Adels, die auf den erst kürzlich aufgefundenen Kupferstichen für den dritten Band wiedergegeben sind. In der altehrwürdigen Universitätsstadt Bologna (S. 127), die seit alters her „la dotta, la grassa", „die gelehrte, die fette" Stadt genannt wurde, hatten sich Johann Georg Volkamer der Ältere wie auch der Jüngere während ihrer Studienjahre aufgehalten. Zu ihren wichtigsten Produktionszweigen gehörte seit dem 17. Jahrhundert die Seidenproduktion. Vielleicht pflegte Johann Christoph daher auch geschäftliche Beziehungen in die zum Kirchenstaat gehörende Stadt. Die ikonische Präsentation der Stadt Bologna (S. 124, 411) lässt sich mit der Nürnbergs im ersten Band vergleichen: oben ein „Cedro dolce", unten die Silhouette der Kirchen und Türme. Volkamer übernahm diese Vedute vom Titelblatt (S. 124) von Giuseppe Maria Mitellis (1634–1718) *Le Arti per Via* (Bologna 1660). In der *Dissertatio* (1713) führt Erhard Reusch – wie bereits erwähnt – zwei bedeutende Bologneser Forscher auf: Ulisse Aldrovandi und den Gelehrten Ovidio Montalbano. Beide befassten sich mit den Agrumen (S. 72). Aldrovandis Sammlungen gingen in das 1711 gegründete Istituto delle Scienze ein, eine der berühmtesten wissenschaftlichen Akademien ihrer Zeit. Die dort tätigen Botaniker, unter anderen Lelio Trionfetti (1647–1722) und sein Nachfolger als Direktor des Botanischen Gartens, Giuseppe Monti (1682–1760), korrespondierten mit den Volkamers in Nürnberg. Monti nennt Nürnberg als einzigen Ort in Deutschland, mit dem er – neben zahlreichen anderen berühmten botanischen Gärten in ganz Europa – im Austausch stehe, und zitiert regelmäßig Johann Georg Volkamers *Flora* sowie Johann Christoph Volkamers Hesperidenwerk.

Der Bologneser Adel hatte sich seit dem späten 16. Jahrhundert in der näheren Umgebung der Stadt, vor allem an und auf den Hügeln im Süden und Südwesten, Landhäuser anlegen lassen. Die Stadtpläne Bolognas aus dem späten 17. Jahrhundert und der Zeit um 1700 (z. B. Agostino Mitellis Stadtplan von 1692) deuten dies an. Diese florierende Villenkultur, die sich in der Literatur und im Theater niedergeschlagen hat, findet allerdings nicht im selben Maße in der Reiseliteratur oder in Stadtbeschreibungen Erwähnung. Im 17. und 18. Jahrhundert hielten die meisten der ausländischen Reisenden auf Grand Tour – der Bildungsreise, die sie zu den politischen und künstlerischen Zentren Florenz, Rom oder Neapel führte – in Bologna an, blieben aber nicht lange. Die Tradition der Reiseführer und der repräsentativen Kupferstich-serien wurde vor allem im päpstlichen Rom gepflegt und von den Verlagen ausgebaut. Bologna gehörte zwar zum Kirchenstaat, hatte aber keine mit Rom vergleichbare Bildproduktion zur Profanarchitektur aufzuweisen. Die frühesten, über Jahrzehnte oft kopierten Bologneser Veduten stammen aus dem topografischen Kartenwerk von Joan Blaeu, der 1663 eine Serie von acht Ansichten von Bologna herausgab. Erst 1732 erschien, beim Augsburger Verleger Johann Georg Merz, die erste umfangreiche Vedutenserie, gestochen von dem schlesischen Kupferstecher Friedrich Bernhard Werner; im späten 18. Jahrhundert folgte die Serie von Pio Panfili. In den genannten Stichserien kommen Villen oder Gärten ebenso wenig vor wie in anderen bolognesischen Veduten des späteren 18. oder 19. Jahrhunderts. In diesem Kontext verdienen die Kupferstiche im dritten Band des Hesperidenwerks Aufmerksamkeit. Paläste und Gärten der großen Bologneser Adelsfamilien werden hier ebenso wiederge-geben wie die als städtische Promenade genutzte Anlage La Montagnola in Bologna (S. 409) und die weithin bekannten Wallfahrtskirchen San Michele in Bosco (S. 424) und, bereits im zweiten Band, Madonna di San Luca (S. 388). Malerisch gelegene, spelunkenartige Gasthäuser auf dem Land (S. 413) wirken auf den ersten Blick wie eine Bühnendekoration für Giuseppe Verdis Oper *Rigoletto*. Einzelmotive mancher Tafeln sind aus verschiedenen Vorlagen zusammengeklaubt – so aus Kupferstichen von Agostino Mitelli und Georg Andreas Böckler – und willkürlich kombiniert. Architekturmotive wie kastellartige, zinnenbekrönte Palazzi, Aquädukte oder Brunnenprospekte werden zu Vedutencapricci mit Bologneser und emilianischem Lokalkolorit zusammengestellt. Am deutlichsten fällt dies bei einer Tafel ins Auge, die Giambolognas Neptunstatue aus der Bologneser Innenstadt kurzerhand in einen fiktiven Garten versetzt (S. 435). Die Bologneser Veduten wirken in der perspektivischen Wiedergabe zwar unbeholfen, sollten aber dennoch als Bilddokumente in Betracht gezogen werden. Die auf den Vorzeichnungen im Germanischen Nationalmuseum (S. 123) verzeichneten Bildtitel stammen jedenfalls von einem ortskundigen Italiener und bezeichnen Bauten und Anlagen, über deren Aussehen sonst keine Informationen erhalten sind. Wer sie

Editorische Anmerkung zu den Tafellegenden: Die botanischen Bezeichnungen und Klassifikationen folgen den Angaben Volkamers. Die Ortsangaben sind auf Englisch in der aktuellen Schreibweise angegeben. Daraus ergeben sich Abweichungen zu den Originalinschriften der Tafeln. Das Ortsregister im Anhang umfasst auch die deutschen und französischen Ortsbezeichnungen.

„nach dem Leben zeichnete", ist leider auch hier unbekannt. War es möglicherweise der Venezianer Vincenzo Coronelli, von dem überliefert ist, er habe im Jahr 1713 beabsichtigt, einen Reiseführer über die Stadt Bologna zu schreiben? Der Nürnberger Architekt Johann Jakob Schübler, dessen Name auf der Rückseite einer der Vorzeichnungen zu finden ist, war es vermutlich nicht.

Die letzten Tafeln des zweiten und dritten Bandes zeigen Veduten von Nazareth, Peking, dem Kap der Guten Hoffnung (S. 128) und Brasilien. Der Horizont des Johann Christoph Volkamer war weit gesteckt und umfing nicht nur Europa. „Mundus in litteris" – die geistige, die wissenschaftliche Welt, in der sich der Kaufmann und Zitrussammler Volkamer bewegte, spiegelt sich in seinem Hesperidenwerk.

Franz Ertinger, **Apparatus for straightening the trunks of potted trees**
Vorrichtung zur Begradigung des Stammes von Kübelpflanzen
Dispositif permettant de redresser le tronc des plantes en pot
Engraving. From: Frans van Sterbeeck, *Citricultura*, Antwerp, 1682, pl. 7
Geneva, Bibliothèque du Conservatoire et Jardin Botaniques

Pages 90/91
Volkamer's orangery at Gostenhof, view and plan
Volkamers Pomeranzenhaus in Gostenhof, Ansicht und Plan
L'orangerie de Volkamer à Gostenhof, vue et plan
From: *Nürnbergische Hesperides*, 1708, vol. 1, plate p. 14

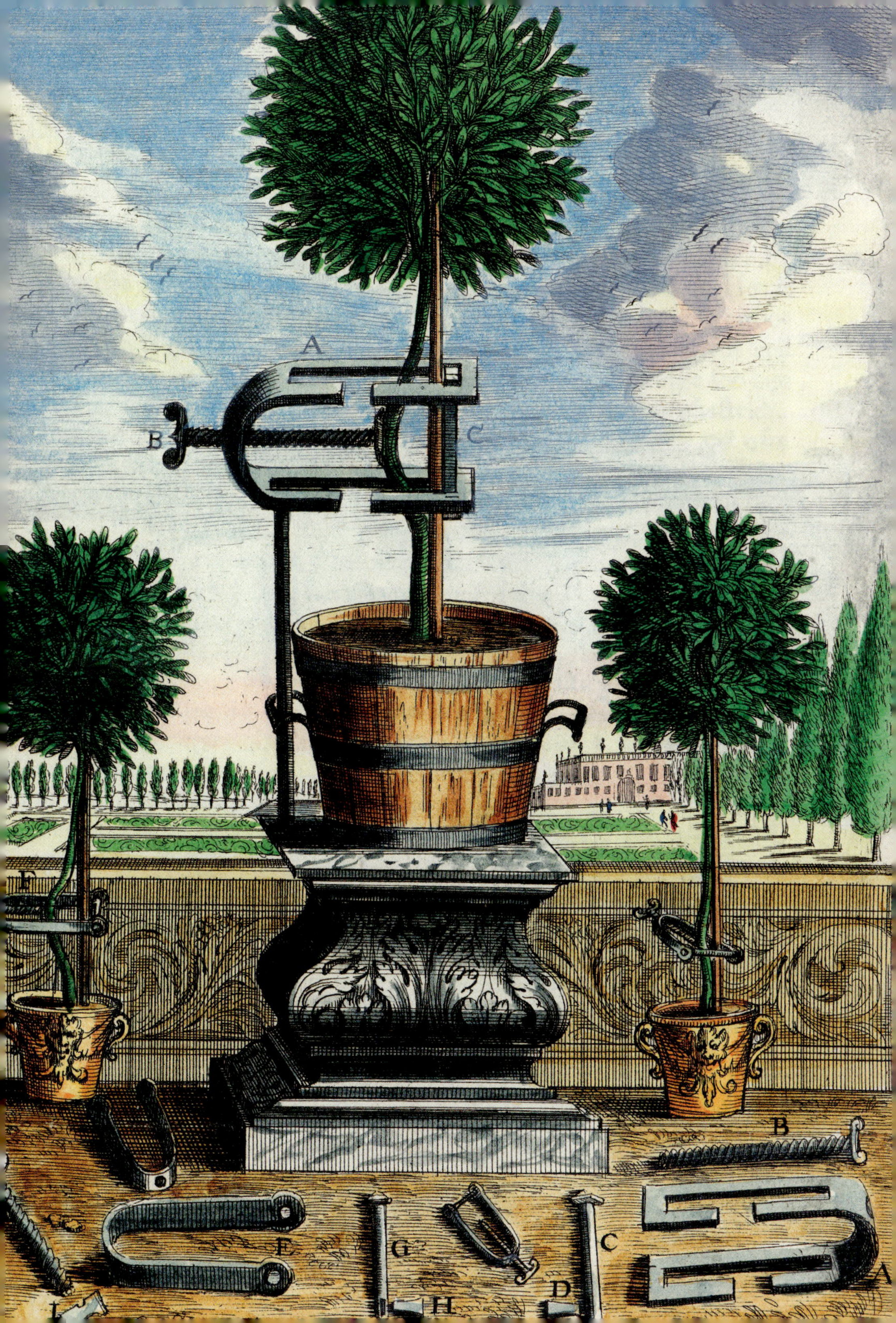
A
B
C
F
B
E
G
C
D
H
A

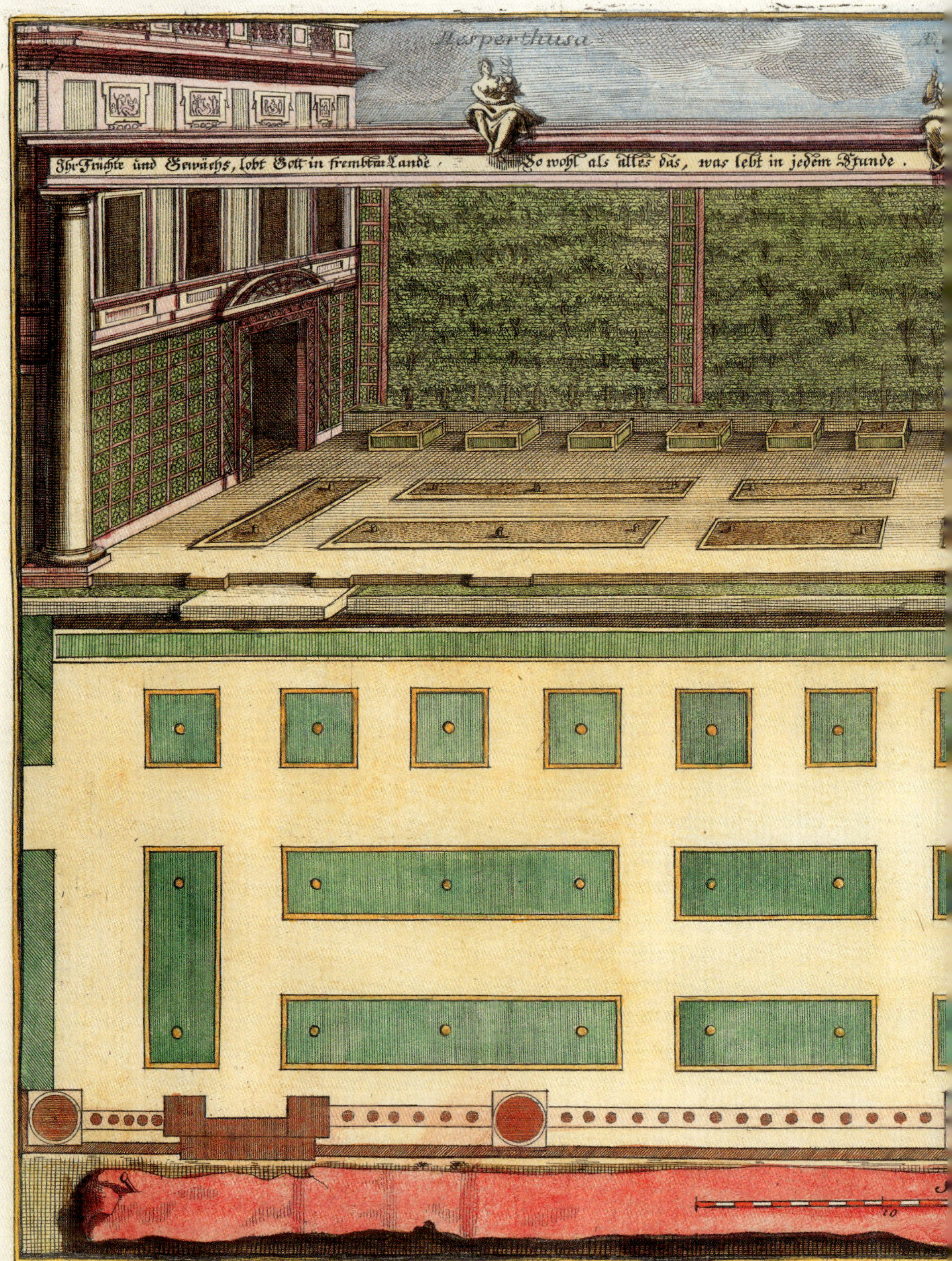
Hesperthusa
Ihr Früchte und Gewächs, lobt Gott in frembten Lande ,
So wohl als alles das, was lebt in jedem Stunde .
10

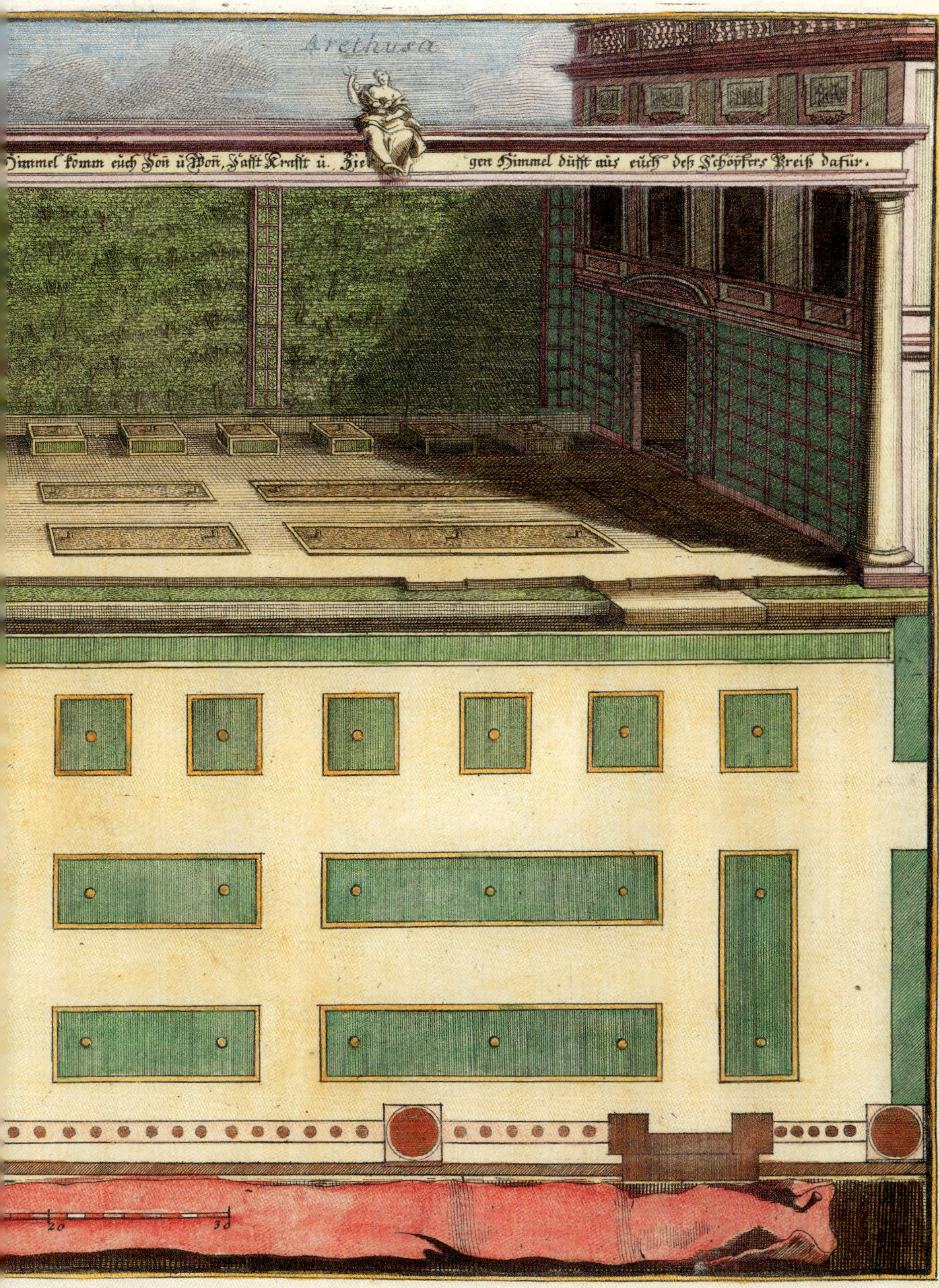

14

Arethusa
Himmel komm euch Son ū Won, Safft Krafft u. Zier
gen Himmel düfft aus euch deß Schöpfers Preiß dafür.
20
30

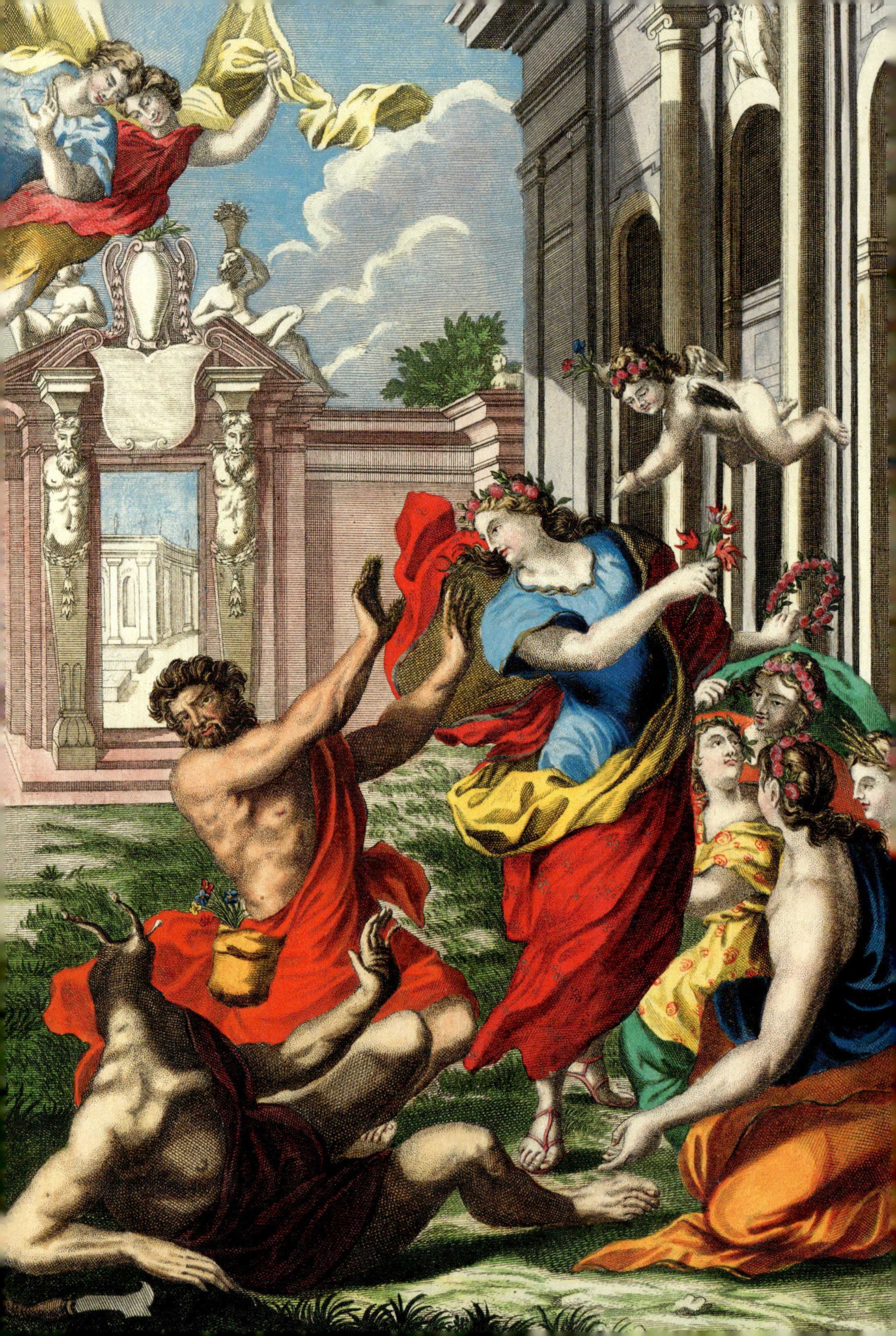

« Des fruits divins » Le livre des *Hespérides* de Johann Christoph Volkamer

IRIS LAUTERBACH

« L'oranger est sans contredit le plus beau de tous les arbres de fleur : sa tige droite, son bois uni, ses grandes feuilles luisantes, ses belles fleurs, ses fruits exquis, sa tête régulière d'un très beau vert, tout en est admirable ; l'on en distingue plusieurs sortes, comme le Citronnier ou Balotin, le Limier ou Limonier, le Bigaradier, le Cédrat, le Riche-dépouille, le Poncyre, le Pommier d'Adam, la Bergamotte, l'Oranger de Chine, etc., leurs différences sont peu considérables : elles ne consistent qu'en ce que les uns font des arbres de tige, et les autres des nains ou buissons, ou parce que le fruit des uns est doux et celui des autres plus aigre ; ils conservent tous leur beau feuillage… »

Antoine-Joseph Dezallier d'Argenville (1680–1765), théoricien du jardinage, résume en ces termes la fascination qu'exercent les agrumes à l'époque baroque, en même temps que l'importance de la tradition de l'orangerie pour le jardin classique à la française. À son ouvrage *La théorie et la pratique du jardinage*, publié à Paris en 1709 (p. 214) et qui connut une large audience, il ajoute dans la deuxième édition, en 1713, deux chapitres sur la culture des agrumes.

Avec leur port élancé, leur somptueux feuillage persistant, leurs fleurs et leurs fruits aux couleurs éclatantes, les agrumes sont un plaisir pour les yeux ; leurs fruits et leurs écorces confites réjouissent le palais de leurs aromatiques saveurs ; le parfum des huiles essentielles extraites des fruits et des fleurs enivre l'odorat. Comme le notent de nombreux auteurs d'ouvrages sur les jardins des XVIIe et XVIIIe siècles, dans les orangeries, ces arbres toujours verts, qui portent à la fois des fleurs et des fruits, évoquent la repré-

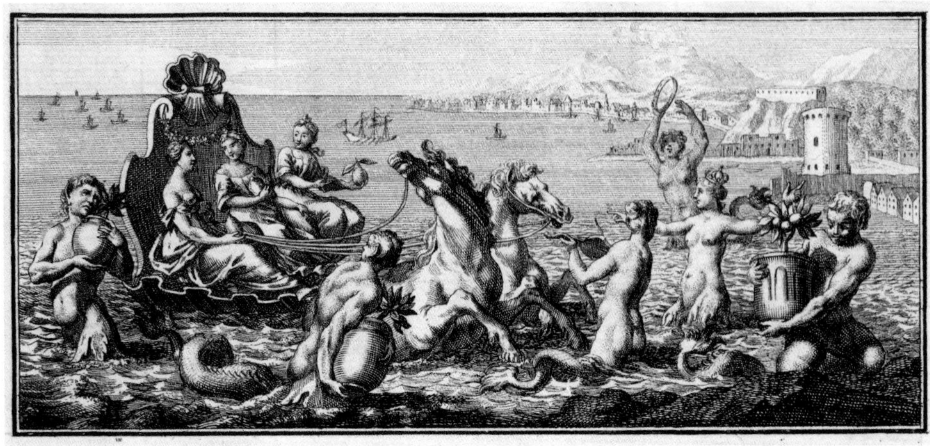

sentation d'une félicité éternelle et paradisiaque: «Car lorsque, au plus fort de l'hiver, le gel et le grand froid ont tué toute végétation, que tout est recouvert d'une épaisse couche de neige, et que le terrible vent du nord souffle avec une telle violence, qu'on a la ferme impression qu'il va détruire et ravager la nature tout entière, on voit dans ce merveilleux jardin du paradis, avec le plus grand émerveillement, les arbustes les plus beaux et les plus rares sous des formes diverses, qui verdoient et fleurissent, l'un a d'adorables fleurs blanches qui sentent délicieusement bon, l'autre des jaunes, le troisième des rouges, le quatrième est pourpre, et ainsi de suite, l'un a des fruits de saison, l'autre hors saison, le tout accompagné des senteurs les plus merveilleuses et les plus pénétrantes, cela donne forcément à un être humain, comme en un éternel printemps, un élan nouveau» (Hesse 1706, p. 35 s.). Les pommes d'or du jardin des Hespérides, dont la dénomination latine *poma aurantia* a donné le nom allemand *Pomeranze*, sont des oranges. Le mythe antique souligne la préciosité de ces fruits, qui peuvent faire ressembler de simples jardins terrestres au paradis. C'est dans le jardin mythique des dieux que se trouve le légendaire

Page 92
Flora punishes two negligent gardeners by transforming them into a snail and a caterpillar
Flora verwandelt zwei nachlässige Gärtner zur Strafe in Schnecke und Raupe
Flora punit deux jardiniers négligents en les transformant en une limace et une chenille
From: *Nürnbergische Hesperides*, 1708, vol. 1, plate p. 80

The arrival of the Hesperides on the coast of Italy
Die Ankunft der Hesperiden am italienischen Gestade / Arrivée des Hespérides sur la côte italienne
Engraving and etching. Vignette for the unpublished third volume of *Nürnbergische Hesperides*, 1714–1720
Universitätsbibliothek Erlangen-Nürnberg, H61/2 RAR.A 35[2, p. 2

arbre aux fruits d'or, gardé par le dragon Ladon et soigné par trois nymphes, les Hespérides Aeglé, Aréthuse et Hesperthuse – filles d'Atlas et de la Nuit. Le nom d'Hespérides provient de l'étoile du soir Hesperos, étoile de Vénus. Le héros Hercule est vainqueur du dragon et obtient ainsi les précieux fruits que lui offrent les Hespérides. Déjà dans le mythe s'expriment à la fois toute la valeur que l'on accorde au genre *Citrus*, arbres et fruits, et le soin particulier que demande leur culture – plantation et entretien.

L'origine des *Citrus*, agrumes, qui font partie des plantes cultivées les plus anciennes, se situe dans différentes régions d'Asie. Au sud de la Chine, on trouve, déjà il y a quatre mille ans, l'orange (*Citrus sinensis* L.). Au XVe ou tout au début du XVIe siècle, des marchands génois et portugais introduisent des variétés cultivées d'orange douce en Italie. L'orange amère ou bigarade (*Citrus aurantium* L.), également issue à l'origine d'Asie, le citron (*Citrus limon* L.) et le limon (*Citrus aurantiifolia* (Christm.) Swingle) furent apportés d'Asie au Proche-Orient, et de là sans doute introduits par les croisés en Italie, tandis que le cédrat (*Citrus medica* L., *Citrus limonimedica* L.) devait être déjà présent en Italie au plus tard au premier siècle avant Jésus-Christ. Connus dans les cultures arabes et maures dès le Moyen Âge, les oranges amères et les citrons furent cultivés en Toscane à partir du XIVe siècle. Le processus millénaire de sélection des agrumes avait produit à la longue un grand nombre de formes et de variétés.

Les agrumes à la cour des princes : motif héraldique et objet de collection

À la cour des princes des premiers temps modernes prit place dans l'iconographie des souverains, à côté d'Apollon, en tout premier lieu Hercule, héros valeureux et par conséquent figure d'identification. Des copies de la célèbre sculpture monumentale d'Hercule de la collection Farnèse, qui tient une poignée de fruits (p. 8), ornent de nombreux jardins de l'époque baroque, évoquant le mythique jardin des dieux gardé par les Hespérides. La culture des agrumes devint, au cours des XVIe et XVIIe siècles, une gageure importante. Les Médicis, famille de négociants qui s'étaient hissés au rang de souverains du duché de Toscane, interprétèrent le nom botanique *malus medica* comme une référence à leur nom de famille, et ils voyaient dans les agrumes des fruits héraldiques ressemblant aux boules dans le blason des Médicis. Aux jardins Boboli de Florence et au jardin de la villa Médicis à Castello se trouvent, aujourd'hui encore, l'une des collections d'agrumes d'Europe les plus anciennes, les plus riches et réunissant le plus grand nombre de variétés. Les agrumes furent montrés dans les jardins comme des joyaux du monde végétal à partir du XVIe siècle ; les fruits – artistiquement reproduits en cire, en céramique et plus tard en porcelaine, ou représentés en peinture (p. 11) – figuraient dans les cabinets de curiosités et étaient exposés dans les collections princières (p. 57). Au XVIIe siècle, l'importance héraldique des fruits pour la Maison d'Orange-Nassau fit de la Hollande, en particulier des jardins botaniques de Leiden et d'Amsterdam, un centre de culture des agrumes.

Les agrumes au nord des Alpes : rêve, économie, science

Les jardins italiens de la Renaissance richement agrémentés de sculptures, de monuments, de fontaines, et de végétaux d'une enivrante sensualité comme les agrumes, ne suscitaient pas seulement l'enthousiasme chez les visiteurs princiers, mais aussi dans le monde des érudits, des écrivains et des marchands. Ainsi le maire de Francfort Johann Schwind déclarait-il sa passion pour l'art des jardins (p. 12) née d'une « puissante étincelle qui avait éveillé cet esprit au cours des voyages qu'il avait faits, quelques années auparavant, en Italie » (Merian 1641). Johann Christoph Volkamer (1644–1720) songeait bien souvent, lui aussi, à son séjour en Italie et se remémorait « avec le plus grand plaisir les palais d'une beauté extraordinaire » (vol. II, Préambule). Goethe dans *Les Années d'apprentissage de Wilhelm Meister* (1795/96) exprime, à travers la célèbre chanson nostalgique de la jeune Mignon, la fascination pour ce pays aux jardins luxuriants qu'est l'Italie : « Connais-tu le pays des citronniers en fleur, / Où luit l'orange d'or dans l'ombre du feuillage ? / La douce brise y naît d'un azur sans nuage, / Là croît le fier laurier, là le myrte rêveur. / Le connais-tu vraiment ? » (*Ballades et autres poèmes,* version française de Jean Malaplate).

Les agrumes étaient connus au nord des Alpes dès le Moyen Âge. Leur utilisation était de tradition très ancienne dans les usages populaires et religieux, en particulier pour les rites funéraires. Dans la religion juive, l'etrog, variété de cédrat, intervient dans la liturgie de la fête des tabernacles *(souccot)*. Volkamer qualifie le fruit du cédratier de « Cedro col Pigolo » ou « pomme-citron des Juifs » (vol. I, p. 121).

Les multiples propriétés médicinales des agrumes furent déjà soulignées par les auteurs de l'Antiquité. À partir du début de l'époque moderne, on utilisa le citron comme remède contre le scorbut, carence qui se manifestait fréquemment chez les navigateurs au cours de leurs longs voyages. Médecins et pharmaciens, qui étaient en même temps d'éminents botanistes, du fait de l'intérêt qu'ils portaient aux plantes pour leurs propriétés curatives, s'intéressaient aussi beaucoup aux agrumes. Depuis le XVIe siècle, les relations commerciales et les échanges entre savants qui étudiaient dans les plus grandes universités italiennes furent essentiels pour la transmission culturelle entre l'Italie et l'Allemagne

Pages 97, 98
After Pietro da Cortona, ***Hercules inter Hesperides Romanis in hortis Midiccorum***
Hercules with the Hesperides / Herkules bei den Hesperiden / Hercule chez les Hespérides
From: *Continuation der Nürnbergischen Hesperidum*, 1714, vol. II, plates pag. 3, 4
Volkamer borrowed the engravings from: / Die Stiche übernahm Volkamer aus: / Volkamer a repris les gravures de : Giovanni Battista Ferrari: *Hesperides, sive de malorum aureorum cultura et usu*, Rome, 1646

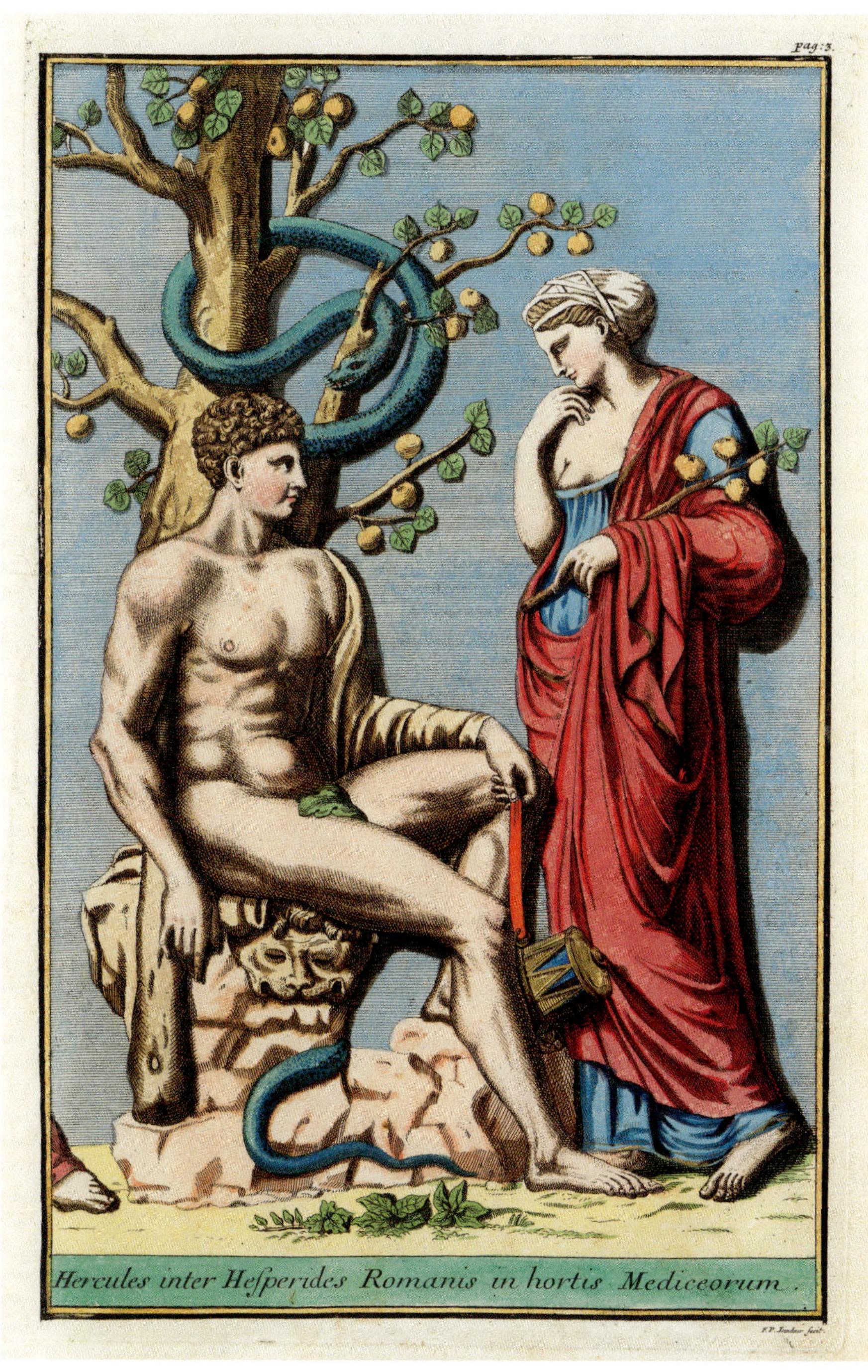
Pag: 3.
Hercules inter Hesperides Romanis in hortis Mediceorum.

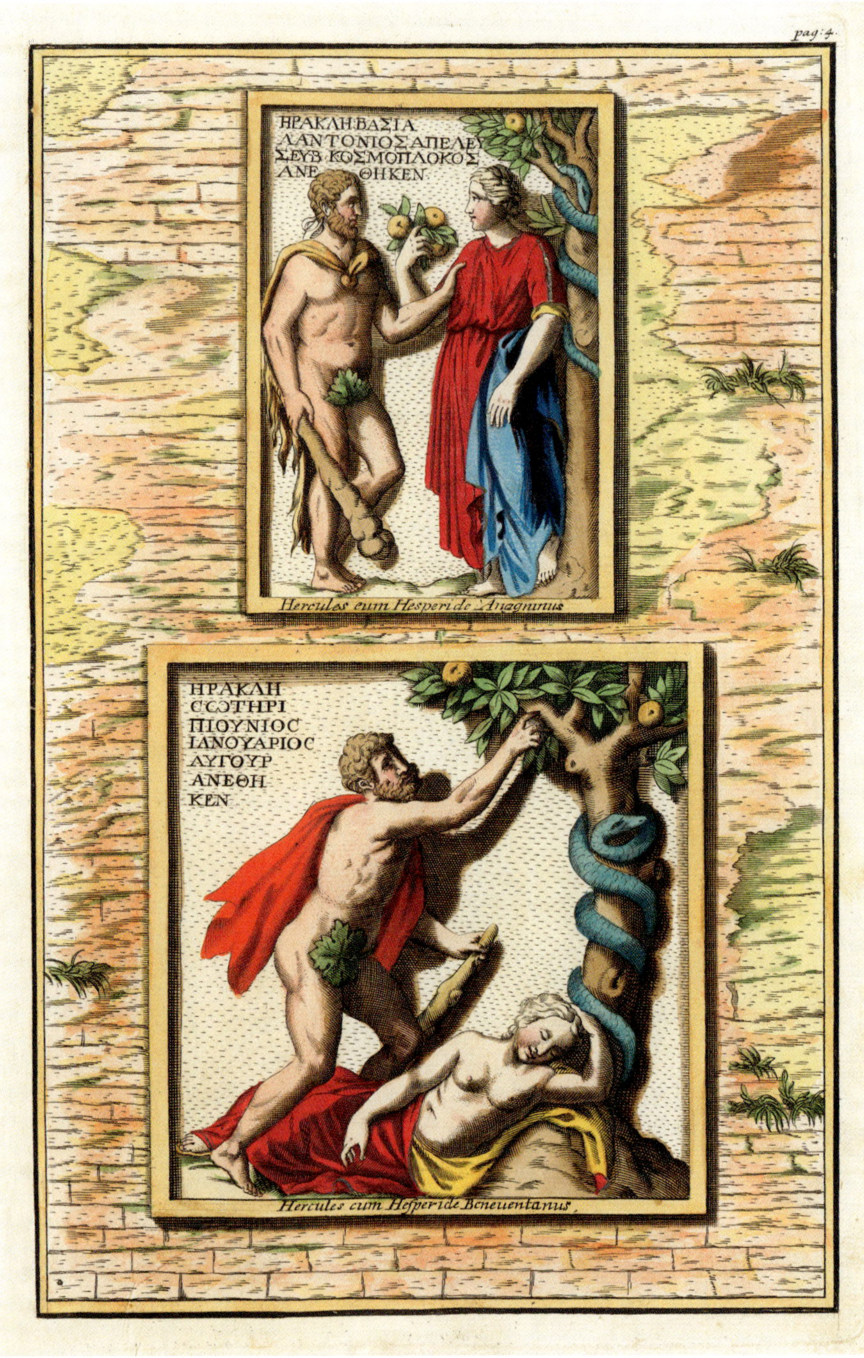
pag: 4.
ΗΡΑΚΛΗ ΒΑΣΙΑ
ΛΑΝΤΟΝΙΟΣ ΑΠΕΛΕΥ
ΣΕΥΒ ΚΟΣΜΟΠΛΟΚΟΣ
ΑΝΕ ΘΗΚΕΝ
Hercules cum Hesperide Anagninus
ΗΡΑΚΛΗ
CCѠΤΗΡΙ
ΠΙΟΥΝΙΟC
ΙΑΝΟΥΑΡΙΟC
ΑΥΓΟΥΡ
ΑΝΕΘΗ
ΚΕΝ
Hercules cum Hesperide Beneuentanus.

en matière d'art des jardins et de botanique. Outre les cours princières comme Vienne, Prague, Munich, Stuttgart ou Dresde, la culture des jardins dans les villes libres d'Empire fut aussi d'une importance capitale pour l'introduction des agrumes en Europe centrale. Il faut mentionner surtout Augsbourg, qui au XVIe siècle, par l'intermédiaire des marchands et banquiers de la famille Fugger, entretint d'étroites relations commerciales avec l'Italie, et Nuremberg, dont le patriciat et la bourgeoisie poursuivaient aussi des échanges actifs avec le nord de l'Italie.

La culture des agrumes dans les régions du nord, où il fallait réussir à ce que les plantes passent l'hiver, ne fut et n'est pas possible sans connaissances approfondies de botanique et de jardinage, dont la transmission compta à partir du XVIe siècle parmi les plus grandes réussites et prouesses techniques de l'art des jardins. À partir du deuxième tiers du XVIe siècle, dans les parcs princiers et les jardins de riches bourgeois et patriciens de Nuremberg, ou de la famille Fugger à Augsbourg, les agrumes furent cultivés, aussi bien en pleine terre que dans des bacs (p. 103).

Lorsque Johann Christoph Volkamer, marchand de Nuremberg, publia en 1708 son ouvrage *Nürnbergische Hesperides,* livre des *Hespérides*, qu'il fit suivre en 1714 d'un deuxième volume sous le titre *Continuation der Nürnbergischen Hesperidum,* exprimant sa passion pour les agrumes, « les plus beaux ornements de l'art des jardins », il s'inscrivait dans une tradition très ancienne. Ce livre des *Hespérides* offre, sur la base de l'état des connaissances de l'époque, une classification extraordinairement vaste des agrumes, par le texte et par l'image. C'est en même temps la première description systématique en langue allemande du genre *Citrus*. Les gravures sur cuivre montrent, par une disposition assez inhabituelle, dans leur partie haute le fruit en taille originale, et dans la partie basse des vues de jardins, de maisons de campagne, de villas et de paysages. On peut aborder le livre des *Hespérides* de Volkamer sous différents angles : la botanique, l'histoire des jardins et de l'architecture ou la topographie. On ne saurait toutefois en faire le tour rapidement, car l'ouvrage, dont l'auteur avait commencé la préparation au plus tard en 1695, et qui devait être complété d'un troisième volume, compte en gros 750 pages et plus de 250 planches.

La famille Volkamer

La clé pour comprendre et apprécier l'ambition scientifique et la perspective internationale du livre des *Hespérides* se trouve dans l'histoire de la famille de son auteur. Johann Christoph Volkamer était issu d'une lignée qui avait « donné au monde nombre d'érudits, gens de cour et valeureux guerriers » (Will, 1758). La confusion facile et fréquente avec la famille patricienne des Volckamer de Nuremberg est commentée et rectifiée dès le XVIIIe siècle. Johann Volkamer (1576–1661), grand-père de notre auteur, qui avait fait fortune grâce à la manufacture de soirie implantée à Rovereto en Italie du Nord

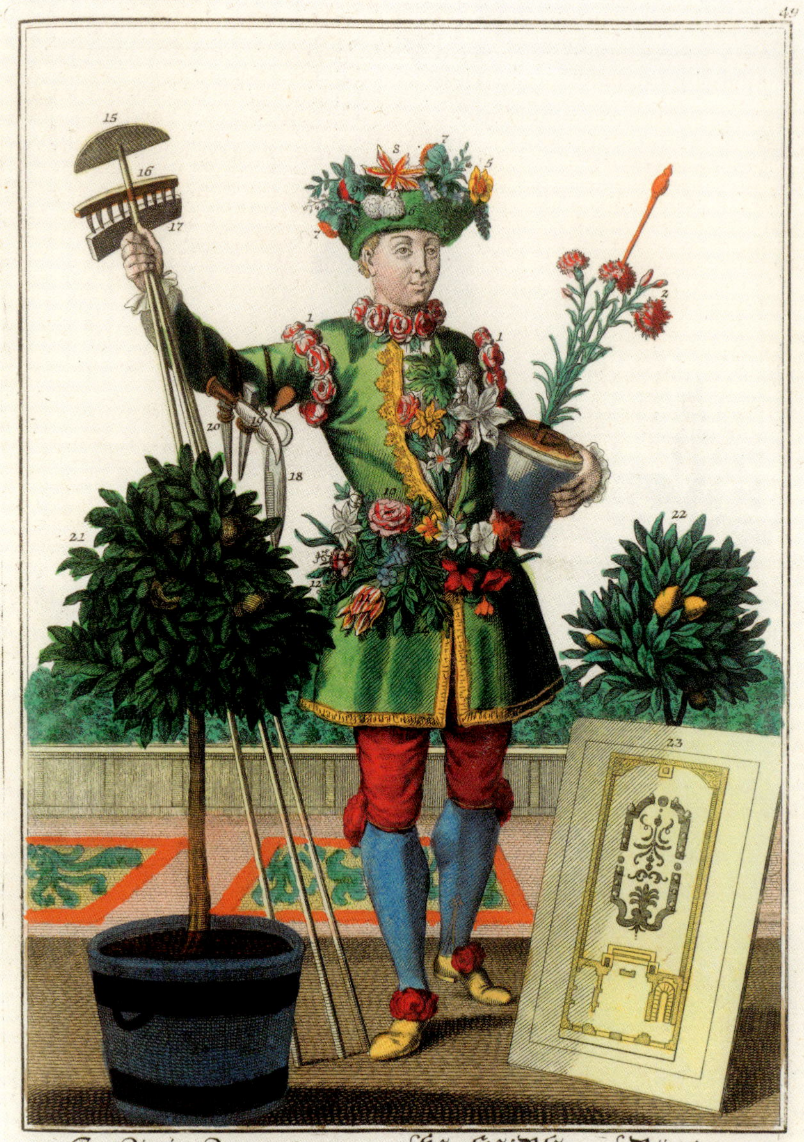

Jardinier de parterre. Künst u: Blumen Gärtner.

1. Roses rouges et blanches. 1. Roth u: weiße Rosen. 2. pie d'oeillets. 2. Nelckhenstockh 3. narcisses. 3. Narzißen 4. lis blancs. 4. Weiße Lilien. 5. Jacinte. 5. gelber Stern. 6. perce neige. 6. schnee ballen 7. fleur Stomacal 7. Ohlmagen. 8 une tulipe fleurie. 8. eine offne Tülipan. 9. Monstreuse. 9. große Monstrosa d.° 10. une Pionne. 10. Beonien Rosen. 11. Tulipe. 11. Tülipan. 12. Marguerites fleuries. 12. Margranten Blüth. 13. coquelicoq. 13. Klaprosen. 14. Laurier. 14. Lorber Blätter. 15. unis.soir. 15. eine Britsche. 16. rateau. 16. ein Rechen 17. Sarcloir. 17. ein stoßeisen den weg zü bützen. 18. Ciseaux. 18. ein Gartenscher. 19. Serpettes. 19. ein Reben meßer. 20. pivot à tirer au cordeau. 20. die eiserne Spitzen zü der Schnüer. 21. Oranger. 21. Pomerantzenbaüm. 22. Citronnier. 22. Zitronen baüm. 23. plan d'un parterre. 23. Aüffriß von einem Garten. 24. Cuvier. 24. ein Gewächs Kübel.

Cum Priv. Maj. Mart. Engelbrecht excud. A.V.

et à son activité commerciale, avait acquis en 1614 un terrain à Gostenhof, faubourg de Nuremberg, pour y installer le jardin dont son petit-fils Johann Christoph poursuivit l'aménagement.

Le père de Johann Christoph, Johann Georg Volkamer (1616–1693) obtint de hautes distinctions scientifiques. Après ses études de médecine à l'université de Iéna, puis d'Altdorf près de Nuremberg et, de 1638 à 1641, à Padoue, il entreprit un voyage d'études de presque deux ans qui le conduisit à Rome puis à Naples en passant par Venise, Ferrare, Bologne, Florence, Pise, Livourne et Lucques, puis à Nice, Marseille et Montpellier, Toulouse, Bordeaux, Orléans et Paris, avant de présenter sa thèse de doctorat en 1643 à Altdorf. Au cours d'un autre voyage en Italie, en 1658, il fut nommé membre de l'Academia Recuperatorum de Padoue. Sa prodigieuse érudition en qualité de naturaliste, astronome, physicien et botaniste, lui valut la célébrité. Il entra en 1676 à l'Académie impériale des naturalistes, la Leopoldina, dont il fut même le président à partir de 1686. Aussi bien en tant que membre de cette Académie que de la société littéraire du Pegnesischer Blumenorden (où il entra en 1646), Johann Georg Volkamer avait choisi le nom d'Helianthus, ou Tournesol. Il s'intéressait aux cadrans solaires, en construisait lui-même et était, à cet égard, à la pointe du progrès de son temps.

C'est le fils aîné de Johann Georg Volkamer qui publia le livre des *Hespérides*: Johann Christoph, né en 1644. Un frère nettement plus jeune, prénommé Johann Georg (1662–1744) comme le père, suivit les traces de celui-ci en devenant médecin et se fit un nom comme « le plus illustre médecin, que l'on tenait pour le plus grand botaniste d'Allemagne » (Will, 1758). Le fils aîné au contraire reprit avec succès la fabrique de soierie du grand-père à Rovereto et continua le commerce de la soie. Il possédait en outre une manufacture de dinanderie à Laufamholz (p. 246). Respecté comme « marchand distingué et révéré », occupant plusieurs charges importantes dans sa ville natale, il acquit une « science exceptionnelle de l'entretien et de la culture des agrumes, des fleurs et plantes de jardin » (Will, 1758). Il vécut à Rovereto de 1660 à 1668 au moins. Il y séjournait pour ses affaires, mais cela allait aussi lui donner la possibilité de visiter les jardins du nord de l'Italie qui l'émerveilleraient pour le restant de ses jours. Beaucoup de choses laissent à penser qu'après les marquantes années de jeunesse passées en Italie du Nord Johann Christoph Volkamer ne franchit plus jamais les Alpes. Il passa le reste de sa vie

Martin Engelbrecht, **"Artist and flower gardener"**
„Kunst u. Blumen Gärtner" / « Jardinier de parterre »
Hand-coloured engraving. From: *L'Assemblage nouveau des manouvries habilles / neu-eröffnete Sammlung der mit ihren eigenen Arbeiten und Werkzeugen eingekleideten Künstlern, Handwerkern und Professionen*, Augsburg, *c.* 1730, pl. 49
Staatliche Kunstsammlungen Dresden, Kupferstich-Kabinett

à Nuremberg, se consacrant à son jardin et à la culture des *Citrus* – et entretenant une correspondance très active avec ses pareils dans le reste du monde.

Histoire éditoriale du livre des *Hespérides*

Volkamer n'avait prévu à l'origine qu'un seul volume intitulé *Nürnbergische Hesperides*. Le livre obtint au mois de mars 1706 le privilège impérial d'impression, mais parut seulement deux ans plus tard, en 1708, chez Endter, éditeur de Nuremberg (p. 6). L'auteur est manifestement intervenu constamment dans l'impression et la composition de l'ouvrage, car les exemplaires de la première édition ne sont pas tous identiques : les motifs de *vedute* de certaines planches ont été modifiés, les signatures des graveurs ajoutées et certaines planches à l'eau-forte reliées dans des états plus tardifs. À la dernière page de la première édition de 1708 figure une liste des fautes d'impression.

La même année parut une deuxième édition de l'ouvrage qui se différencie de la précédente, entre autres, par la page de titre et le frontispice. Le nom de l'auteur apparaît désormais en toutes lettres, et la mention de l'éditeur et du libraire a changé. Le nouveau frontispice est une copie inversée du premier, dont il diffère par quelques détails. La plaque du premier frontispice (p. 2) avait donc manifestement déjà été réutilisée, on ne comptait pas l'employer pour des rééditions. Les châssis carrés des initiales de la première édition sont remplacés par des châssis rectangulaires que l'on retrouvera dans le deuxième volume. La liste d'errata, corrigés entre-temps, a été supprimée.

Sur les instances des spécialistes étrangers, Volkamer commanda au philologue et juriste Erhard Reusch (1678–1740) une traduction latine du premier volume, qui parut en 1713. L'auteur n'hésita donc pas à payer un certain prix pour sa notoriété internationale, d'autant que la facture du volume latin n'a rien à envier à celle de la première édition. Il reprend le frontispice de la deuxième édition de 1708. Le texte latin et les planches correspondent à l'édition allemande jusque dans la pagination. Le traducteur a ajouté un rapport de recherche sur la culture des *Citrus*.

Le privilège d'impression du volume suivant est daté du 21 août 1714, et le livre nettement plus volumineux paraît cette fois plus rapidement, à savoir la même année, sous le titre *Continuation der Nürnbergischen Hesperidum* à Francfort-sur-le-Main et à Leipzig.

Le livre des *Hespérides* n'est dédié à aucun dignitaire, pas plus par exemple au conseil de cette ville libre d'Empire qu'est Nuremberg qu'à aucun patricien en particulier, ce qui aurait délibérément favorisé sa diffusion dans les cercles correspondants. Volkamer semble avoir été assez fortuné pour n'avoir pas eu besoin de la gratification que valait une dédi-

Citrus planter / Zitruskübel / Pot et bac à agrumes
From: *Nürnbergische Hesperides*, 1708, vol. 1, p. 35

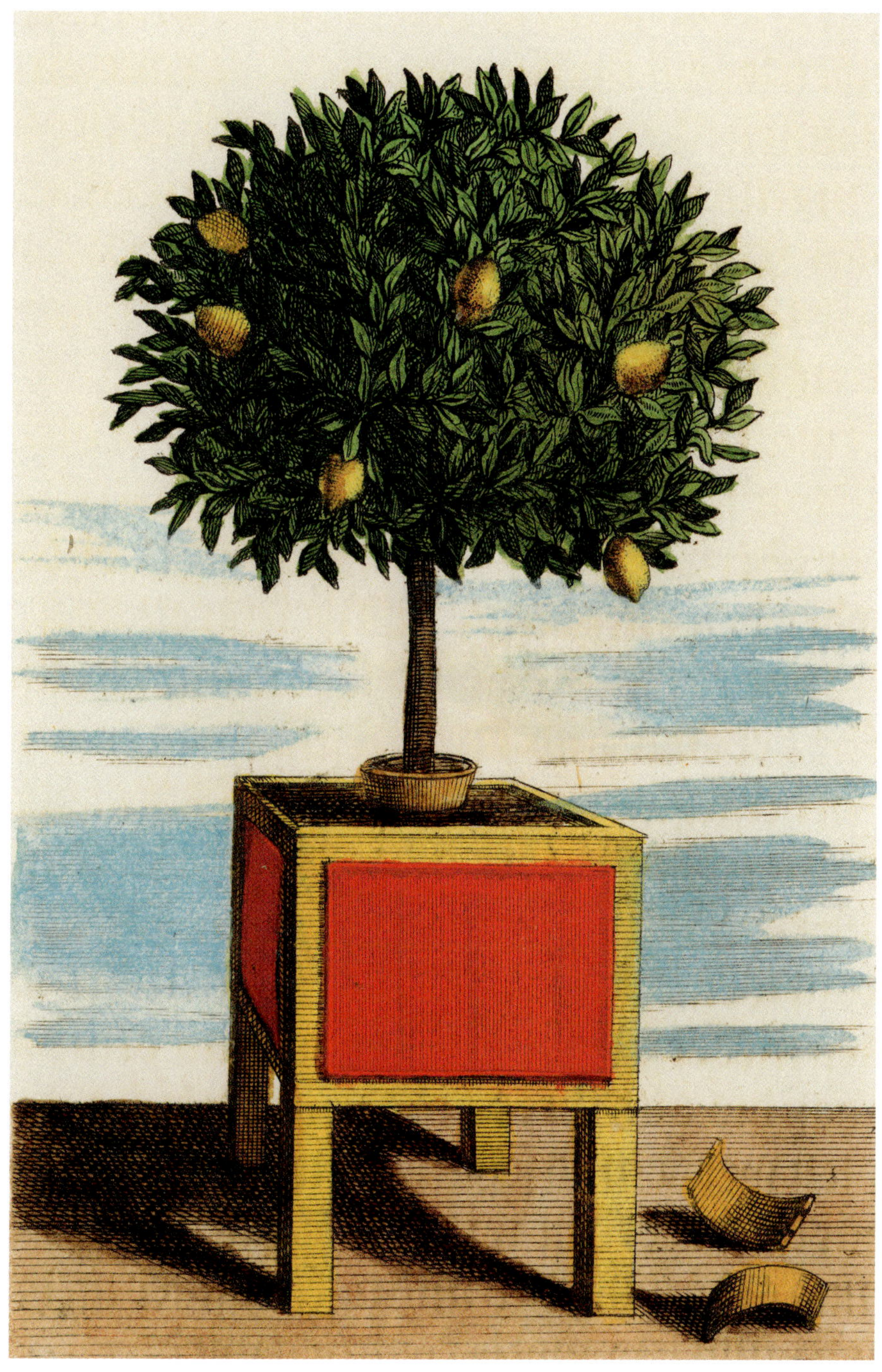

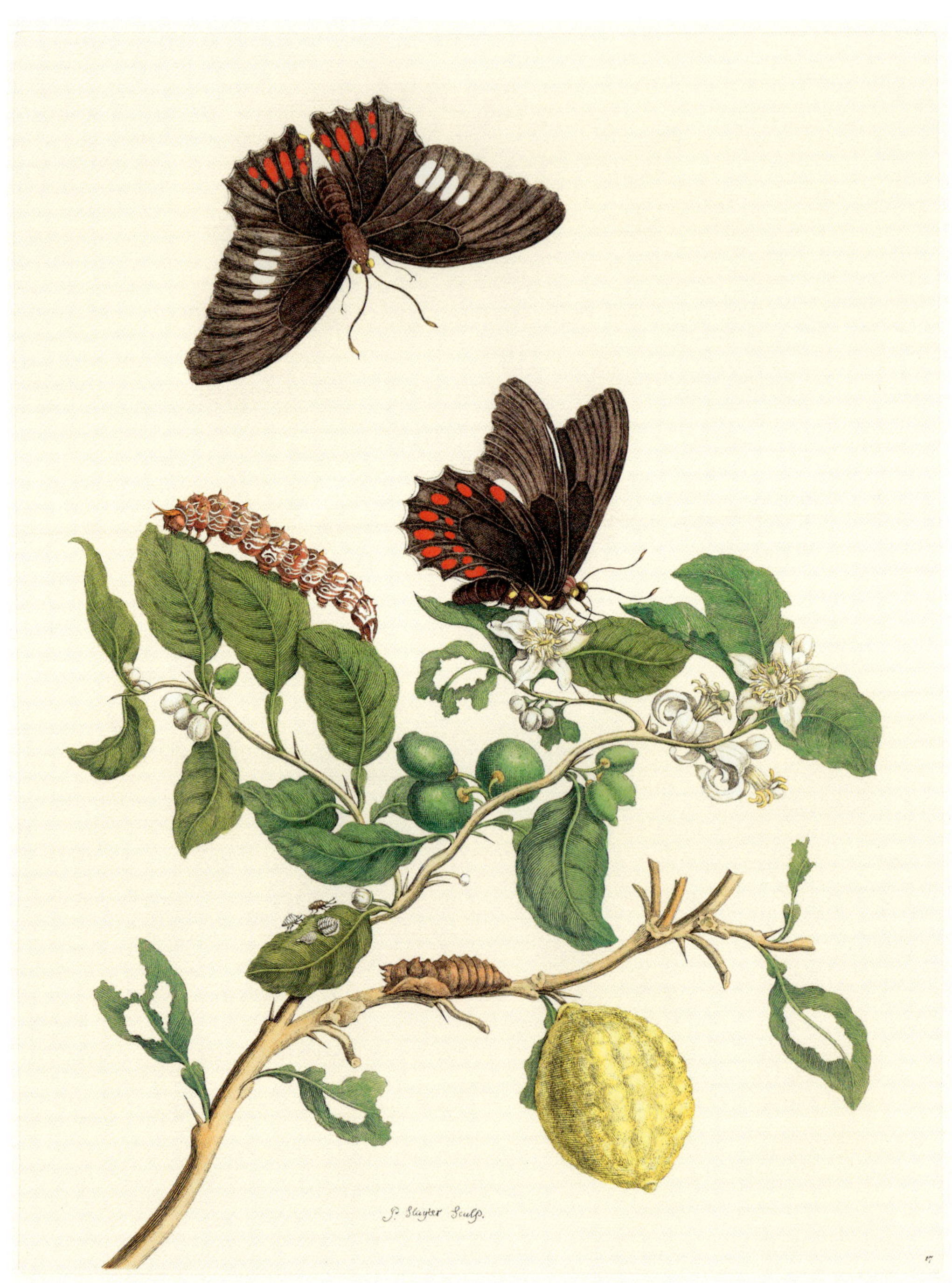
P. Sluyter Sculp.
17

Pages 104–107
Maria Sibylla Merian
Metamorphosis Insectorum Surinamensium,
Amsterdam, 1705
Basel, Universitätsbibliothek Basel

Citrus aurantiifolia
Mexican lime / Saure Limette / Limette
Hand-coloured copperplate engraving, pl. 17

Citrus maxima
Pomelo / Pampelmuse / Pomelo
Hand-coloured copperplate engraving, pl. 28

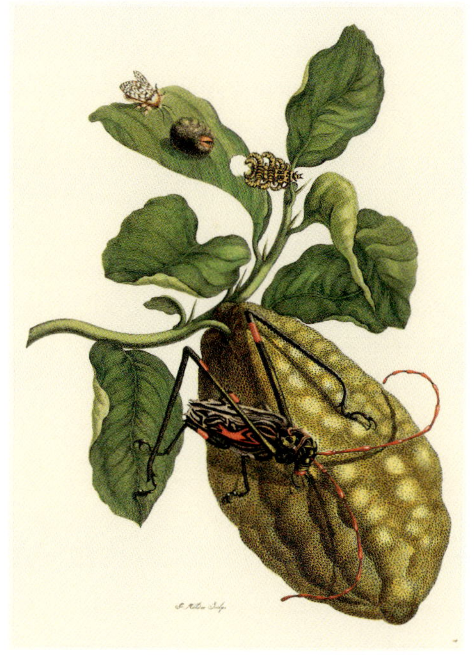

cace. Il se félicite constamment de n'avoir économisé ni son argent ni sa peine, et exprime toute sa fierté « que nul autre avant lui n'ait jamais décrit de façon aussi exhaustive et diversifiée ces ornements extraordinaires de l'art des jardins en donnant à voir les gravures correspondantes » (vol. II, Préambule). L'histoire éditoriale montre que l'auteur et l'éditeur furent tous deux étonnés du succès de la première publication en 1708. L'écho du premier volume s'étant révélé positif, Volkamer en publia pour commencer une deuxième édition, puis sa traduction latine suivie de la version en langue allemande de la *Continuation*. La traduction latine du deuxième volume, qui était prévue et devait être augmentée d'une longue description des représentations du mythe des Hespérides dans la sculpture et sur les gemmes antiques, ne fut pas publiée.

Même après la parution du deuxième volume, Volkamer, qui avait alors plus de soixante-dix ans, continua de se consacrer à la culture des agrumes dans son jardin de Gostenhof. Il collectionna du matériel et entretint une correspondance avec ses collègues étrangers afin de compléter son œuvre magistrale. Il ne réussit toutefois pas à faire mettre sous presse un troisième volume avant sa mort en 1720. Le matériel préparatoire réuni à cet effet est conservé au Germanisches Nationalmuseum de Nuremberg (p. 19). Une découverte récente nous permet de savoir ce qu'aurait été le contenu de cette suite. L'Universitätsbibliothek Erlangen-Nürnberg possède un volume de 62 planches, qui sont les tirages des gravures pour le troisième volume des *Nürnbergische Hesperides*. Outre des gravures réunissant comme à l'habitude des représentations de fruits et des vues générales, l'ouvrage d'Erlangen contient le frontispice (p. 16), trois vignettes (p. 19, 50, 94), une gravure montrant l'orangerie du comte Neithardt à Wroclaw (p. 78) et une « Vue du jardin et du château royal de Berlin » (p. 20). Cette vue témoigne d'un projet d'extension du château de Berlin dont le dessinateur Paul Decker le Jeune (1685–1742) était sans doute informé par son frère aîné. Ce dernier travailla en effet jusqu'en 1706 à la construction de ce château auprès d'Andreas Schlüter. Une « Vue du château et du jardin de Charlot[t] enburg à une heure de Berlin », du même auteur, nous a aussi été conservée (p. 32) ; et cette dernière aurait sans doute aussi été gravée pour le troisième volume du livre des *Hespérides*. Le *terminus ante quem* pour la datation de ces œuvres destinées au troisième volume est 1718, date de la disparition du graveur Joseph a Montalegre dont elles portent la signature.

Le jardin de Volkamer à Nuremberg – *quasi centrum Europae*

Le jardin de Volkamer à Gostenhof, faubourg de Nuremberg, est représenté sur plusieurs planches du livre des *Hespérides* : dans le premier volume par une vue à vol d'oiseau (p. 46/47), et par plusieurs autres dans le deuxième volume, dont le frontispice (p. 48) et une vue à vol d'oiseau de plus grandes dimensions de ce même jardin, réaménagé entretemps (p. 272/273). Ces différentes illustrations permettent de constater que Volkamer cultivait ses agrumes en pleine terre et en pots. L'hiver, ils étaient protégés des intempéries par une construction en bois installée entre la maison d'habitation et l'orangerie, dispositif que l'on démontait au printemps (p. 26/27, 90/91). Ces serres amovibles sont de nos jours encore utilisées couramment sur les rives du lac de Garde. Volkamer en fournit le modèle sur une autre gravure (p. 134/135). Les trois statues des Hespérides disposées sur la charpente semblent veiller à la prospérité des agrumes et autres plantes exotiques (p. 90/91).

La vue à vol d'oiseau du jardin – en vérité cultivé en large partie comme potager – qui se trouve dans le deuxième volume du livre des *Hespérides* est intitulée en latin *Viridarium Suburbaneum Johan Cristoffori Volckameri in Norimberga*. Par ce titre inspiré de l'Antiquité romaine, Volkamer espérait attirer l'attention internationale. Et avec les gravures de bas-reliefs et de sculptures antiques sur le mythe d'Hercule qu'il inclut au deuxième volume, il s'inscrit aussi dans une tradition romaine (p. 97, 98), à laquelle l'art et la culture de Nuremberg au XVIIe siècle étaient étroitement liés – transfert culturel que le

Ananas comosus
Pineapple / Ananas / Ananas
Hand-coloured copperplate engraving, pl. 1

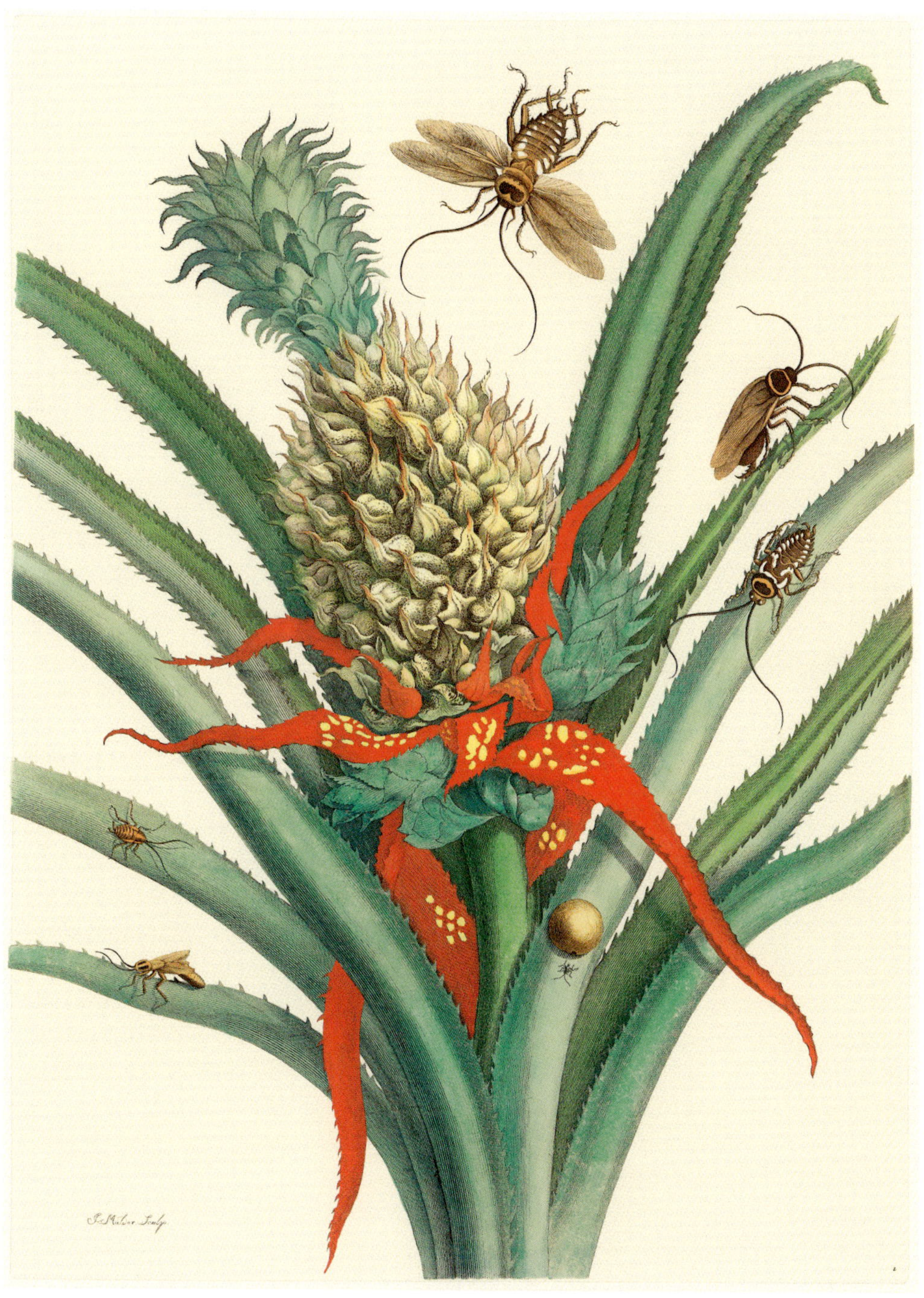

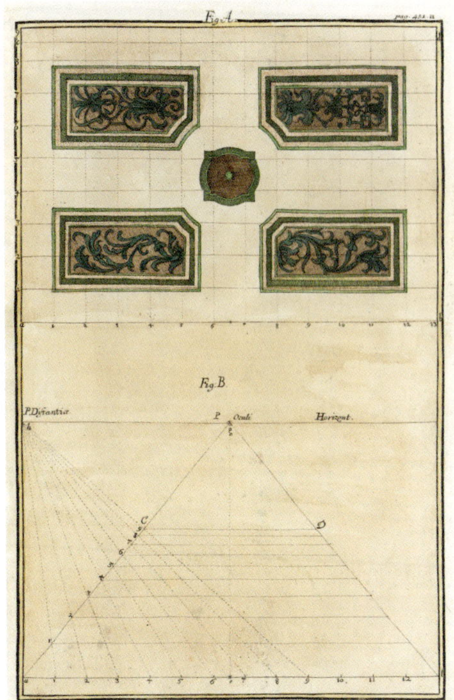

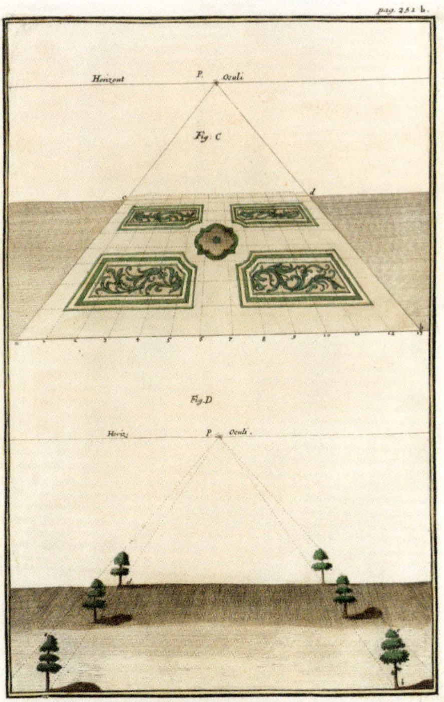

peintre, graveur et éditeur Joachim von Sandrart (1606–1688) renforça sensiblement avec la publication de sa *Teutsche Academie.*

Les liens avec Rome et Florence existaient déjà depuis l'époque de Johann Georg Volkamer père, et le frère de notre auteur s'était aussi rendu dans ces deux villes en 1685. Johann Christoph spéculait peut-être sur une sorte d'affinité entre sa propre famille qui travaillait dans la fabrication de la soie, et dont les membres les plus renommées à l'échelle internationale étaient des médecins – *medici,* en italien – et la famille Médicis, qui avait tiré sa fortune du commerce des étoffes. Peut-être même Johann Christoph Volkamer transposait-il à sa propre famille la fonction héraldique des agrumes pour les Médicis. Il qualifie constamment le jardin de son père Johann Georg de jardin de plantes médicinales et il abrège la formule latinisante *Horto Medico Volckameri* en *H. M. V.*

Volkamer connaissait certainement la série de gravures de Giovanni Battista Falda (1643–1678) *Li Gardini di Roma* (Rome 1683), dont une édition allemande parut en 1695 chez l'éditeur Sandrart à Nuremberg. On voit sur le frontispice, *Gli Esperidi Romani,* les Hespérides romaines, veillant sur la prospérité des jardins et agrumes de la ville (p. 28). Falda montre, entre autres, le jardin de la villa Médicis (p. 31) avec son obélisque et sa multitude de sculptures antiques. Dans le labyrinthe de son jardin de Gostenhof (p. 38), notre marchand de Nuremberg Johann Christoph Volkamer fit, en juillet 1709, lui aussi remplacer une statue équestre par une copie réduite à un tiers de l'*Obeliscus Constantinopolitanus* que Théodose Ier avait fait ériger à Constantinople en l'an 390. Pour son interprétation des hiéroglyphes, Volkamer se réfère, entre autres, au jésuite érudit Athanasius Kircher qui vivait à Rome et avait publié des ouvrages sur l'*Obeliscus Pamphilius* en 1650 et sur l'*Obeliscus Aegyptiacus* en 1666. En 1713 parut la description par Volkamer de l'obélisque de 7 mètres de haut (p. 37), qui se trouve aujourd'hui dans l'historique cité industrielle Hammer, à Laufamholz, dans la banlieue de Nuremberg. Ce traité fut relié avec le deuxième volume du livre des *Hespérides* ou adjoint a posteriori au premier volume. Dans l'exemplaire de Fürth présenté ici, il se trouve dans le premier volume. Il vient s'ajouter avec son titre latin aux nombreuses publications de la deuxième moitié du XVIIe siècle sur les obélisques antiques. L'auteur concluait la description de ce monument surmonté d'une colombe de la paix en exprimant le souhait de cette « paix sûre et constante si ardemment espérée et désirée jusqu'alors par toute l'Europe » (relié au vol. 1, p. 16). Cette aspiration fut satisfaite par la paix d'Utrecht, qui mettait fin en 1713 à la guerre de Succession d'Espagne.

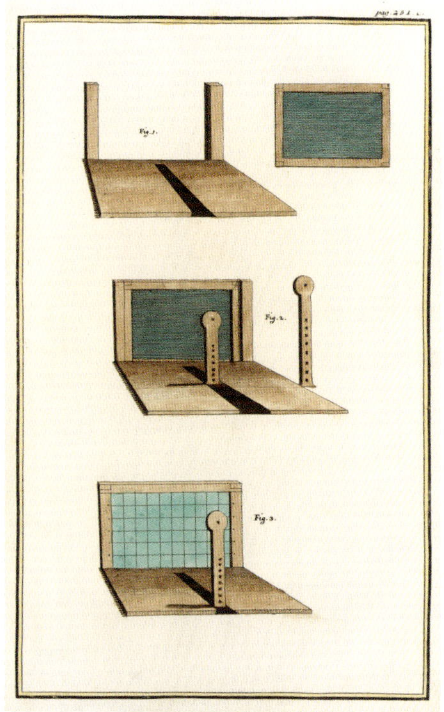

L'auteur décrit aussi de façon exhaustive la construction, en 1696, du cadran solaire en buis dans le jardin de Gostenhof (p. 41 ; vol. 1, p. 245–248), ainsi que la *Columna Milliaria* érigée en 1697 (p. 45 ; vol. 1, p. 253–255). Le modèle de ce monument était le *milliarium aureum* antique du forum romain, à partir duquel étaient mesurées et indiquées les distances des localités importantes de l'empire. À Gostenhof, il y avait aussi, disposées

Instructions for a garden design with perspective
Anweisungen zum perspektivischen Gartenentwurf / Instructions pour le dessin d'un jardin en perspective
From: *Nürnbergische Hesperides*, 1708, vol. 1, plates pp. 251a, 251b and 251c

sur quatre colonnes supportant un baldaquin et une cinquième colonne indépendante au centre, des cartes géographiques qui, par une sorte d'anamorphose cartographique imposaient à la topographie de l'Europe, de Lemberg, Gotland, Salisbury en passant par Perpignan et jusqu'à Bari, une perspective centrée sur Nuremberg. La désignation de Nuremberg comme le centre du commerce du continent – *quasi centrum europae* – devenue depuis la fin du XVe siècle l'un des thèmes majeurs de l'apologie de la ville, trouve une expression forte dans ce monument à colonnes du négociant Volkamer.

Agrumes et patriotisme local

Le format in-folio, la longueur du texte et le nombre de planches illustrées justifient le prix de 12 thalers, prix élevé pour les deux volumes du livre des *Hespérides*, qui surclassaient aussi par là les nombreuses publications de moindre envergure sur les jardins de la même époque. L'ouvrage en plusieurs volumes du patricien de Nuremberg Wolf Albrecht Stromer von Reichenbach, paru chez le même éditeur sous le titre *Garten-Wissenschafft* (Science des jardins) ne coûtait par exemple qu'un thaler et huit groschen. Chez les éditeurs d'Augsbourg et de Nuremberg avaient paru dans les dernières décennies du XVIIe siècle de nombreux livres sur les jardins, qui témoignent de l'essor économique qui avait suivi la fin de la guerre de Trente Ans et du vif intérêt que l'on portait à la culture des jardins dans les villes libres d'Empire. Volkamer connaissait un grand nombre de ces ouvrages et en cite quelques-uns, par exemple ceux d'Agostino Mandirola, Wolfgang Jakob Dümler et Stromer von Reichenbach.

C'est par une accumulation de superlatifs que Johann Christoph Volkamer dédie sa publication sur les agrumes à sa ville natale de Nuremberg, « reine des cités allemandes ».

« À ma patrie / la noble cité de Nuremberg, / les Allemands comme les étrangers, / reconnaissent tout naturellement la gloire/ d'être la mieux située, / construite avec la plus grande beauté, / la mieux pourvue de tout l'Empire allemand pour répondre non seulement à tous les besoins, / mais pour offrir aussi tous les plaisirs. Parmi ces derniers il faut compter / à plus juste titre / les jardins d'ornement et d'agrément / qui se présentent avec une beauté et une grâce aussi exceptionnelles / que le sont leur taille et leur nombre/ à l'intérieur et hors des murs. »

Volkamer concevait son ouvrage sur les agrumes comme un hommage à sa ville natale, ce qu'illustrent jusque dans leurs détails les frontispices de Paul Decker l'Ancien (1677–1713) et de son frère cadet du même nom (p. 2). C'est à la personnification de Nuremberg, la fière Noris, que les Hespérides offrent leurs fruits, assistées de Mercure, dieu du commerce, dans le premier volume, et d'Hercule dans les autres. Le décor topographique, à l'arrière-plan, montre dans le premier volume la ville de Nuremberg, et dans le second le jardin de Volkamer à Gostenhof (p. 48). Sur le frontispice du premier volume

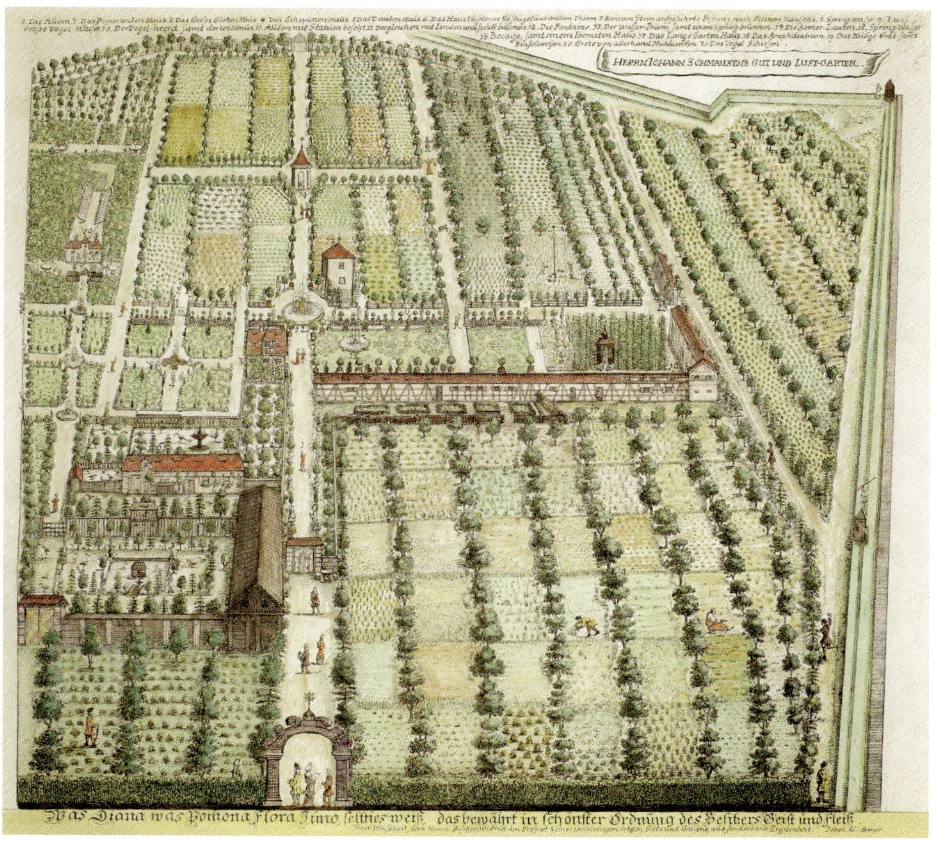

s'élève du bouquet derrière Mercure une couronne impériale, *Fritillaria imperialis*, qui est sans aucun doute une allusion au rôle historique de la ville en tant que lieu où étaient conservés les joyaux de l'Empire, et par conséquent aussi la couronne impériale.

Les jardins privés des XVIIe et XVIIIe siècles sont souvent représentés sur l'arrière-plan de la ville (p. 54). Les descriptions de la culture des plantes et de l'art des jardins, de la végétation et de la flore se prêtent à l'expression du patriotisme local. Elles montrent l'identification du citoyen avec sa florissante cité et sont interprétées aux XVIIe

Johann Alexander Boener, **Johann Schmaus's garden, known as the "Schmausengarten", in Mögeldorf**, *c.* 1700
Garten des Johann Schmaus, sog. Schmausengarten in Mögeldorf
Jardin de Johann Schmaus, dit Schmausengarten, à Mögeldorf
No. 2 indicates a temporary orangery / Nr. 2 bezeichnet ein abschlagbares Pomeranzenhaus / N° 2 montre une orangerie démontable
Hand-coloured engraving. Nuremberg, Stadtbibliothek, B. II 14

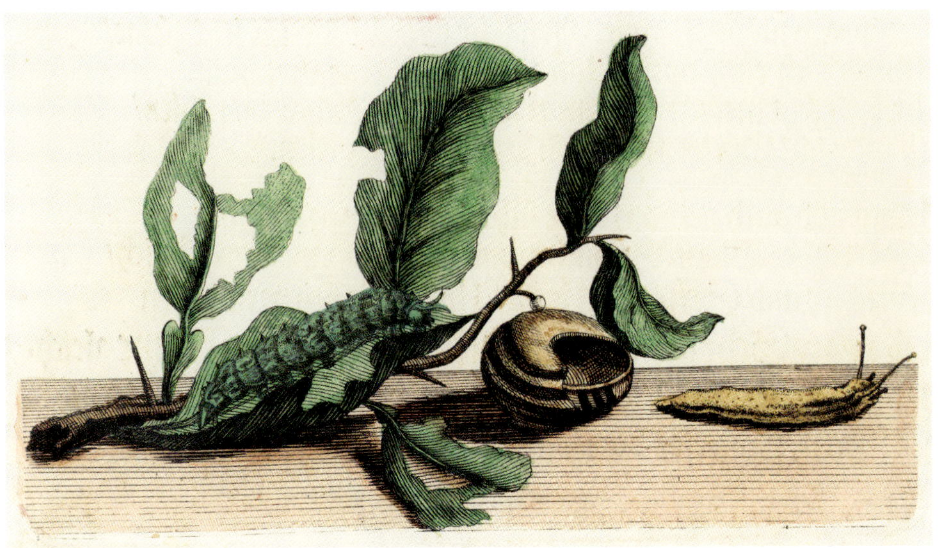

et XVIIIe siècles, dans de nombreuses chroniques de villes, comme des conquêtes municipales. Ainsi la première planche de la deuxième partie du livre des *Hespérides* avec le grand *Cedro grosso Bondolotto* surplombant la ville libre d'Empire de Nuremberg (p. 150) doit-elle être comprise comme une affirmation du patriotisme local. Cela vaut aussi pour le catalogue d'agrumes de Caspar Wilhelm Scultetus (s. l. 1731) influencé par le livre des *Hespérides* et publié à Wroclaw, ou pour les publications sur le jardin de Caspar Bose à Leipzig (p. 34). Volkamer entretint d'ailleurs une correspondance avec Bose (1645–1700), dont le jardin jouissait d'une grande réputation pour la rareté de ses plantes exotiques, et dont la précieuse collection d'agrumes fut qualifiée en 1686 de *Hesperides Bosianae.*

Négociant et savant

La famille Volkamer, composée de commerçants prospères et de savants de renom international, établie à Nuremberg depuis la fin du XVIe siècle, ne faisait certes pas partie du patriciat, mais était bien ancrée dans les instances sociales et administratives de la ville où elle jouissait d'un grand prestige. D'une façon générale, la ville libre d'Empire de Nuremberg devait en partie sa réputation aux productions de ses artistes et aux savants qui travaillaient dans la ville et à l'université d'Altdorf.

Citrus branch with caterpillar and snail
Zitruszweig mit Raupe und Schnecke / Branche d'agrume avec une limace et une chenille
From: *Nürnbergische Hesperides*, 1708, vol. 1, p. 80

Le livre des *Hespérides* reflète à divers égards les intérêts, les relations personnelles et les connaissances non seulement de son auteur, mais aussi de la famille dans son ensemble – du grand-père qui avait de multiples centres d'intérêt, du père qui disposait d'une vaste érudition, et du frère cadet, savant renommé, à qui l'auteur devait beaucoup. Le frère Johann Georg s'était fait une réputation internationale avec la publication, en 1700, de son traité de botanique de 407 pages, *Flora Noribergensis Sive Catalogus Plantarum in Agro Noribergensi Tam sponte nascentium, quam exoticarum* (Nuremberg, 2e éd. 1718). Il y consacre seulement deux pages aux oranges, citronats et citrons (p. 276 s.). Les rares planches que comporte l'ouvrage montrent pour la plupart des plantes exotiques que Johann Georg Volkamer cultivait dans son jardin, mais pas d'agrumes. Si l'on se demande ce qui peut avoir incité le frère aîné de près de vingt ans, Johann Christoph, à poursuivre inlassablement la préparation des volumes de son œuvre originale sur les agrumes, l'un après l'autre, à les financer et à les publier, la réponse est la suivante : les *Nürnbergische Hesperides* sont l'ouvrage scientifique d'un « marchand distingué et considéré » et en même temps d'un amateur passionné, qui apporte ainsi sa contribution à une noble compétition d'érudition et à l'émulation à l'intérieur de la famille. Johann Christoph Volkamer eut lui aussi finalement, six mois avant sa mort, au début de l'année 1720, à l'âge de 76 ans, la satisfaction d'être admis, comme avant lui son père et son frère, à l'Académie impériale des naturalistes.

Le père et le frère écrivaient leurs traités scientifiques en latin. Johann Christoph Volkamer au contraire écrit pour ses pareils, amateurs des jardins – il écrit en allemand, même s'il cite des textes latins et maîtrise cette langue ancienne aussi bien que l'italien. De ce point de vue, le livre des *Hespérides* est le fruit d'un remarquable effort de transposition. Se voulant scientifique et systématique d'une part, mais de l'autre, compréhensible pour tous, rédigé en langue allemande, il revêt une forme hybride. La somptueuse édition par Basilius Besler (1561–1629) du *Hortus Eystettensis* (s. l. 1613) qui recherche une reproduction picturale fidèle et l'exactitude de la description, et qui fut sans doute l'un des modèles de Volkamer, ou lui était en tout cas connu (p. 59), est en latin. Le livre des *Hespérides* s'inscrit au contraire dans le courant qui, à partir du milieu du XVIIe siècle, s'efforça de faire accéder la langue allemande au statut de langue scientifique. À Nuremberg, l'Ordre des fleurs de la Pegnitz, société littéraire fondée en 1644 dont fit partie Johann Georg Volkamer senior, joua sur le plan linguistique un rôle de premier plan. Si l'ouvrage de Giovanni Battista Ferrari (1584–1655) sur les agrumes (1646) était encore rédigé en latin, la plupart des ouvrages de la deuxième moitié du XVIIe siècle sur le même sujet sont écrits dans les langues nationales respectives de leurs auteurs ; cela vaut par exemple pour Commelin (1676), Sterbeeck (1682), les traités français et les ouvrages de références d'auteurs allemands. Se fondant sur une expérience et une observation de longue durée et sur une analyse précise, Volkamer nous livre, avec sa description et classification des agrumes, une contribution originale à la « noble science de la botanique et des herbes » (vol. 1, p. 4 s.). Bien qu'il ait été marchand et non savant, son ouvrage s'inscrit au plus haut niveau des publications de botanique de son temps.

Ce livre figure, aujourd'hui encore, parmi les références pour la classification des agrumes. Et, par exemple, dans leur *Histoire naturelle des Orangers* (Paris 1818/19), les botanistes Joseph-Antoine Risso et Alexandre Poiteau dénomment une espèce d' Oranger « Bigaradier de Volcamer / Melangolo de Volcamerio » (p. 60).

Les modèles : publications sur les agrumes

Le livre du père jésuite Ferrari, paru en 1646 à Rome sous le titre *Hesperides, sive de malorum aureorum cultura et usu,* est la première publication qui propose une classification des *Citrus.* L'ouvrage montre sur de nombreuses gravures les fruits, les branches et les fleurs (p. 71) ainsi que des orangeries, et contient en outre d'admirables représentations artistiques du mythe des Hespérides, exécutées par les plus brillants artistes qui se trouvaient alors à Rome, entre autres Pierre de Cortone (p. 68), l'Albane et Nicolas Poussin. Ferrari, jardinier et botaniste des Barberini à Rome, avait accès aux descriptions botaniques du « Museo Cartaceo », collection de notices et dessins du mécène érudit Cassiano dal Pozzo (1588–1657, p. 75). Il s'était déjà assuré une renommée internationale avec sa *Flora overo cultura dei fiori* (1632 Rome : en latin, 1638 Rome : en italien). La famille Volkamer possédait aussi bien ce dernier ouvrage que le livre de Ferrari sur les *Citrus,* et tous deux sont fréquemment cités tant par le frère cadet, Johann Georg, que par son aîné Johann Christoph. Les frontispices et vignettes sur le mythe des Hespérides reprennent les thèmes des gravures du livre de Ferrari. Outre ce dernier, il faut citer Jan Commelin (1629–1692), « l'incomparable botaniste d'Amsterdam » (vol. 1, p. 17), auteur des *Nederlantze Hesperides* (Amsterdam, 1676), autorité à laquelle Volkamer se réfère souvent dans son propre livre des *Hespérides* (p. 77). Le frère cadet Johann Georg avait connu personnellement Commelin à Amsterdam.

Erhard Reusch, traducteur du premier volume du livre des *Hespérides*, ajouta au texte de Volkamer une analyse critique de 24 pages in-folio, des ouvrages anciens et modernes sur le genre *Citrus,* intitulée *Dissertatio Epistolica de Praecipuis Hesperidum Scriptoribus, iisque tam Antiquis quam Recentioribus.* Cette *Dissertatio* confère au livre des

Insecta malorum Arantiorum et Limoniorum
Lemon branch infested with scale insects; at the bottom, scale insects as seen through a microscope
Zitronenzweig, von Schildläusen befallen; am unteren Rand Schildläuse in mikroskopischer Vergrößerung
Branche de citronnier infestée de cochenilles ; en bas de page, cochenilles vues au microscope
From: *Nürnbergische Hesperides*, 1708, vol. 1, introduction, plate p. 66

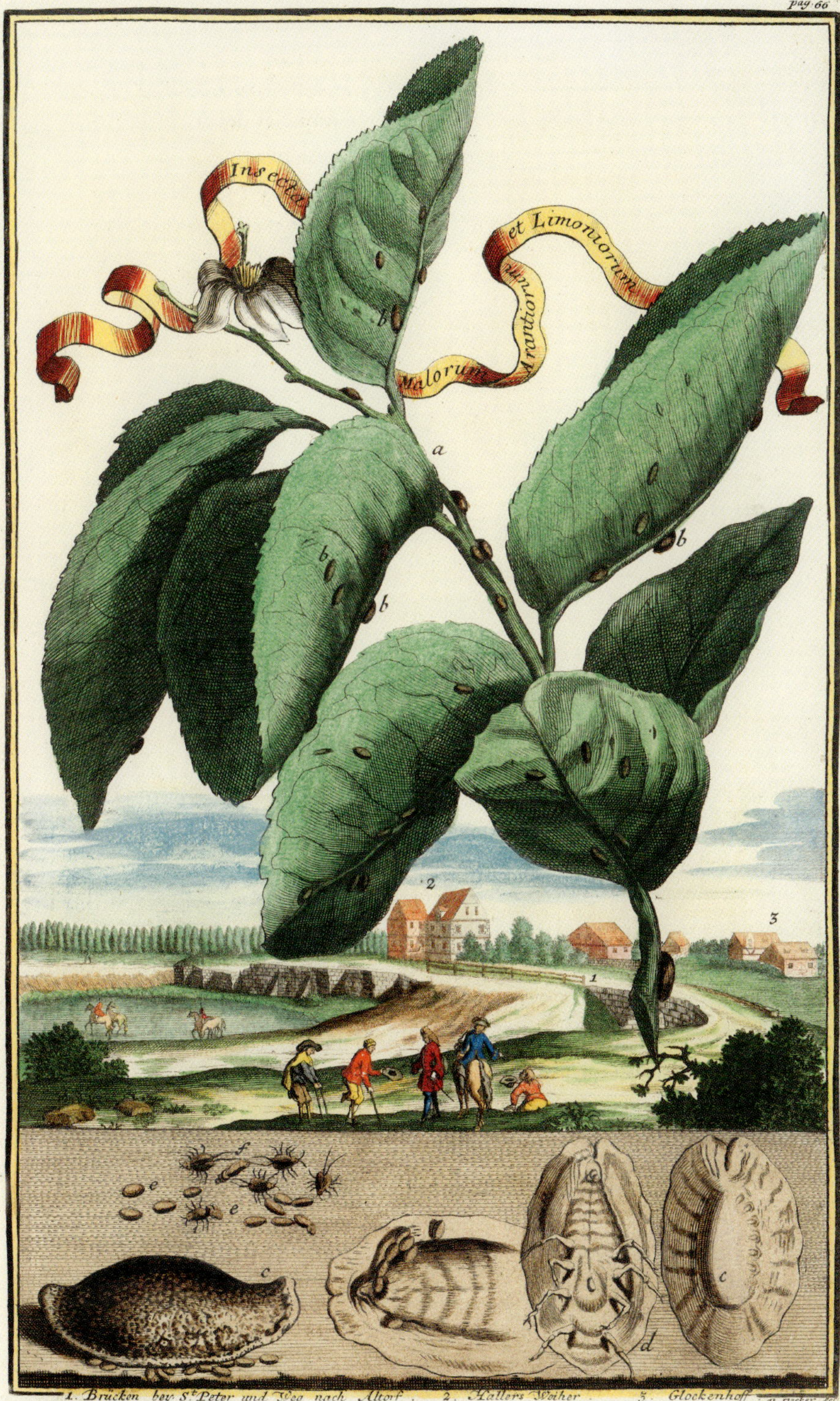
Insecta Malorum Arantiorum et Limoniorum
a
b
c
d
e
f
1
2
3
1. Brücken bey S.t Peter und Weg nach Altorf . 2. Hallers Weiher . 3. Glockenhoff
P. Decker fec.

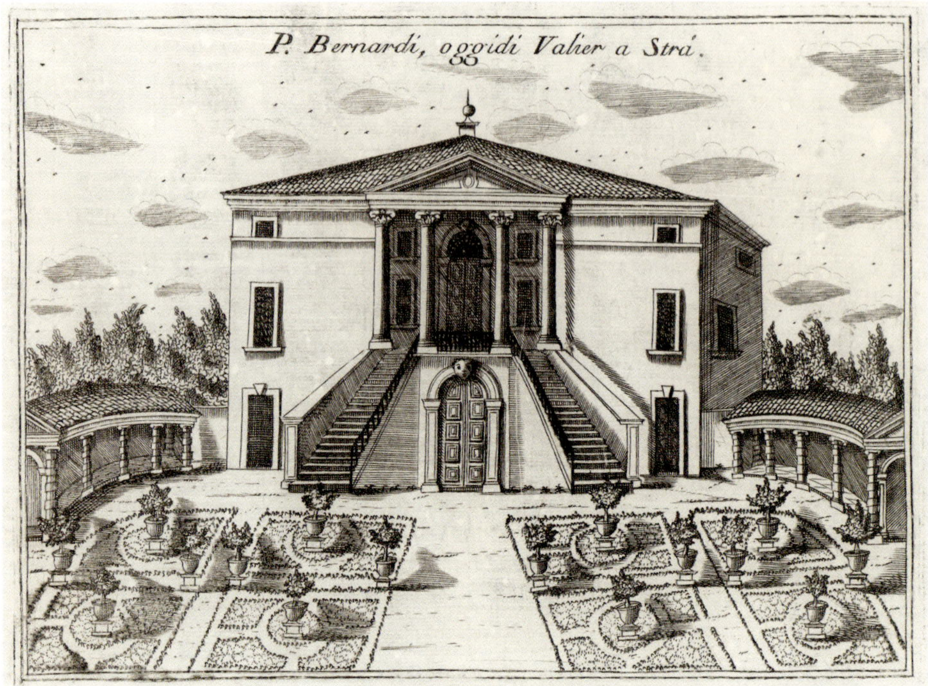

Hespérides la posture académique qui fait défaut aux exposés de Volkamer et à son choix d'écrire dans la langue populaire. Reusch cite d'emblée Giovanni Pontano (1429–1503), Ferrari et Commelin, et rapporte ensuite longuement ce que les auteurs de l'Antiquité grecque et romaine depuis Théophraste ont eu à dire sur le genre *Citrus.* Il évoque la mythologie, l'étymologie et même les écrits de savants arabes. Procédant chronologiquement, il arrive aux débuts de l'époque moderne, se référant là aussi à une série d'autorités de toute l'Europe qui ont écrit sur les agrumes en latin, italien, français, néerlandais, anglais ou allemand. Hormis Pontano, Ferrari et Commelin, Reusch fait référence entre autres, classés par nationa-lité et par langue, aux auteurs suivants : les médecins, poètes et érudits italiens Battista Fiera, Celio Calcagnini, Pietro Nato et Giuseppe Lanzoni ; le naturaliste Ulisse Aldrovandi (1522–1605), qui avait fondé en 1568 le jardin botanique de Bologne, et le savant bolognais Ovidio Montalbano (1601–1672), qui avait publié les

Vincenzo Coronelli, **View of the Villa Bernardi Valier in Stra**
Ansicht der Villa Bernardi Valier in Stra / Vue de la villa Bernardi Valier à Stra
From: Vincenzo Coronelli, *Singolarità di Venezia, Terza Parte: La Brenta, quasi Borgo della Città di Venezia, Luogo di Delizie de' Veneti Patrizj*, Venise, [1711], pl. 80
Göttingen, Niedersächsische Staats- und Universitätsbibliothek

recherches d'Aldrovandi sur les arbres (1668) ; Agostino Mandirola, auteur du *Italiänischer Blumen- und Pomeranzen-Garten* (Nuremberg, 1679). Les livres des botanistes français René Rapin et Pierre Morin sont présentés de même que le *Nouveau traité des orangers et citronniers* (Paris, 1692) et le *Traité de la culture des orangers, citronniers, grenadiers et oliviers* (Paris, 1676). Les écrits du célèbre jardinier de Versailles Jean-Baptiste de La Quintinie (1626–1688) font l'objet d'un long éloge, de même que ceux des auteurs anglais et hollandais. Mis à part Commelin, ce sont essentiellement Frans van Sterbeeck (1631–1693), dont le livre *Citricultura* (Anvers, 1682) fut certainement un modèle pour Volkamer (p. 15, 81, 89), et Henrik van Oosten, auteur de *De Nederlandsen Hof, beplant met Bloemen, Ooft en Orangerijen* (Leyde, 1703). En ce qui concerne l'Allemagne, Reusch mentionne non seulement des auteurs, mais aussi des partenaires qui se sont illustrés plutôt par leur correspondance et l'échange de graines et de plantes que par leurs propres publications, par exemple Otto von Münchhausen (1643–1717) dont le château et jardin Schwöbber, près de Hamelin, est représenté sur plusieurs planches du livre des *Hespérides* comme modèle de la culture de plantes exotiques (p. 23, 274). Reusch fait référence à de bien plus nombreux ouvrages que Volkamer n'en mentionne lui-même dans son texte. On peut toutefois partir du principe que les auteurs et les œuvres cités étaient également familiers à l'auteur. Le niveau de l'ouvrage de Volkamer découle très clairement de la littérature qu'il cite, où c'est la plupart du temps le texte qui domine. Le petit nombre de gravures que l'on trouve chez Commelin et Sterbeeck visent une reproduction à la fois précise et décorative. Seul l'ouvrage de Ferrari adjoint au texte la documentation d'illustrations scientifiques gravées: branches et feuilles, fleurs, fruits entiers ou ouverts sont artistiquement entourés d'un bandeau portant l'inscription de leurs noms et classifications (p. 71). Cette recherche de la précision dans la reproduction, Volkamer la partage avec Ferrari, mais il le dépasse par le nombre de variétés de *Citrus* qu'il traite et montre.

Le public de Volkamer : « Pour le plaisir des amateurs curieux et des jardiniers désireux de s'instruire »

Volkamer écrit pour de riches propriétaires de jardins, pouvant se ménager le temps et les moyens de s'intéresser intensivement à leurs jardins et à la botanique. L'auteur avoue avoir investi dans l'étude des agrumes de nombreuses heures de loisir pour son plus grand plaisir (vol. II, Préambule). Se fondant sur sa propre expérience poursuivie pendant de longues années, il consacre l'intégralité des deux volumes à la culture des végétaux du genre *Citrus*: construction d'orangeries démontables ainsi que de serres, soins à apporter aux végétaux, enrichissement de la terre et moyens de surmonter l'hiver ; multiplication et taille, traitement des maladies, protection contre les parasites comme la cochenille qu'il observe au microscope et qu'il reproduit fortement grossie (p. 115).

Volkamer – se plaçant du point de vue du propriétaire – consacre plusieurs chapitres aux qualités exigées d'un bon jardinier (p. 85) : « d'où l'on comprend qu'il ne faut ni d'un sot ni d'un fainéant pour faire un jardinier / et il lui faut aussi bonne science et connaissance (…) Il le faudra aussi circonspect et réfléchi (…) Enfin un jardinier doit être appliqué et persévérant » (vol. 1, p. 71 s.). Il semble n'avoir pas connu d'expérience très heureuse avec ses propres jardiniers, car il ne cesse de se lamenter sur de « méchants coquins de jardiniers sans honneur et impies » (vol. 1, p. 75), sur les vols et le mauvais entretien des plantes.

Dans son langage familier, il emploie un certain nombre de tournures populaires, par exemple sa mise en garde contre les jardiniers prétentieux qui ne comprennent rien à leur ouvrage : « Ne sont pas tous bon cuisiniers ceux qui portent des couteaux » (vol. 1, p. 73 ; « On voit bien là que l'habit ne fait pas le moine »). Volkamer retranscrit en vers une fable que Ferrari contait déjà dans son ouvrage sur la Flore. Deux fripons négligent le jardin dont on leur a confié l'entretien ; pour les punir, la déesse Flore les transforme en une limace et une chenille – les fléaux des jardins. Chez Volkamer, la métamorphose se traduit par deux anagrammes : Schnecke devient Schenck (limace) et Raupe Paur (chenille). L'illustration des planches correspondantes (p. 92) est plus brutale que chez Ferrari, car la transformation de Paur en chenille se voit – à la différence du modèle italien – par les mains qui commencent à se couvrir de poils, tandis que Schenck, difforme, se tord en rampant déjà sur le sol à la manière d'un mollusque.

Des fruits célestes

Fleurs et fruits, de grande ou de petite taille, sont représentés grandeur nature dans le livre des *Hespérides* : l'Oreille d'ours aussi bien que la Noix de coco, l'Ananas et les Pamplemousses. Quelques-unes des gravures présentent une claire séparation entre la représentation du fruit qui occupe la partie supérieure et, au-dessous, la partie illustrée en trompe-l'œil avec les vues générales (ex. p. 211, 360). Ce schéma ne pouvait toutefois pas être appliqué systématiquement en raison de la taille variable des fruits, et conduit à une disposition qui évoque la technique du collage, pour laquelle l'œuvre de Volkamer est célèbre, mais qui avait aussi des précurseurs chez les auteurs d'ouvrages sur les fleurs publiés à Nuremberg aux alentours de 1700, et même dans d'autres livres de botanique (p. 82).

Le lecteur doit attendre le vingt-troisième chapitre du premier volume pour trouver la première illustration de fruits et de fleurs du genre *Citrus* (p. 67). Au-dessous de la représentation détaillée des fruits, et des fleurs fortement grossies (uniquement sur cette

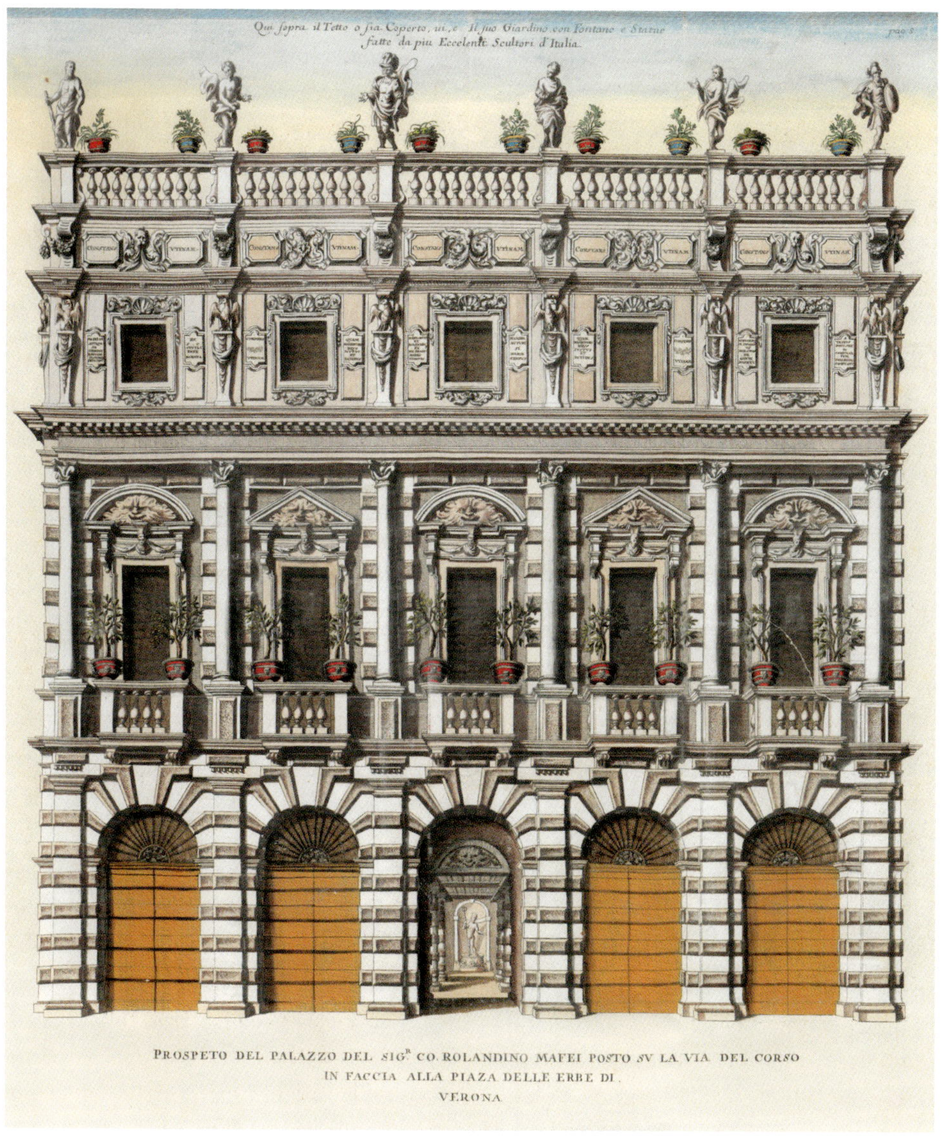

Façade of the Palazzo Maffei on the Piazza delle Erbe in Verona
Fassade des Palazzo Maffei in Verona an der Piazza delle Erbe
Façade du Palazzo Maffei à Vérone près de la Piazza delle Erbe
From: *Continuation der Nürnbergischen Hesperidum*, 1714, vol. II, plate p. 224
Vienna, Österreichische Nationalbibliothek

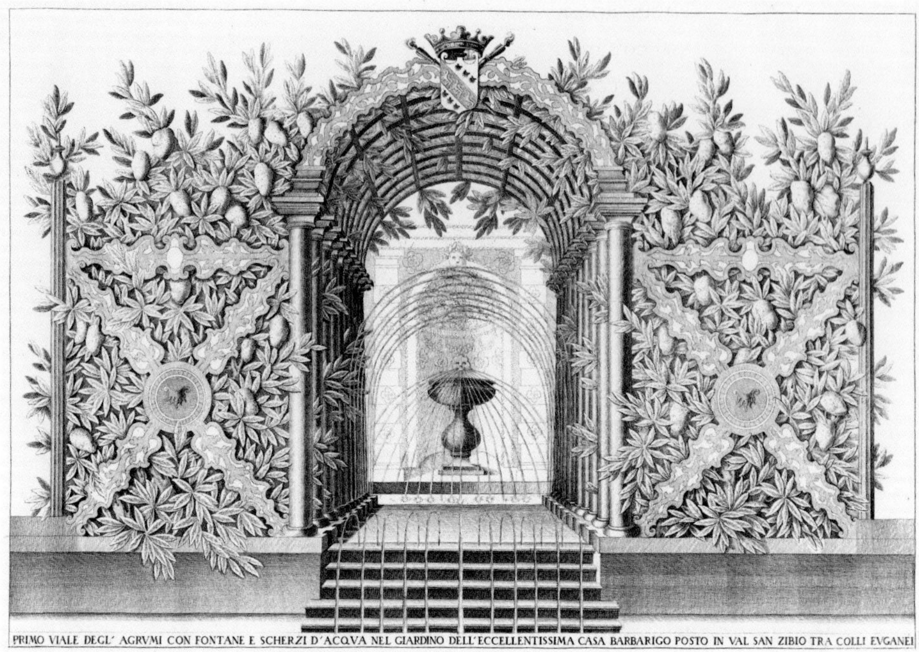

planche), Volkamer montre le célèbre observatoire de Nuremberg, qui avait été construit en 1678 par l'astronome et graveur Georg Christoph Eimmart sur l'un des bastions des remparts de la ville. Cet observatoire public connut une forte affluence au mois de mai 1706 à l'occasion d'une éclipse solaire totale. La planche faisant figurer les agrumes au-dessus de l'observatoire exprime l'approche scientifique de l'auteur et illustre la méthode par laquelle il entend aller au fond des choses : tout au long de son ouvrage, il tient à préciser qu'il se sert d'un « microscopium » ou d'un « verre grossissant ». La confrontation significative du proche et du lointain, du microscope et de la longue-vue explique en même temps la stratégie suivie dans la composition des planches. La technique bifocale de collage présente dans la partie supérieure, grandeur nature et vu de près, le fruit, et dans la partie inférieure, à distance, la *veduta.* La planche de Volkamer traduit en outre l'intérêt qu'il porte aux constellations, intérêt qu'il partageait avec son père et beaucoup de ses compa-

Primo viale degl'agrumi con fontane e scherzi d'acqua
Citrus-covered arbour at the Villa Barbarigo in Valsanzibio
Mit Zitrus überwachsener Laubengang in der Villa Barbarigo in Valsanzibio
Pergola formée d'agrumes à la villa Barbarigo à Valsanzibio
From: Domenico Rossetti, *Fabbriche e giardini dell'Eccellentissima Casa Barbarigo*, Verona, 1702
Padua, Biblioteca Civica di Padova

triotes de Nuremberg. La juxtaposition de l'observatoire avec le grossissement du microscope peut sans doute aussi être interprétée comme l'invention de ces gravures du livre des *Hespérides*: finalement, les précieux fruits apparaissent comme d'énormes astres célestes brillant au firmament, au-dessus de la ville, du paysage et du jardin.

Dans les trois volumes de l'ouvrage de Volkamer, le genre *Citrus* est divisé en cédrats (*Citrus medica* L., *Citrus limonimedica* L.), citrons et limons (*Citrus limon* L., *Citrus aurantiifolia* (Christm.) Swingle) oranges amères ou bigarades, oranges douces et pamplemousses (*Citrus aurantium* L., *Citrus sinensis* L., *Citrus grandis* L.). Suivant en cela Ferrari et d'autres auteurs faisant référence au mythe antique, Volkamer attribue aux trois Hespérides différentes catégories de fruits et leur culture dans différentes régions d'Italie: Aeglé est censée s'être appliquée à la culture du cédrat autour du lac de Garde, sa sœur Aréthuse aurait apporté le citron sur la côte de Ligurie, et Hesperthuse les oranges en Calabre. Les trois parties correspondantes du premier volume sont illustrées de représentations allégoriques d'un jardin avec, en arrière-plan, un lac ou la mer. Dans le deuxième volume, les trois pages d'introduction portent le nom de chacune des Hespérides dans une couronne de feuillage; aucune représentation figurative du même ordre ne nous a été conservée pour le troisième volume.

Volkamer s'efforce de décrire chacune des espèces du genre Citrus en fournissant les indications exactes de taille, de forme de développement et de couleur, avec la senteur de l'arbre, des feuilles, des fleurs et des fruits, l'époque de maturité, l'origine des fruits, la culture de l'arbre. La multiplication à partir des graines, de rejets, de feuilles et même d'une épine (« aiguillon ») retient tout particulièrement son attention. Le principe scientifique de l'autopsie est la règle suprême de sa démarche. Volkamer transmet les connaissances qu'il a tirées de ses cultures dans son propre jardin, et se plaint fréquemment, se référant à Ferrari ou à Commelin, de la classification controversée et du manque d'homogénéité de la nomenclature botanique. La description des différentes espèces de *Citrus* commence à chaque fois par une description générale et une énumération des « propriétés et de l'utilisation » des fruits. L'auteur renvoie à maintes reprises au *Vollständiges Nürnbergisches Koch-Buch* (Nuremberg 1691), livre de cuisine qui contient une foule de recettes sucrées et salées dans lesquelles sont utilisés les citrons, cédrats et oranges. À la table des princes et des bourgeois aisés, les agrumes frais ou confits ne devaient pas manquer. Leur emploi pour la fabrication des eaux de senteur, si appréciées à l'époque baroque, était indispensable. Volkamer montre sa « chambre odorante » à l'orangerie de Gostenhof, par la fenêtre de laquelle pénètre le parfum des fleurs d'oranger (p. 243, 258/259).

Du fait de la tendance des espèces du genre *Citrus* à de fortes modifications et de leur culture intensive, on vit se répandre au XVIIe siècle une grande variété d'arbres, de fleurs, de feuilles et de fruits, que les jardiniers et botanistes enregistrèrent, décrivirent, et s'efforcèrent de reproduire – dans toute la mesure du possible. Volkamer énumère de nombreux fruits qui ne se trouvent pas chez Ferrari. Le *corpus* de son ouvrage présente une pluralité d'espèces jusqu'alors inconnue des ouvrages de référence. Il parle de monstrueuses « bizarreries » ou qualifie « d'avortons » les fruits inhabituels qu'il pense être le résultat de mutations fortuites ou de greffes, de même que Ferrari, chez qui certaines formes de fruits pleins d'excroissances ou curieusement fourchus, font un effet particulièrement déconcertant (p. 71). Il présente à plusieurs reprises des fruits eux-mêmes « fructifères » *(fetifero)*, des fruits « engrossés », par exemple l'extraordinaire « Cedro con frutto in frutto » du troisième volume, ou les fruits qualifiés d'hermaphrodites en raison des éperons de leur écorce. Il ne semble pas avoir connu les oranges sanguines. Quant à la Mandarine *(Citrus reticulata Blanco)*, elle fera son apparition seulement au XIXe siècle, importée d'Asie du Sud-Est.

« Jaune soufre » et « couleur citron » : botanique et représentation

Volkamer indique très clairement, au fil de ses descriptions, les diverses colorations des feuilles, fleurs, branches et fruits, striés, flammés, hachurés ou tachetés, qui varient fréquemment : par exemple, « la coloration extrêmement sombre et vert-noir » des Pomi d'Adamo (vol. 1, p. 167) également dénommées « citrons noirs », les « rayures jaune soufre et vertes » des Bigarades ou le jaune safran, « tirant légèrement vers le jaune soufre, mais plutôt citron » de l'Aranzo fiamato (vol. 1, p. 196), ou « les nombreuses stries sensiblement verdâtres » des fruits qualifiés de Bizarrerie (vol. 1, p. 172). Les dessins de fruits par Volkamer, dont pas un seul ne semble malheureusement nous avoir été conservé, étaient certainement coloriés. Les gravures de fruits tentent de donner par le moyen du graphisme une impression nuancée de la coloration et du dessin des feuilles et des fruits. Les planches destinées au troisième volume n'ayant pas été coloriées, le lecteur de cette réimpression pourra se faire une idée des différences d'effet et d'expression des gravures par comparaison avec les planches en couleurs des deux premiers volumes.

Plusieurs exemplaires et planches séparées coloriés nous sont parvenus : leurs couleurs diffèrent néanmoins. L'exemplaire reproduit ici provient de la famille Holzschuher et a été colorié dès le XVIIIe siècle, alors que l'ouvrage était encore entre les mains de cette famille patricienne de Nuremberg. Le coloriage estompe, à vrai dire, les nuances du dessin des feuilles et des fruits. Coloriés uniformément en jaune, orange, ou jaune clair, les fruits sont réunis par groupes, les feuilles et les branches sont vert turquoise. Certains spécimens rayés ou flammés sont toutefois spécialement mis en valeur par le coloriage. Contrairement aux coloriages ultérieurs, qui n'utilisent généralement plus de couleurs vives et veillent à la discrétion des dégradés, dans le présent exemplaire la couleur l'emporte sur la composition de l'illustration. Elle souligne la proximité (le fruit) et le lointain

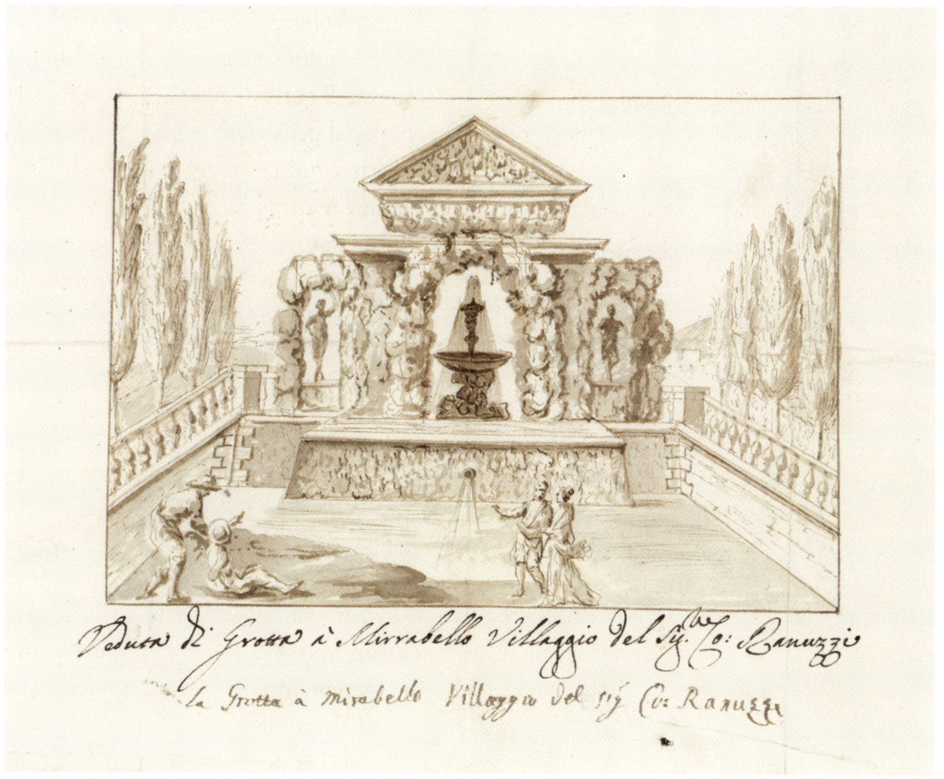

(Veduta), le haut et le bas, puisque dans la plupart des cas le ciel et les nuages sont en bleu et blanc, coupant en deux les planches. Les vives tonalités des façades de villas vénitiennes par exemple – turquoise, rose, pourpre, ou jaune citron – ne correspondent pas à la réalité. Mais ces couleurs éclatantes s'adressent directement au plus noble des organes sensoriels, l'œil. Elles produisent un effet d'ensemble extrêmement décoratif et séduisant : cela vaut pour les gravures, les vignettes, et par conséquent le livre des *Hespérides* tout entier. À travers ce coloriage s'opère la transmutation décisive du savant traité de botanique de Volkamer sur le genre *Citrus* en ouvrage représentatif de la science.

L'auteur distingue les agrumes dont on lui a seulement fait parvenir des feuilles et des fruits de ceux qu'il cultive, réussit à faire fleurir et fructifier lui-même dans son jardin. Il

***Veduta di Grotta à Mirabello Villaggio del Sig[nore] Co[nte] Ranuzzi**, c. 1714/15*
View of the grotto at Mirabello / Ansicht der Grotte von Mirabello / Vue de la grotte à Mirabello
Preliminary drawing for an engraving for the unpublished third volume of *Hesperides*, 1714–1720
Pen and brush in brown, 22.4 × 33.7 cm (8 ⅞ × 13 ¼ in.)
Nuremberg, Germanisches Nationalmuseum, Graphische Sammlung, ZR 3196 Kaps 726 Cont. II, Nr. 12

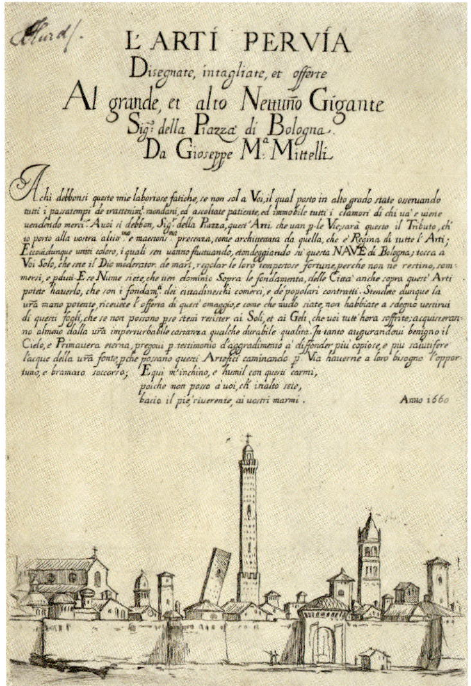
L'ARTI PERVIA
Disegnate, intagliate, et offerte
Al grande, et alto Nettuno Gigante
Sig.re della Piazza di Bologna.
Da Gioseppe M.a Mitelli.

A chi debbonsi queste mie laboriose fatiche, se non sol a Voi, il qual posto in alto grado state osseruando tutti i passatempi de trattenim.ti mondani, ed ascoltate patiente, ed immobile tutti i clamori di chi ua' e uiene uendendo merci. A uoi si debbon, Sig.r della Piazza, quest'Arti che uan p. le Vie; sarà questo il Tributo, ch' io porto alla uostra altiss.ma e maestosiss.ma presenza, come architettata da quella, che è Regina di tutte l'Arti; Eccoui dunque uniti coloro, i quali sen uanno fluttuando, e tondeggiando su questa NAVE di Bologna; tocca a Voi Solo, che sete il Dio moderator de mari, regolar le loro tempestose fortune, perche non ne restino, sommersi, e p.duti. E se Nume siete, che tien dominio Sopra le fondamenta, delle Citta' anche sopra quest'Arti potete hauerlo, che son i fondam.ti dei cittadineschi comerci, e de' popolari contratti. Stendete dunque la u.ra mano potente, riceuete l'offerta di quest'omaggio, e come che nudo siate, non habbiate a sdegno uestirui di questi fogli, che se non possono p.se stessi resister ai Soli, et ai Geli, che uoi tutt'hora soffrite; acquisteranno almeno dalla u.ra imperturbabile costanza qualche durabile qualita. In tanto augurandoui benigno il Cielo, e Primauera eterna, pregoui p. testimonio d'aggradimento a' diffonder più copiose, e più salutifere l'acque della u.ra fonte, p.che possano questi Artefici caminando p. Via hauerne a loro bisogno l'opportuno, e bramato soccorso; E qui m'inchino, e humil con questi carmi,
poiche non posso a uoi, ch' in alto sete,
bacio il piè riuerente, ai uostri marmi.

Anno 1660

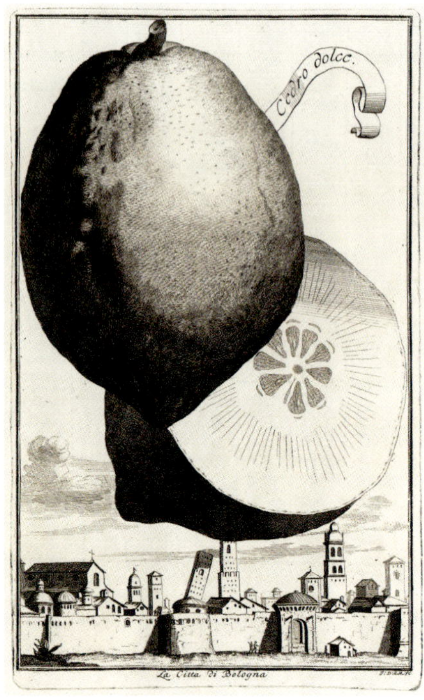

se vante d'avoir reproduit tous ces fruits « de sa propre main, d'après nature avec la plus grande application » (vol. 1, p. 7). Il y eut dès le XVIIe siècle à Nuremberg une tradition bien établie de peinture et de dessin d'après nature, par des artistes amateurs bourgeois ou patriciens. Lorsque Volkamer prend lui-même sa plume et son crayon, il s'inscrit tout à fait dans la tradition locale. La seule exception – selon ses propres dires – est le pamplemousse cueilli en 1705 dans le jardin de Bose à Leipzig, dont il n'y aurait eu qu'un seul exemplaire, de sorte qu'il aurait dû s'en faire envoyer un dessin (vol. 1, p. 173, 189).

On était loin de pouvoir se procurer une aussi grande variété de *Citrus* en Allemagne qu'au sud des Alpes. Il était donc courant de faire venir les agrumes directement d'Italie

Giuseppe Maria Mitelli, **Title-page with view of Bologna**
Titelseite mit der Ansicht von Bologna / Page de titre avune vue de Bologne
28.5 × 20 cm (11 ¼ × 7 ⅞ in.). From: *Le Arti per Via*, Bologna, 1660
London, British Museum

"Cedro dolce" above the veduta of Bologna / „Cedro dolce" über der Stadtansicht von Bologna
« Cedro dolce » au-dessus de la vue de la ville de Bologne
Engraving and etching. Plate for the unpublished third volume of *Nürnbergische Hesperides*, 1714–1720
Universitätsbibliothek Erlangen-Nürnberg, H61/2 RAR.A 35[2, p. 25

ou de les acheter aux foires de Francfort ou de Leipzig. Volkamer dresse dans le premier volume une liste d'espèces que l'on pouvait se procurer au bord du lac de Garde (vol. I, p. 107 s). Il y recommande la culture des agrumes telle qu'elle se pratique là et présente sur une gravure un exemple de « limonaia », l'un des modèles de serres démontables encore couramment en usage aujourd'hui sur les rives du lac (p. 134/135). Il mentionne certes aussi Gênes, qu'il connaissait d'après le récit de voyage en Italie de Joseph Furttenbach *Newes Itinerarium Italiae* de 1627 (vol. II, fol. 78r), et montre, sur des gravures en grand format, le paysage parsemé de villas s'élevant au-dessus de la mer autour de Gênes et de la toute proche Nervi, mais on peut se demander s'il s'y est jamais rendu lui-même.

Primevère, Pistache et Ananas

Volkamer cultivait et décrivit en même temps que les agrumes d'autres plantes méridionales ou exotiques (p. 133) auxquelles il consacre la fin de chacun des volumes, traitant par exemple, dans le troisième volume, du caféier (p. 463). Au premier volume s'ajoute pour terminer une cinquième partie intitulée *Flora Noribergensis, Oder Nürnbergische Flora,* exposé qu'il doit à son frère, mais qui n'est toutefois pas identique avec le gros ouvrage dudit frère portant le même titre. Aux 66 « Oreilles d'ours » (*Primula auricula* L.), particulièrement appréciées comme fleurs d'agrément dans les jardins de l'époque, et aux 49 Primevères (*Primula veris* L.) font suite des fleurs particulièrement intéressantes et spectaculaires du jardin du frère de l'auteur. Parmi les plantes du jardin de Gostenhof, Johann Christoph Volkamer décrit, entre autres, l'Olivier, le Laurier et l'Arbousier, le Pistachier et l'Aubergine, que l'on pensait nuisible parce qu'elle était censé rendre « sot ou fol » (vol. I, p. 243). Dans le deuxième volume suivent les descriptions de différents palmiers, du Dragonnier et du Cotonnier, mais surtout de l'Ananas, « roi des fruits », qui était cultivé dans les serres d'Europe depuis la fin du XVIIe siècle. Le médecin et naturaliste de Nuremberg Michael Friedrich Lochner (1662–1720), qui avait fait ses études en Italie en 1684/85 et acheté en 1691 le domaine de Hummelstein près de Nuremberg, où il cultivait des plantes méridionales et exotiques, publia en 1716 un traité sur l'Ananas qui fut ensuite relié à un certain nombre d'exemplaires du livre des *Hespérides (Commentatio de Ananasa sive nuce pinea Indica, vulgo Pinhas).*

Pour la représentation de fruits comme l'Ananas ainsi que du Colibri, du Cancrelat et de la Tarentule, Volkamer s'inspire des publications de Maria Sibylla Merian (1647–1717), qui était à peu près du même âge que lui et avait vécu à Nuremberg de 1670 à 1681. La célèbre naturaliste connaissait la famille Volkamer, avec qui elle avait des relations familiales et scientifiques, et entretint des échanges avec Johann Georg junior à propos de ses recherches sur les plantes et insectes du Surinam. C'est en 1705 que parut son étonnant ouvrage *Metamorphosis Insectorum Surinamensium* (p. 104, 105, 107). Johann Christoph

Volkamer connaissait, lui aussi, la célèbre observatrice du monde des insectes au Surinam. Du Surinam il reçut en 1706, via Amsterdam où vivait Merian, un pamplemousse.

Réseaux de botanistes

Johann Christoph Volkamer – de même que son père et son frère – était en rapport intense et permanent avec de nombreux propriétaires de jardins et jardiniers en Allemagne et à l'étranger. De Hamelin, Hambourg, Leipzig, Dresde, Breslau, la Bohême, la Hollande, l'Italie, l'Espagne, l'Amérique du Sud (Surinam, Curaçao) et du Cap de Bonne-Espérance en Afrique, ainsi que de nombreux autres endroits, il recevait des informations, et on lui envoyait des fruits, des boutures et même des plantes adultes, que ce soit à racines nues ou en motte. Ses correspondants italiens travaillaient dans des endroits où son père et son frère s'étaient rendus au cours de leurs études (Padoue, Bologne, Rome, Naples, etc.). Les lettres de Johann Christoph Volkamer ne nous ont malheureusement pas été conservées, et il ne mentionne nommément qu'un petit nombre de ses correspondants dans son livre des *Hespérides*. Le plus souvent, il les qualifie globalement de «bons amis».

Dans les premiers temps modernes, la recherche fonctionnait pourtant grâce à de vastes réseaux internationaux. L'une des plus importantes collections de correspondances sur la médecine, la botanique et les sciences naturelles fut réunie par le médecin et botaniste de Nuremberg Christoph Jakob Trew (1695–1769), lui aussi descendant d'une famille d'érudits et qui connaissait la famille Volkamer. Les savants Johann Georg Volkamer senior et junior sont largement présents dans la collection de Trew; ils ont eu d'importantes relations épistolaires avec des correspondants internationaux. Ils échangeaient des informations avec des jardiniers et botanistes, dont les jardins et lieux d'activité figurent aussi dans le livre des *Hespérides*. En rapprochant systématiquement ces mentions de la correspondance du père et du frère, on arrive à identifier sans trop de difficulté un certain nombre de ces « bons amis» de Johann Christoph Volkamer. Par exemple, lorsqu'il est question d'un jardinier de Château Schwöbber, il s'agit de Johann Friedrich Berner, dont la correspondances des années 1712 à 1717 nous a été conservée.

Même les catalogues de plantes et d'agrumes sont présentés comme les annexes à des correspondances adressées à la famille Volkamer, par exemple un répertoire d'agrumes envoyé en 1717 à Nuremberg par Giorgio Cornaro de Padoue. Dans de nombreuses lettres adressées à Johann Georg, il est question de son frère Johann Christoph, à qui les expéditeurs veulent faire plaisir en lui offrant des plants ou des fruits du genre *Citrus.* La collection Trew montre clairement que Johann Christoph Volkamer a utilisé pour ses recherches sur les agrumes les contacts établis au sein de sa famille et des cercles scienti-

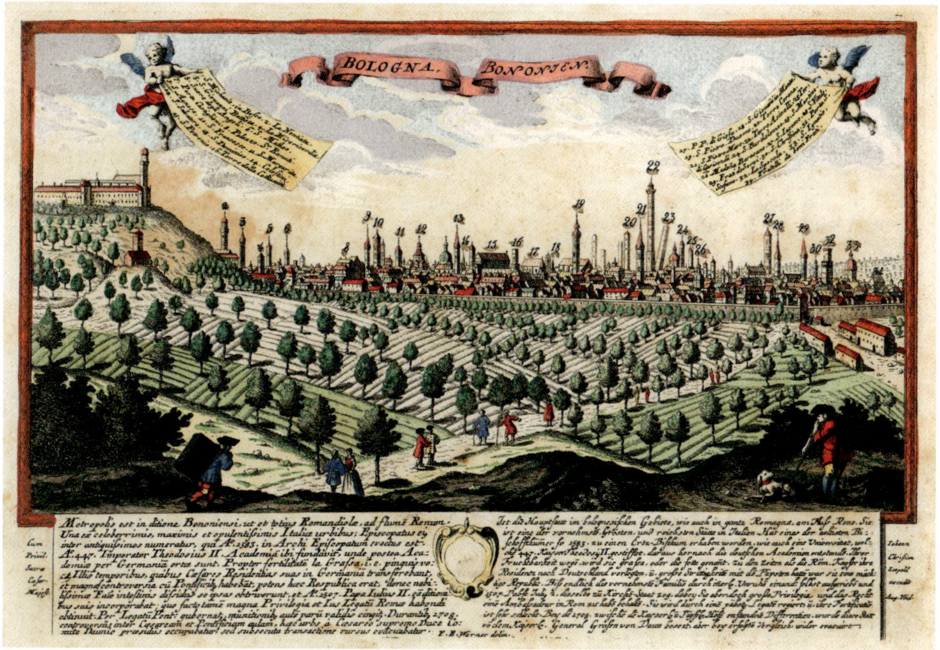

fiques de Nuremberg. Pour l'étude de ces réseaux, le livre des *Hespérides* est donc à la fois une mine et un défi.

Mundus in litteris – le monde dans le livre : Nuremberg, Padoue, Bologne, Pékin, Le Cap, Curaçao

« Pour mon premier *Hesperidibus* de Nuremberg, j'ai fait/ figurer au-dessous des dessins de fruits, / nombre de vues et de jardins, d'ici, de la région de Nuremberg / représentés d'après nature. Mais comme / au cours de la préparation de cet ouvrage, / j'ai dû bien souvent penser à l'Italie, / me remémorant avec le plus grand plaisir, / les palais d'une extrême beauté / que possèdent les nobles de Venise / tout le long de la Brenta / de Padoue jusqu'à Venise, / dressés ou étalés, / j'ai pris la décision / de faire graver dans le cuivre, / ces édifices même / et aussi d'autres bâtiments d'exception qui sont érigés là / et de montrer au-dessous des fruits reproduits / de somptueuses vues et palais d'Italie. Cela n'a pas été

Johann Christian Leupold, **Veduta of Bologna**, *c.* 1720
Stadtansicht von Bologna / Vue de la ville de Bologne
Hand-coloured engraving after Friedrich Bernhard Werner, Augsburg
Bologna, Biblioteca comunale dell'Archiginnasio,
Gabinetto Disegni e Stampe, Raccolta Piante della Città, cart. 3, n. 22a

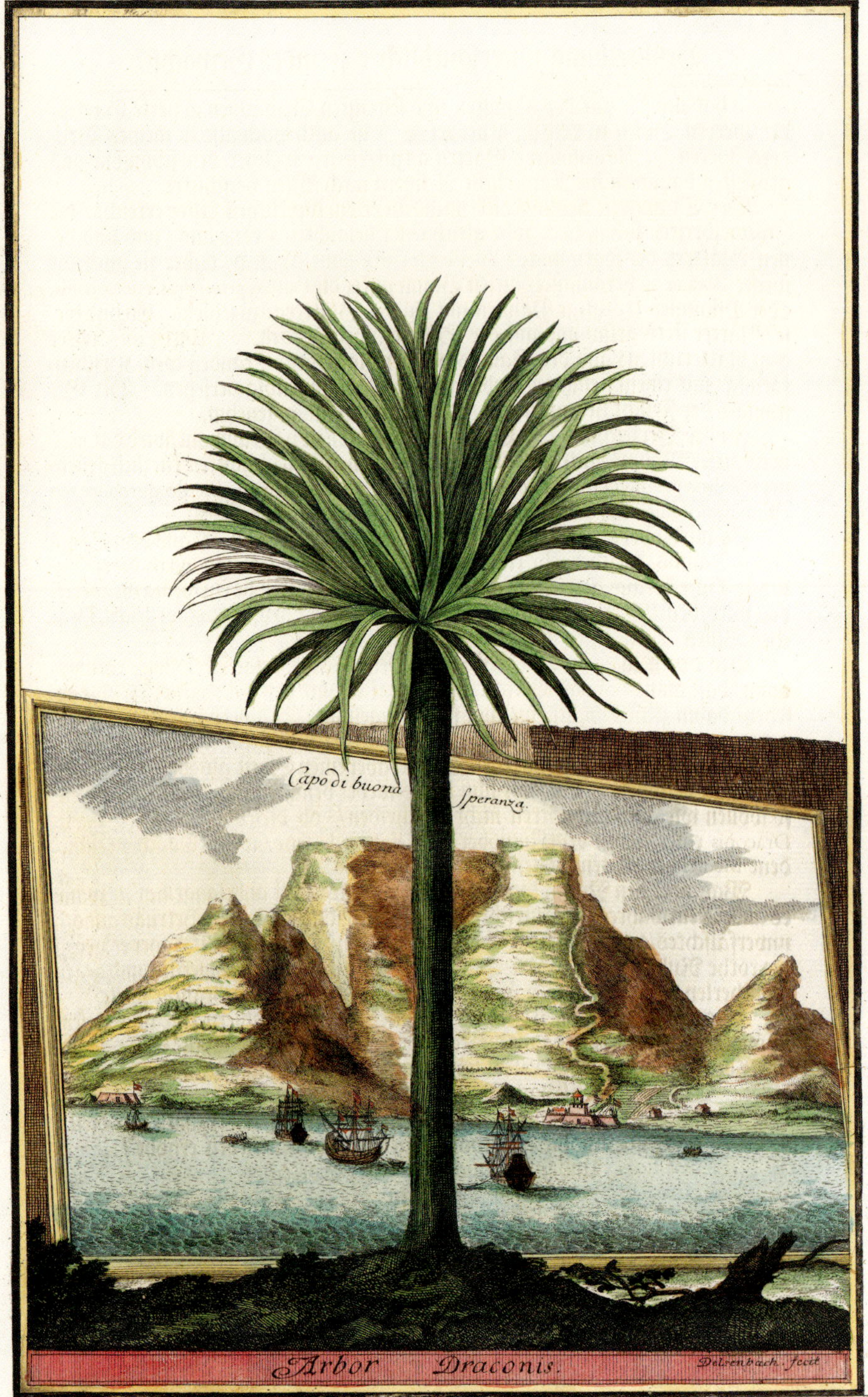

Arbor Draconis.

sans peine, / que j'ai fini par trouver un bon ami / qui, parcourant ces mêmes contrées, / a pu exécuter la suite d'esquisses, dessinées avec la plus grande précision, d'après nature; auxquelles se sont ajoutées en même temps celles de Vérone et Bologne. J'ai donc finalement réussi, / et pu ainsi satisfaire mon désir / d'embellir la présentation de chacun des fruits / par la vue d'une riche demeure / ou de quelque autre belle vue d'Italie. » (vol. II, Préambule) Le livre des *Hespérides* de Volkamer est aussi instructif du point de vue topographique que botanique. D'une façon générale, il n'y a pas de correspondance entre le fruit et les lieux représentés. Volkamer a au contraire manifestement ordonné les vues de façon pragmatique en fonction de leur dimension. Les *vedute* sont groupées par région et apportent une touche de couleur locale.

Le fait que soient représentés dans le premier volume des manoirs, châteaux et jardins de Nuremberg et de la région, ainsi qu'à la fin de l'ouvrage des paysages environnants, s'explique par l'attachement de l'auteur à sa ville natale. Beaucoup des vues de Nuremberg sont inspirées des gravures de Johann Alexander Boener (1647–1720) qui était en relation avec Volkamer et dont la période d'activité la plus féconde se situa dans la dernière décennie du XVIIe et la première du XVIIIe siècle (p. 111). Si au contraire certains jardins célèbres de Nuremberg n'apparaissent pas dans le livre des *Hespérides*, c'est vraisemblablement qu'il n'en existait pas de modèle de gravure de Boener qui ait pu être adapté aux planches des *Hespérides*. Ses *vedute* n'ont sans doute pas été remaniées par ses propres soins, mais par chacun des graveurs qui les ont mises au format du livre de Volkamer, modifiées dans l'ensemble des proportions, le plus souvent étendues en largeur et accompagnées d'un premier plan pittoresque et d'un arrière-plan paysager tout aussi fictif. Il faut noter qu'il fournit lui-même une indication sur la façon de transposer le plan d'un jardin en perspective (p. 108, 109; vol. I, p. 249–251). Pour ces *vedute* – contrairement aux représentations de fruits – Volkamer concédait toutefois une marge d'interprétation formelle à la qualité picturale de la représentation. Les vues en grand format de Nuremberg par le dessinateur et graveur Johann Adam Delsenbach (1687–1765) ne parurent qu'à partir de 1715, elles n'existaient donc pas encore lorsque fut mis sous presse le premier volume de l'ouvrage de Volkamer.

Pour le deuxième volume du livre des *Hespérides*, Delsenbach fournit une vue de St Georgen près de Bayreuth (p. 264/265) et une vue à vol d'oiseau du château et du jardin de Schönbrunn (p. 262/263). Volkamer a fait graver les vues en grand format des jardins d'Erlangen (p. 266–269), de Château Schwöbber (p. 23, 274) et de Passau (p. 276, 277)

Dragon tree and Cape of Good Hope
Drachenbaum und Kap der Guten Hoffnung / Dragonnier commun et le cap de Bonne-Espérance
From: *Continuation der Nürnbergischen Hesperidum*, 1714, vol. II, plate p. 234

d'après des œuvres des frères Decker et d'autres dessinateurs. Quelques-uns des graveurs du livre des *Hespérides* travaillèrent aussi pour le grand livre d'architecture de Paul Decker l'Ancien, *Fürstlicher Baumeister* (Augsbourg 1711–1713). Les vues de la villa Allegri à Cuzzano di Grezzana (p. 270/271) ainsi que d'autres villas et jardins des bords de la Brenta, à Padoue (p. 63), Vérone (p. 24, 119) et dans les monts Euganéens, et deux vues de Bologne s'ajoutent au deuxième volume du livre des *Hespérides.* En tant que collectivités souveraines, la République de Venise et Nuremberg, ville libre d'Empire, étaient des entités comparables. La *villeggiatur*a, lieu de séjour à la campagne de la noblesse de Venise et de Padoue pendant l'été, et la retraite bucolique des patriciens et de la bourgeoisie citadine de Nuremberg n'étaient pas le fait d'une société de cour, mais d'une noblesse et d'une bourgeoisie urbaines qui avaient une certaine culture de la vie à la campagne. On ignore qui a représenté « d'après nature » les villas vénitiennes où l'on cultivait aussi des agrumes. Le dessinateur qui travaillait pour Volkamer devait, en tout cas, être proche du cartographe et frère mineur franciscain Vincenzo Coronelli (1650–1718). Coronelli publia en 1711 une série de *vedute* des villas de la Brenta, dont la composition ressemble étonnamment à celle des planches de Volkamer (p. 116). Le choix n'est toutefois pas identique. Et comme certains édifices ne se trouvent que chez Volkamer, son ouvrage constitue une source importante pour l'histoire de l'architecture des villas vénétiennes.

Il en va à peu près de même des villas de la noblesse bolognaise reproduites sur les planches destinées au troisième volume et découvertes récemment. Johann Georg Volkamer senior et junior avaient tous deux séjourné au cours de leurs études dans cette très ancienne université de Bologne (p. 127), surnommée depuis bien longtemps « la dotta, la grassa », la ville docte et riche. Elle comptait parmi ses principales activités, depuis le XVIIe siècle, la production de la soie. Peut-être est-ce aussi l'une des raisons pour lesquelles Johann Christoph entretenait des relations sociales dans cette ville qui faisait partie des États pontificaux. On peut comparer la représentation iconographique de la ville de Bologne (p. 124, 411) avec celle de Nuremberg dans le premier volume : dans la partie supérieure un « Cedro dolce », au-dessous la silhouette des églises et des clochers. Volkamer a emprunté ces vues à la page de titre (p. 124) de l'ouvrage de Giuseppe Maria Mitelli (1634–1718) *Le Arti per Via* (Bologna 1660). Dans sa *Dissertatio* (1713), Erhard Reusch cite deux grands savants de Bologne : Ulisse Aldrovandi et l'érudit Ovidio Montalbano. Tous deux se sont consacrés à l'étude des agrumes (p. 72). Les collections d'Aldrovandi ont été reprises par l'une des académies des sciences les plus réputées de son temps : l'Istituto delle Scienze fondé en 1711. Les botanistes qui exerçaient dans cet institut, entre autres Lelio Trionfetti (1647–1722) et celui qui lui succéda à la direction du jardin botanique, Giuseppe Monti (1682–1760), entretinrent une correspondance avec les Volkamer de Nuremberg. Monti dit de Nuremberg qu'elle est la seule ville d'Allemagne avec laquelle il entretienne des échanges – à côté de nombreux autres célèbres jardins botaniques de toute l'Europe –, et il cite régulièrement la *Flora* de Johann Georg Volkamer et le livre des *Hespérides* de Johann Christoph Volkamer.

La noblesse bolognaise s'était fait construire depuis la fin du XVIe siècle des villas de campagne aux environs immédiats de la cité, et surtout au pied des collines ou sur ces collines du sud et du sud-ouest de la ville. Les plans de la ville de Bologne, à la fin du XVIIe siècle et autour de 1700 (par exemple, le plan d'Agostino Mitelli en 1692), le montrent. Cette florissante tradition des villas, qui se reflète dans la littérature et le théâtre de l'époque, est également présente dans les récits de voyage et les descriptions de la ville. Aux XVIIe et XVIIIe siècles, la plupart des voyageurs étrangers qui faisaient leur « grand tour » – voyage d'éducation qui les conduisait dans les centres politiques et artistiques de Florence, Rome et Naples – s'arrêtaient à Bologne, mais n'y séjournaient pas longtemps. La tradition des guides de voyages et des séries de gravures représentatives fut surtout entretenue à Rome et développée par les maisons d'édition. Bologne faisait partie certes des États pontificaux, mais elle n'avait pas de production iconographique comparable à celle de Rome en matière d'architecture profane. Les premières *vedute* de Bologne, souvent reproduites au fil des décennies, provenaient de l'ouvrage topographique de Joan Blaeu, qui avait publié en 1663 une série de huit vues de Bologne. Il fallut attendre 1732 pour que parût chez l'éditeur d'Augsbourg Johann Georg Merz la première importante série de vues générales, exécutées par le graveur silésien Friedrich Bernhard Werner ; vint ensuite, à la fin du XVIIIe siècle, la série de Pio Panfili. Dans ces séries de gravures, les villas ou jardins ne sont pas plus présents que dans les vues de la fin du XVIIIe ou du XIXe siècle. C'est pourquoi les gravures prévues pour le troisième volume du livre des *Hespérides* méritent de retenir l'attention. Les palais et jardins des grandes familles de la noblesse bolognaise y sont représentés au même titre que l'espace dit La Montagnola in Bologna (p. 409), qui était l'une des promenades de la ville, la célèbre église de pèlerinage San Michele in Bosco (p. 424) et, déjà présente dans le deuxième volume, la Madonna di San Luca (p. 388). Dans leur cadre pittoresque, les auberges de campagne plus ou moins louches (p. 413) font au premier abord l'effet d'un décor de théâtre pour l'opéra de Verdi *Rigoletto.* Les différents motifs de certaines planches sont empruntés à différentes sources – par exemple, à des gravures d'Agostino Mitelli et de Georg Andreas Böckler – et combinés de façon arbitraire. Les éléments architecturaux, palais aux murs crénelés, aqueducs ou fontaines, sont réunis pour donner des *vedute capricci,* d'allure bolognaise, de l'Émi-

---

Note éditoriale concernant les légendes des planches : Les appellations et classifications botaniques sont conformes aux indications de Volkamer. Les localisations sont mentionnées en anglais selon l'orthographe actuelle. Il en résulte quelques divergences par rapport aux inscriptions originales des planches. L'Index des lieux en appendice inclut également les appellations de lieux allemandes et françaises.

lie. Cela apparaît plus clairement que partout ailleurs sur une planche qui transporte sans ambages la statue de Neptune par Jean Bologne du centre de la ville de Bologne dans un jardin imaginaire (p. 435). Les *vedute* de Bologne font certes un effet un peu maladroit dans leur transposition en perspective, elles n'en constituent pas moins des documents iconographiques à prendre en compte. Les titres inscrits sur les cartons qui se trouvent au Germanisches Nationalmuseum sont en tout cas d'un Italien autochtone (p. 123) et désignent des constructions et des jardins sur l'aspect desquels aucune information ne nous a par ailleurs été conservée. Là encore, nous ne savons malheureusement pas qui les a « dessinés d'après nature ». Ce pourrait être le Vénitien Vincenzo Coronelli, dont il nous est dit qu'il aurait eu, en 1713, l'intention de composer un guide de voyage sur la ville de Bologne. Ce ne fut probablement pas l'architecte de Nuremberg Johann Jakob Schübler, dont le nom est inscrit au dos d'un des dessins. Les dernières planches des deuxième et troisième volumes montrent des vues de Nazareth, Pékin, du Cap de Bonne-Espérance (p. 128) et du Brésil. L'horizon de Johann Christoph Volkamer était vaste, il ne s'arrêtait pas aux limites de l'Europe. *Mundus in litteris* – le monde des lettres et des sciences dans lequel évoluait le marchand et collectionneur d'agrumes Johann Christoph Volkamer se reflète dans son livre des *Hespérides*.

Johann Georg Puschner, ***Aloe americana florens in horto Volcameriano***, 1726
Agave in bloom in the Volkamer garden at Gostenhof
Blühende Agave im Garten der Familie Volkamer in Gostenhof
Agave en fleur dans le jardin de la famille Volkamer à Gostenhof
Hand-coloured engraving. Nuremberg, Museen der Stadt Nürnberg, Graphische Sammlung

Pages 134/135
Temporary orangery at Salò on the shores of Lake Garda
Abschlagbares Pomeranzenhaus in Salò am Ufer des Gardaseea
Orangerie démontable à Salò sur les rives du lac de Garde
From: *Nürnbergische Hesperides*, 1708, vol. 1, plate p. 20

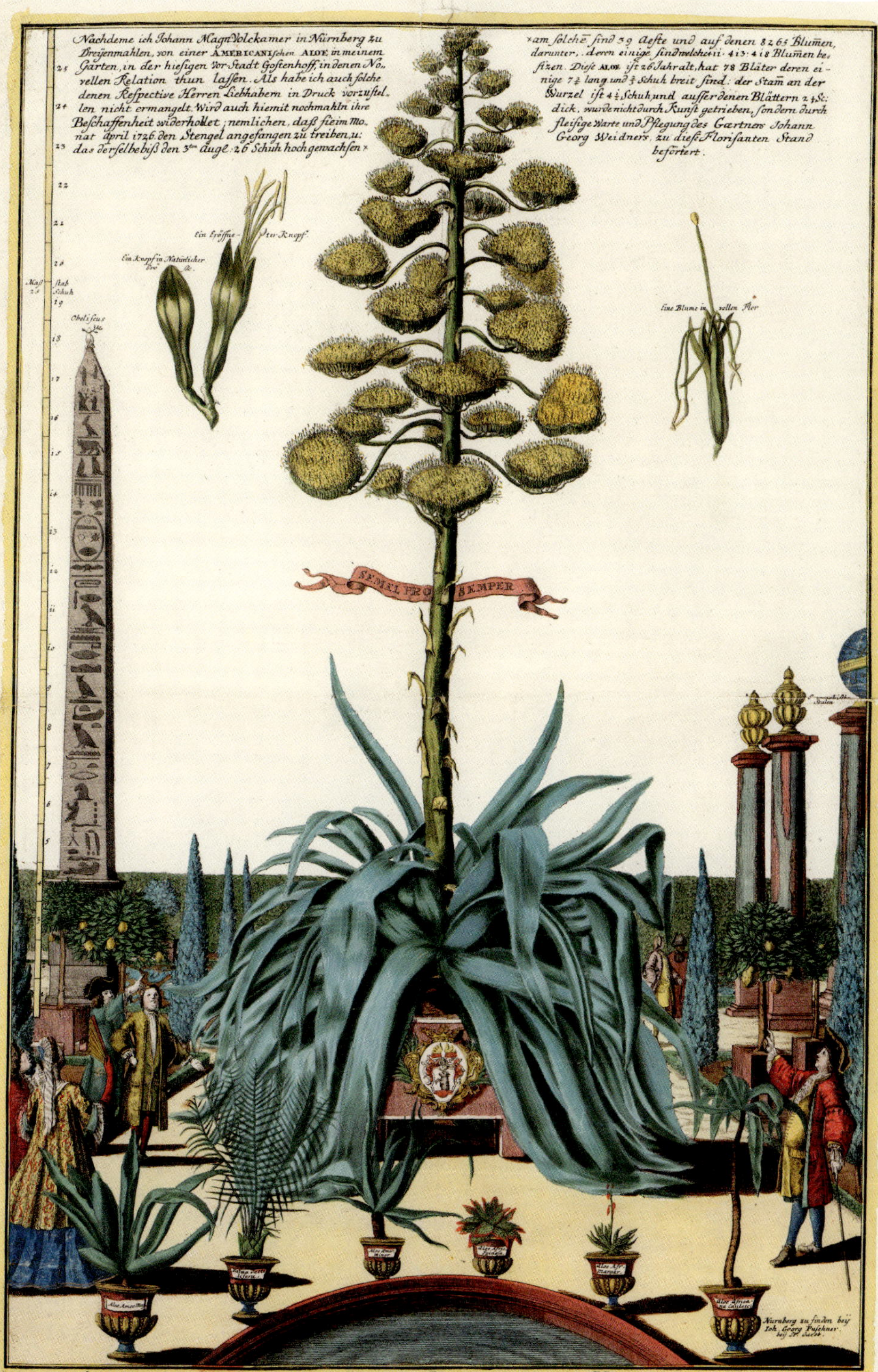
Nachdeme ich Johann Magn. Volckamer in Nürnberg zu Dreÿenmahlen, von einer AMERICANIschen ALOE in meinem Garten, in der hiesigen Vor-Stadt Gostenhoff, in denen Novellen Relation thun lassen. Als habe ich auch solche denen Respective Herren Liebhabern in Druck vorzustellen nicht ermangelt. Wird auch hiemit nochmahln ihre Beschaffenheit widerhollet; nemlichen, daß sie im Monat April 1726 den Stengel angefangen zu treiben, u: das derselbe biß den 3ten Augl: 26 Schuh hoch gewachsen ×
× am solchē sind 39 Aeste und auf denen 8265 Blumen, darunter, deren einige sind welche 411 · 413 · 418 Blumen besizen. Diese ALOE ist 26 Jahr alt, hat 78 Bläter deren einige 7½ lang und ¾ Schuh breit sind: der Stam̄ an der Wurzel ist 4½ Schuh und ausser denen Blättern 2¼ St: dick, wurde nicht durch Kunst getrieben, sondern durch fleisige Warte und Pflegung des Gærtners Johann Georg Weidners, zu diese Florisanten Stand befördert.
Ein Eröffne-ter Knopf
Eine Blume in vollen Flor
SEMEL PRO SEMPER
Nürnberg zu finden bey
Joh. Georg Puschner
ALOE AMERICANA FLORENS IN HORTO VOLCAMERIANO NORIMBERGÆ·A·MDCCXXVI

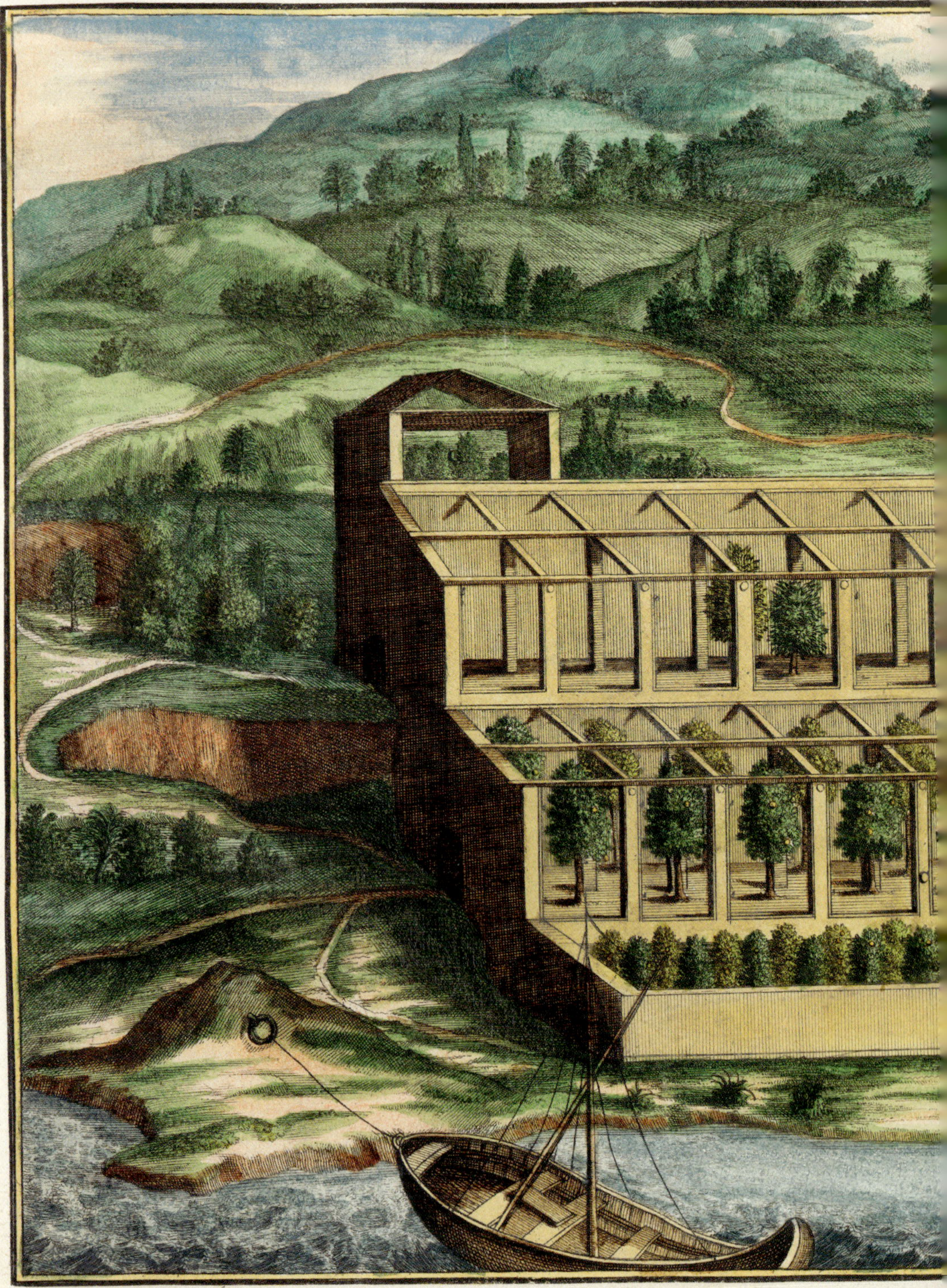

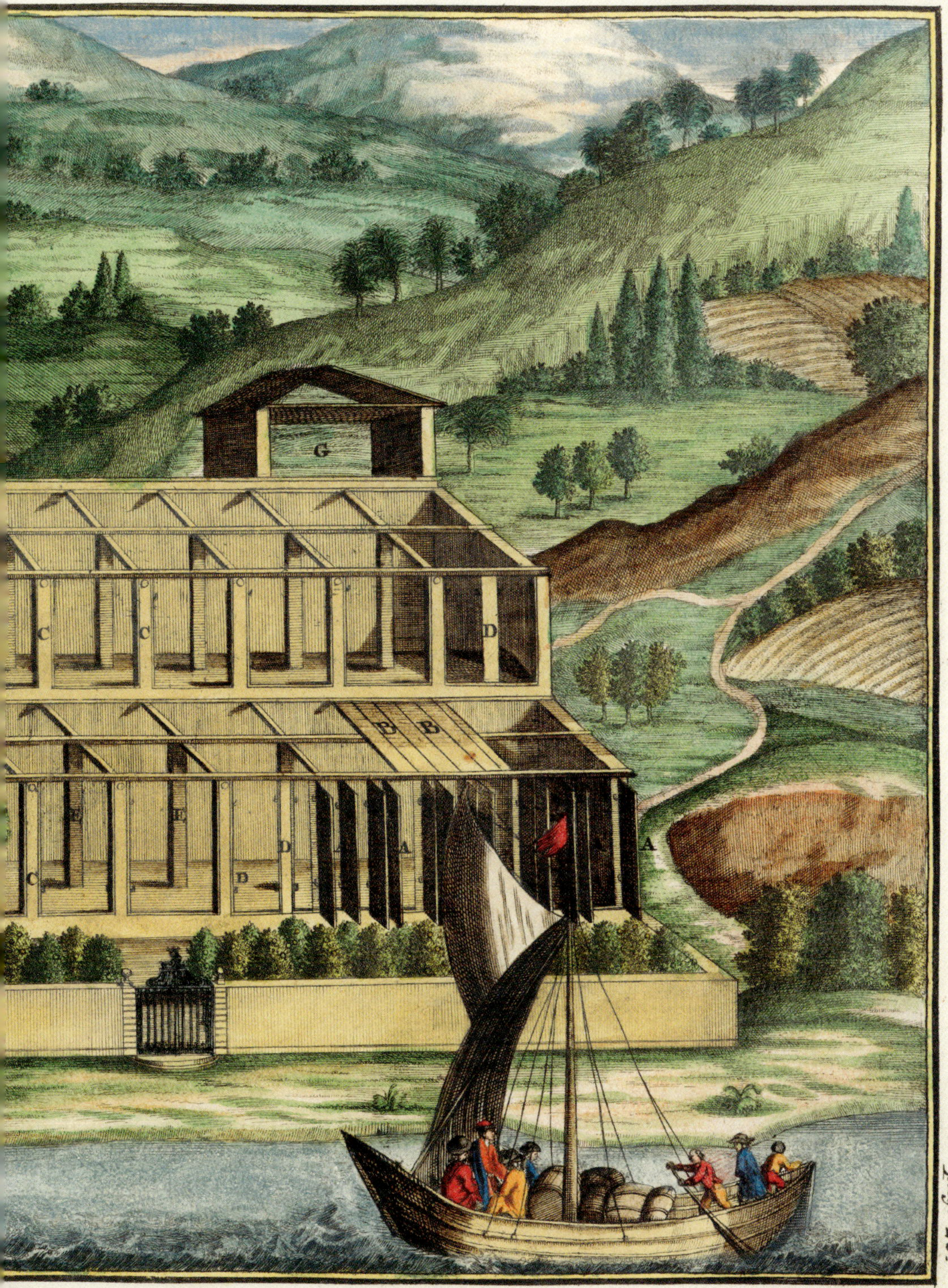

pag. 20.

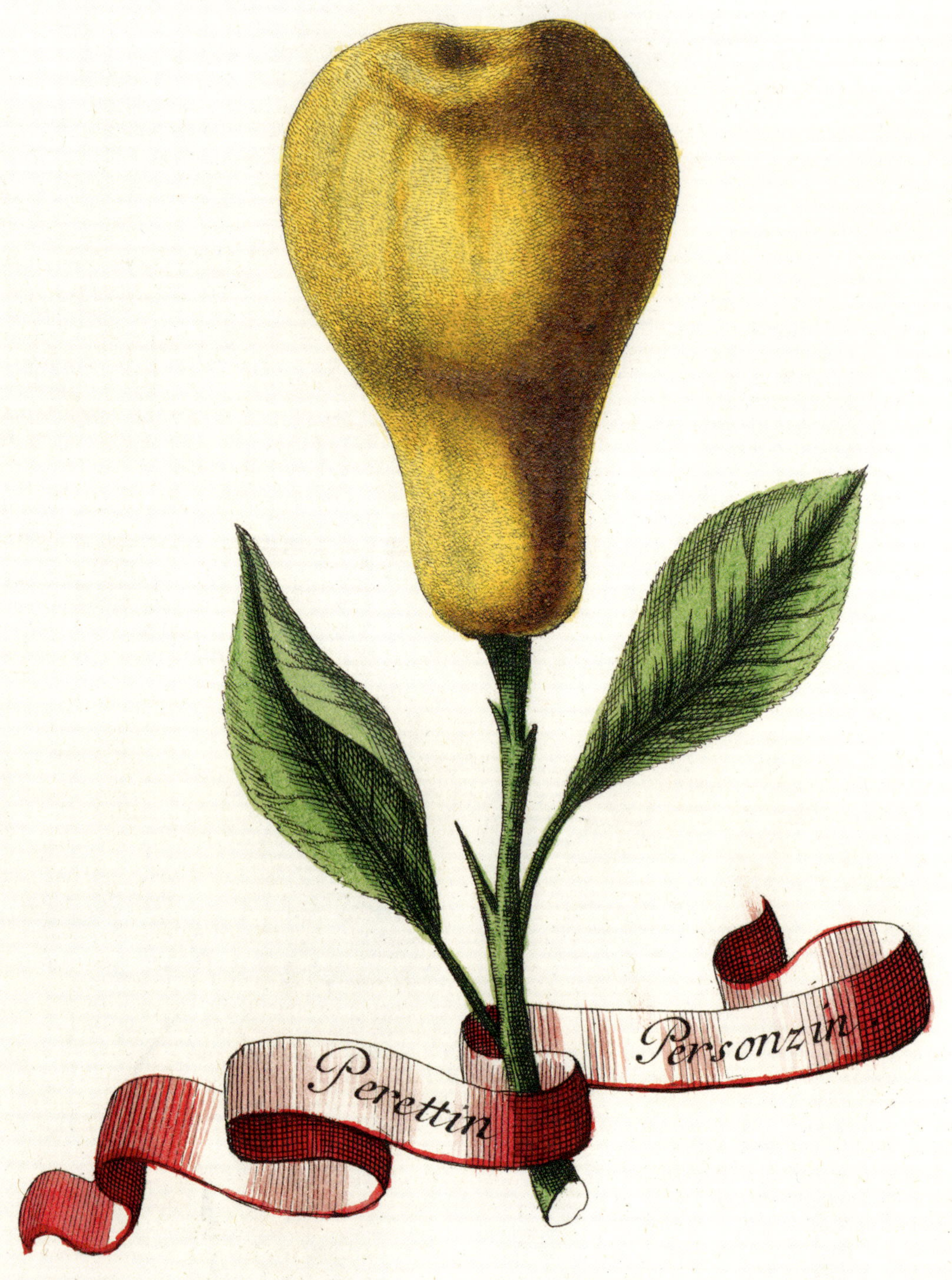
Perettin
Personzin

Volume I

The Nuremberg Hesperides, or: A detailed description of the noble fruits of the citron, lemon and bitter orange; how these may be correctly planted, cared for and propagated in that and neighbouring regions; including a detailed description of most varieties, some of which presently grow in Nuremberg and others which were brought here from various foreign places; engraved in copper with the greatest accuracy, divided into four parts and explained with useful comments. In addition, The Flora, or: A remarkable presentation of various rare flowers, together with numerous other plants, and an extensive description concerning how a sundial may be correctly positioned in a box-hedge garden, also how to break up gardens a little according to perspective, along with a description of the Colvmnis Milliaribvs constructed in the author's garden
Edited by J. C. V. 1708

Nürnbergische Hesperides, Oder Gründliche Beschreibung Der Edlen Citronat, Citronen, und Pomerantzen-Früchte, Wie solche, in selbiger und benachbarten Gegend, recht mögen eingesetzt, gewartet, erhalten und fortgebracht werden, Samt einer ausführlichen Erzehlung der meisten Sorten, welche theils zu Nürnberg würcklich gewachsen, theils von verschiedenen fremden Orten dahin gebracht worden, Auf das accurateste in Kupffer gestochen, in Vier Theile eingetheilet und mit nützlichen Anmerckungen erkläret. Beneben der Flora, Oder Curiosen Vorstellung Verschiedener raren Blumen, Samt Einer Zugabe etlicher anderer Gewächse, und ausführlichem Bericht, wie eine richtig-zutreffende Sonnen-Uhr im Garten-Feld von Bux anzulegen, und die Gärten nach der Perspectiv leichtlich aufzureissen, Wie auch einem Bericht von denen in des Authoris Garten stehenden Colvmnis Milliaribvs Herausgegeben von J. C. V. 1708
(Original German text of the title-page)

Les Hespérides de Nuremberg, ou : La description détaillée de ces nobles fruits, citrons, limons et oranges amères ; comment ceux-ci peuvent être correctement plantés, soignés et répandus dans cette même région et dans la région avoisinante ; avec une description détaillée de la plupart des variétés, certaines poussant réellement à Nuremberg tandis que d'autres ont été importées de divers pays étrangers ; soigneusement gravées sur cuivre, divisées en quatre parties et expliquées en commentaires judicieux. De plus, la Flore, ou: Une remarquable présentation de diverses fleurs rares, ainsi que de nombreuses autres plantes et un exposé approfondi sur le positionnement adéquat dans un jardin d'un cadran solaire en buis et sur l'infime morcellement des jardins en fonction de la perspective ainsi qu'un rapport sur les Colvmnis Milliaribvs érigées dans le jardin de l'auteur
Édité par J. C. V. 1708

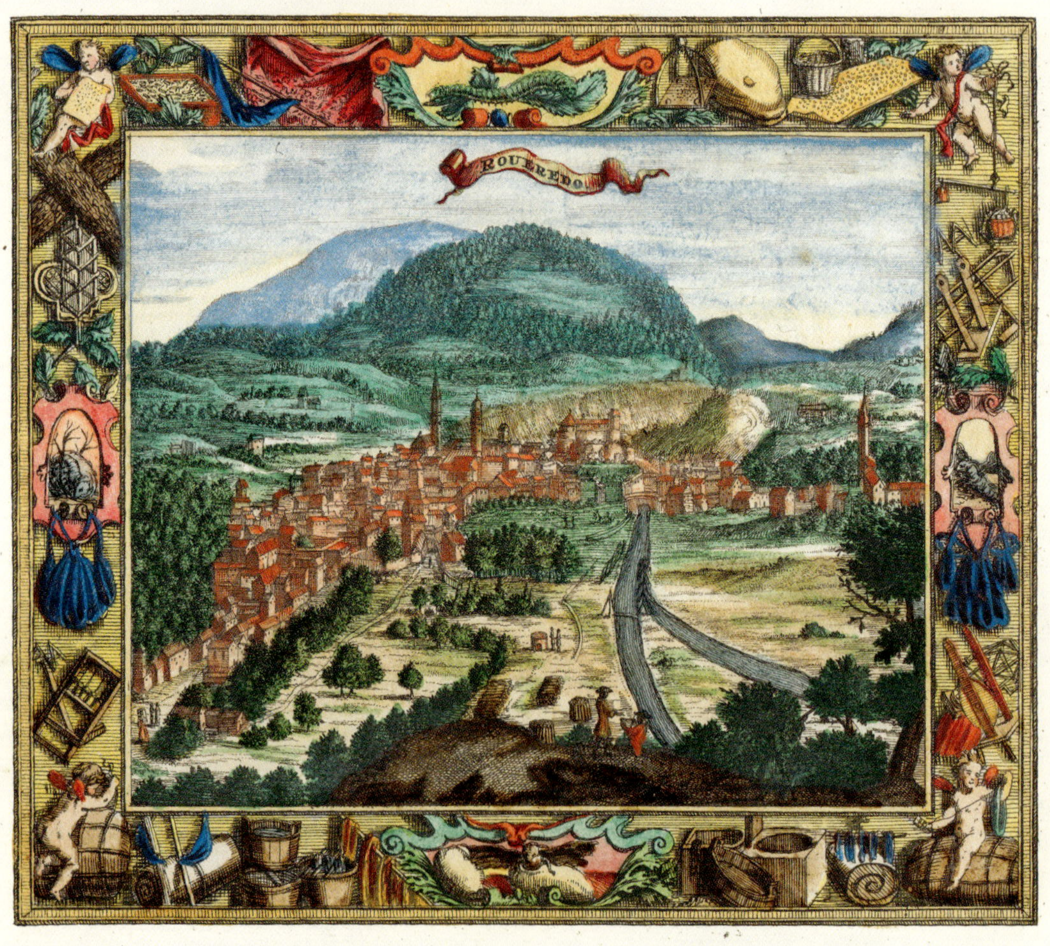

Page 136 Perettin Personzin, detail (see p. 175) *Above* Rovereto (Trentino) *Page 139* Unknown garden *Pages 140/141* Lake Garda *Pages 142/143* Genoa, Nervi *Pages 144/145* San Pietro d'Arena, a suburb of Genoa and its main port *Pages 146/147* Genoa – Garden and Palazzo del Principe Doria

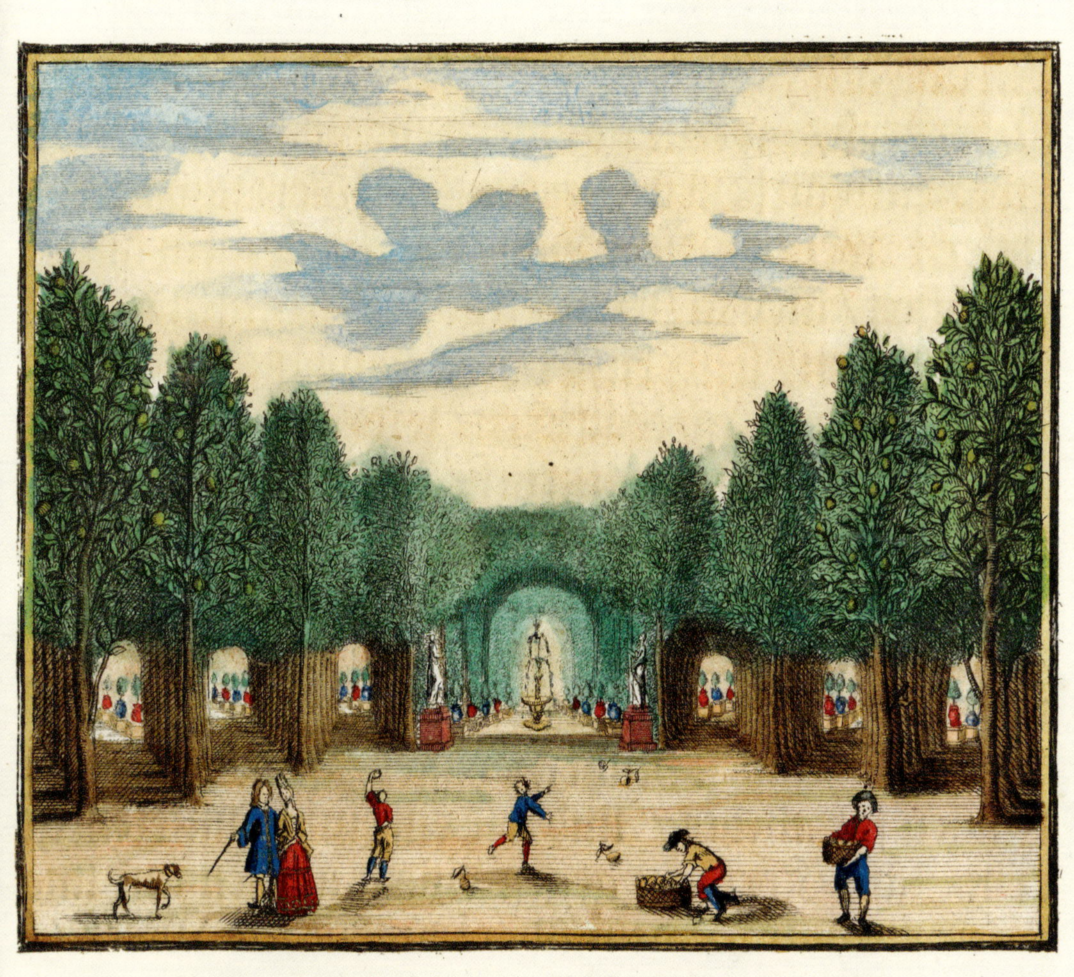

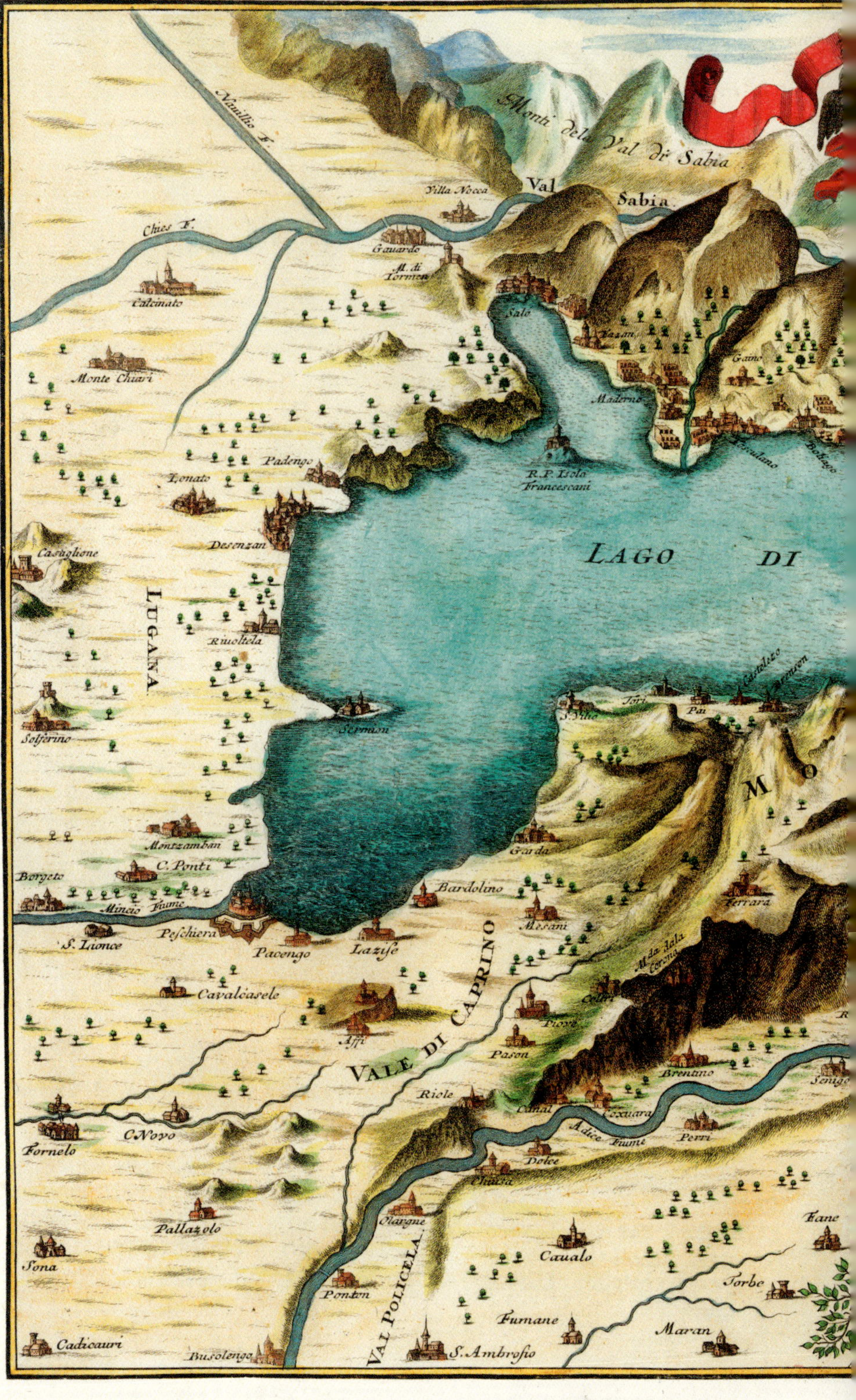

Monti de la Val di Sabia
Val
Sabia
Villa Nocca
Naviglio F.
Chies F.
Gauardo
M. di Tormen
Calcinato
Salò
Bazan
Gaino
Maderno
Monte Chiari
Padengo
Lonato
R.P. Isola Francescani
Desenzan
Casaglione
LAGO DI
LUGANA
Riuoltela
Solferino
Sermion
S. Vilio
Tori
Pai
Brenzon
M O
Montzamban
C. Ponti
Garda
Borgeto
Mincio Fiume
Bardolino
Peschiera
Ferrara
S. Lionce
Pacengo
Lazise
Mesani
Cavalcasele
VALE DI CAPRINO
Caprin
Affi
Pason
Piove
Brentino
Riole
Canal
Pescuara
Adice Fiume
Perri
C. Novo
Fornelo
Dolce
Chiusa
Olargne
Pallazolo
Sona
Caualo
Fane
Ponton
Torbe
VAL POLICELA
Fumane
Maran
Cadicauri
Busolengo
S. Ambrosio

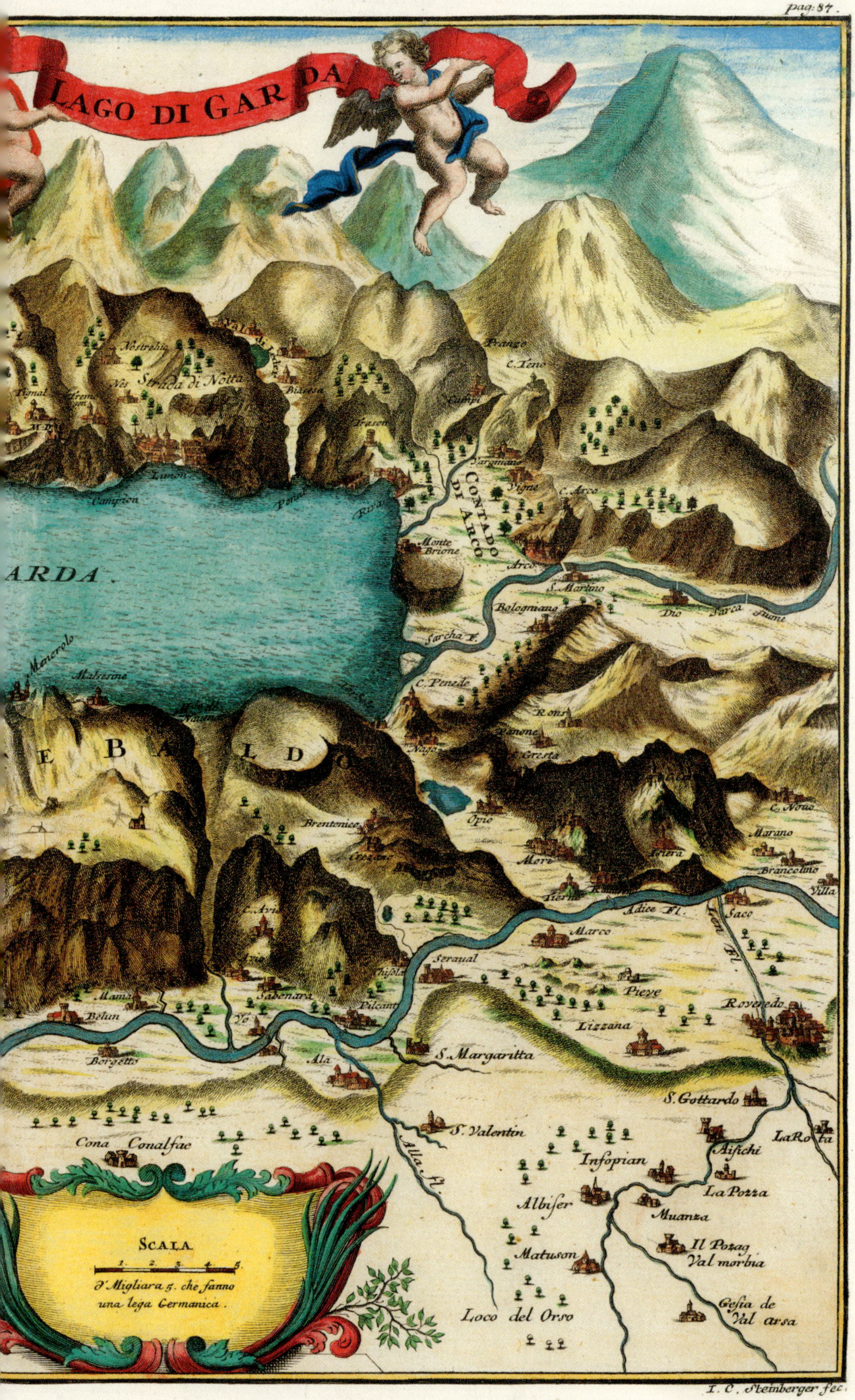

LAGO DI GARDA

ARDA.

CONTADO DI ARCO

Monte Brione

Arco

S. Martino

Bolognano

Sarca fiume

Sarcha F.

C. Penede

Nago

Brentonico

Mori

Adice Fl.

Saco

Marco

Seraual

Roveredo

Pieve

Lizzana

S. Margaritta

Ala

Borgetto

Belun

S. Gottardo

S. Valentin

Infopian

Albiser

Matuson

Loco del Orso

La Pozza

Muanza

Il Pozag Val morbia

Gesia de Val arsa

Cona Conalfac

Alla fl.

SCALA

1. 2. 3. 4. 5.

5 Migliara 5. che fanno una lega Germanica.

I. C. Steinberger fec.

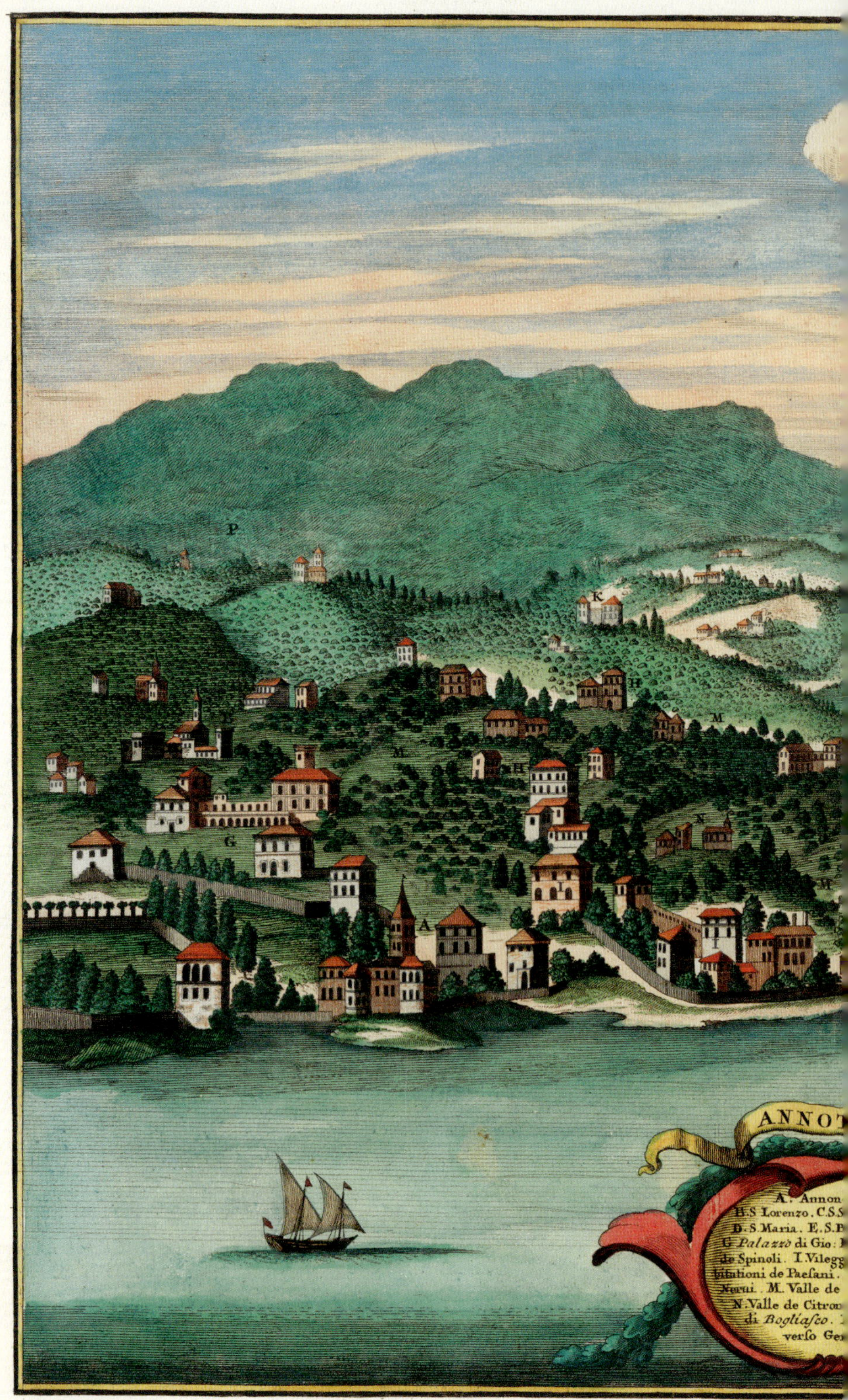
ANNOT
A. Annon
B.S Lorenzo. C.S.S
D. S.Maria. E. S.B
G Palazzo di Gio:
de Spinoli. I.Vilegg
bitationi de Paesani.
Nerui. M. Valle de
N.Valle de Citron
di Bogliasco.
verso Ge

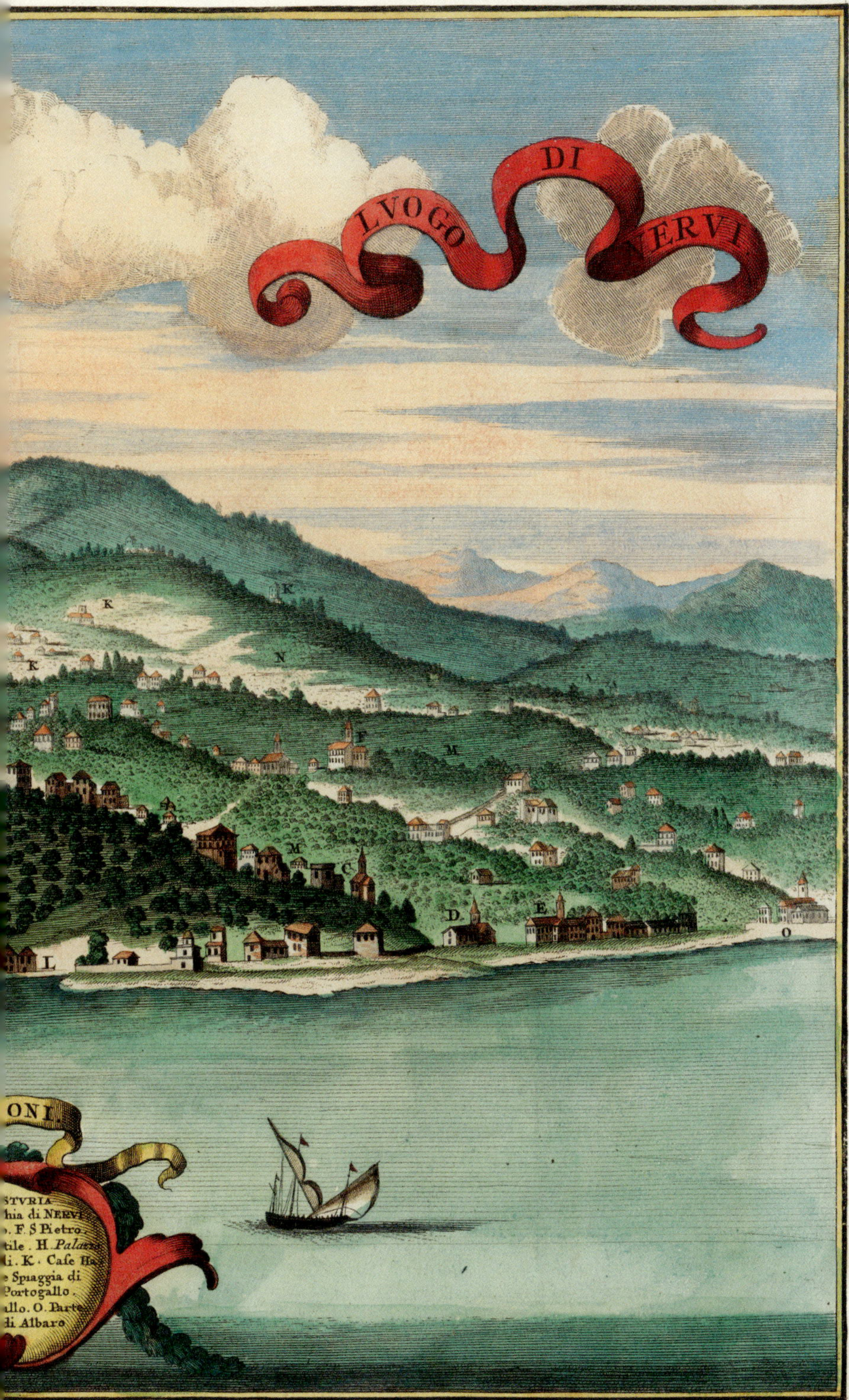

C. F. Krieger fecit aquaforti.

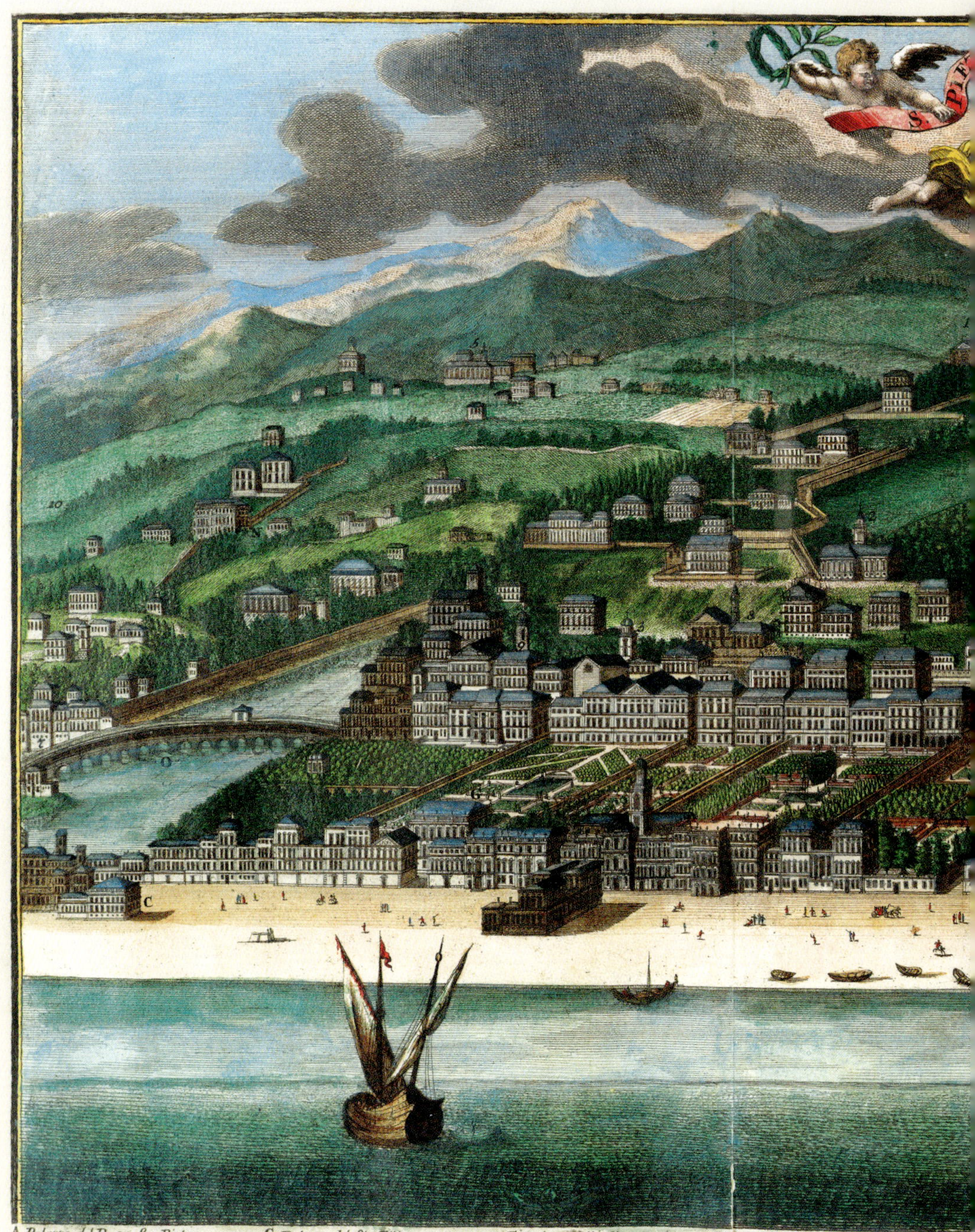

A. Palazzo del Duca San Pietro . C. Palazzo del Sig. Filippo Cattaneo . E. Palzzo delli Sig: Doria . G. Pal: del Prencipe Centurione . L. Pal. del
B. Palazzo del Sig Francesco M.a Imperiale . D. Palaz: del Sig Nicolo M.a Pallauicino . F. Pal: del Sig. Paris M.a Saluago . K. Palazzo de Sig. Pallauicini . M. Palazzo

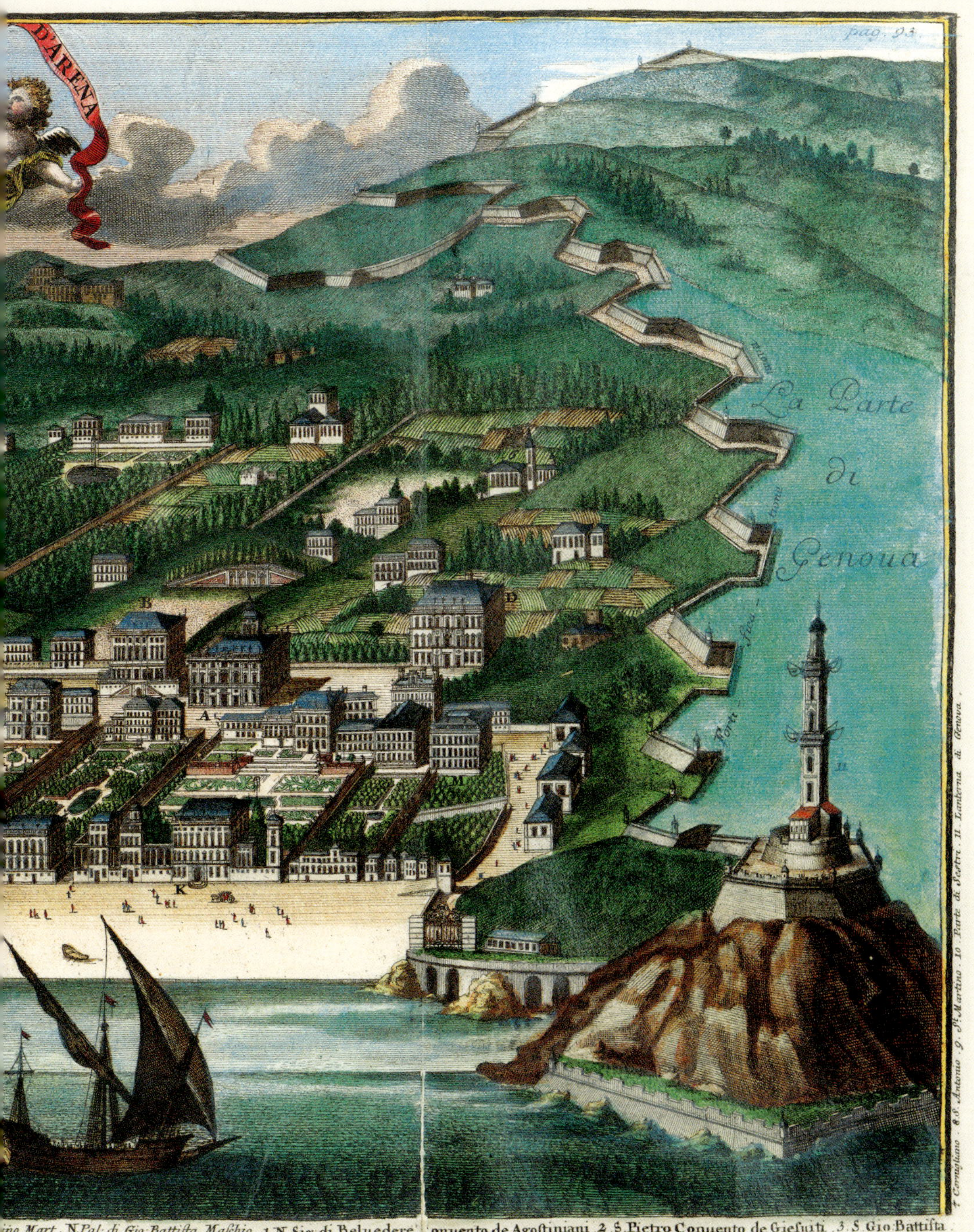

D'ARENA
pag. 93.
La Parte di Genoua
Forti ficationi
A
B
D
K
11
ino Mart. N. Pal: di Gio: Battista Maschio. 1 N. Sig: di Beluedere Conuento de Agostiniani. 2. S. Pietro Conuento de Giesuiti. 3. S. Gio: Battista.
rimaldi. O. Polceuera Riuiera. G. de Teatini. 4. La Cel. e G. de Agostiniani. 5. N. Sig: Incoronata. 6. S. Bartolomeo della Costa.
7 Cornigliano. 8 S. Antonio. 9 St. Martino. 10 Parte di Sestri. 11 Lanterna di Genova.

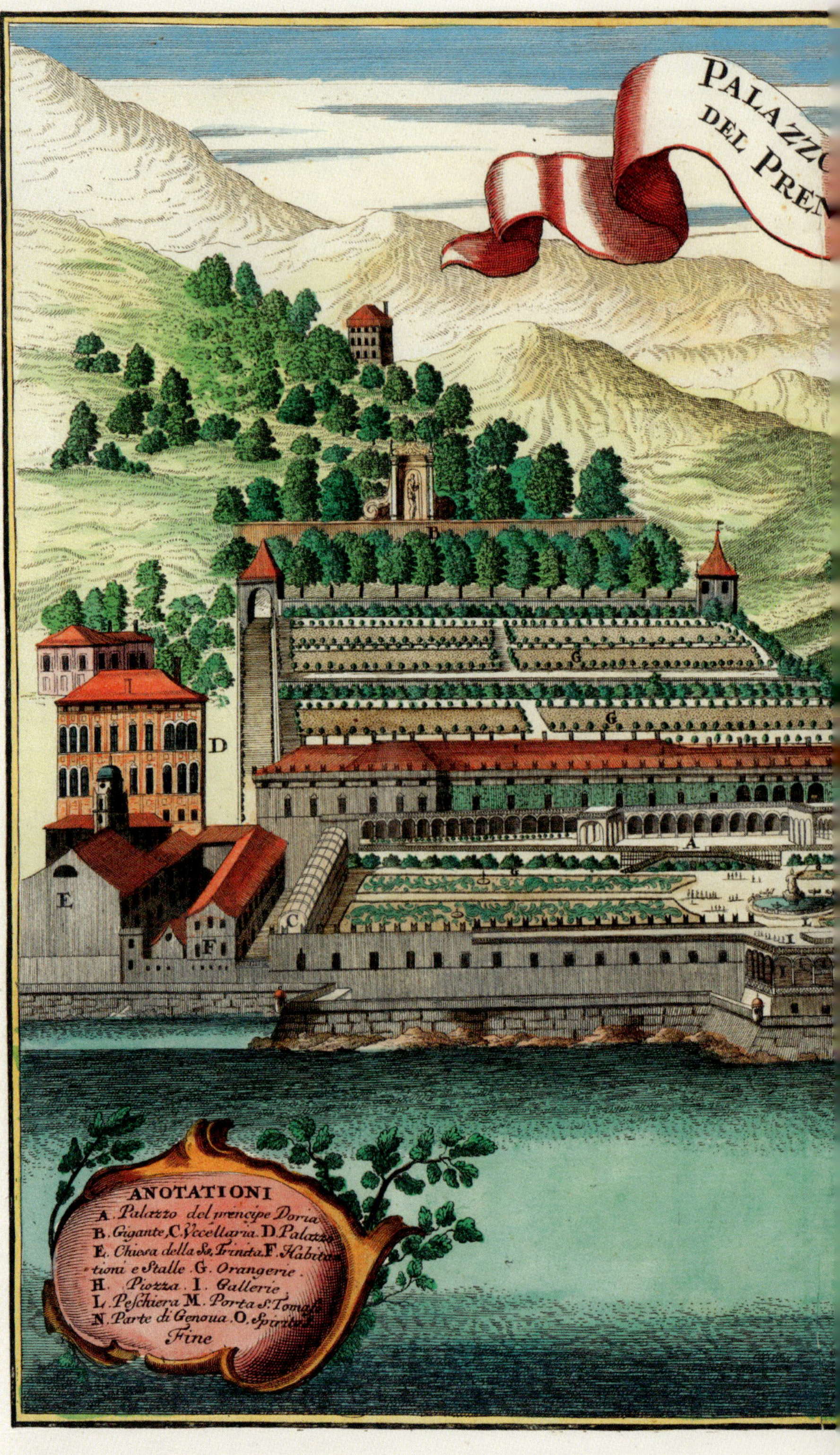
PALAZZO
DEL PREN
ANOTATIONI
A. Palazzo del prencipe Doria
B. Gigante, C. Vccellaria. D. Palazz
E. Chiesa della Ss. Trinita. F. Habita-
tioni e Stalle. G. Orangerie.
H. Piozza. I. Gallerie
L. Peschiera M. Porta S. Toma
N. Parte di Genoua. O. Spirit
Fine

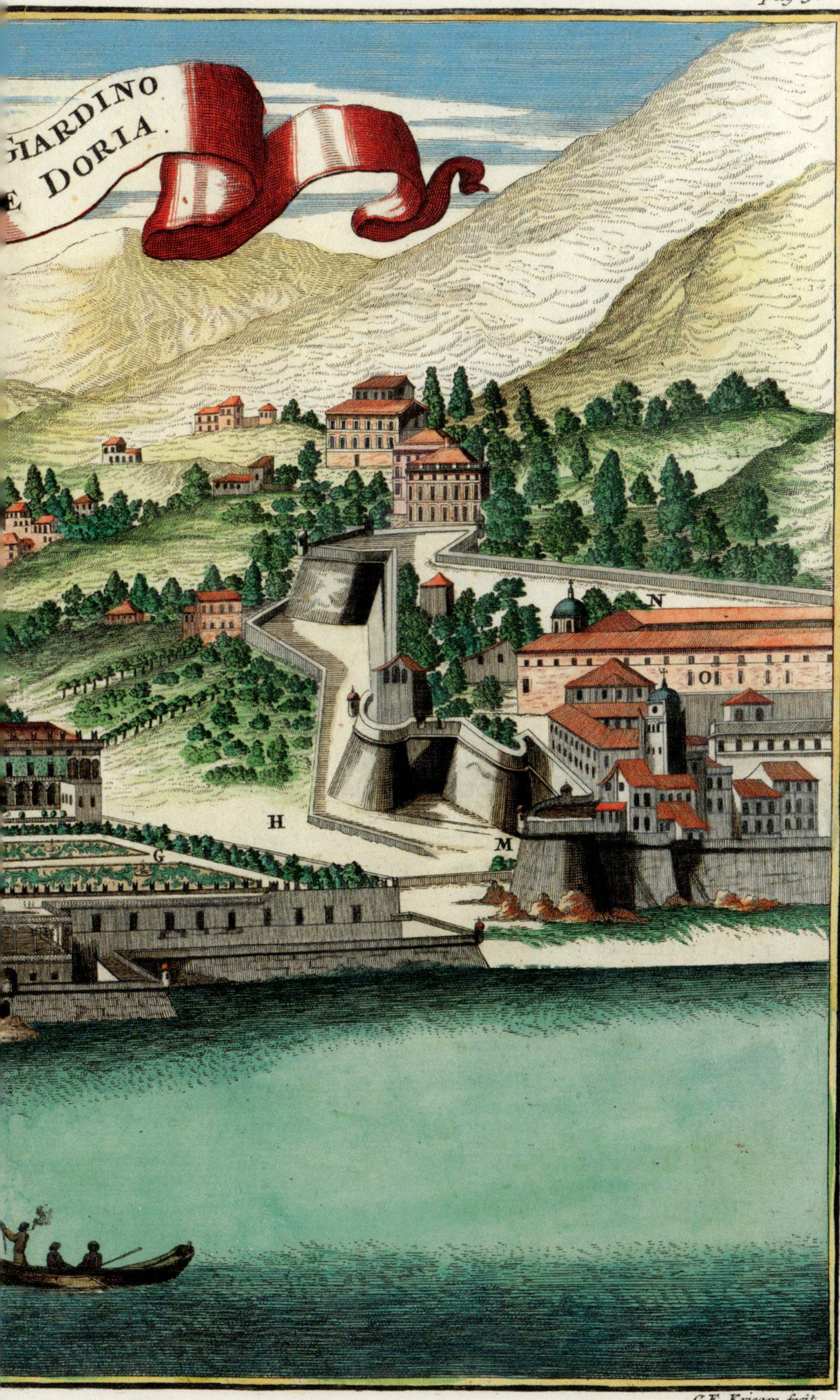

C.F. Krieger fecit

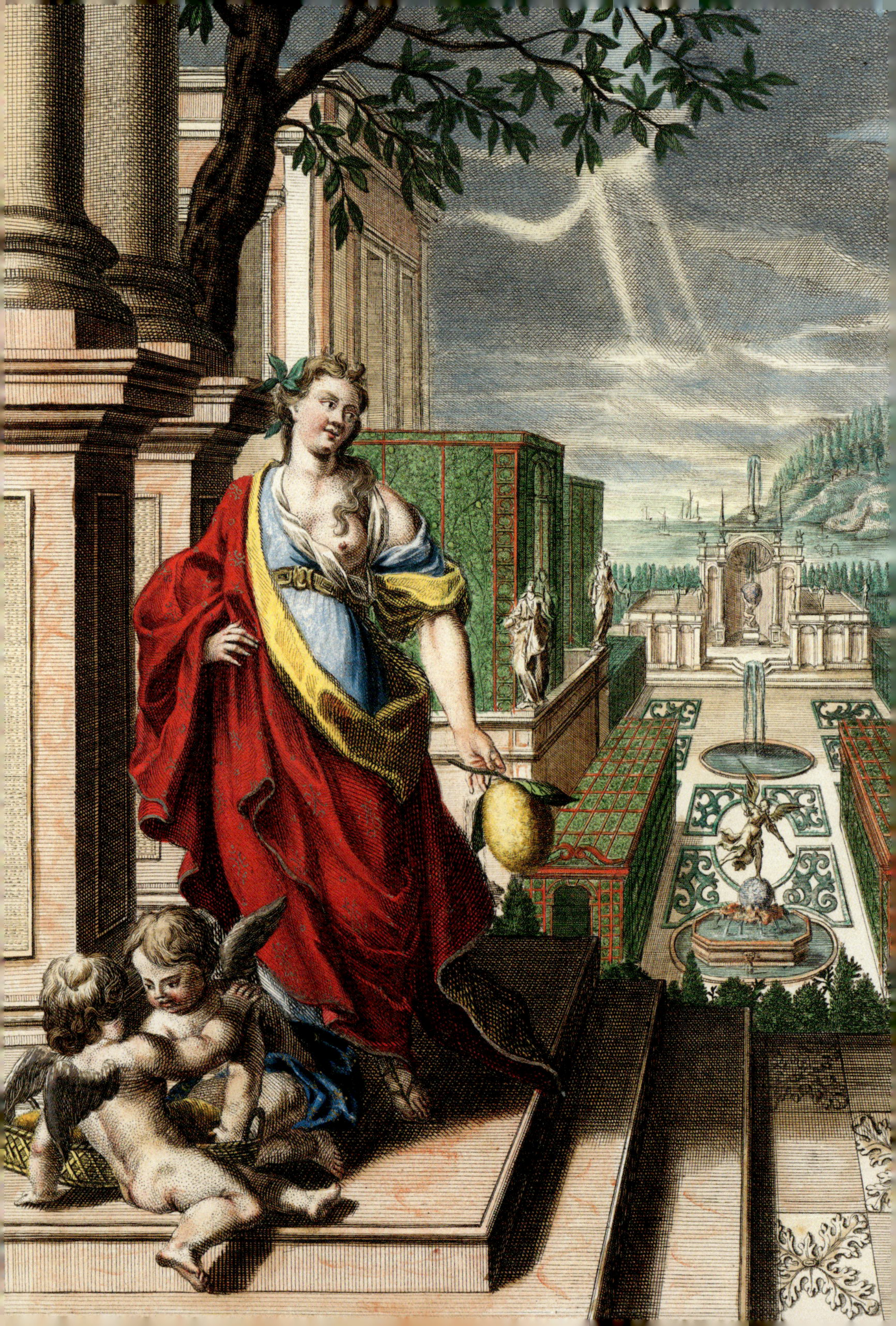

Der Nürnbergischen HESPERIDUM Anderer Theil/ ÆGLE.

* * * * *
* * * *

Das Erste Capitel.

Von denen Citronaten insgemein.

EGLE, die älteste unter den dreyen Schwestern der Hesperidum, als sie die Pforte ihres vortrefflichen Gartens eröffnete/ stunde ich voller Verwunderung ausser mir selbsten/ nicht wissend / ob ich die Anmuthigkeit der gantzen Gegend/ so sich um und um präsentirte/ zu erst betrachten/ oder/ ob ich meine Augen auf die bunde und so zierlich von der Natur in ein ander geflochtene Spallier wenden solte/ dann sie bestunden aus lauter lebendigem Gesträuche/ von Lorbeern und Granaten; da dann jener grünes Laub einen angenehmen Geruch von sich gab / und die hohe Scharlach-Farb der gefüllten Granaten-Blühe die Augen ungemein ergötzete. Gegen Mittag und Abend umfloß das Ufer oder die Grentze dieses Gartens ein anmuthig- und Fisch-reicher See/ weil diese Gewächse solche Oerter gerne lieben/ wo sie eine feuchte Lufft mit warmen Sonnenschein verwechseln können/ wie dann gemeiniglich an diesen Orten die schönste Gärten solcher edlen Früchte zu finden/ wie mit dem Exempel des Gard- und Genueser-Sees zu beweisen. Hinter diesem Garten stehen viele Berge/ so mit denen höchst-nutzbaren Oel-Bäumen häuffig besetzet sind / welche die rauhe Nord- und diesen so zarten Gewächsen sehr schädliche Ost-Winde abhalten. Wann man in diesen herrlichen Frucht-Garten weiter hinein spatzirte/ sahe man schöne lange Gänge und Geländer von Latten gemachet/ woran die köstlichste Citranaten mancherley Arten/ theils rund/ theils ablang/ theils unzeitig/ theils groß/ theils klein/ in grosser Menge hiengen/ welche mit ihrer schönen Blühe auch dann und wann vermischt zu sehen waren.

Es zeigte uns die Garten-Patronin Ægle dabey an/ daß diese Früchte nach Art der Bäume sich nicht wol wolten in die Höhe zu wachsen gewöhnen lassen/ sondern füglicher an Geländern angehänget/ aufgezogen würden/ woran sie öffters/ zumal wann sie groß/ müssen bevestiget und angebunden werden/ widrigen falls sie/ wegen ihrer Schwehre/ gantze Aeste abbrechen würden/ daher auch nicht wol ein formlicher Baum daraus gezogen werden könte/ sondern je niedriger sie an der Erden wüchsen/ je schöner blüheten sie/ und je vollkommnere Früchte pflegten sie zu tragen / zudeme wäre es ihnen sehr nutzlich/ wann sie zugleich etwas tieff in der Erden stünden: Und dieses habe ich nachgehend wahr zu seyn befunden/ da ich einen etwas hochstehenden Citronat-Baum

 mit

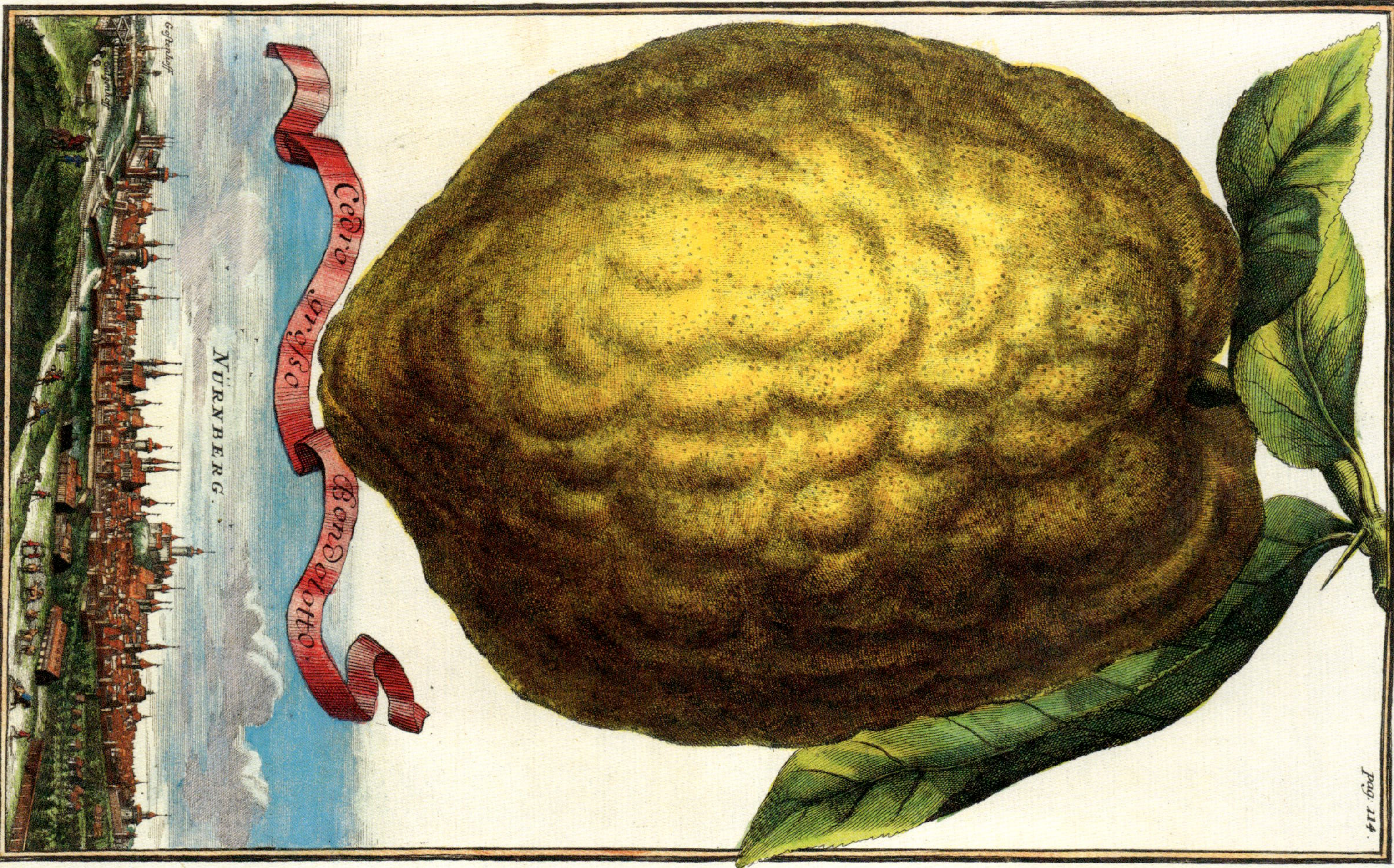

Nuremberg. *Pages 148/149* Personification of Aegle, and beginning of the second section of vol. I

Cedro grosso Bondolotto

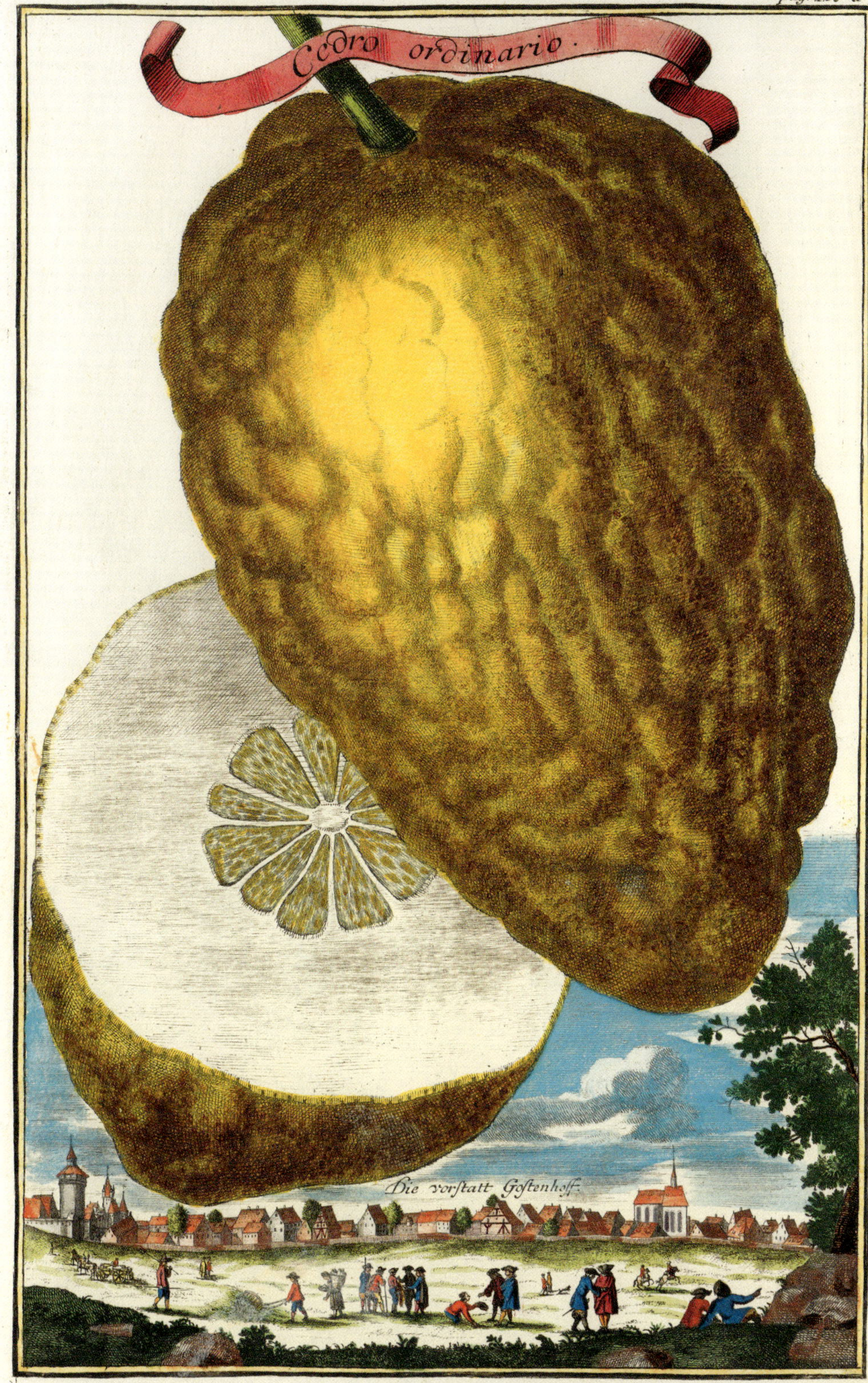

Cedro [Genovese] ordinario

Nuremberg, Gostenhof

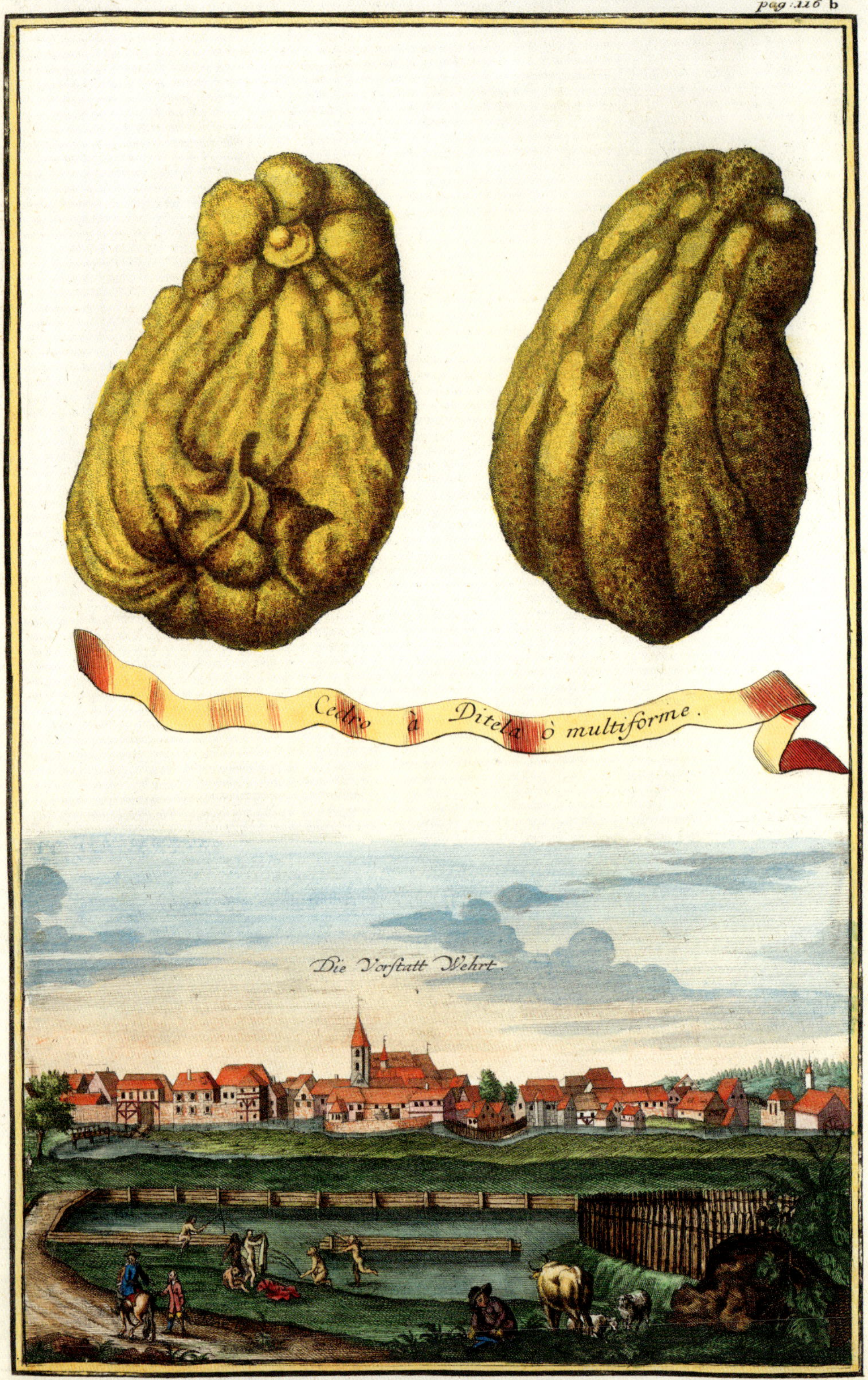

Cedro a Ditela o multiforme

Nuremberg, Wöhrd

Cedro a Dittela

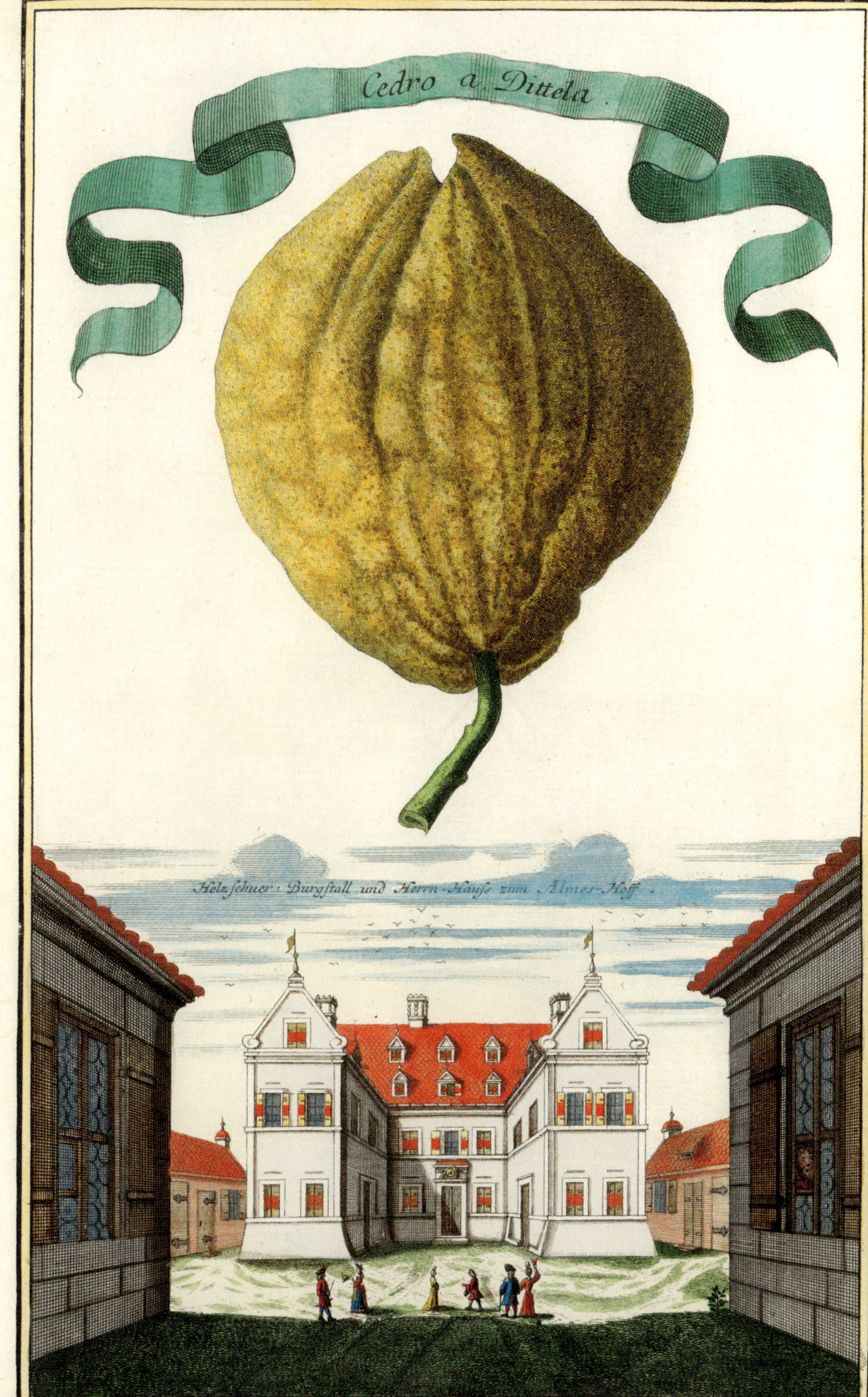

Nuremberg, Almoshof – Holzschuher Castle

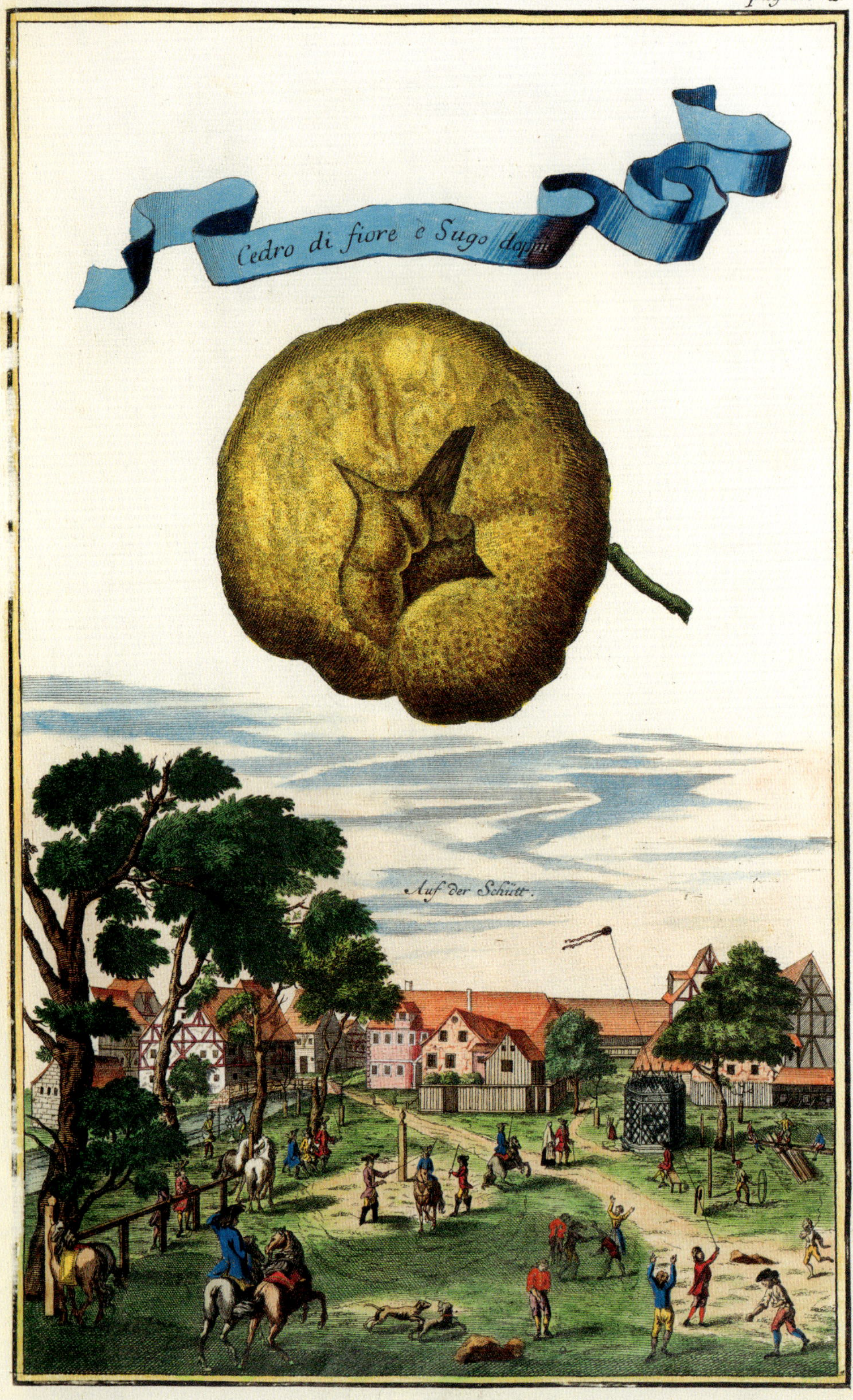

Cedro di fiore e Sugo doppio

Nuremberg, Schütt Island on the River Pegnitz

Cedro di fior e Sugo doppio

Nuremberg, Gleißhammer

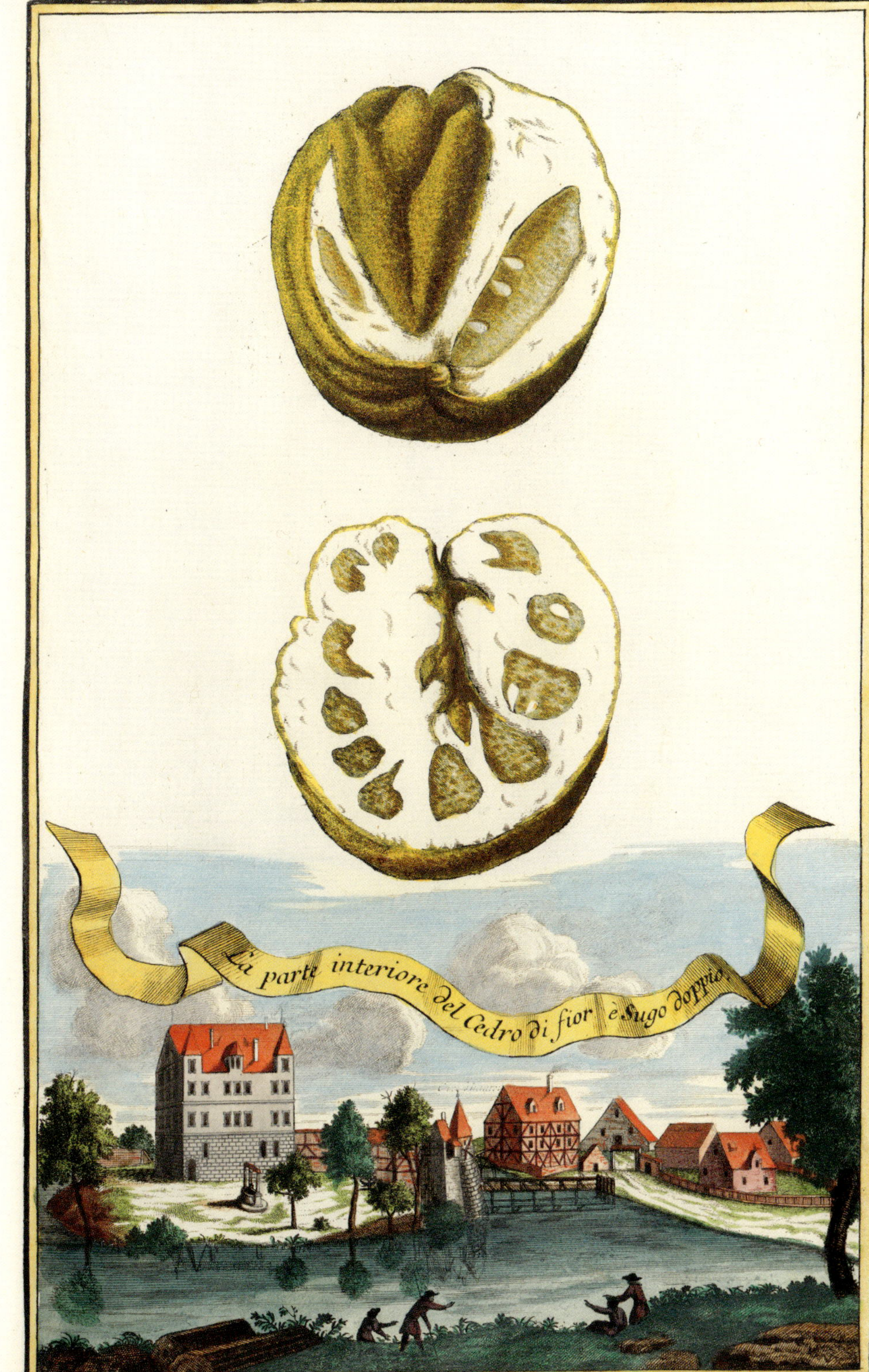

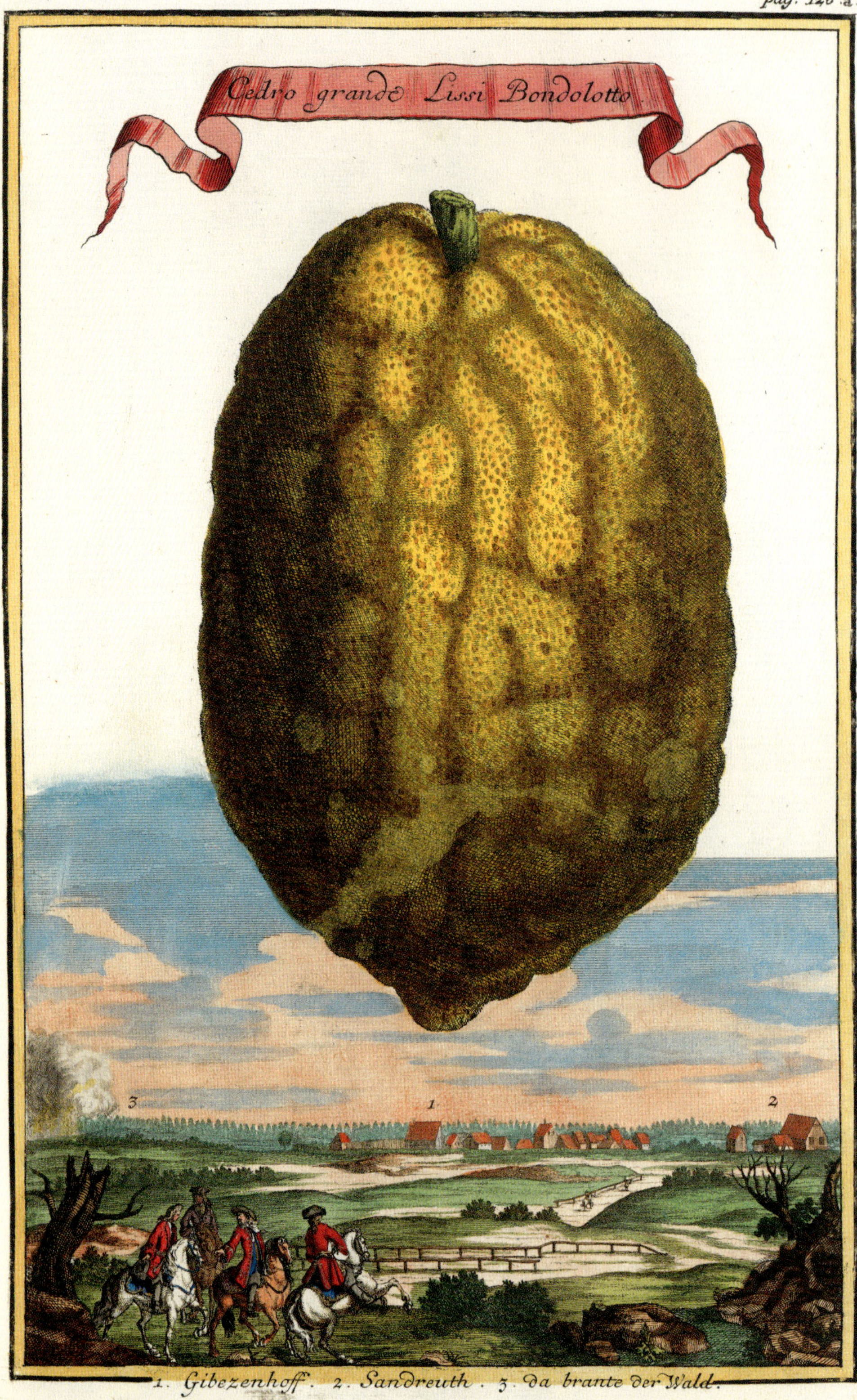

Cedro grande Lissi [liscio] Bondolotto

Nuremberg, Gibitzenhof and Sandreuth

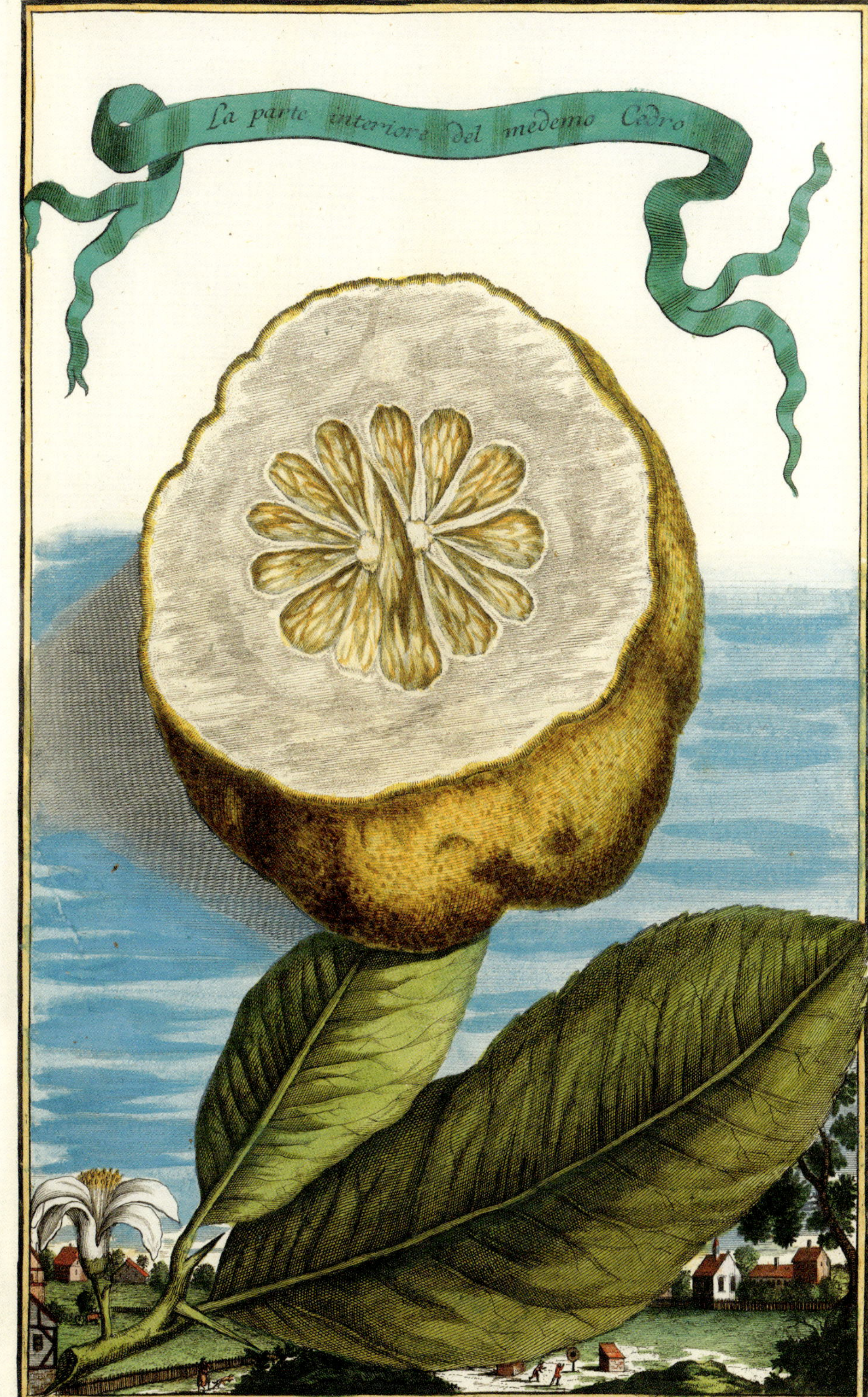

Nuremberg, Wöhrd – Shooting Range and Churchyard

Cedro grande Lissi [liscio] Bondolotto

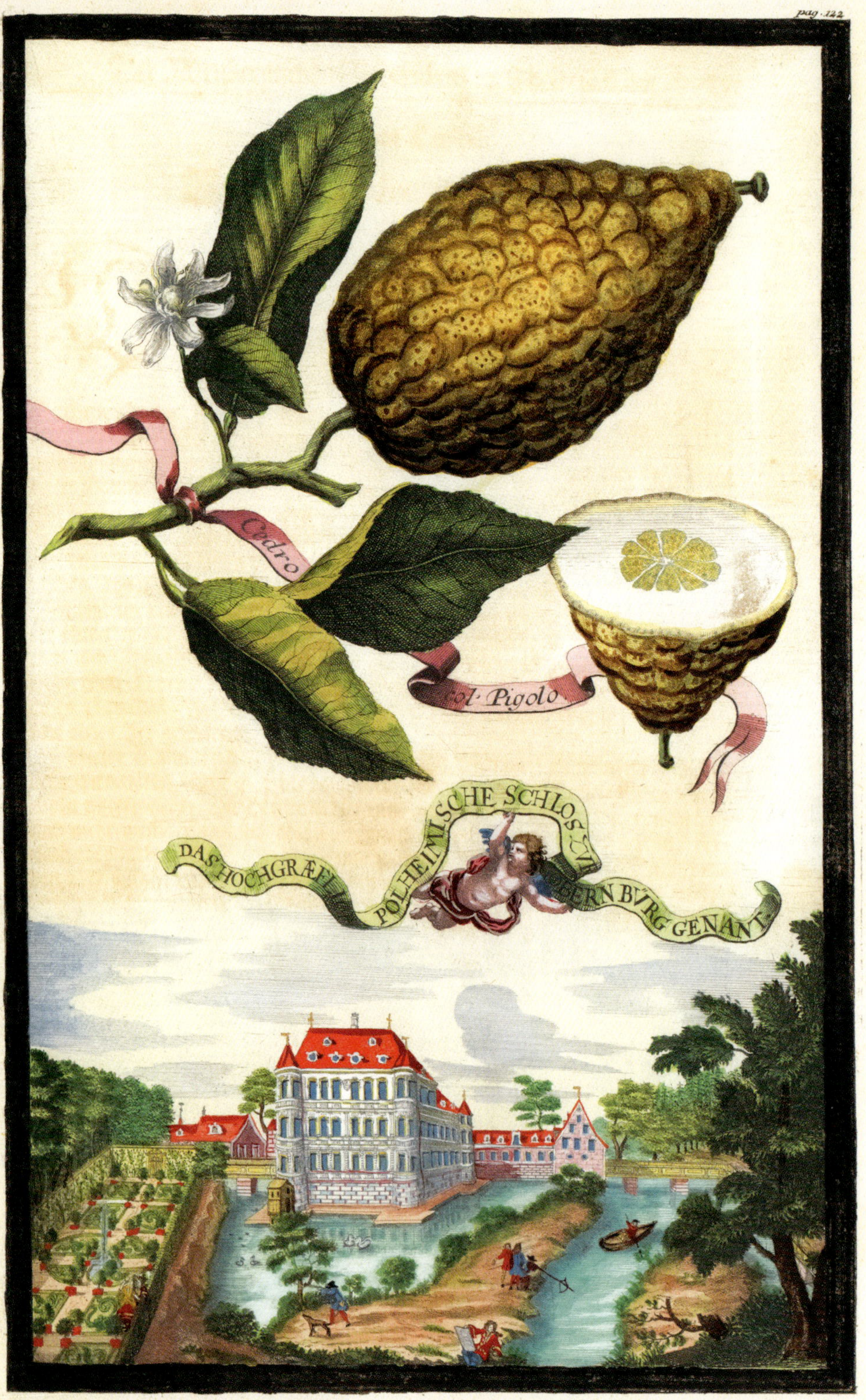

Cedro col Pigolo

Nuremberg, Oberbürg – Castle of Count von Polheim

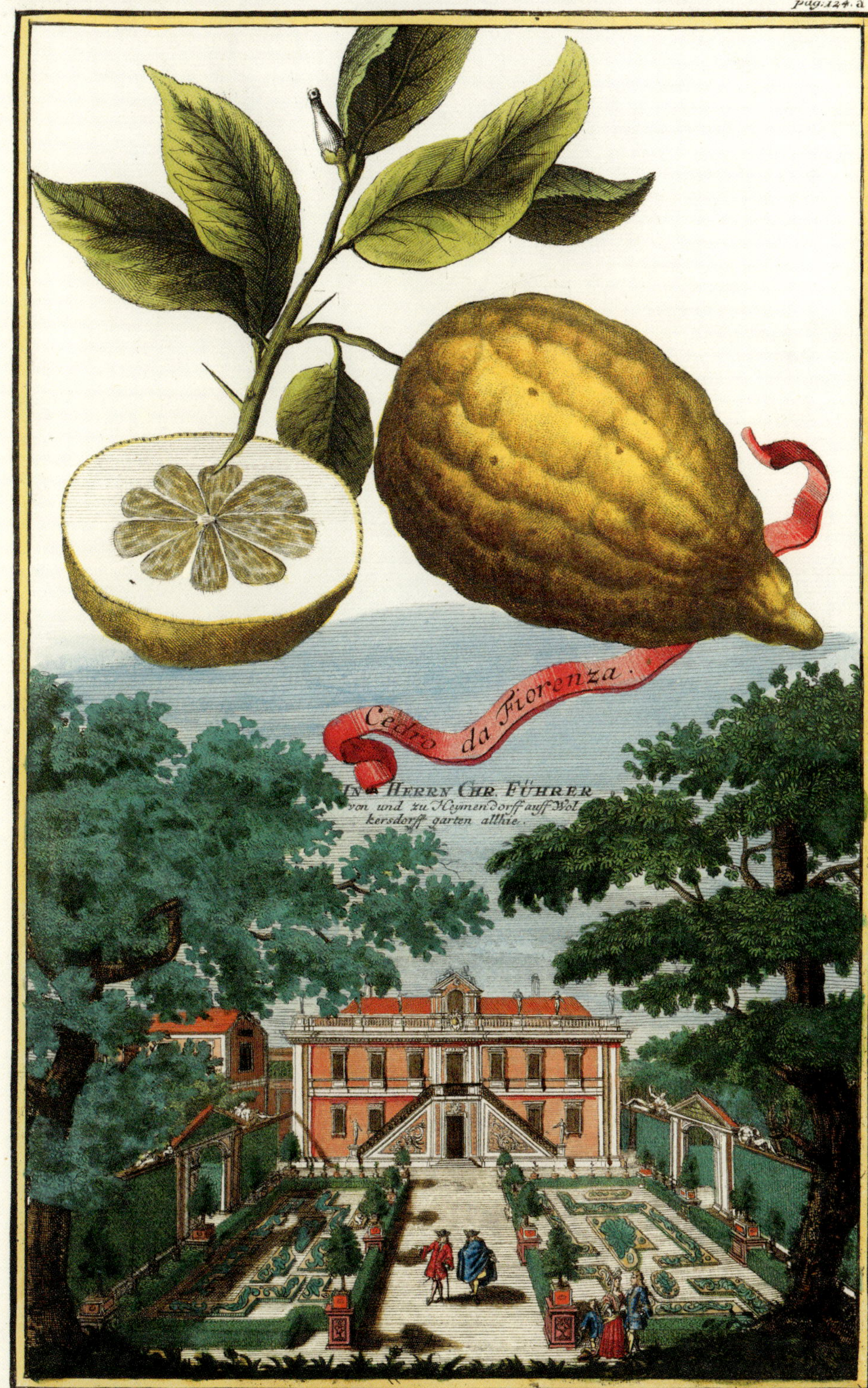

Cedro da Fiorenza

Schwabach, Wolkersdorf – Garden of Christoph Fürer von Haimendorf

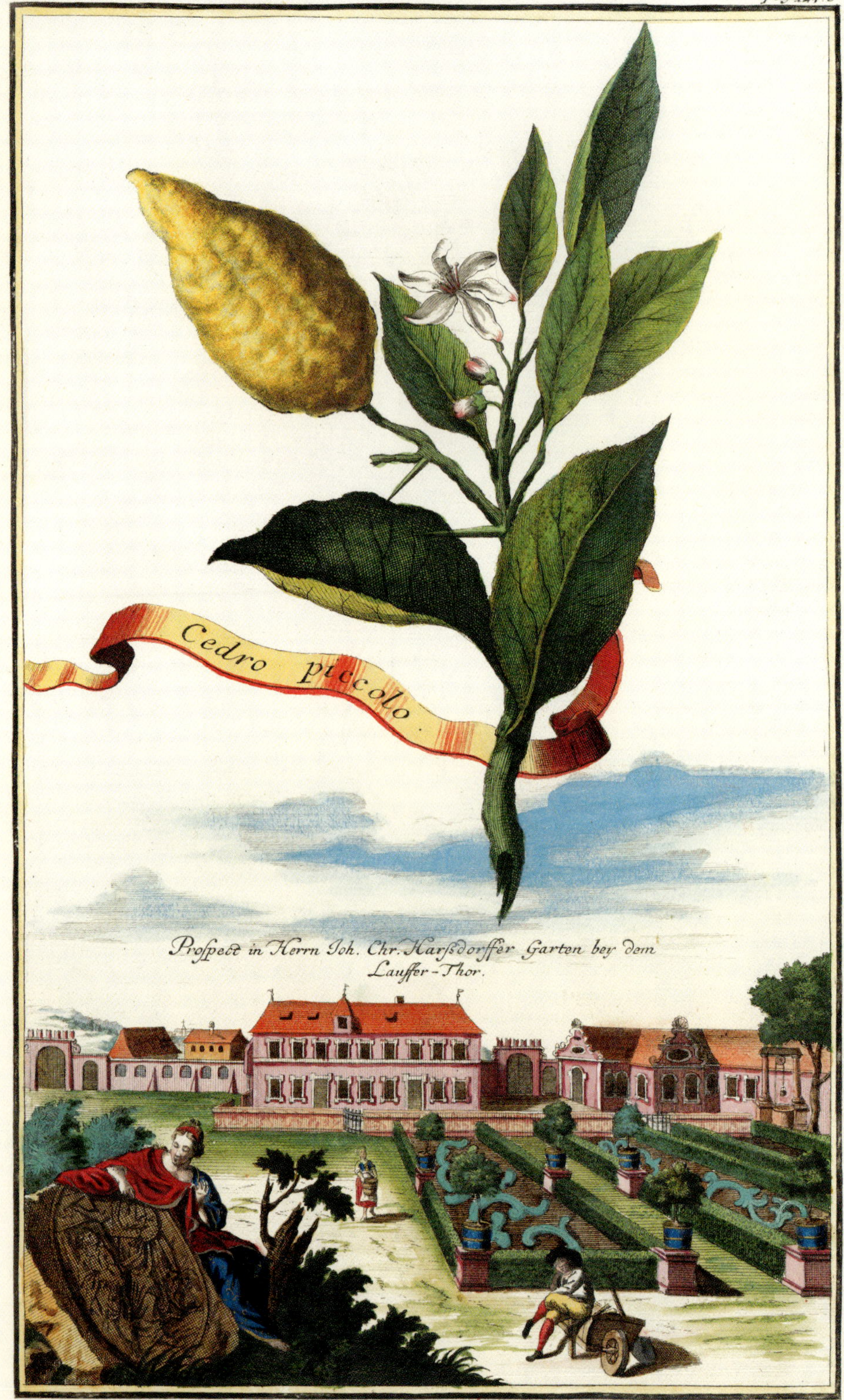

Cedro piccolo

Nuremberg – Laufer Tor and Garden of Johann Christoph Harßdörrfer

Das Zehende Capitel.

Von dem Cedro picolo ordinario.

DIesen kleinen Citronat nennen die Einwohner am Gard-See Cedro nostrano picolo. P. Ferrarius heiset solchen am 58. Blat Citreum vulgare parvum. Es kan diese Art und der Baum wol auch für ein Zwerg-Bäumlein gehalten werden/ dann er bleibet niederträchtig/ hat kleinere Blätter als die andere Citronaten/ vornenher wol zugespitzt/ und gekerbt/ an der Farb dunckelgrün/ mit vielen kleinen Stacheln an Aesten bey sich führend. Also ist auch die Blühe klein/und nicht gar starcken Geruchs. Die Früchte werden hie zu Lande nicht grösser/ als der hiebey seyende Abriß/ welche Frucht vor einem Jahr gewachsen: Und scheinet dieser Baum dauerhaffter gegen andern Citronaten zu seyn/ weil er alle Jahre Früchtlein bringet/die gegen das folgende neue Jahr zeitig werden/ seyn ein wenig hochfärbig Citronen-farb/ und gleichet/ dem Geschmack nach/ andern Citronaten/ ist aber dabey etwas scharff und säuerlicht/und die Schelffe bis auf die Helffte hinein dick.

E N D E
des
Andern Theils.

End of the second section of vol. I. *Pages 162/163* Schwabach, Wolkersdorf – Garden of Christoph Fürer von Haimendorf, detail (see p. 159)

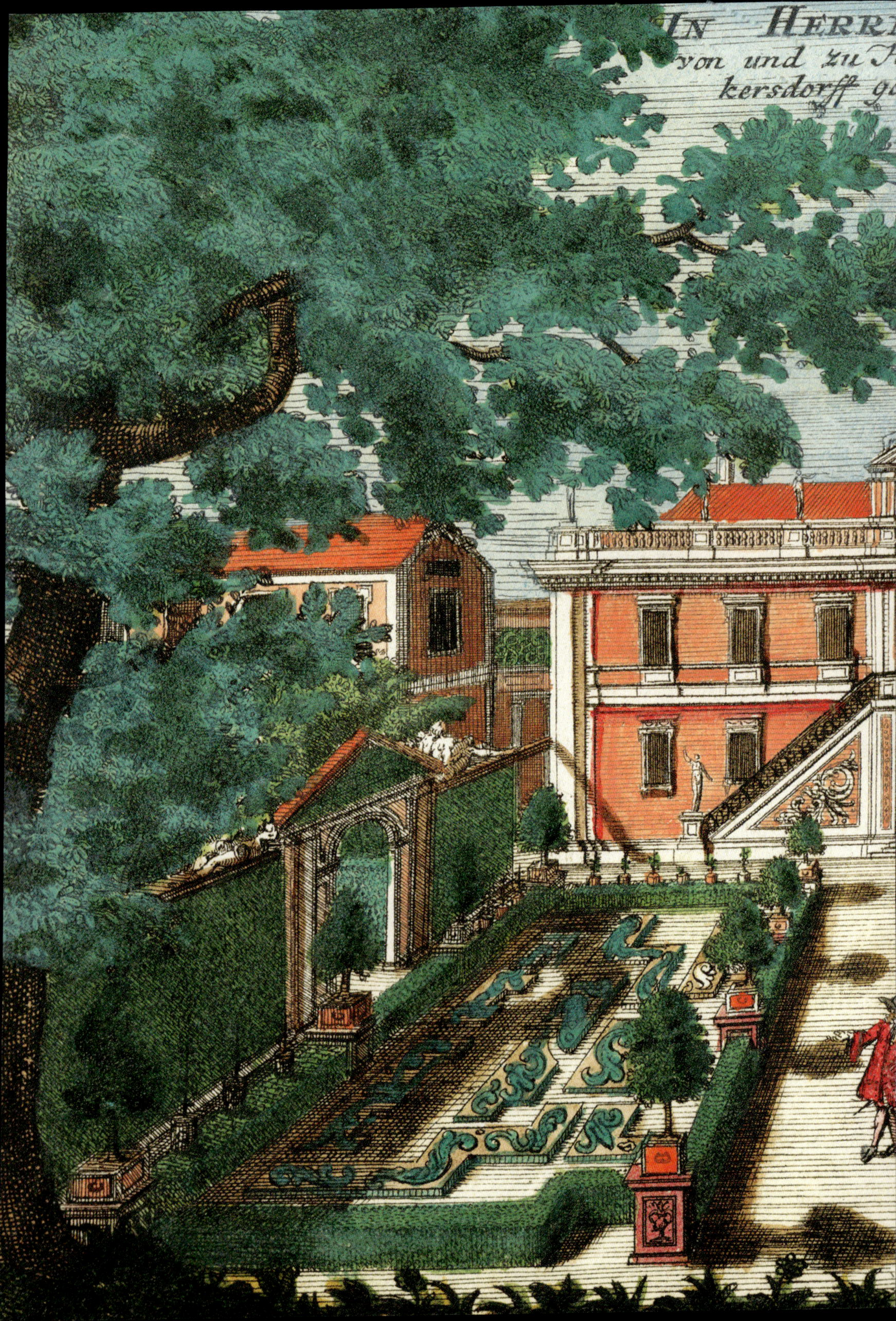
IN
von und zu
kersdorff

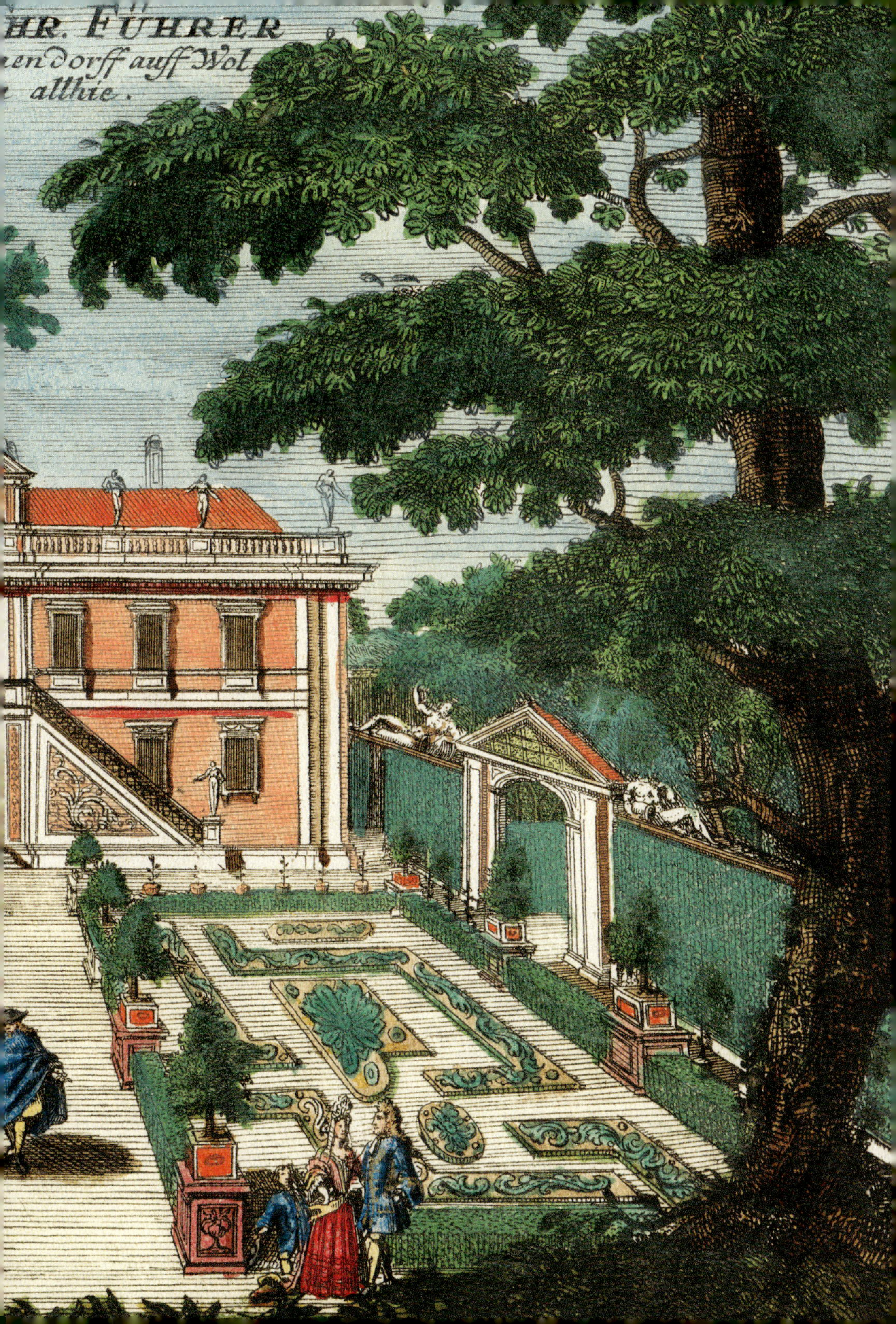
HR. FÜHRER
endorff auff Wol
allhie.

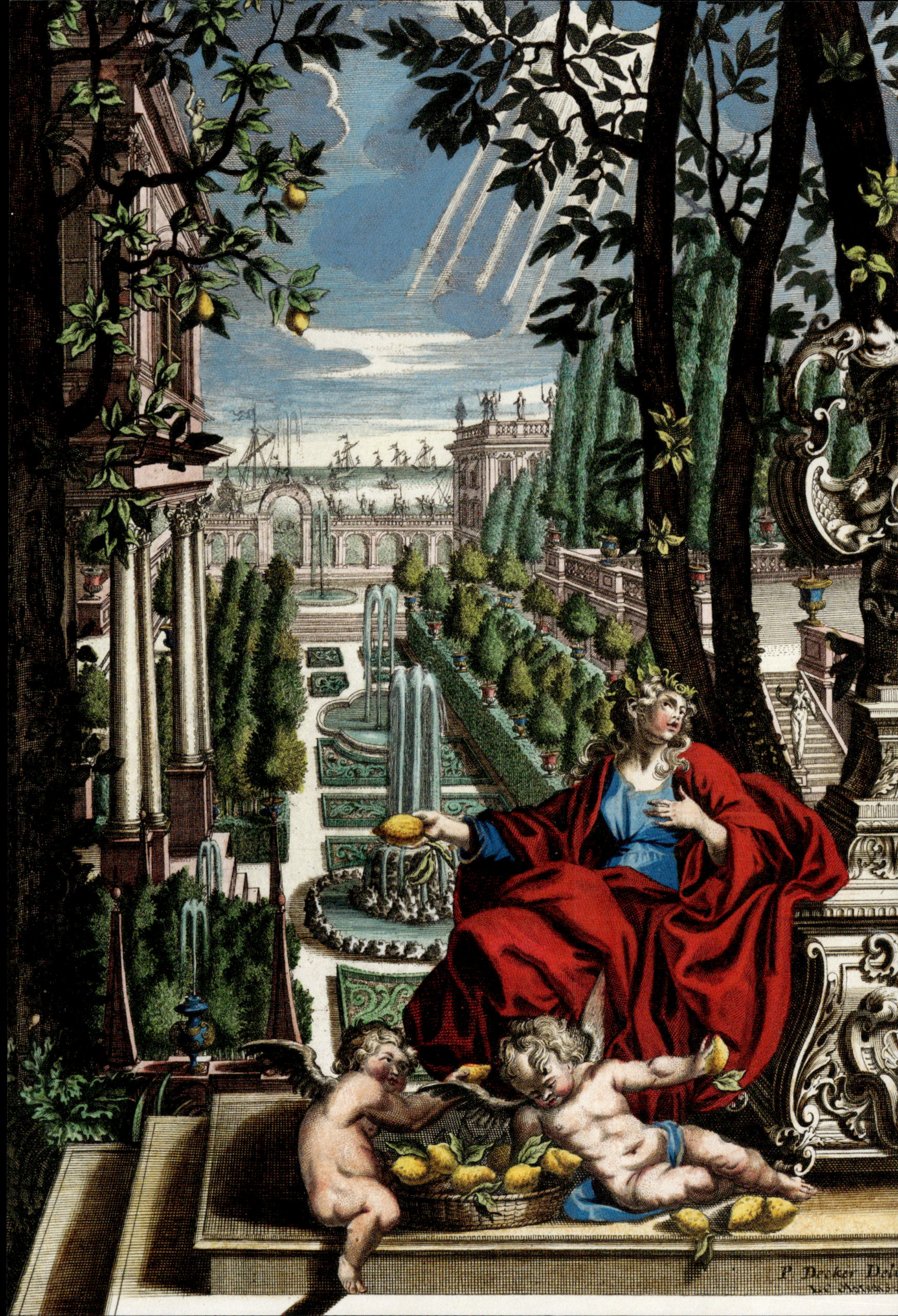
P. Decker Del

Der Nürnbergischen HESPERIDUM Dritter Theil/ ARETHUSA.

Das Erste Capitel.

Von denen Citronen insgemein.

Weil die Citronen und Citronaten so nahe mit einander verwand seyn / daß die mehriste der Botanicorum, und die in Untersuchung der Natur und Eigenschafften der Kräuter und Gewächse best-erfahrne alte Medici, selbige unter eine Classe gebracht/ und vor einerley Frucht gehalten/ auch diejenige/ so heut zu Tage in solchem Studio vor andern floriren/ annoch selbst zweiffelhafftig seyn / indeme sie eine und die andere Frucht einen Citronat nennen/ welche andere unter die Citronen zählen / ist es kein Wunder/ wann die Gärten dieser beeden Frucht-Arten etwas nahe beysammen stehen/ zu malen beede Schwestern/ Ægle und Arethusa, welche von ihrem Vatter/ dem Hespero, Hesperides genennet / die Aufsicht und Versorgung solcher Gärten auf sich genommen haben. Nachdeme wir nun von der Ægle, nach Besichtigung dero Garten/ uns beurlaubet/ waren wir so kühn/ nach dem Citronen-Garten der Arethusæ zu wandern / welche nicht minder als ihre Schwester den Eintritt mit aller Höfflichkeit uns vergönnete ; da dann der erste Anblick wegen des vortrefflichen Prospectes und der zierlichen Einrichtung uns nicht weniger bestens vergnügte/ als der Citronat-Garten ihrer Schwester der Ægle, dann wir stunden gleich anfangs in einer schönen Alleé zu beeden Seiten mit stets-grünenden in schönster Ordnung gepflantzten Cypressen-Bäumen besetzet. So bald wir selbige hindurch spatziret / kamen wir auf einen grossen ebenen Platz/ welcher von allen Seiten mit denen annehmlichsten Citronen-Wäldern

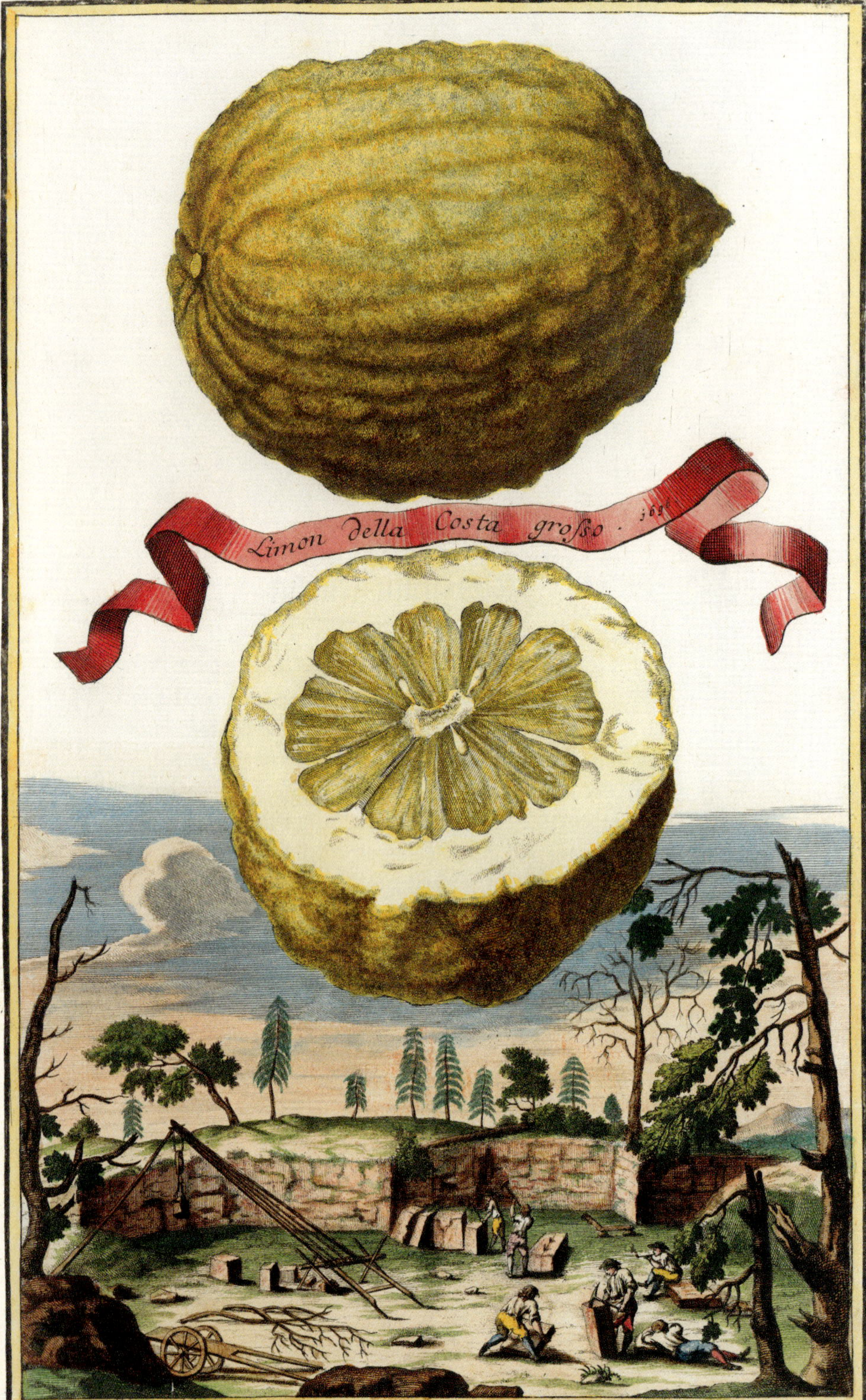

Limon della Costa grosso

Nuremberg – Quarry. *Pages 164/165* Personification of Arethusa, and beginning of the third section of vol. I

Limon da Portugal dolce

Nuremberg, Hallerwiese – Imhoff Cottage

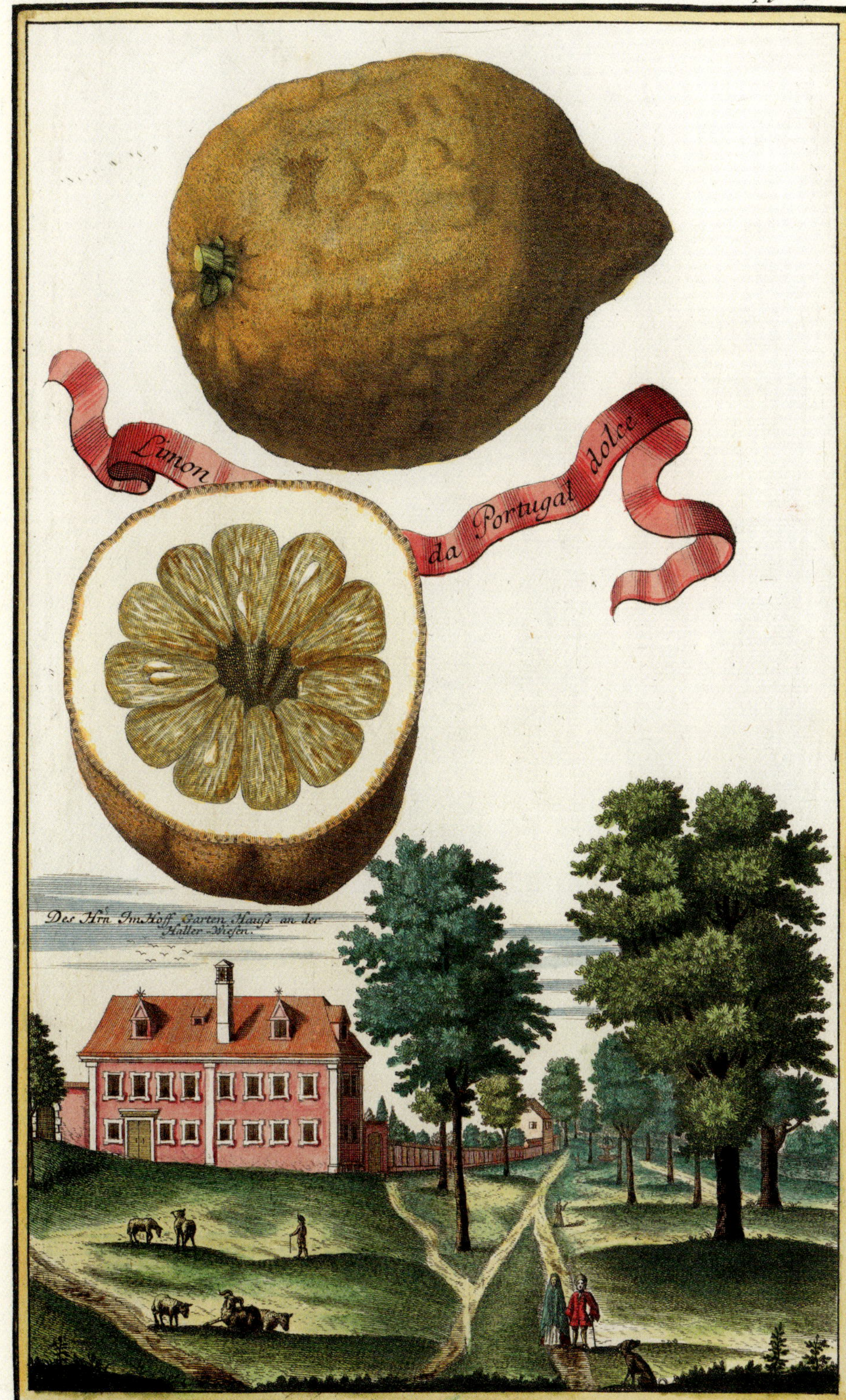

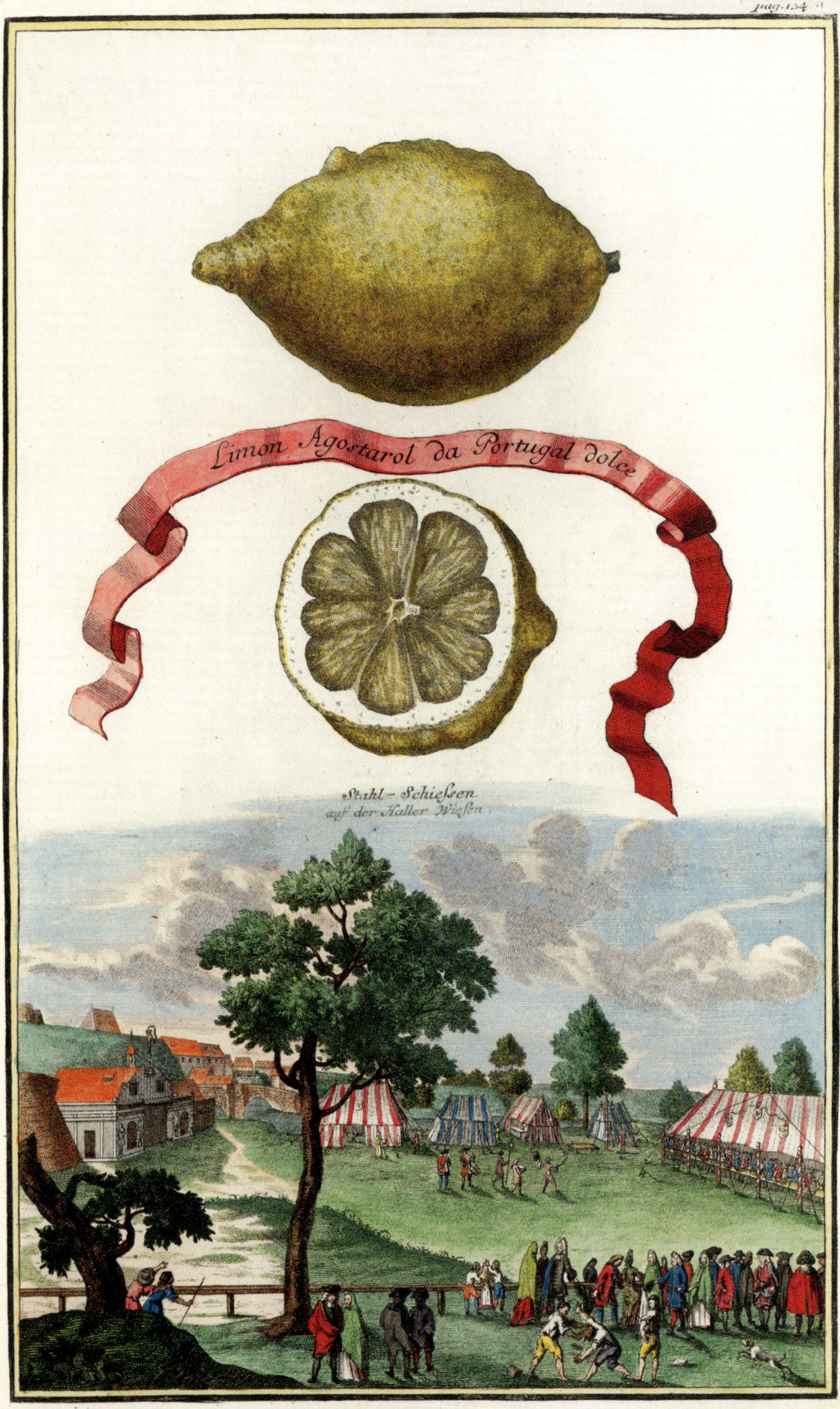

Limon Agostarol[o] da Portugal dolce

Nuremberg, Hallerwiese – Crossbow Range

Limon Zucherino dolce

Nuremberg, Erlenstegen – Ebner Manor House

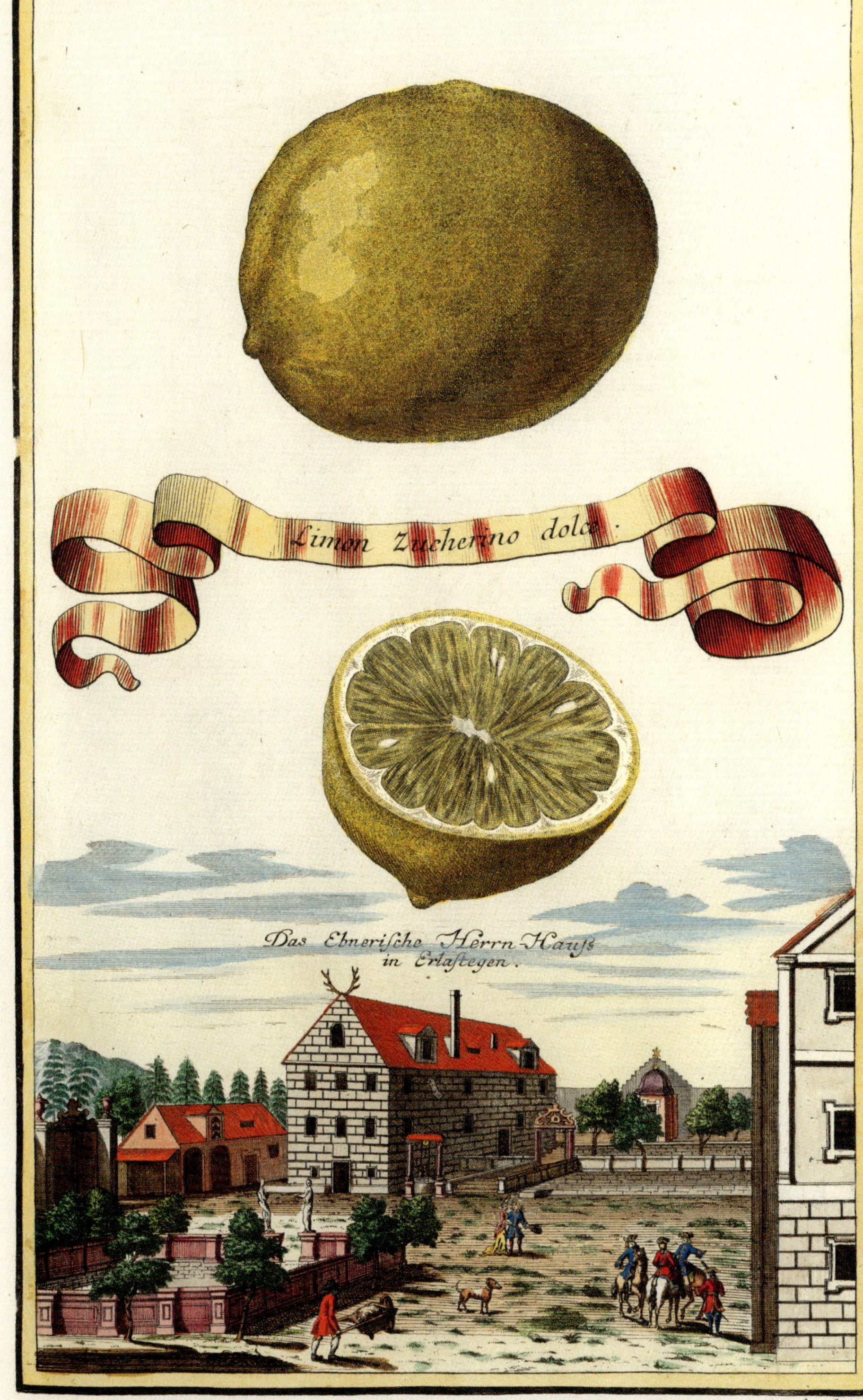

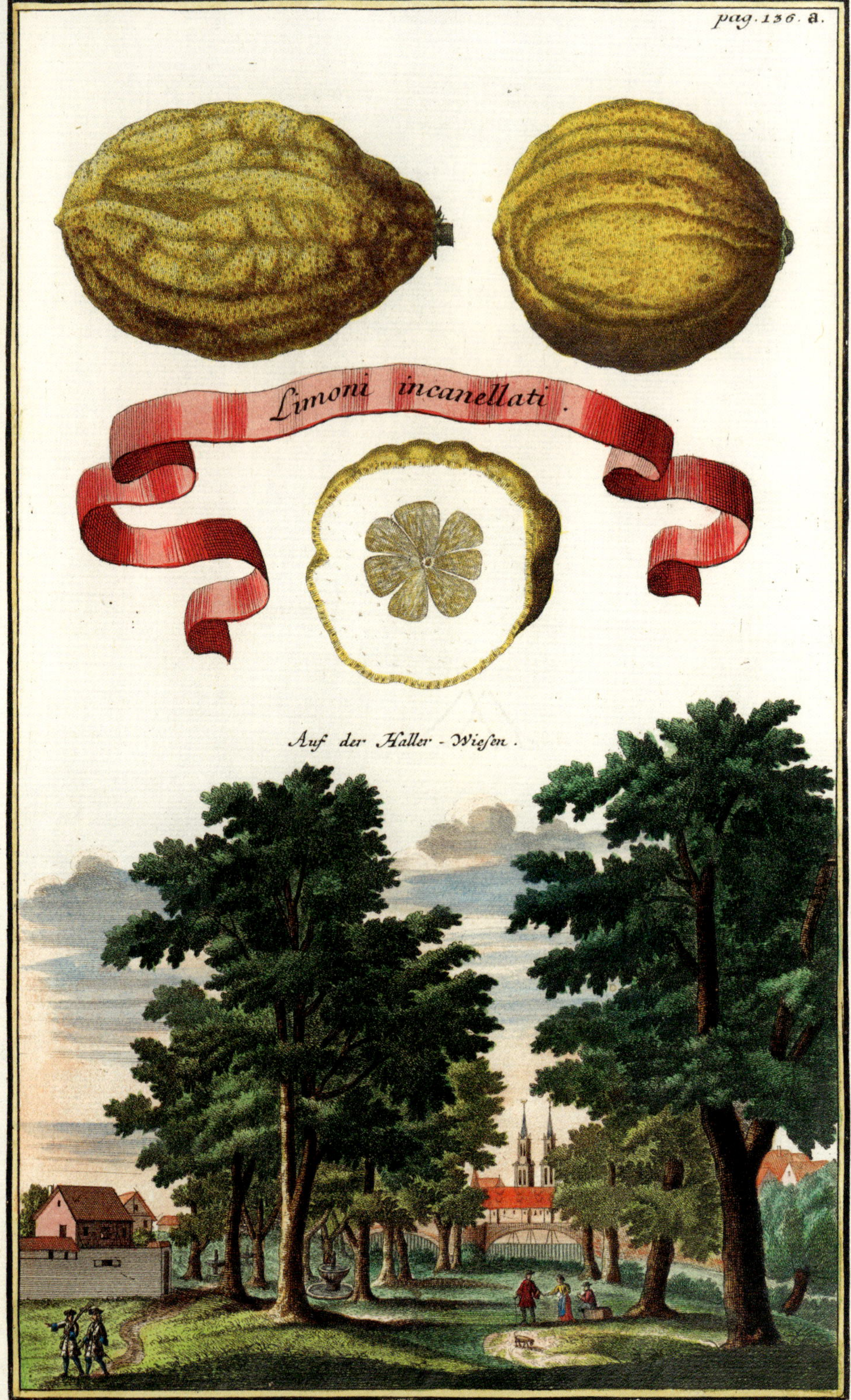

Limoni incanellati

Nuremberg, Hallerwiese

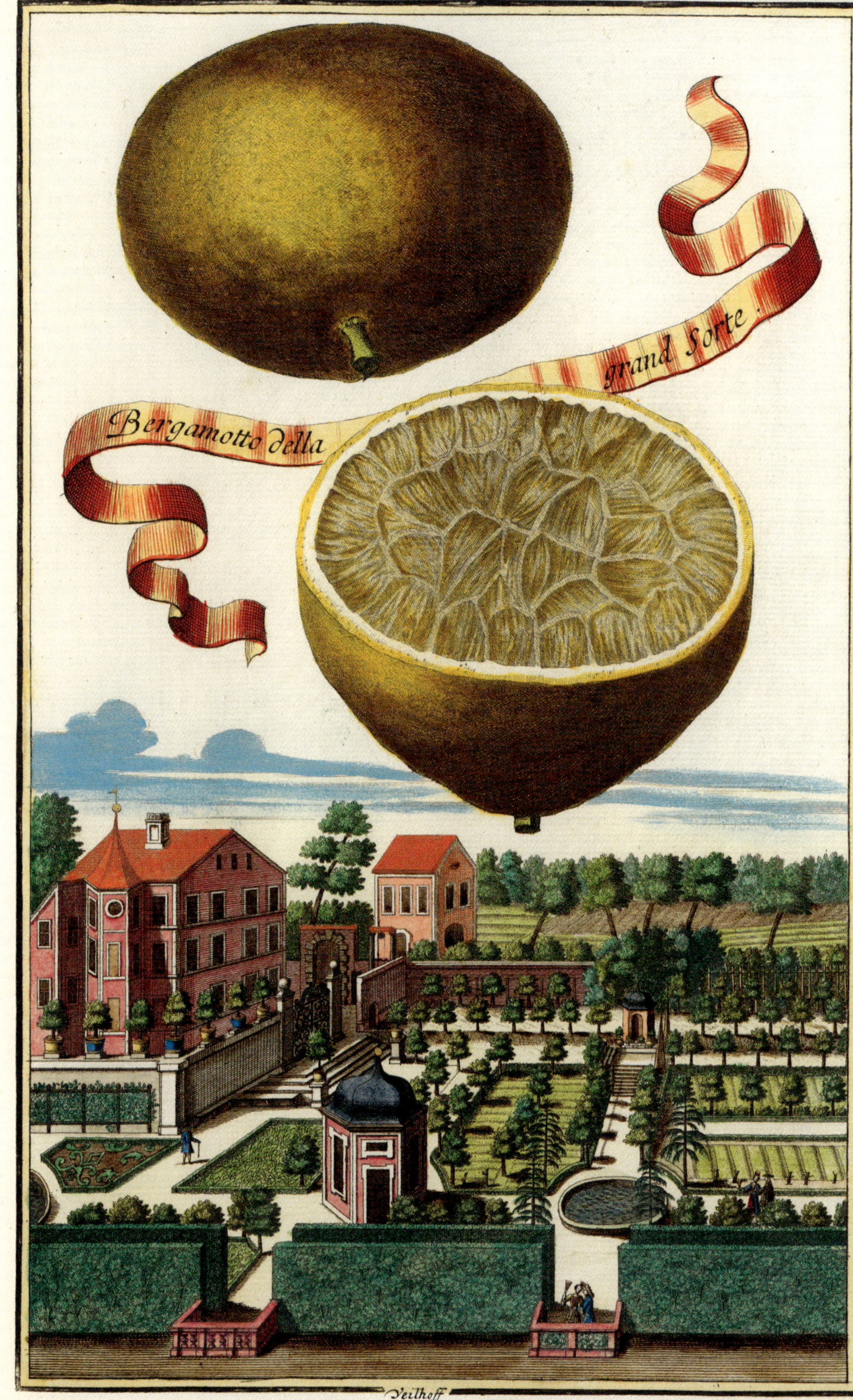
pag. 136. b
Bergamotto della grand Sorte
Veilhoff

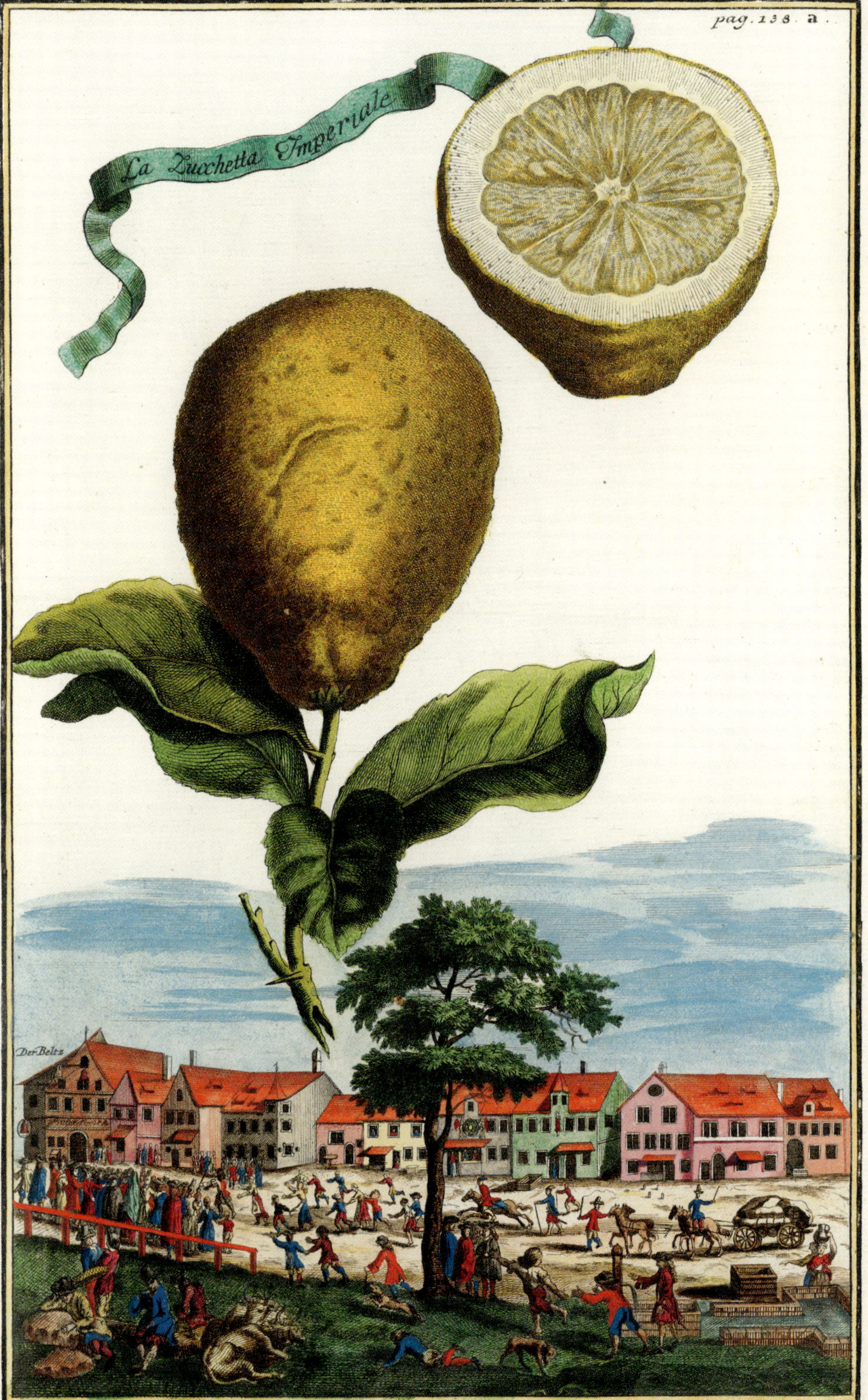

Nuremberg, Gostenhof – Church Festival

[Limon] La Zucchetta Imperiale

Lumia & Limon a Zucheta

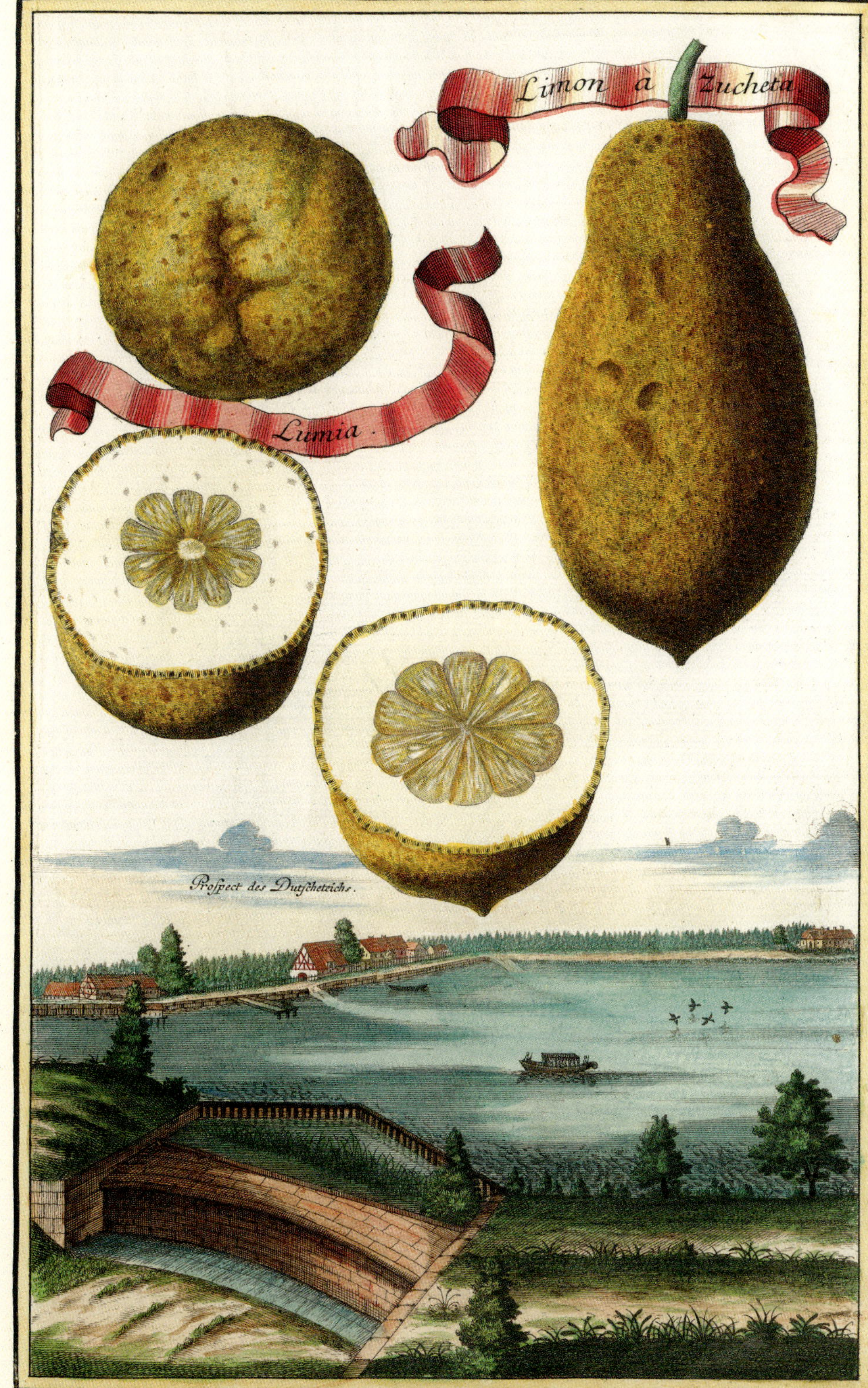

Nuremberg, Dutzendteich

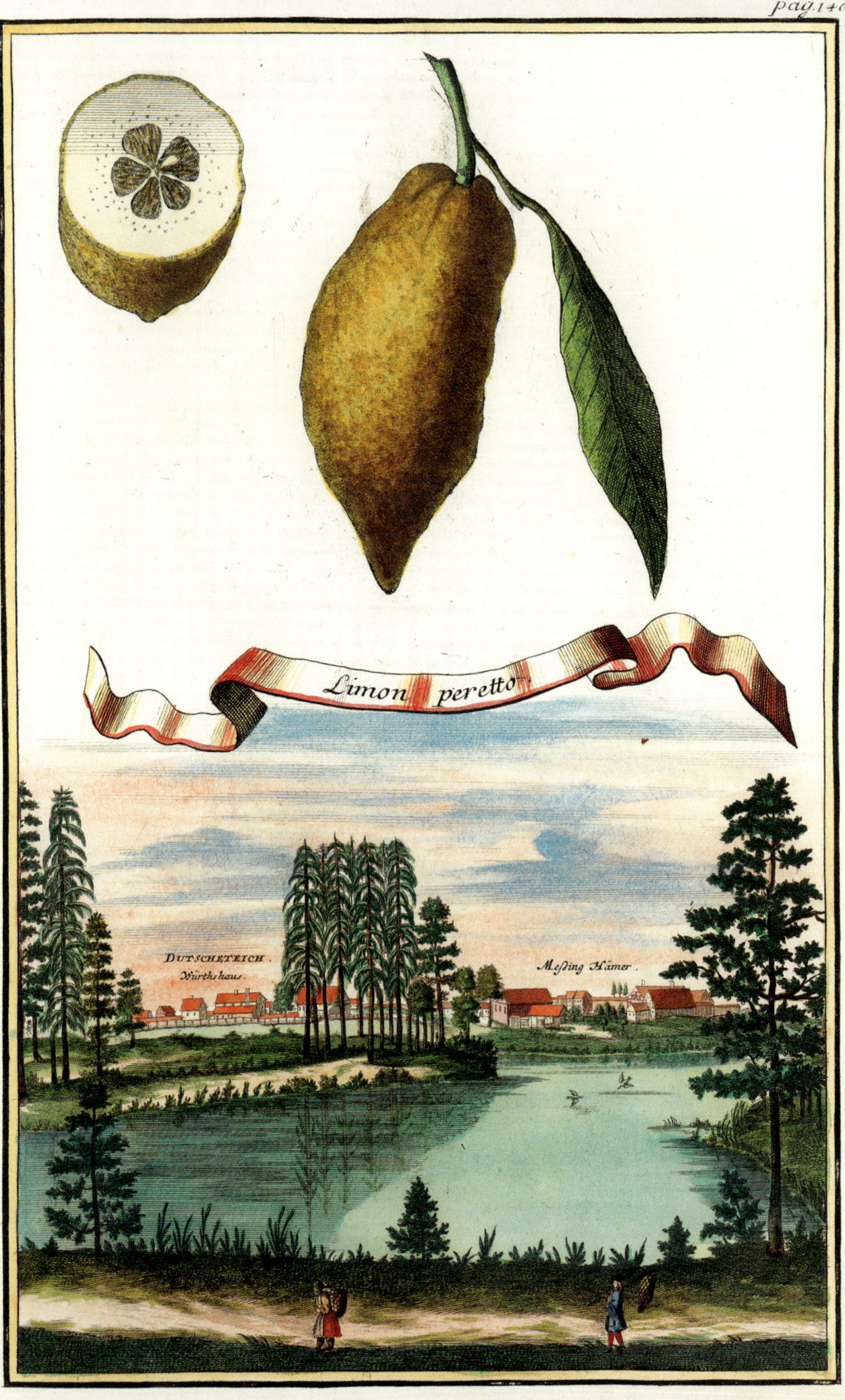

Limon Peretto

Nuremberg, Dutzendteich – Inn and Hammer Industrial Estate

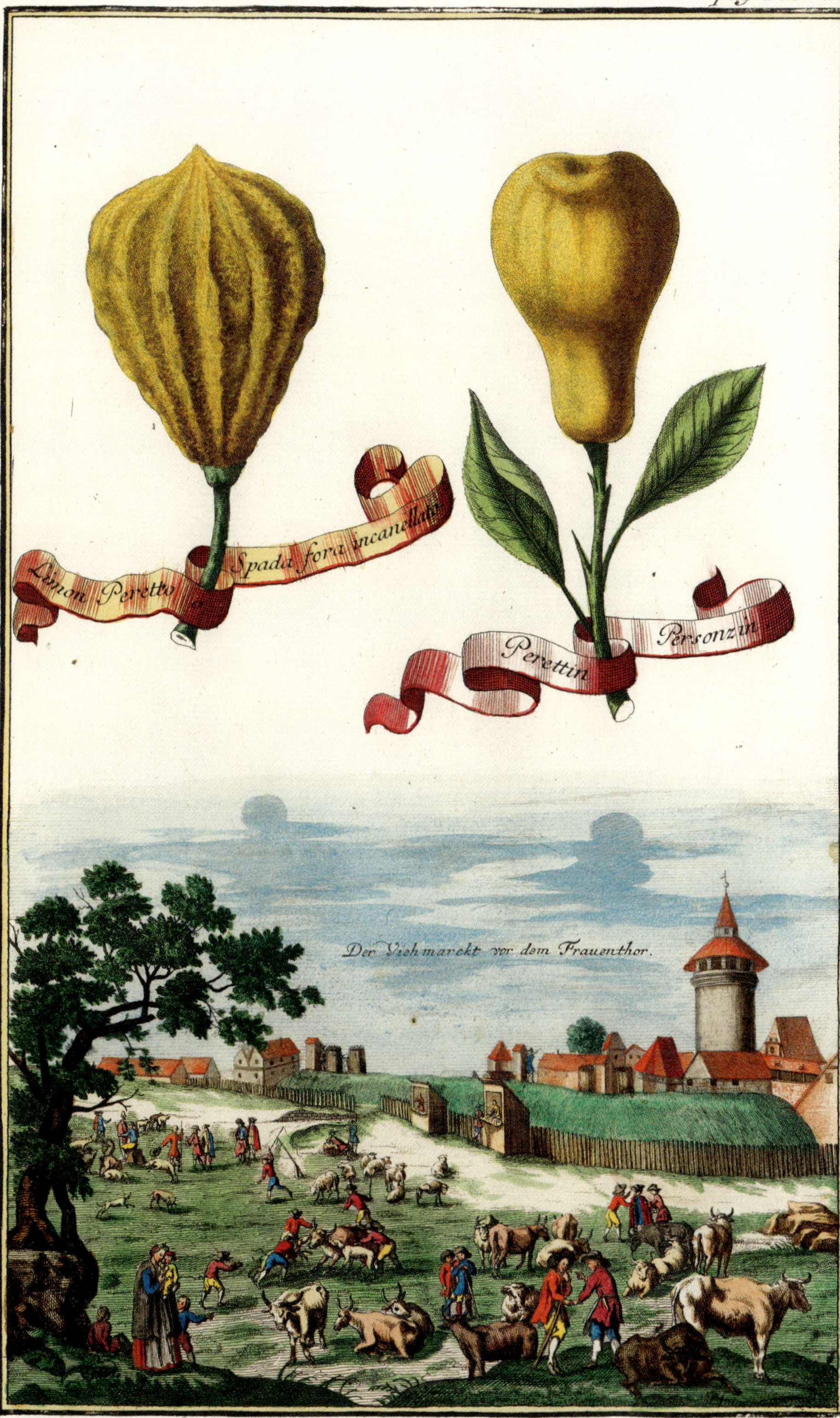

Limon Peretto o Spada fora incanellato & Perettin Personzin

Nuremberg – Frauentor and Cattle Market

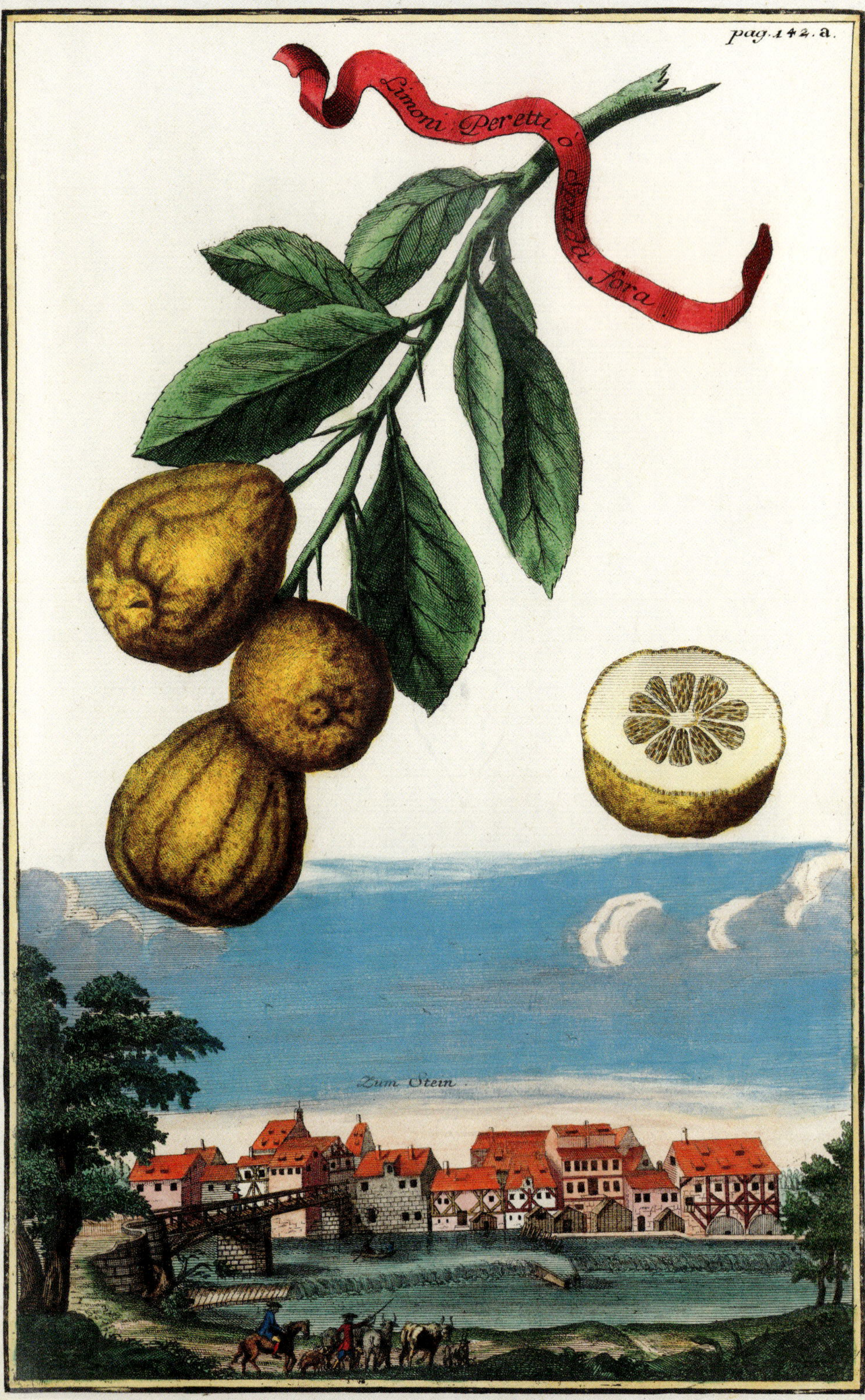

Limoni Peretti o Spada fora

Nuremberg, Stein

Limoni da Roma

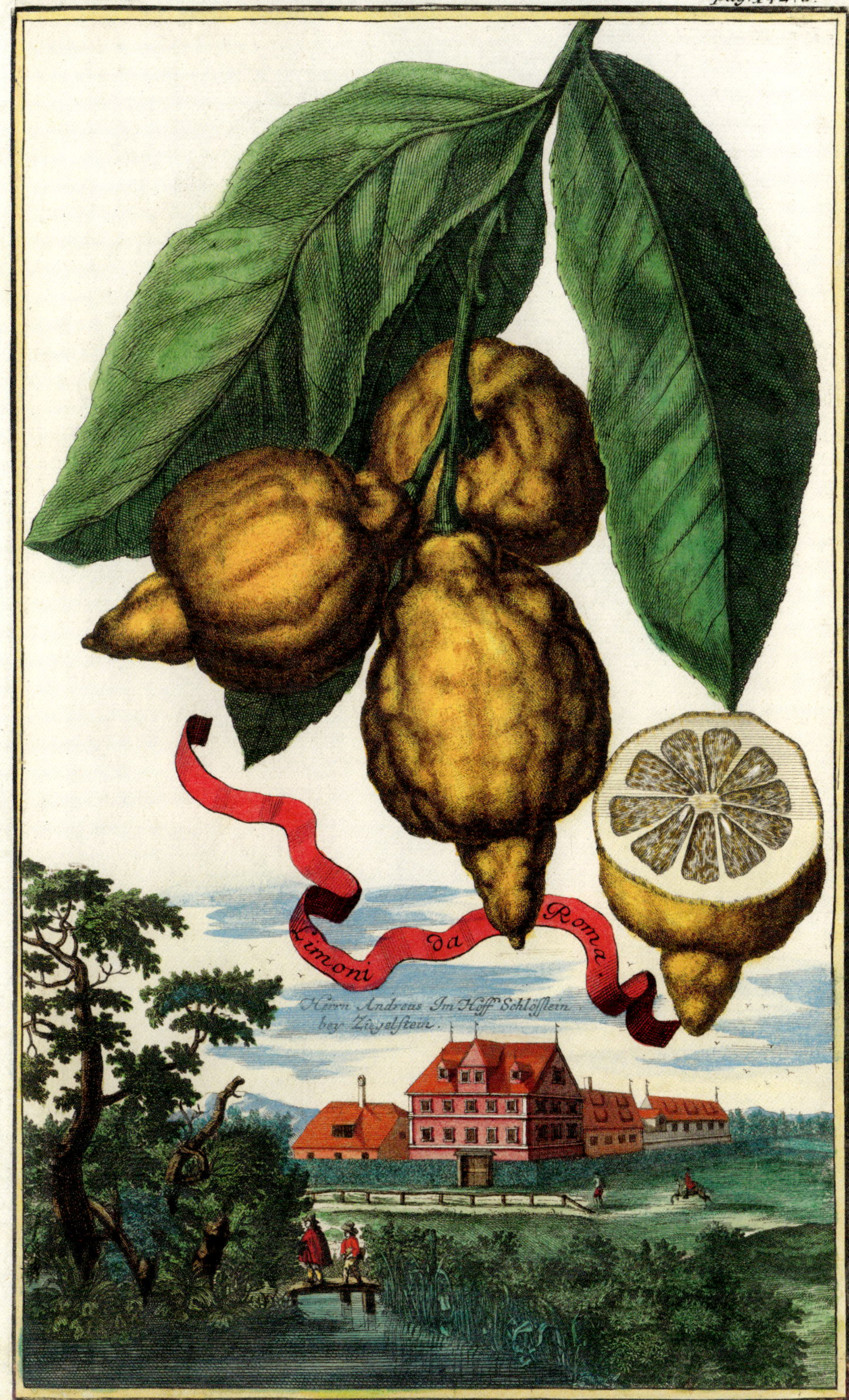

Nuremberg, Ziegelstein – Imhoff Manor

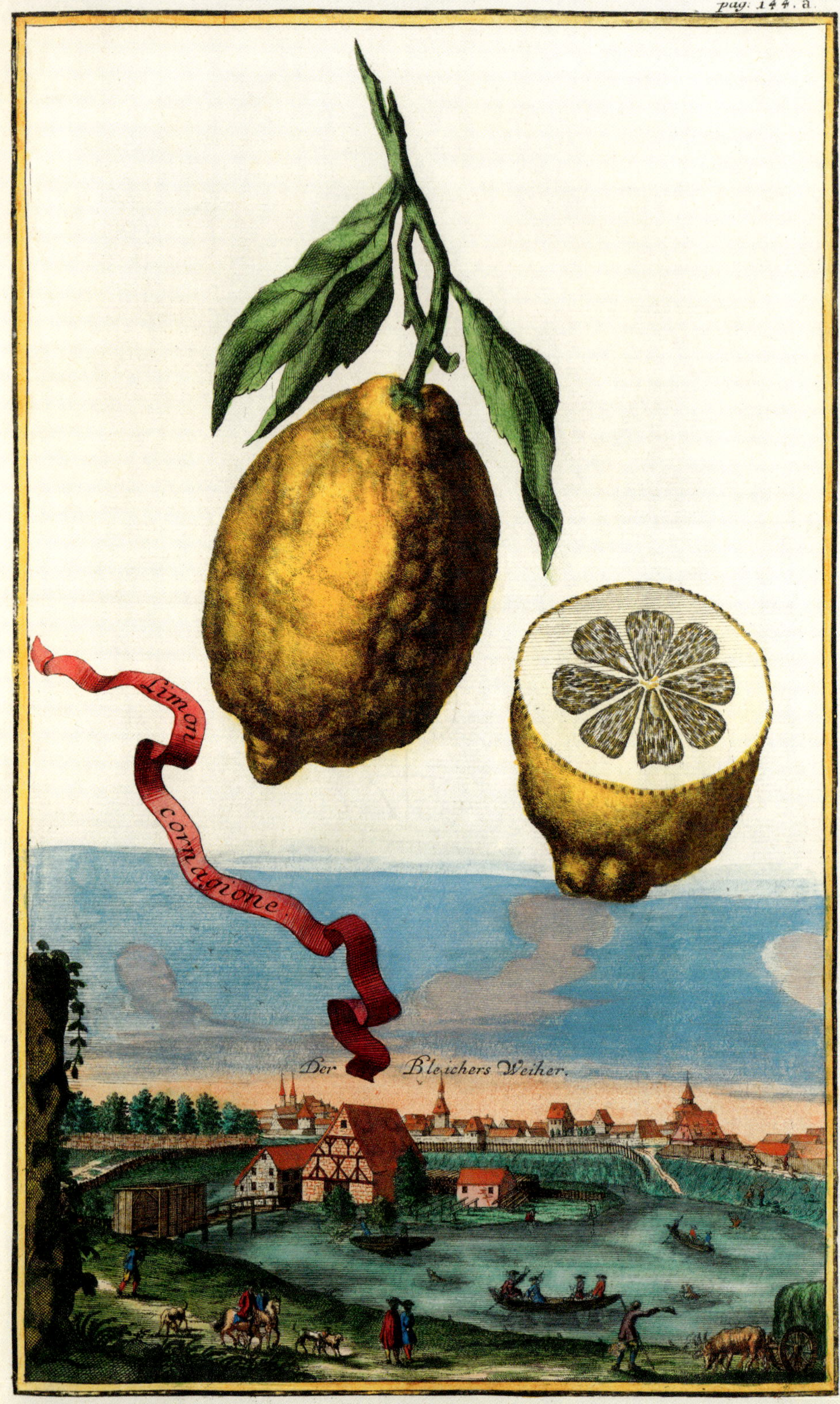

Limon cornagione

Nuremberg, Rosenau – The Bleichersweiher Pond

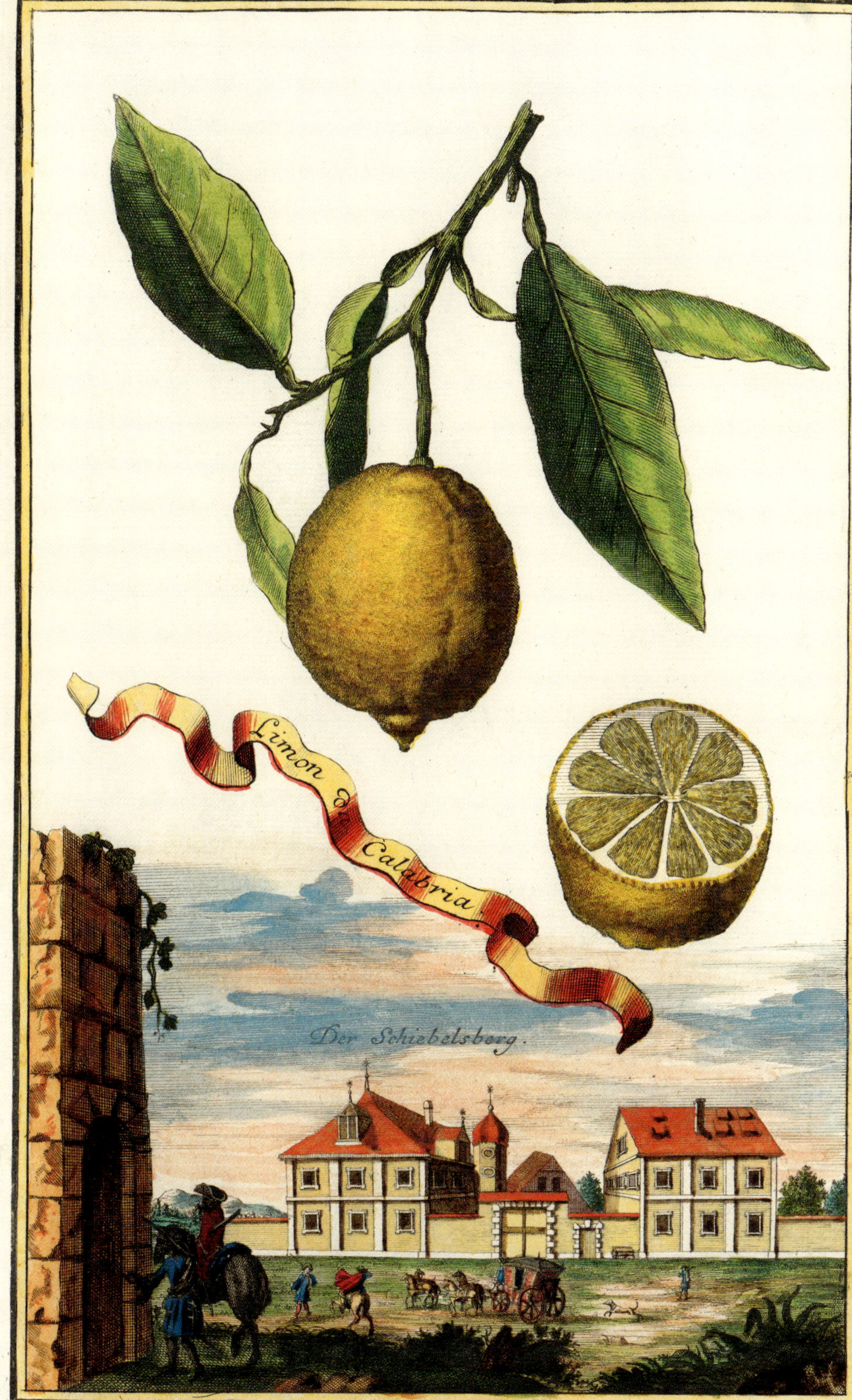

Limon da Calabria

Nuremberg, Schübelsberg

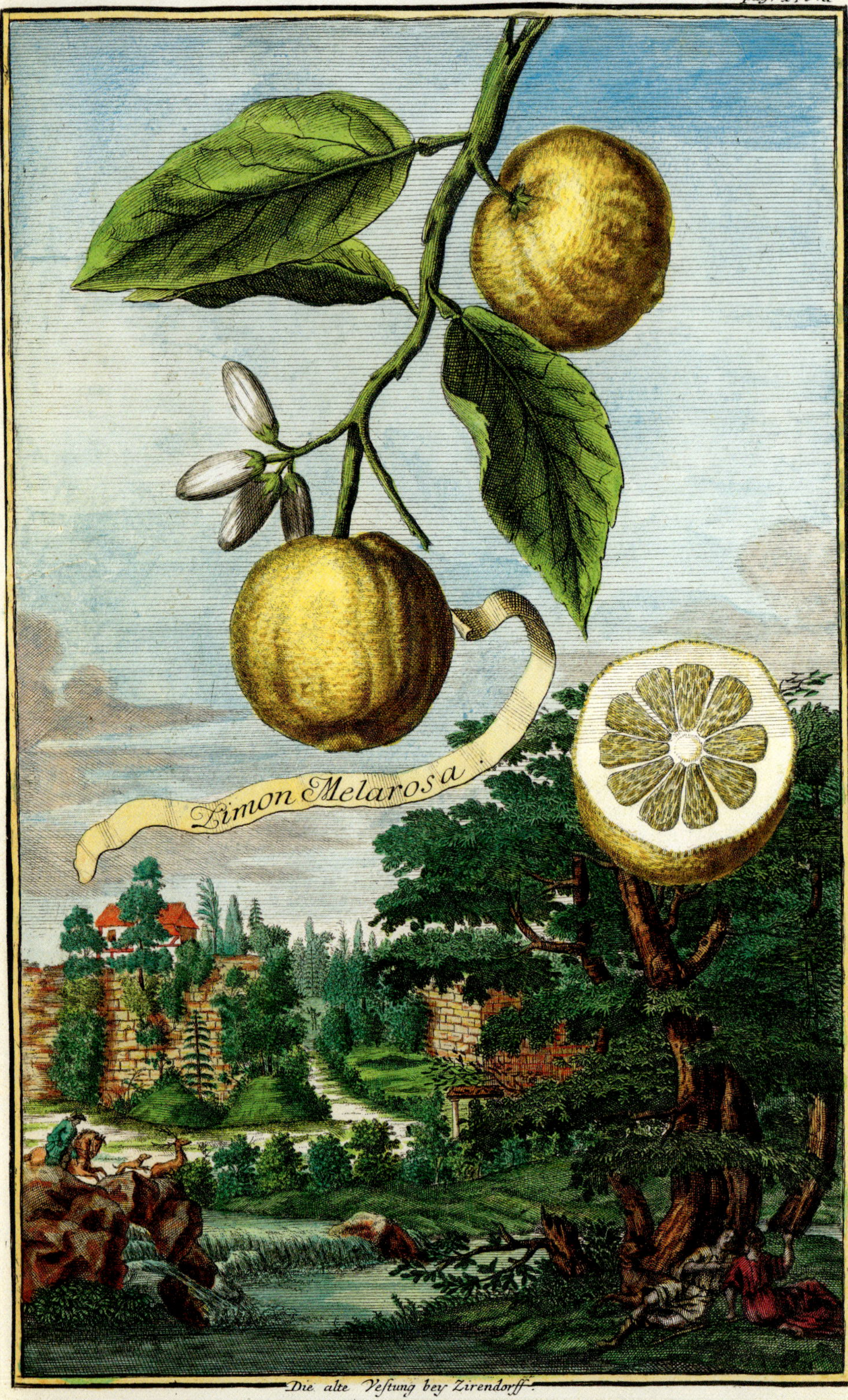

Limon Melarosa

Zirndorf, near Fürth – Old Fortress

Limon Zattelle

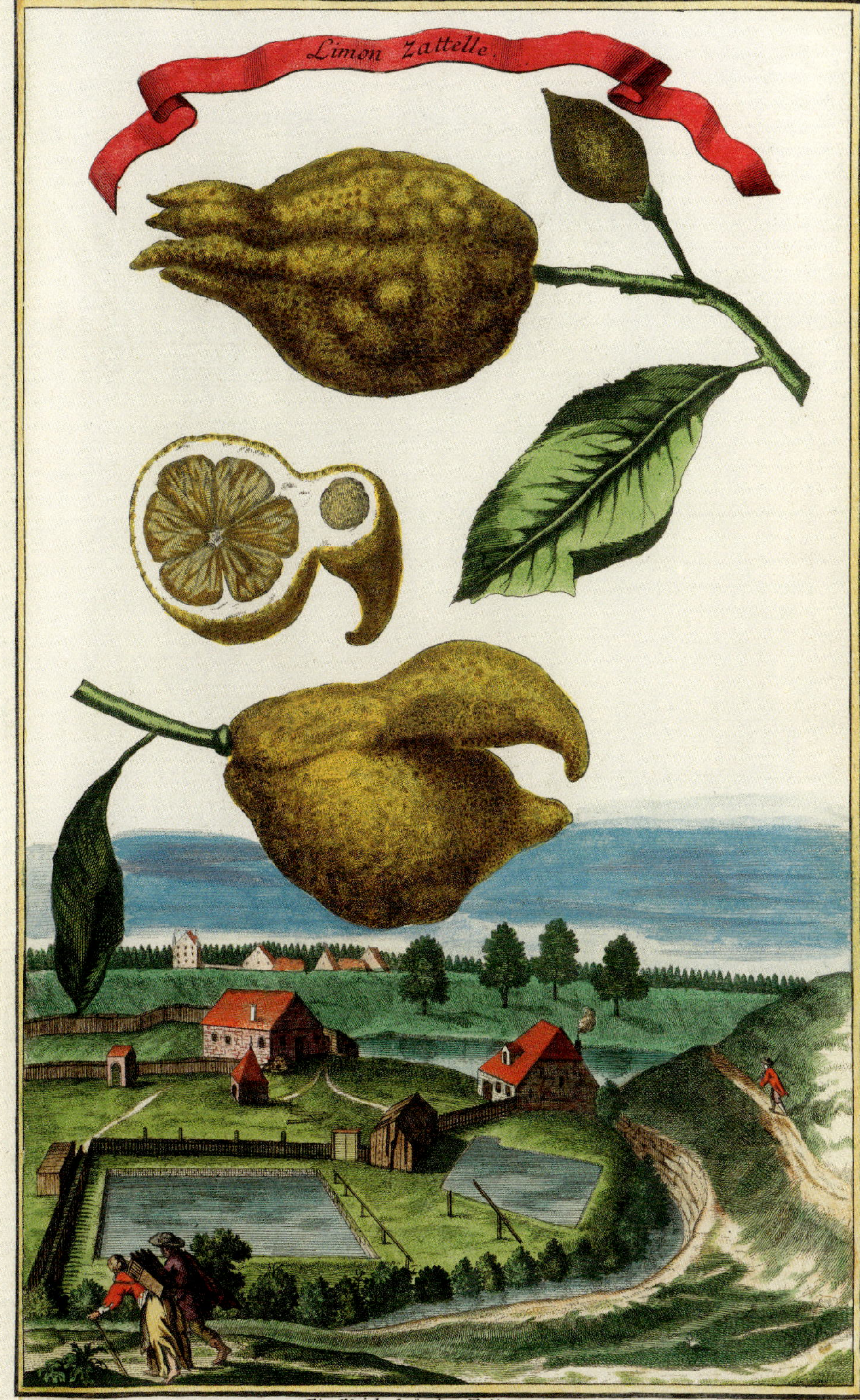

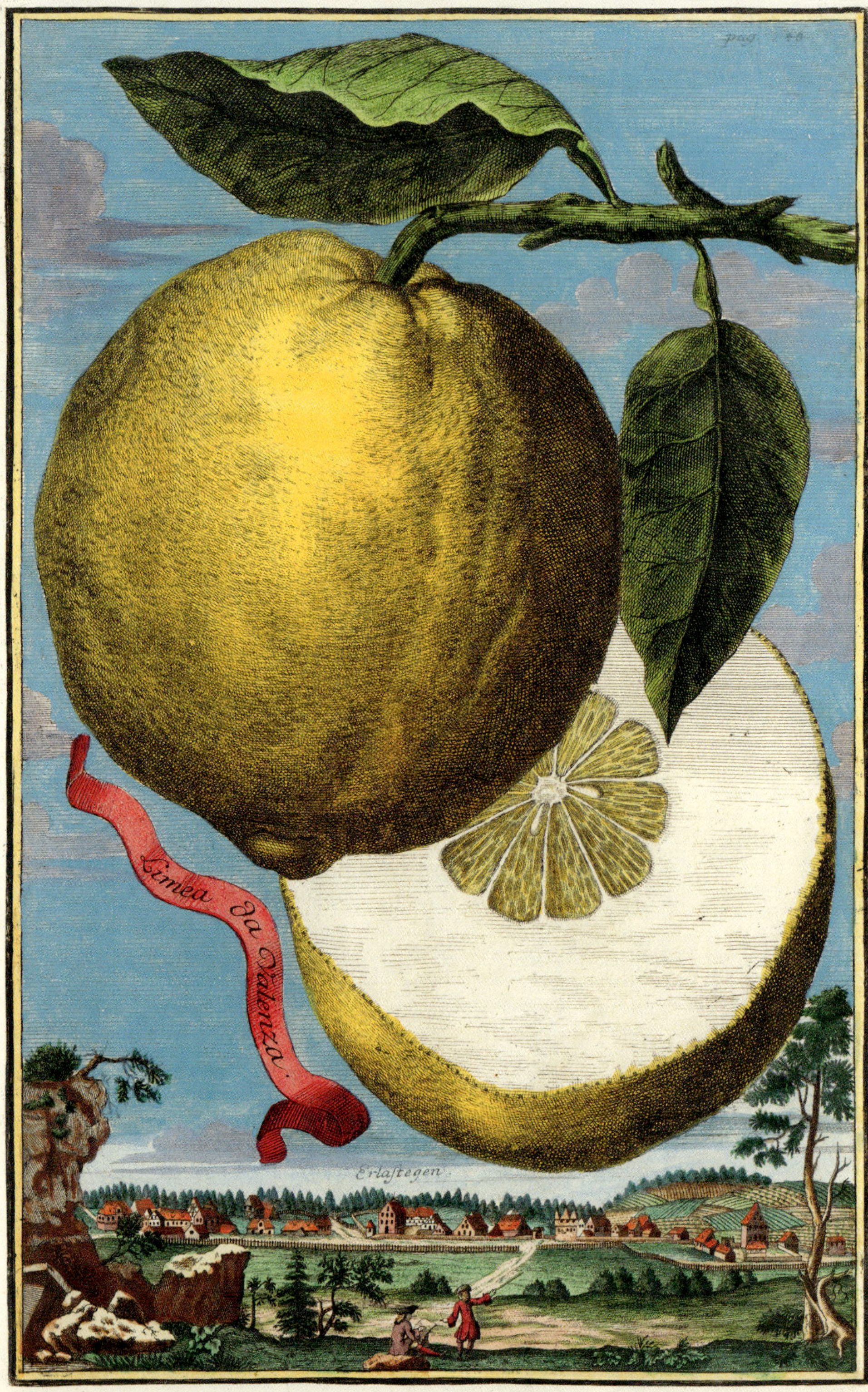

Limea da Valenza

Nuremberg Erlenstegen

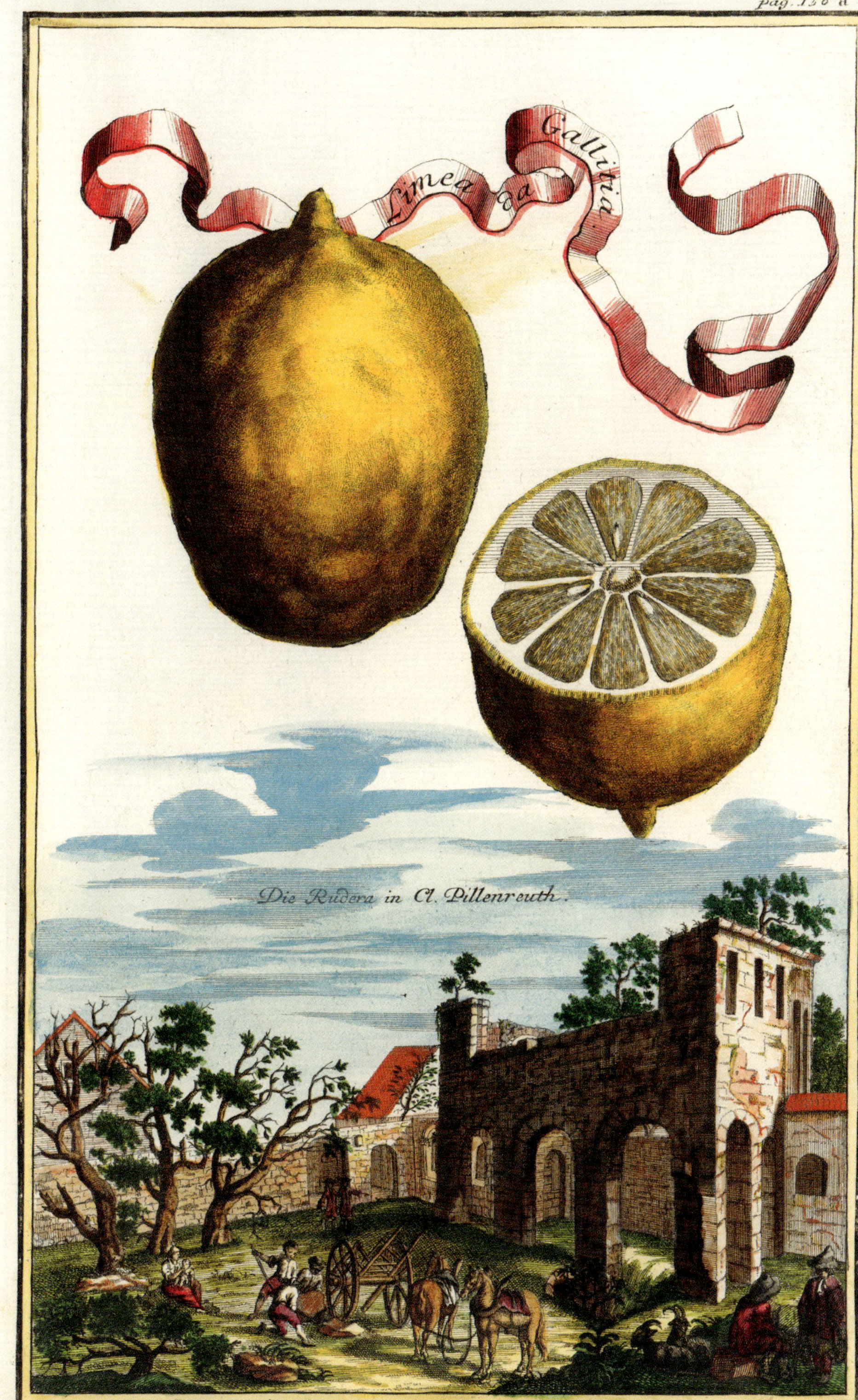

Limea da Gallitia

Nuremberg, Pillenreuth – Ruins of the Monastery

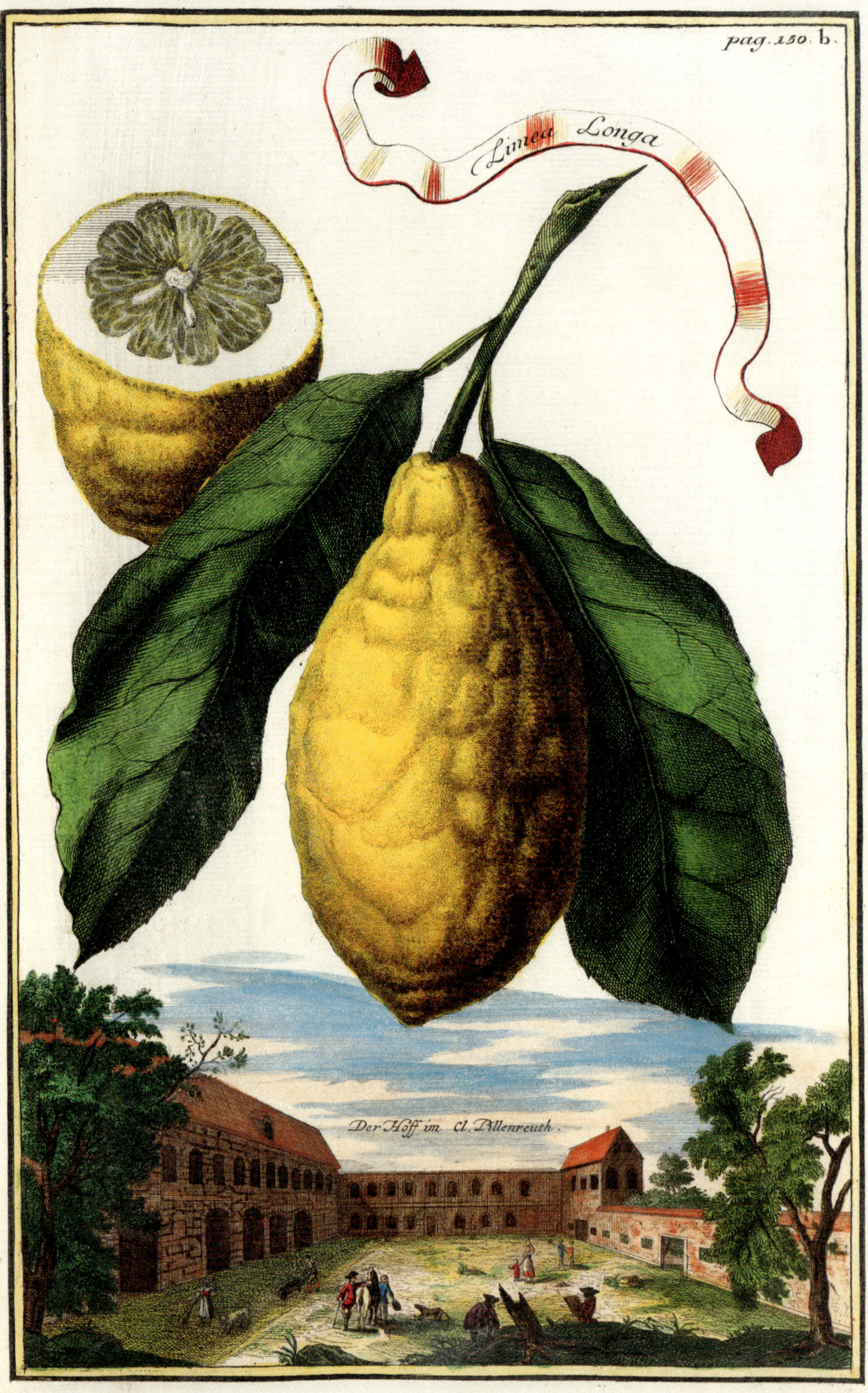

Limea Longa

Nuremberg, Pillenreuth – Monastery Courtyard

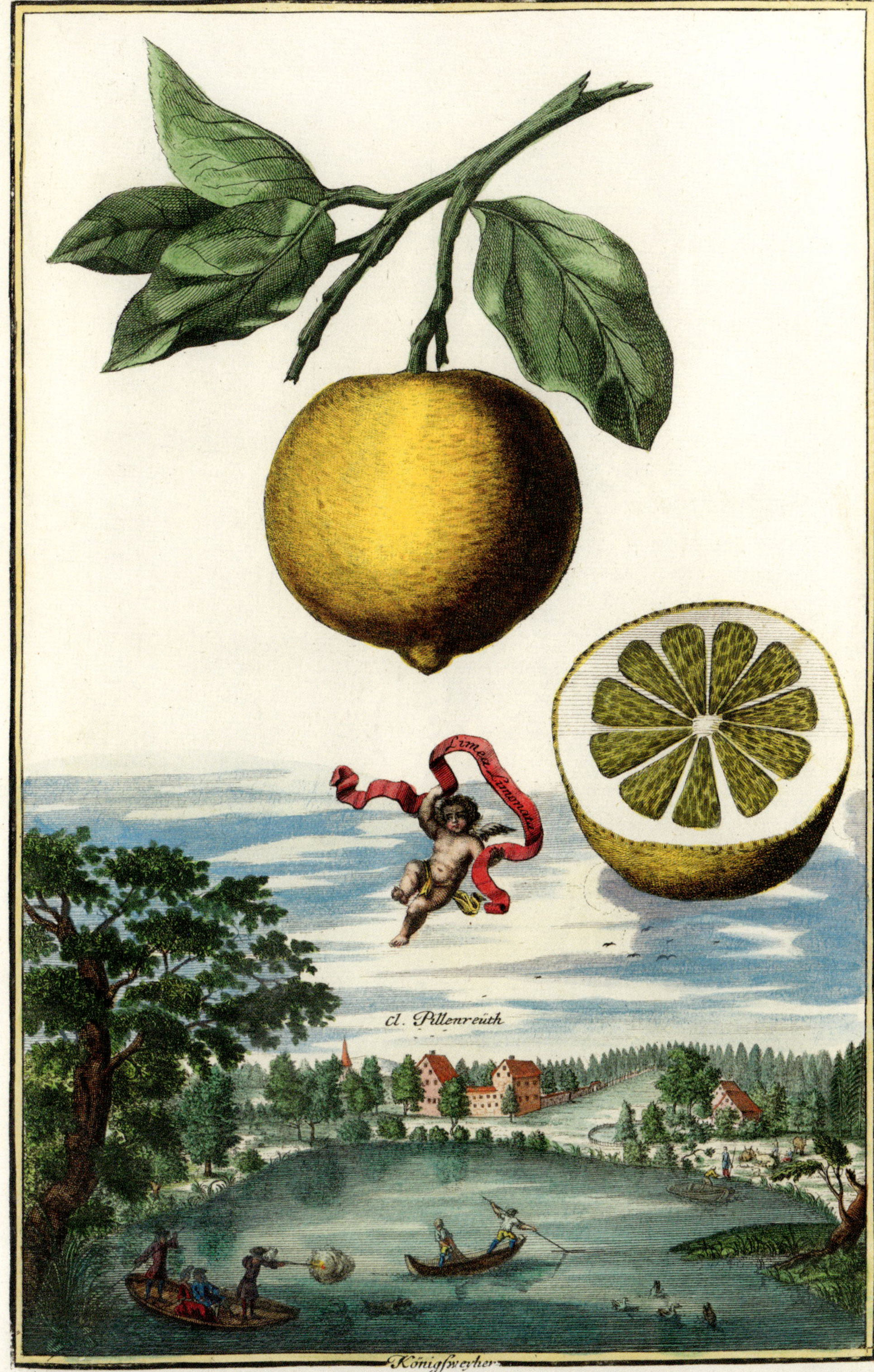

Limea Limonata

Nuremberg, Pillenreuth – Monastery and King's Pond

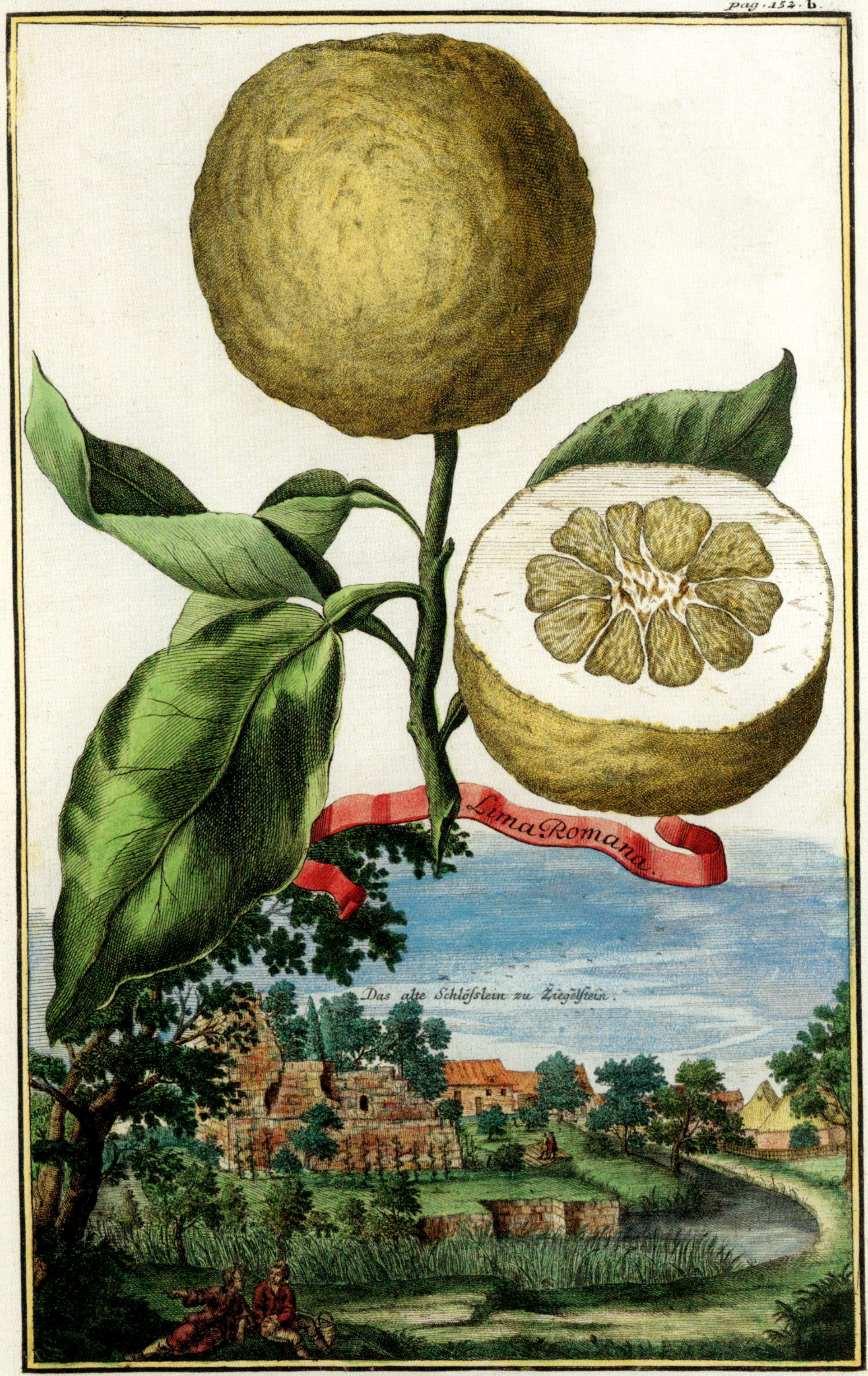

Lima Romana

Nuremberg, Ziegelstein – The Old Castle

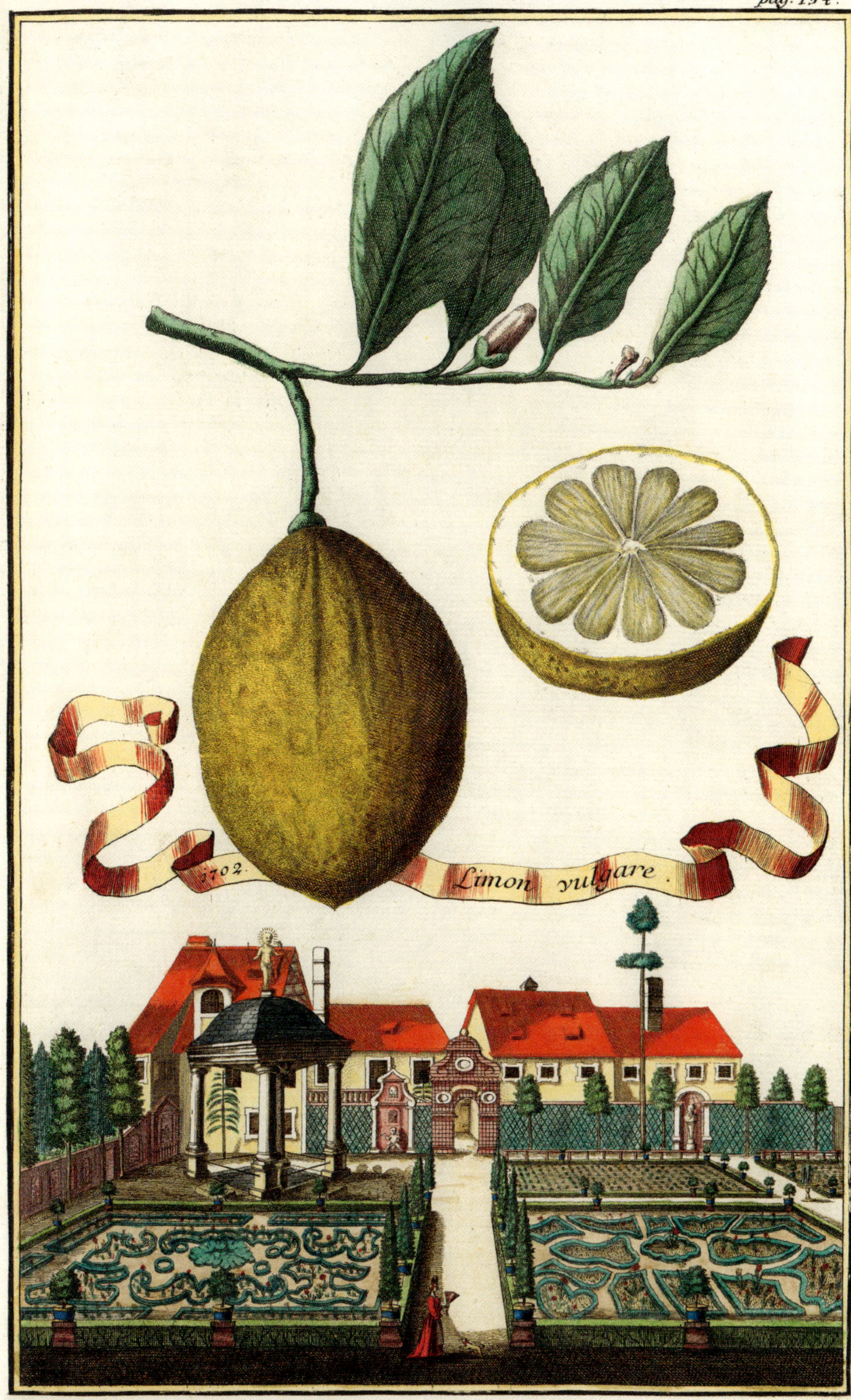
pag. 154.
1702.
Limon vulgare.

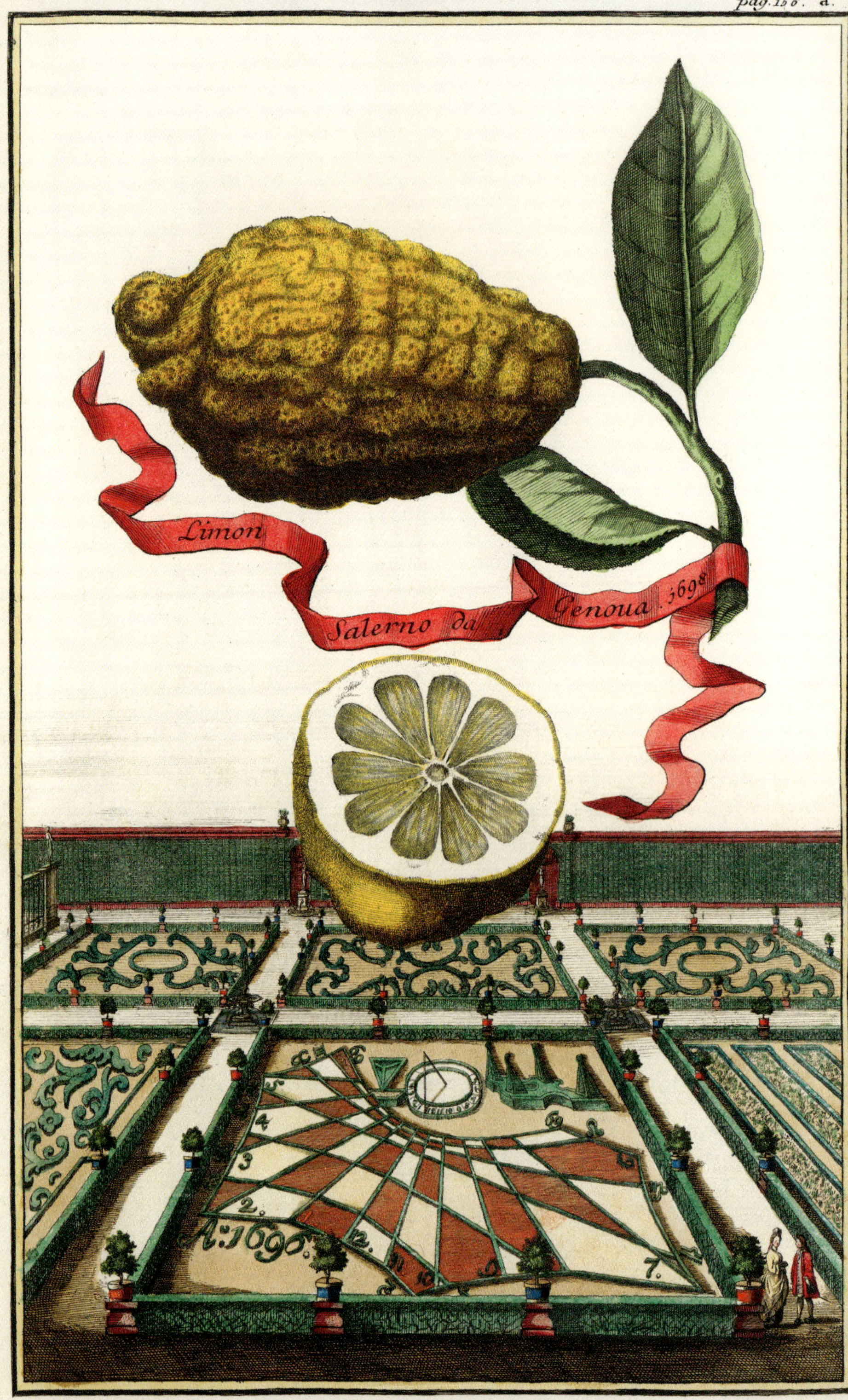

Limon Salerno da Genova

Nuremberg, Gostenhof –
Johann Christoph Volkamer's Garden

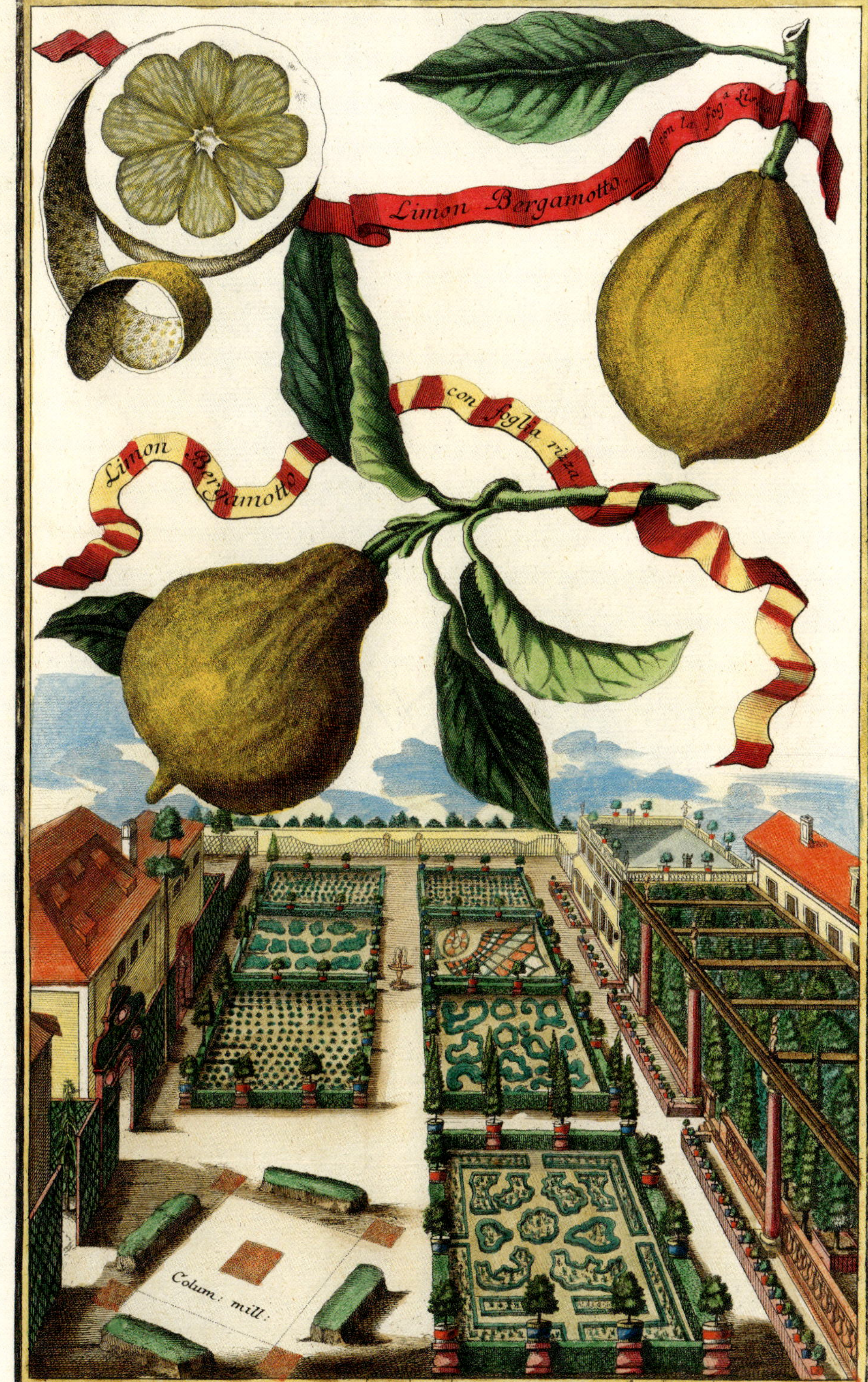

Limon Bergamotto con la foglia Liscia & Limon Bergamotto con foglia rizza

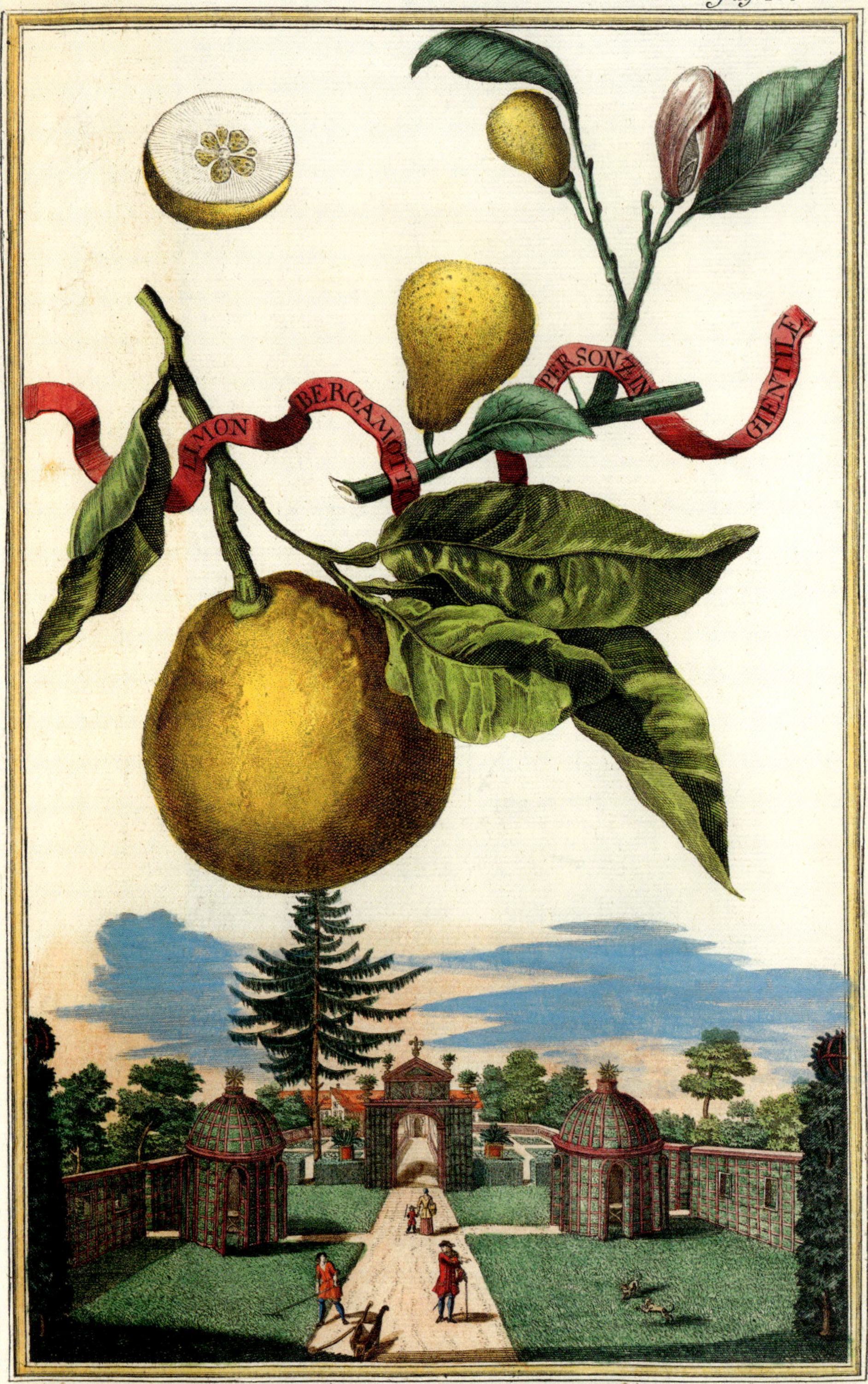

P.D fecit.

PROSPECT IN HERRN C.W. TVCHERS GARTEN.

Limon Bergamotto Personzin Gientile

Nuremberg, St Sebald – Garden of C. W. Tucher

Limon dolce ordin[ario]

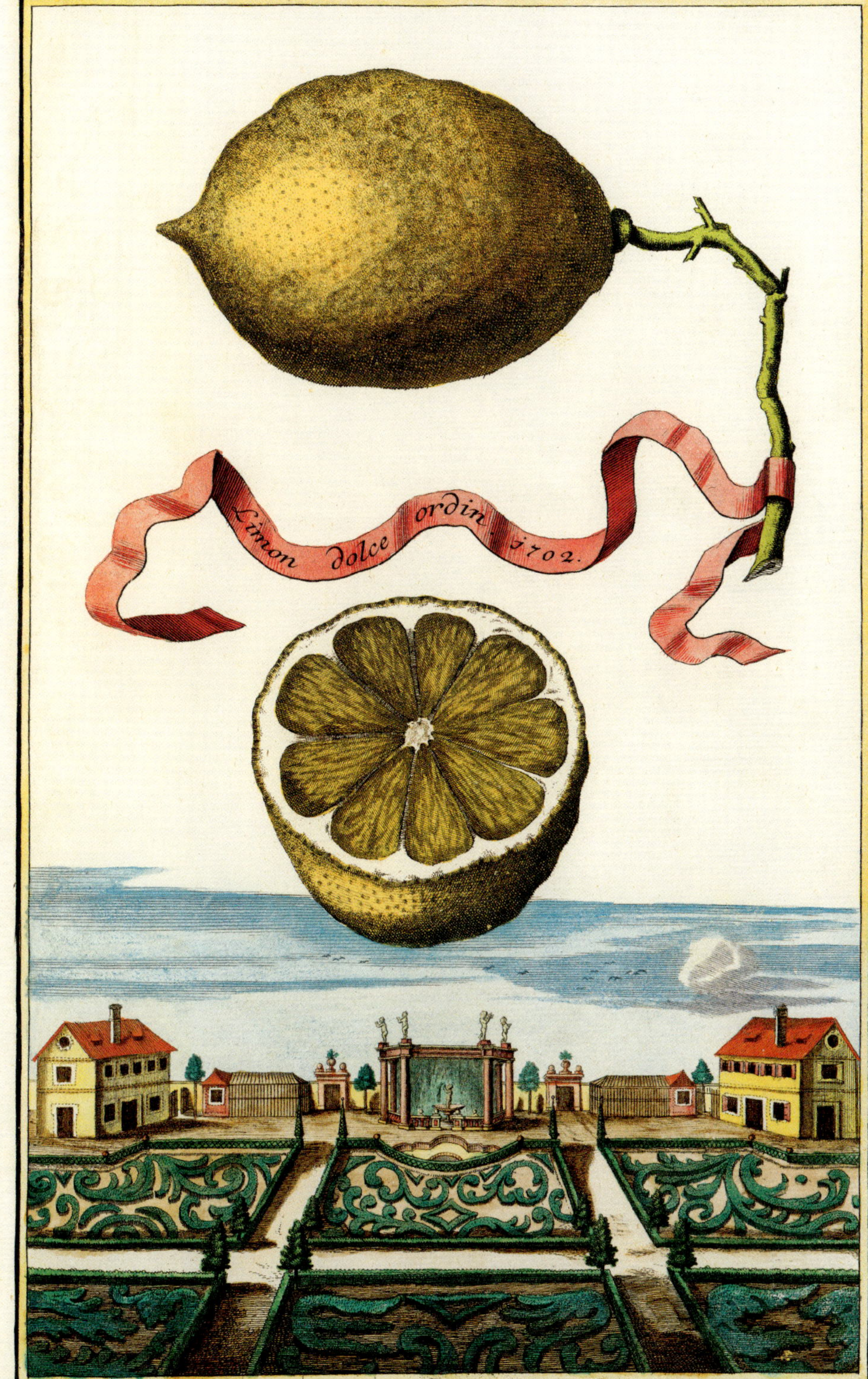

Nuremberg, Gostenhof –
Johann Christoph Volkamer's Garden

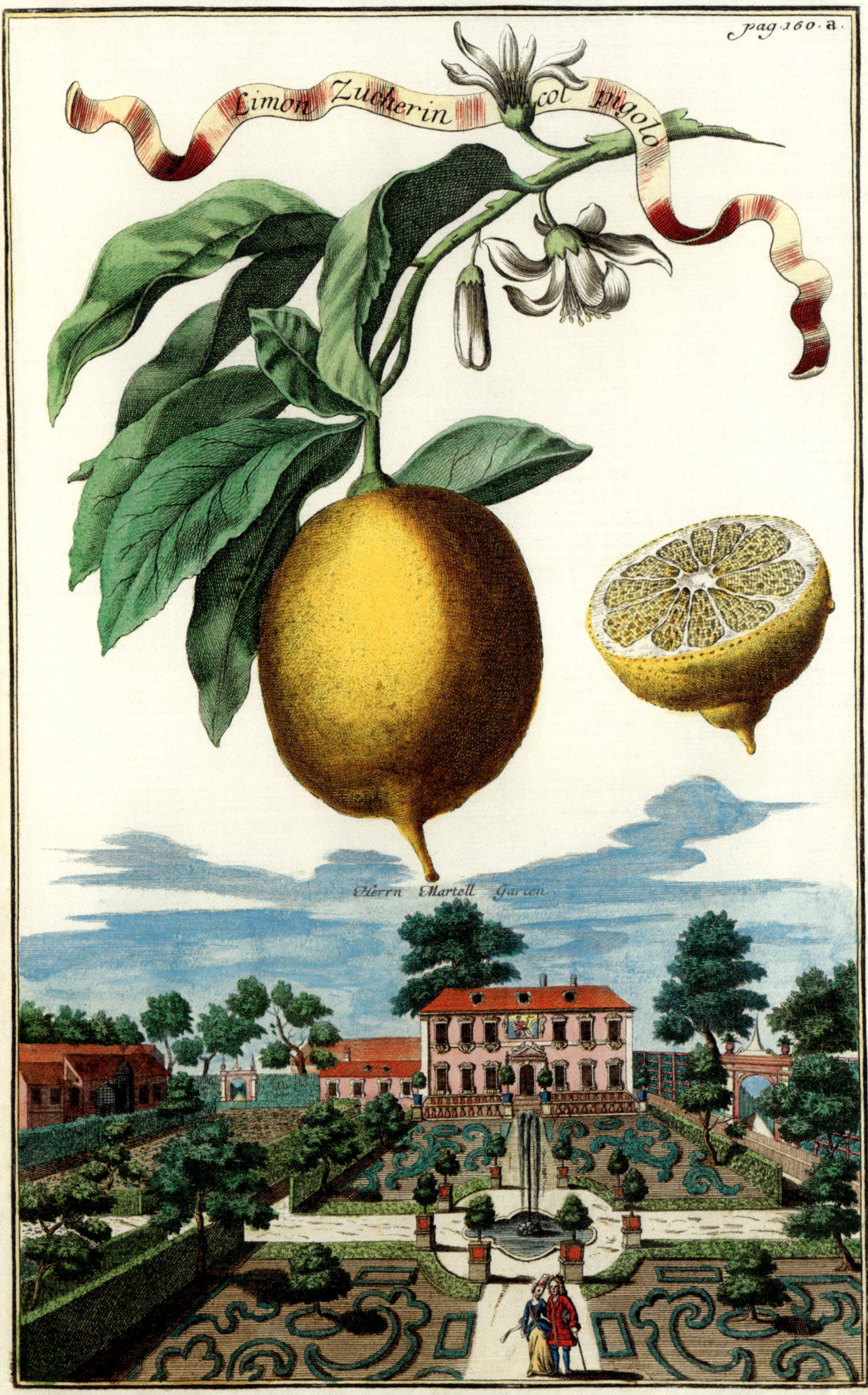

Limon Zucherin col pigolo

Nuremberg, St Johannis – Garden of Mr Martell

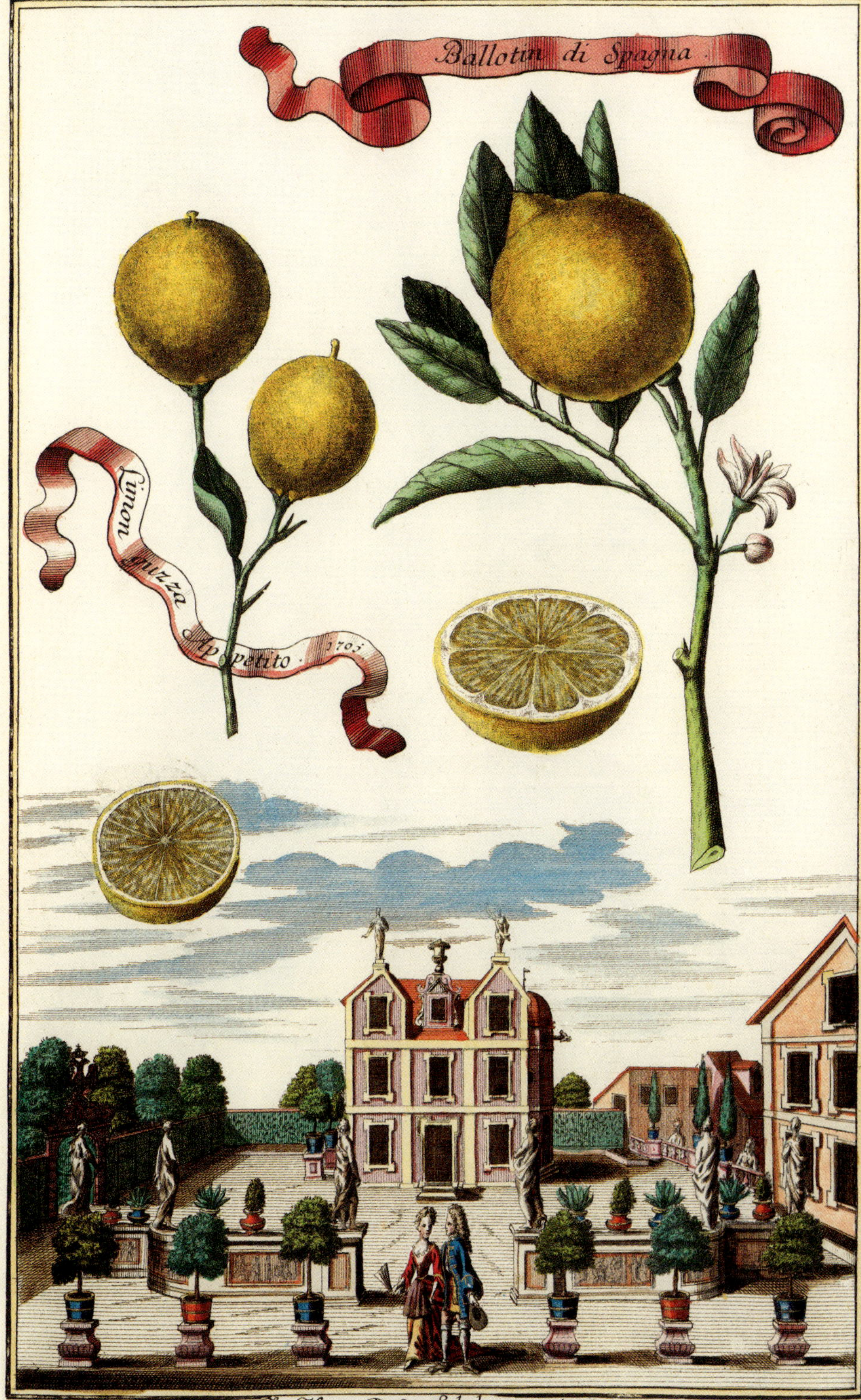

Ballotin di Spagna & Limon guzza Appetito

Nuremberg, Wöhrd – Garden of Dr Schober

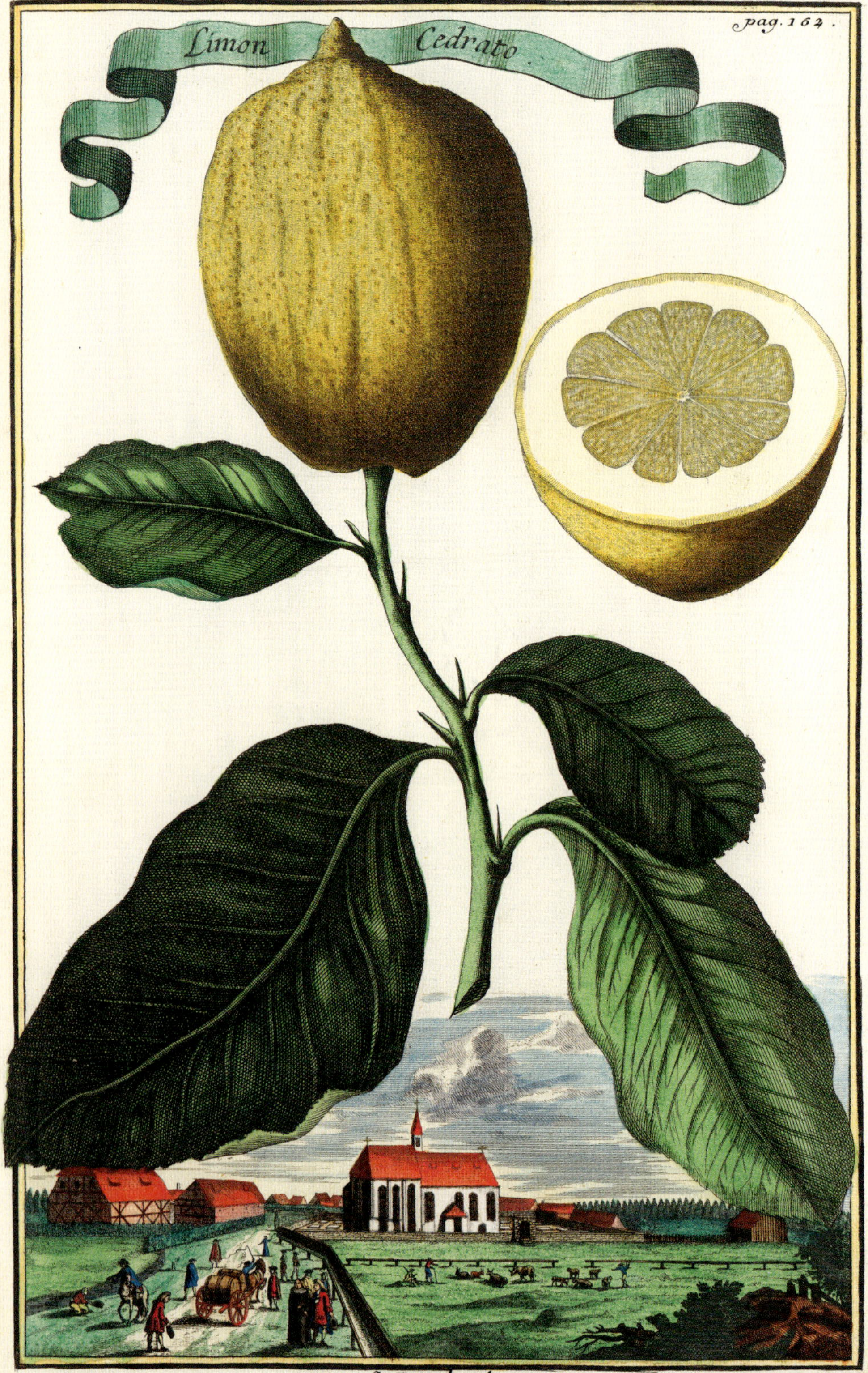

Limon Cedrato

Nuremberg, St Leonhard

Limon Cedrato

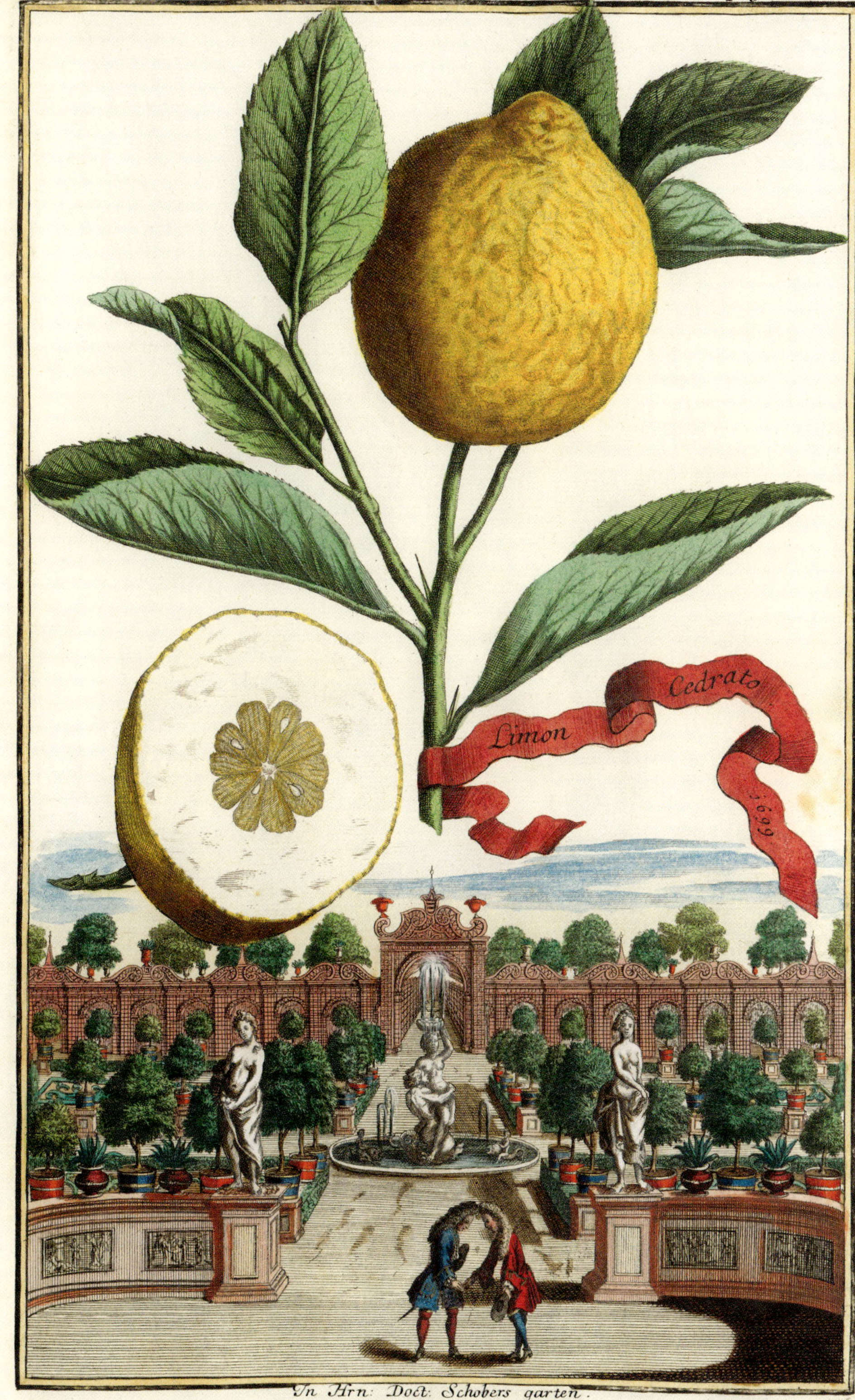

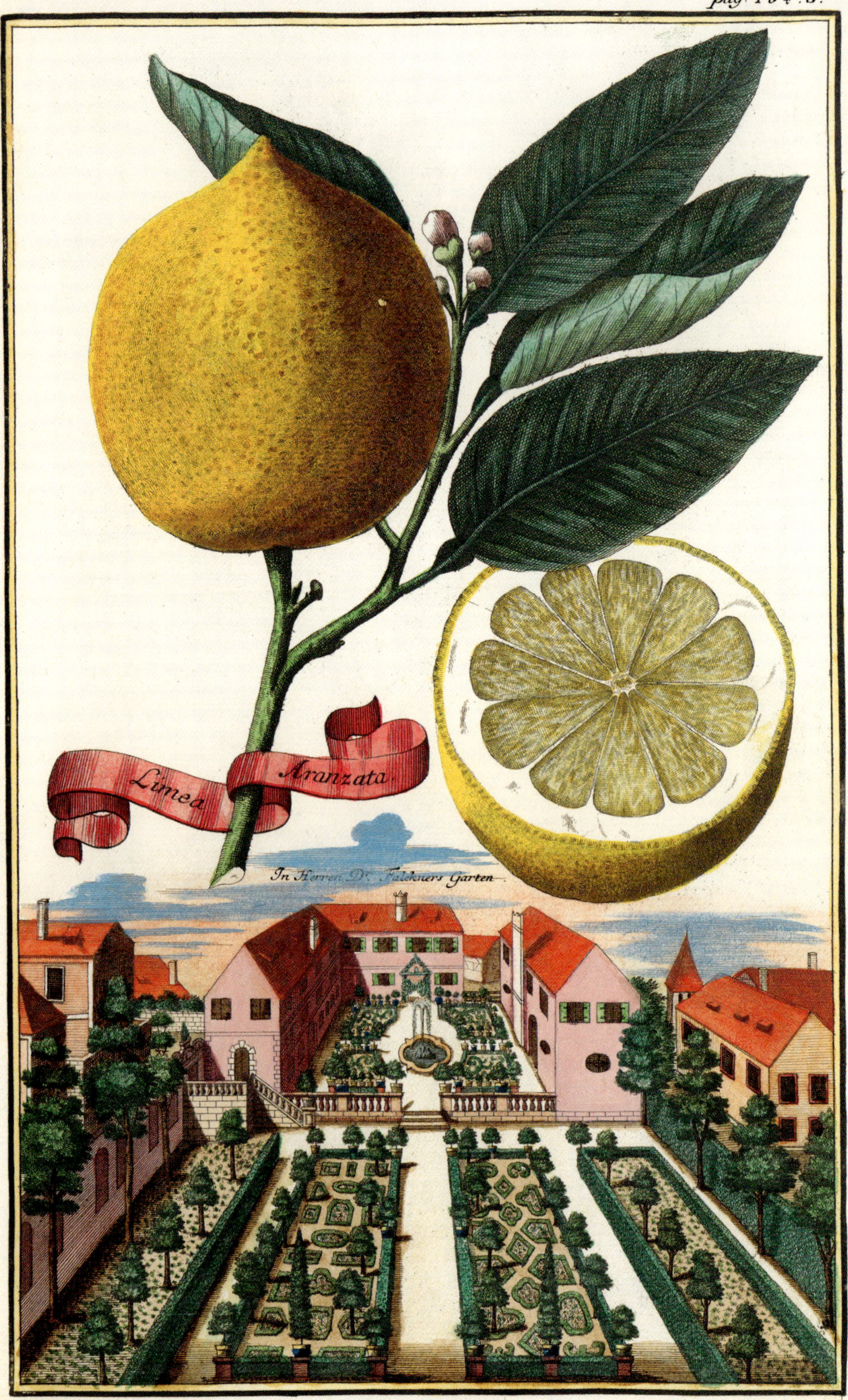

Limea Aranzata

Nuremberg, Wöhrd – Garden of Dr Falckner

Lima dolce

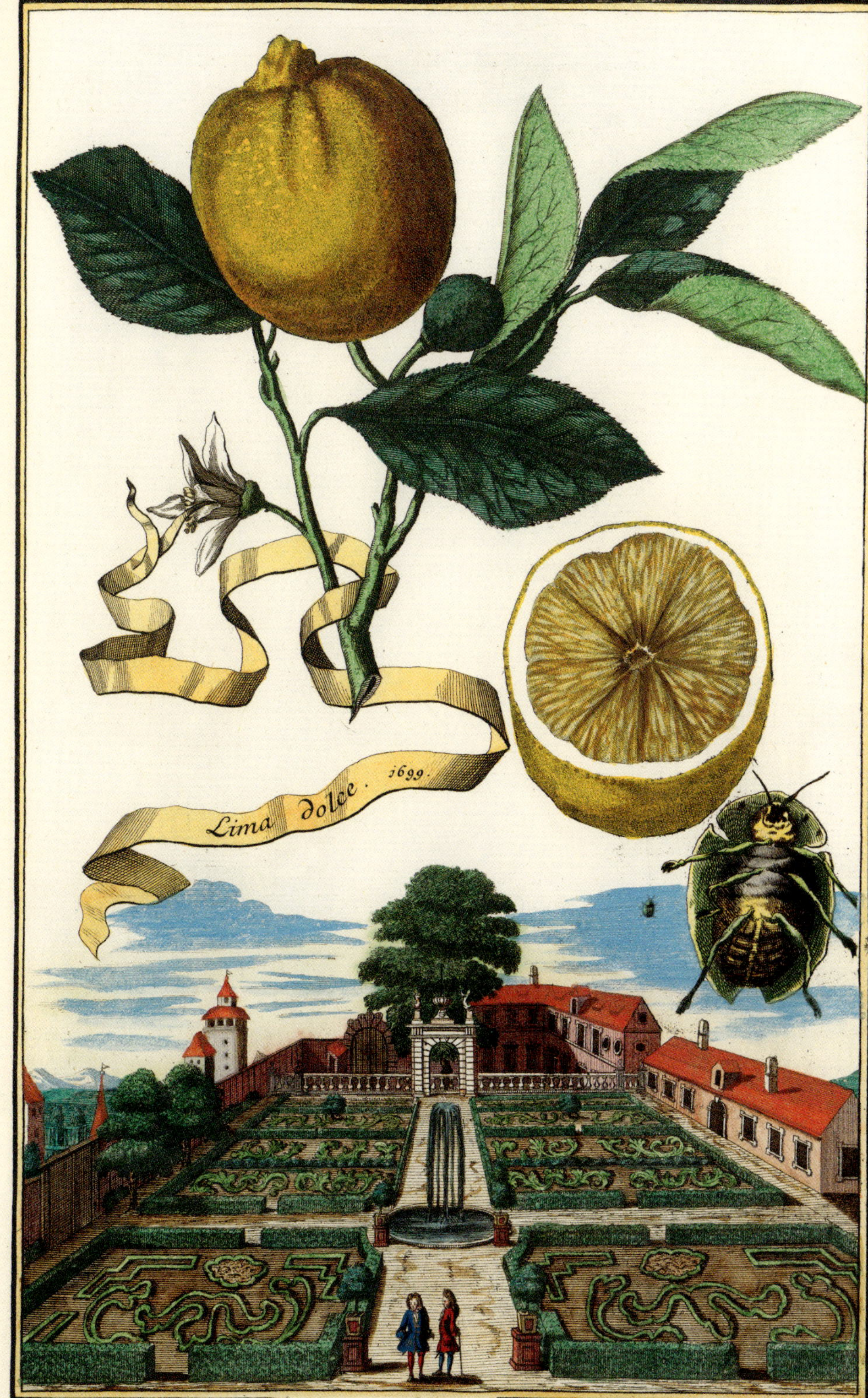

Nuremberg, Wöhrd – Garden of Dr Silberrad

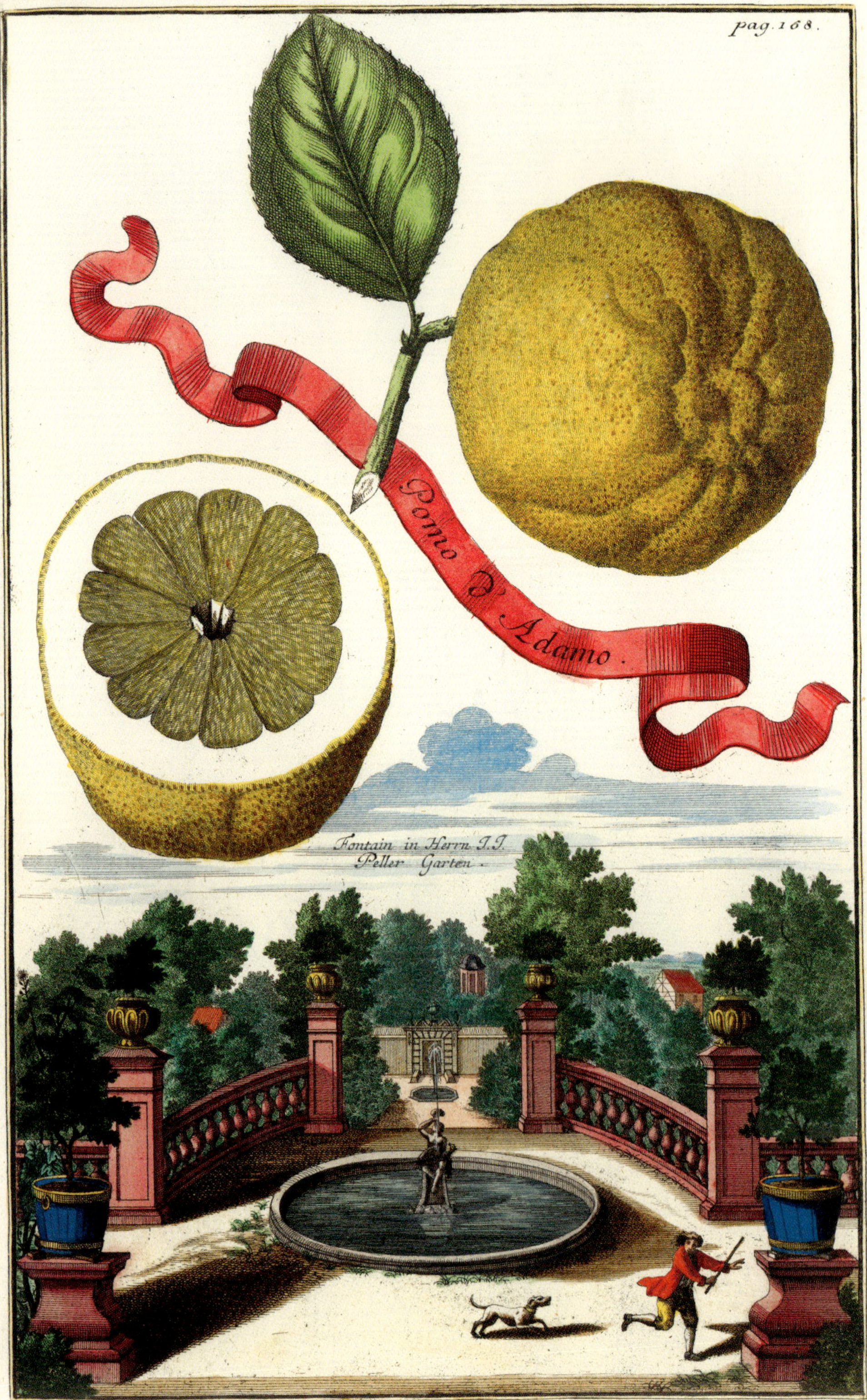

Pomo d'Adamo

Nuremberg, St Johannis – Garden of J.J. Peller

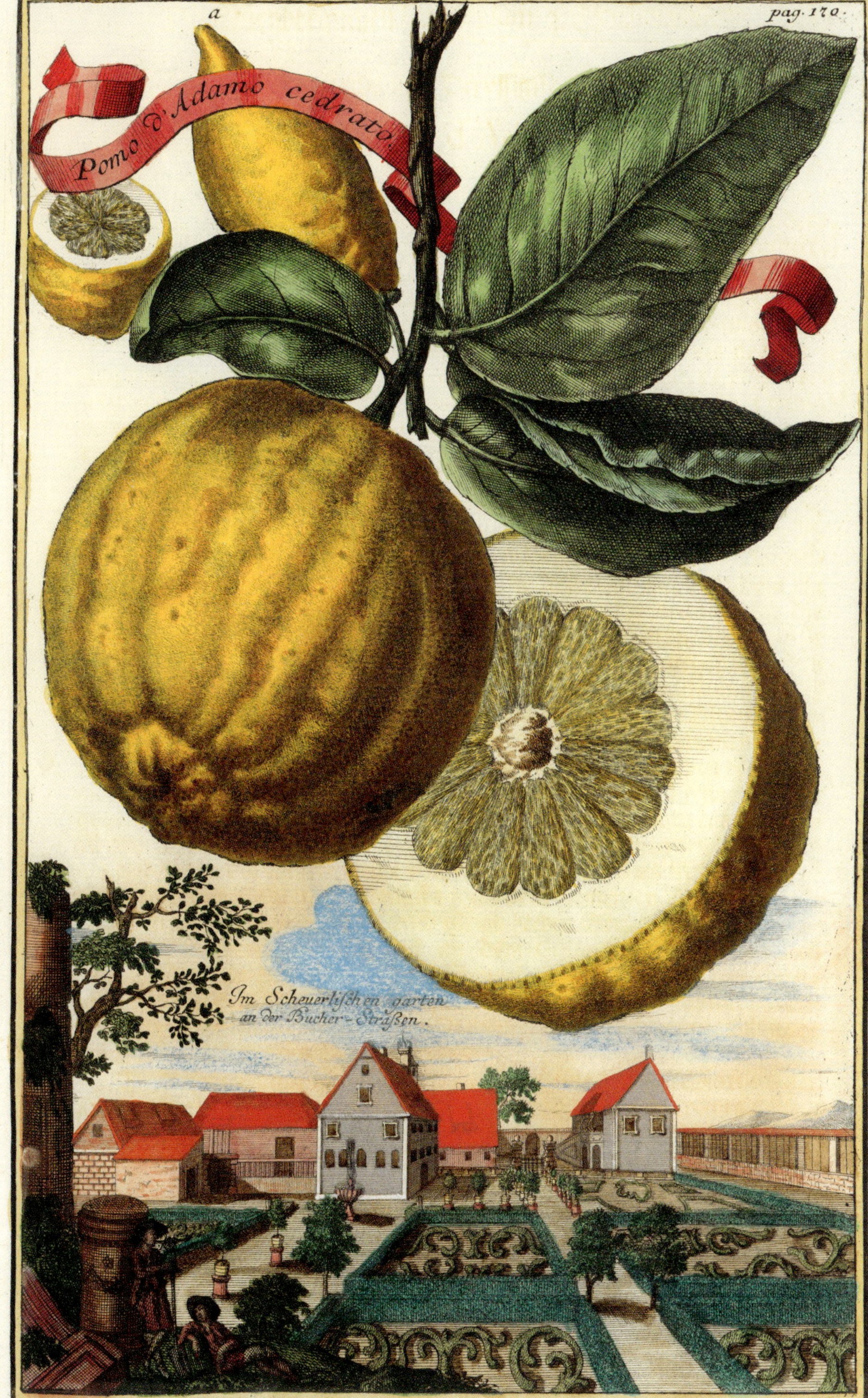

Pomo d'Adamo cedrato

Nuremberg – Garden of Mr Scheurl

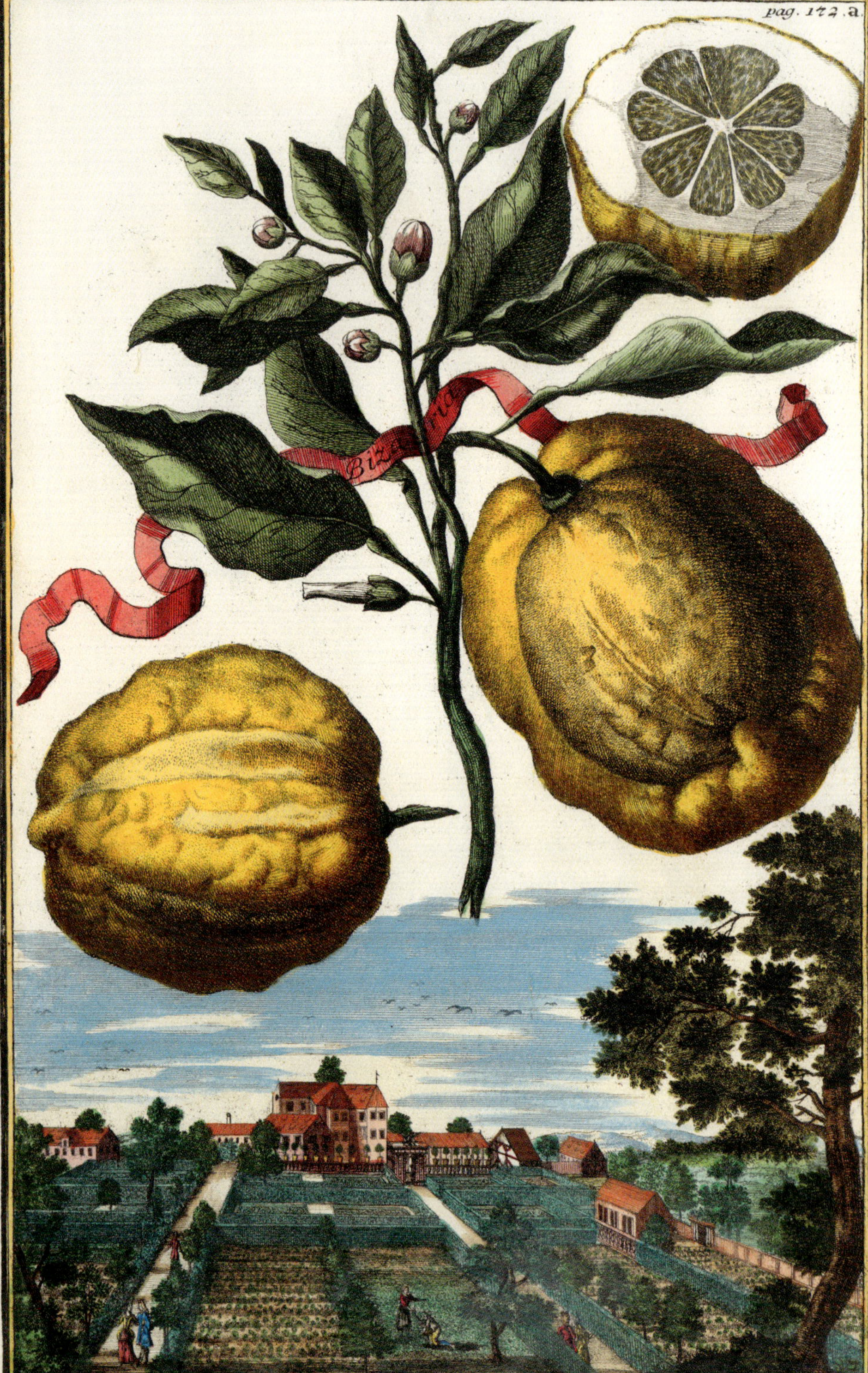

Biz[z]aria

Nuremberg, Wöhrd – Garden of Mr Buirette (formerly Blumert)

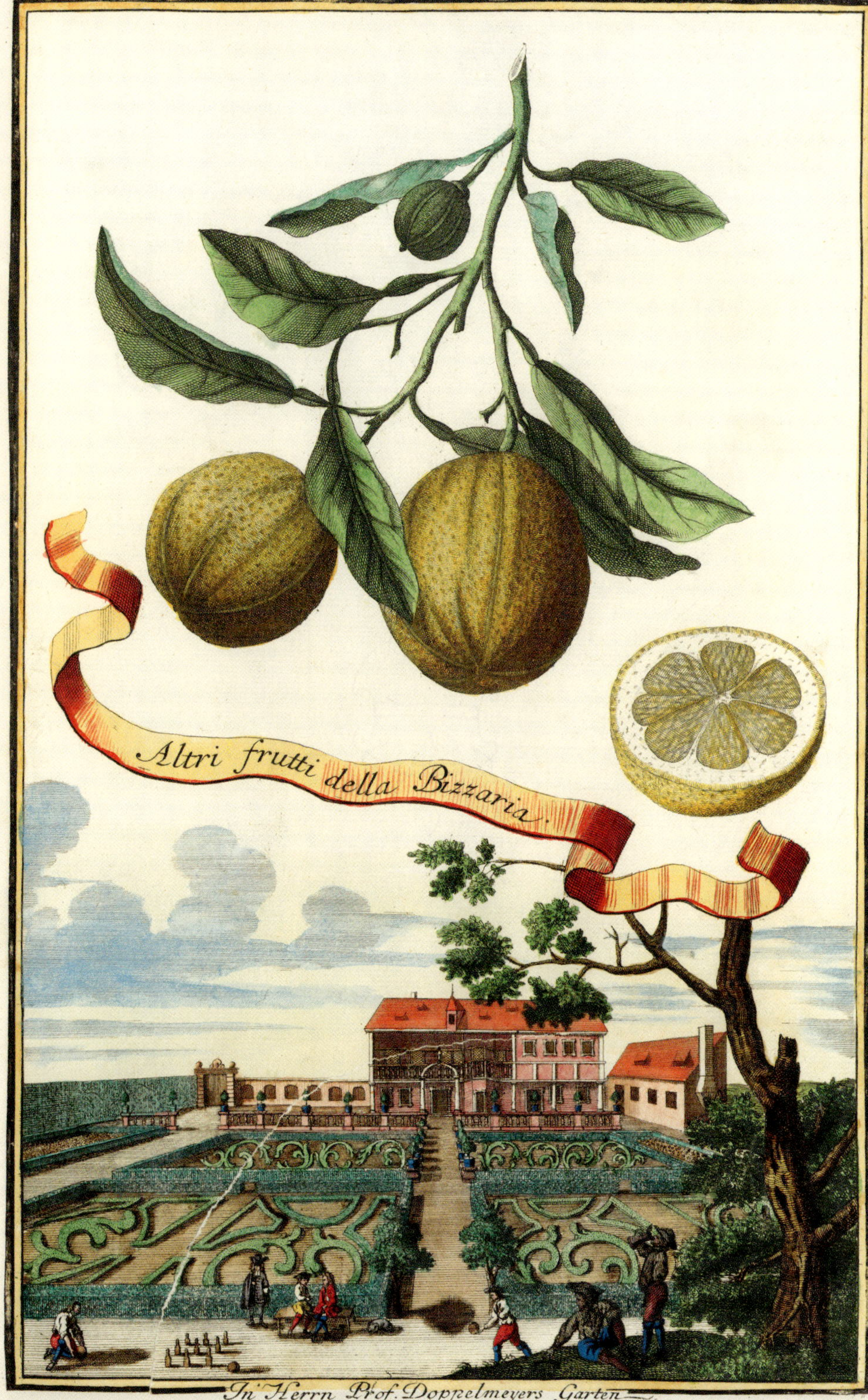

Altri frutti della Bizzaria

Nuremberg, St Johannis –
Garden of Prof Johann Gabriel Doppelmayr

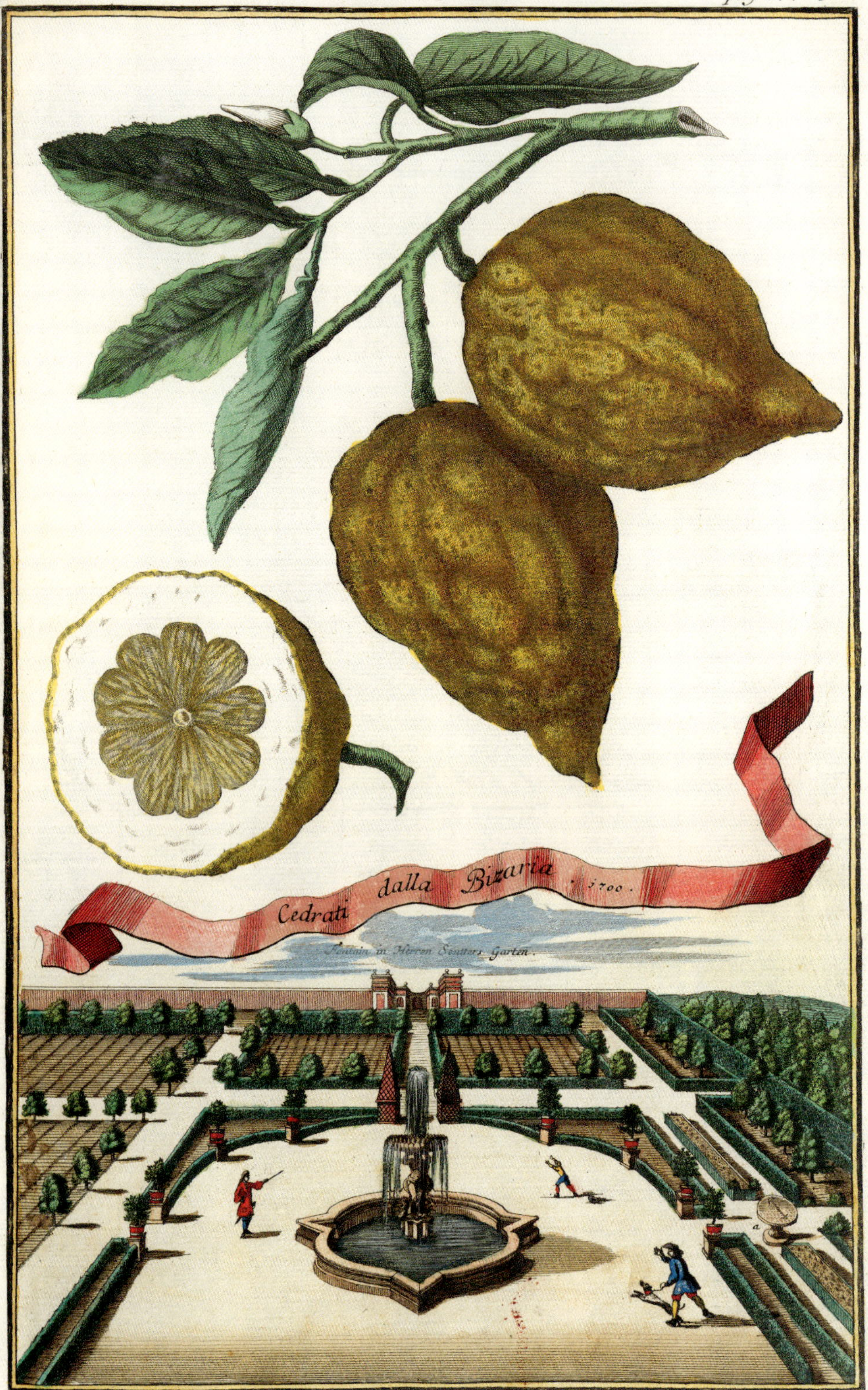

Cedrati dalla Biz[z]aria

Nuremberg, Wöhrd – Garden of Mr Seutter

Cedrati dalla Biz[z]aria

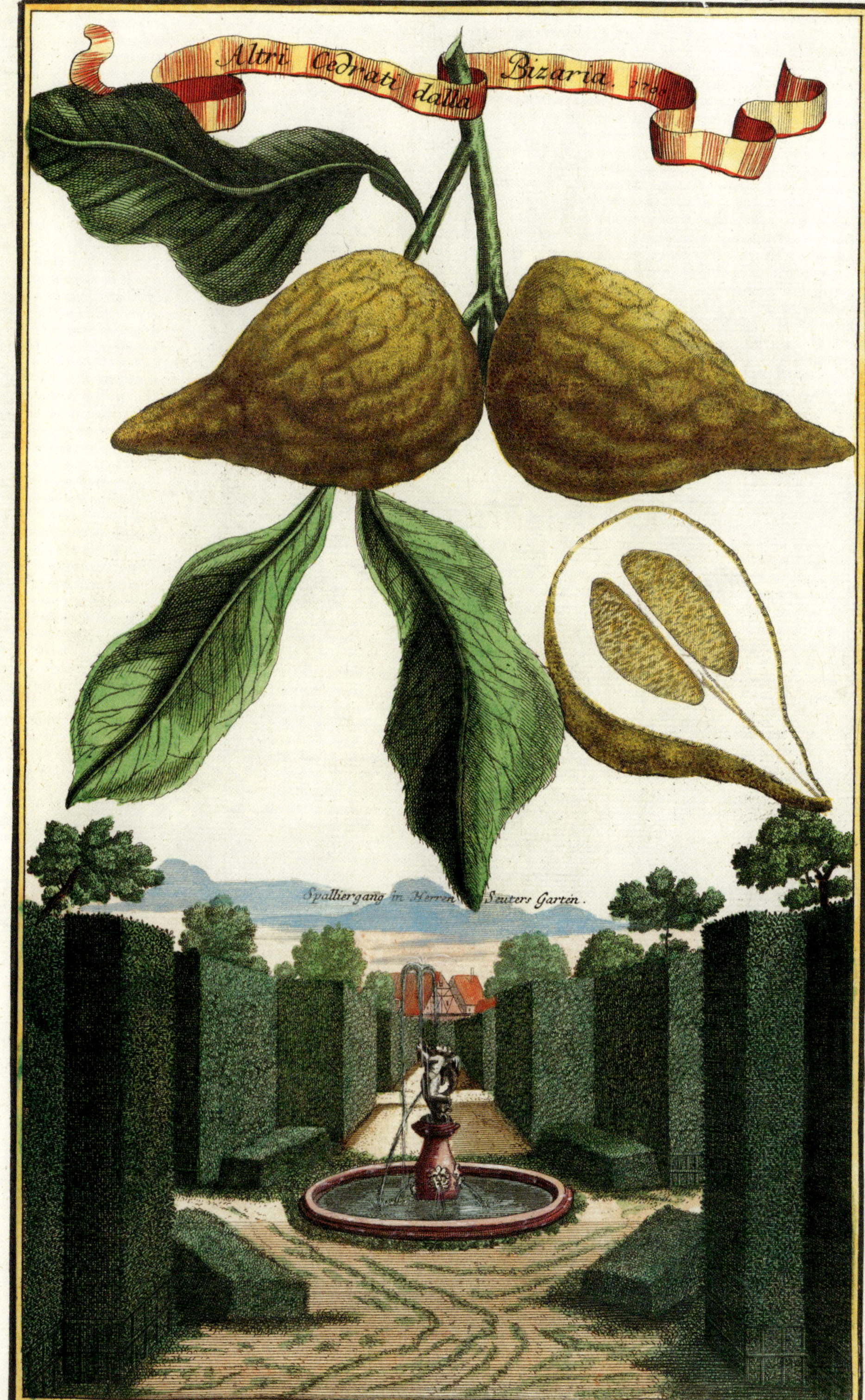

Nuremberg, Wöhrd – Garden of Mr Seutter

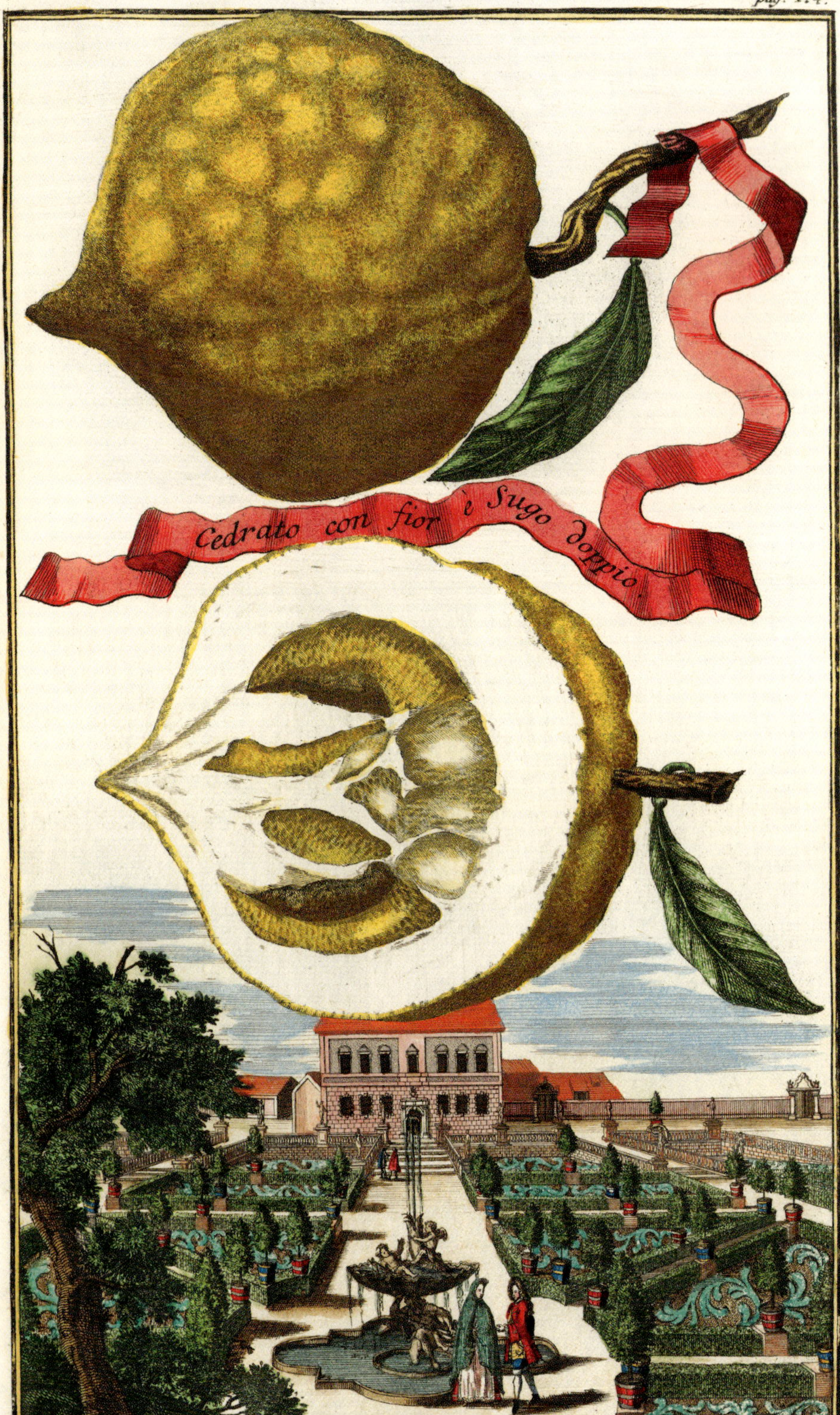

Cedrato con fior e Sugo doppio

Nuremberg, Wöhrd – Garden of Dr Falckner

Cedrato col Pigolo e Sugo doppio

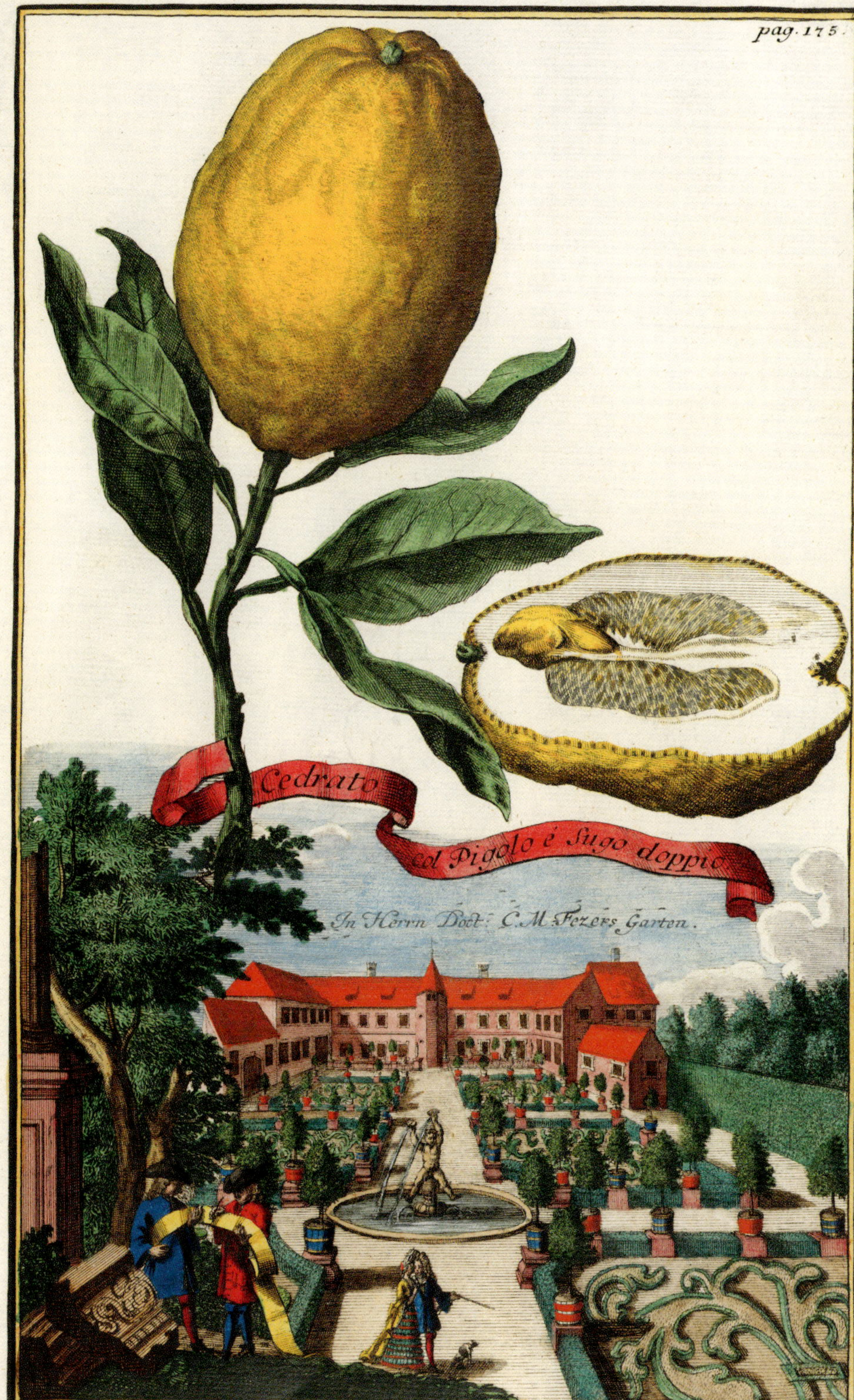

Nuremberg, St Johannis –
Garden of Dr Christoph Magnus Fetzer

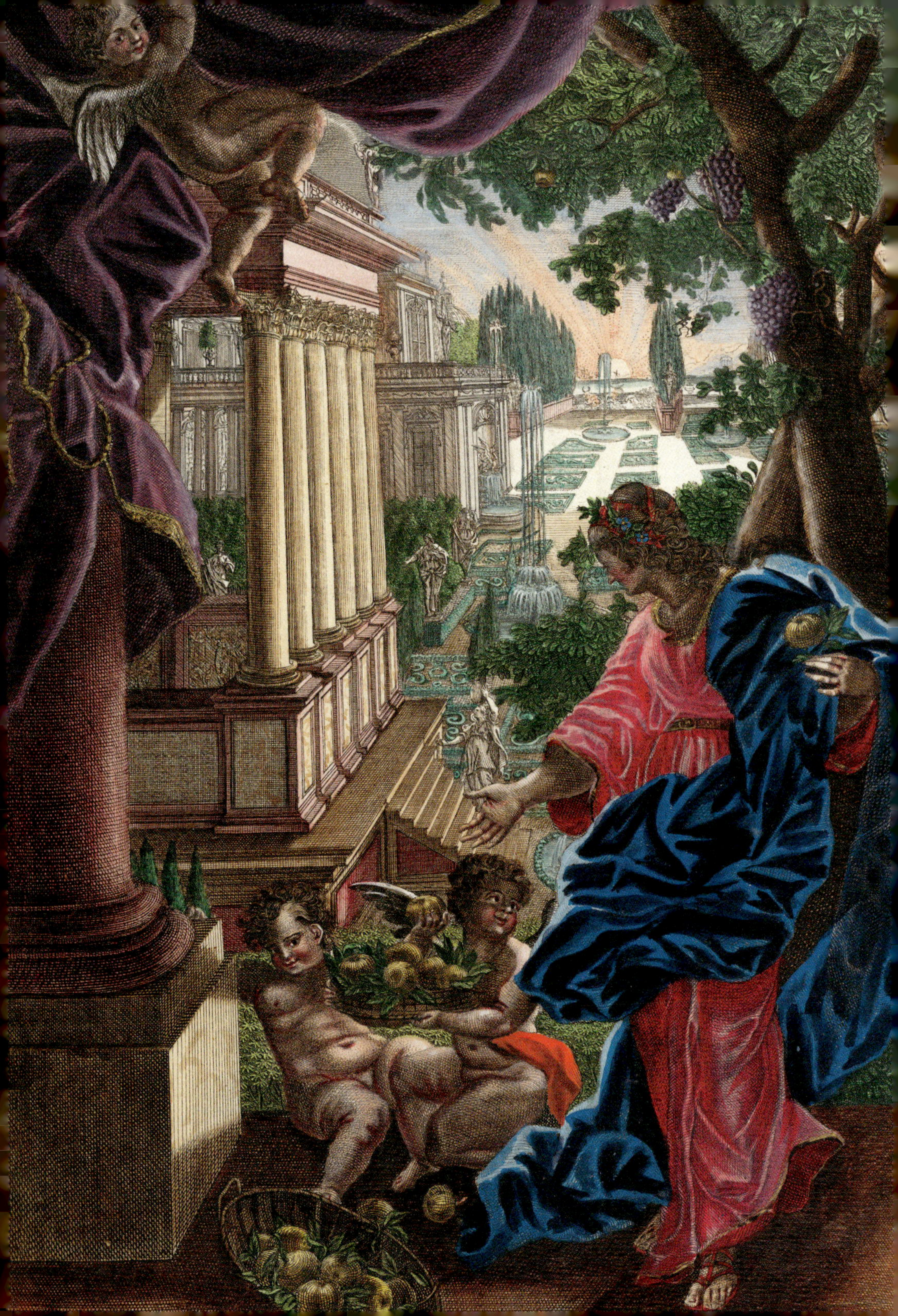

Der Nürnbergischen HESPERIDUM Vierdter Theil/ HESPERTHUSA.

* * * * * * *

Das Erste Capitel.

Von denen Pomerantzen insgemein.

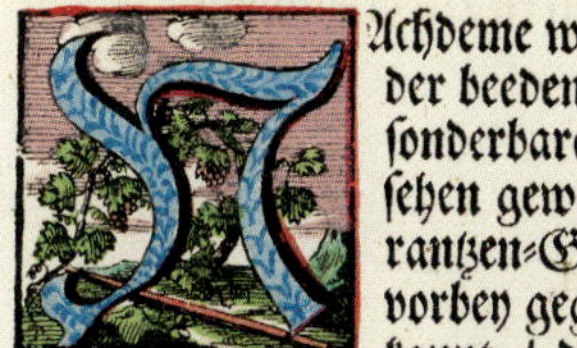

Achdeme wir die berühmteste Citronat- und Citronen-Gärten der beeden Hesperidum Ægle und Arethusæ besuchet/ und mit sonderbarem Vergnügen besehen haben/ wäre es ein übles Versehen gewesen / wann wir den dritten/ und zwar den Pomerantzen-Garten/der dritten Schwester Hesperthusæ allerdings vorbey gegangen und unbesucht gelassen hätten / zumal bekannt / daß selbiger nicht minder berühmt / und an seiner Ordinantz denen andern nichts bevor lasse / auch die Hesperthusa denen Fremden nicht weniger/als ihre Schwestern/mit möglichster Höflichkeit zu begegnen pflege/ daher wir dann nicht ermangelten/ folgenden Tages uns auch daselbsthin am frühen Morgen zu verfügen/ geziemender massen anmelden zu lassen / und von der Hesperthusa selbst/ auf das freundlichste empfangen zu werden: Gleich bey dem ersten Eintritt stunde lincker Seiten ein wol und zierlich-erbauter Palast/ der erstreckete sich von selbigem am Prospect in der schönsten Ebene sehr weit hinaus/ biß an einen breiten und Schiff-reichen See/ welchen die eben dazumal erst kurtz zuvor aufgegangene Sonne/ mit ihrem Gold-Purpur/auf das schönste bemahlte / und mit dem Glantz ihrer Strahlen auf das zierlichste beleuchtete/ die Alleen waren theils mit Spaliern und Wänden von Myrten/und theils Cypressen bekleidet / anbey mit dazwischen stehenden herrlichen Statuen gezieret/ und in der Mitte des Haupt-Gangs / wie auch der zierlichen Blumen-Felder/ sahe man das helleste Wasser der schönsten Fontainen hoch in die Höhe spritzen/ der artigen Grotten-Wercke zu geschweigen; die Pomerantzen-Bäume verschiedener Arten sahe man in unglaublicher Menge Zeil-weiß beysammen in der Erde/ theils auch in Geschirren hier und dar vertheilet stehen/und mit ihren güldenen Aepffeln und Gold-farben Früchten prangen / welches um so viel desto zierlicher stunde/ und das Auge um so mehr ergötzete / als diese Bäume auf verschiedene Art entweder an der Cron rund gewöhnet / oder mit der Stutz-Scheer spitzig / nach Art der Cypressen und Pyramiden / zugeschnitten und also zierlich fortzuwachsen gezogen worden / ja es ist fast nicht wol zu glauben / welch einen starcken und lieblichen Geruch die annoch an denen Bäumen hangende Blühe von sich dufftete/ daß man auch solches an ziemlich weit entfernten Orten/und so

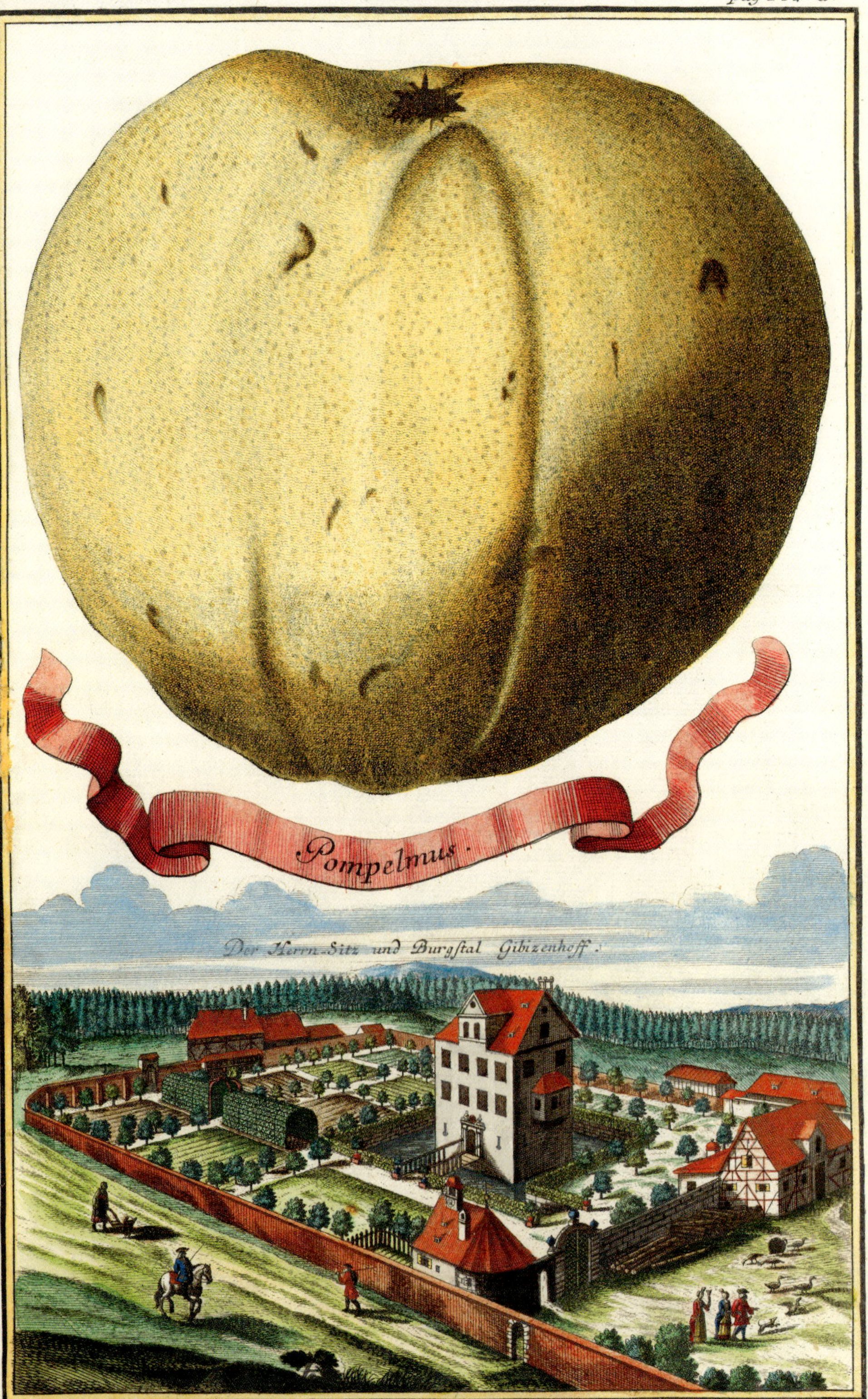

Pompelmus

Nuremberg, Gibitzenhof – The Manor. *Pages 206/207* Personification of Hesperia, and beginning of the fourth section of vol. I

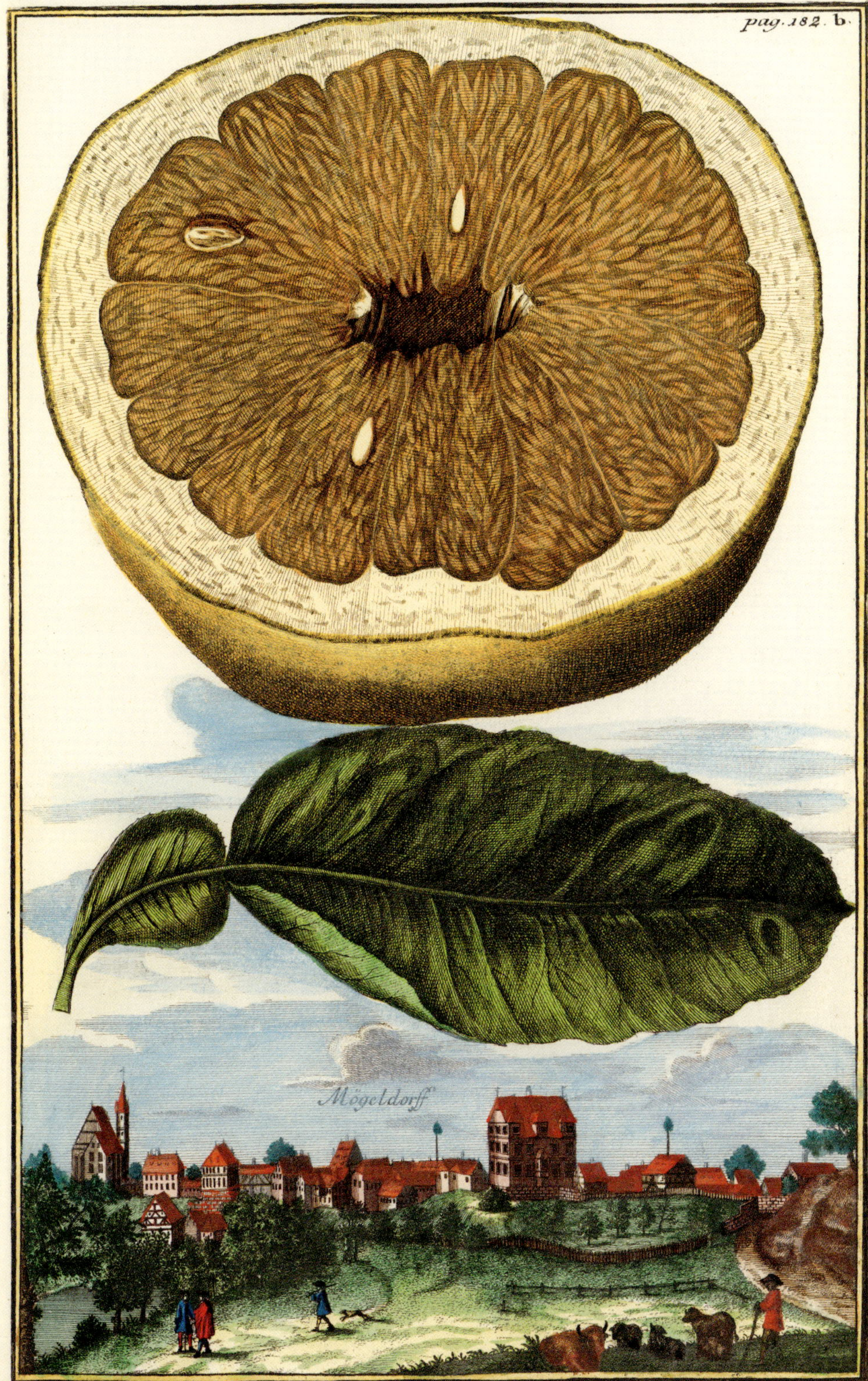

Pompelmus

Nuremberg, Mögeldorf

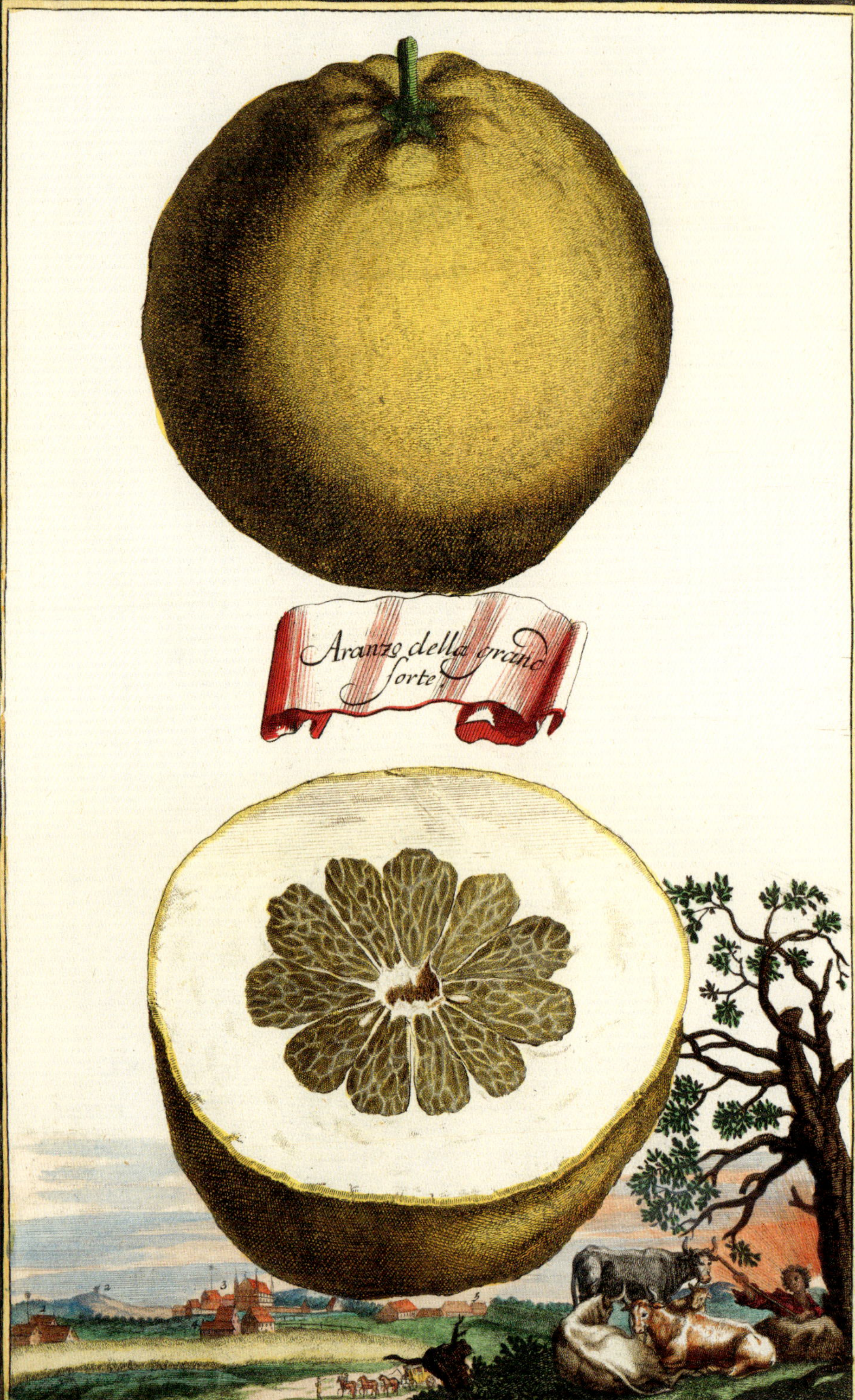

1. Herrn-hütten 2. Spitalhoffen. 3. Schoppershoffen. 4. Mäierhoff. 5. Schibelberg.

Aranzo della grand Sorte

Nuremberg, 1. Herrnhütte 2. Spitalhof 3. Schoppershof 4. Meierhof 5. Schübelsberg

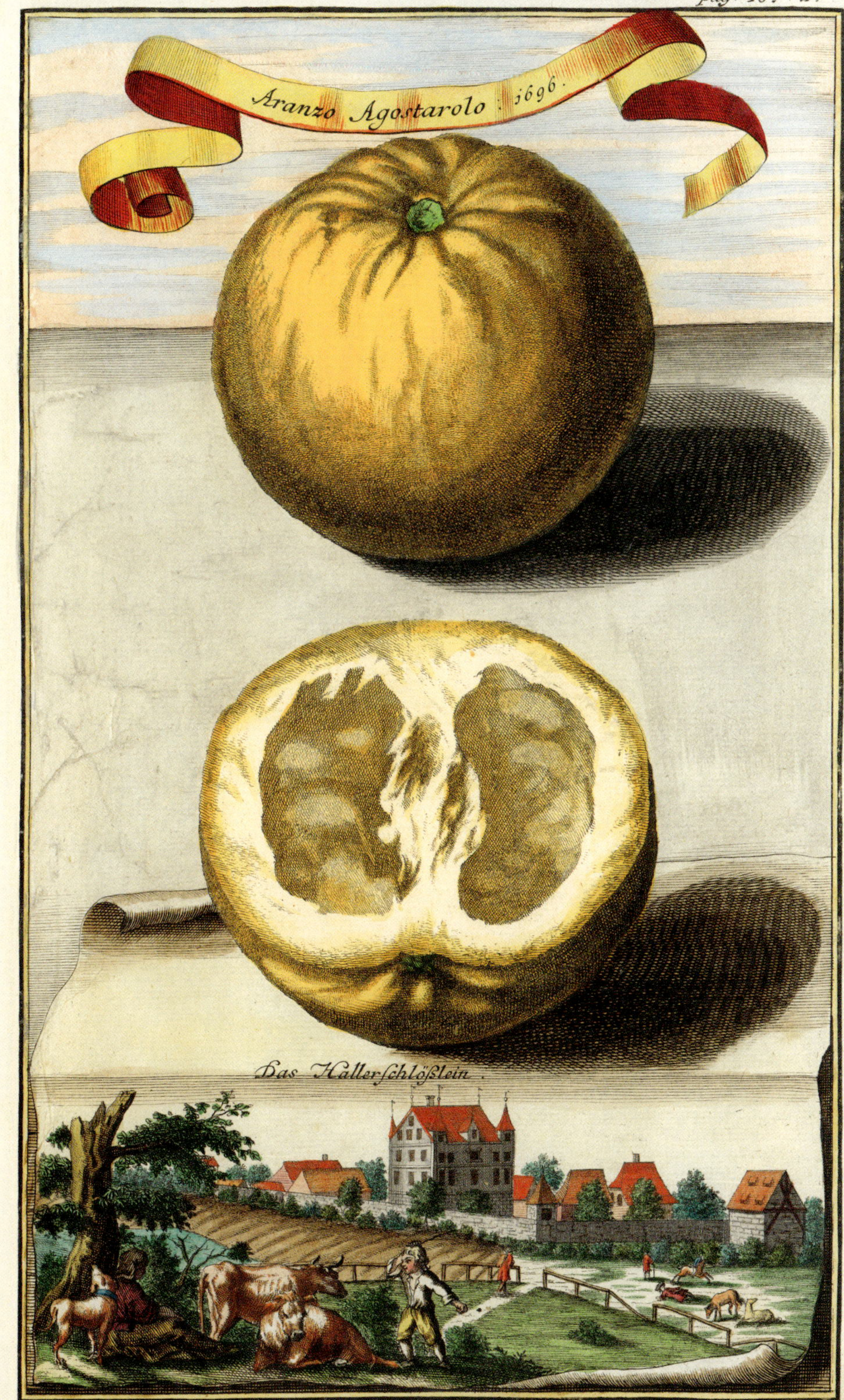

Aranzo Agostarolo

Nuremberg, Mögeldorf – Haller Manor

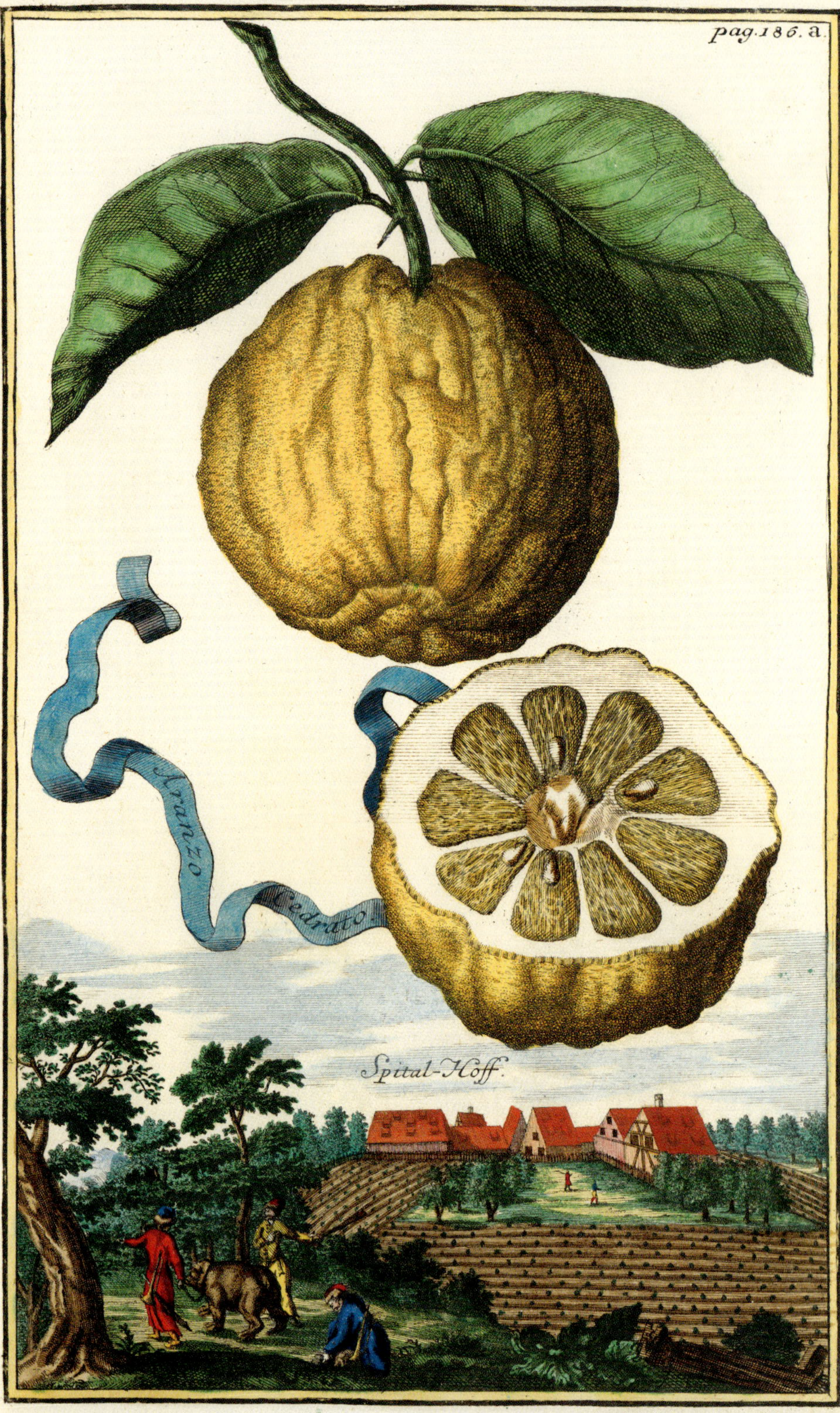

Aranzo Cedrato

Nuremberg, Spitalhof

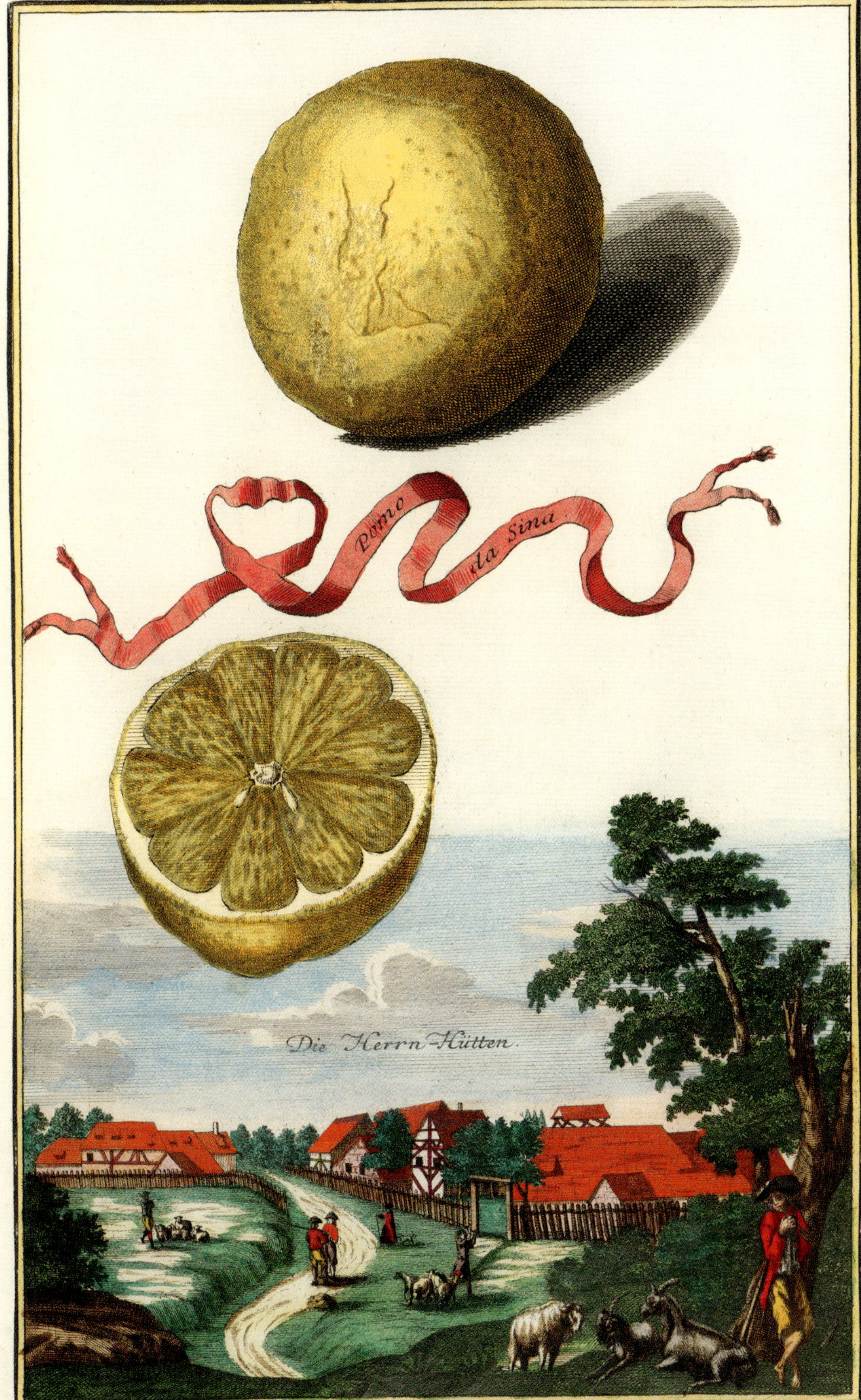
pag. 186 b.
Pomo da Sina
Die Herrn-Hütten.
P. Decker fecit.

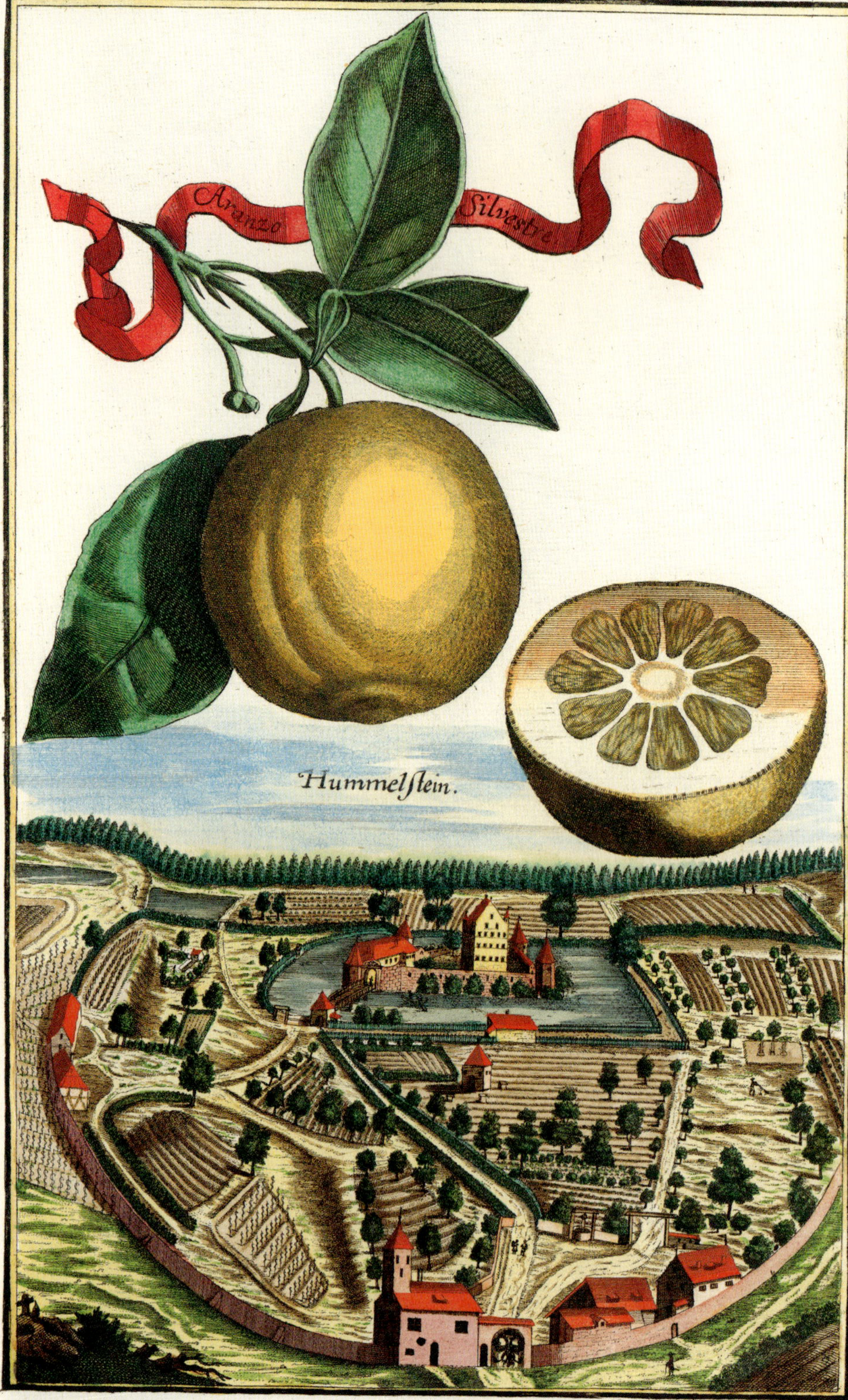

Aranzo Silvestre

Nuremberg, Hummelstein

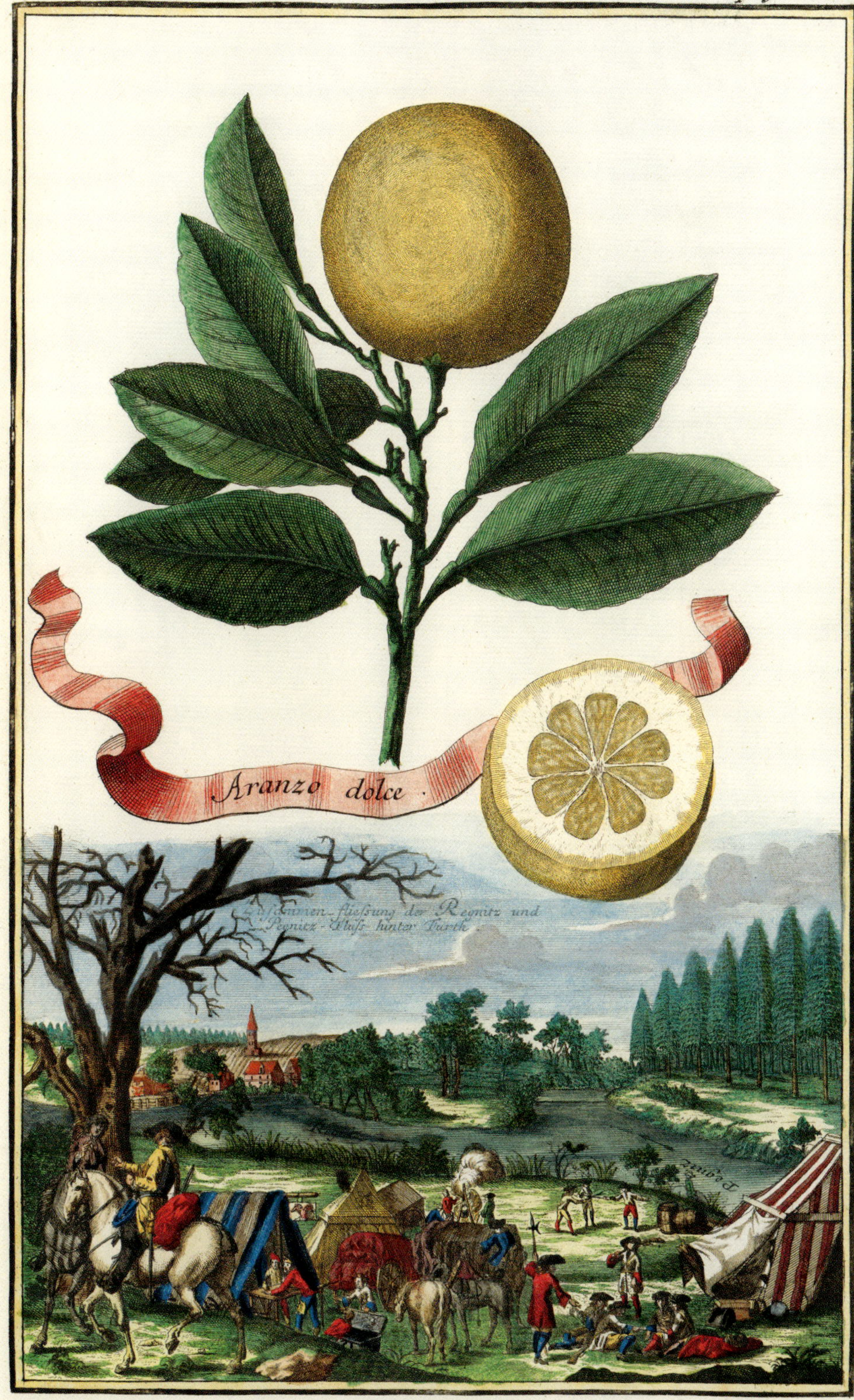

Aranzo dolce

Fürth – Confluence of the Rednitz and Pegnitz Rivers

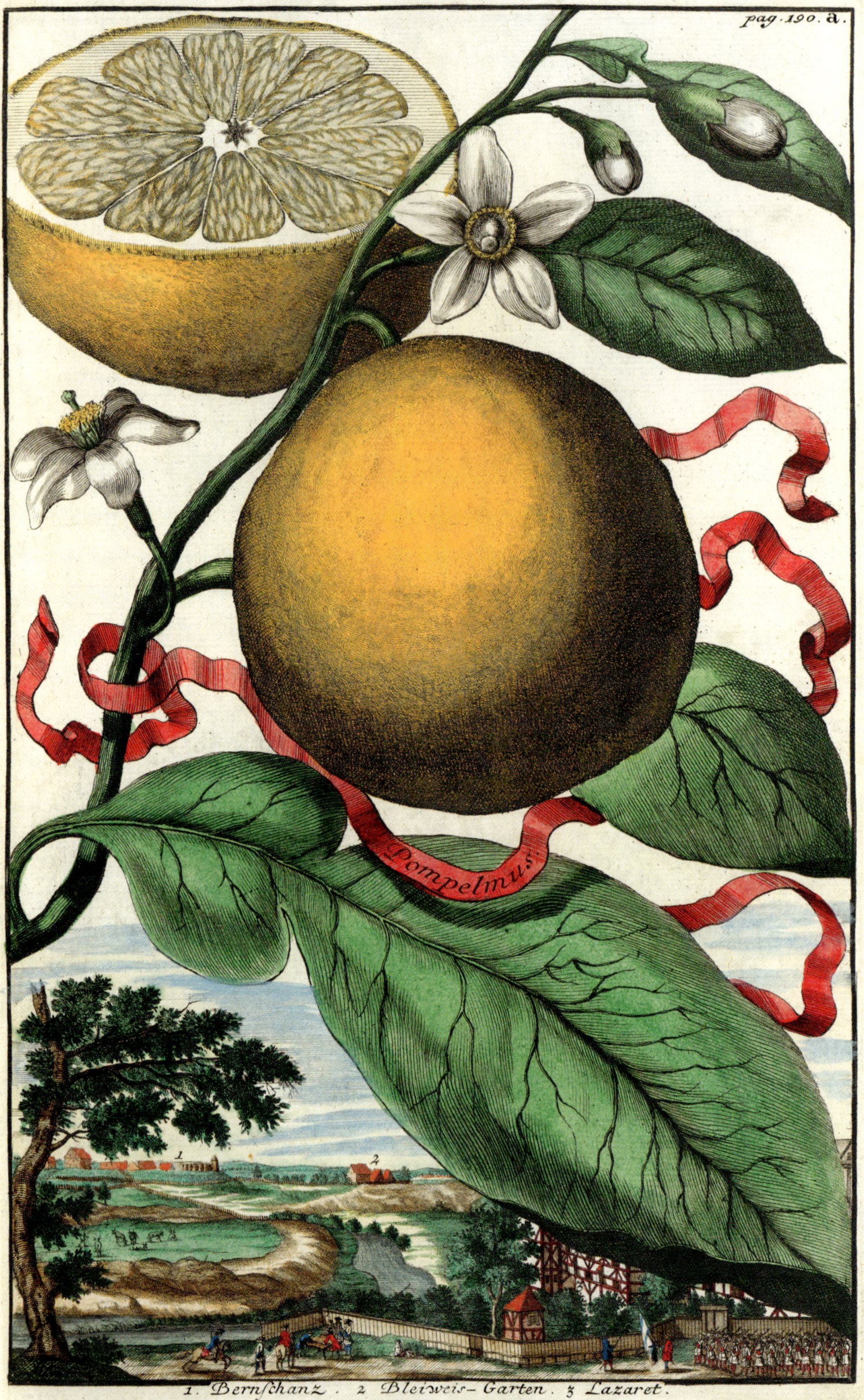

Pompelmus

Nuremberg, 1. Bärenschanze 2. Bleiweiß 3. Infirmary

Aranzo con foglia rizza

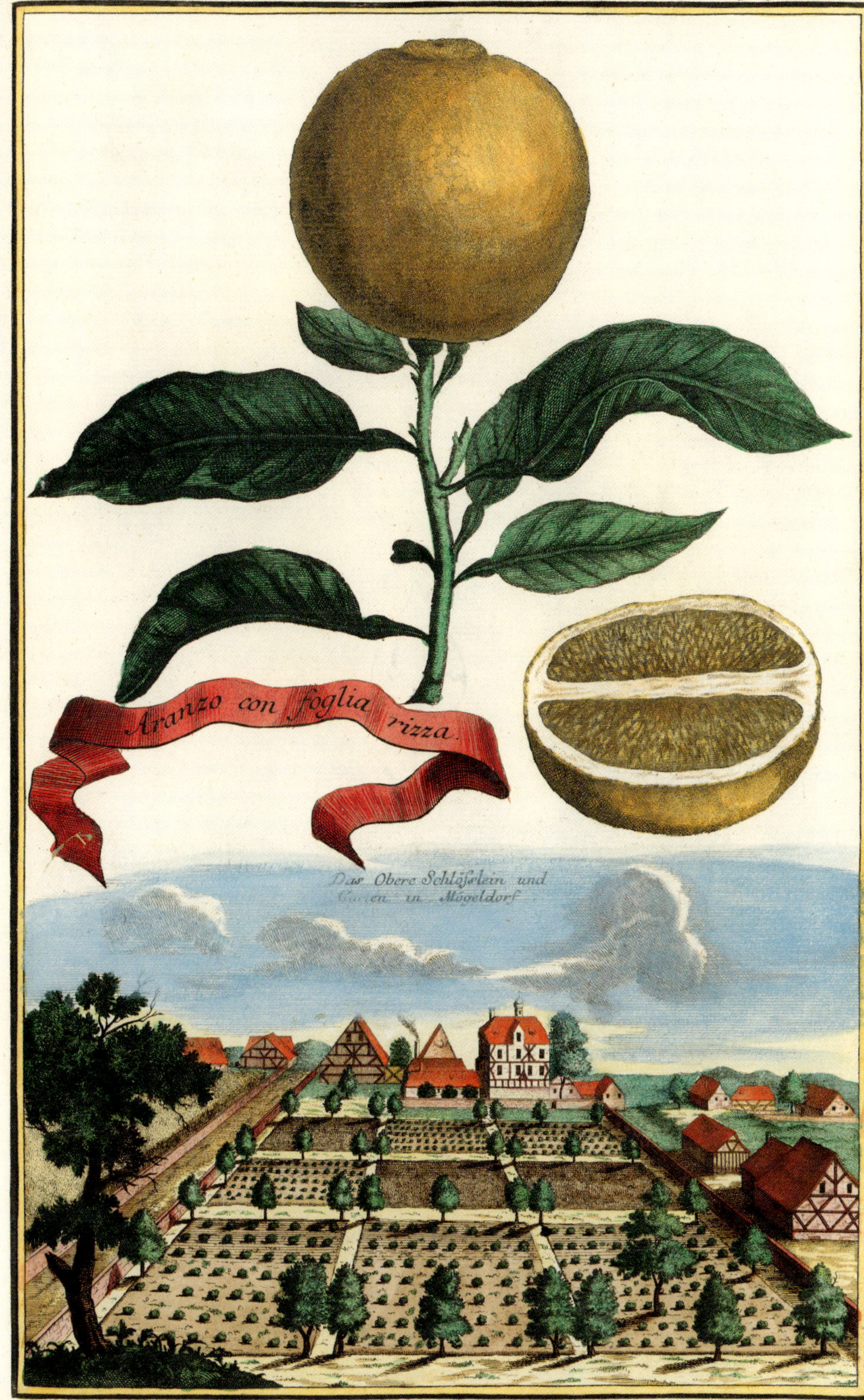

Nuremberg, Mögeldorf – Former Link Castle

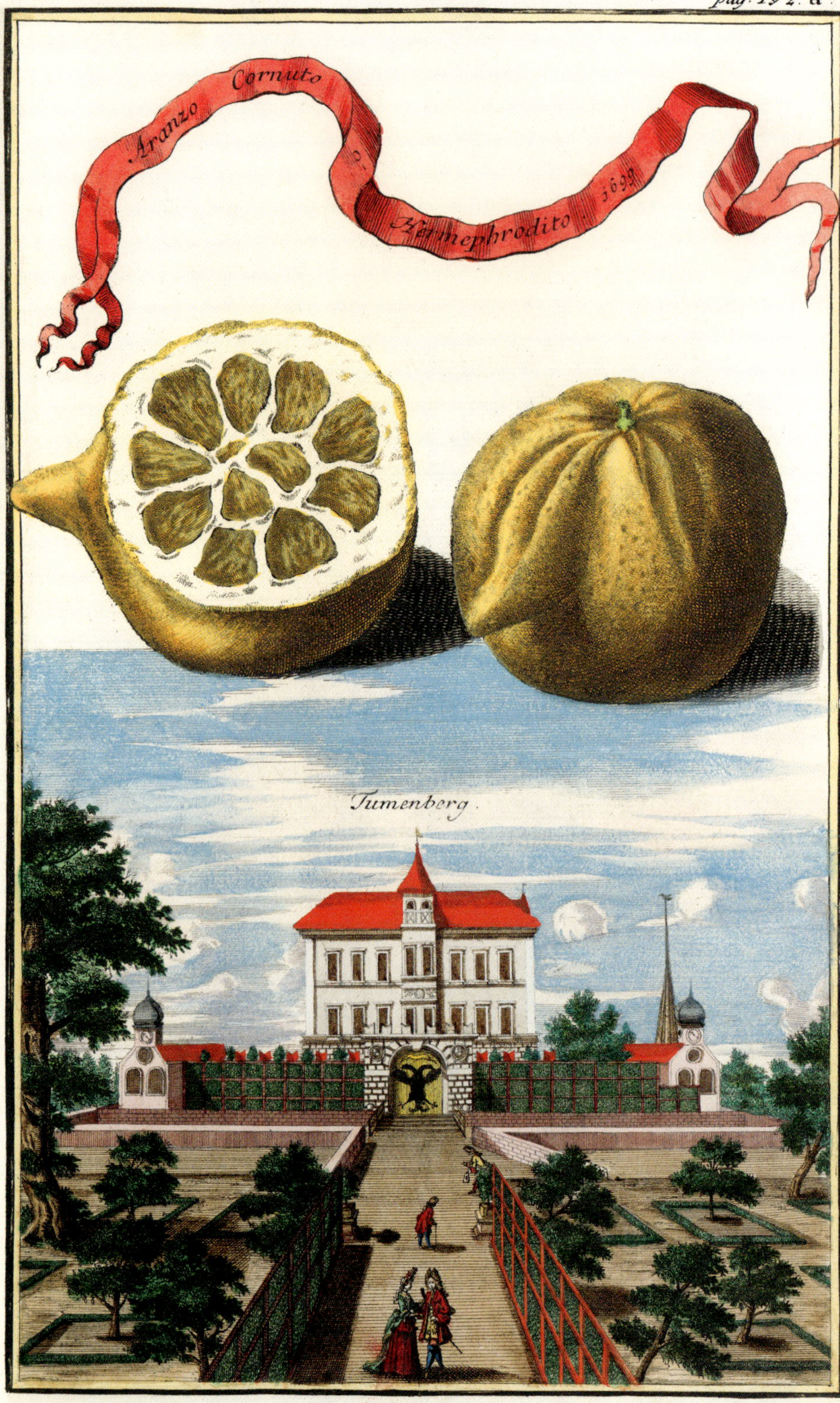

Aranzo Cornuto o Hermephrodito

Nuremberg, Thumenberg – The Manor

Aranzo Cornuto incanellato

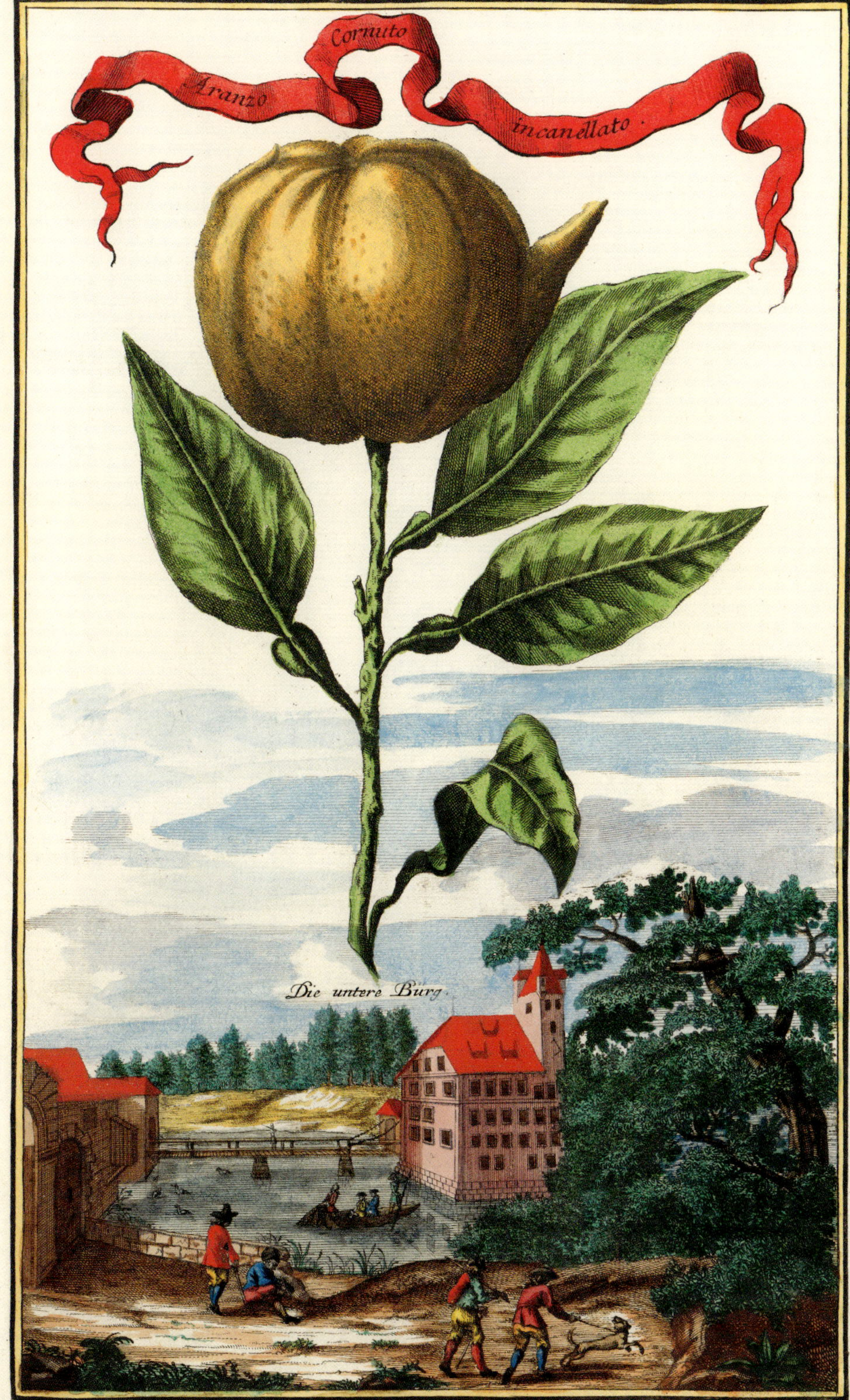

Nuremberg, Laufamholz – Unterbürg Manor

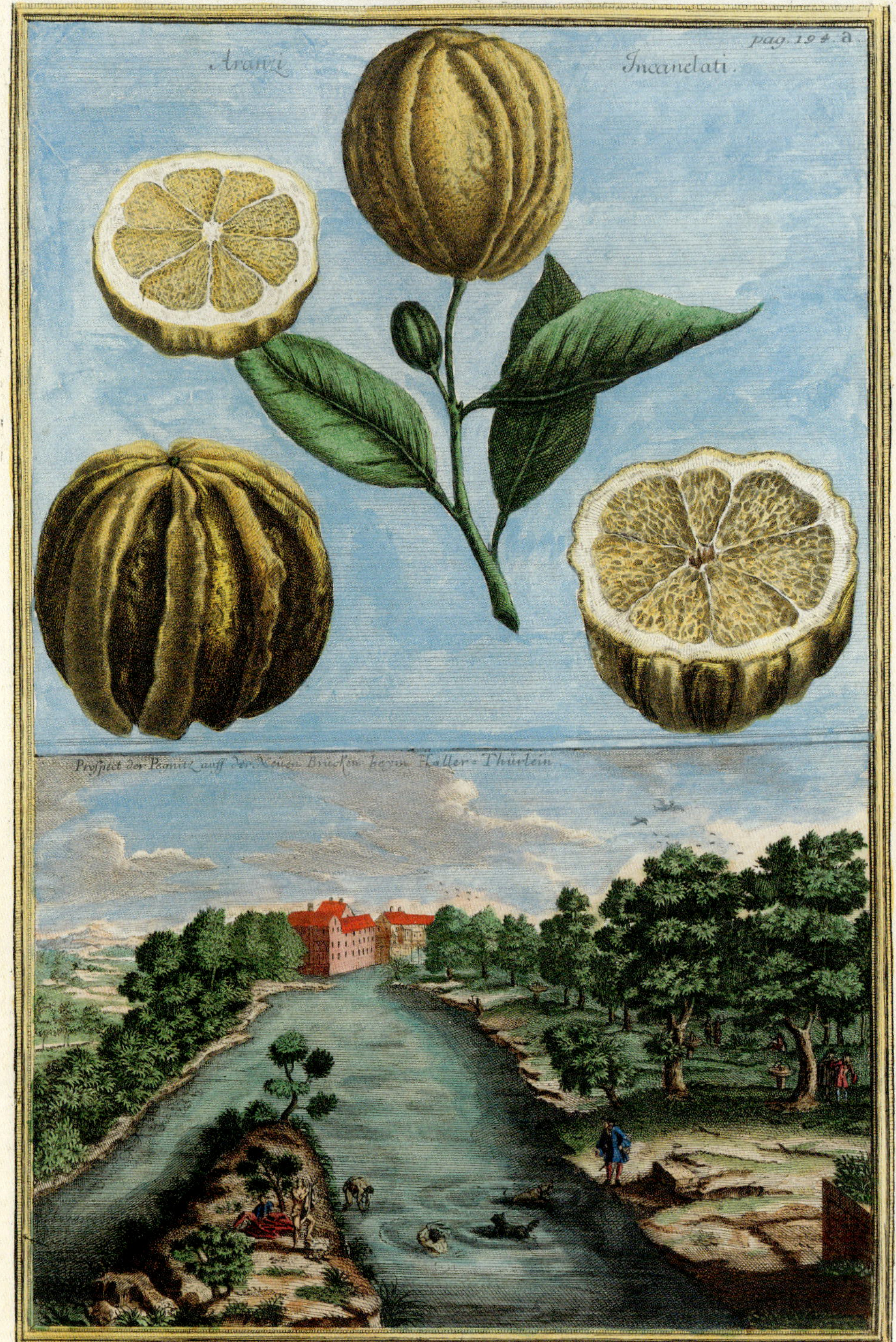

Aranzi Incanelati

Nuremberg, St Johannis – Hallertor and the River Pegnitz

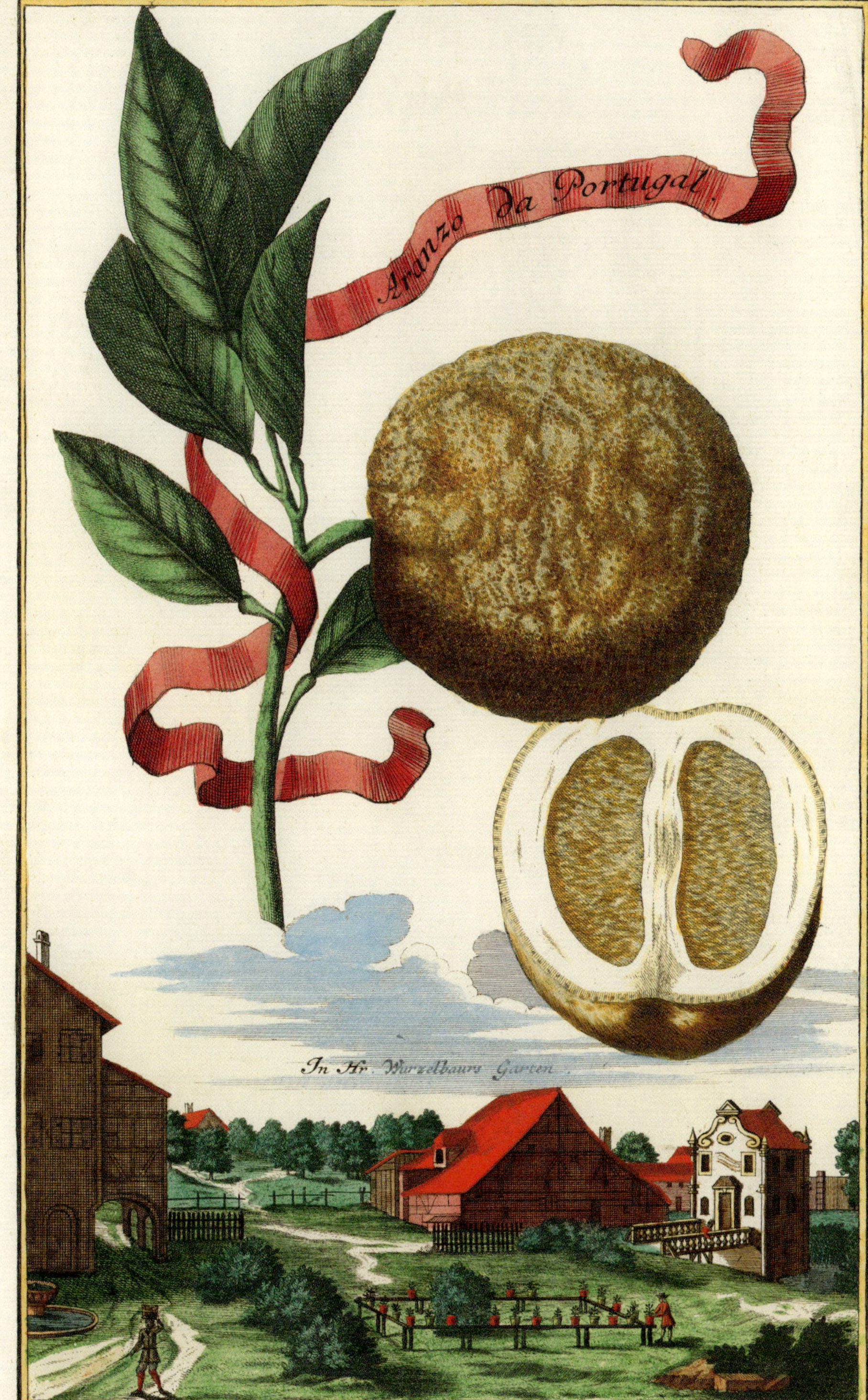

Aranzo da Portugal

Nuremberg, Kleinweidenmühle – Garden of Johann Friedrich Wurzelbauer

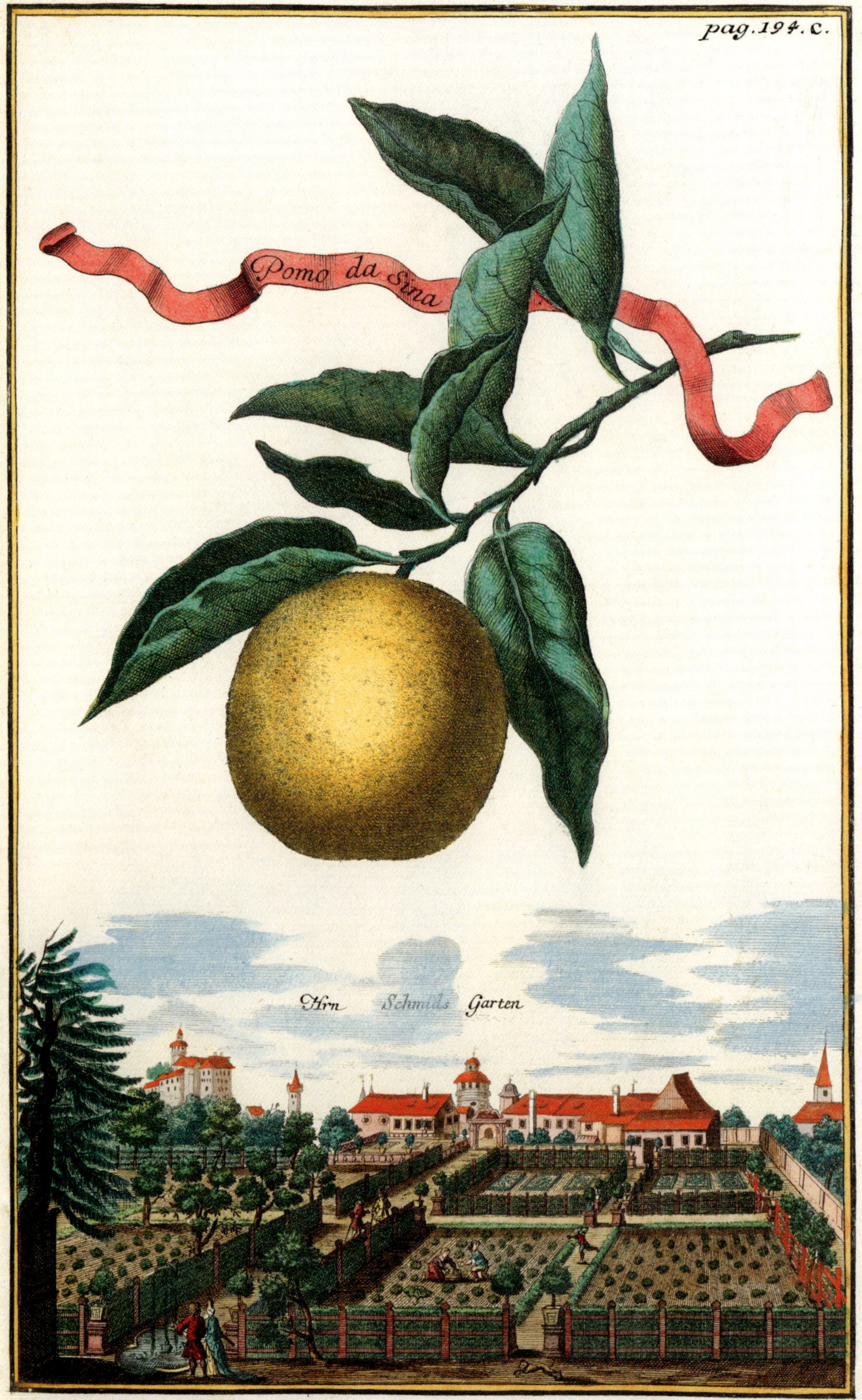

Pomo da Sina

Nuremberg, St Johannis – Garden of Mr Schmidt

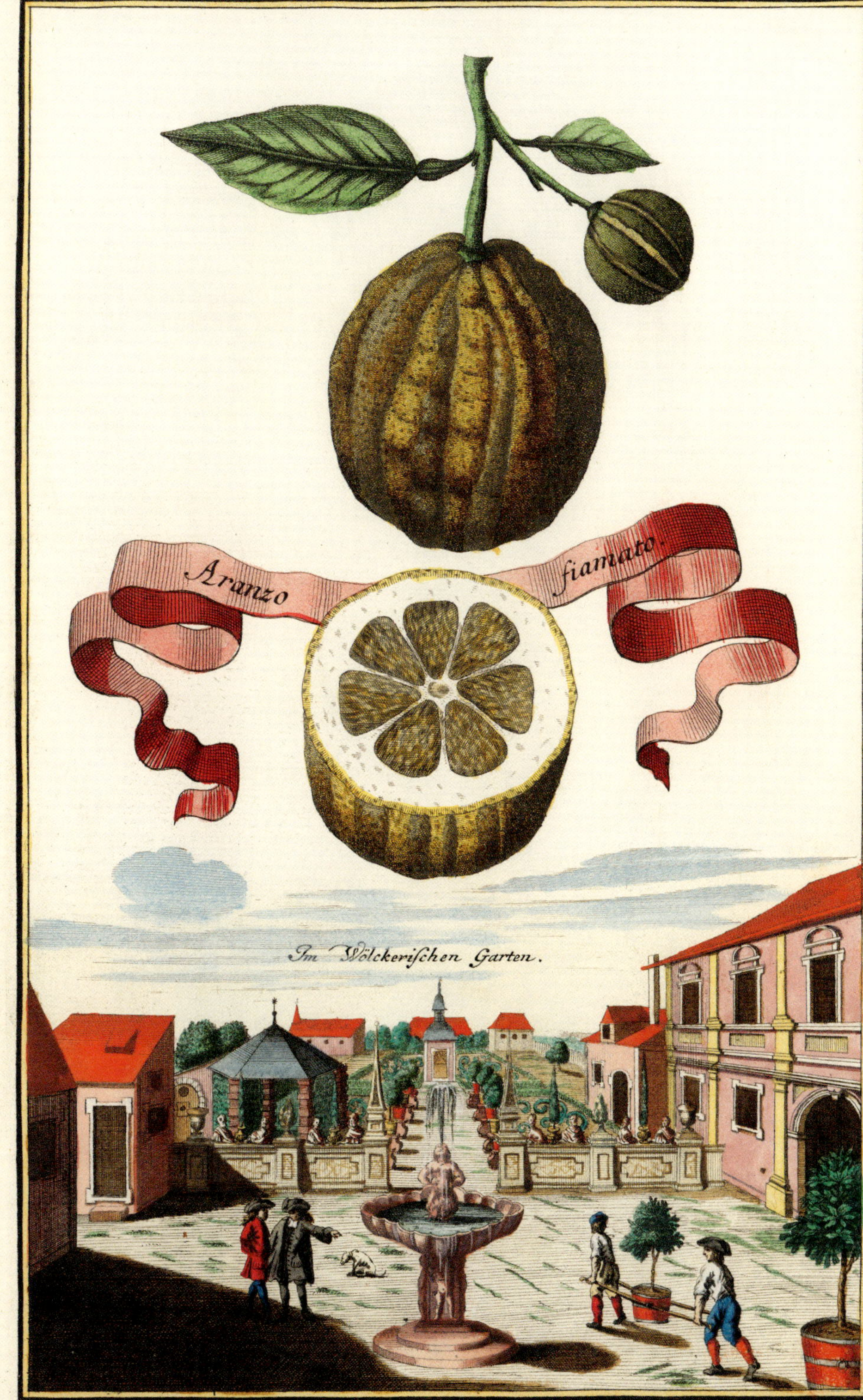

Aranzo fiamato

Nuremberg, St Johannis – Garden of Mr Wölcker

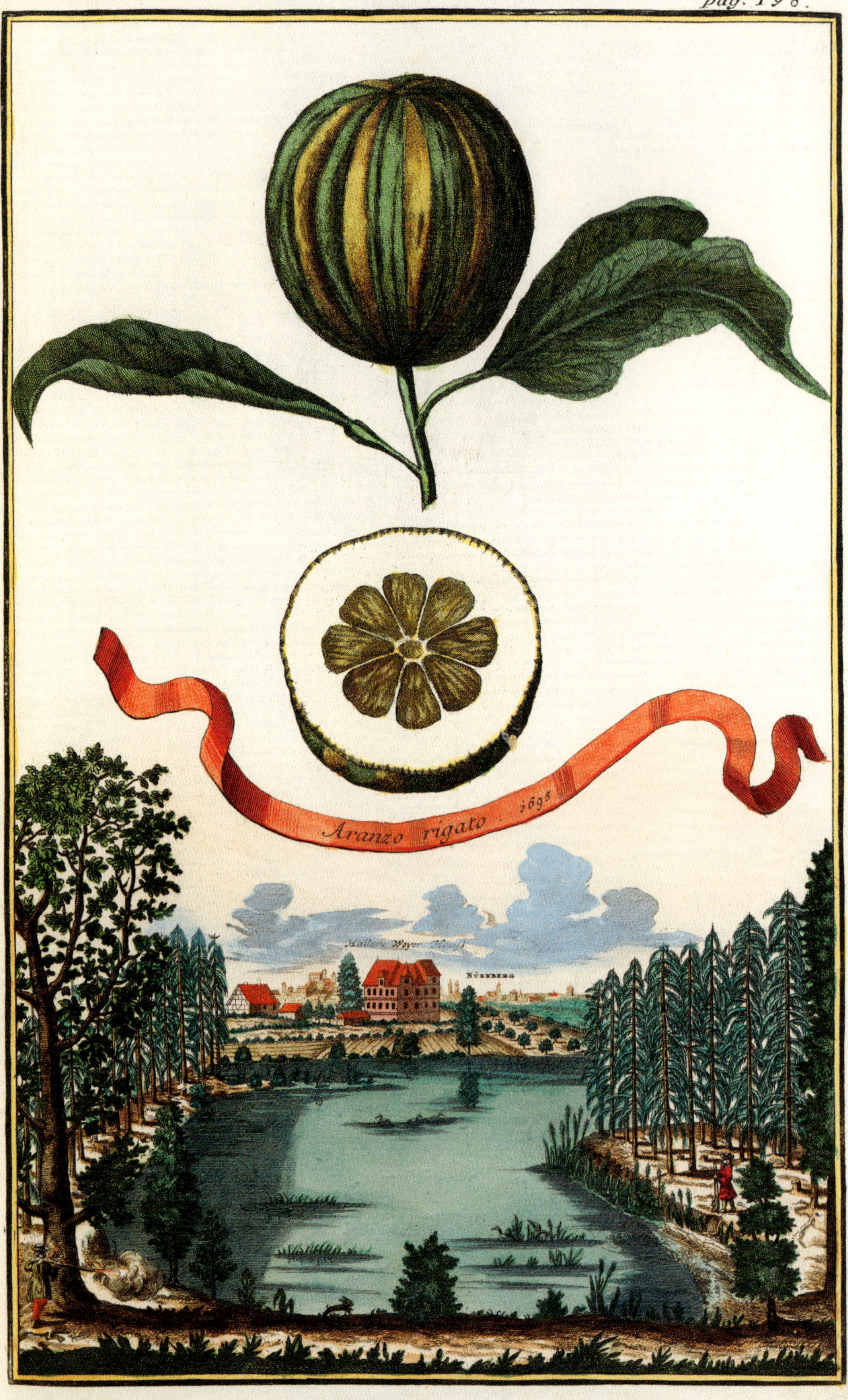
pag. 198.
Aranzo rigato 1695
NÜRNBERG

Aranzo rigato con foglia larga

Nuremberg – Garden of Mr M. Vatter

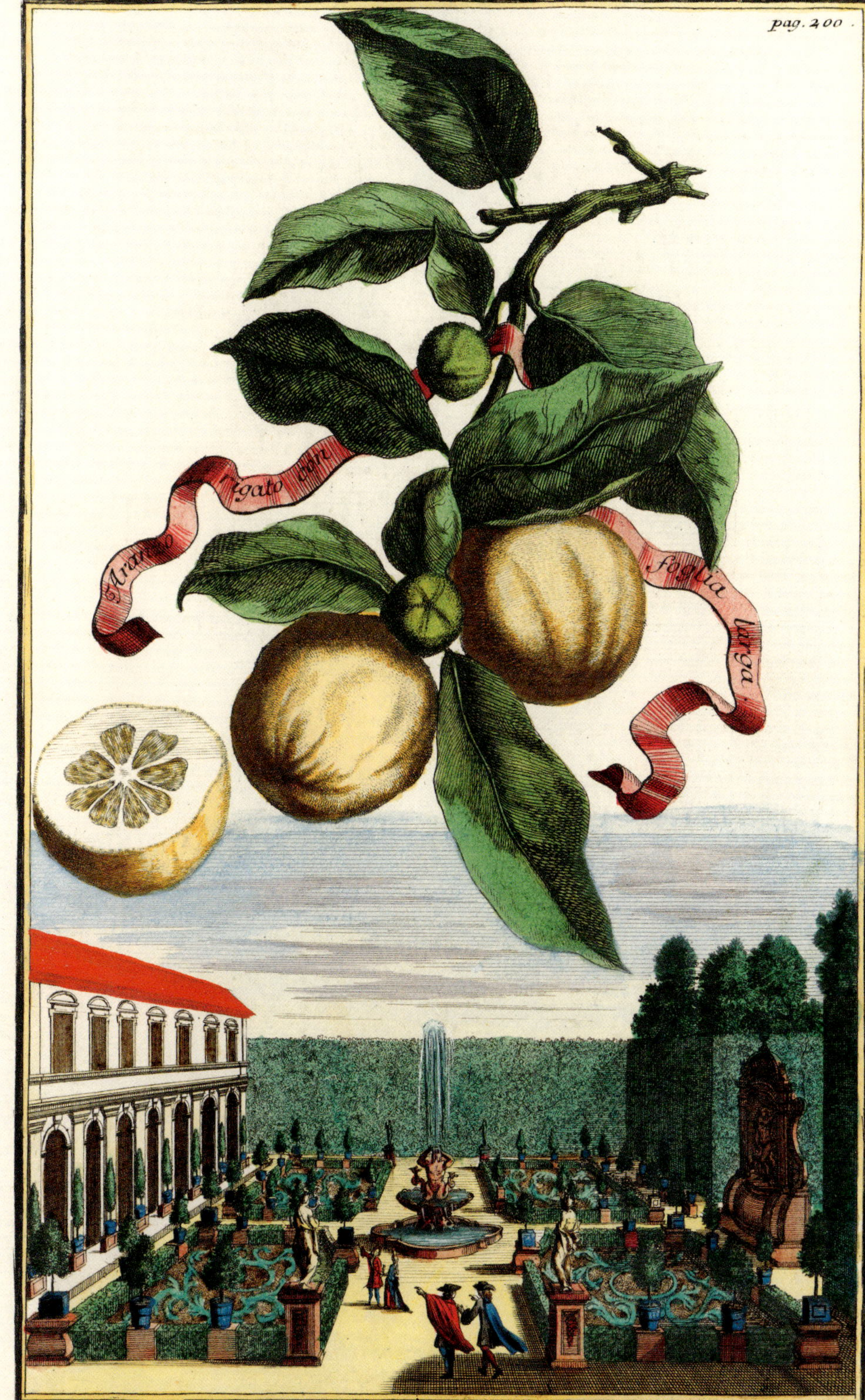

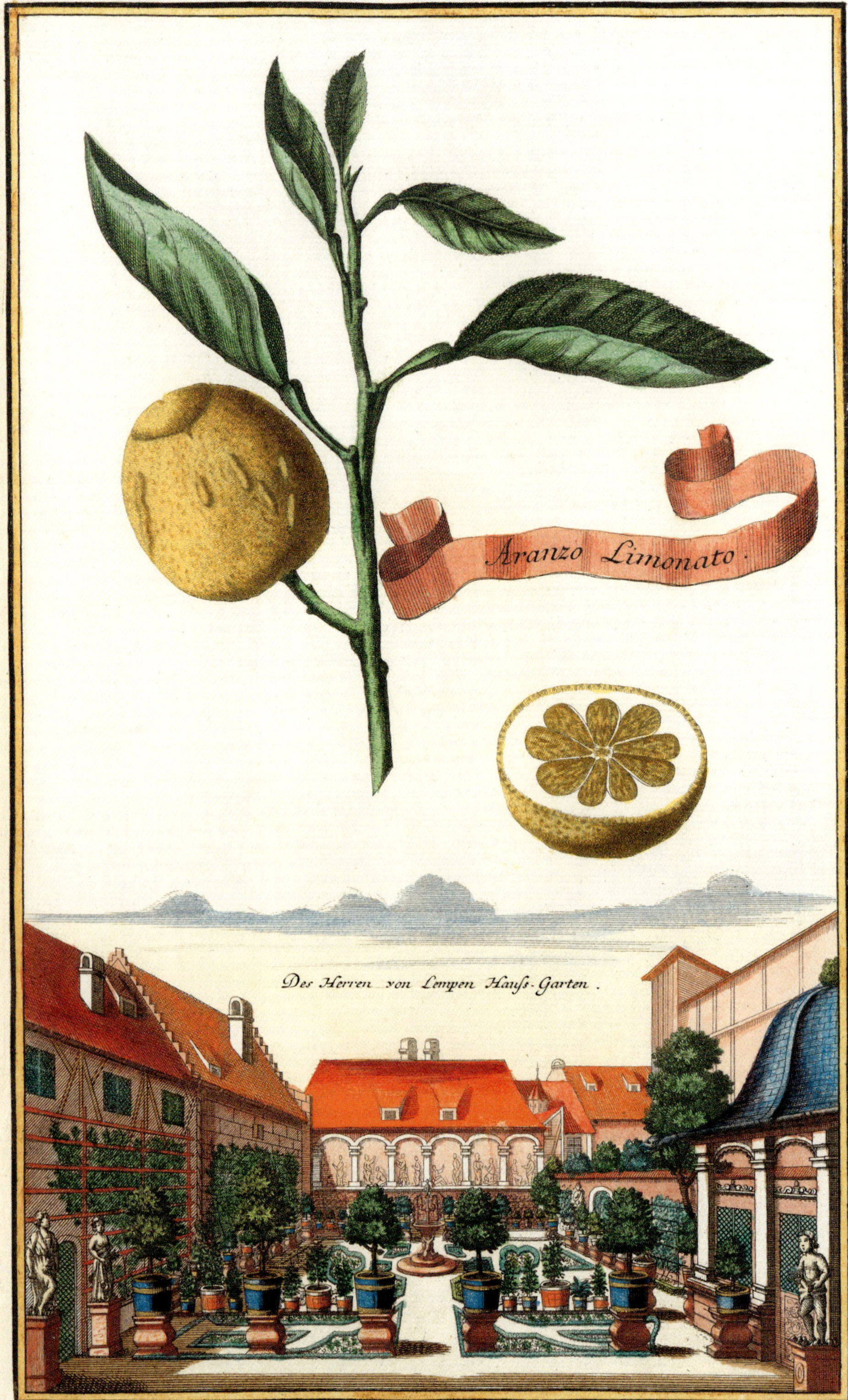

Aranzo Limonato

Nuremberg – Garden of Mr Lempen

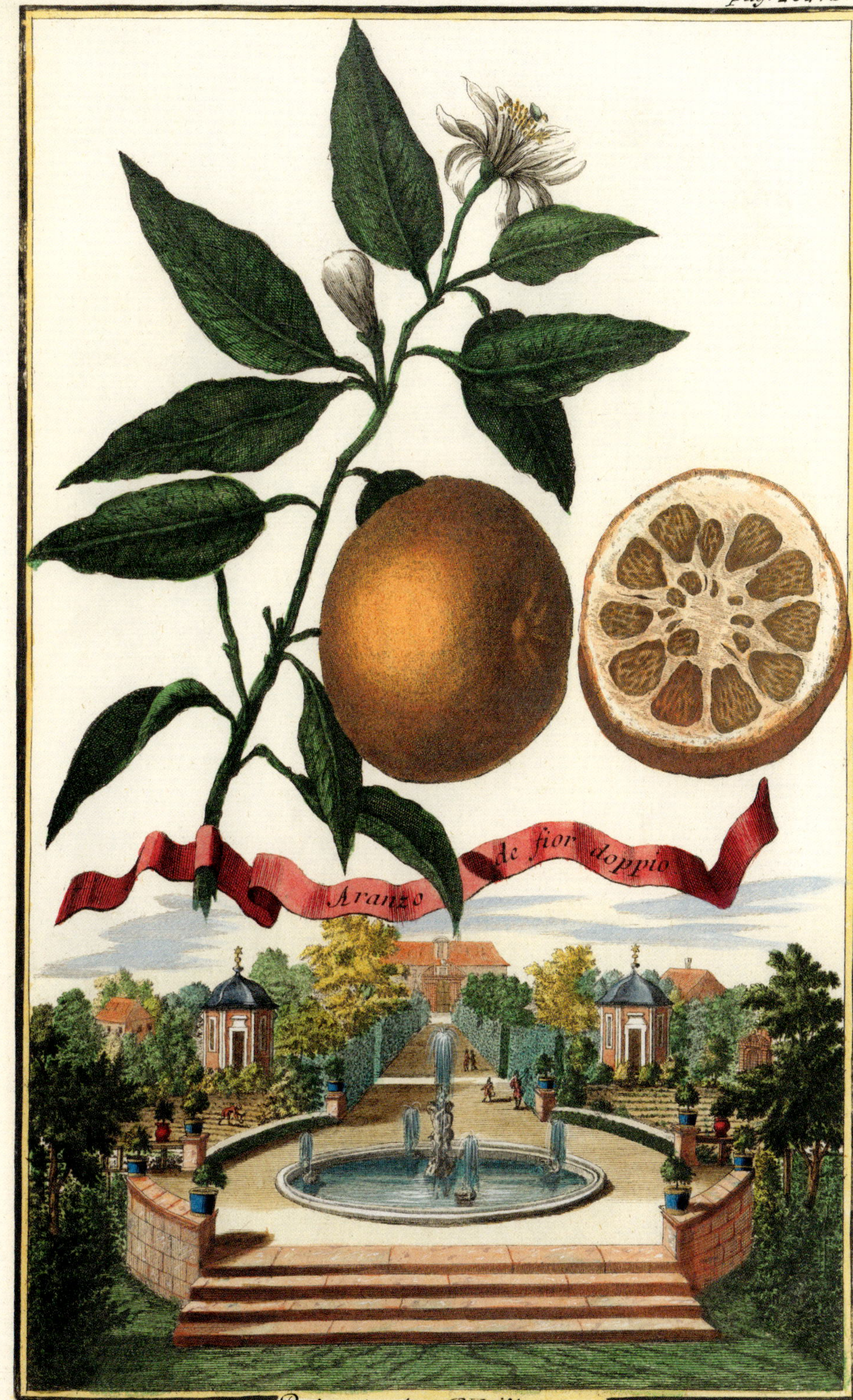
pag. 202. b.
Aranzo de fior doppio
Proſpect in dem Röſleriſchen Garten.

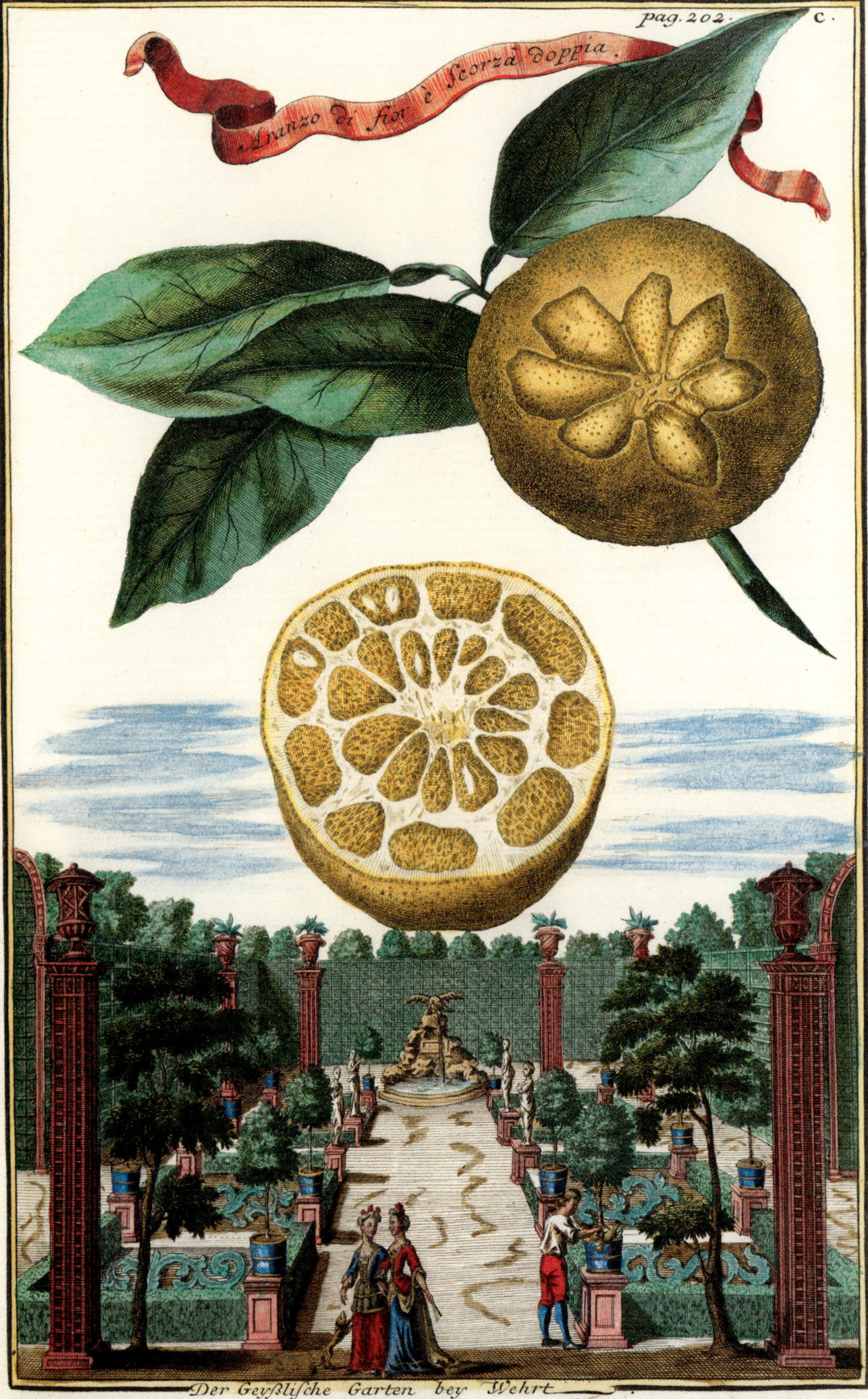

Aranzo di fior e Scorza doppia

Nuremberg, Wöhrd – Garden of Mr Geyßel

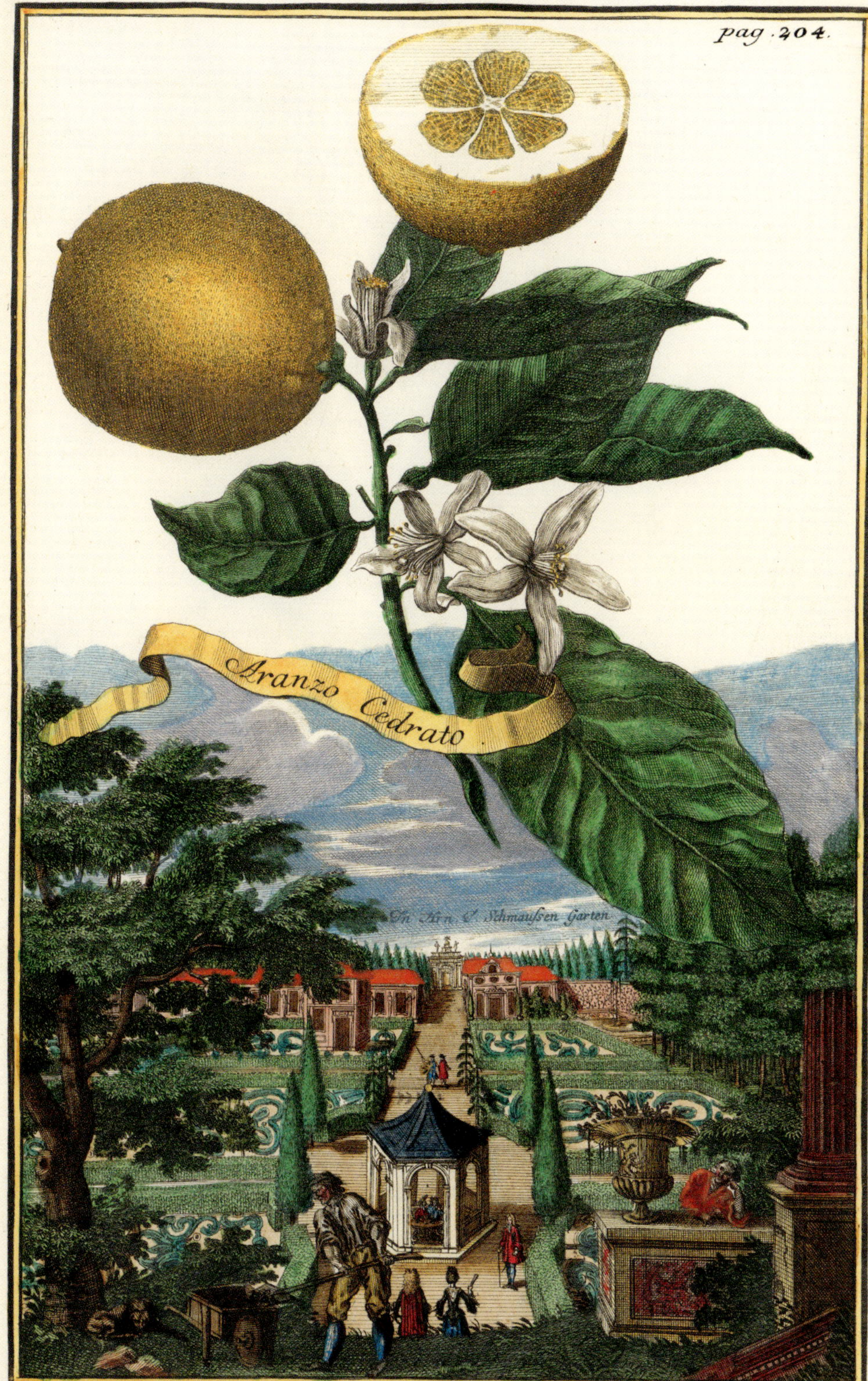

Aranzo Cedrato

Nuremberg, Mögeldorf – Garden of Mr Schmaus

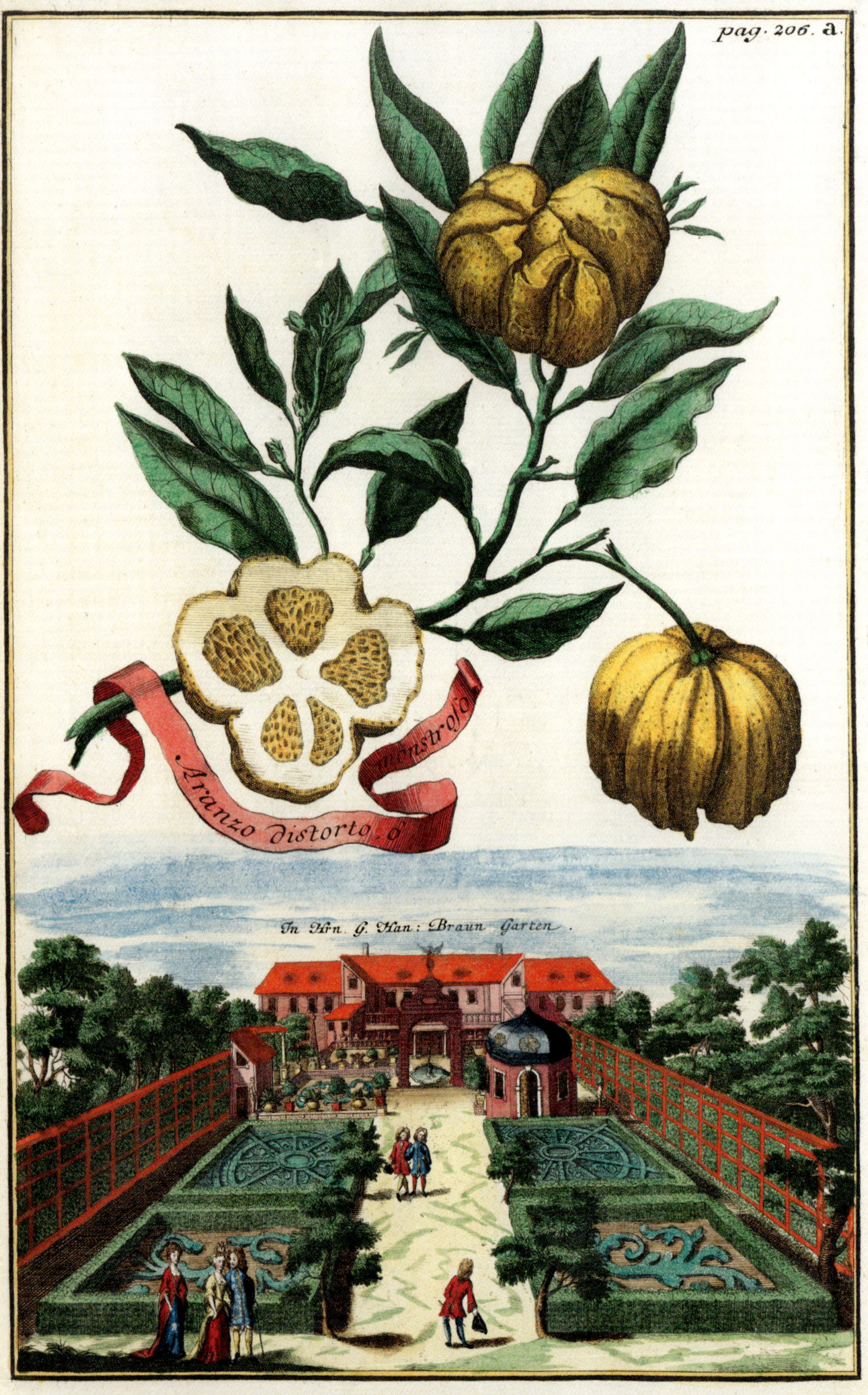

Aranzo distorto o monstroso

Nuremberg, St Johannis – Garden of G. Han. Braun

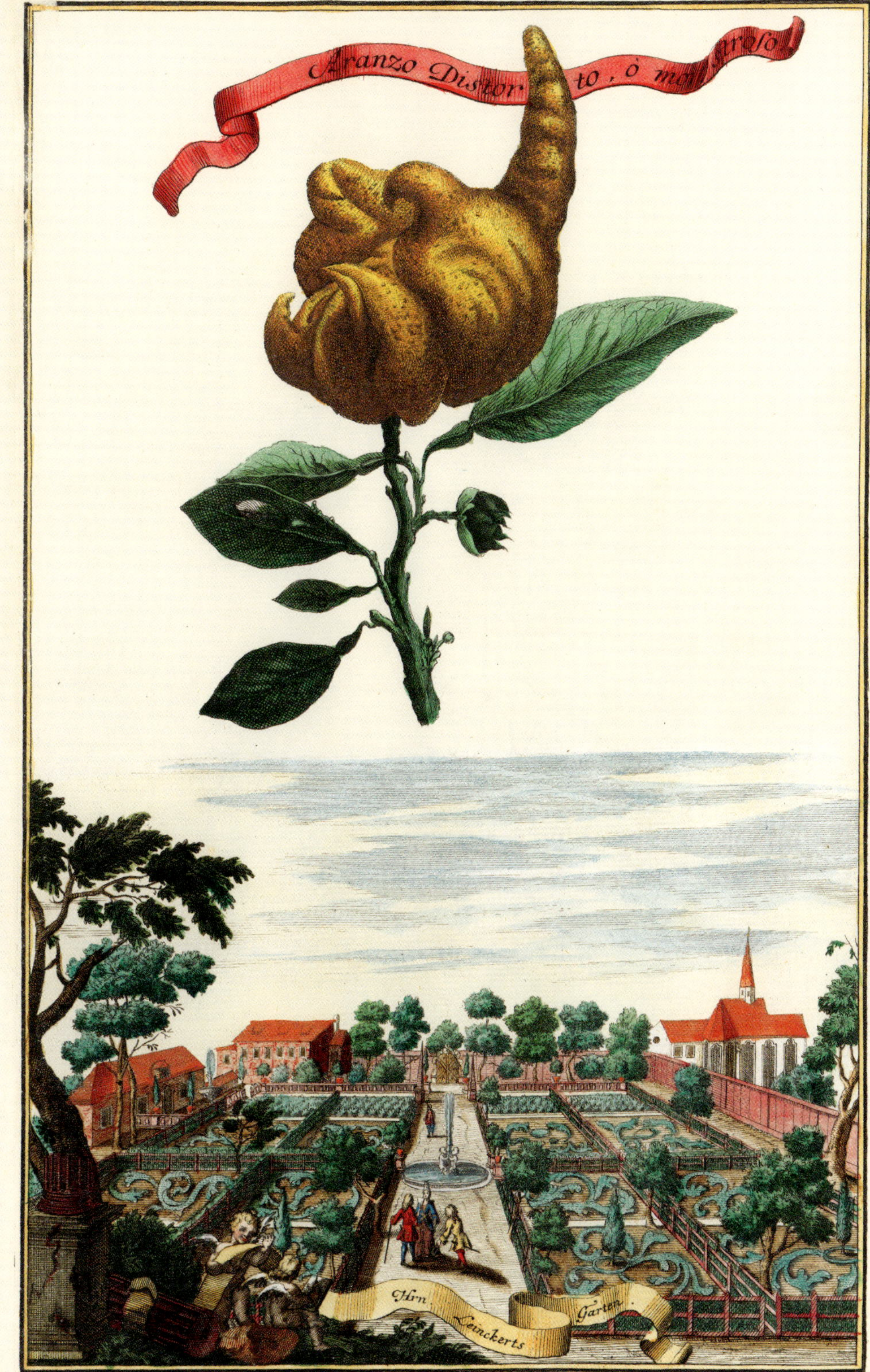

Aranzo distorto o monstroso

Nuremberg, St Johannis – Garden of Mr Leinckert

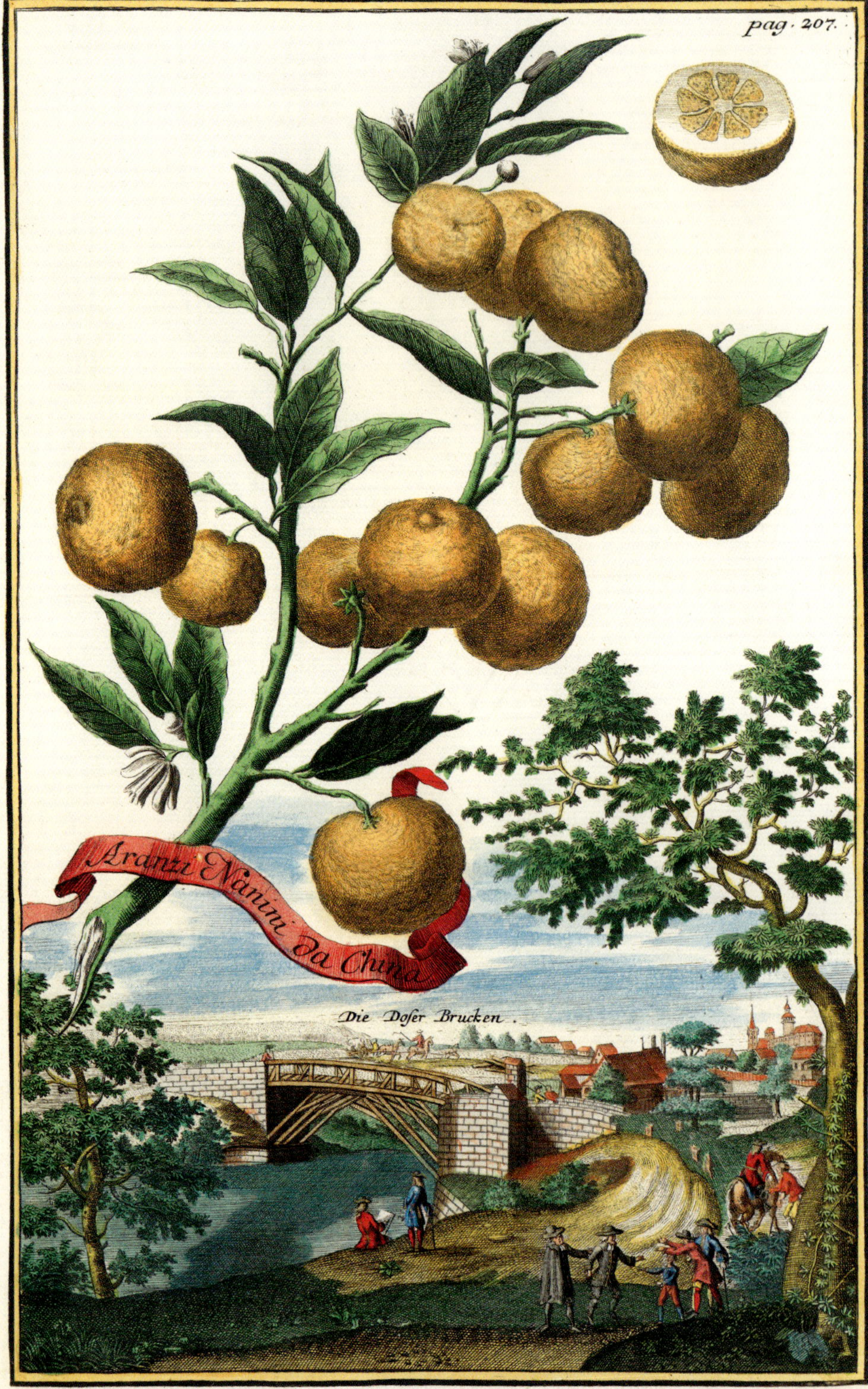

Aranzi Nanini da China

Nuremberg, Muggenhof – Doos Bridge

Das Zwey und Zwantzigste Capitel.

Von dem Aranzo Nanino da China.

Allhie werden diese Bäume die Zwerch-Bäum oder Pomerantzen-Zwerchlein / vom Ferrario aber pag. 430. Arantium Sinense genennet / in dem diese Art aus Sina oder China, oder wie gedachter Ferrarius will / vielmehr aus Goa und denen Saltz-Insuln heraus gebracht worden seyn solle: Diese Bäumlein bleiben gerne niederträchtig / und wollen viel lieber in Geschirren / als im Erdboden in Pomerantzen-Häusern stehen / wie ich solches aus eigener Erfahrung bezeugen kan / dann nachdem ich einige solche Zweiglein über drey Jahre in dem Pomerantzen-Hauß stehend hatte / habe doch nicht mercken können / daß sie im geringsten etwas höher oder grösser worden / so haben sie auch gar wenig geblühet / noch viel weniger Früchte getragen / und behalten / ja ich glaube / daß sie lieber in denen Geschirren und in dem freyen Lufft darum stehen / weil von der Sonnen Hitze die Geschirre von aussen / und die Erd und Wurtzel einwendig wol erwarmen / mithin das Wachsthum desto besser befördern kan: Manche kauffen solche Zwerch-Bäumlein / und stellen sie gerne vor die Fenster ihrer Häuser / weil sie klein und artig bleiben / allein sie schlagen denen wenigsten wol an / dann ob sie schon ein paar Jährlein gedauret / schön gegrünet / auch endlich geblühet / auch ein und anderes Früchtlein gebracht / nehmen sie doch nachmal immer zu von Zeit zu Zeit ab / biß sie endlich verderben / sonder Zweiffel / weil sie nicht genugsam die frey-durchstreichende Lufft zu geniessen haben. Es haben diese Bäumlein viele knockerigte Aeste / welche nicht anders anzusehen / als ob sie meist Augen wären / deren künfftig hervor wachsenden Blärlein / ja es wachsen solche Aestlein mit ihren dunckel-grünen zugespitzten Laub gantz dick ineinander / tragen viele Blühe / welche doch kleiner ist / als an den andern Pomerantzen-Bäumen / solchen aber doch gleichwol an dem Geruch nichts bevor lässet; die Früchtlein bleiben auch klein / und wann sie groß werden / so übertreffen sie doch die Grösse einer Welschen Nuß nicht wol / wann sie dann zeitigen / wird ihre grüne Schelffe recht hoch Pomerantzen-färbig / und so man sie aufschneidet / findet man einwendig den Safft und das Marck / gleich in denen andern Pomerantzen / welches aber etwas säuerlicht / die Schelffe aber nicht allzu bitter ist. Die jenige / welche viele dergleichen Früchtlein bekommen / pflegen sie in Zucker einzumachen / und auf verschiedene Weise zu den Speisen zu gebrauchen. Wann diese Zwerch-Bäumlein mit denen daran hangenden Früchtlein aus der Winterung kommen / pflegen solche Früchtlein gar bald zu wachsen anzufangen / und sich ehe als die grosse Pomerantzen zu färben / wie sie dann öffter schon im Julio und Augusto zeitigen / alsdann kan man sie bald abnehmen / weil sie um solche Zeit annoch sehr safftig sind / wann sie aber länger an dem Baum hangend bleiben / vertrocknet der einwendige Safft / gleich so gehet es auch mit denen Früchtlein / welche sich erst zu färben beginnen / wann man die Bäumlein in die Winterung setzet / dann sie pflegen gemeiniglich schwartze Flecken zu überkommen / und werden gantz schwelck / einwendig aber trocken zu seyn.

Es sollen auch dergleichen Zwerch-Bäumlein gefunden werden / welche süsse Früchte bringen / allein / ob ich wol sehr darnach getrachtet / habe ich doch weder der-

gleichen

Beginning of the fourth section of vol. I, chapter 22.
Pages 234/235 Nuremberg, Thumenberg – The Manor, detail (see p. 218)

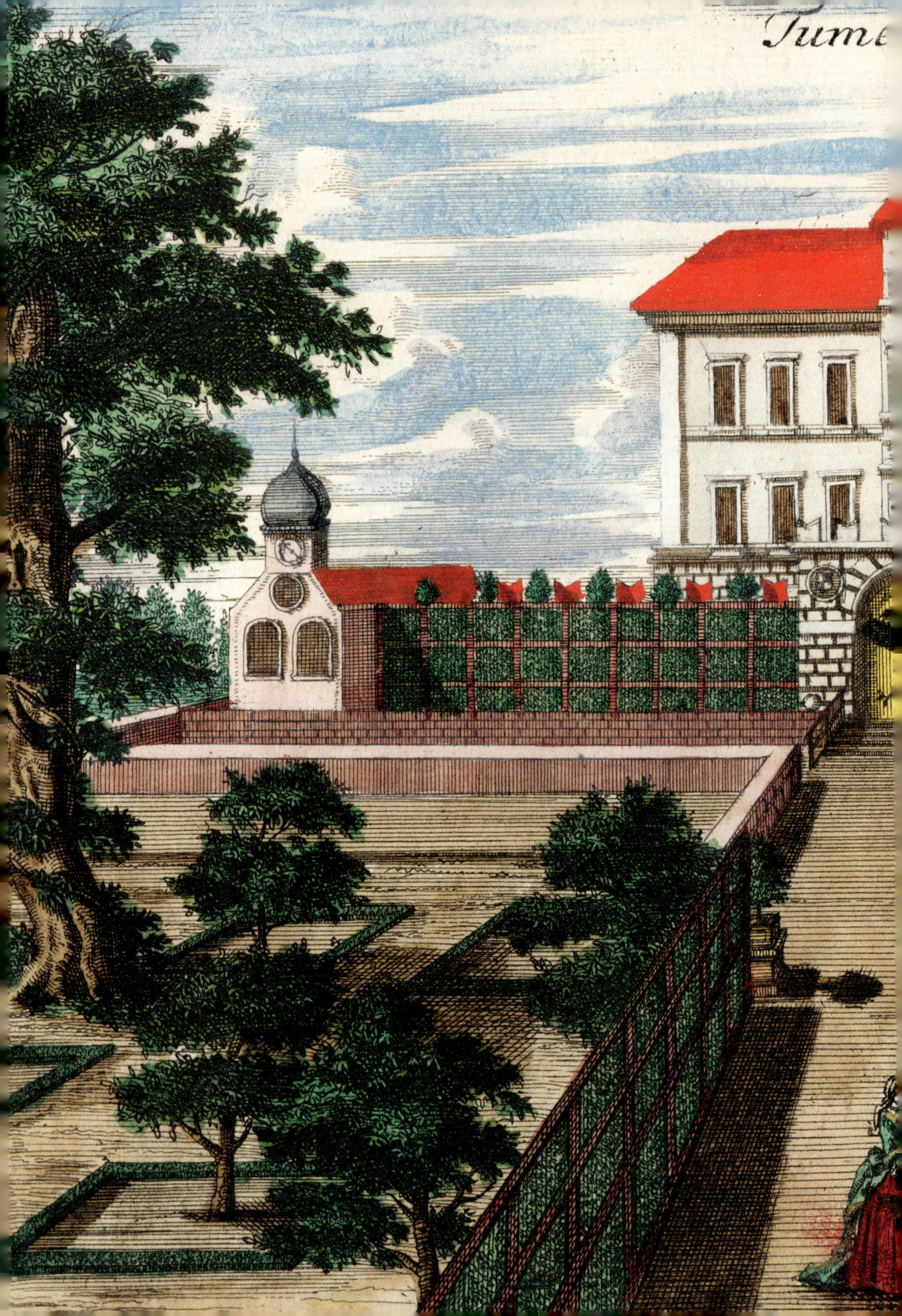

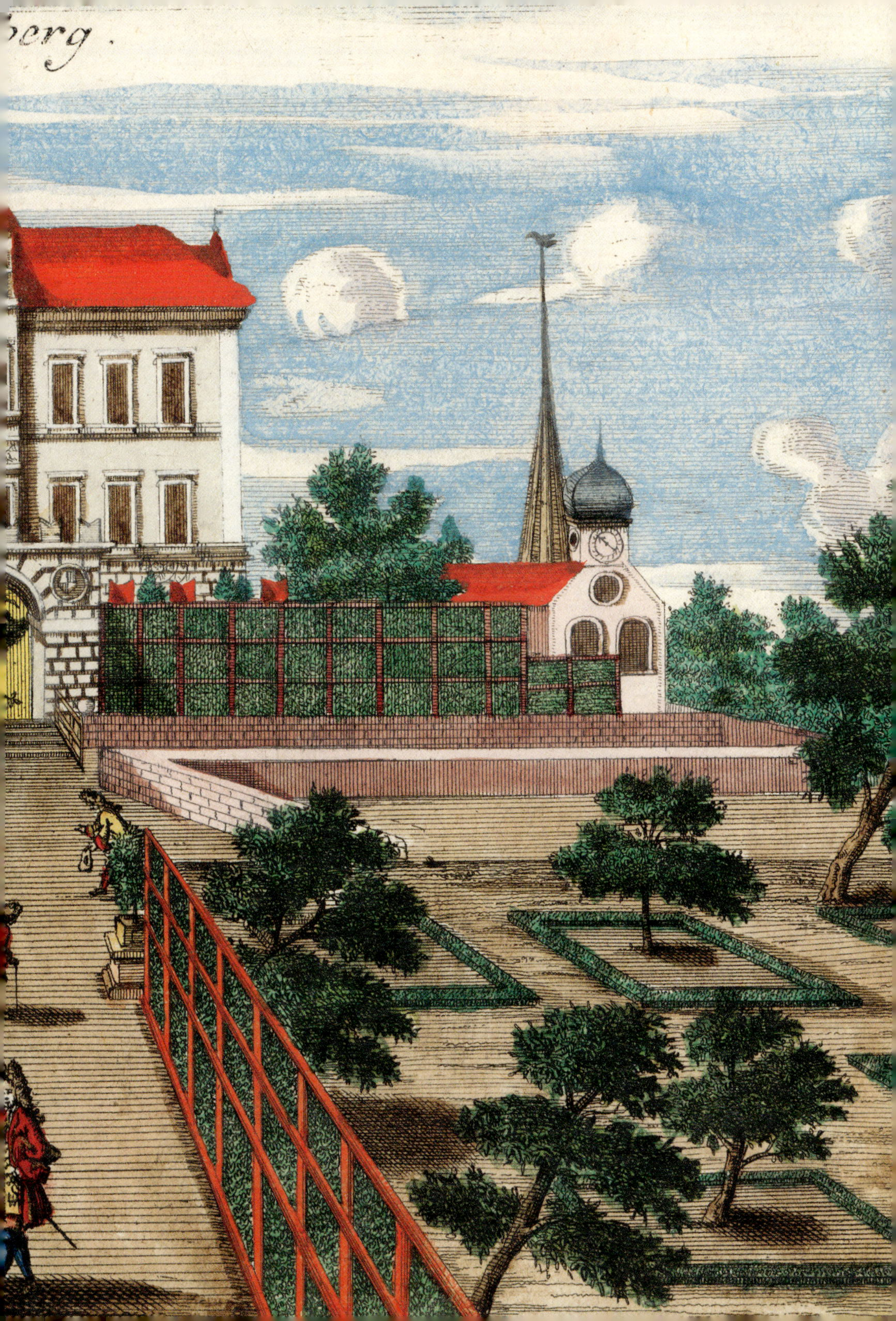

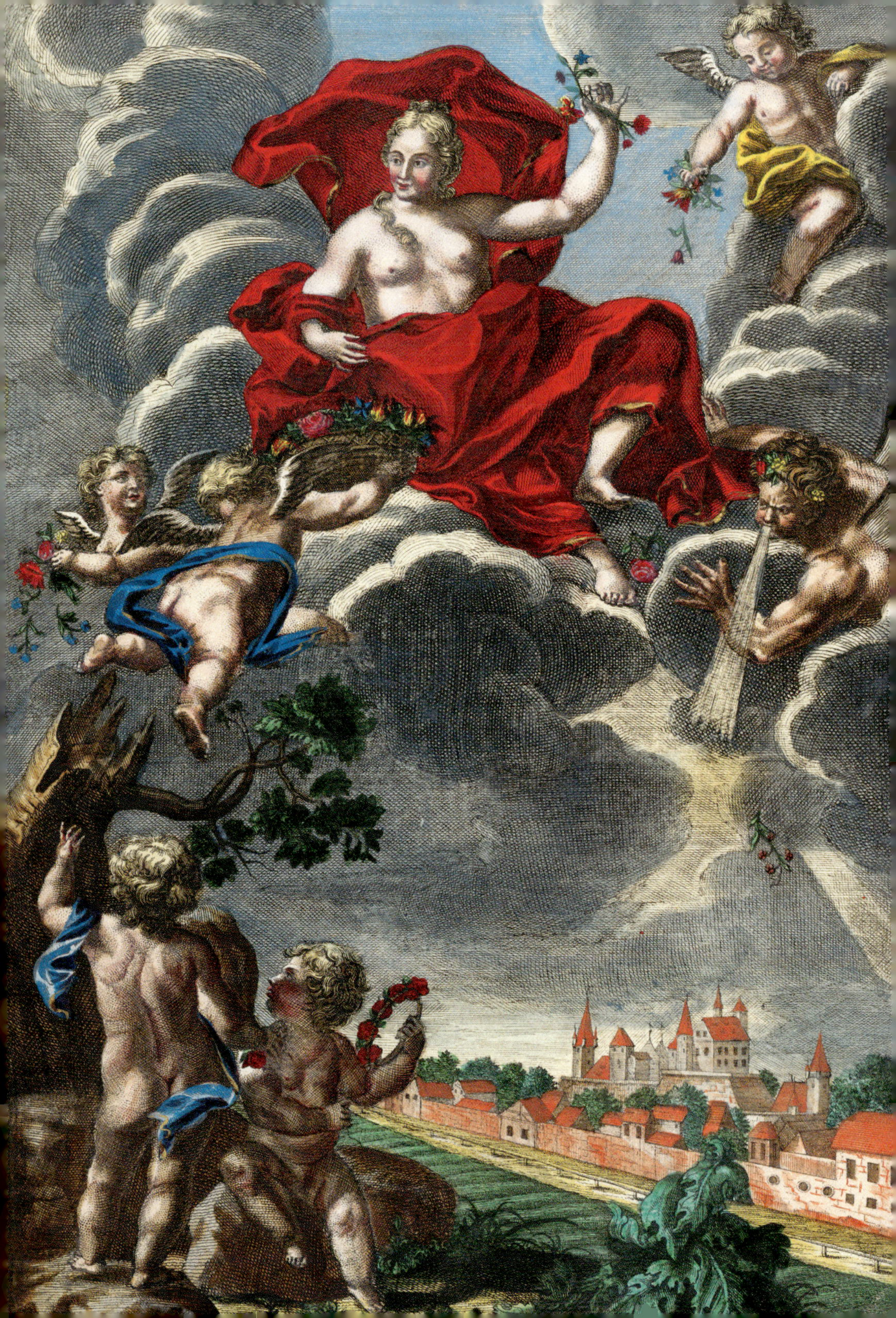

FLORA NORIBERGENSIS, Oder Nürnbergische FLORA.

Wie geneigt die Hesperides gegen die edle Noris sich erzeiget / so günstig erweiset sich auch die Flora gegen dieselbe / und wie freygebig das Klee-Blat jener Schwestern/ mit Austheilung ihrer herrlichen Früchte / sich aufgeführet / so reichlich hat sie die Flora mit der Zierde ihrer Blumen beschencket ; es war ihnen nicht genug / die Pomerantzen / Citronen und Citronaten aus weit entlegenen Landen der Noris in Uberfluß zuzuschicken / um die unter dero Schutz und Schatten lebende / so Gesund- als Krancke / damit zu ergötzen / zu laben und zu erquicken / sondern sie machte den in solchen Früchten erhaltenen Saamen noch über dieses so fruchtbar / daß er / in die Erde gestecket / sich reichlich mehret / mithin die an Anzahl solcher köstlicher Frucht-Bäume vergrösserte / weil es aber sehr langsam zugehet / biß solche aus denen Kernen erzogene Bäume / blühen / Früchte tragen und vom neuen sich besaamen / als haben sie nicht nur sehr viele Liebhabere an sich gezogen / welche sich äusserst bemühet / solche aus dem Saamen erzogene rohe Bäumlein zu äugeln / zu beltzen / und mit Setzung der Augen auf besondere Stämmlein gantz neue Arten derselben zu erzielen. Ja / was noch mehr / so haben offt besagte Hesperides bereits schon tragbare Bäume / der von ihnen so sehr geliebten Noris zugeschicket / daß sie auch nunmehr daselbst in Menge blühen / und in ziemlicher Anzahl gesegnete Früchte bringen. Nicht minder hat die bey den Heyden also genannte Blumen-Göttin Flora, aus sonderbar tragender Neigung zu der edlen Noris, selbige mit dem ungemeinen Garten-Pracht ihrer Blumen beschencket; Nun waren zwar dero Gärten schon von langen Zeiten nicht wenig berühmt / daß sie mit schönen und seltenen Blumen in Menge prangeten / allein wann wir selbige zu dieser unserer Zeit beschauen / müssen wir gestehen / daß sich die Zeiten mercklich verändert haben / und was wir ehemalen vor die schönste und rareste Blumen-Arten gehalten / nur eintzeln gesehen / und als etwas ungemeines bewundert / nun als die gemeineste Sorten kaum ansehen mögen und vor nichts achten / dahingegen mit allerley unsern Vorfahren gantz unbekannten Blumen und Gewächsen unsere Gärten dermalen angefüllet sehen ; Ich will darunter nicht zehlen die vielerley Arten der Nelcken / deren heut zu Tag keine geachtet werden / in welchen sich nicht zum wenigsten viererley Farben / zierlich ineinander vermischet / zeigen / nichts von denen Hyacinthen / welche nichts taugen / wo sie nicht mit grossen und vielen Blumen schön von Farb auf einem dicken Stengel wachsen / nichts von denen vielerley schön und bund-gestreimten Tulpen / nichts von denen wolriechenden Tazzetten und Jonqvilien / und andere mehr / sondern ich will bloßhin etlicher solcher Blumen und Gewächse einige

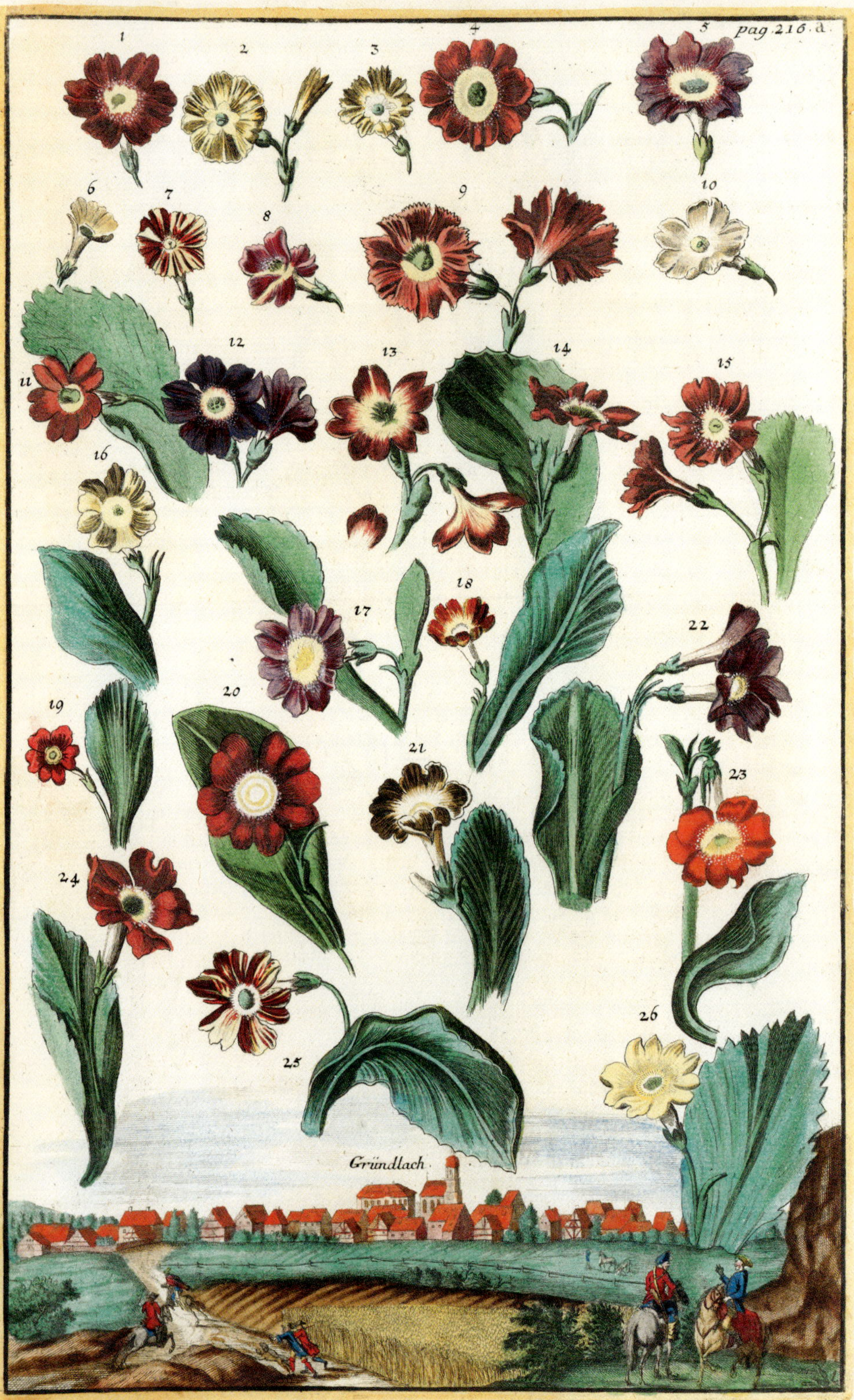

Primula auricula L.

Nuremberg, Großgründlach. *Pages 236/237* Personification of Flora, and beginning of the fifth section of vol. I

Primula auricula L.

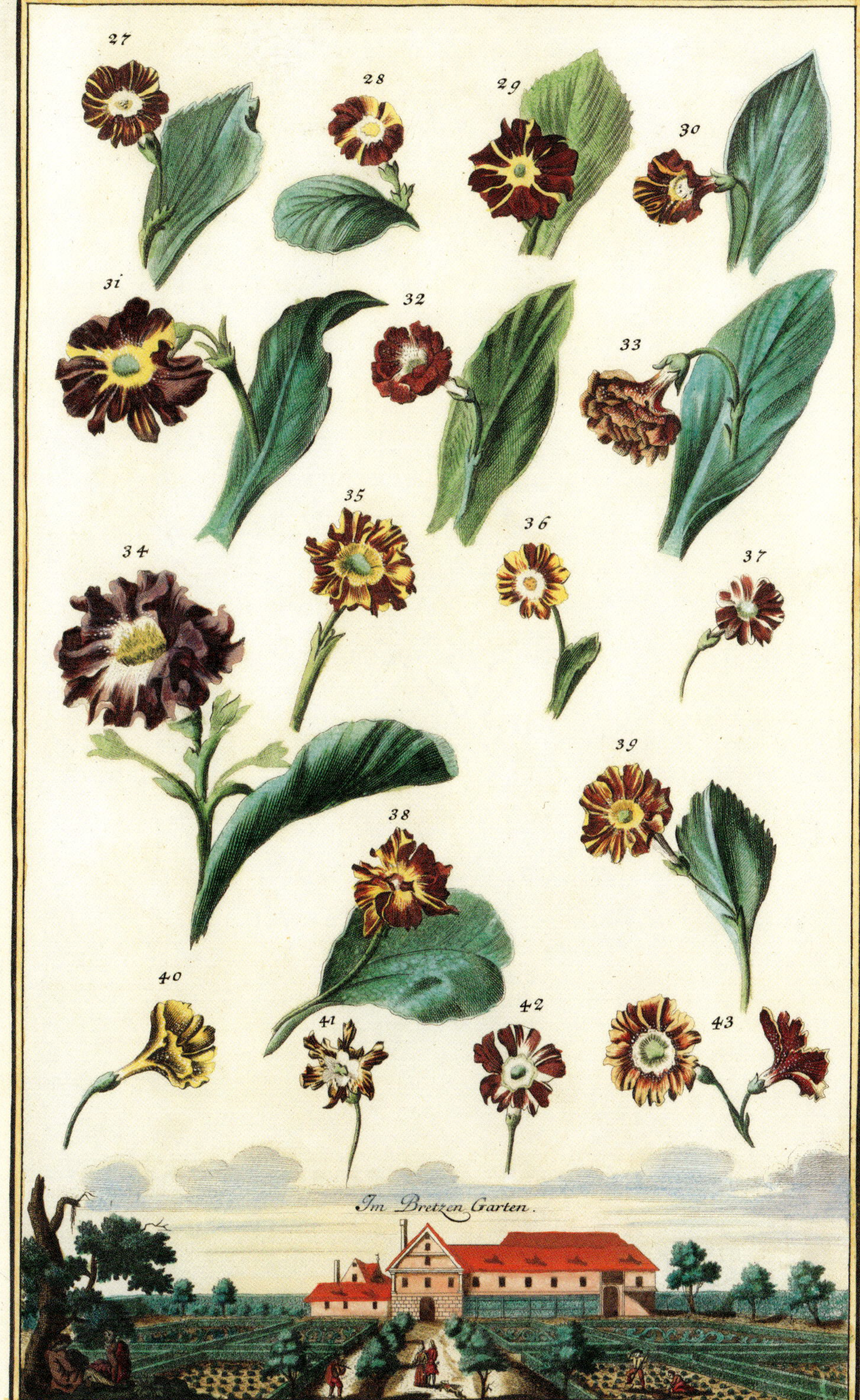

Nuremberg, Bretzengarten

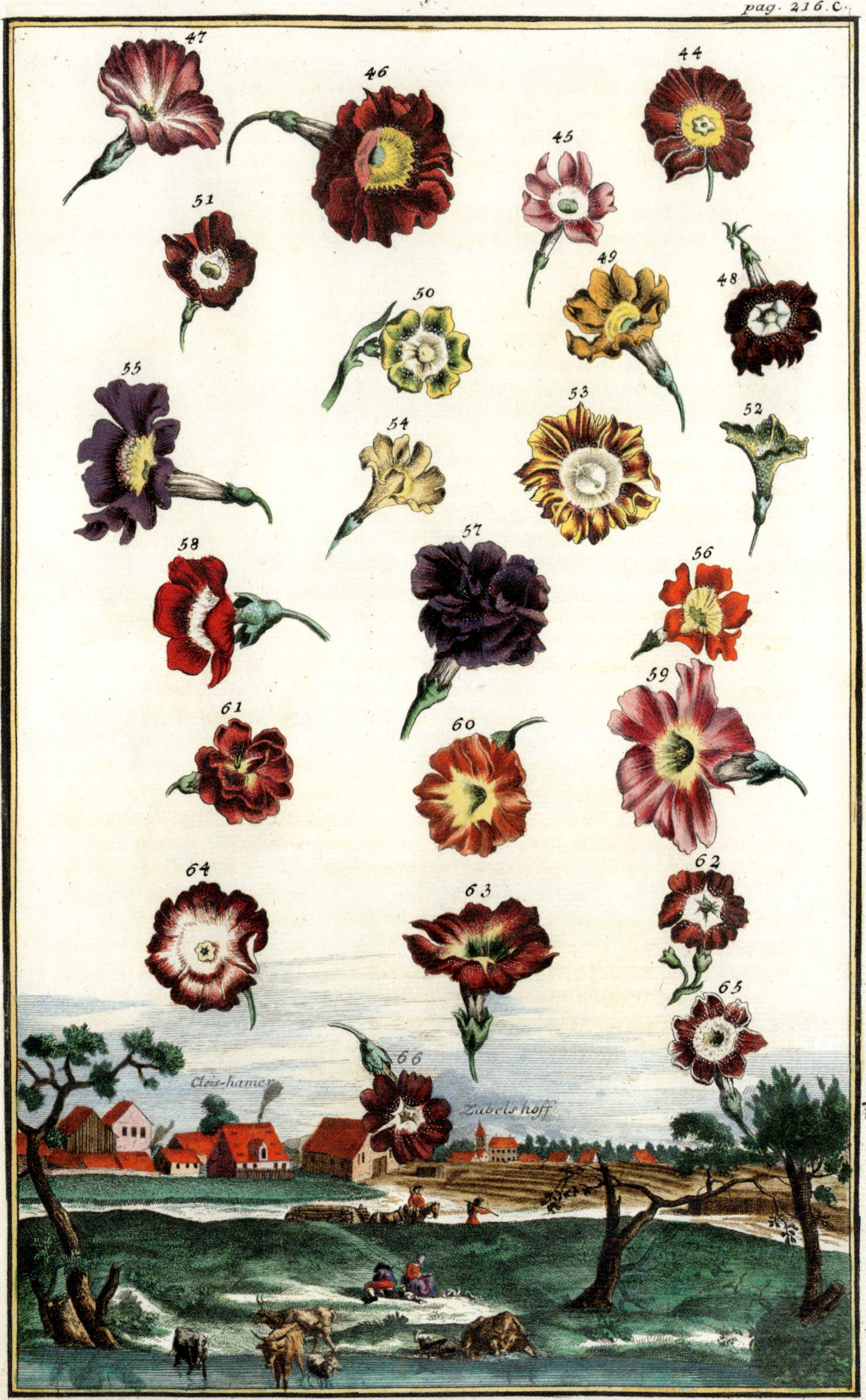

Primula auricula L.

Nuremberg, Gleißhammer and Zerzabelshof

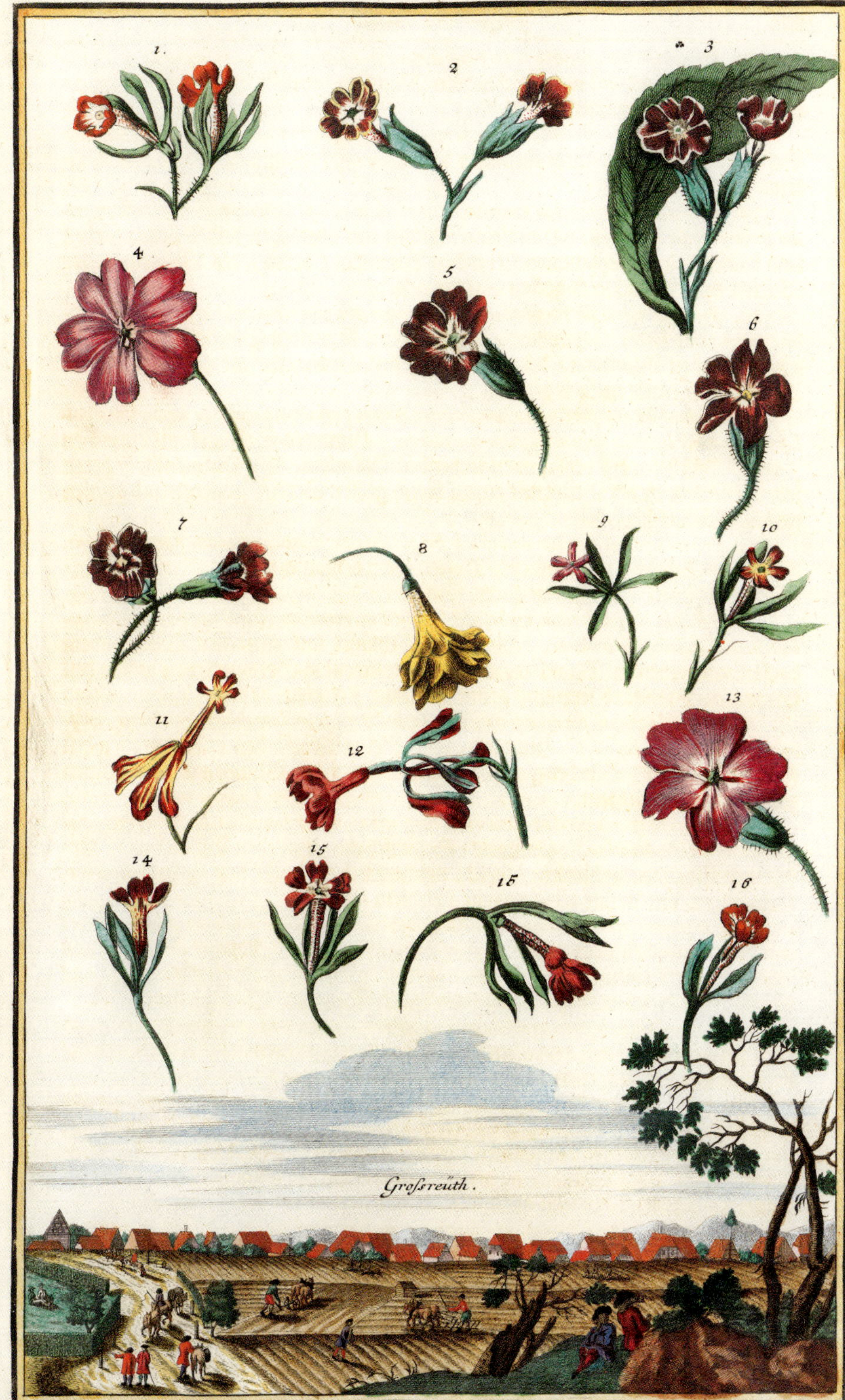

Primula veris L.

Nuremberg, Großreuth

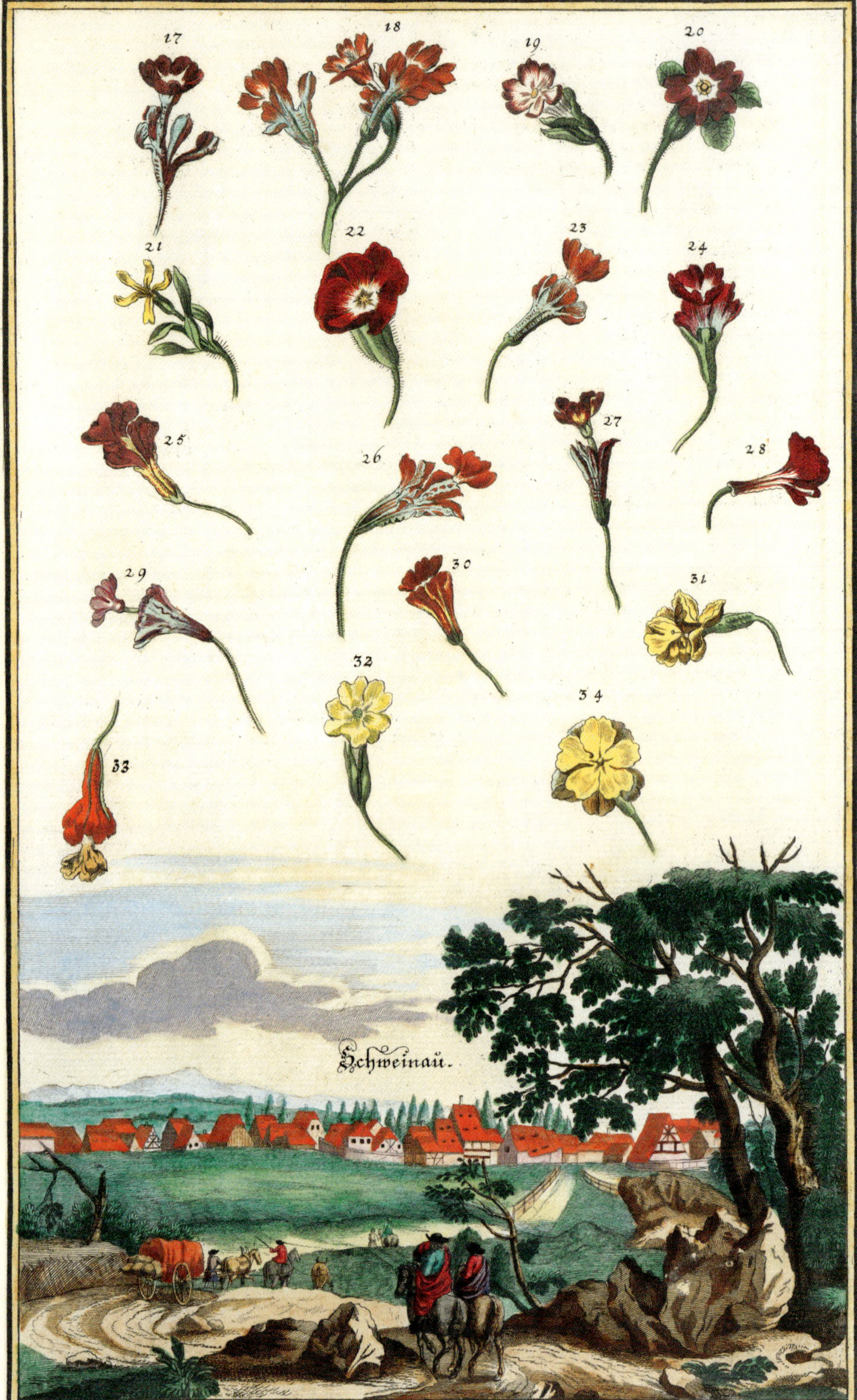

Primula veris L.

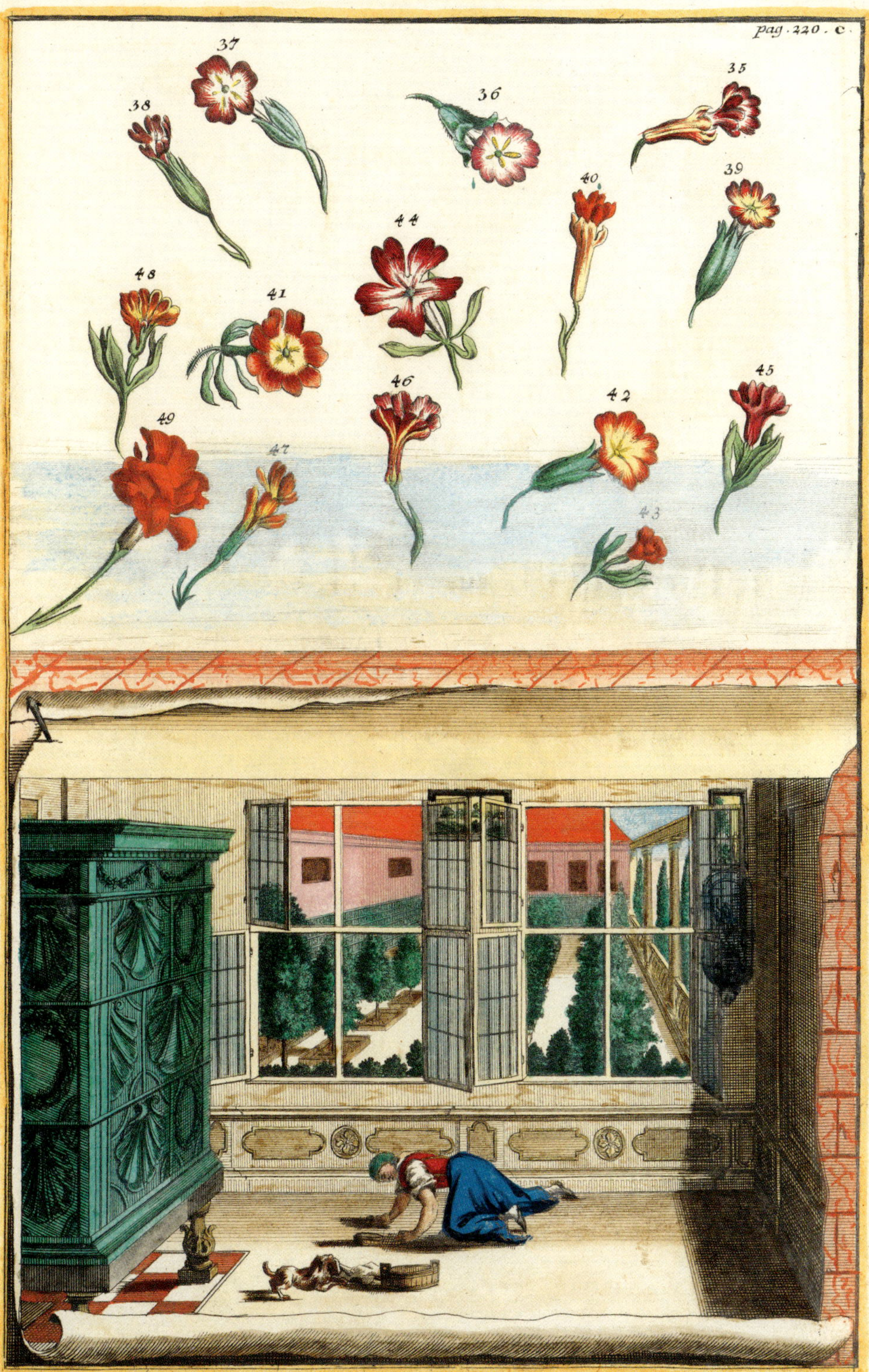

Nuremberg, Gostenhof – Johann Christoph Volkamer's House and Orangery, the 'Scent Room' next to the Orangery

Primula veris L.

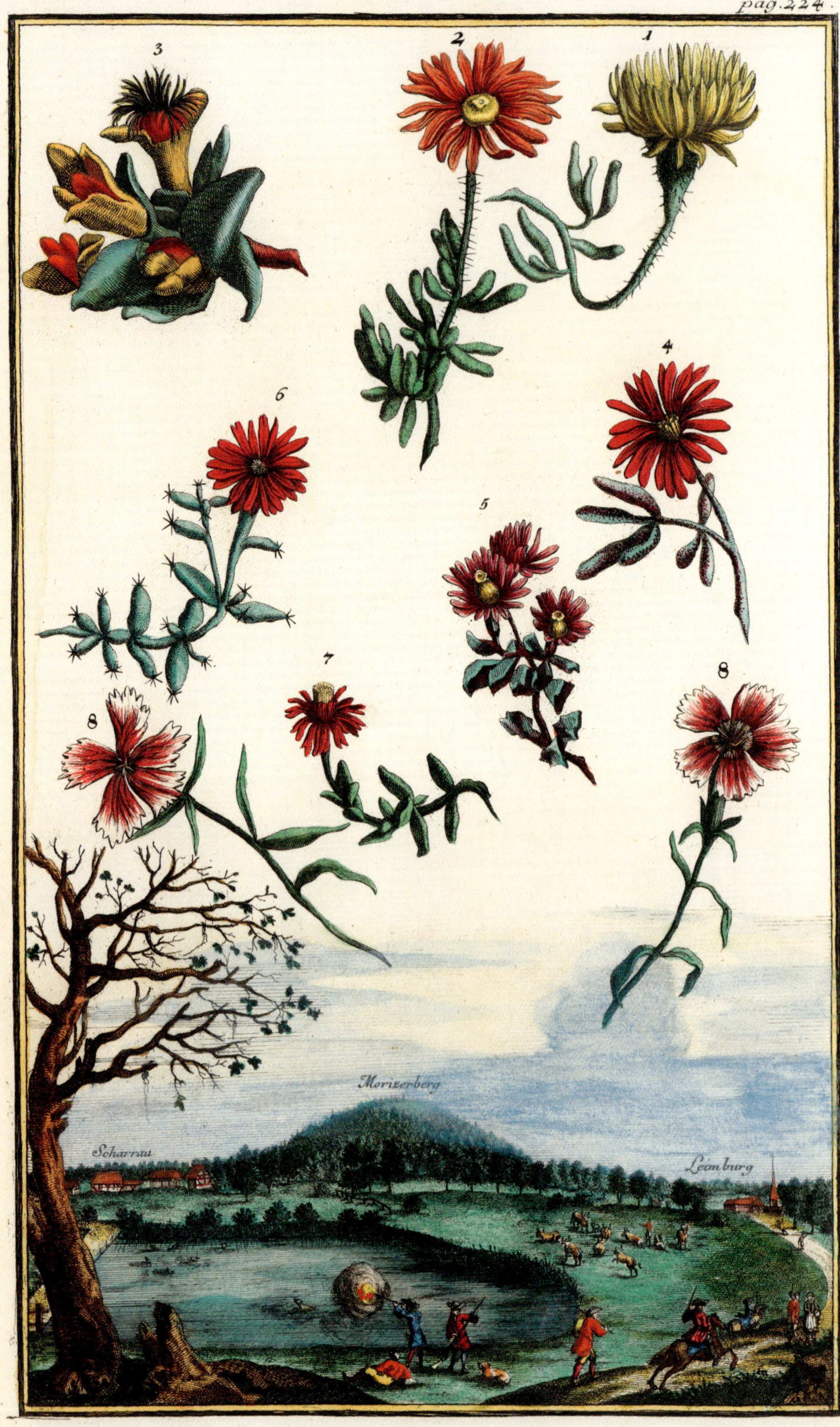

Leinburg, near Nuremberg– Scherau and Moritzberg | Ficus aizoides & Dianthus chinensis | Nuremberg Flora / Nürnbergische Flora / La flore de Nuremberg

Apocynum Curassavicum seu Americanum

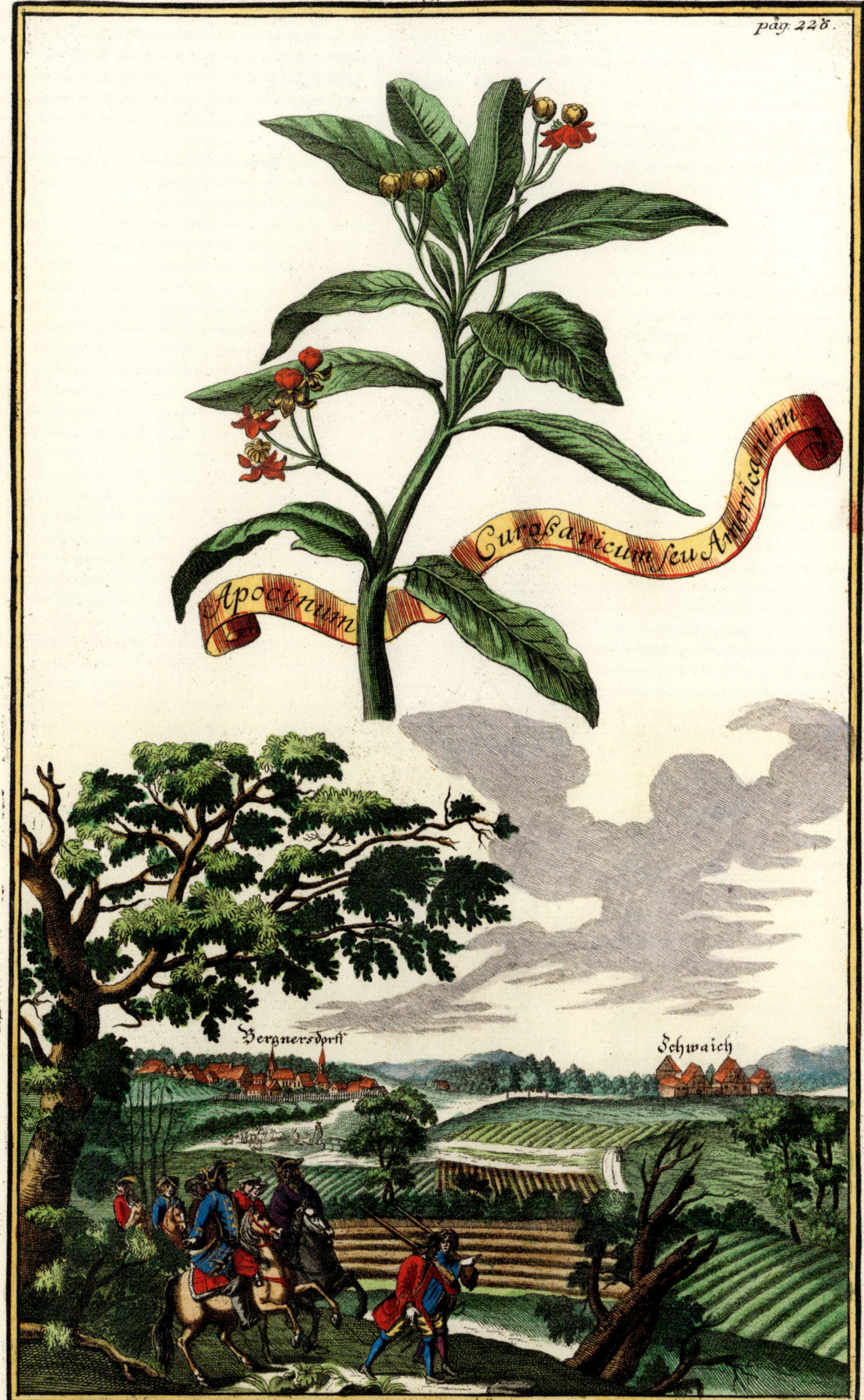

Schwaig and Behringersdorf, near Nuremberg

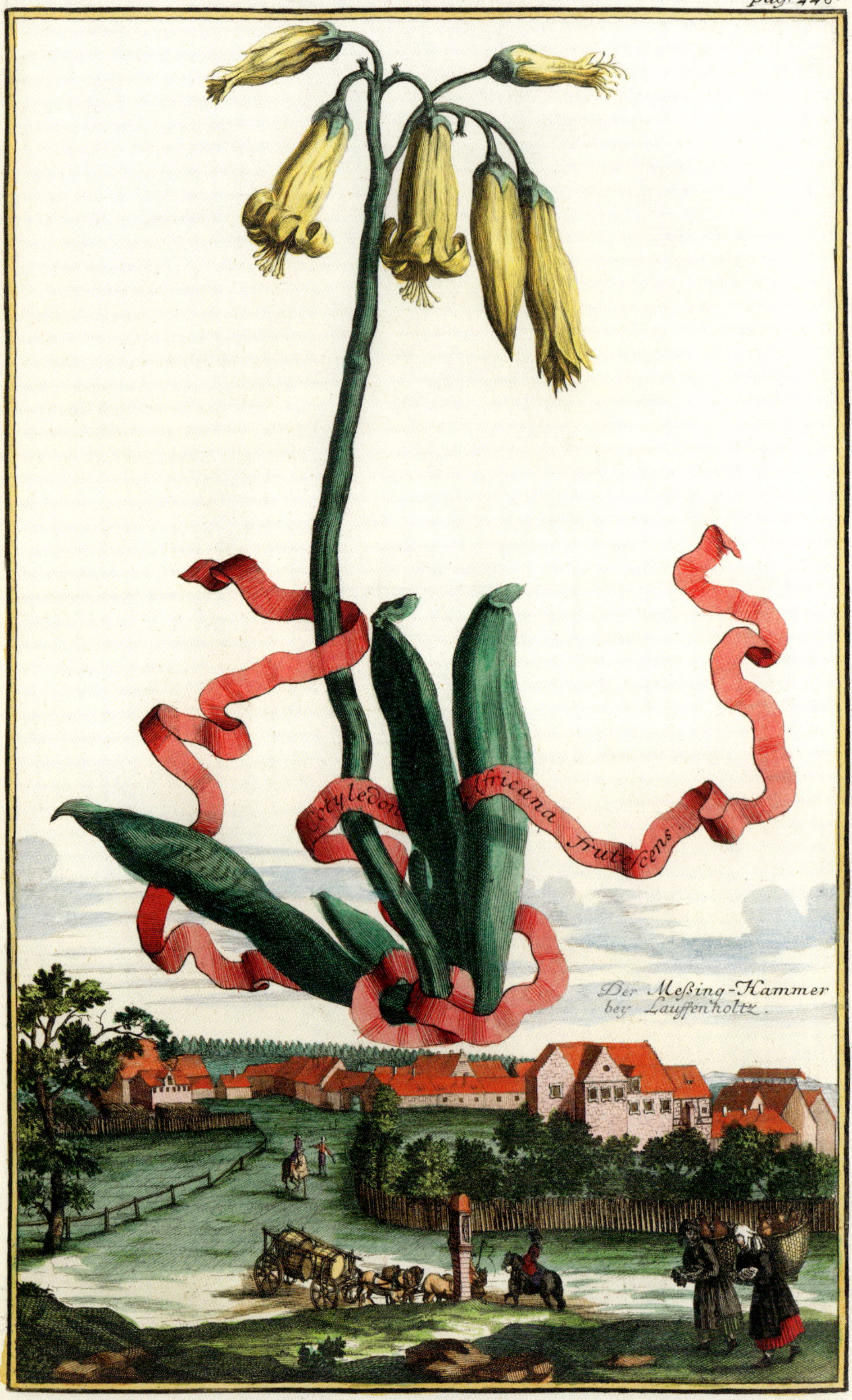

Cotyledon Africana frutescens

Phaseolus Indic[us] cochleatus

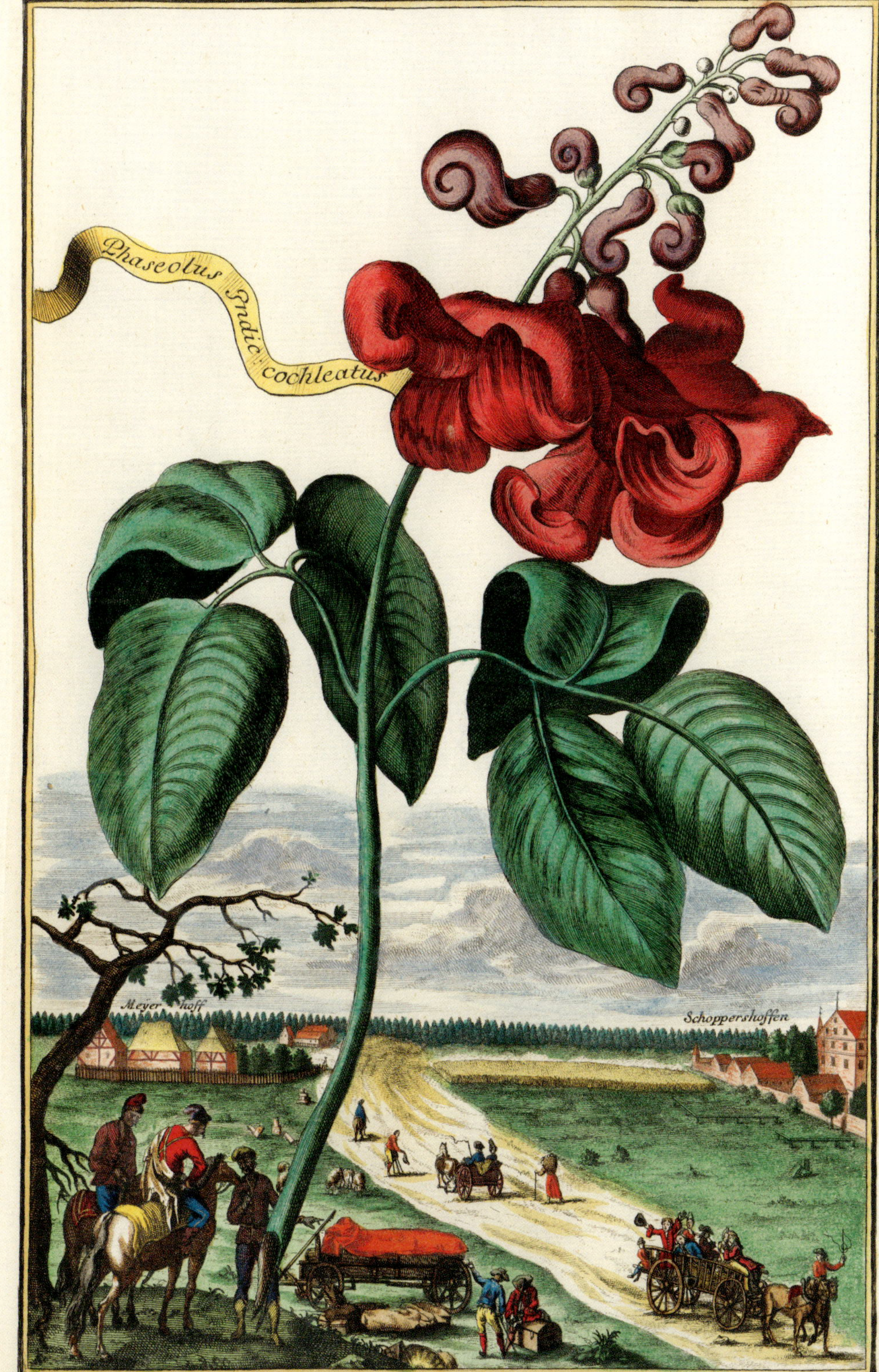

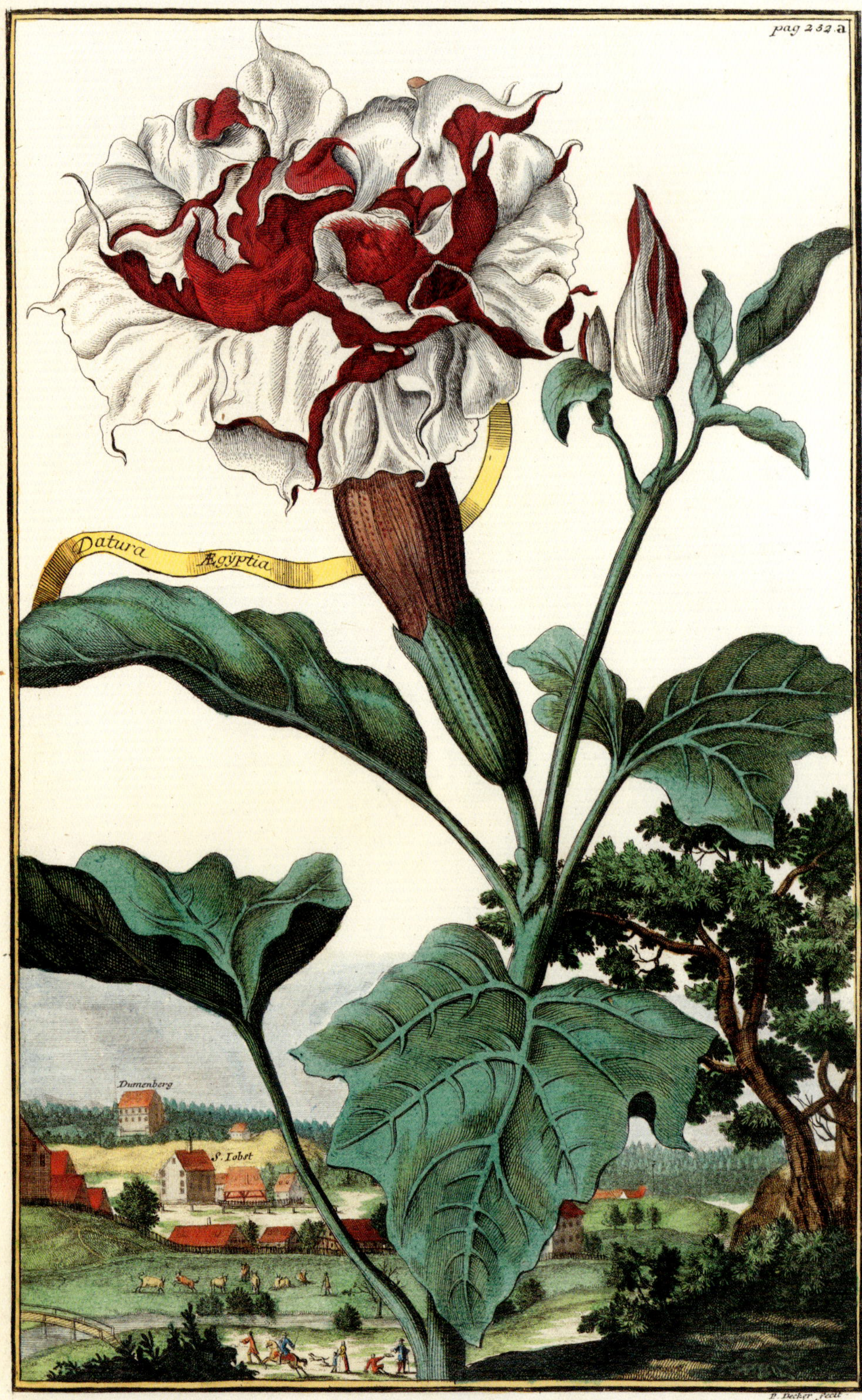

Datura Aegyptia

Nuremberg, St Jobst and Erlenstegen – Thumenberg Manor

Leonurus

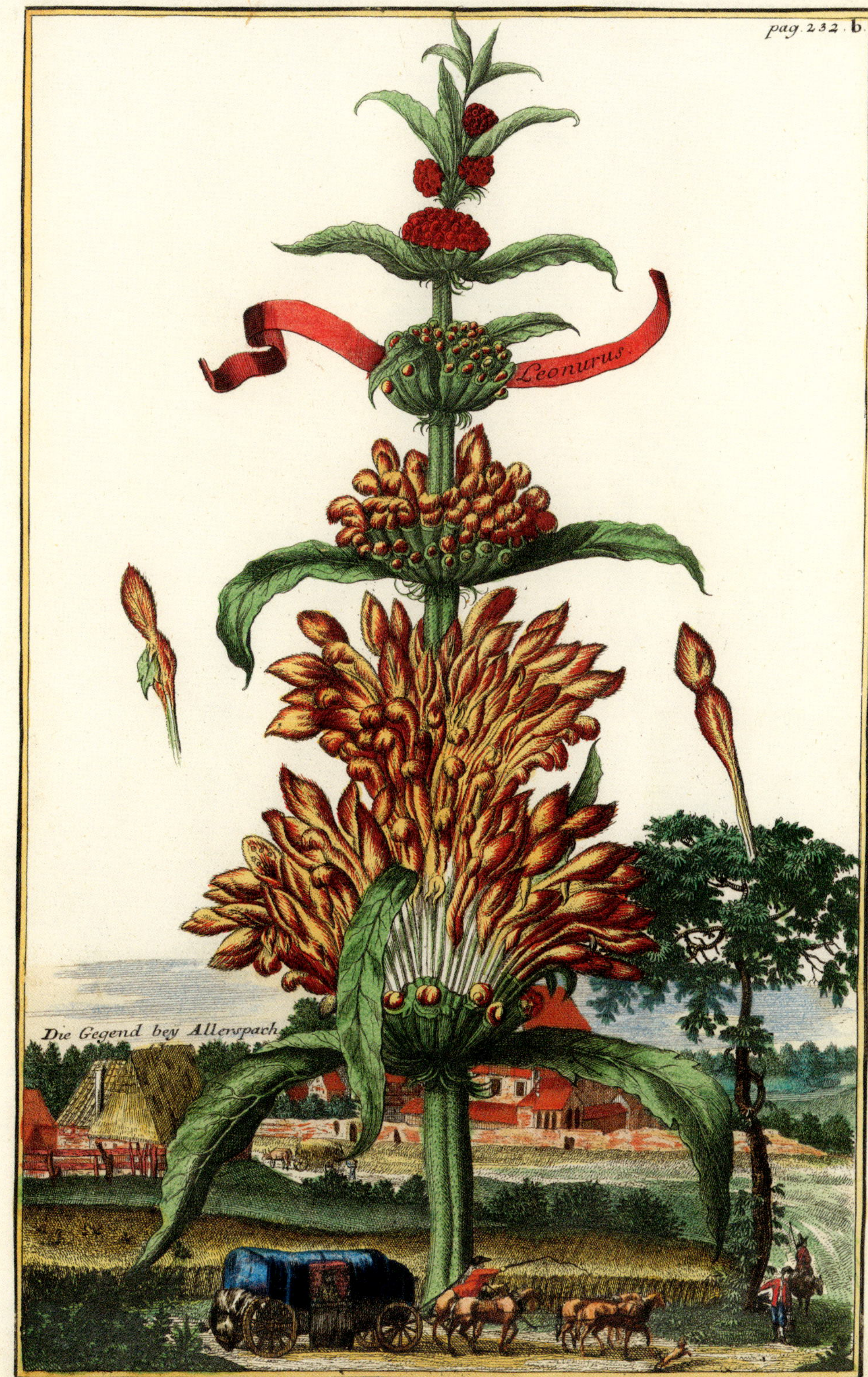

Allersberg, near Nuremberg

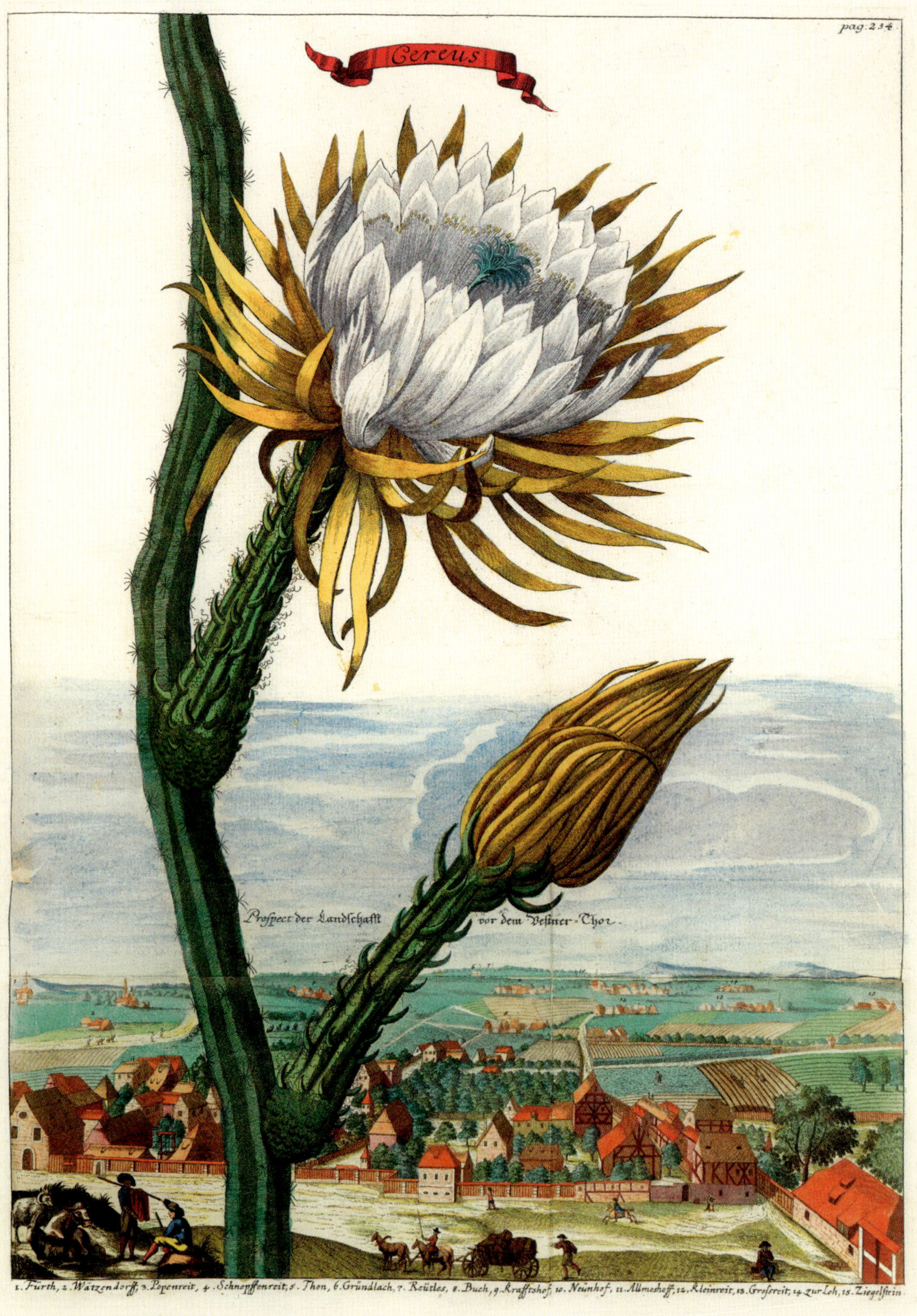

Cereus

Countryside near the Vestnertor

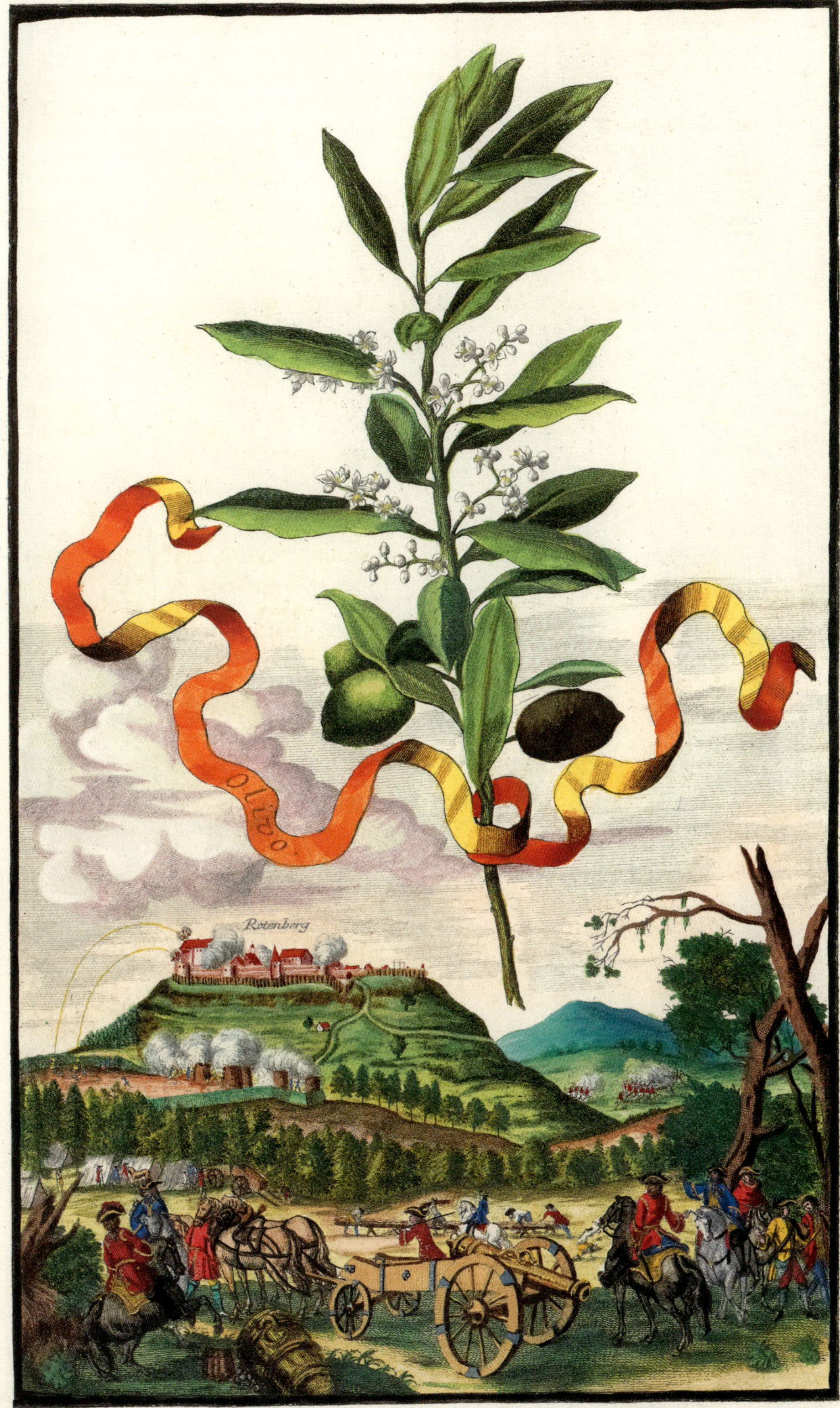

Olivo

Schnaittach, near Nuremberg – Rothenberg Fortress

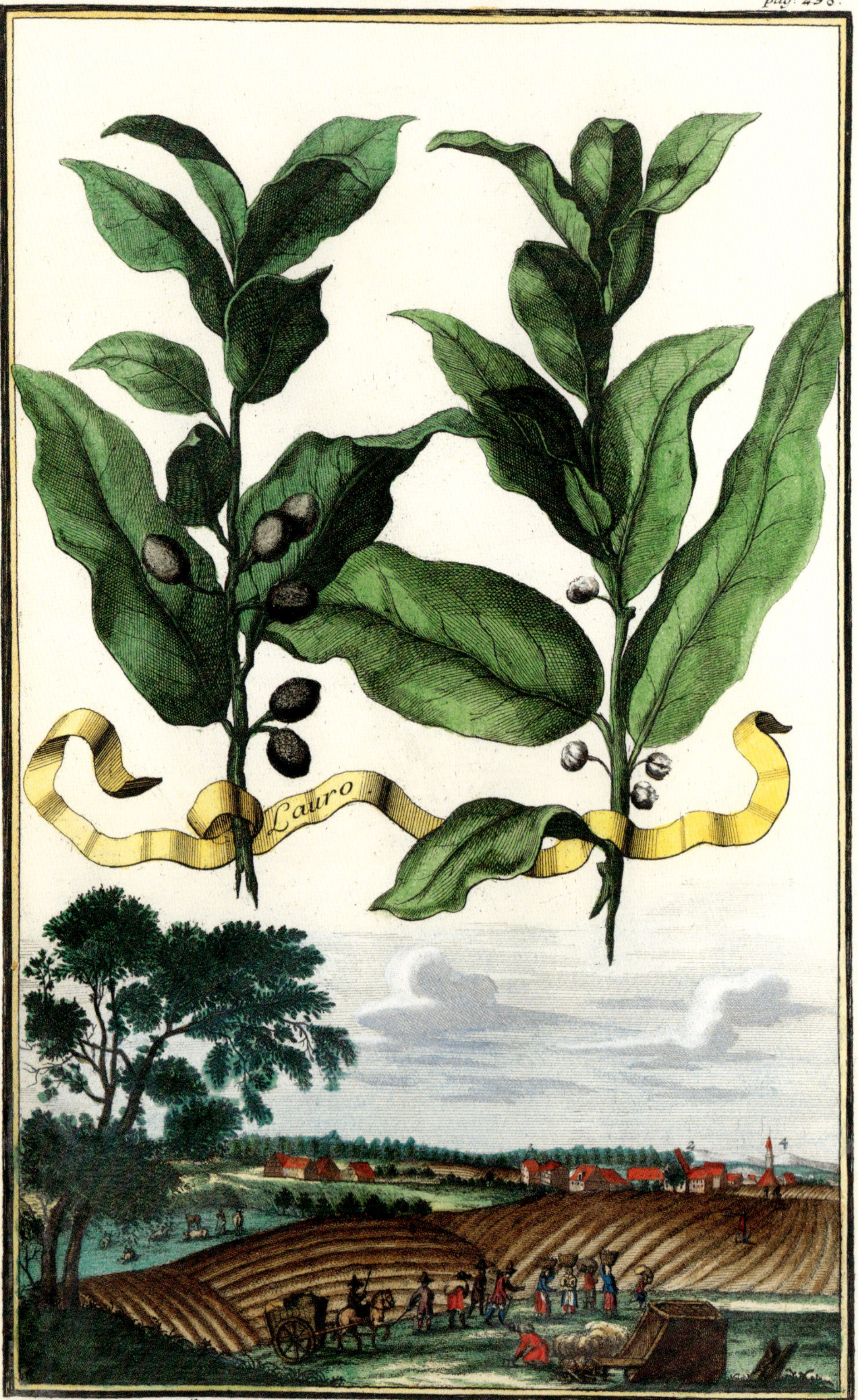

Lauro

Nuremberg. 1. Muggenhof 2. Schniegling 3. Doos 4. Fürth

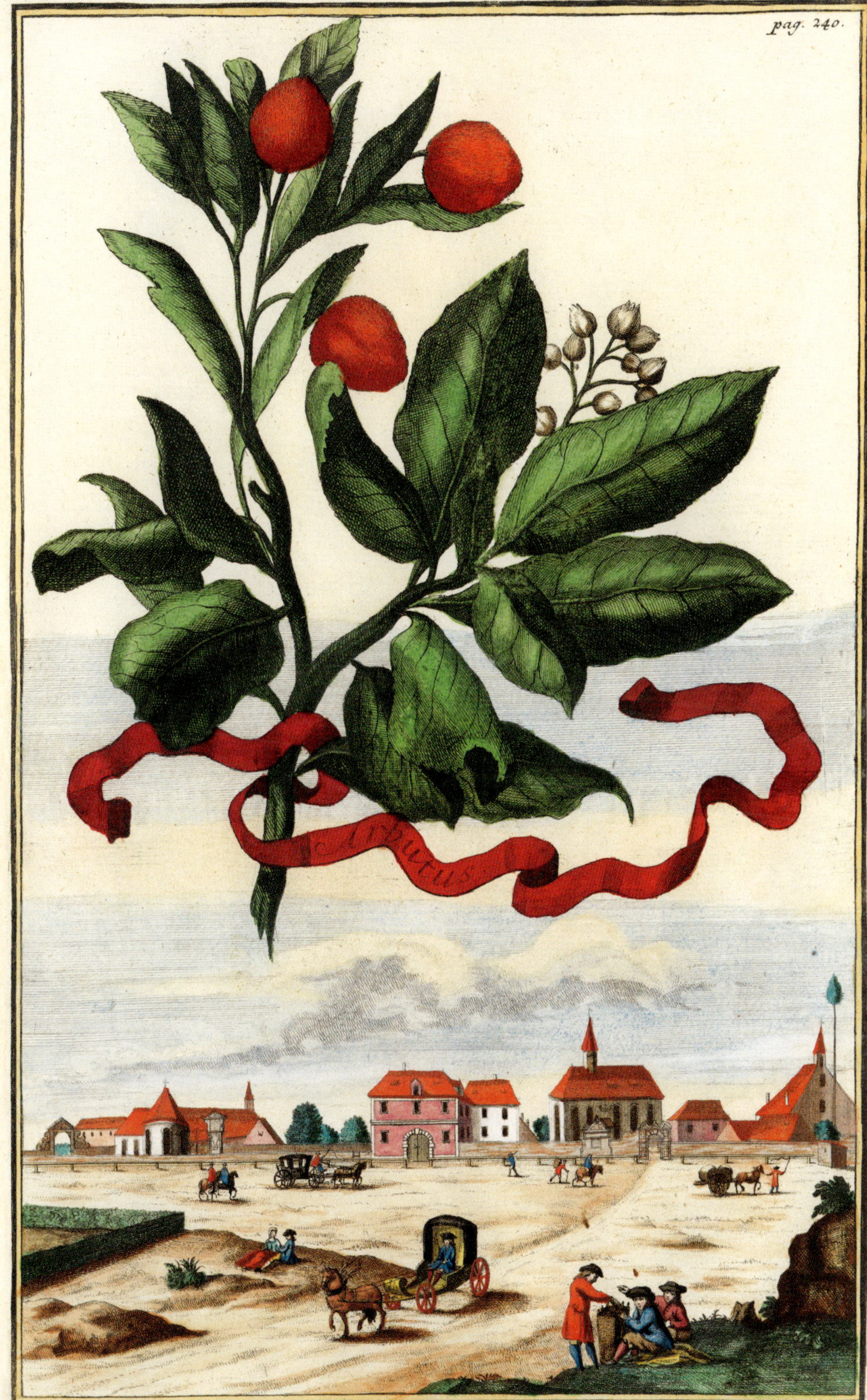
pag. 240.
Arbutus
St Iohannes Kirchhoff.

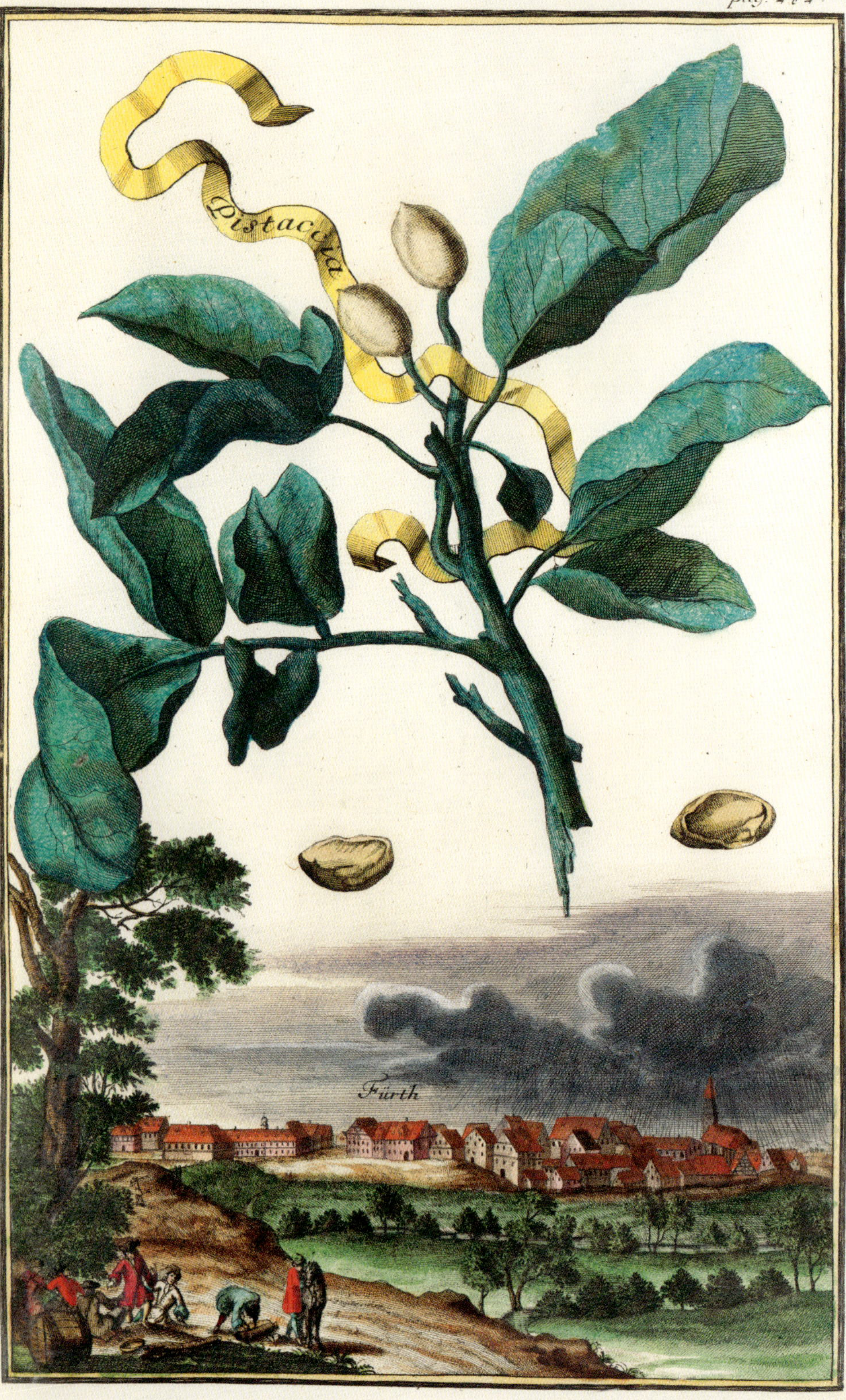

Pistaccia

Fürth

Melanzana

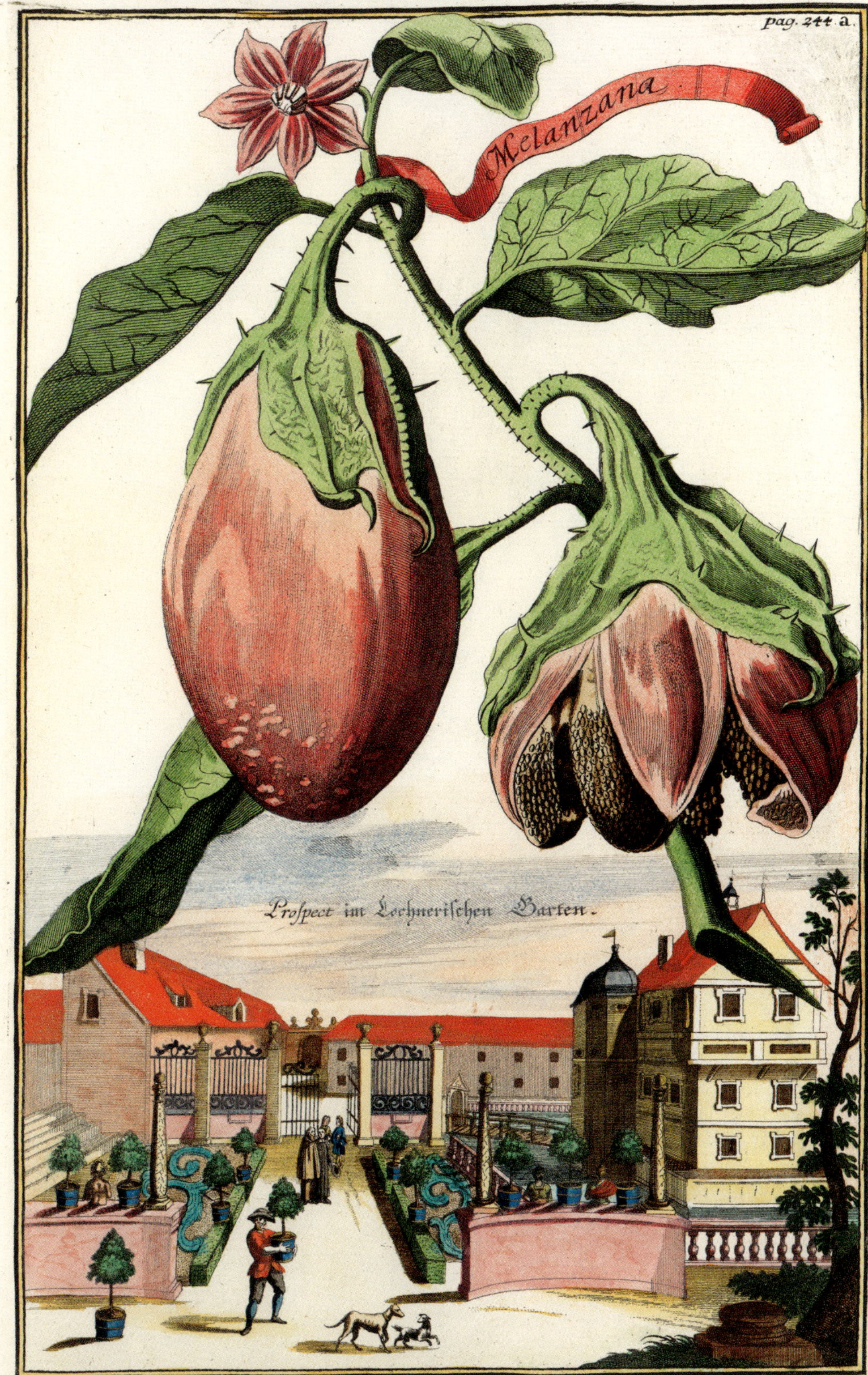

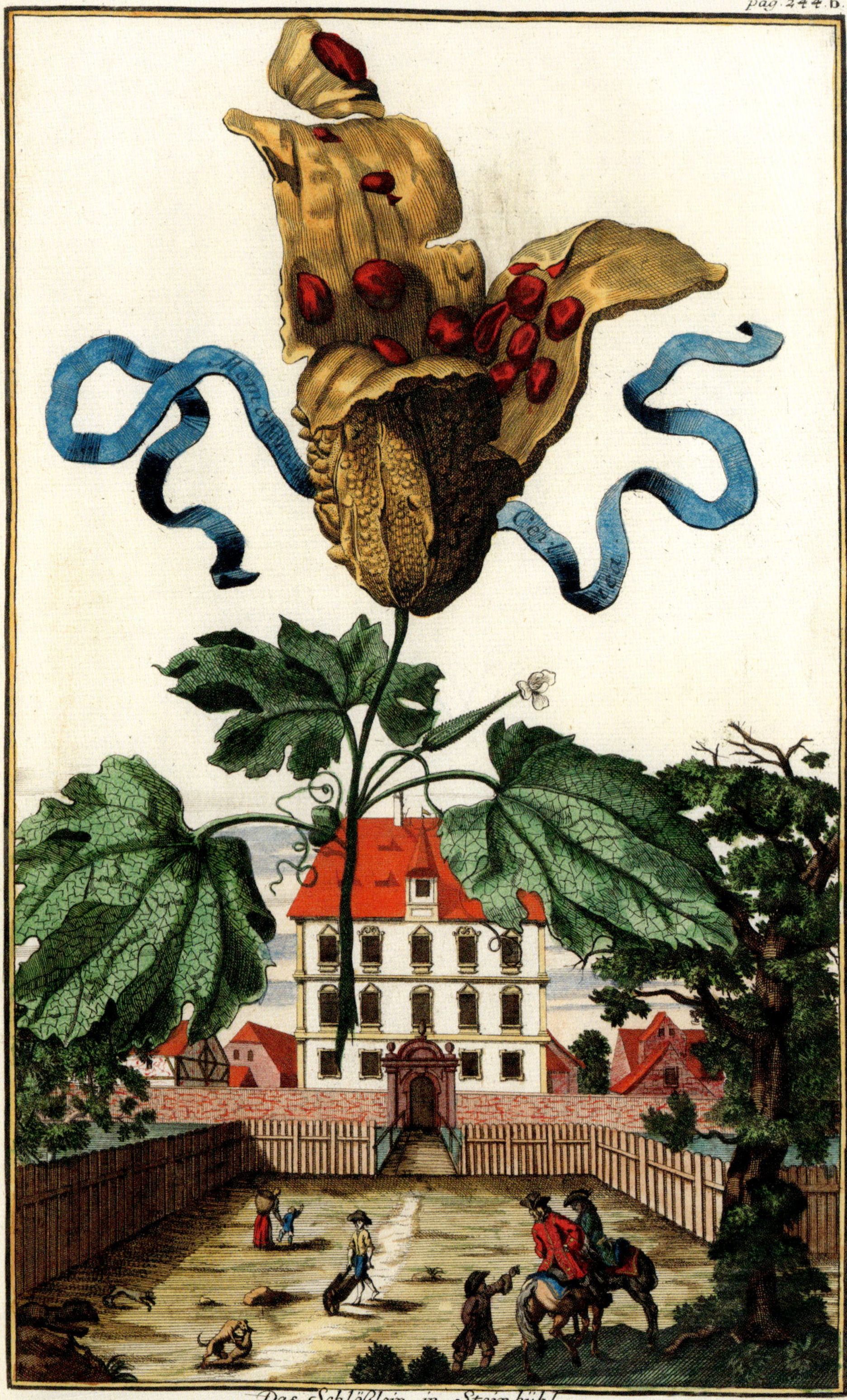

Momordica Ceylandica

Nuremberg, Steinbühl – The Manor

MELANZANA.

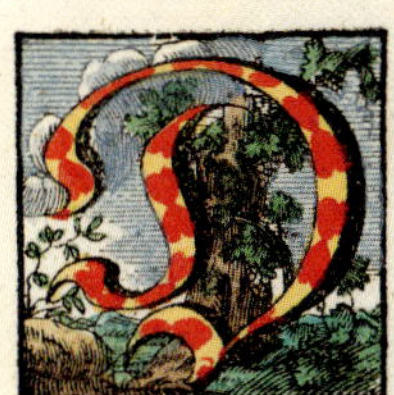

Diese Frucht wächset mehrentheils in Italien und sonderlich in Rom/ von dar ich einigen Saamen bekommen/ werden sonst Mala insana genannt/ weil sie nicht gar gesund seyn/ indeme sie den Kopff einnehmen / und wie thumm oder doll machen sollen/ sie geben sie aber dannoch einen weg / wie Sig.r Vicenzo Tanara in seiner Oeconomia berichtet / dem Gesind zu essen / am meisten aber bedienen sich dessen die Juden. Hie zu Lande kan man die Frucht wol zuweg bringen / so man den Saamen aus Italien bekommt / doch wird hie zu Land solcher Saame selten reiff und gut/ es gibt aber zweyerley Arten dieser Früchte/ eine ist blaß-gelb/ in der Form/ wie fast eine grosse Pflaume/ von dem Stiel an/hat sie dünne und was lang-zugespitzte Blätter/ welche um die Frucht biß fast an die Helffte gehen/ auf welchen Blättern kleine Stacheln zu sehen / welche sich auch an dem Stiel einfinden. Und also ist auch die andere Art beschaffen / welche wie Fleisch-farb an einer Seiten / an der andern aber hoch Purpur-färbig ist / wann sie lang im Feld oder Geschirren stehen/ springet endlich die Frucht auf/ wie an der einen in diesem Kupffer-Druck zu sehen / ist aber gantz dick und das Fleisch hart / wie an einem Apffel/ daran hangen die Saamen-Körnlein/ welche anfänglich weißlicht/ hernach braun werden/ aber wie gedacht/ gar selten zeitigen. Es hat diese Frucht ein schönes Blümlein / welches Rosen-farb / mit Purpur-farben Striemen/ welche einen Stern præsentiren / und träget dabey grosse breite Blätter.

Von der Momordica Ceylanica.

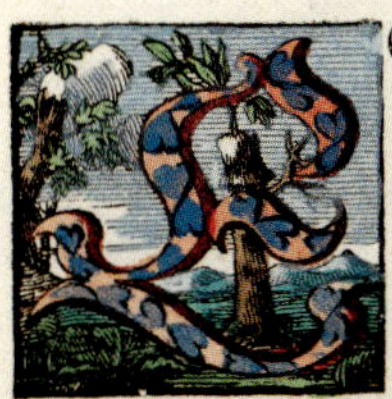

Es gibt wol zweyerley Momordicas , deren die erste und gemeine Art auch Balsamina von etlichen genennet wird/ wächset nicht gar groß / rundlicht / und oben zugespitzt / an der Farb Pasteil-gelb und röthlicht durcheinander. Diese Art aber/ welche aus Ceylan heraus kommen / von daher sie auch den Namen hat / wird etwas ablang / fast wie die Gurcken und Kümmerlinge / geräth aber nicht allemal in solcher Grösse/ wie die in hiebey gemachtem Abriß/ vor einem Jahr gewachsen/ abgezeichnet worden/ wann sie recht zeitig wird/ springet sie auf/ und theilet sich etwas voneinander / darinnen die Saamen-Körner liegen / welche schön Blut-roth anzusehen/ die Blühe ist klein/ ein wenig gelblicht von Farbe/ die Blätter seyn etwas groß/ und fast formirt wie Sterne/ anbey voller kleinen Aederlein/ man brauchet auch diese/ absonderlich aber die ordinari Momordica, in denen Apothecken zu unterschiedlichen Heil- und Hülff-Mitteln.

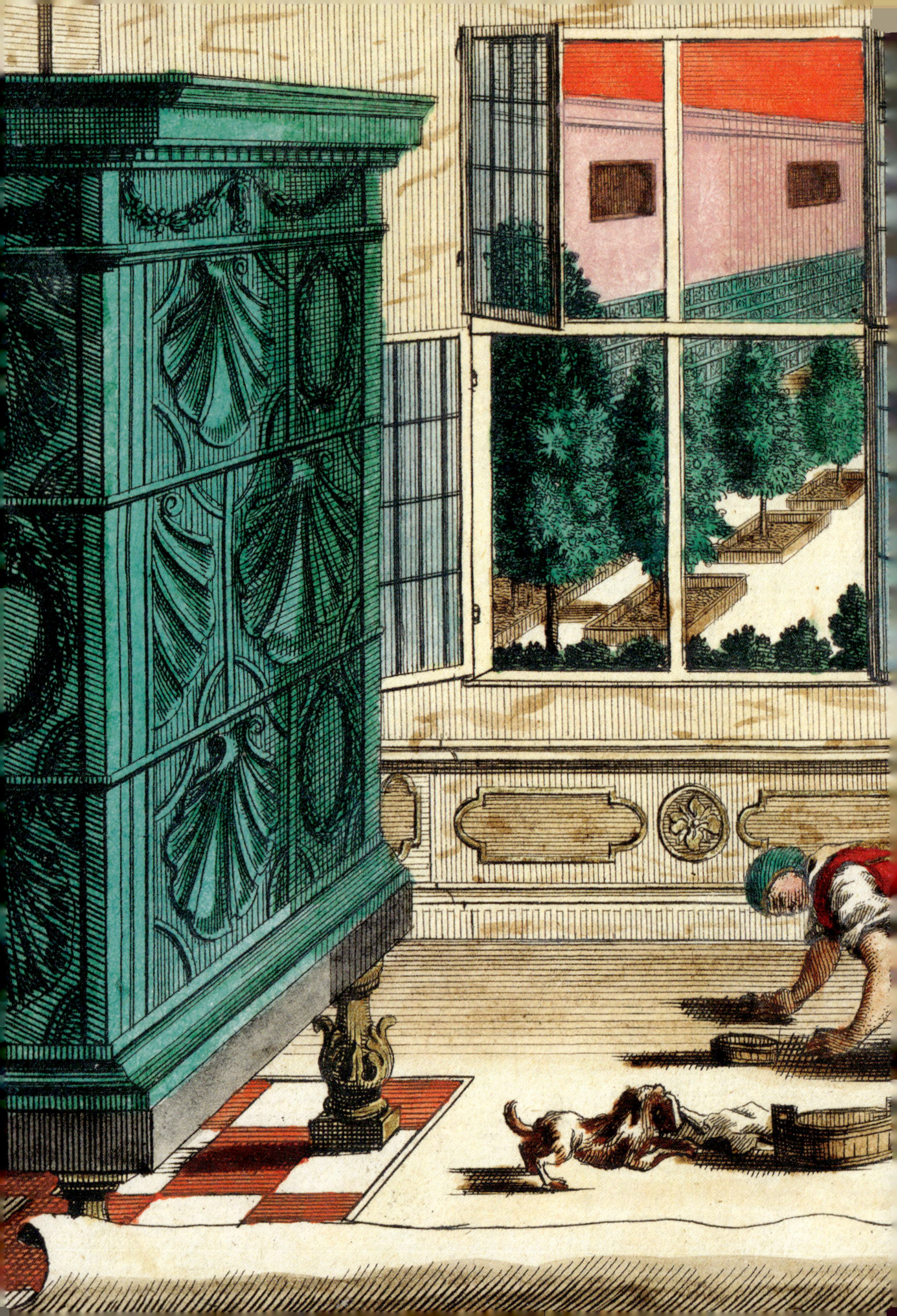

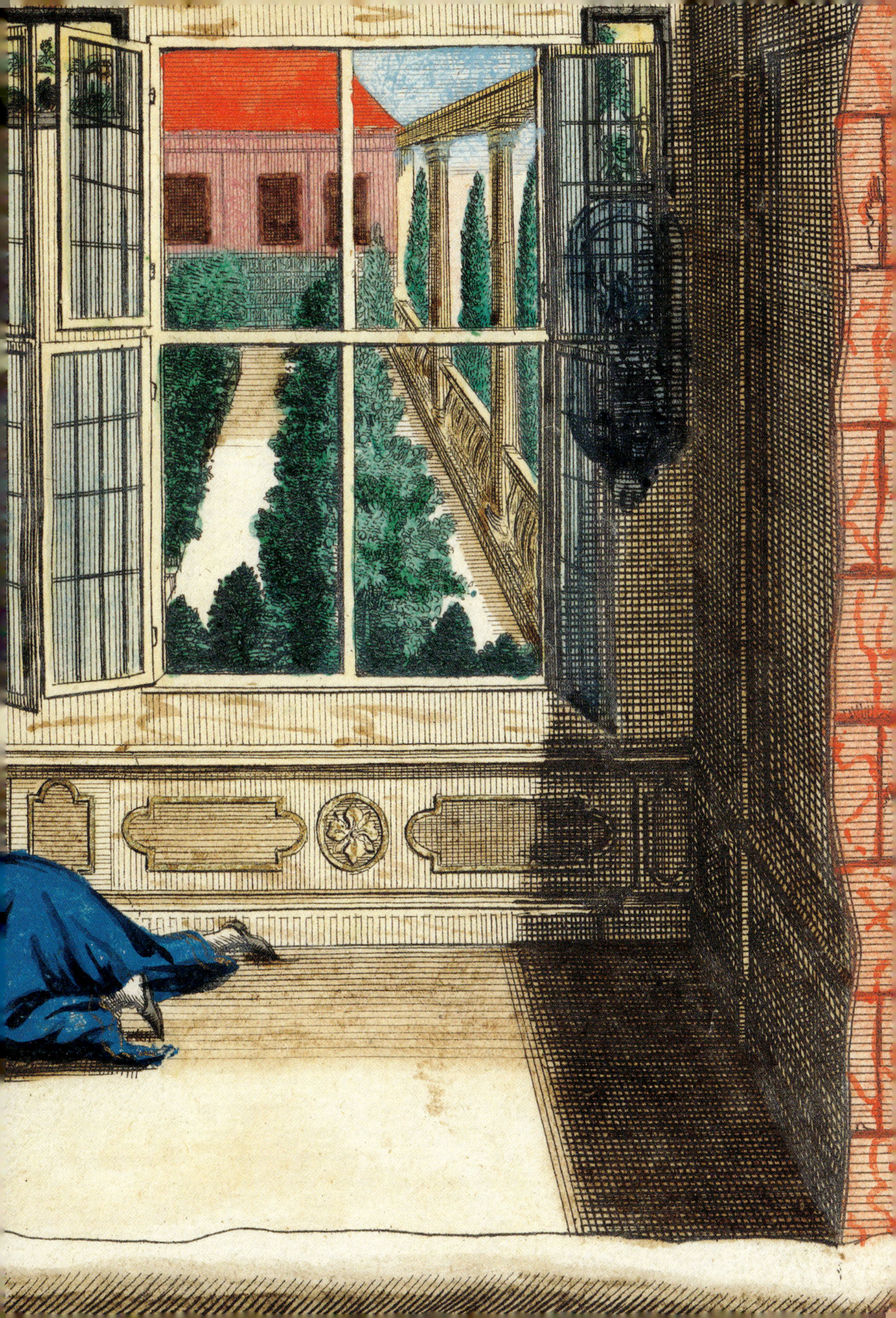

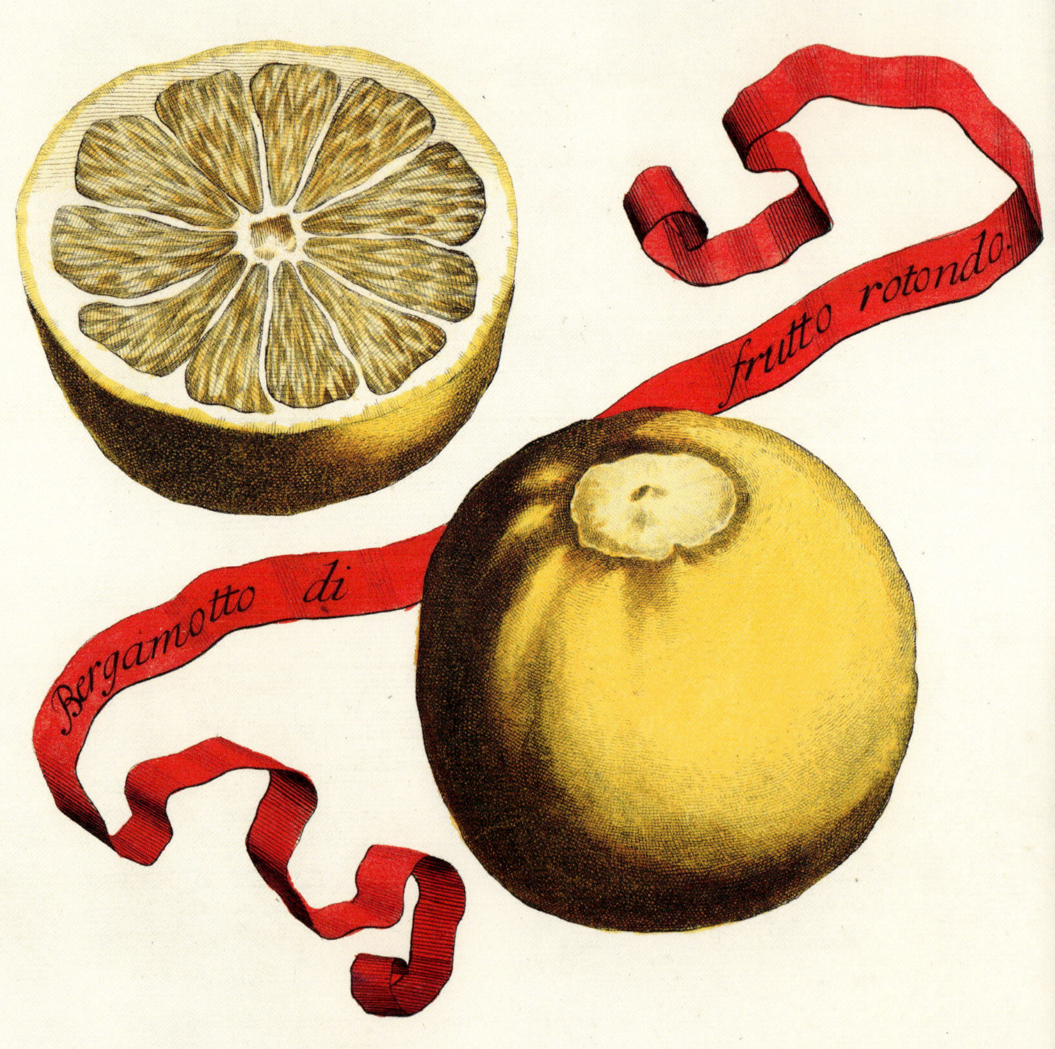
Bergamotto di
frutto rotondo.

Volume II

Continuation of the Nuremberg Hesperides, or: Further detailed descriptions of the noble fruits of the citron, lemon and bitter orange, together with extensive notes on how these may best be planted and cared for; whereby the varieties which either grow in Nuremberg or which have been brought there from various foreign places have with the greatest accuracy been engraved in copper and traced; also divided into four parts, and explained with relevant comments; in addition, an appendix presents several rare and exotic plants, such as the pineapple, palm tree, coconut, cotton etc., which are also represented in copper engravings; edited by Johann Christoph Volkamer. 1714

Continuation der Nürnbergischen Hesperidum, Oder: Fernere gründliche Beschreibung der Edlen Citronat-, Citronen- und Pomeranzen-Früchte, mit einem ausführlichen Bericht, wie solche am besten zu warten und zu erhalten seyn; Worbei diejenigen Sorten, so theils zu Nürnberg gewachsen, theils von verschiedenen fremden Orten dahin gelanget, auf das accurateste in Kupffer gestochen und nachgezeichnet worden; abermals in vier Theile eingetheilet, und mit gehörigen Anmerkungen erläutert; Benebenst einem Anhang von etlichen raren und fremden Gewächsen, als Der Ananas, des Palm-Baums, der Coccus-Nüsse, der Baum-Wolle u. a. m., welche ebenfalls in Kupffer-Rissen vorgestellet sind; herausgegeben von Johann Christoph Volkamer. 1714
(Original German text of the title-page)

Continuation des Hespérides de Nuremberg, ou : Autre description minutieuse de ces nobles fruits, citrons, limons et oranges amères ; Avec un récit détaillé de comment ceux-ci peuvent être correctement soignés et conservés ; les variétés, qui poussent à Nuremberg ou importées de divers pays étrangers, ont été méticuleusement gravées et tracées sur cuivre ; Également divisées en quatre parties et expliquées en commentaires judicieux ; De plus, un appendice répertoriant de nombreuses plantes rares et exotiques, comme l'ananas, le palmier, la noix de coco, le coton etc., présentées également sous forme de gravures sur cuivre ; Édité par Johann Christoph Volkamer. 1714

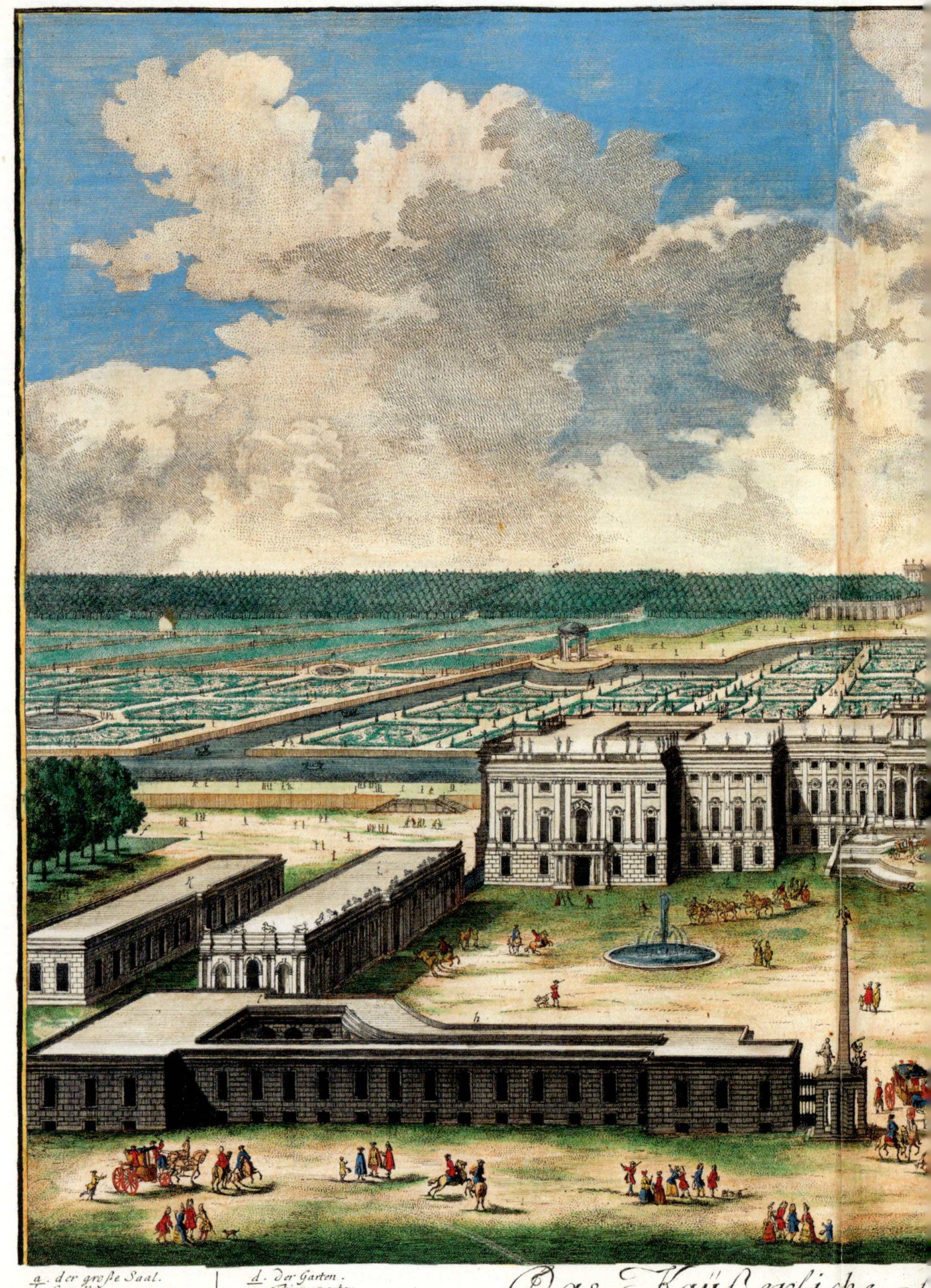
a. der große Saal.
b. Capelle.
c. Eingang zum Lust=garten.
d. der Garten.
e. Thier=garten.
f. der fasanen wald.
Das Kayßerliche

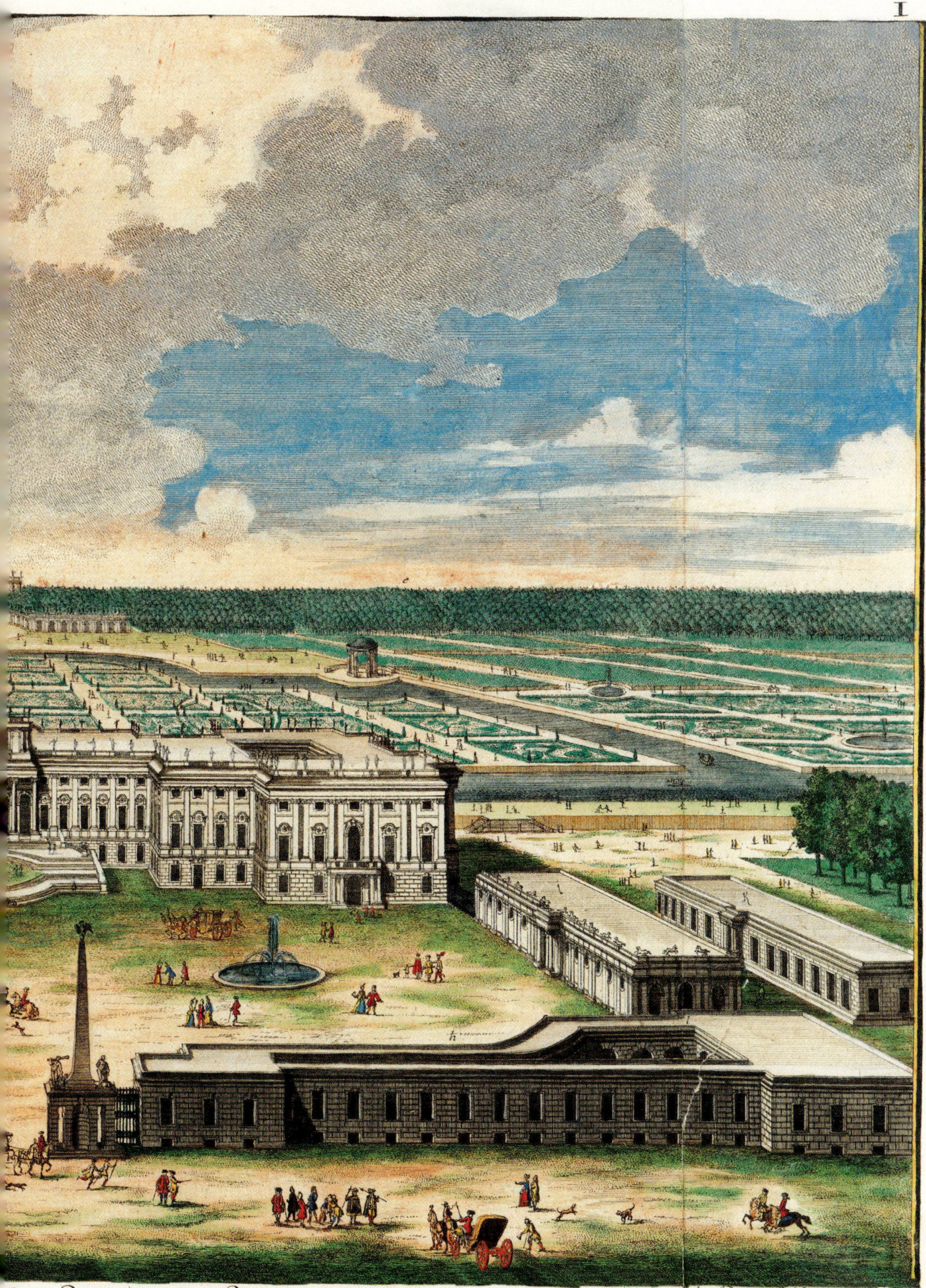

Schloß, Schönbrunn

Joh: Adam Delsenbach. fecit.

g. der Tournier platz.
h. Wohnung der bedienten.
i. Ställe vor die Kaiserspferde.
K. Ställe der bedienten pferde.
l. Schupfen vor die wägen.

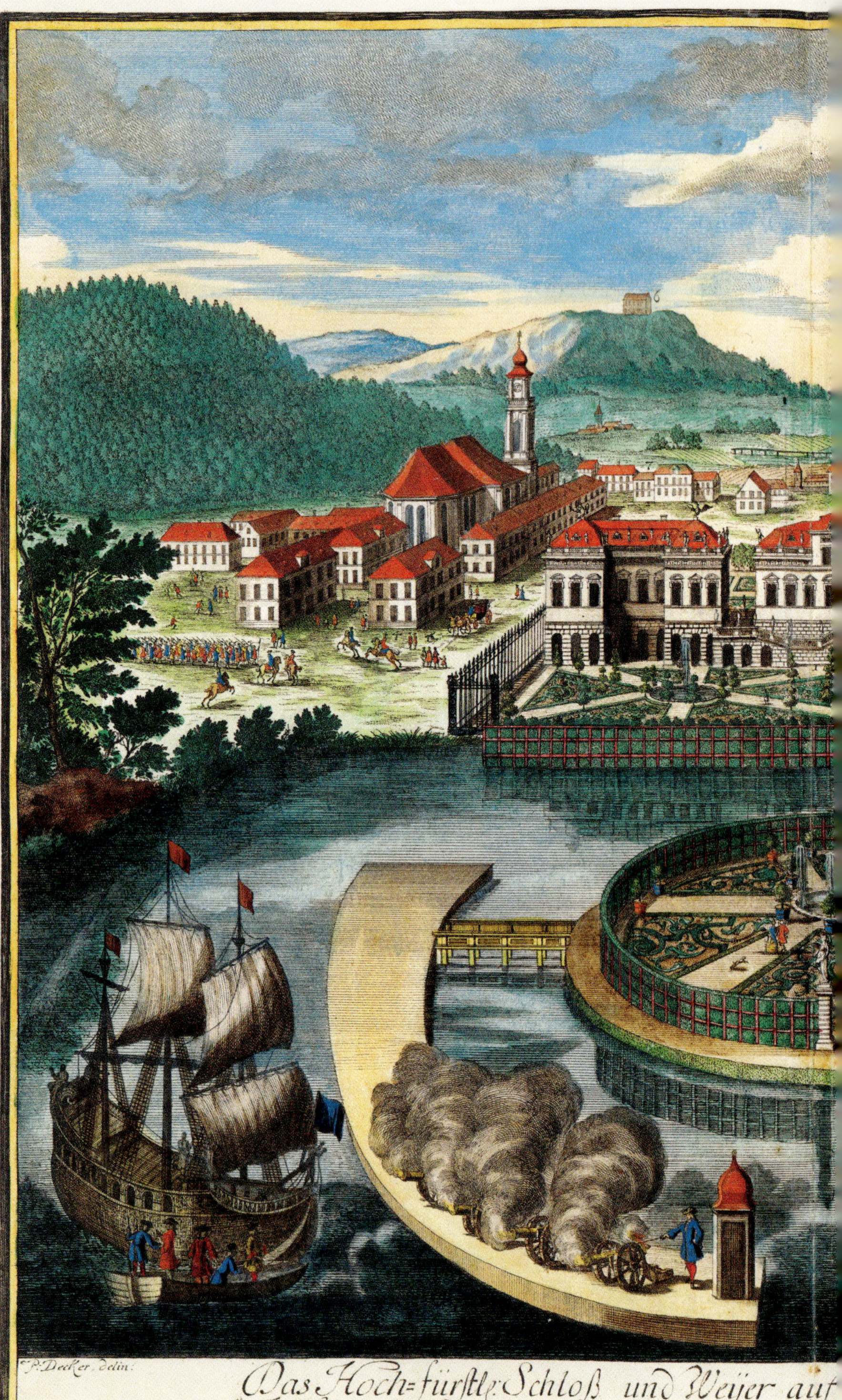
P. Decker, delin.
Das Hoch=fürstl. Schloß und Weijer auf
1 Das Fürstl. Schloß 2 Comedien=haus. 3 Schiffer=häußlein 4 die Neü=an

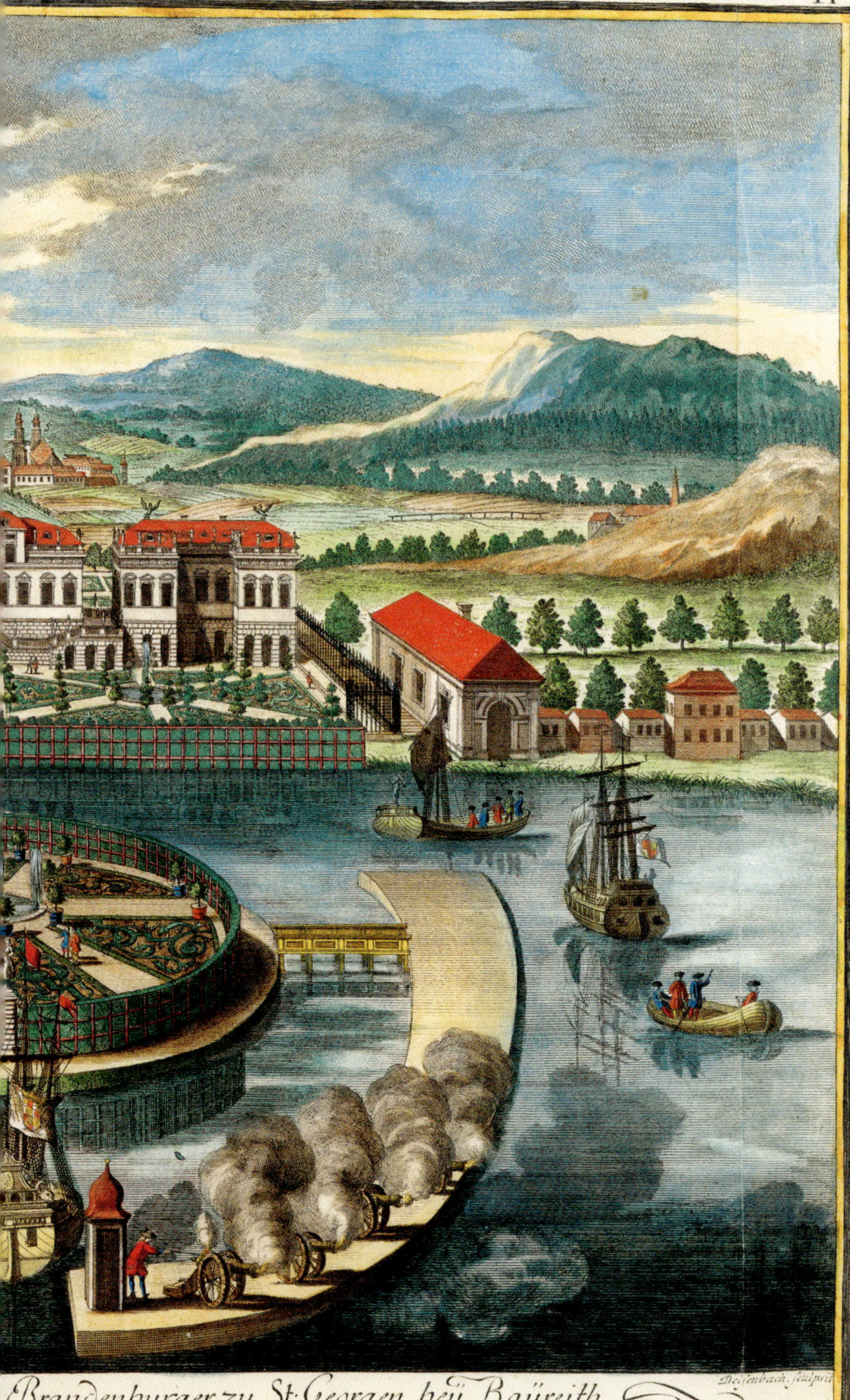

Brandenburger zu St: Georgen bey Bayreith
te Stadt samt der Kirchen 5. Bayreith 6. Sophienberg 7. die Casernen

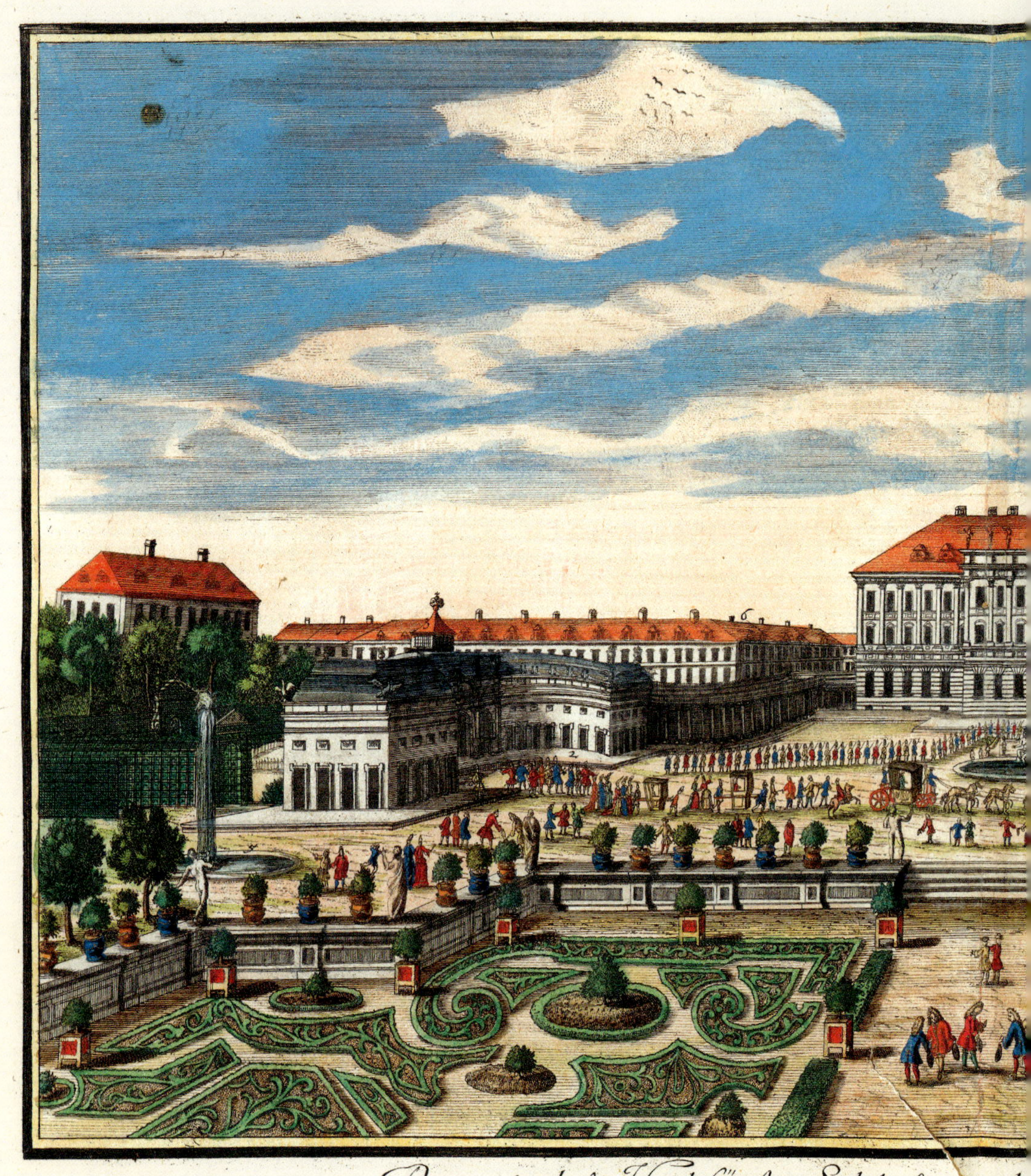

Prospect deß Hochfürstl: Schloß = und

1. Das Schloß.
2. Orangerien.
3. Schloß=Capelle.
4. die große fontaine.

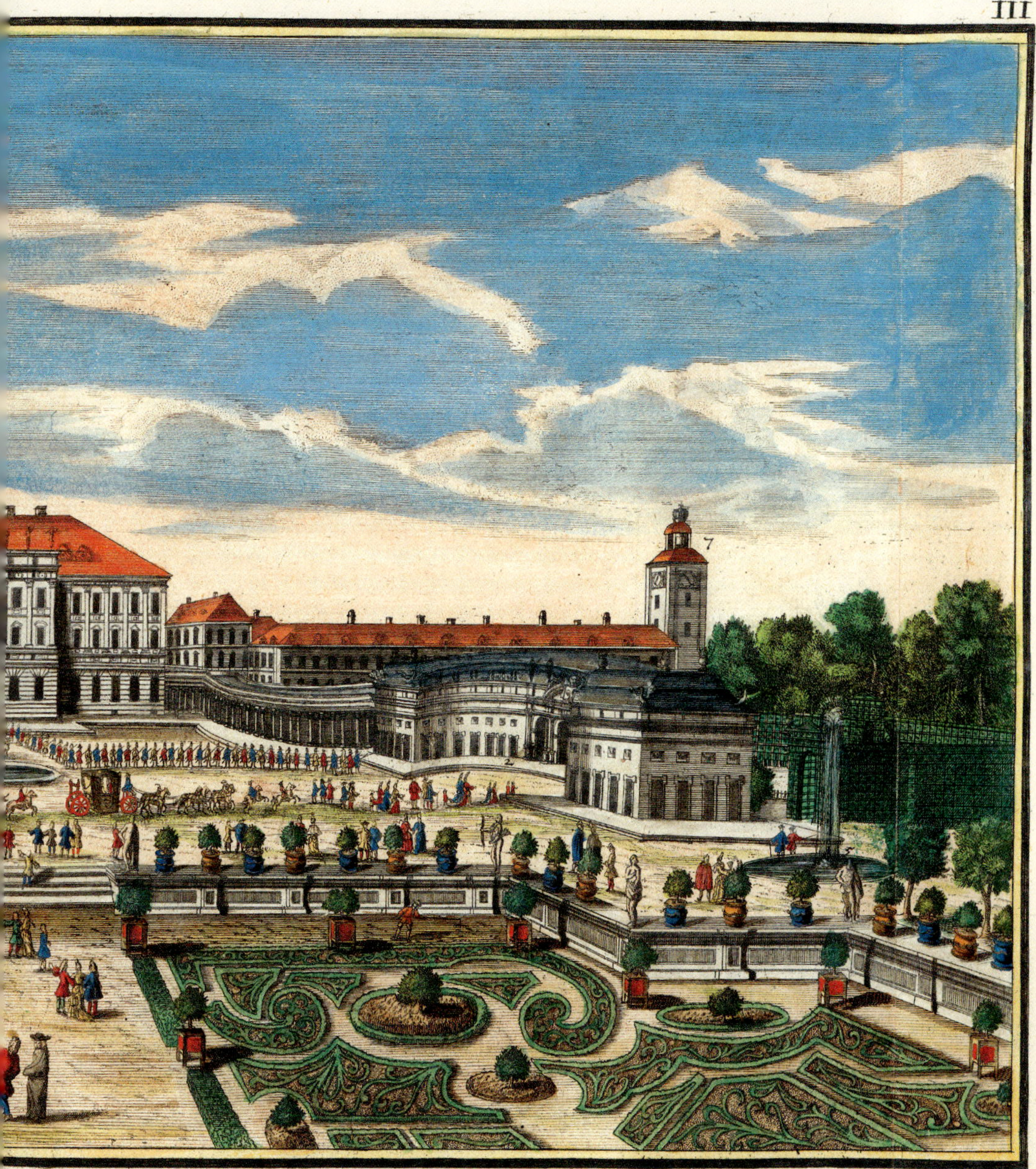

rtens zu Chriſtian Erlang.

5. die Kleinen fontainen.
6. die Küche.
7. der Waſser Thurn.

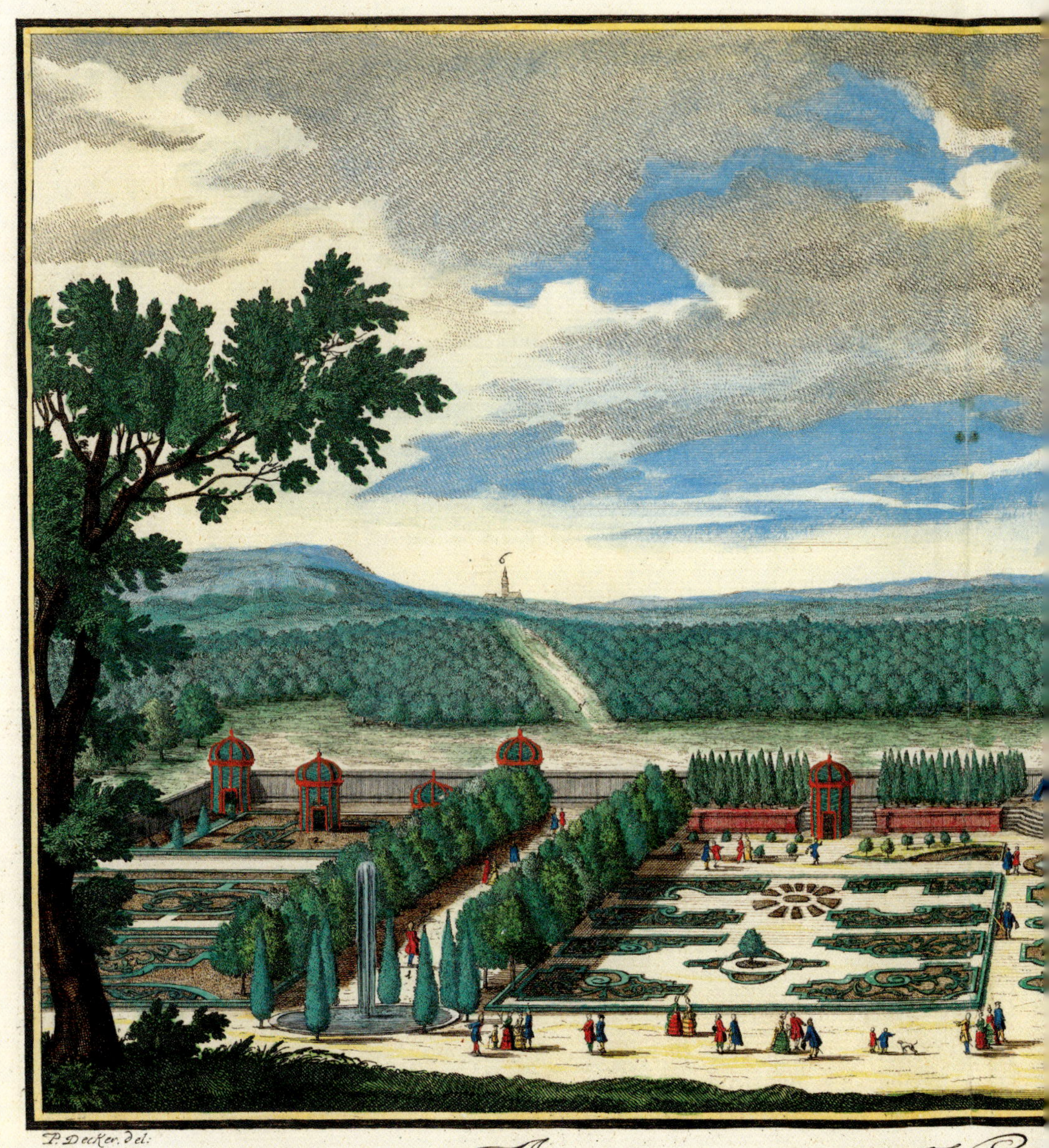

P. Decker. del:

1. Doppelte Alléen von frucht-bäumen.
2. Lust-Häußer, allwo auf einer seiten der Irrgarten auf der andern die fasanereÿ zu sehen.
3. Theatrum.

Anderer Prospect deß Hochfü
gegen Morg

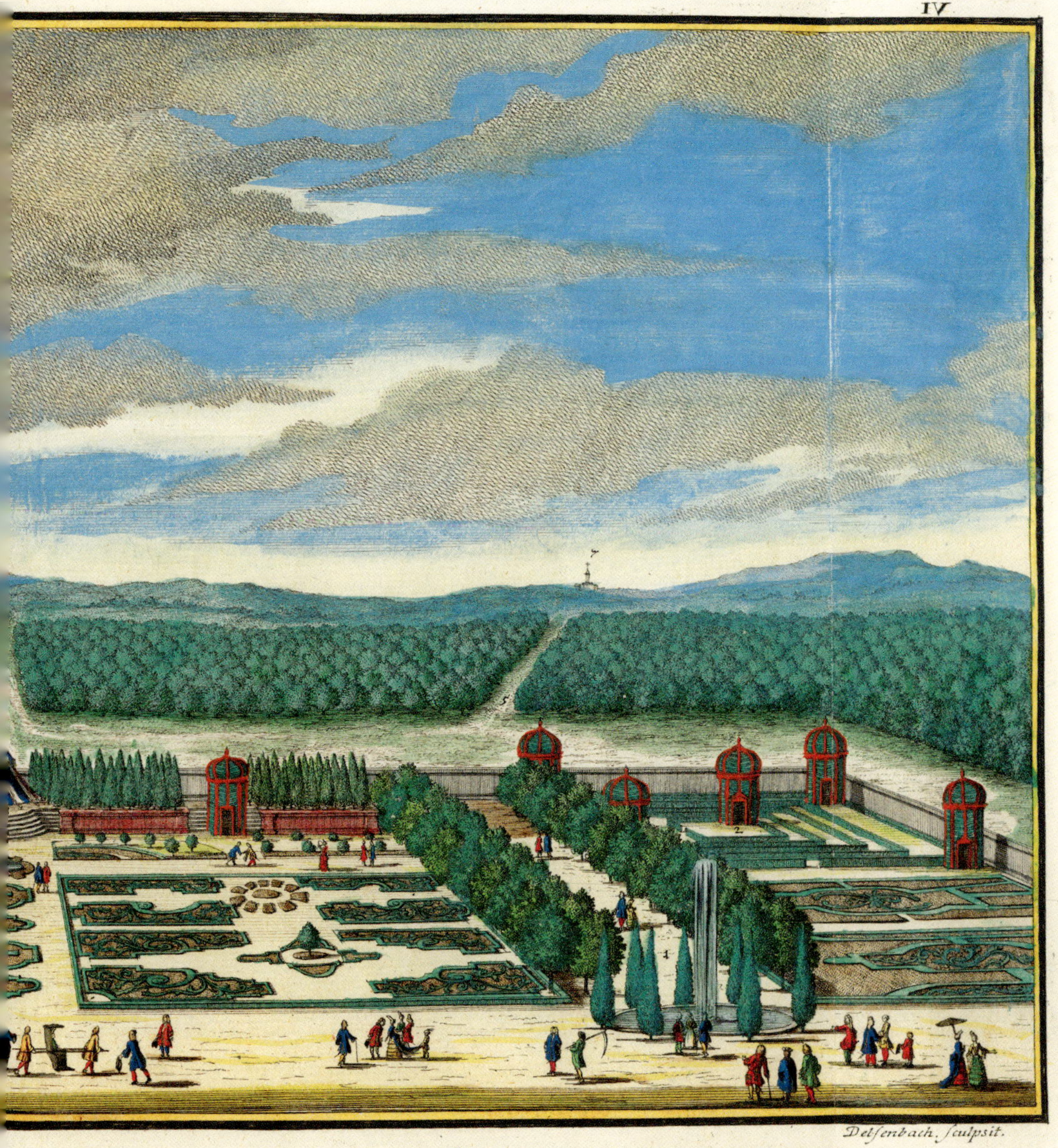

Gartens zu Chriſtian Erlang, anzuſehen

4. Statua des verſtorbenen Churf. zu Brandenburg.
5. Wald-Alléen.
6. Marclavſtein.
7. Huttenreuth.

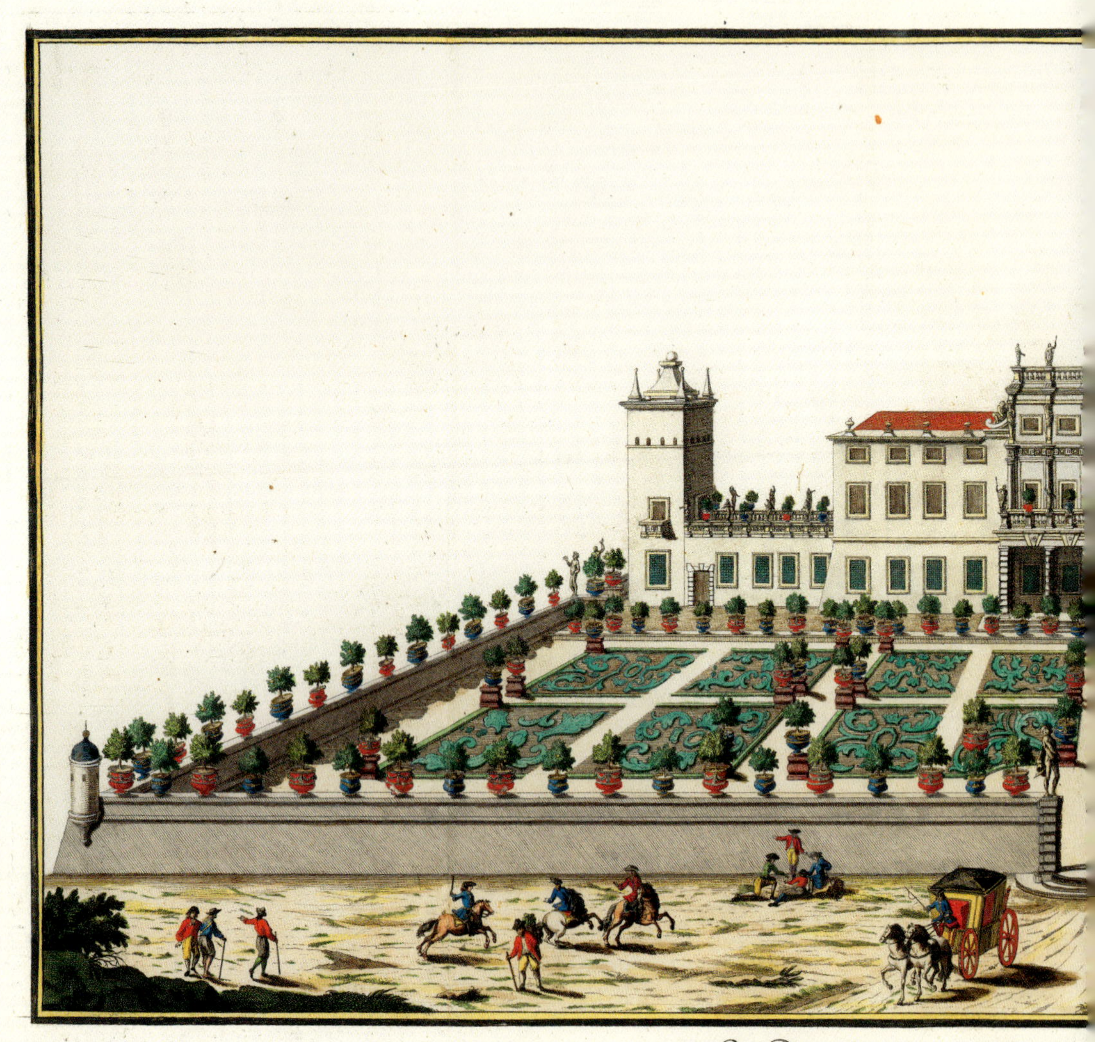

Il Palazzo, con il Giardi

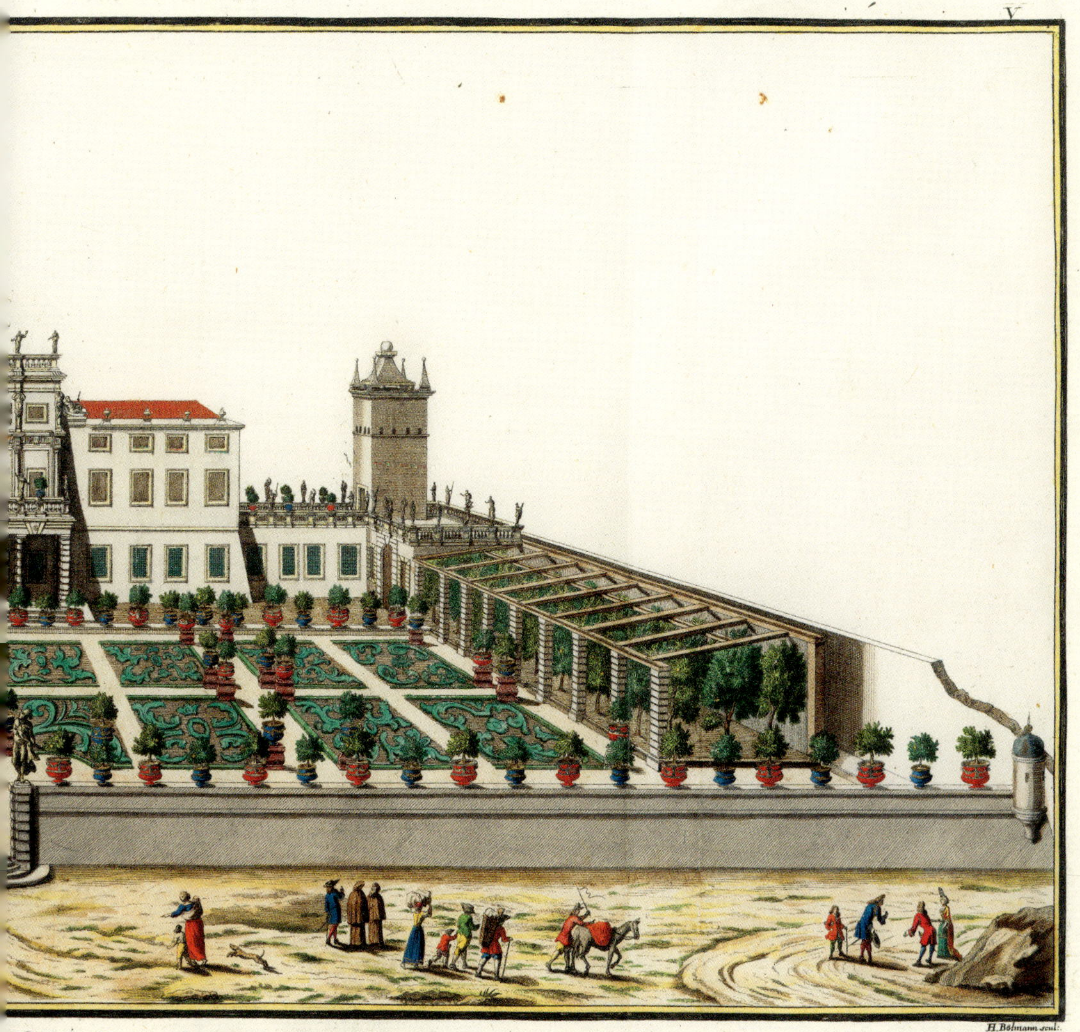

H. Bölmann sculp.

S. S.ri Conti Allegri in Cucciano.

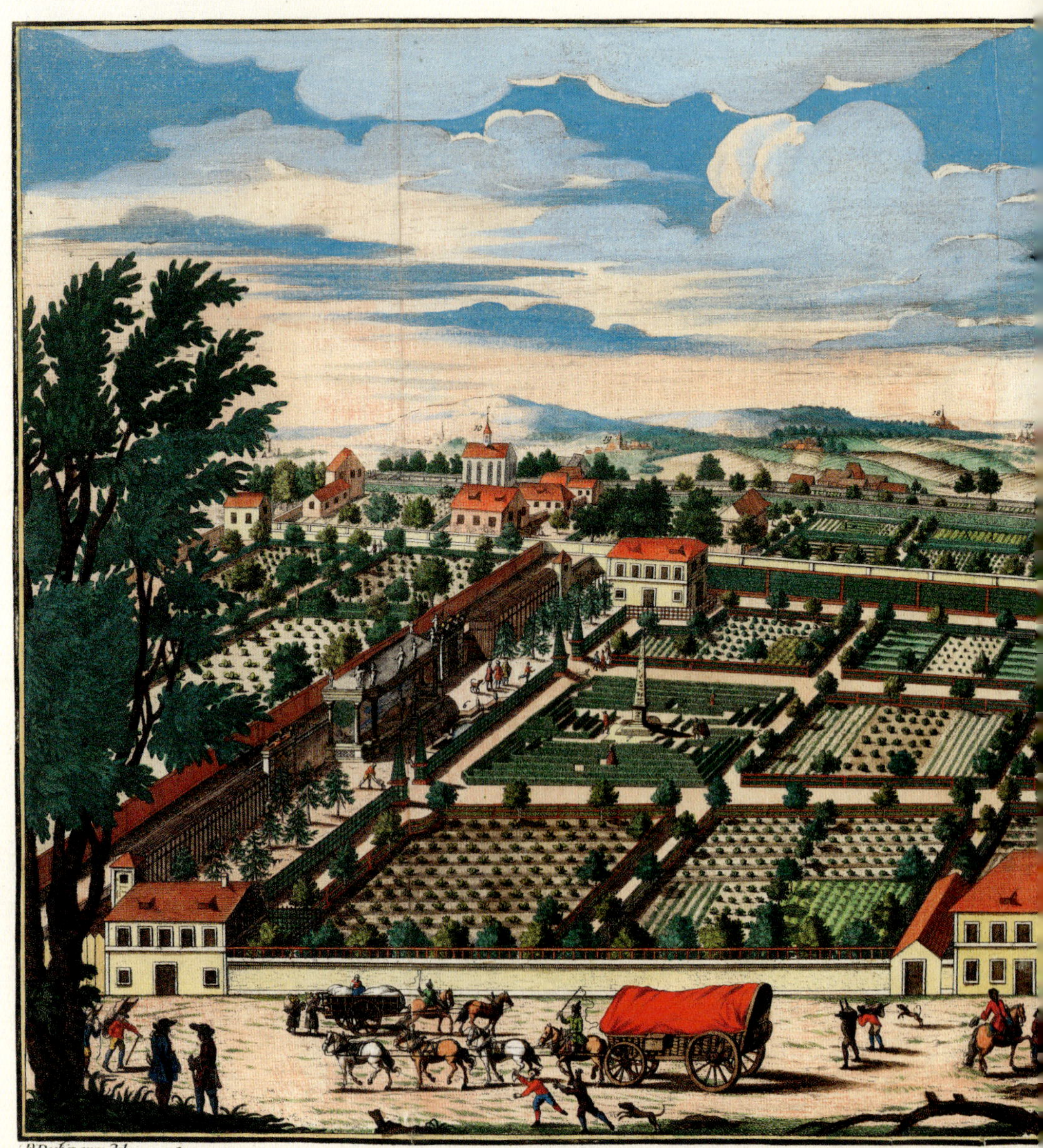

P. Decker jun: del:

1 Das Waſſer-Rad. 2 Platz der fünff Columnen milliarien. 3 Das Pomerantzen-Hauß. 4 Die Sonnen-Uhr von Bux. 5 Der Irrgarten. 6
Garten. 10 St. Rochus. 11 etwas von der Statt. 12 Schwein-ſtell und Weyer. 13 Bern-ſchantz. 14 St. Johan
Viridarium Suburbaneum Johan: Crist

IX.

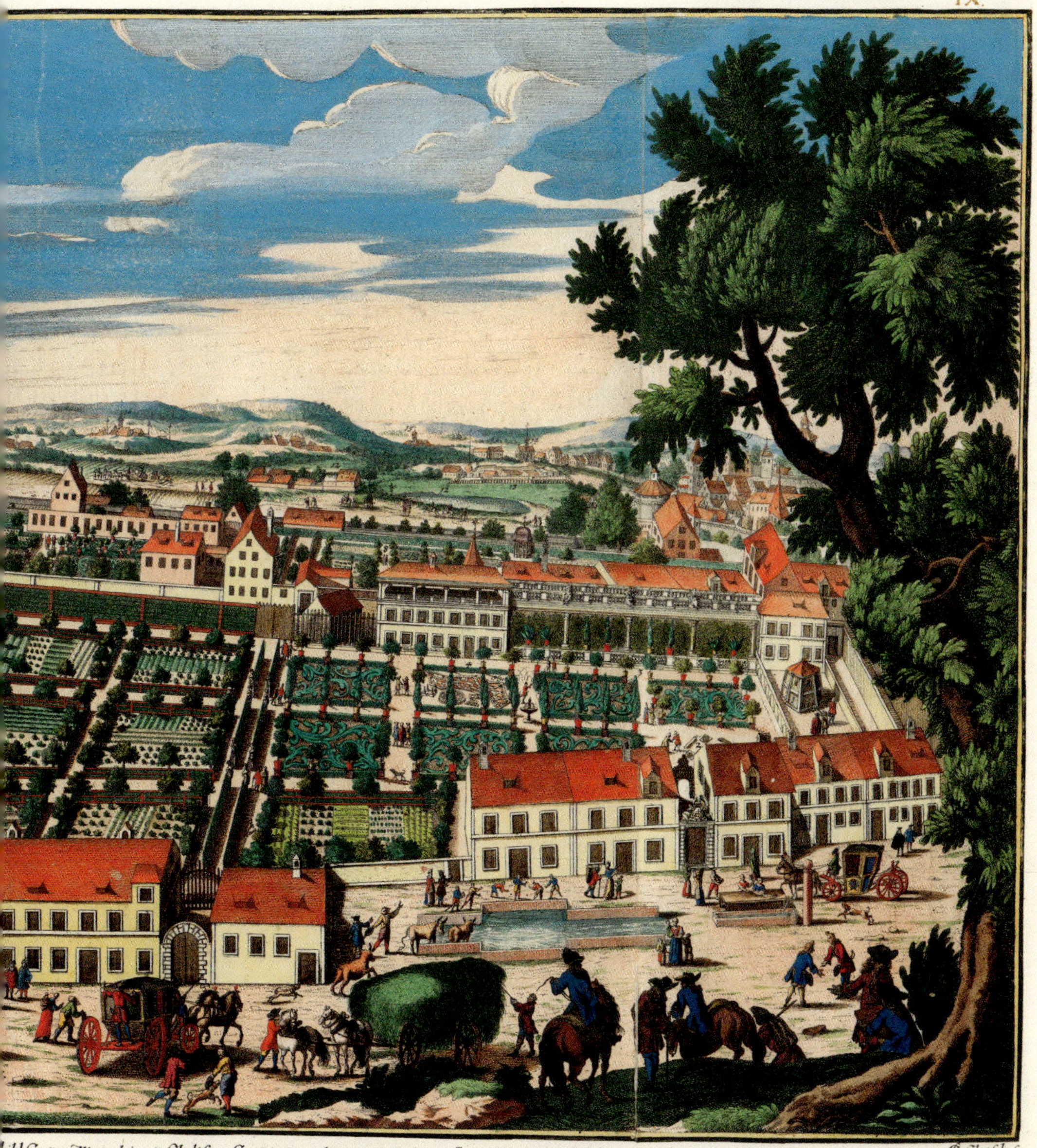

hild Crotten Weyerlein. 7 Obeliscus Constantinopolitanus auß einem Stuckstein 20½ Schuh lang. 8 Reyerischer Garten. 9 Seuschabischer „ C. Flotsch sc
Grindlach: 16. Poppenreuth. 17 Fürth. 18 Farrnbach. 19 Zürndorff.
Folckameri in Norimberga

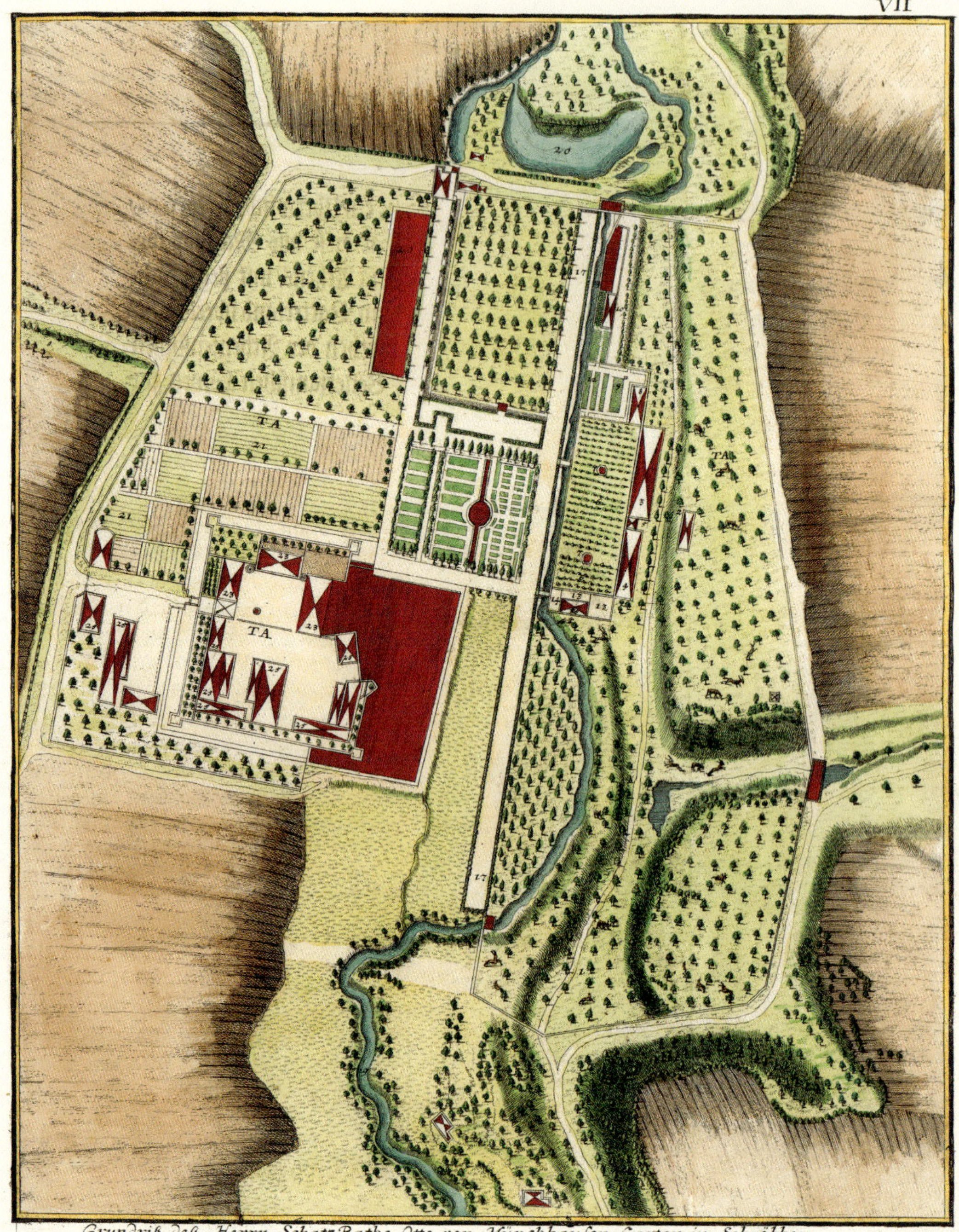

Grundriß deß Herrn Schatz Raths Otto von Münchhausen Garten in Schröbber

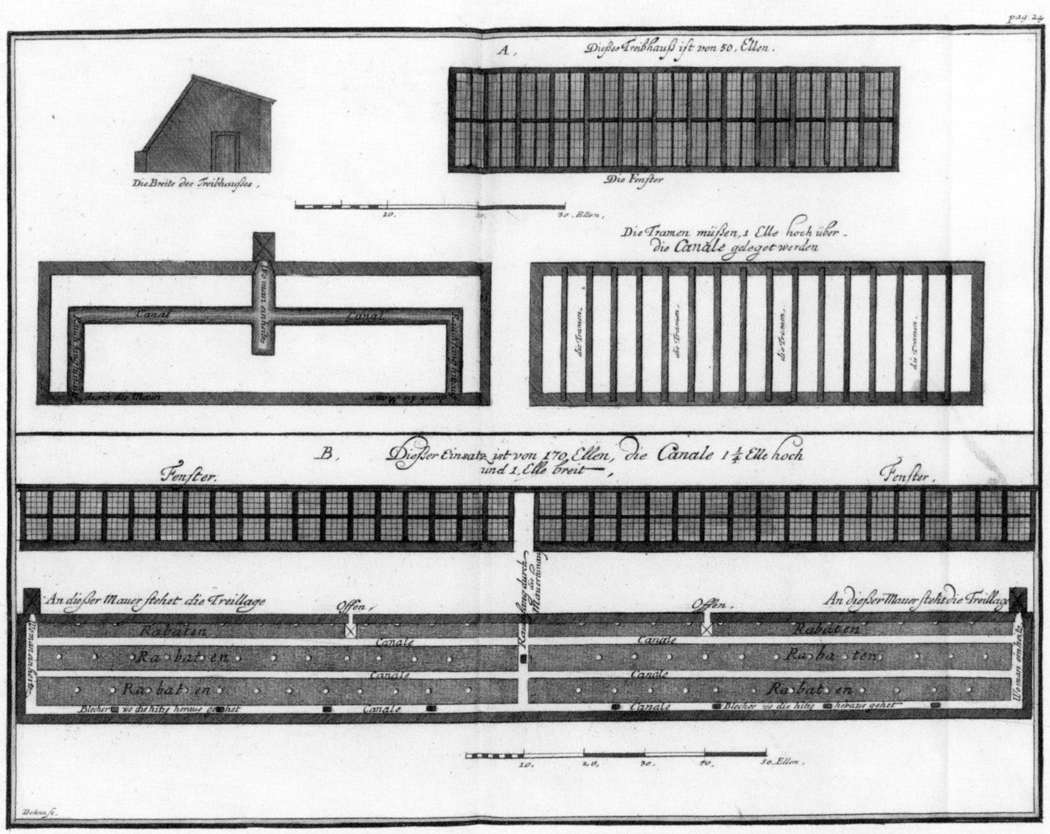

Page 260 Bergamotto di frutto rotondo, detail (see p. 346) *Pages 262/263* Vienna, Hietzing – Schönbrunn Palace and Gardens *Pages 264/265* Bayreuth, St Georgen – Palace and Pond at Brandenburger Straße *Pages 266/267 & 268/269* Erlangen – The Palace and Gardens *Pages 270/271* Cuzzano di Grezzana (Verona) – Villa Allegri, later Arvedi *Pages 272/273* Nuremberg, Gostenhof – Johann Christoph Volkamer's Garden *Page 274* Aerzen, near Hamelin-Pyrmont – Plan of the Schwöbber Palace and Gardens of Otto von Münchhausen *Above* Nuremberg, Gostenhof – Johann Christoph Volkamer's Garden, Ground plans of glasshouses *Pages 276 & 277* Passau, St Georgsberg – Residence and Garden of the Prince-Bishops of Passau

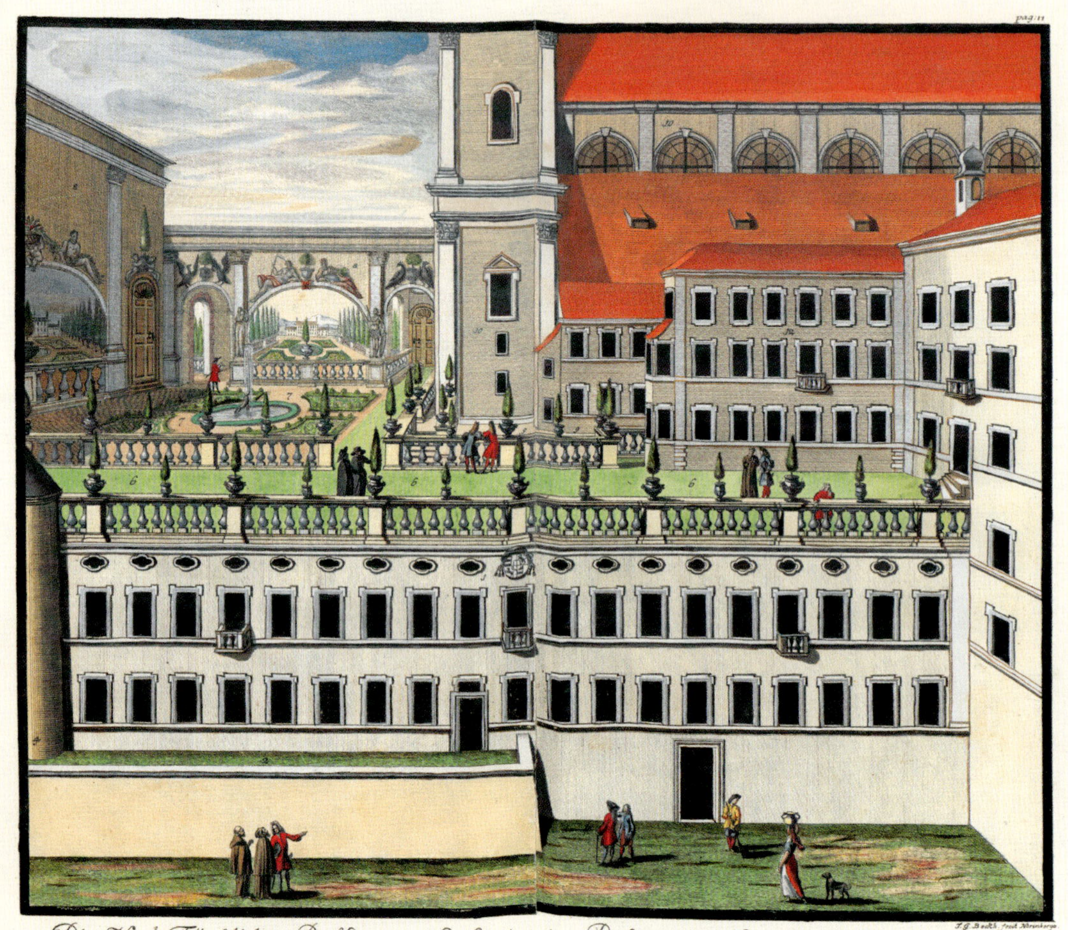

J. G. Beckh fecit Nürnberg

Die Hoch-Fürstliche Residentz und Garten zu Passau auf den St. Georgenberg.

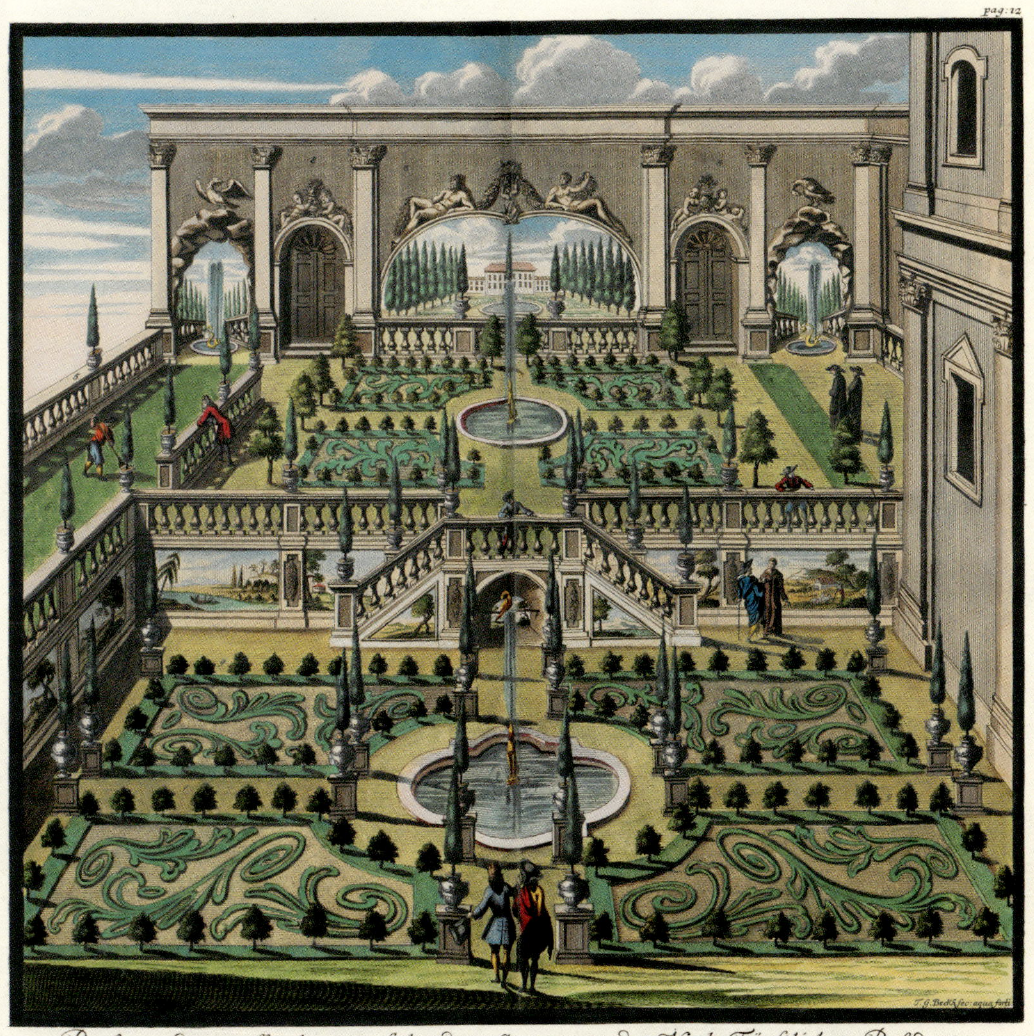

Prospect des auffgebauen stehenden Garten an der Hoch=Fürstlichen Residentz wie er von dar aus zu sehen ist.

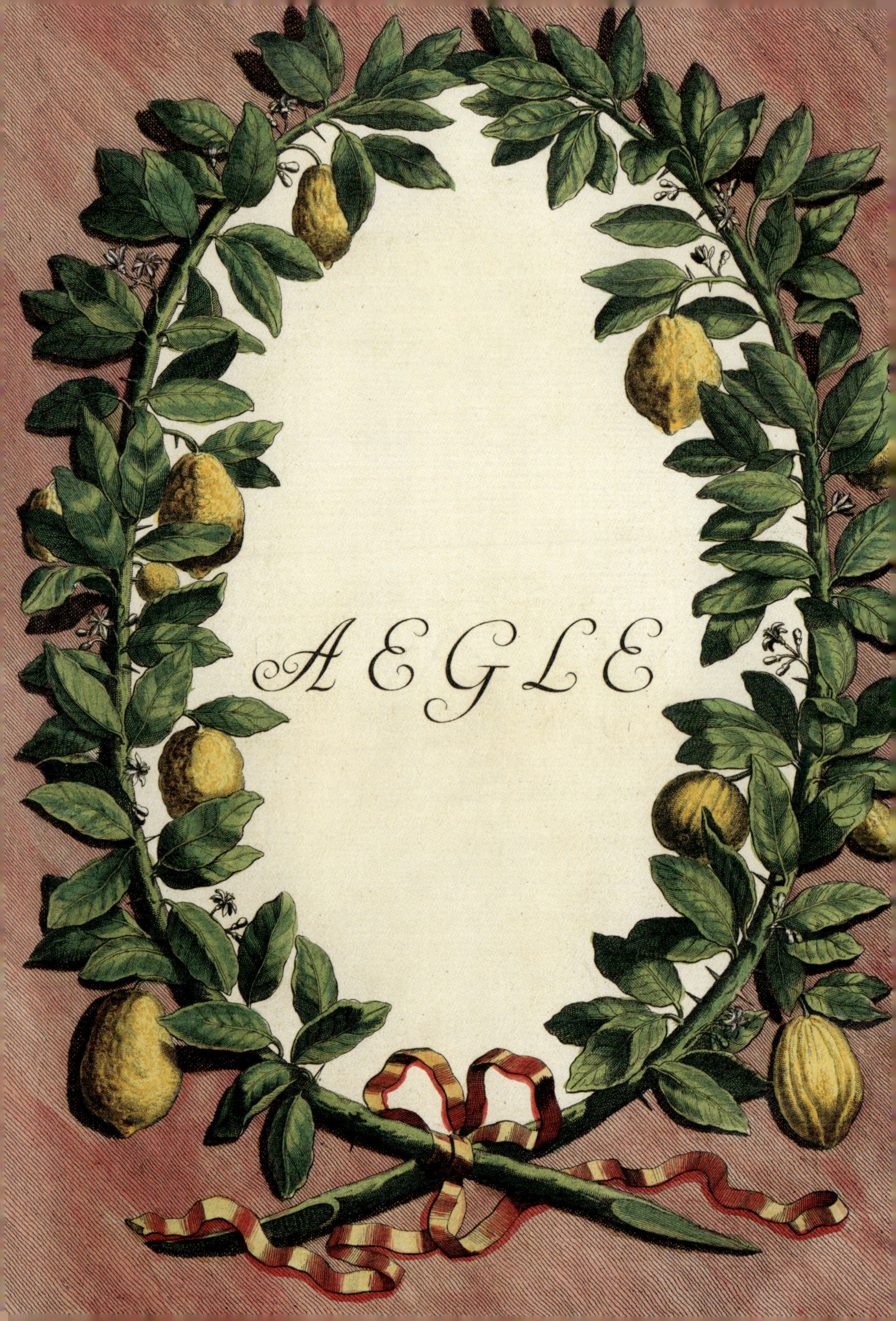
AEGLE

Der andere Theil der CONTINVATION der Nürnbergischen HESPERIDVM.

AEGLE.

❧ ❧ ❧

Das erste Capitel.

Von denen Citronaten.

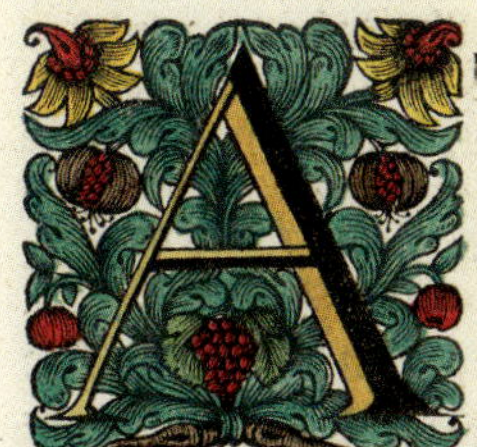

Egle, als die erste unter den Schwestern der Hesperidum, hat uns/ vor etlichen Jahren allbereit/ ihren Wunder- und Schönheit-vollen Garten/ von allerhand raren und delicaten Citronaten/ gezeiget/ und der vorige Theil meines herausgegebenen Werkes/ hat davon eine gehörige Erzehlung abgestattet; anjetzo aber hat sie denselbigen wiederum aufs neue eröffnet/ und will uns darinnen noch mehrere dergleichen fürtreffliche Früchte/ und also den wunderbaren Reichthum der gütigen Natur/ und ihres Garten schönste Zierde vor Augen legen. Sie hat zwar auch in dem vorigen uns schon eine Nachricht/ die fleissige Wartung derselben betreffend/ ertheilet/ vor dißmal aber unterlässt sie nicht/ alsobalden zu bedeuten/ man solle die Beschneidung dieser Bäume ja sorgfältig vornehmen/ und zusehen/ daß man nur bloß von dem alten Holz das überflüssige wegschneide/ und dargegen des jung-gewachsenen Holzes auf das Beste schone. Man wird nicht leichtlich sehen/ daß die Italianer anderst mit ihren Stämmen verfahren/ dieweilen das junge Holz viel eher und lieber/ dann das ältere und stärkere/ die Blüth-Knöpfe treibet/ und man also auf diese Weise sein Vergnügen und seinen Wunsch hieran erhält. Wo man auch von dem jungen Holz Reiser in die Erden setzet/ so werden dieselbigen gar gern und leicht anschlagen/ und man neue Stämme dardurch aufzuziehen vermögen; so man nur diß einzige vor allen dabei in Obacht nimmt/ daß dieselbigen eingesteckten Reiser immerzu müssen feucht gehalten/ und vor der Sonnen so lang verwahret werden/ bis man augenscheinlich siehet/ daß sie gerathen und an-

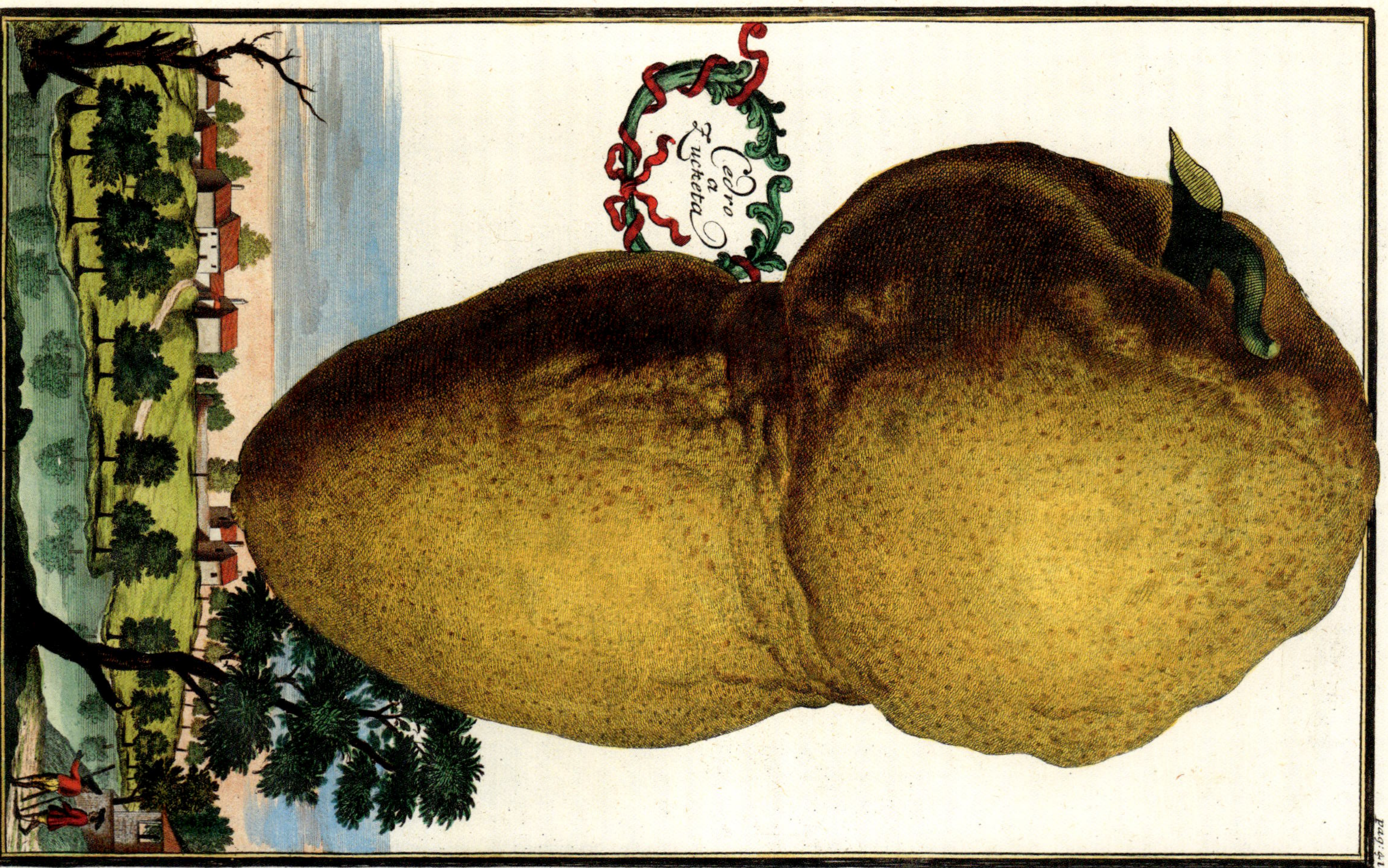

San Vito (Verona). *Pages 278/279* Cartouche and beginning of the second section of vol. II

Cedro a Zucheta

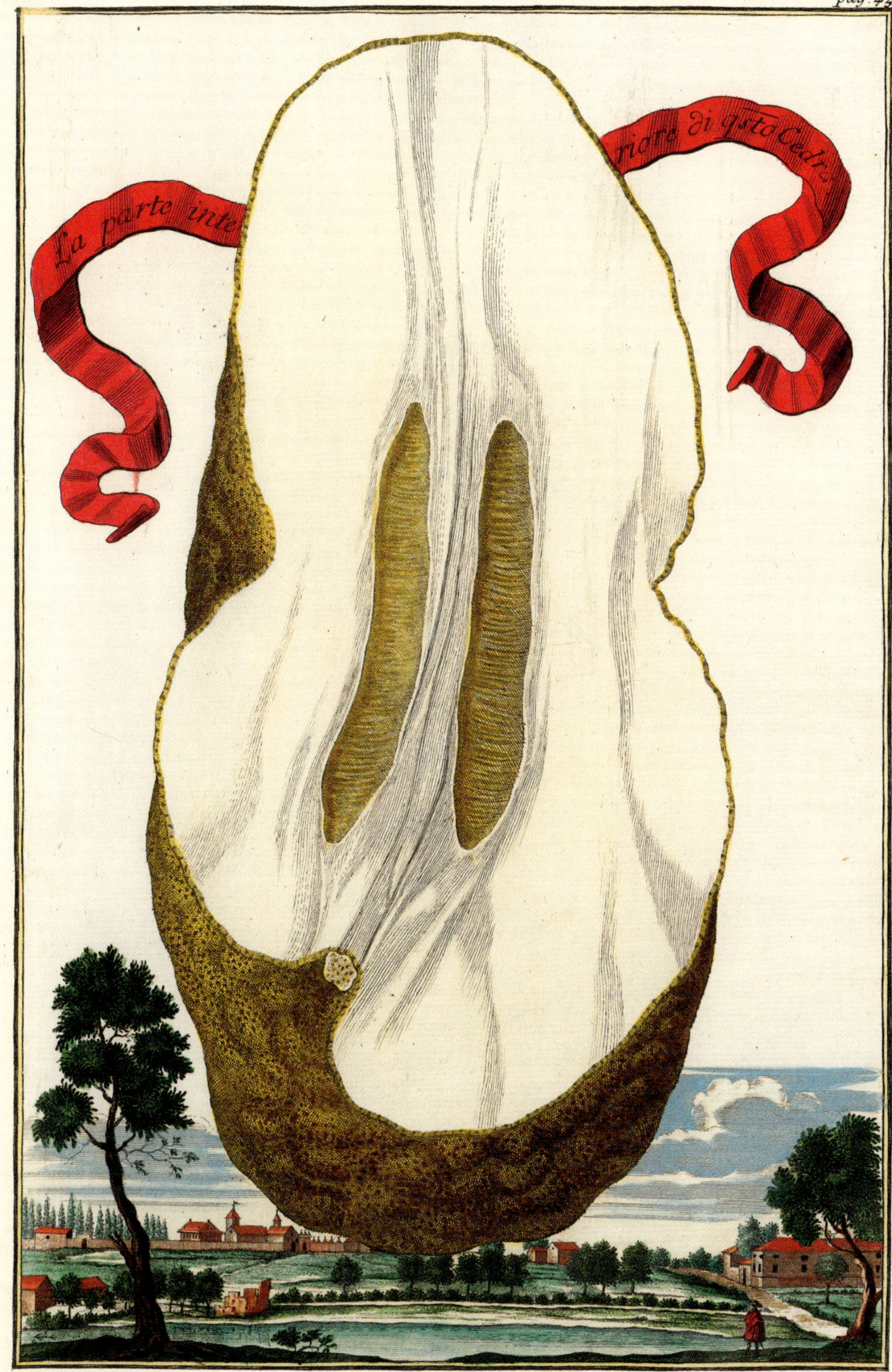

Il Corno; lontano di Verona miglia 4.

Verona – (Il) Corno Alto

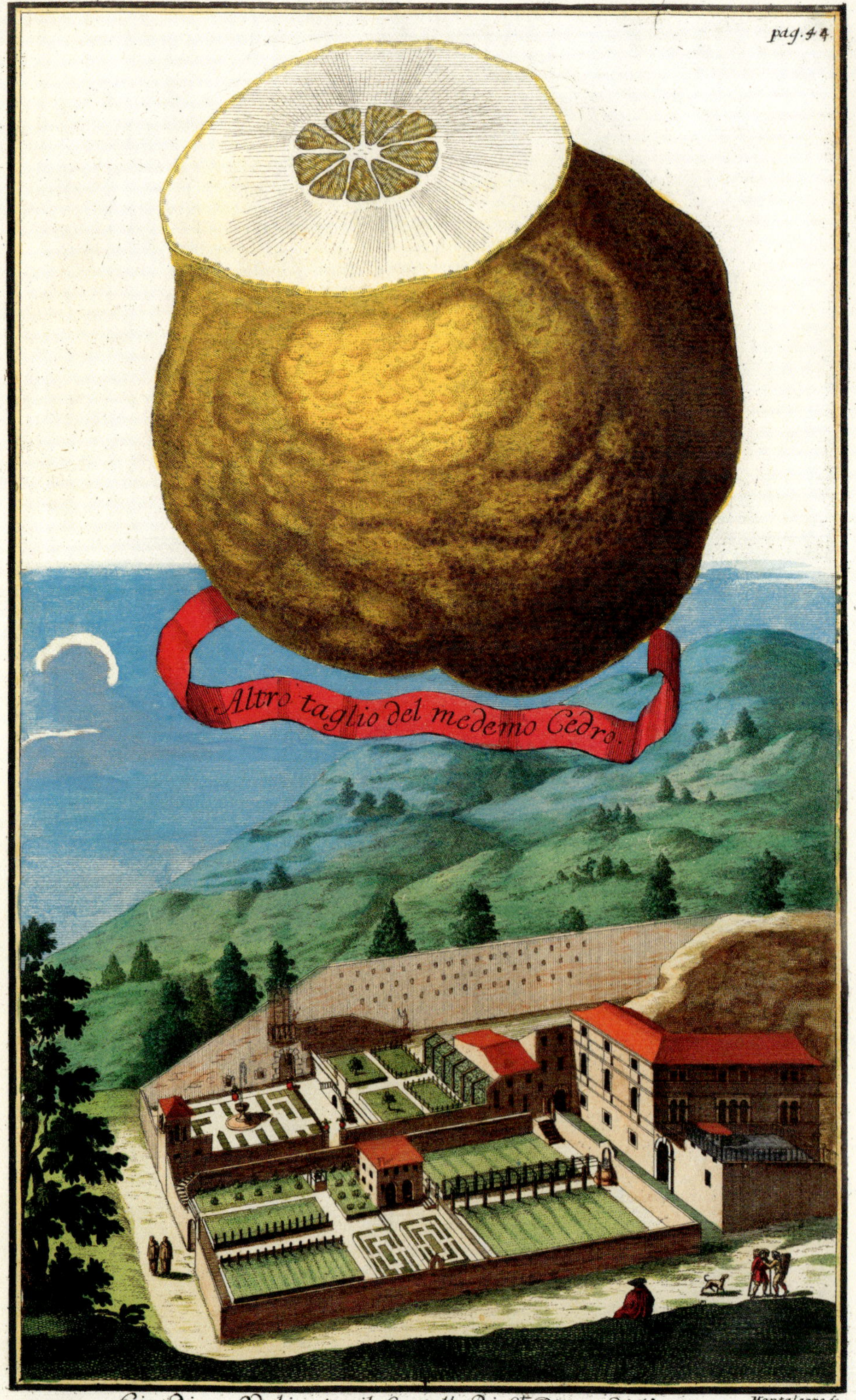

Giardino Odoli sotto il Castello di S.t Pietro di Verona.

Cedro della Ghianda

Monteforte d'Alpone (Verona)

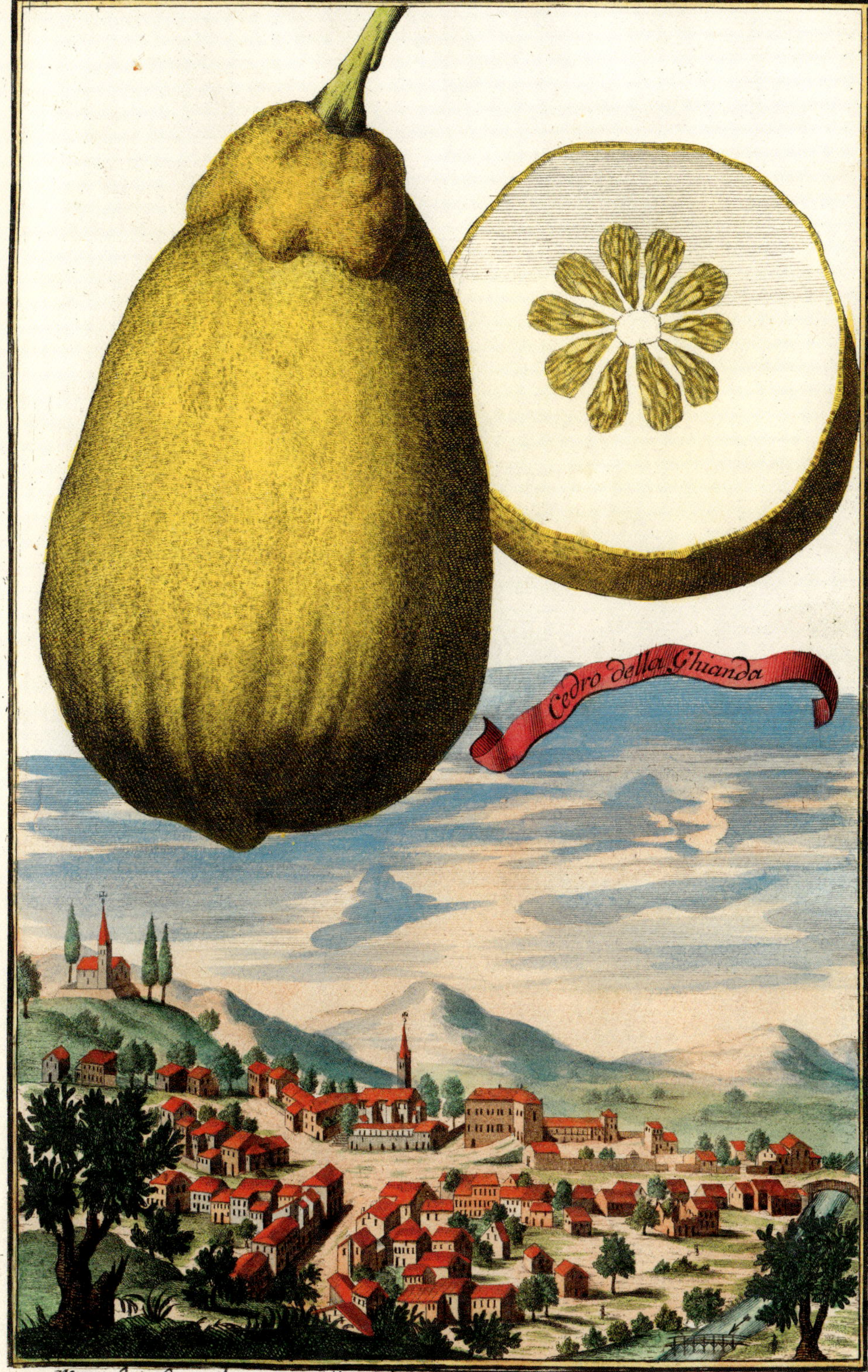

Monteforte ſopra il torrente Albon diſtate dalla Citta di Verona Miglia, 16.

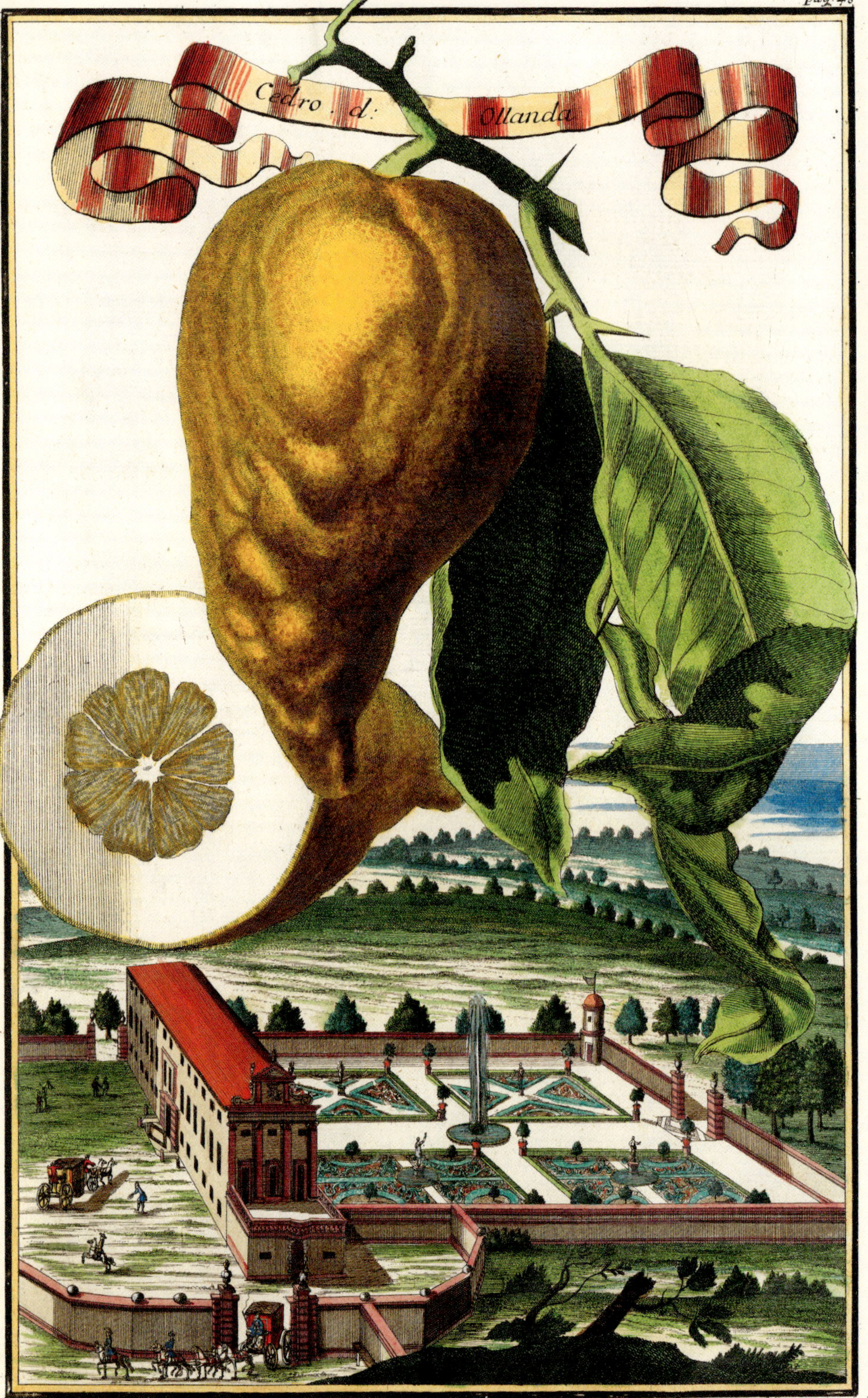

Cedro d'Ollanda

Affi (Verona) – Villa da Persico (Palazzo Vecchio)

Cedro ordinario

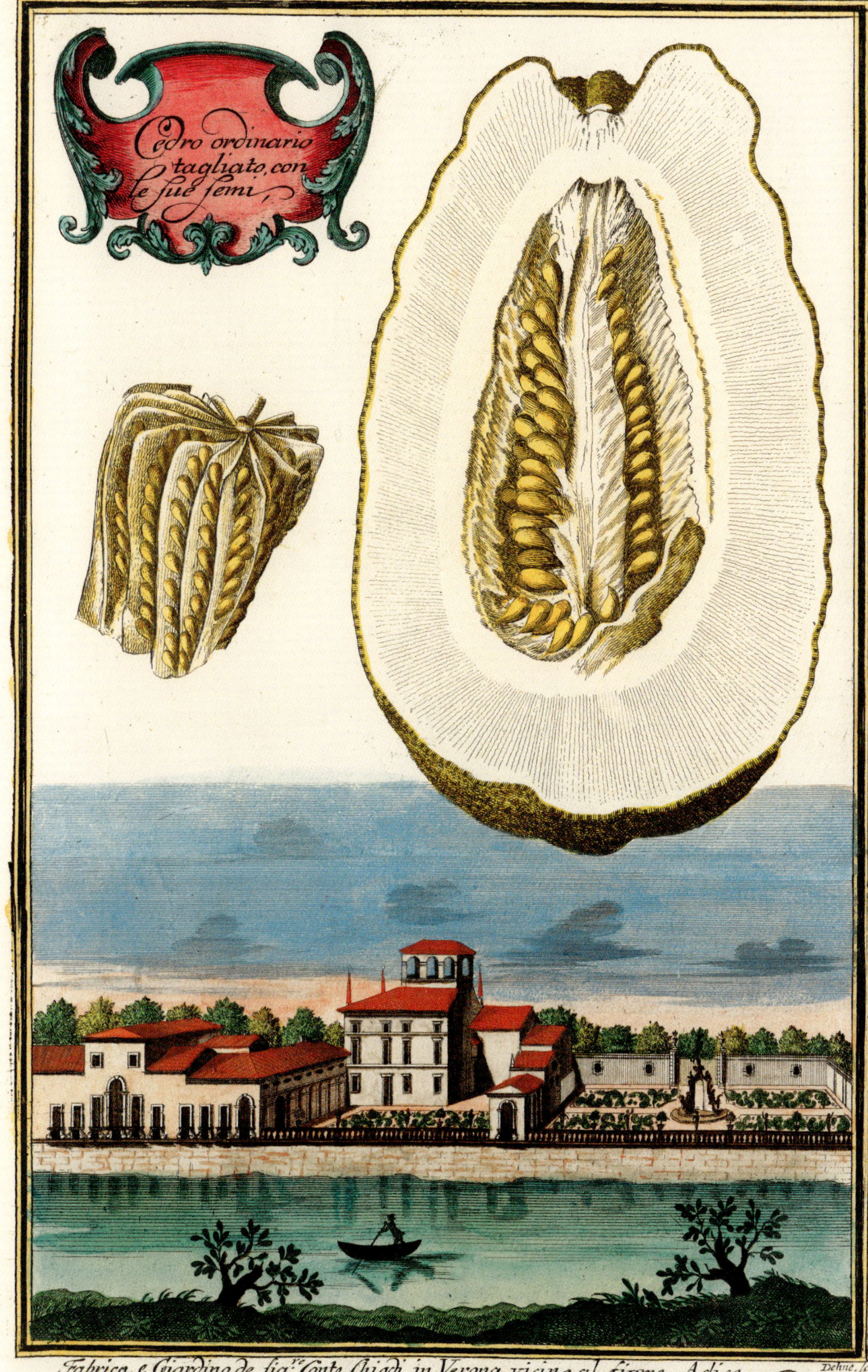

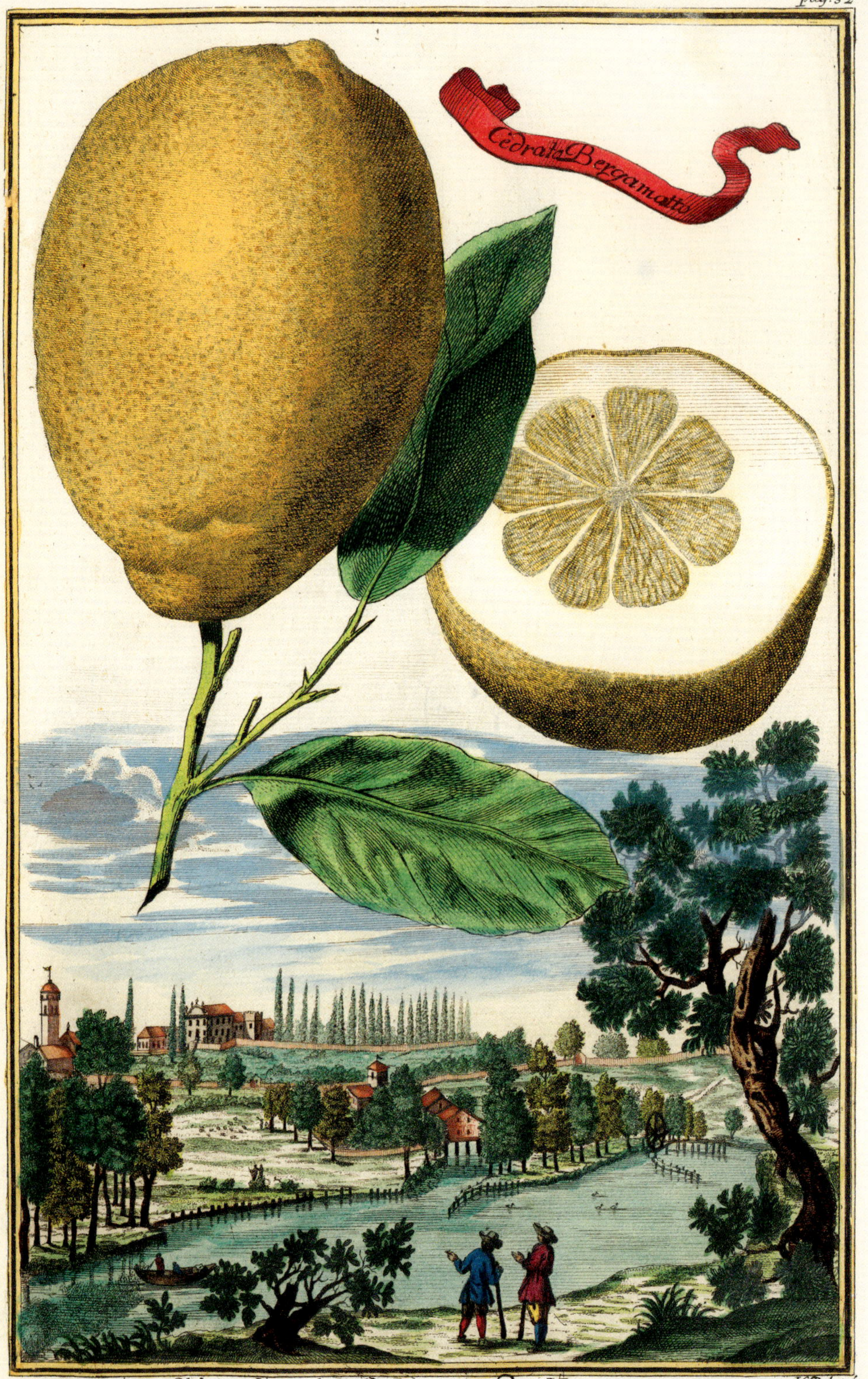

Cedrato Bergamotto

Verona, Chievo

Cedrato monstroso di Fiorenza

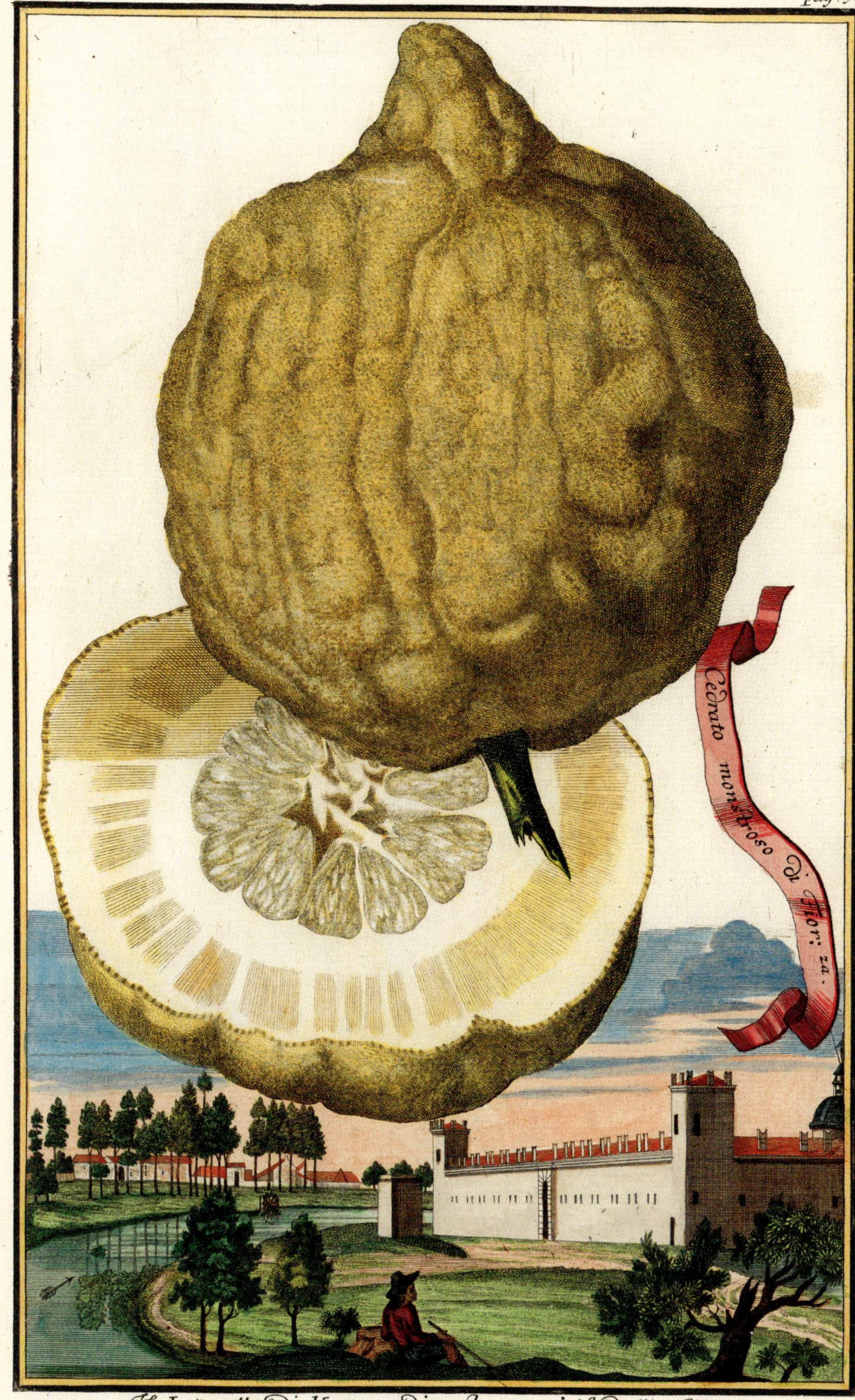

Verona – The Hospital

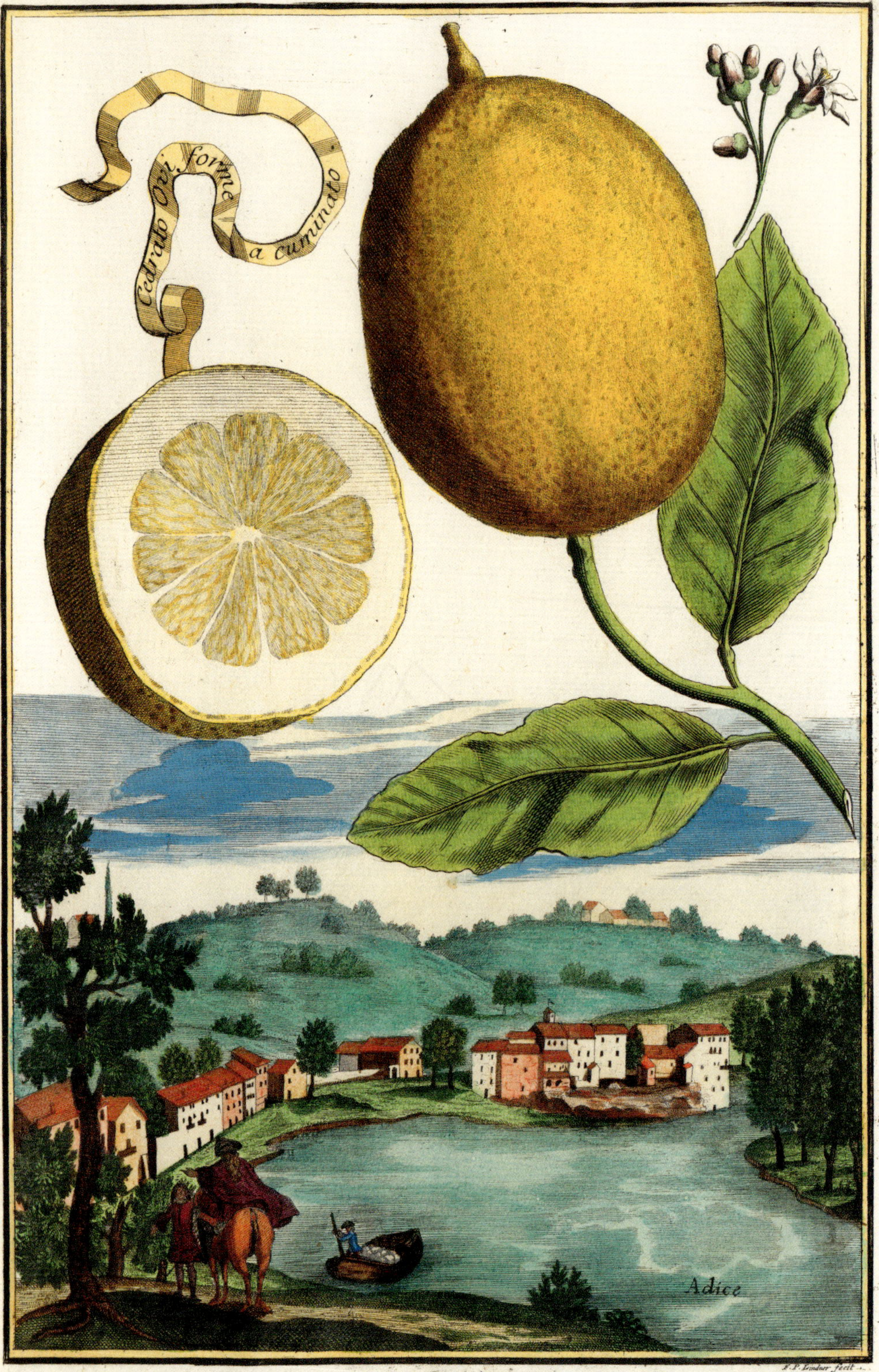

Cedrato oviforme a cuminato

Parona di Valpolicella (Verona)

Cedrato ordinario

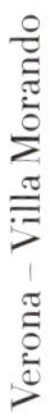

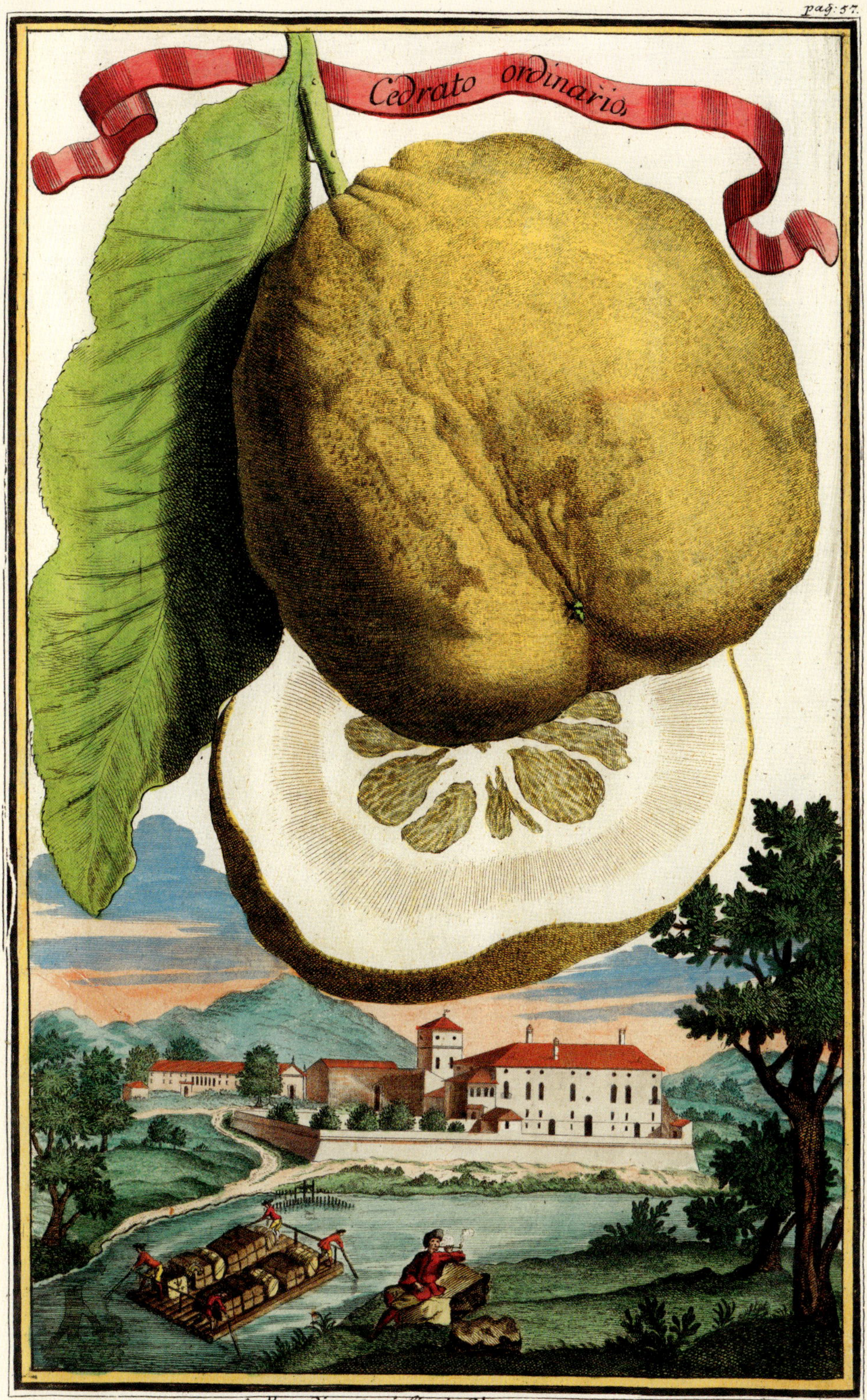

Verona – Villa Morando

pag: 57.

Cedrato ordinario

La Morandina 3½ miglia da Verona.

I.C.Dehne, fe.

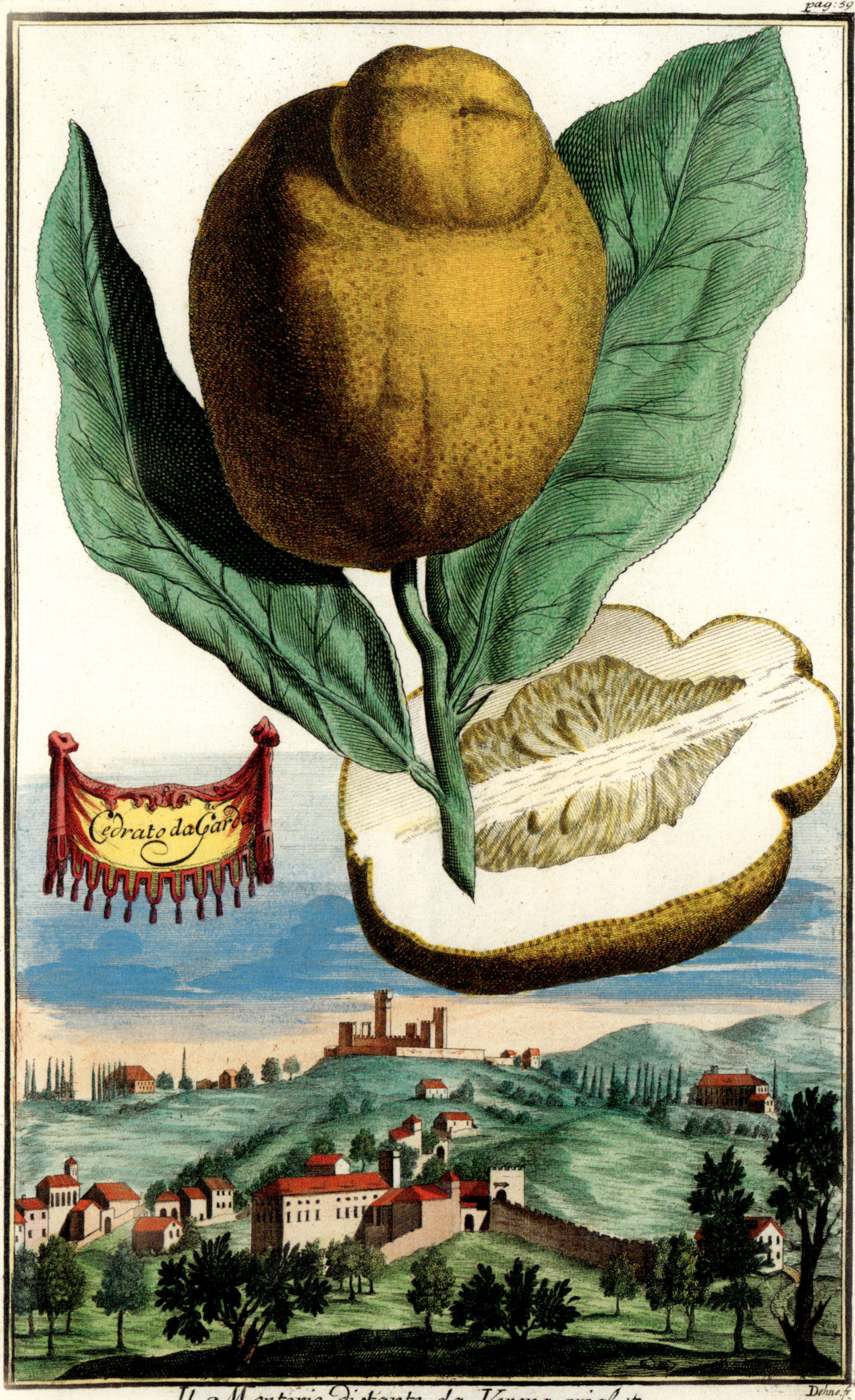

Cedrato da Garda

Montorio (Verona)

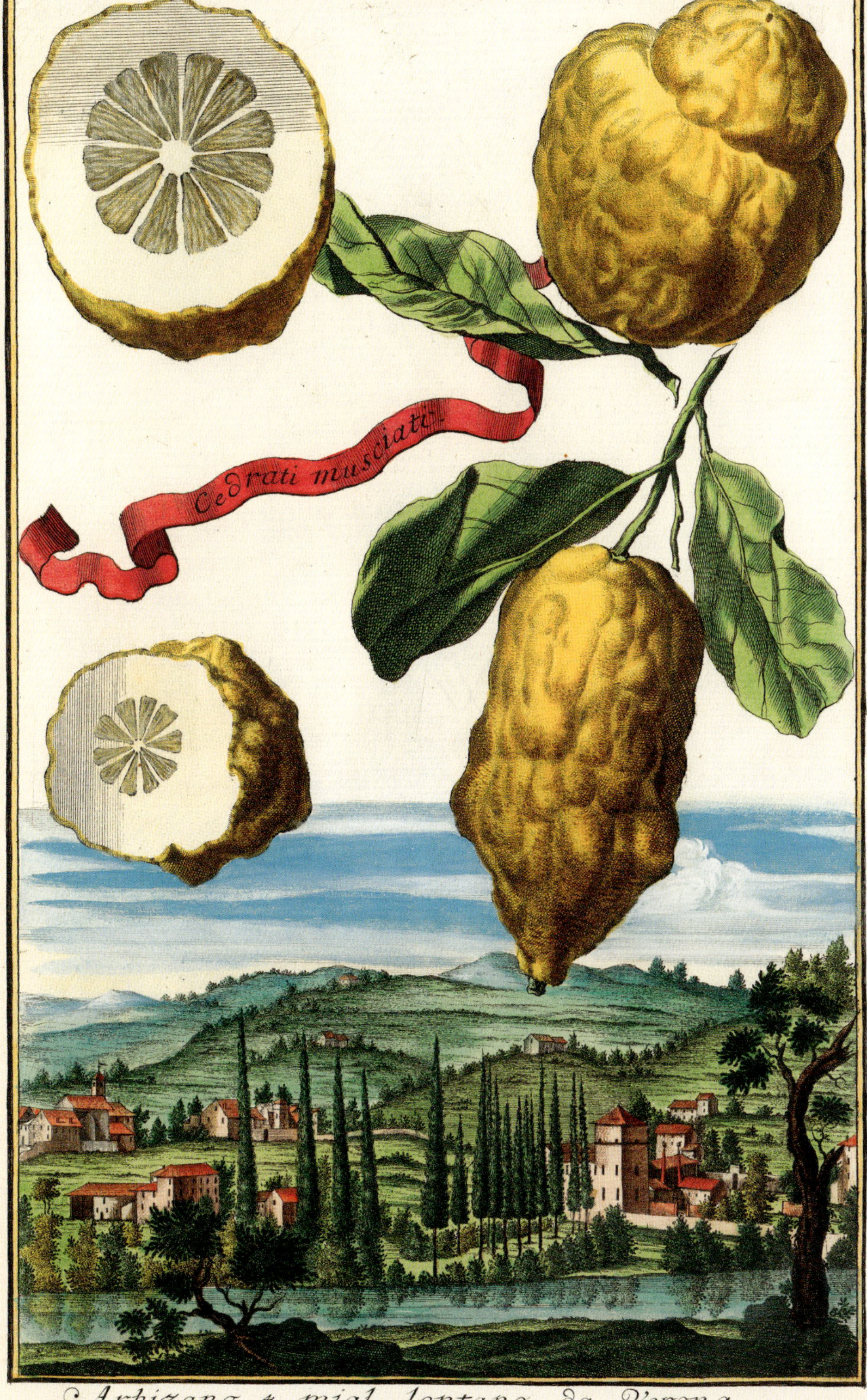
pag: 61
Cedrati musciati
Arbizano 4 migl. lontano da Verona.

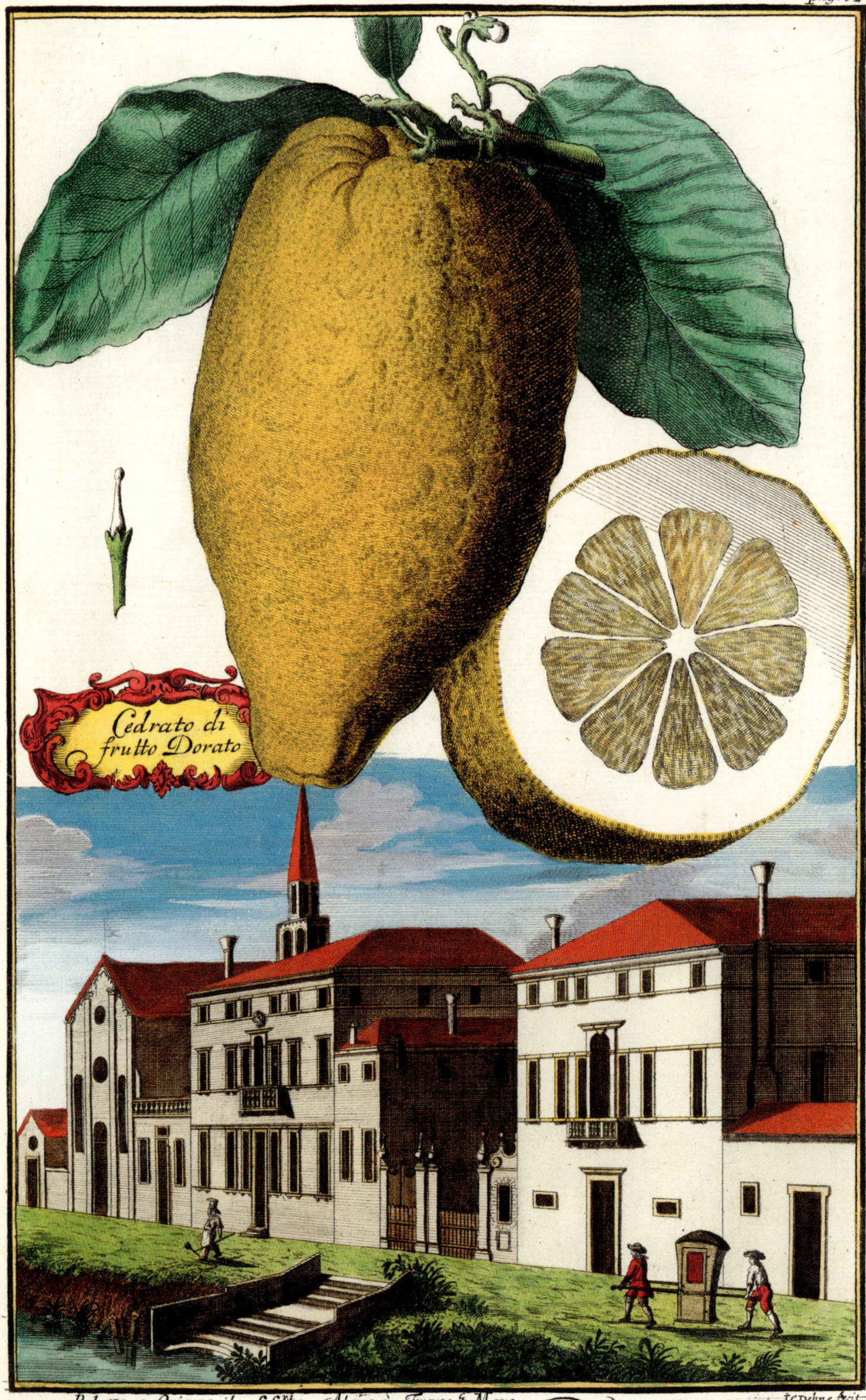

Cedrato di frutto Dorato

Oriago di Mira (Venice) – Villa Moro

hohen Goldfarb an diesem Gewächs / bei dem Namen eines Cedrato di frutto d'orato bewenden. Die Blüthe dieser Frucht wächst / nach Art der Citronaten/ an dicken und kurtzen Stielen Traubenweis beisammen / und schildert sich von aussen röthlicht. Die Blätter sind stark / fett / in etwas gekerbt / wol grün/ und einige unter ihnen sind mit gelben Dupfen besprengt. Die Aeste zeigen hier und dar ihre scharffe Stacheln. Die Schelfe mag man schon zart und glatt heissen / sie hat jedoch dabei etwas Knorrichtes an sich/ und ist / dem Geschmack nach/ ein wenig süß. Die Dicke des Fleisches/ trägt einen guten quer-Finger aus / und besitzt eine kleine Bitterkeit. Ob schon das Mark / wann man es geniesst / noch so fein und anmuthig zu essen ist / so ist es doch zugleich härtlich und säuerlich/ und an der Farb hell schweffelgelb. Die ganze Frucht / welche im Kupfer sich abgebildet hat / ist nach dem hiesigen Gewicht 27. Loth schwehr gewesen.

Ende des andern Theils.

Der

End of the second section of vol. II. *Pages 294/295*
Noventa Padovana (Padua) – Villa Fonte, detail (see p. 377)

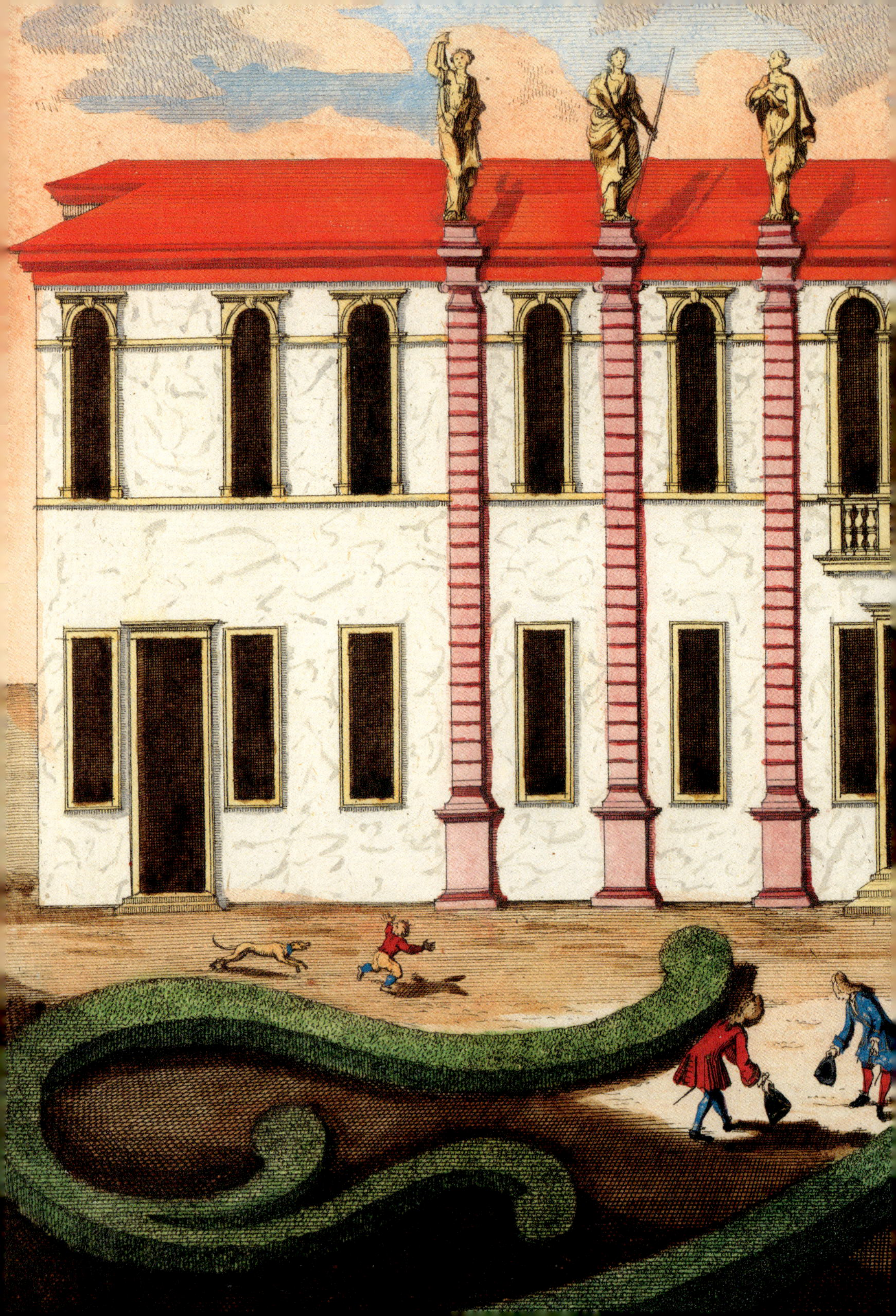

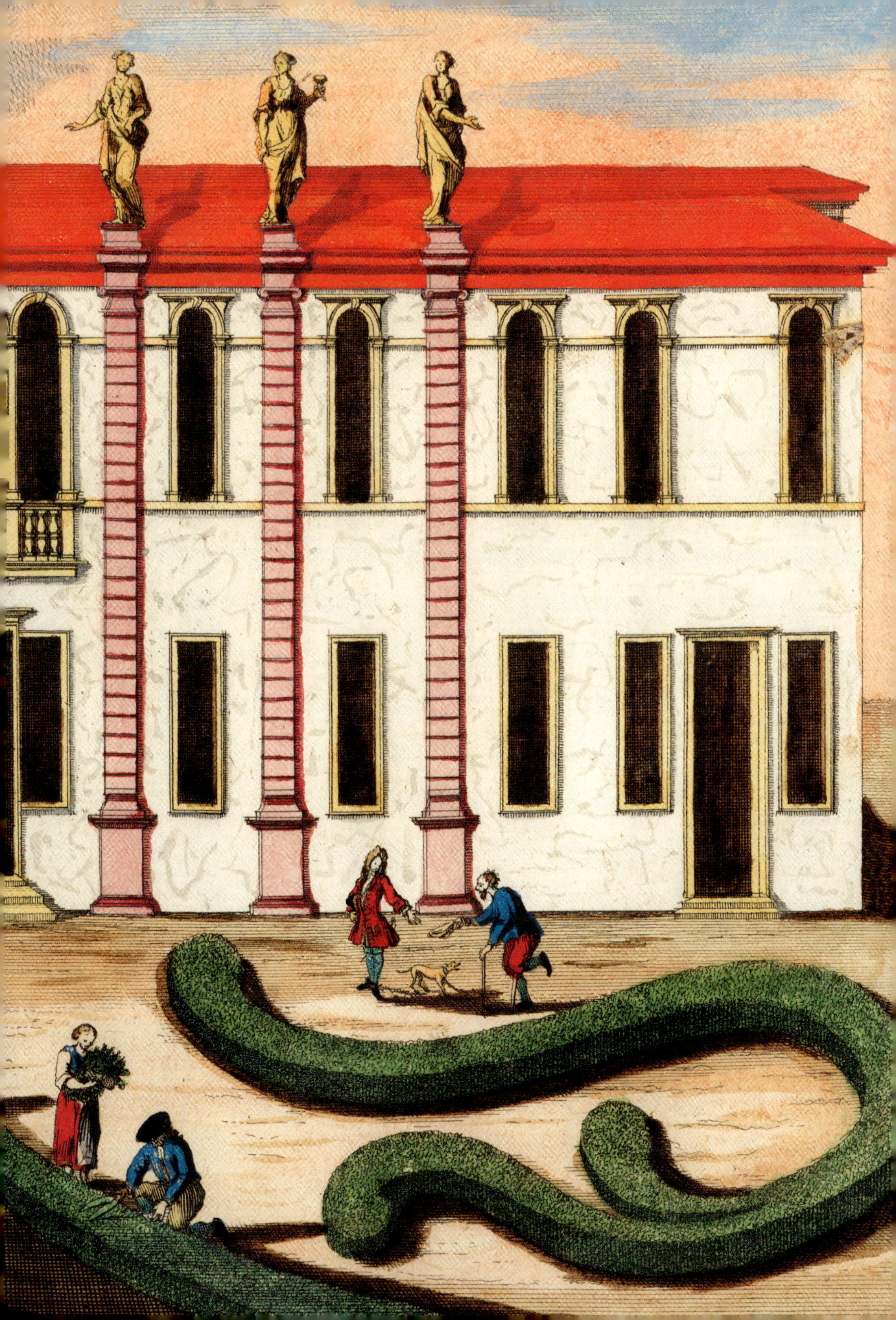

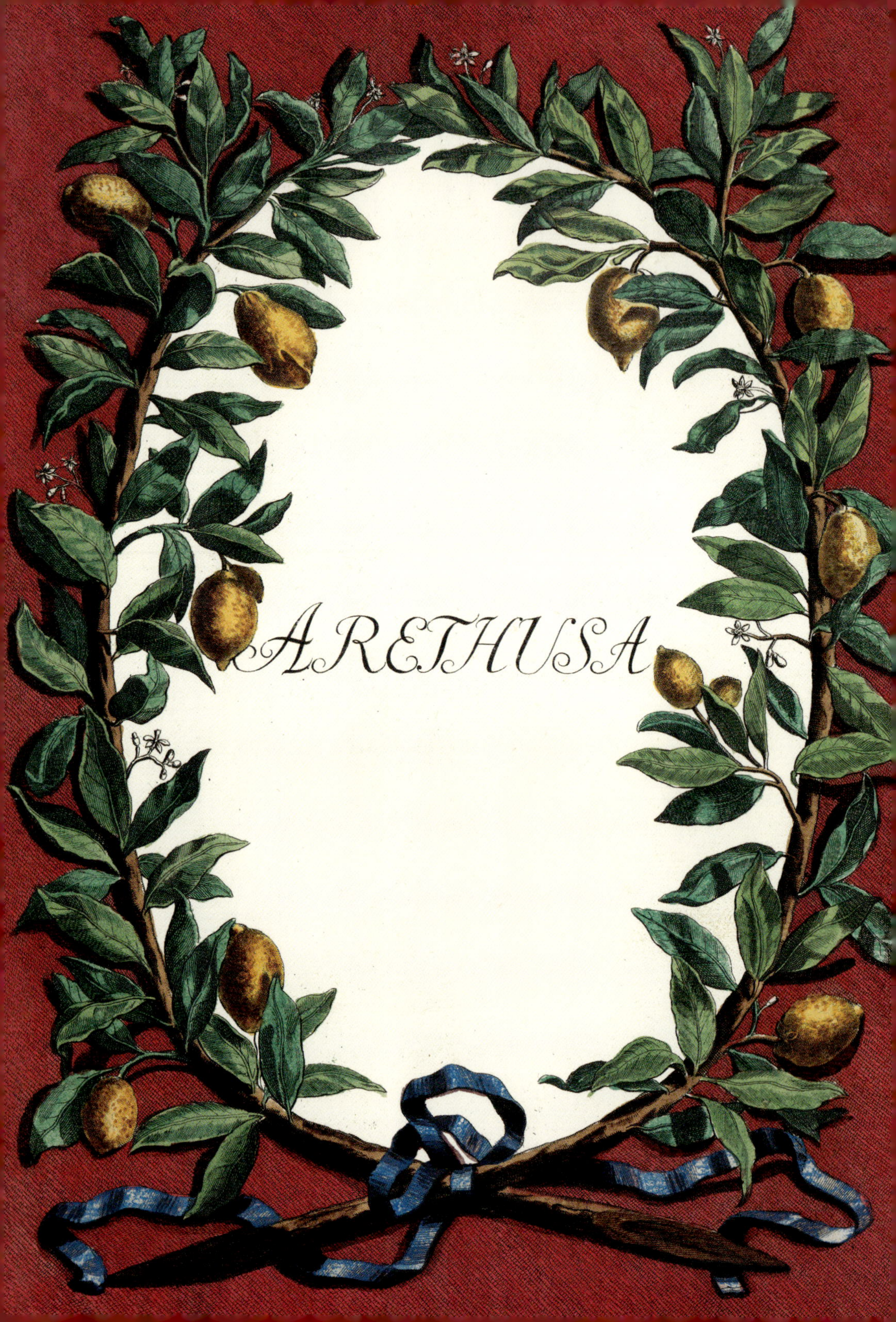
ARETHUSA

Der CONTINVATION der Nürnbergischen HESPERIDVM Dritter Theil.

ARETHVSA.

❁ ❁ ❁

Das erste Capitel.

Von den Citronen insgemein.

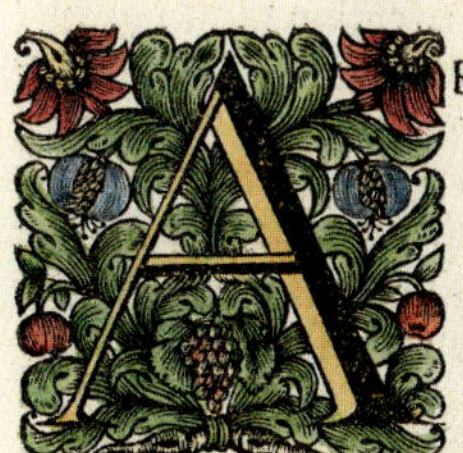

Rethusa, die zweite Schwester unter den Hesperidibus, hat uns/ bei dem Austritt aus ihrer Schwester Ægle Citronat-Garten/ mit ungemeiner Freundlichkeit alsobalden bewillkommet/ und uns bei der Hand in ihren Citronen-Garten geführet. Haben wir nun ehedem schon einmal das Vergnügen gehabt/ viele und mannichfaltige Sorten der Citronen zu beschauen / so sind wir vor dißmal ganz erstaunet geblieben/ als uns eine grosse Anzahl zu Gesicht gekommen / die wir / bei der ersten Durchgehung dieses übertrefflichen Gartens / nicht gesehen / auch nicht betrachten haben können / weil zur selbigen Zeit / nicht alle Stämme mit ihren zeitigen Früchten gezieret gewesen. Dann von diesen raren Gewächsen / kan man nicht alle Jahr / nach Wunsch und Belieben/ gute und zeitige Früchte bekommen / sondern sie wechseln in ihrer Fruchtbarkeit öffters ab / und ist immer ein Jahr daran ergiebiger als das andere / nachdem zumal die Witterung sich anlässt; welche / wann sie nicht besonders gut / geschlacht / und mit einem durchdringenden Sonnenschein begleitet ist / hierinnen einen grossen Schaden verursachet. Und ist nicht nur unser kaltes Teutschland / diesem Unstern unterworffen / sondern dem lieblichen und warmen Italien / schadet ebner Massen eine ungleiche und unstete Witterung/nicht selten ein merkliches / an der Fruchtbarkeit solcher Bäume. Unser Verwundern / über die reiche Menge der uns vorhin unbekandten Früchte (die sich / in dieser meiner Fortsetzung der Nürnbergischen Hesperidum, insgesamt im Kupfer vorstellen werden) hat sich noch mehr vergrössert / als wir von unsrer liebreichen Führerin

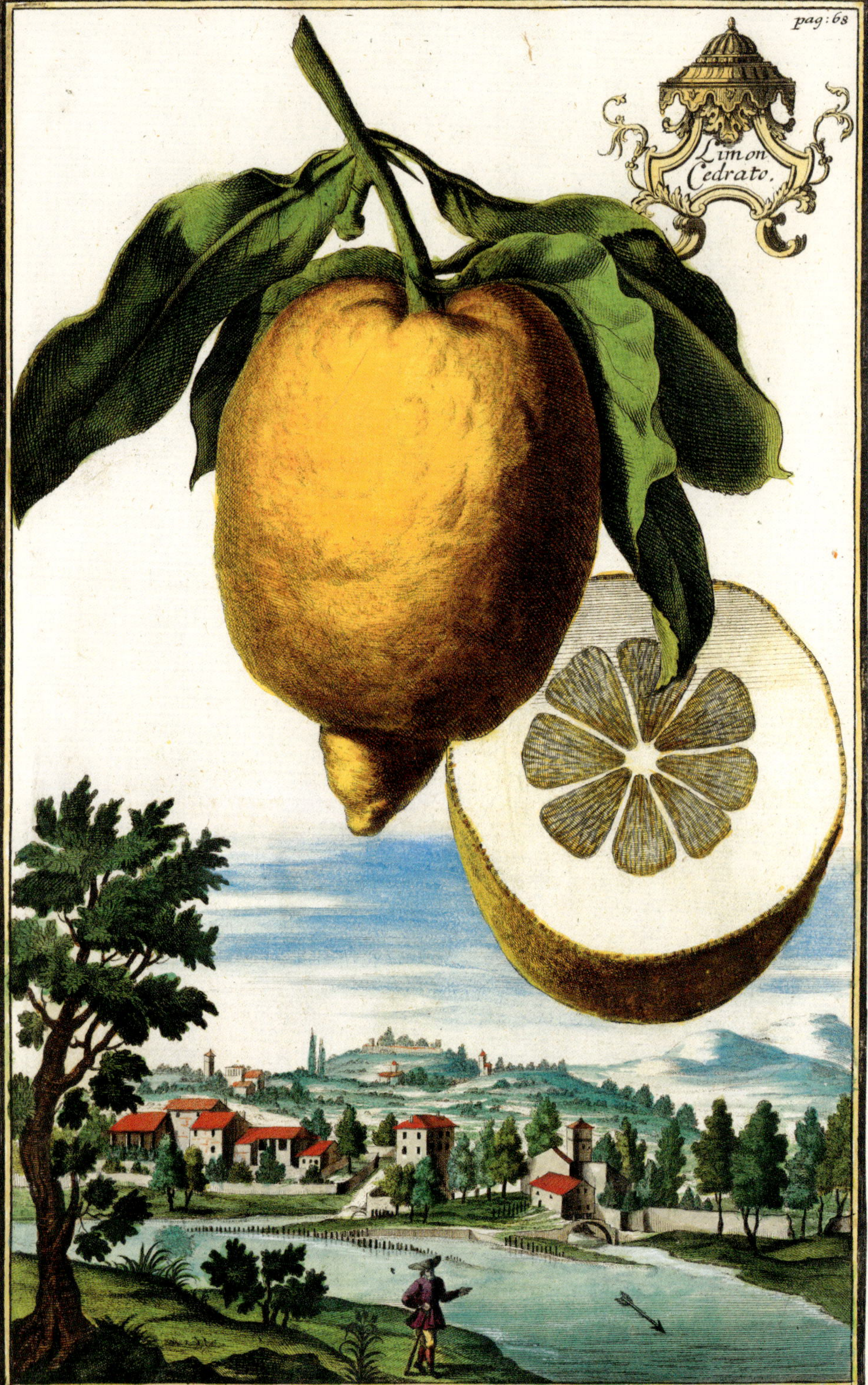

Il Nassar sopra il Fiume Adice distante dalla Citta' di Verona miglia tre, è mezzo.

Limon Cedrato

Nassar di San Pietro in Cariano (Verona). *Pages 296/297*
Cartouche and beginning of the third section of vol. II

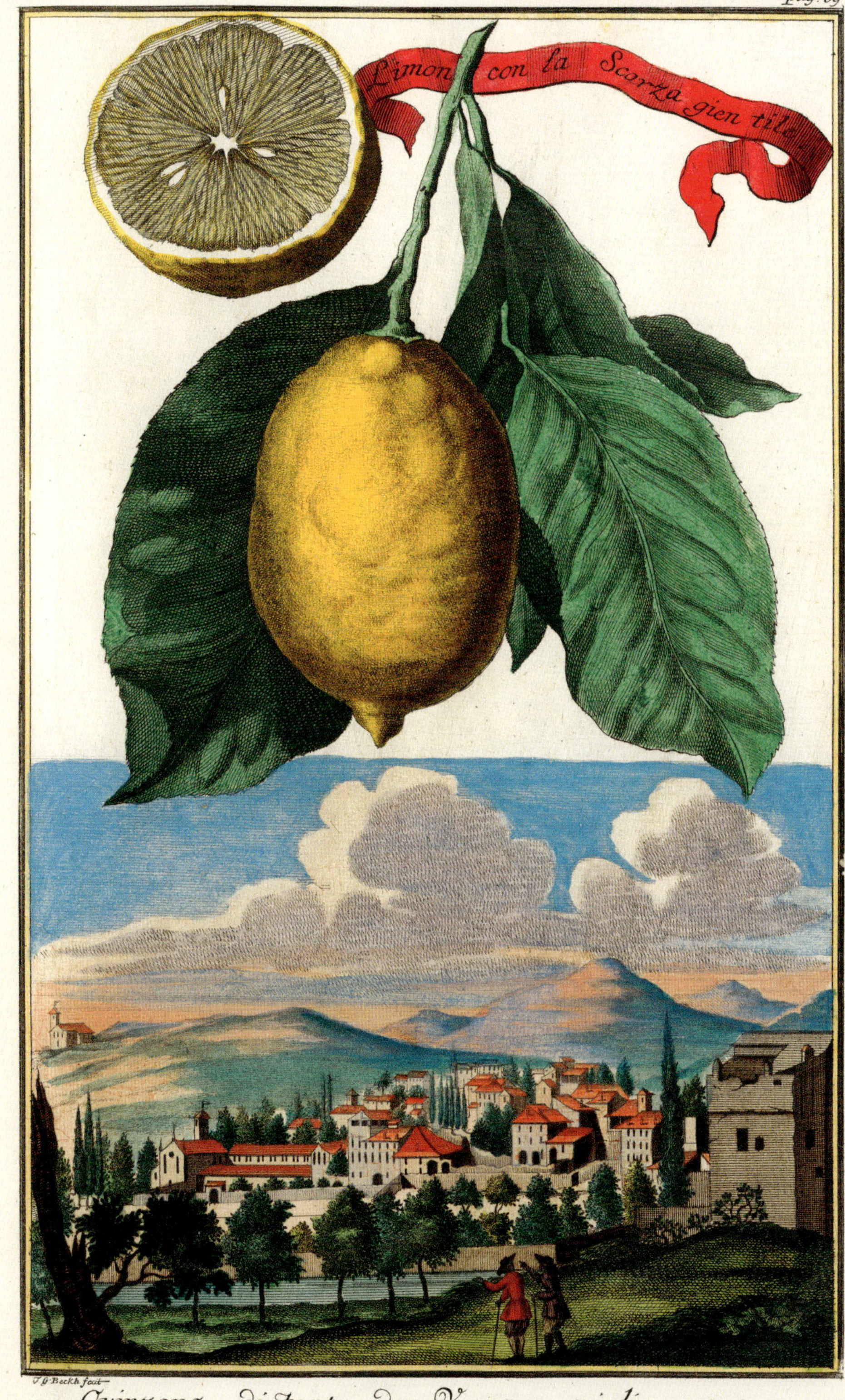

Limon con la Scorza gientile

Quinzano (Verona)

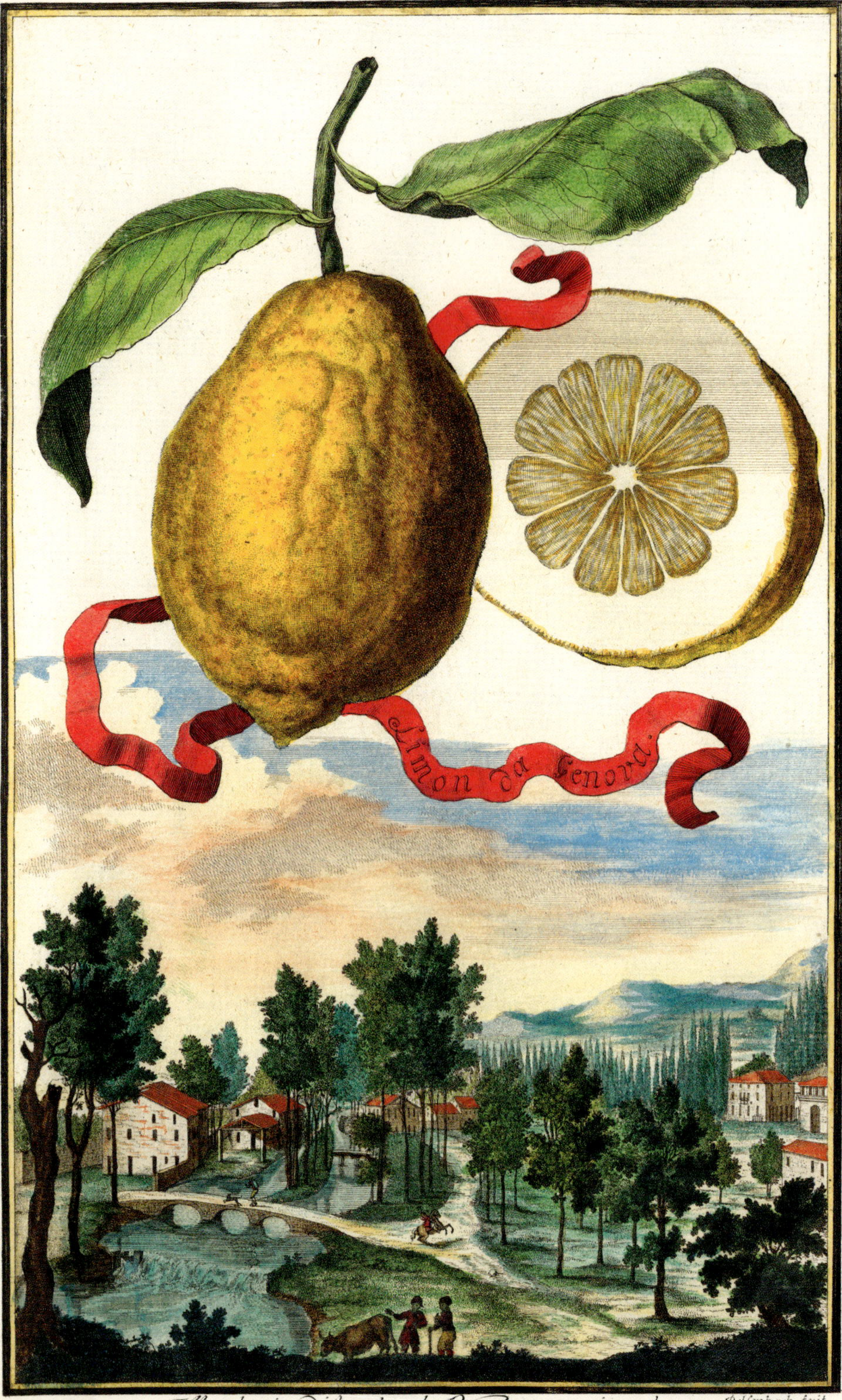

Limon da Genova

Montorio (Verona) – Olive Grove

Limon [di] Salerno

Settimo di Pescantina (Verona)

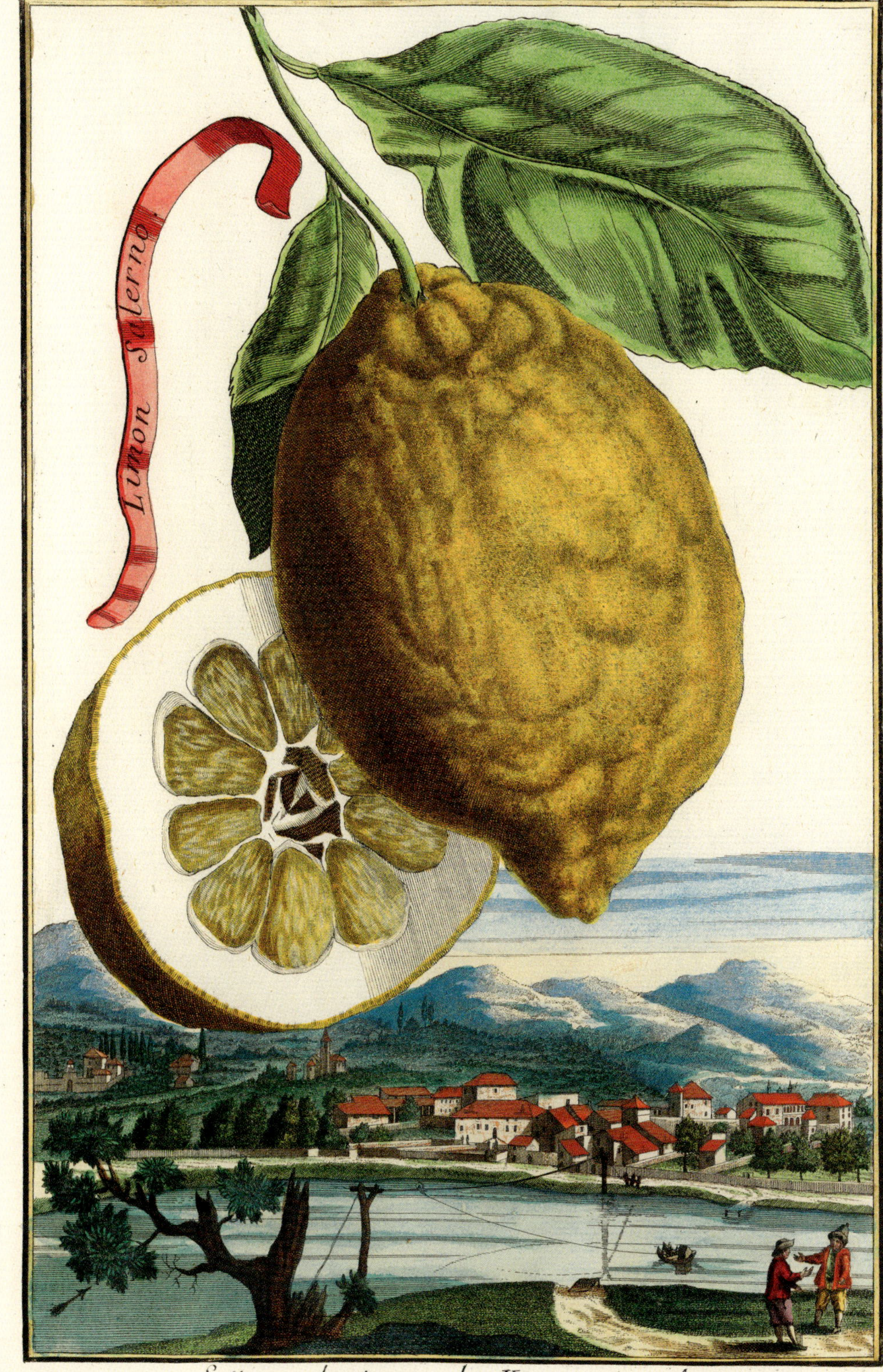

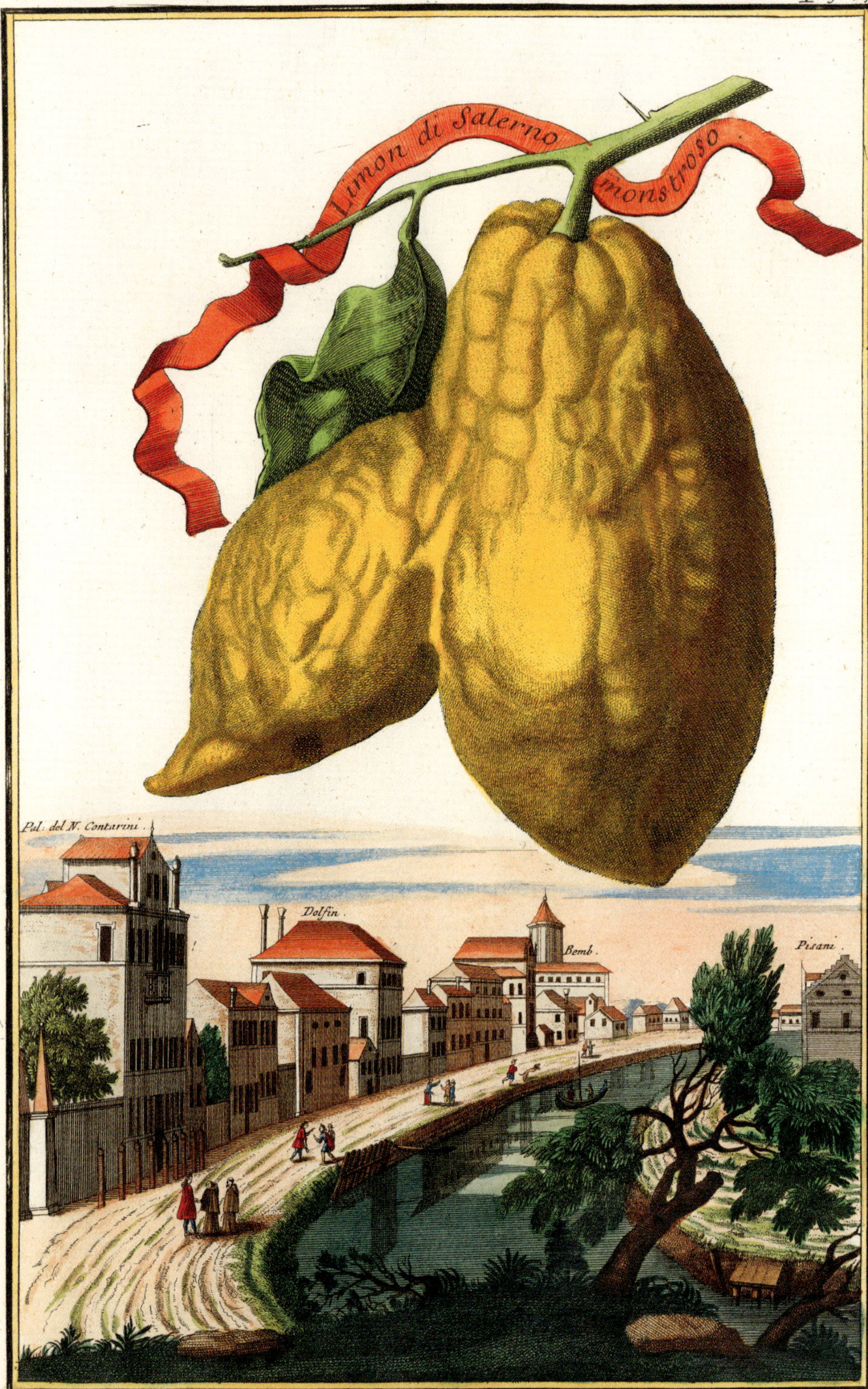

Veduta alla Mira dalla parte delle Gambarare .

Limon di Salerno monstroso

Gambarare di Mira (Venice) – Villa Contarini, Villa Dolfin, Villa Bembo, Villa Pisani

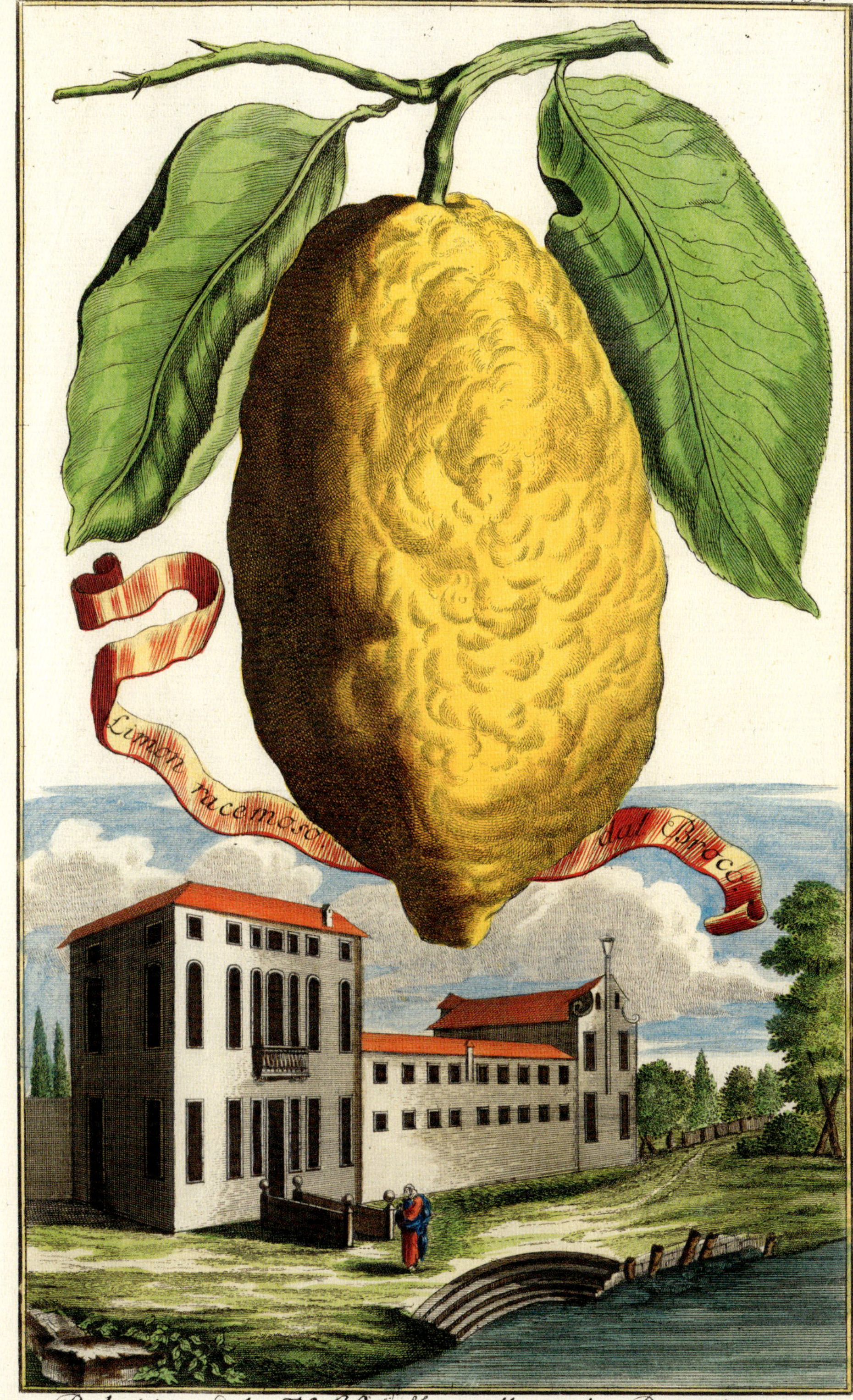
pag. 76.
Limon racemoso dal Broco
Palazzo del N.H. Marcello al Botegin.

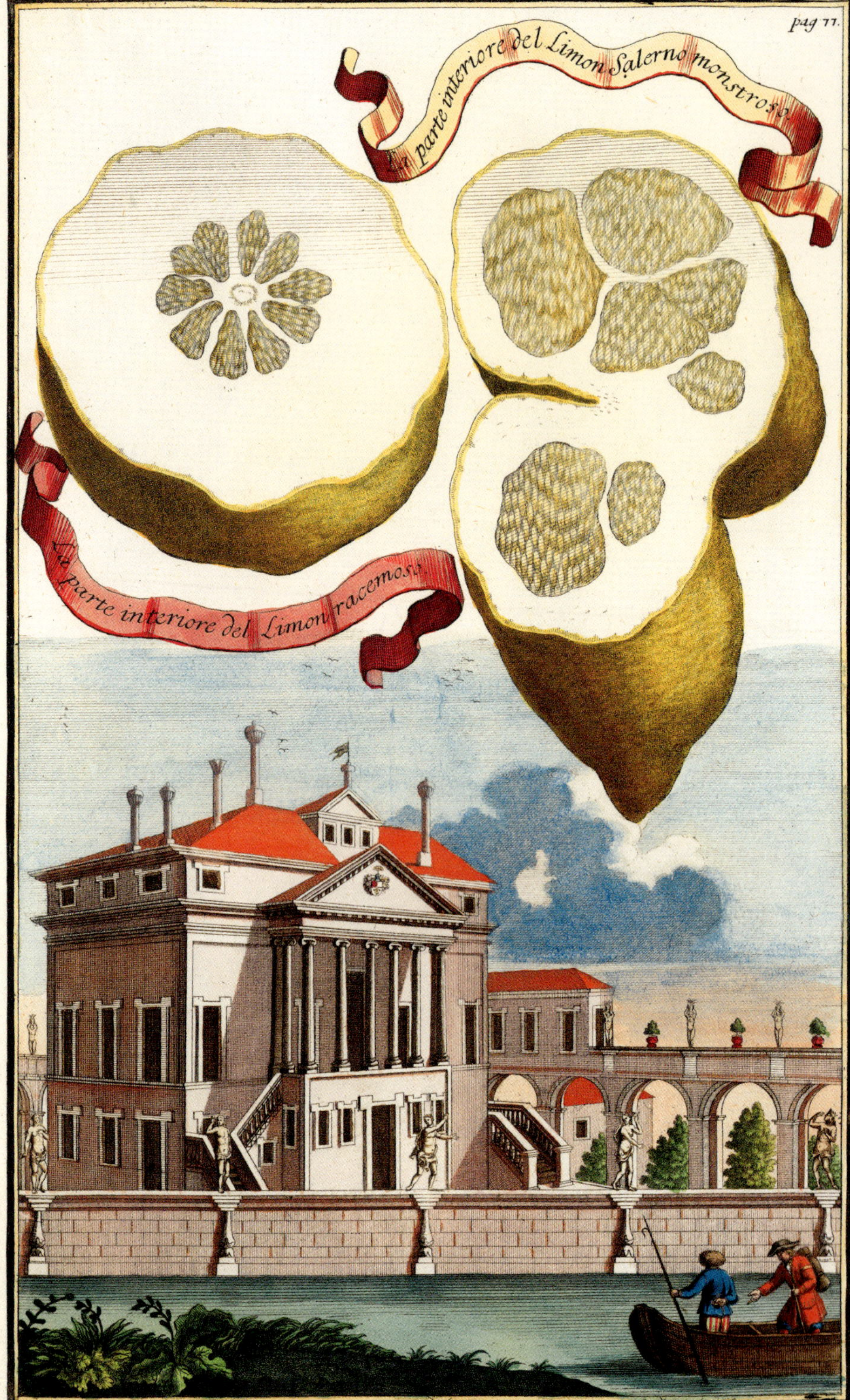

Limon [di] Salerno monstroso & Limon racemoso

Mira (Venice) – Villa Foscari (La Malcontenta)

Limon di S. Remo

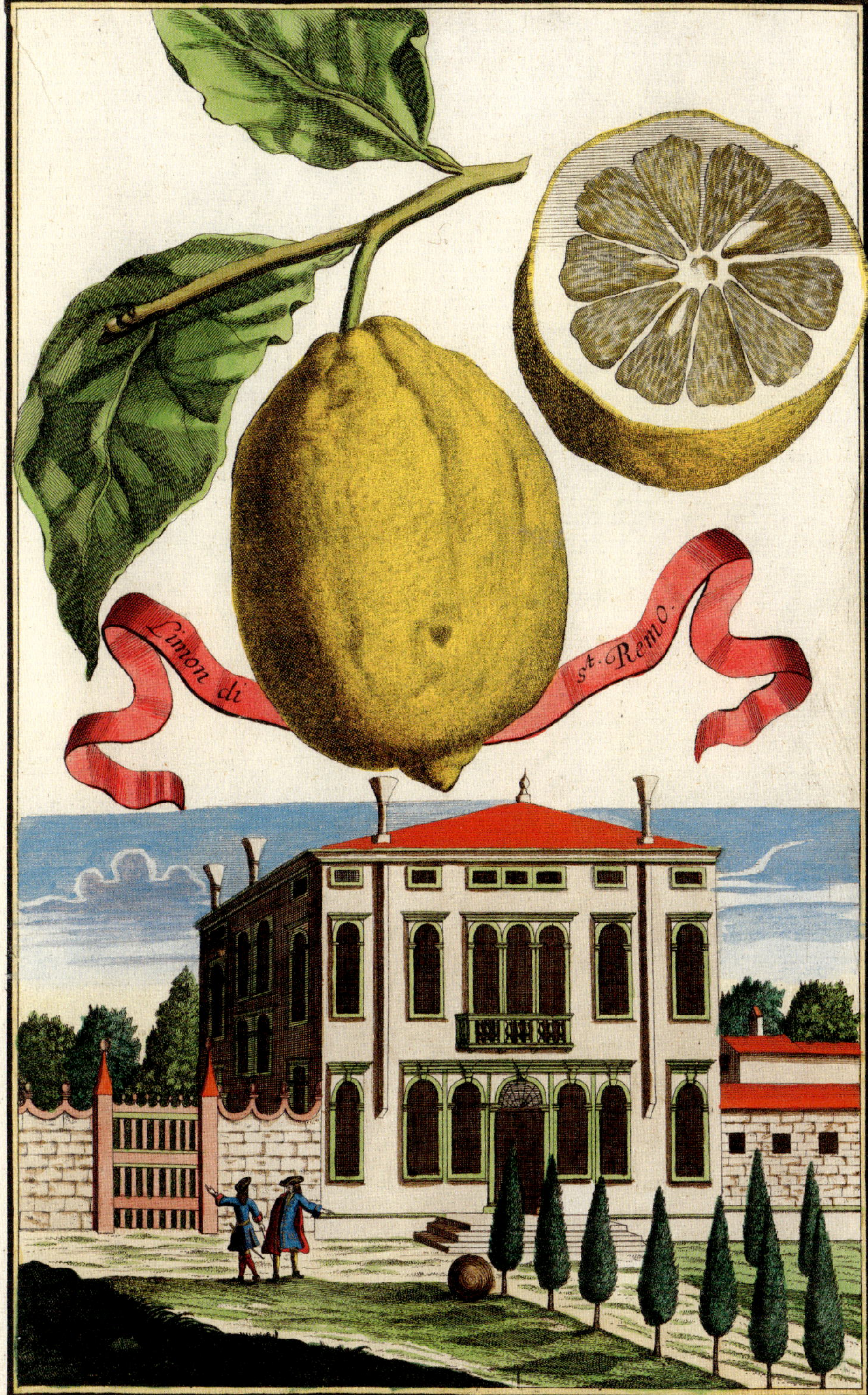

Gambarare di Mira (Venice) – Villa Capello

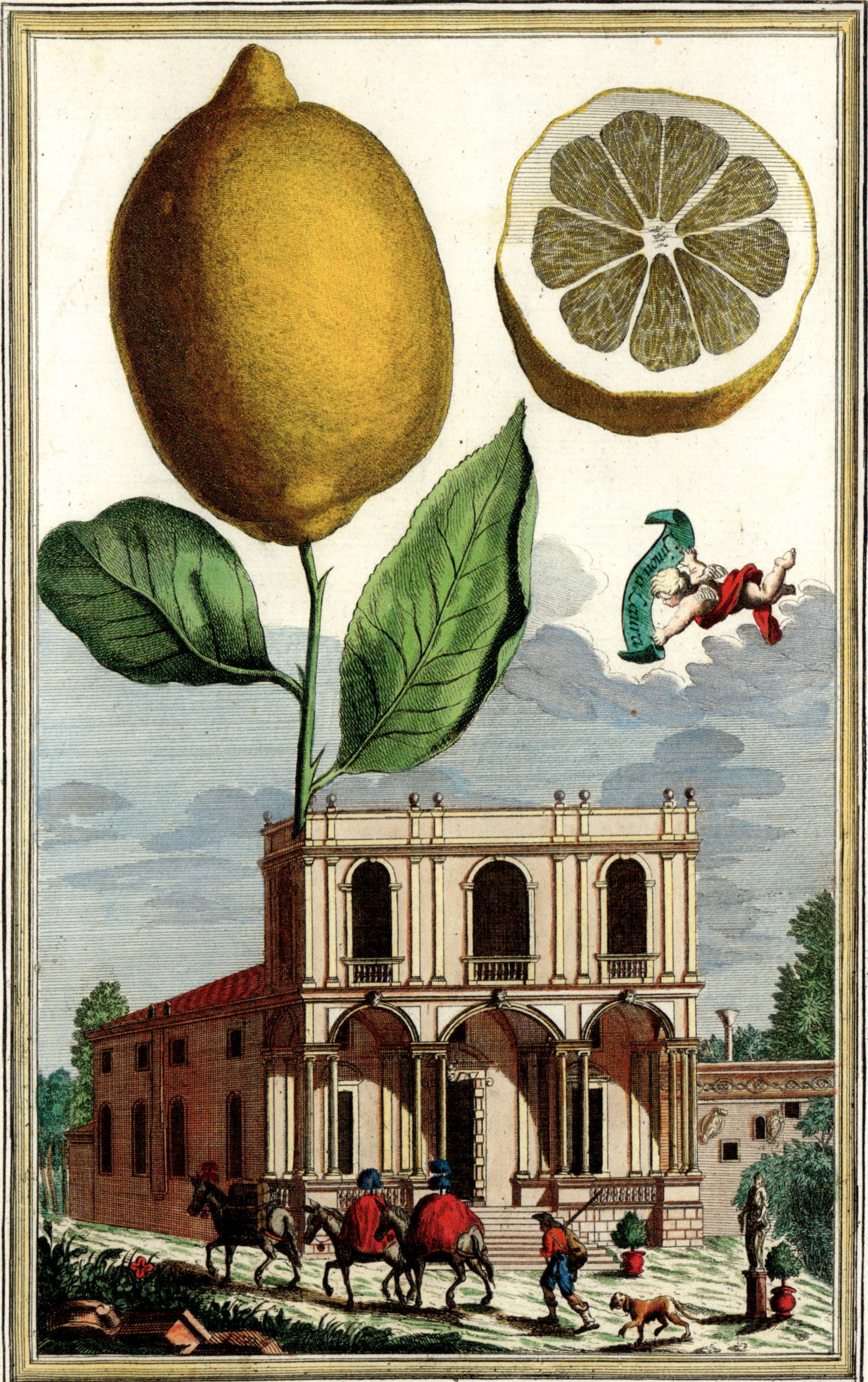

Limon a Laura

Oriago di Mira (Venice) – Villa Priuli

Limon da Gaetta

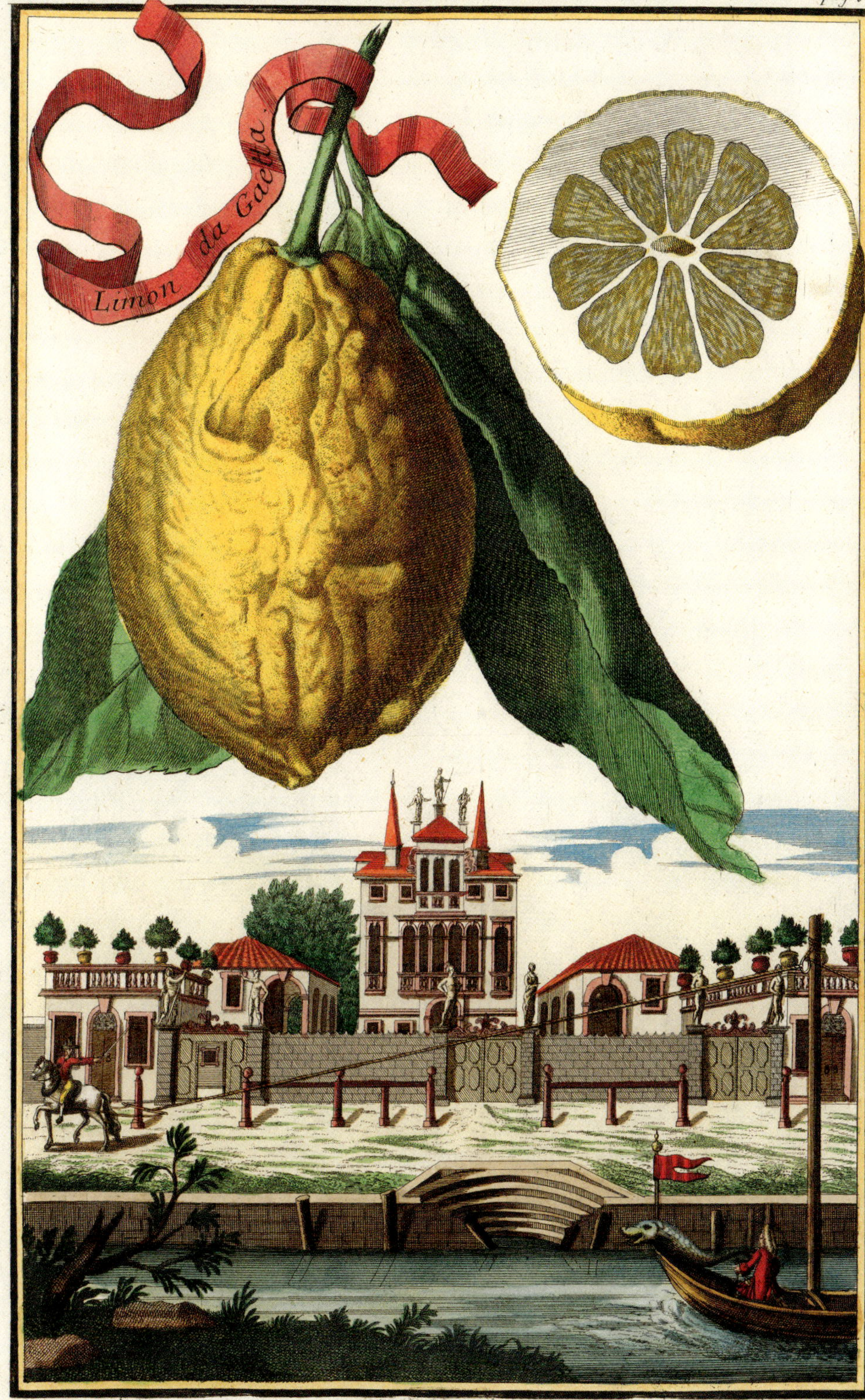

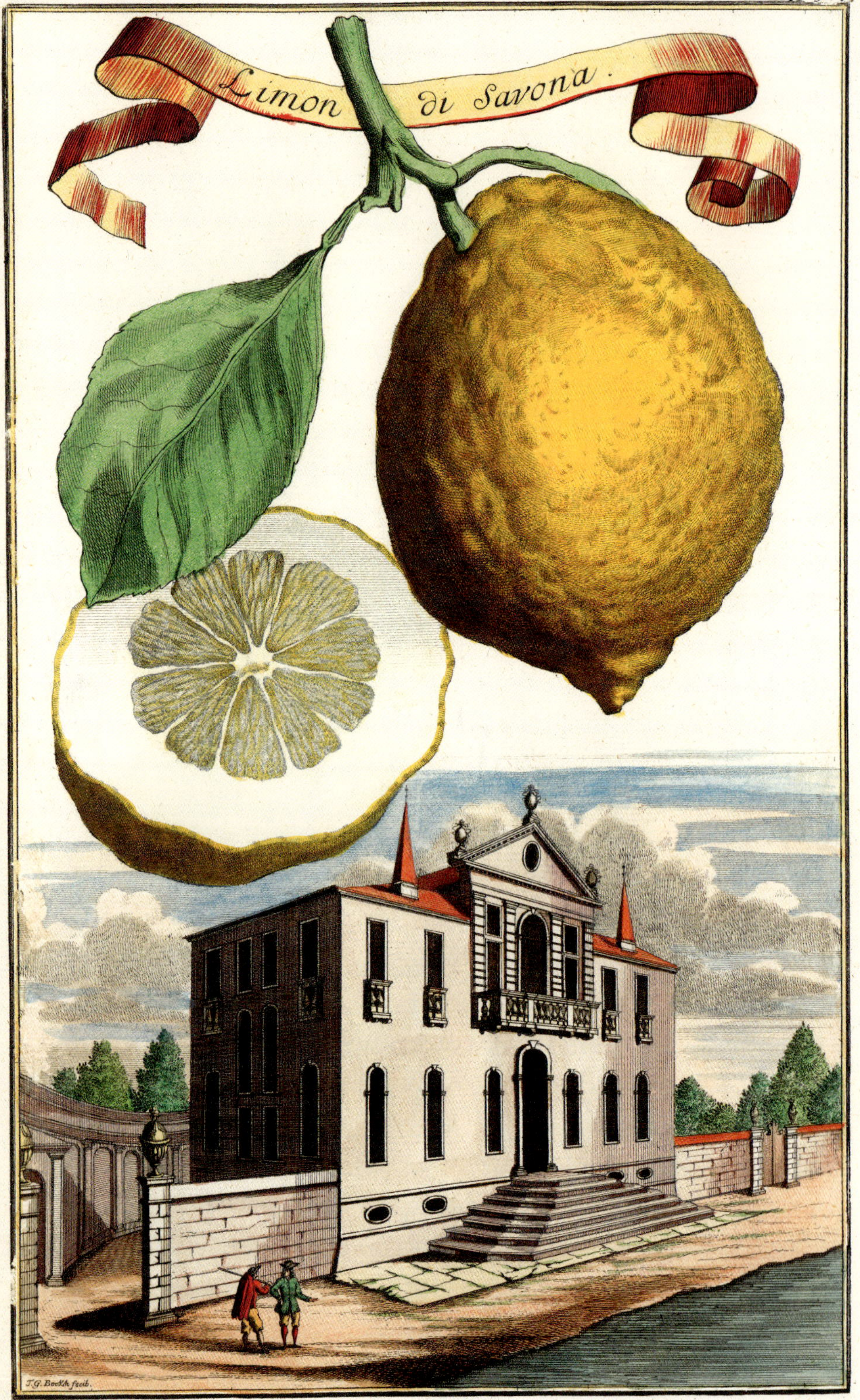

Palazzo del N. H: Gradenigo alla Mira.

Limon di Savona

Mira (Venice) – Villa Franceschi

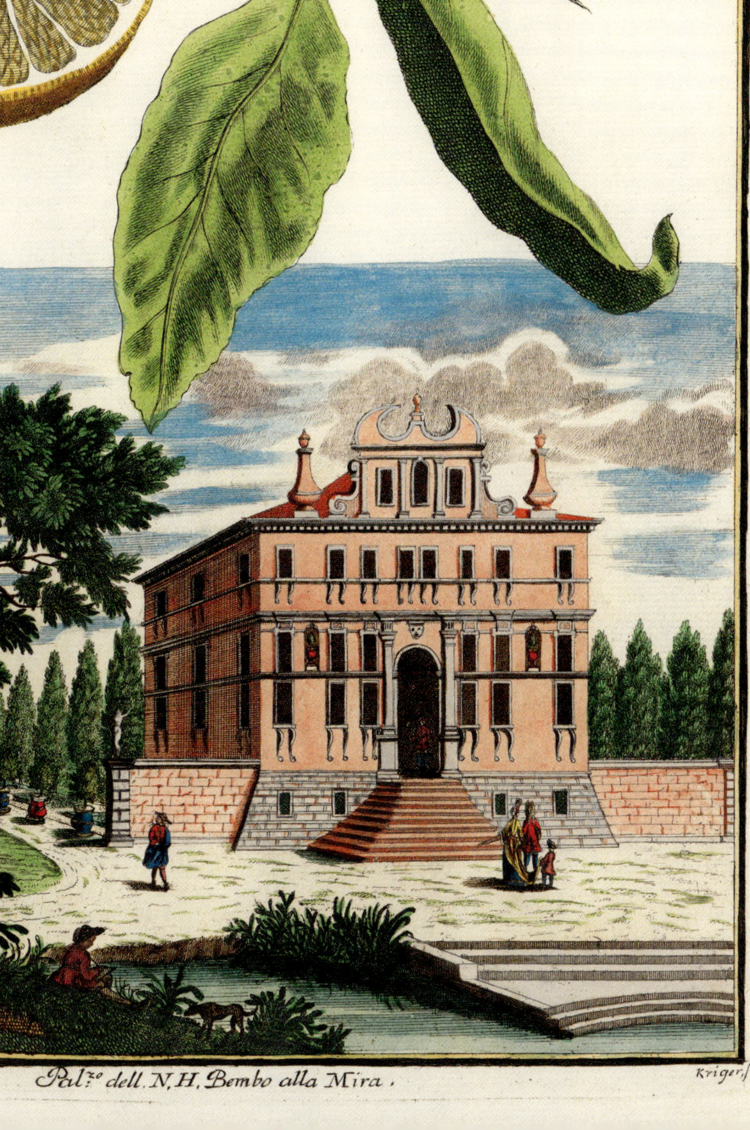
pag. 85.
Limon da Canea
Pal.zo dell. N.H. Bembo alla Mira.
Kriger. fc

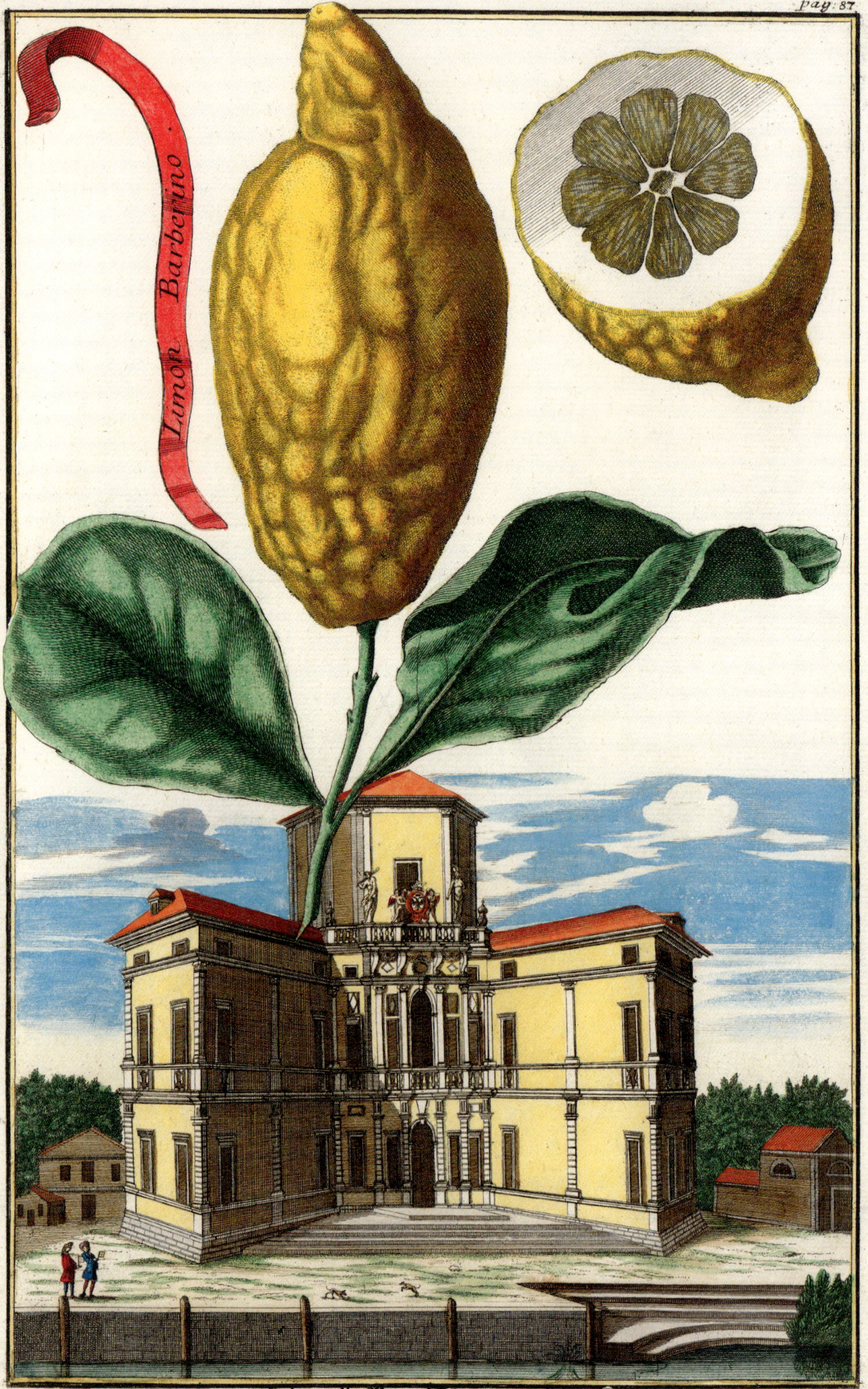

Limon Barberino

Mira (Venice) – Villa Contarini "delle quattro torri"

Limon Rosolino

Mira (Venice) – Villa Contarini dei Leoni

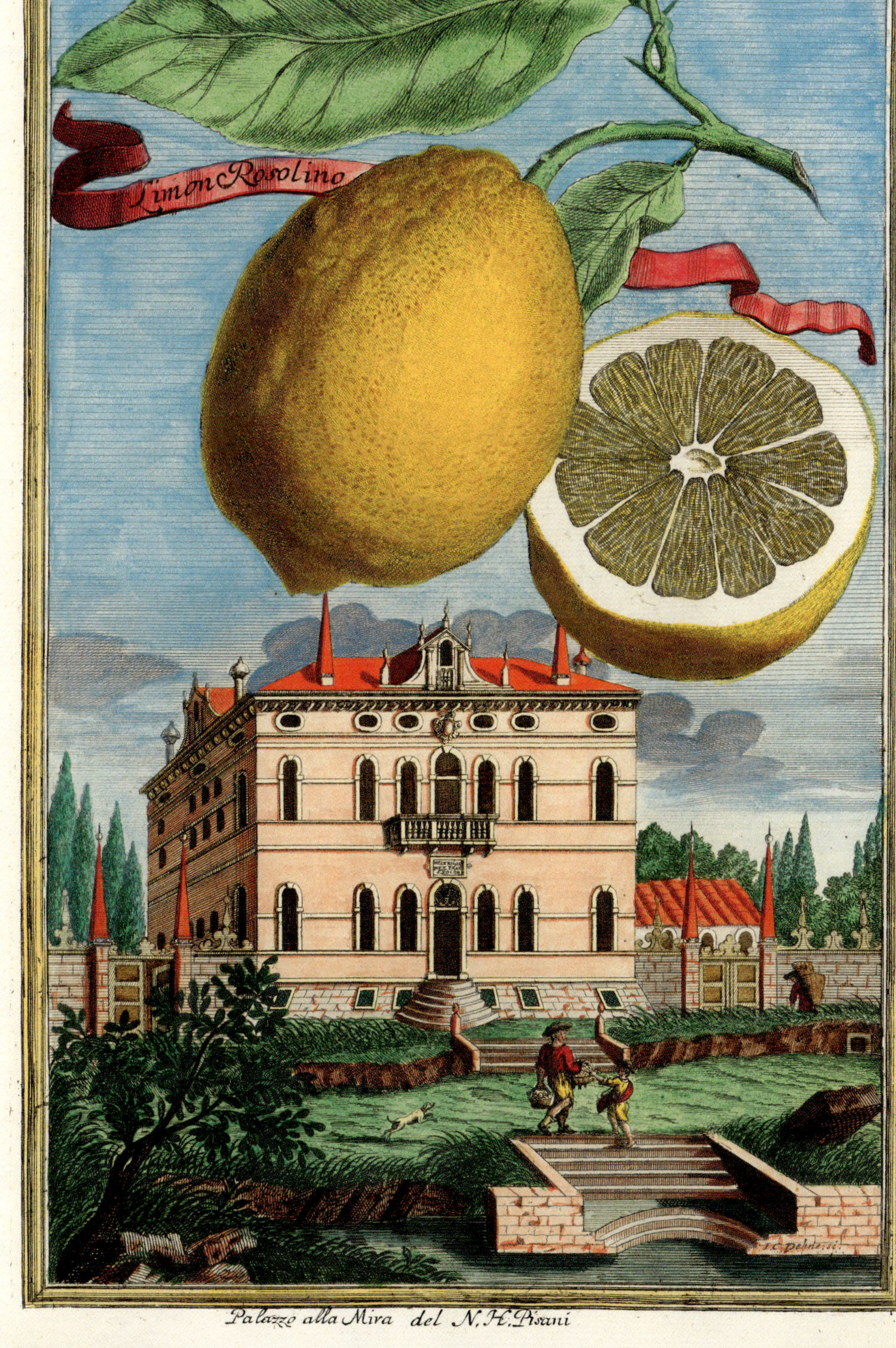

Limon di fior doppio

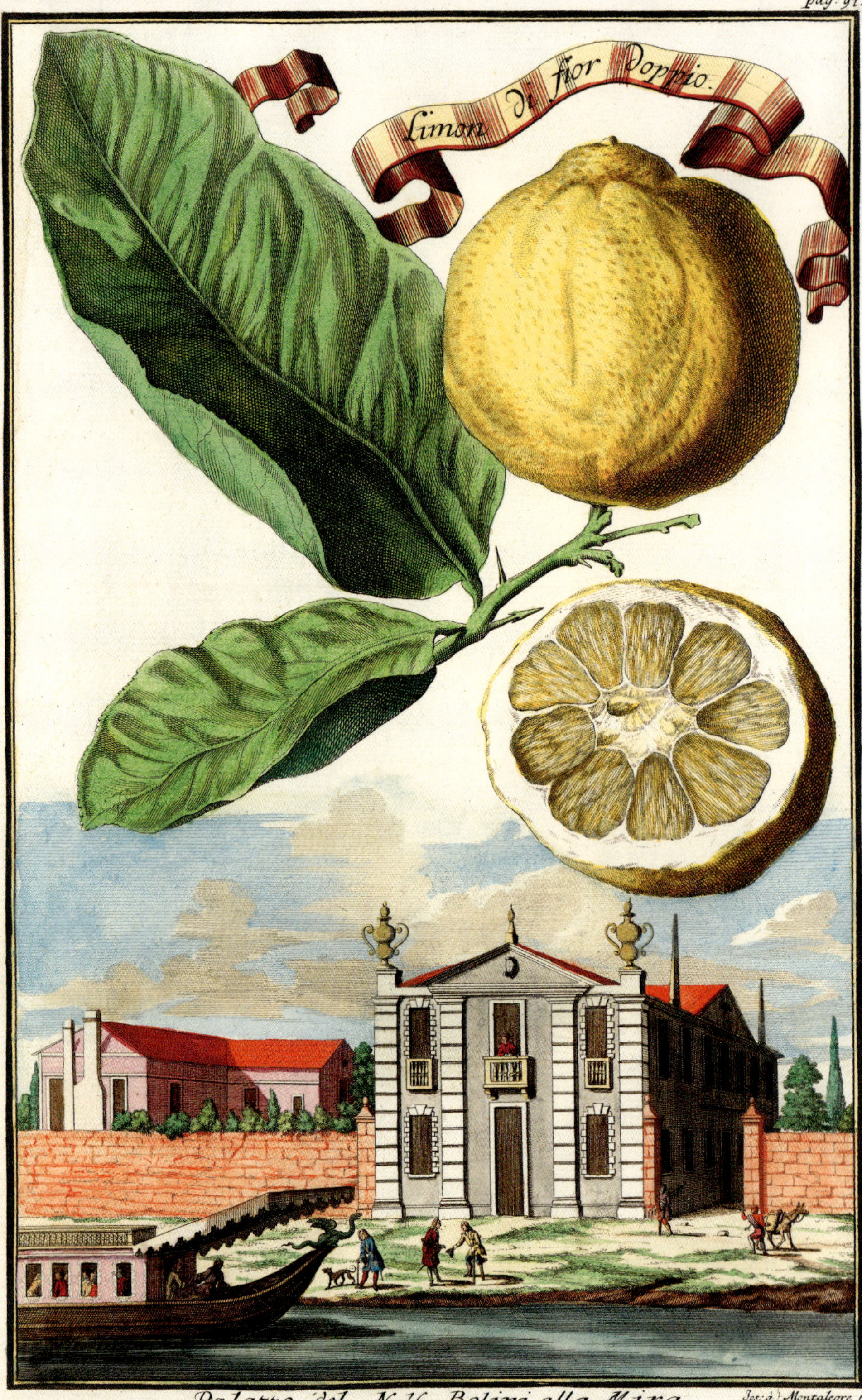

Mira (Venice) – Villa Bon

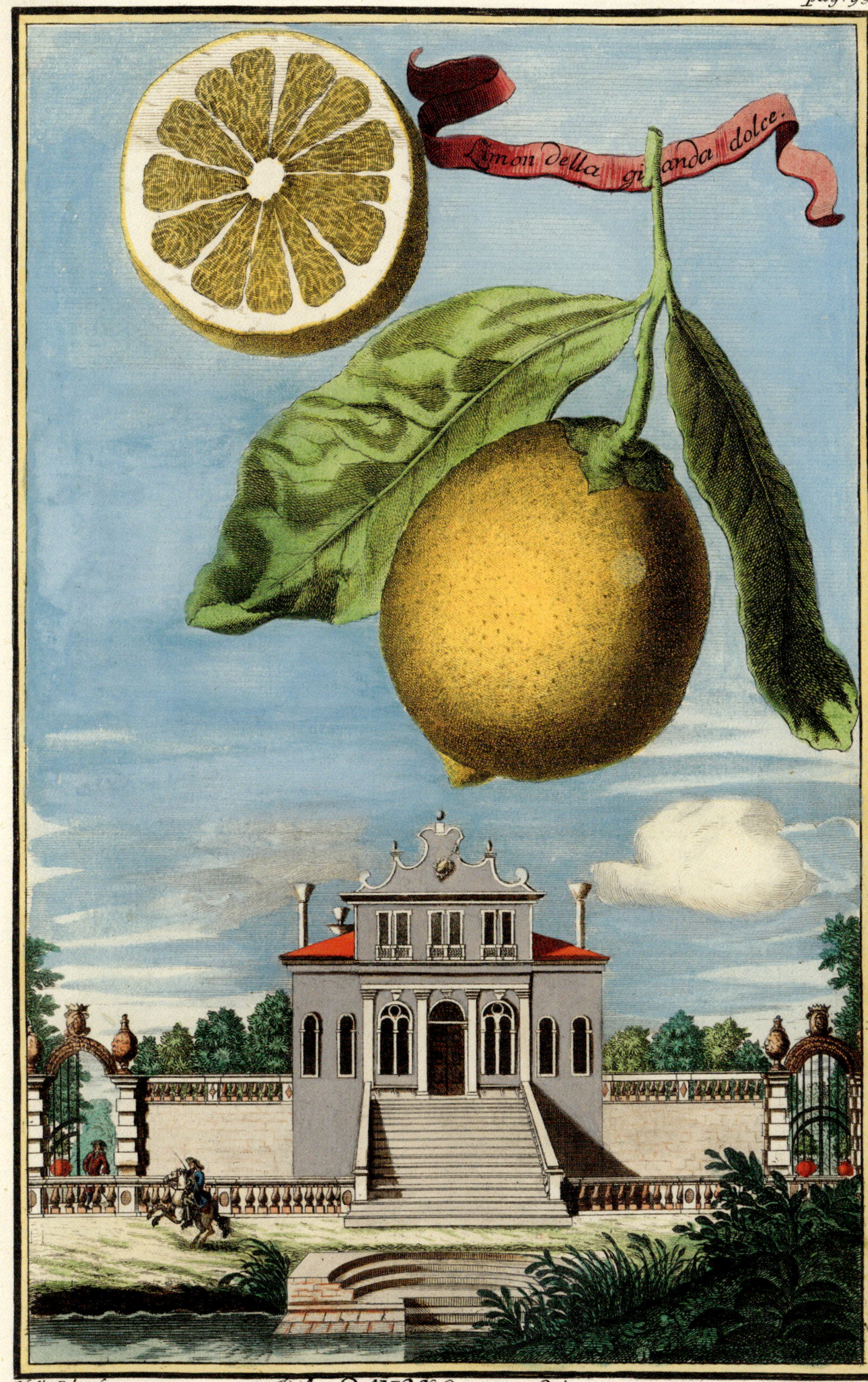
pag: 93
Limon della ghianda dolce.
Joh. Chr. Dehne. fc
Palazo del N.H. Cornaro a Oriago

Limon dolce multiforme

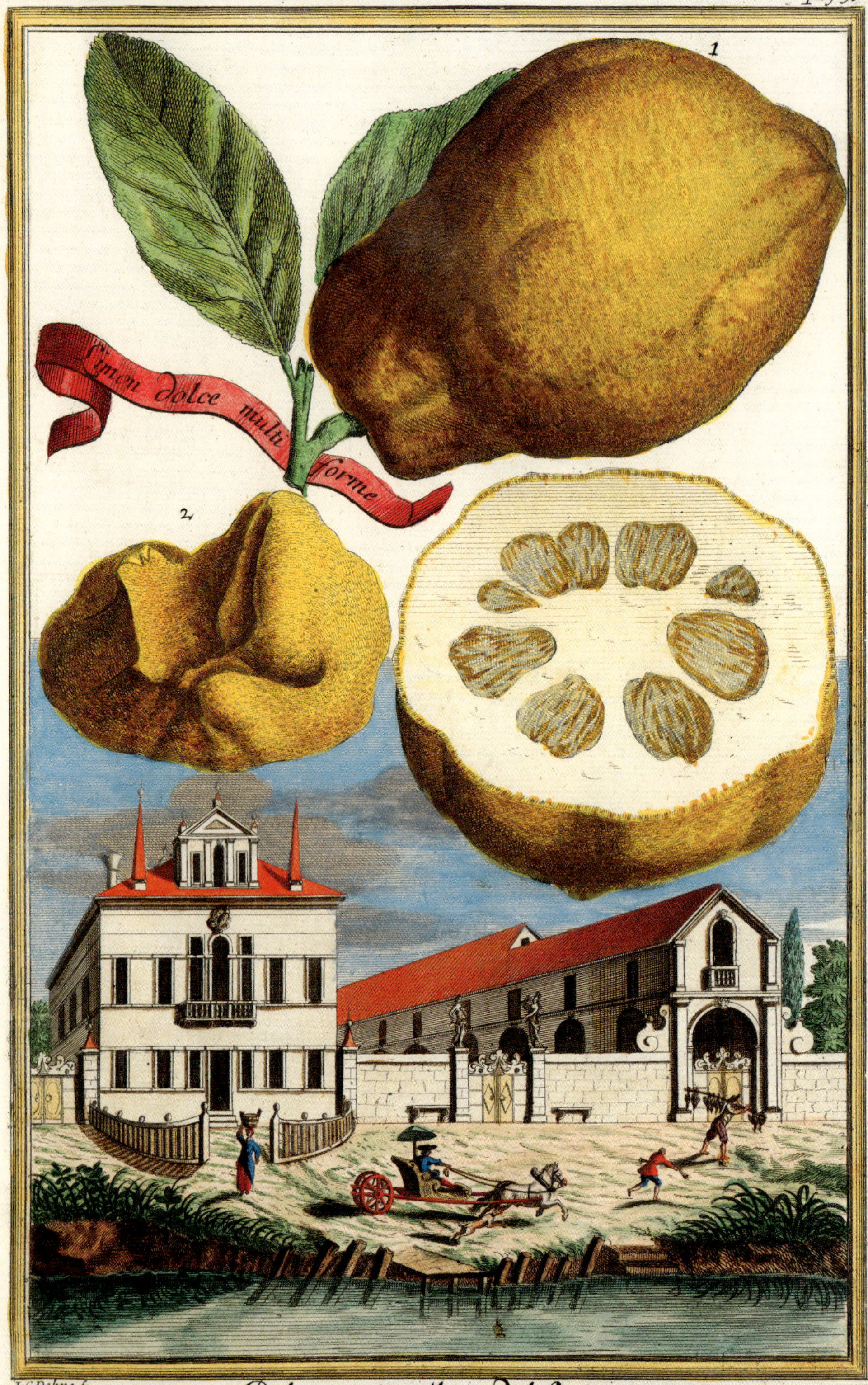

Mira (Venice) – Villa Alessandri

Limon dolce multiforme

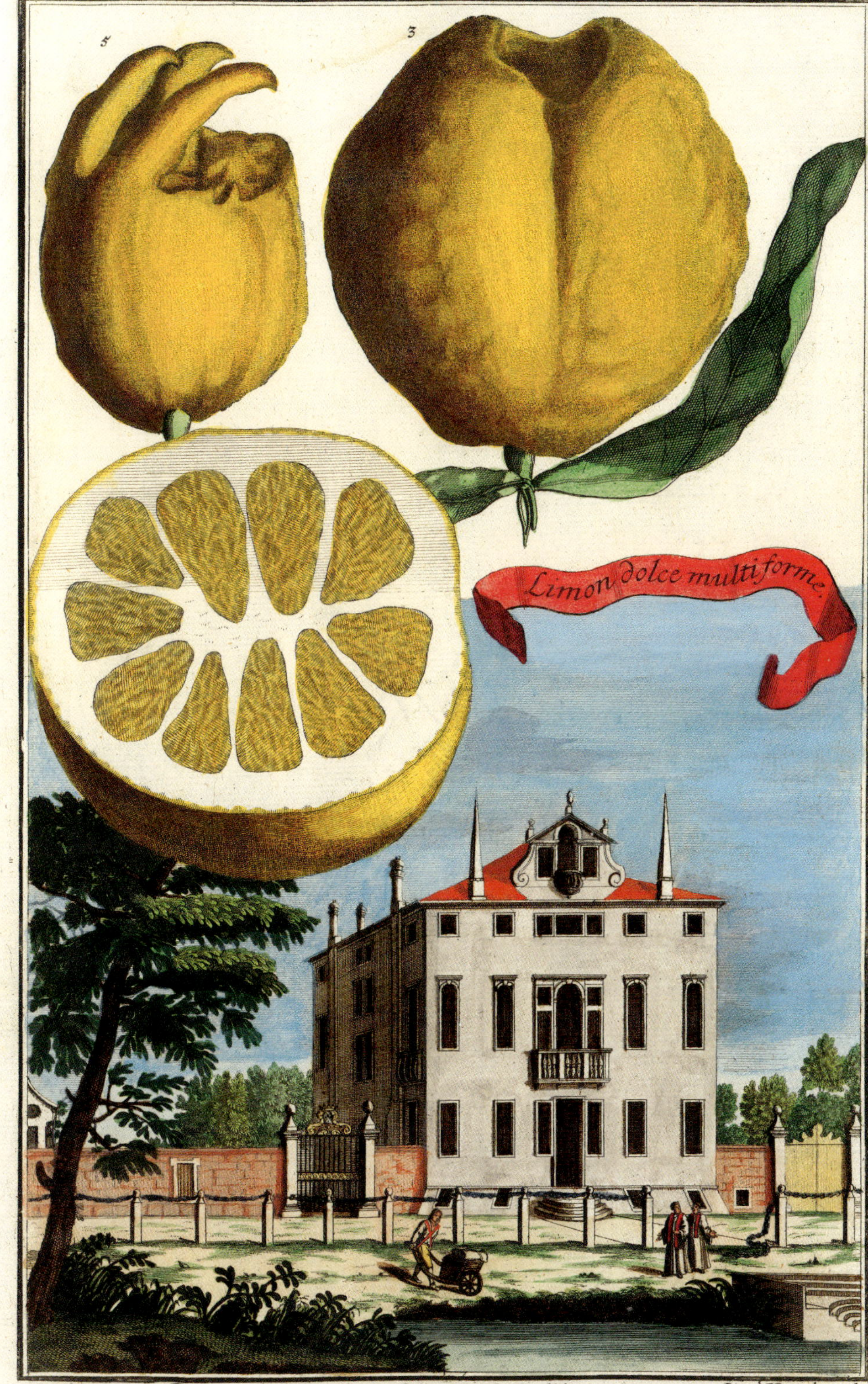

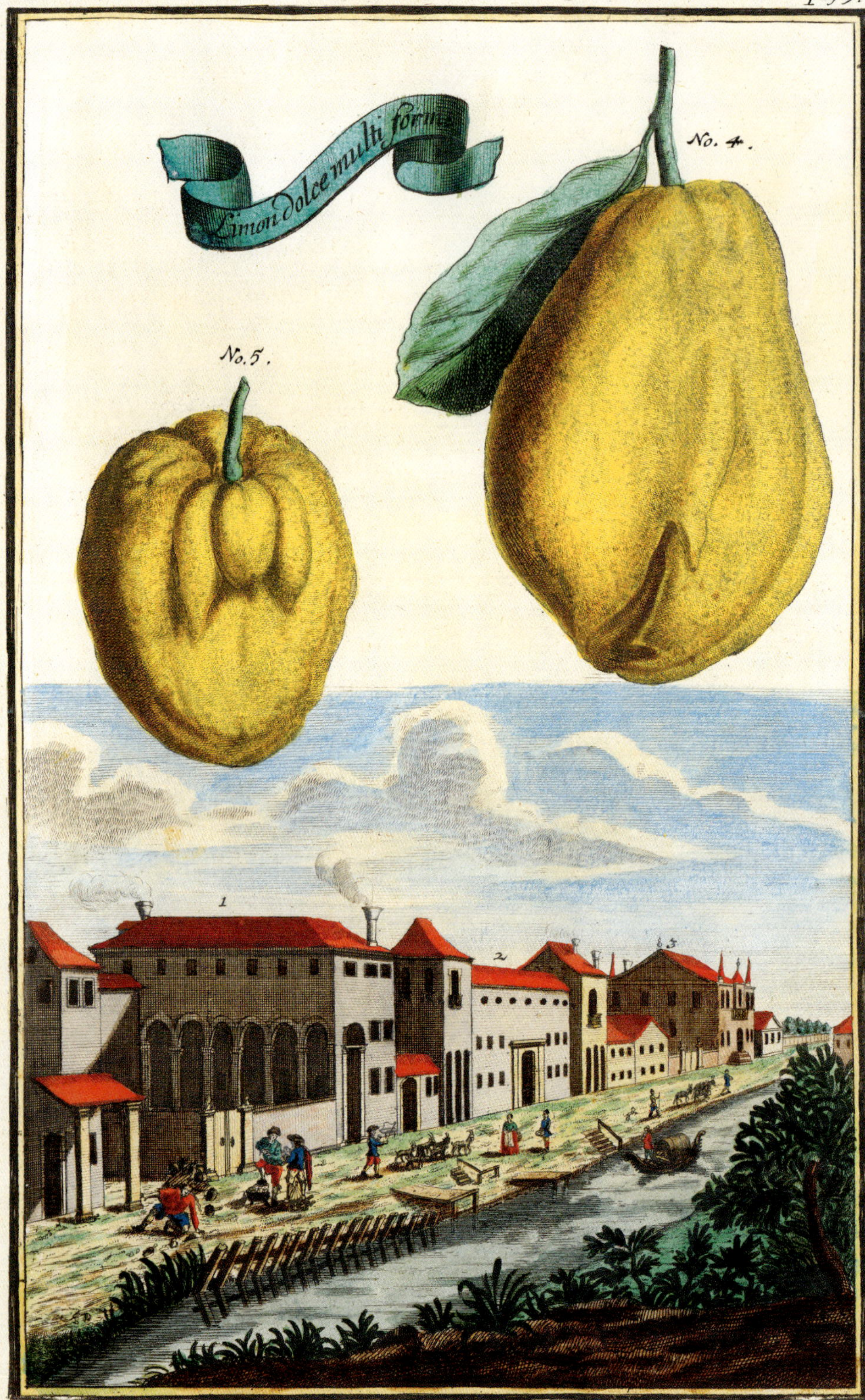

Limon dolce multiforme

Gambarare di Mira (Venice) – Villa Barbarigo, Villa Valier, Villa Franceschi

Limon incomparabile

River Brenta – Villa alli Aringari

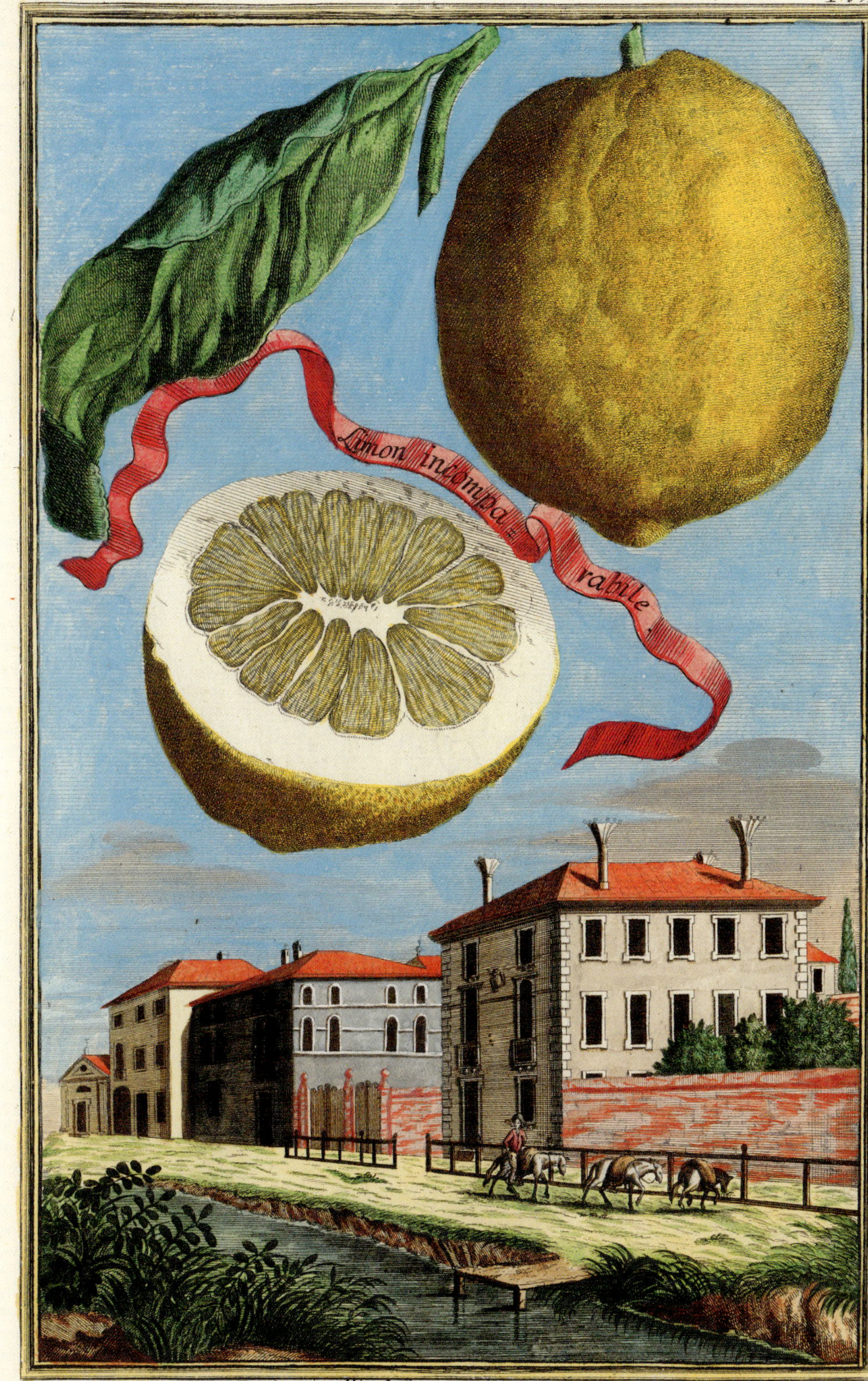

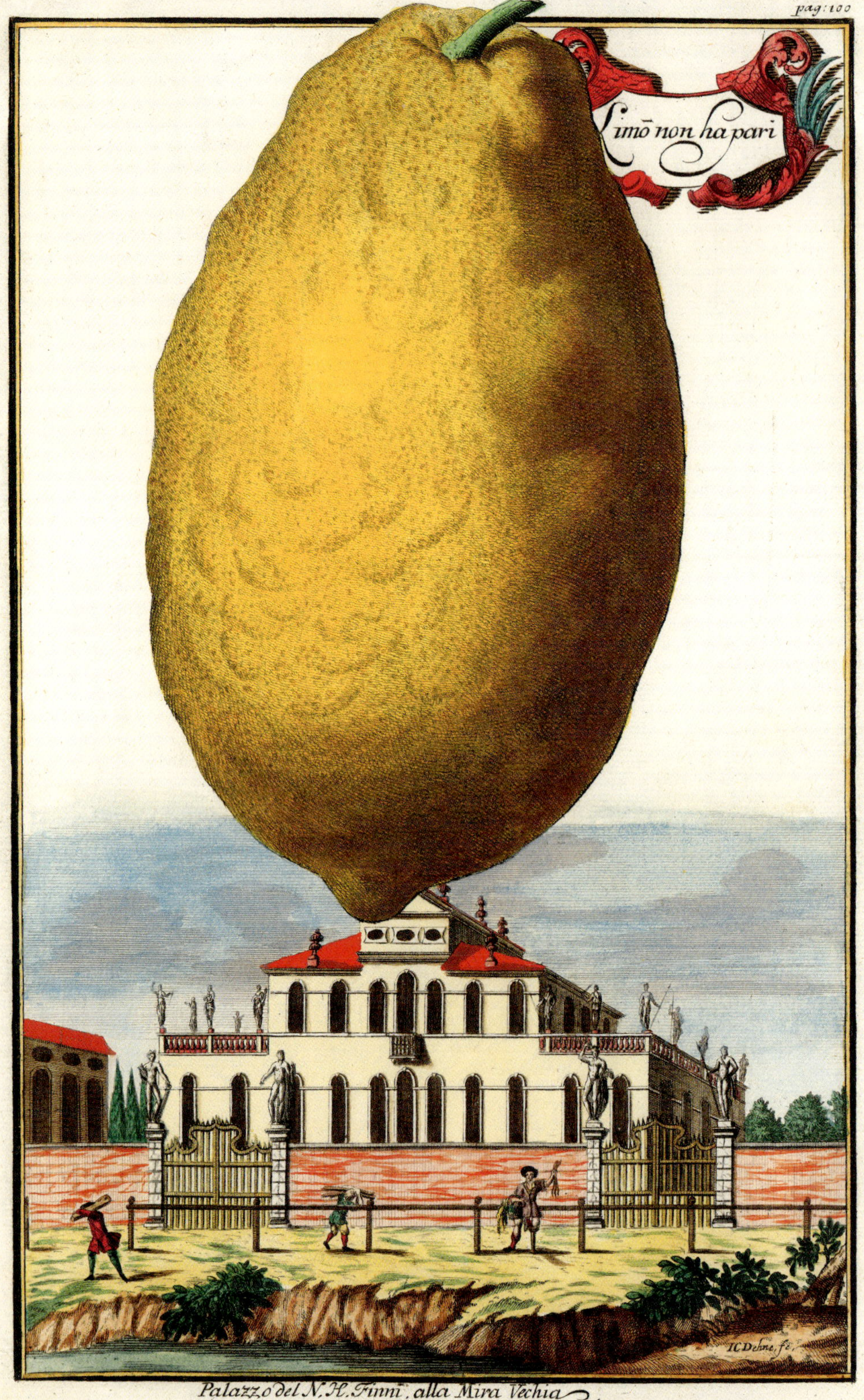

Limon non ha pari

Mira Vecchia (Venice) – Villa Fini

Limon non ha pari

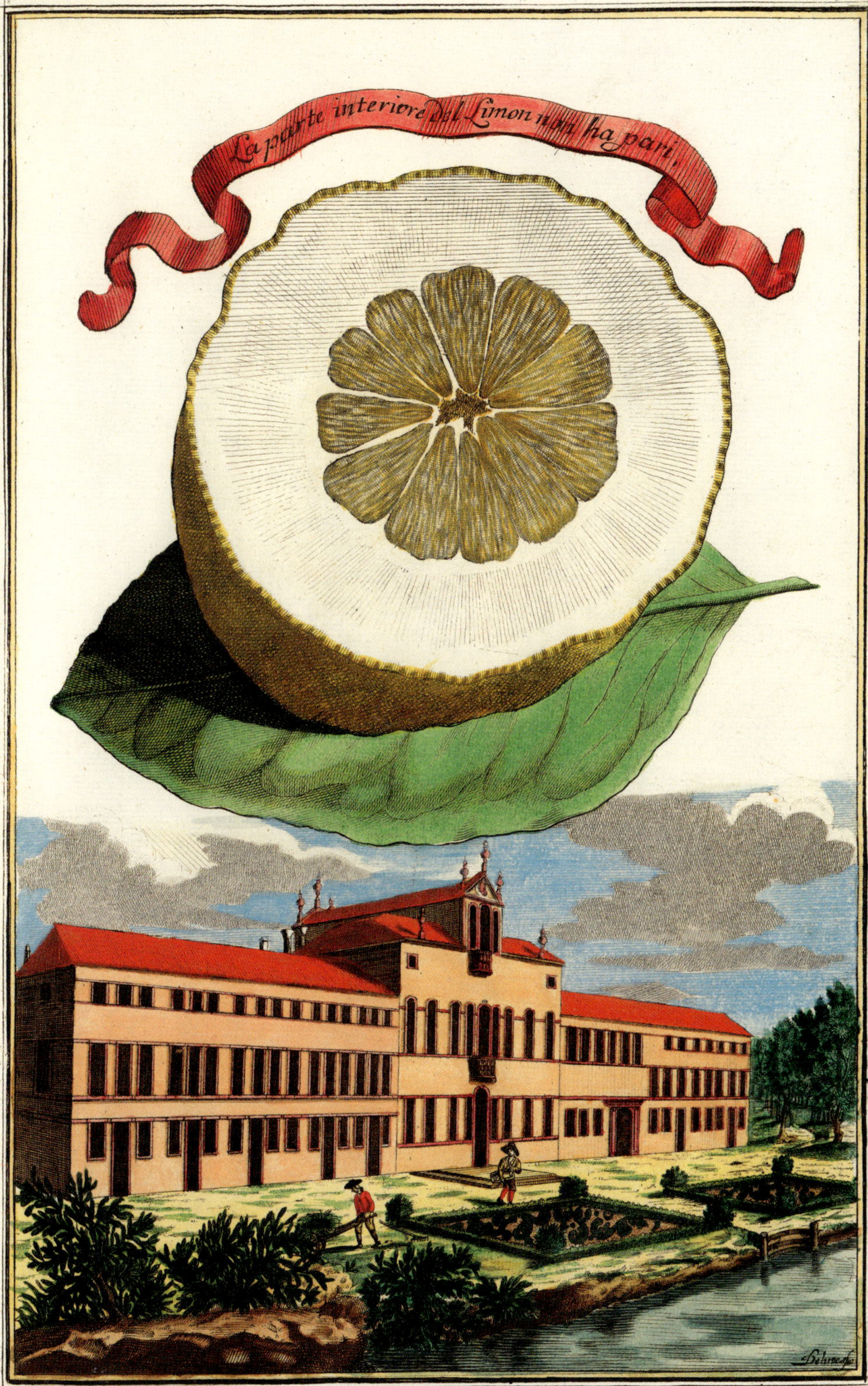

Mira Vecchia (Venice) – Villa Molin

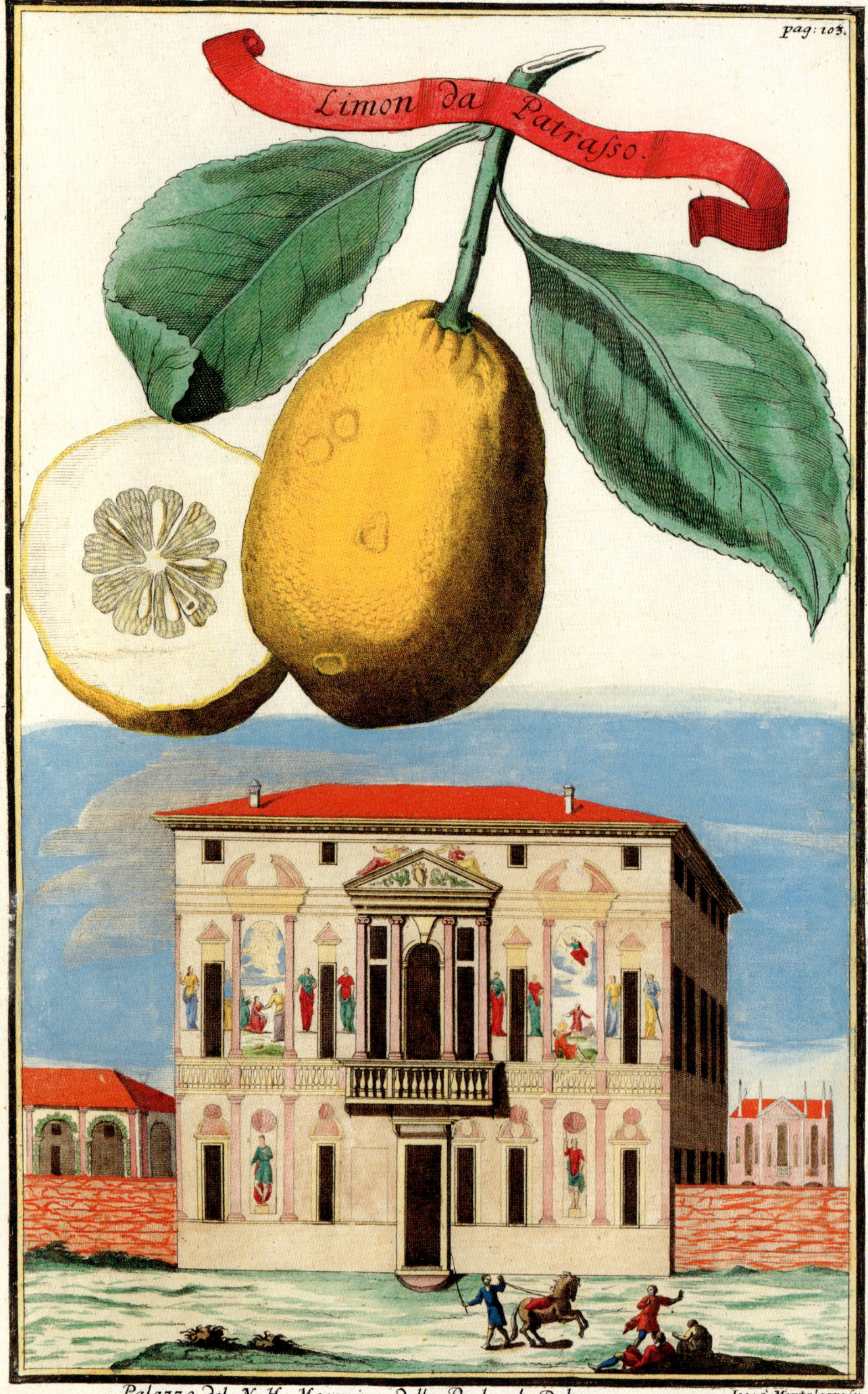

Limon da Patrasso

Mira Vecchia (Venice) – Villa Mocenigo delle Perle

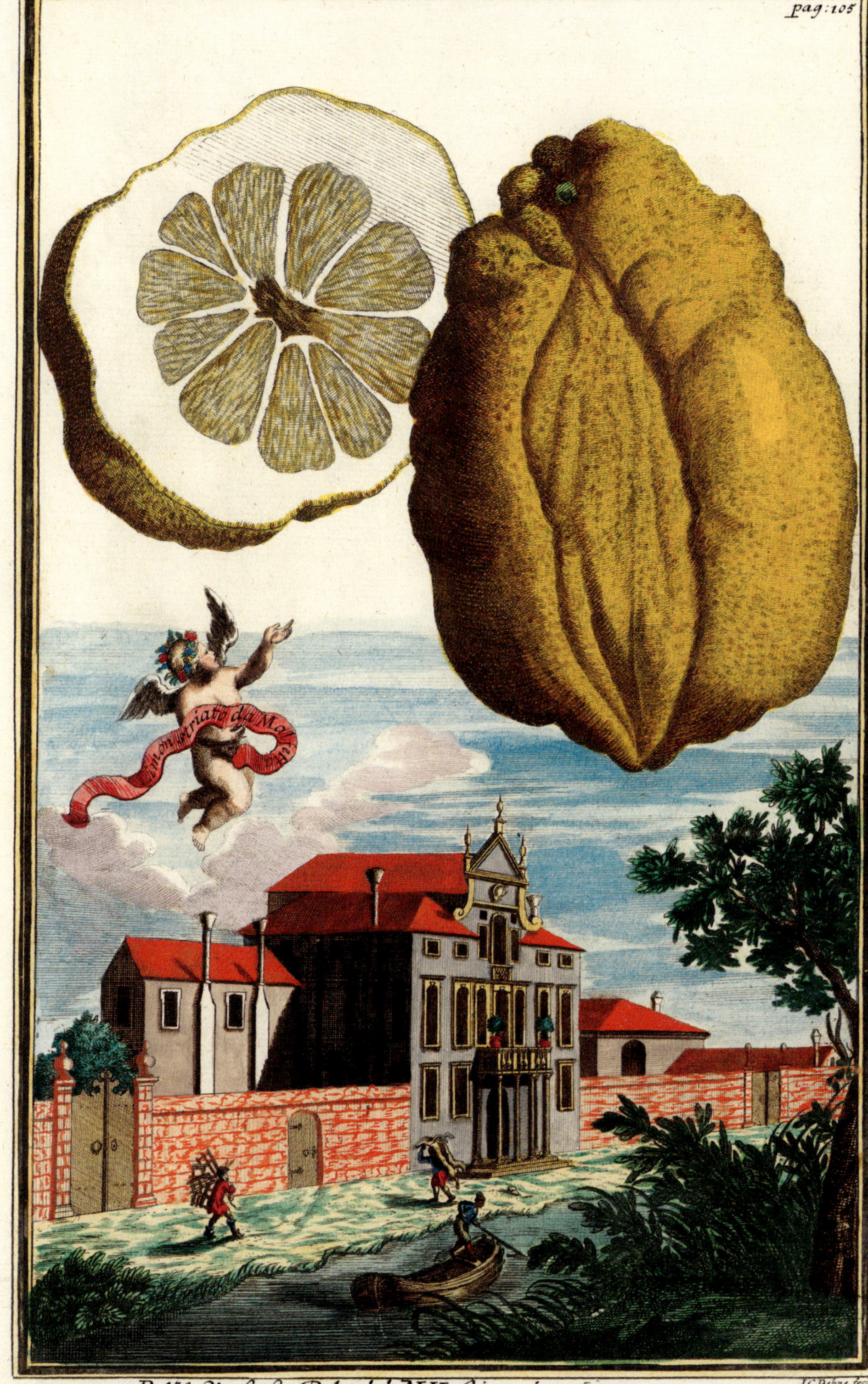

Limon striato da Malfetta

Mira Vecchia (Venice) – Villa Grimani, later Migliorini

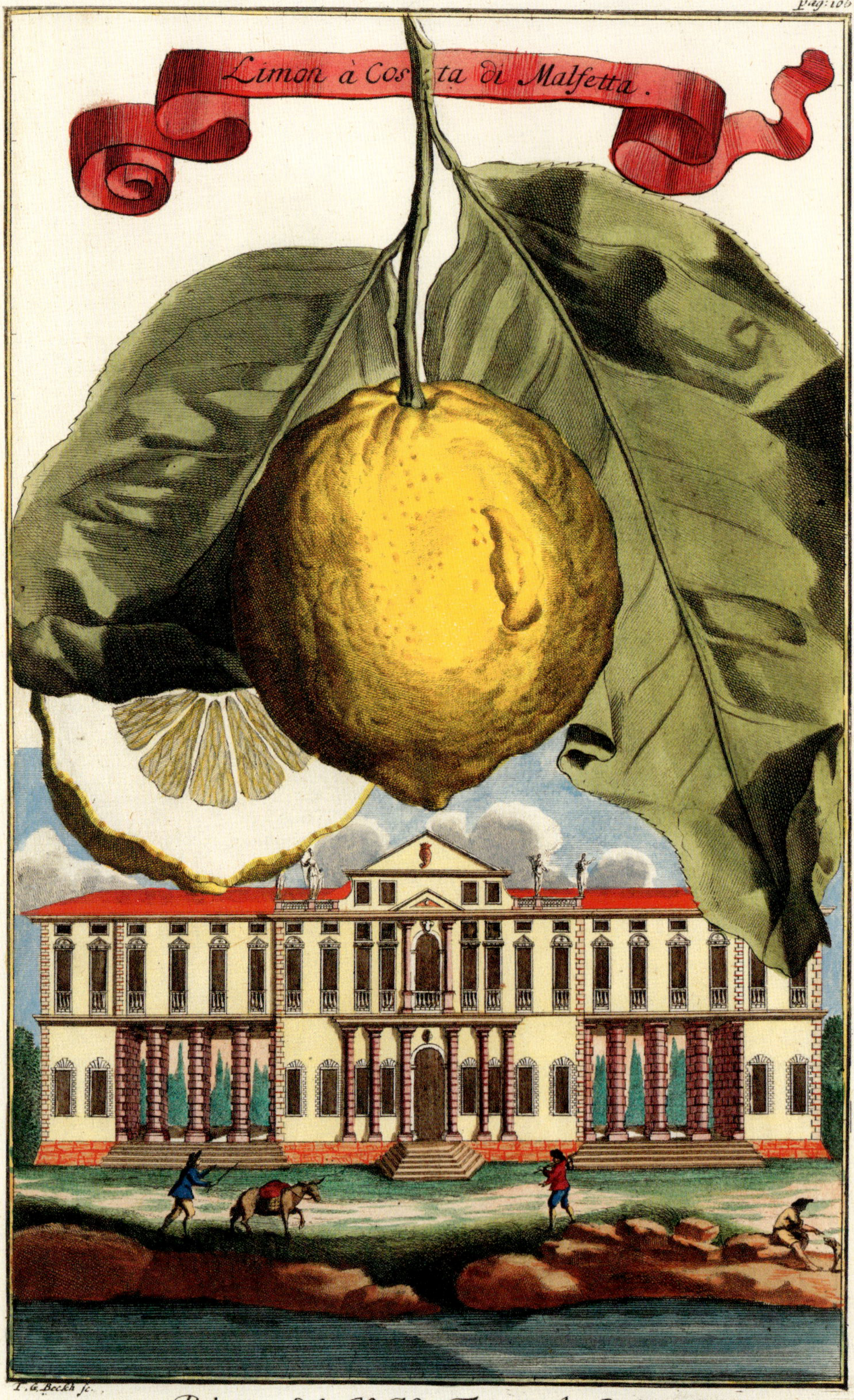

Limon a costa di Malfetta

Dolo (Venice) – Villa Tron

Limon monstroso di Malfetta

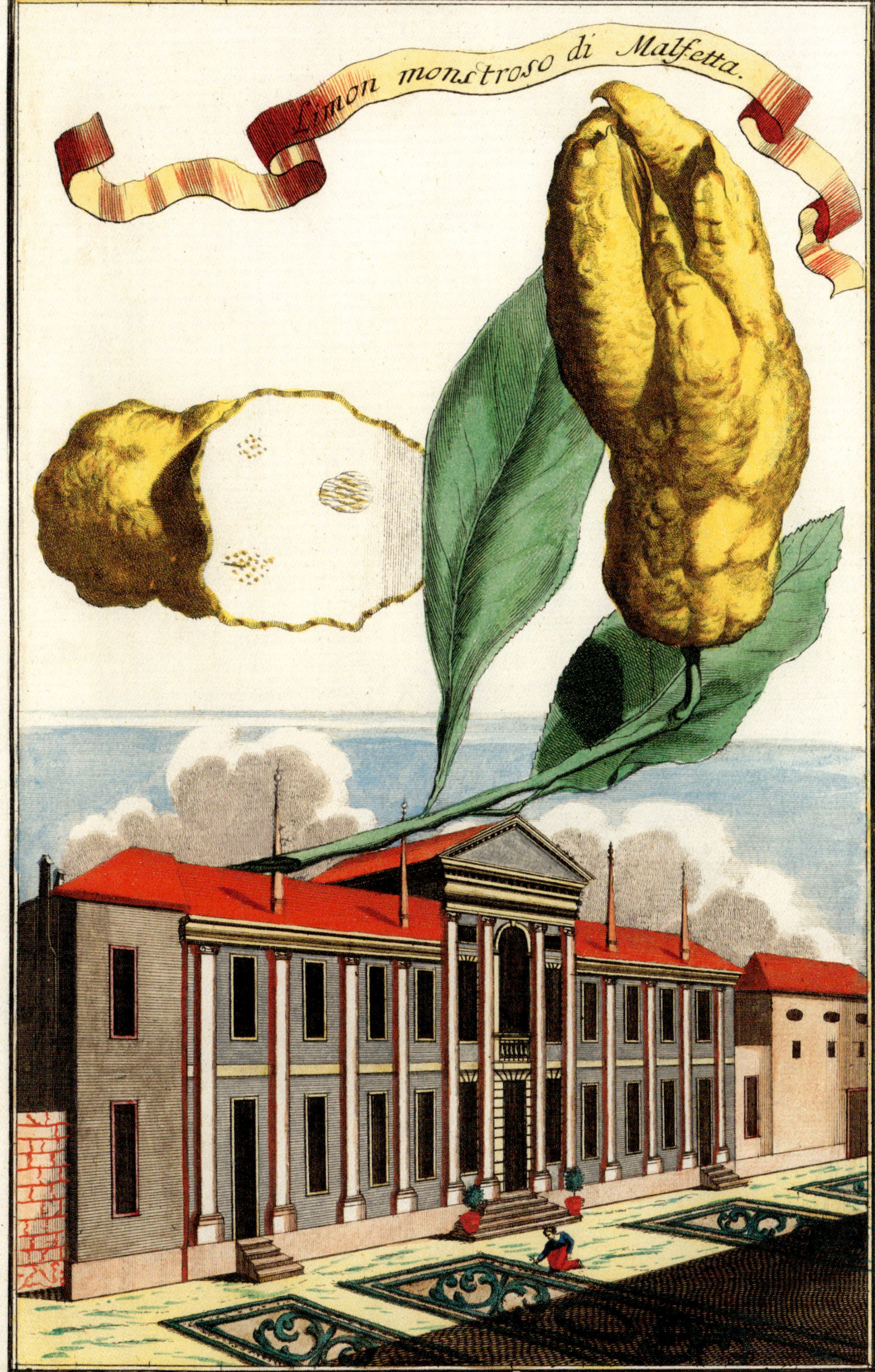

Dolo, Sambruson (Venice) – Villa Ferretti Angeli

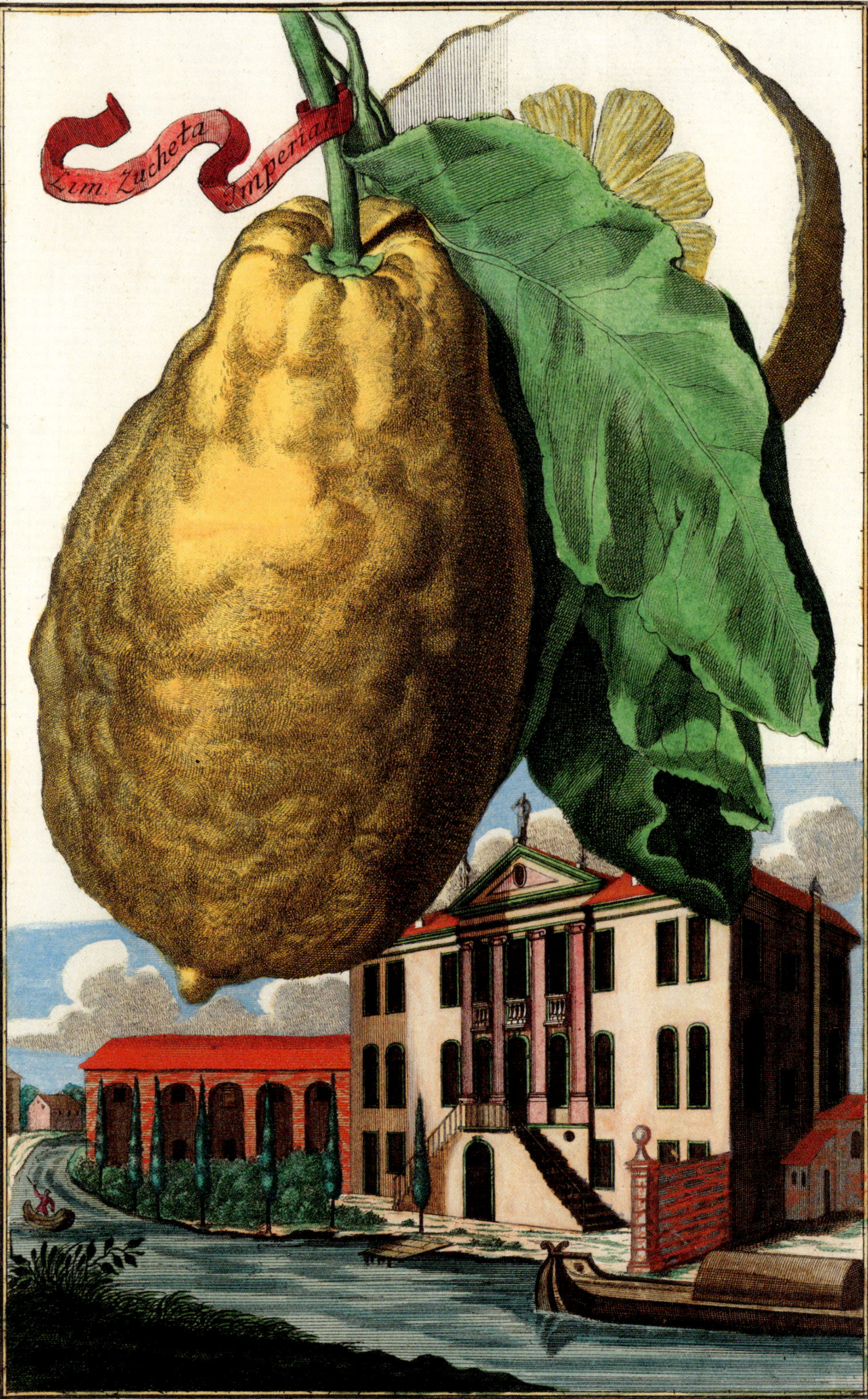

Lim[on] Zucchet[t]a Imperiale

Dolo (Venice) – Villa Andreuzzi

Limon Cucurbitato

Dolo (Venice) – Villa Mocenigo da San Samuele

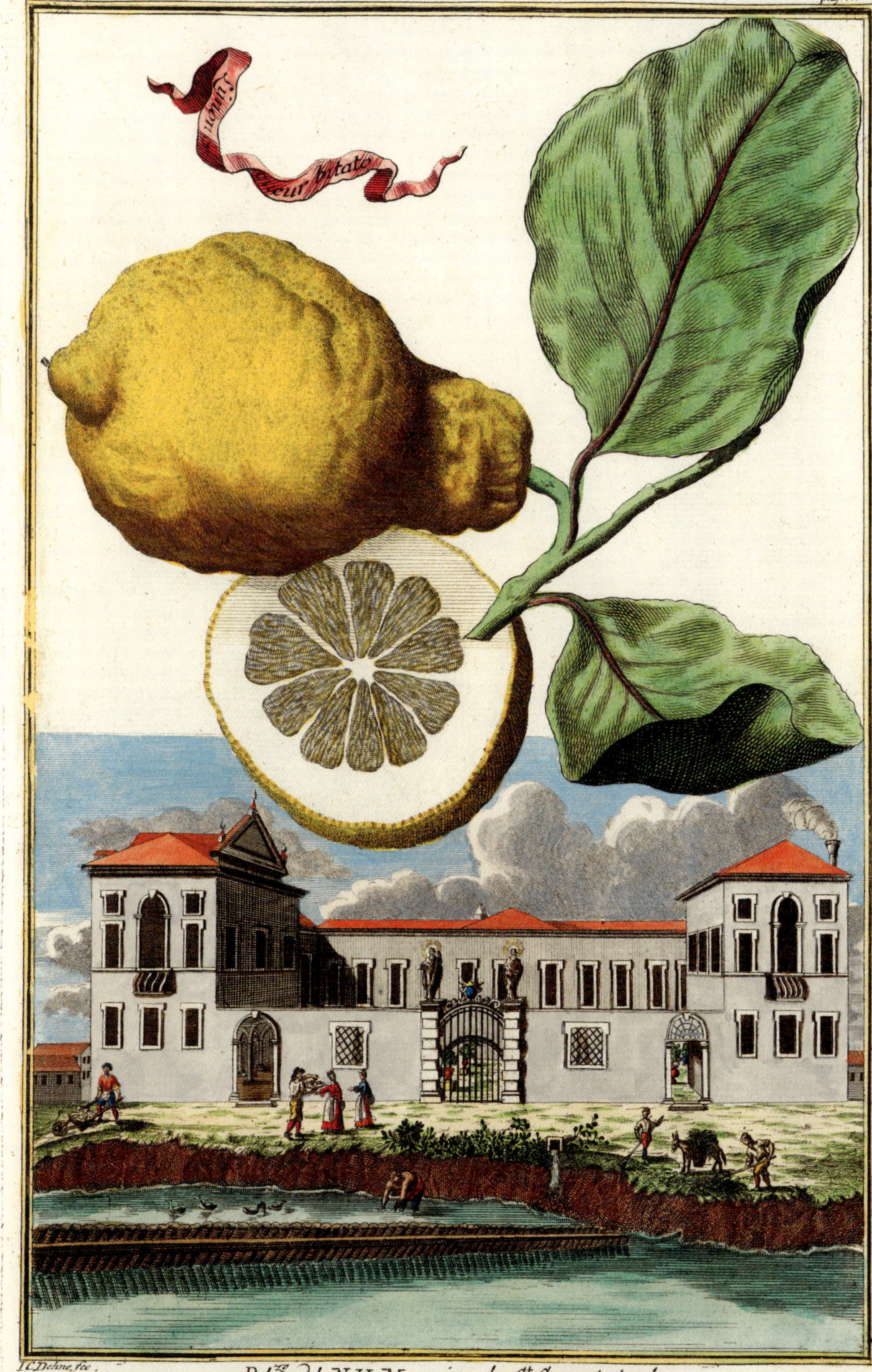

Limon a costa grande da Calabria

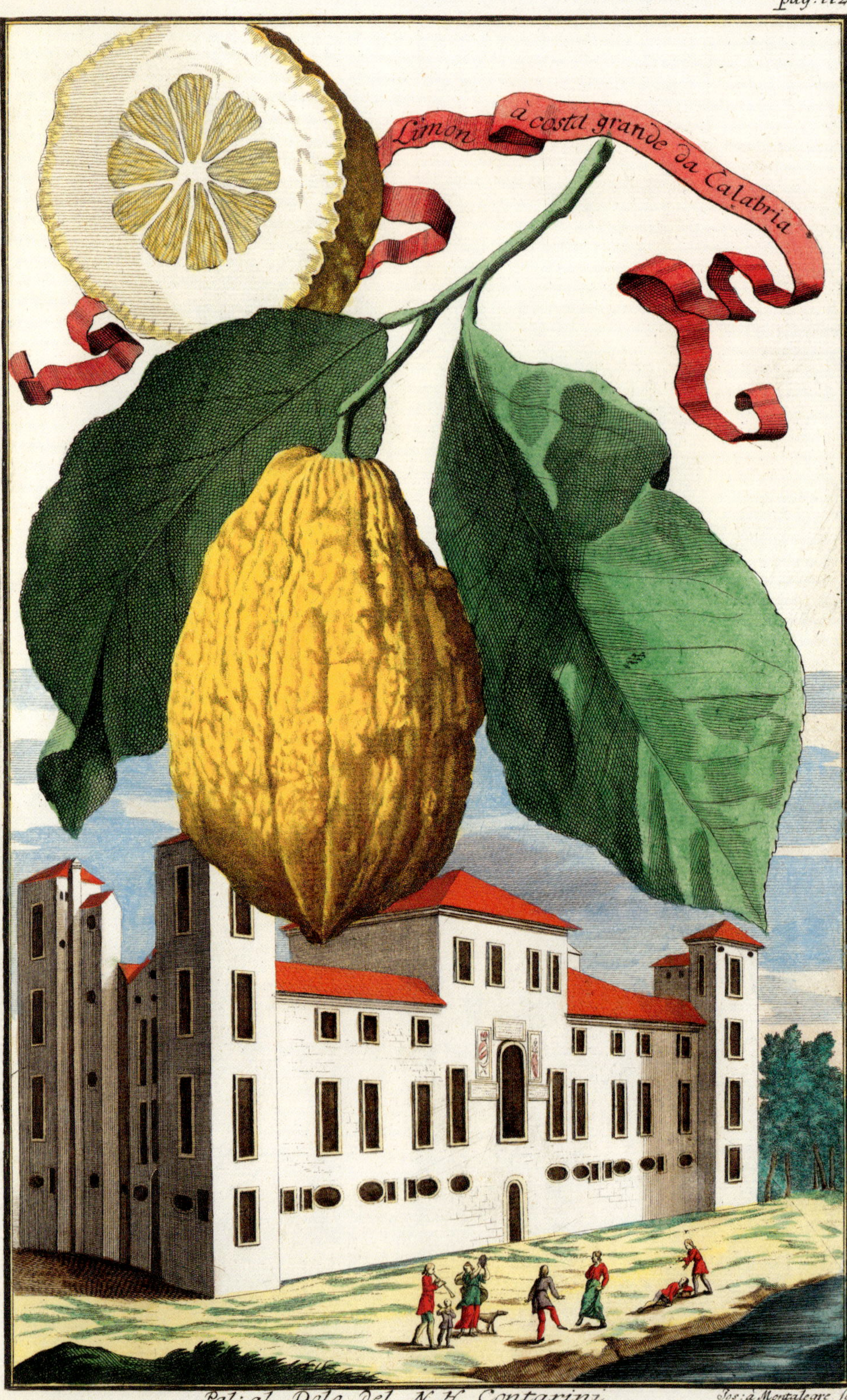

Dolo (Venice) – Villa Contarini, later Donà

Limonet[t]a da Calabria

Stra (Venice) – Villa Contarini

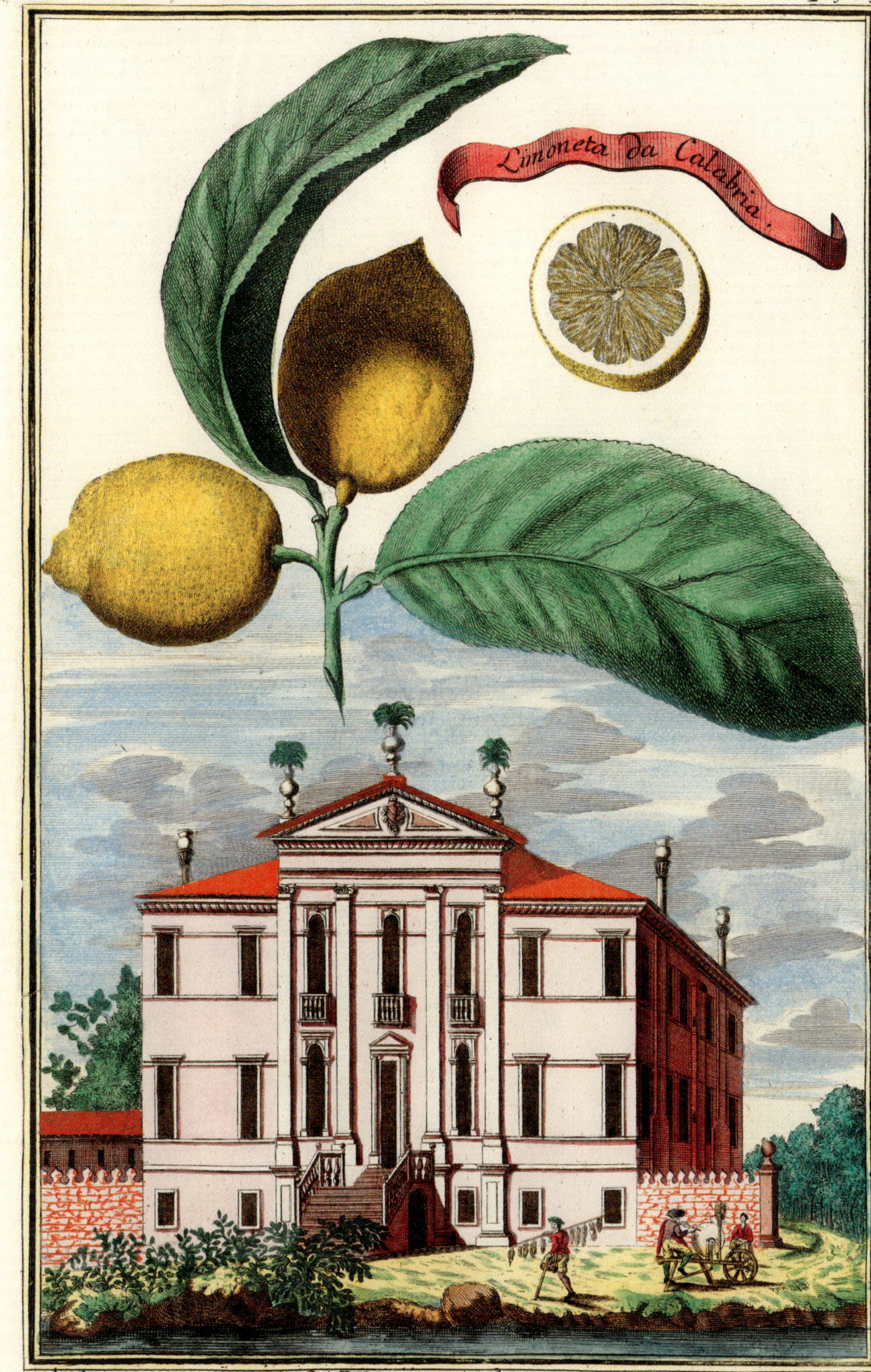

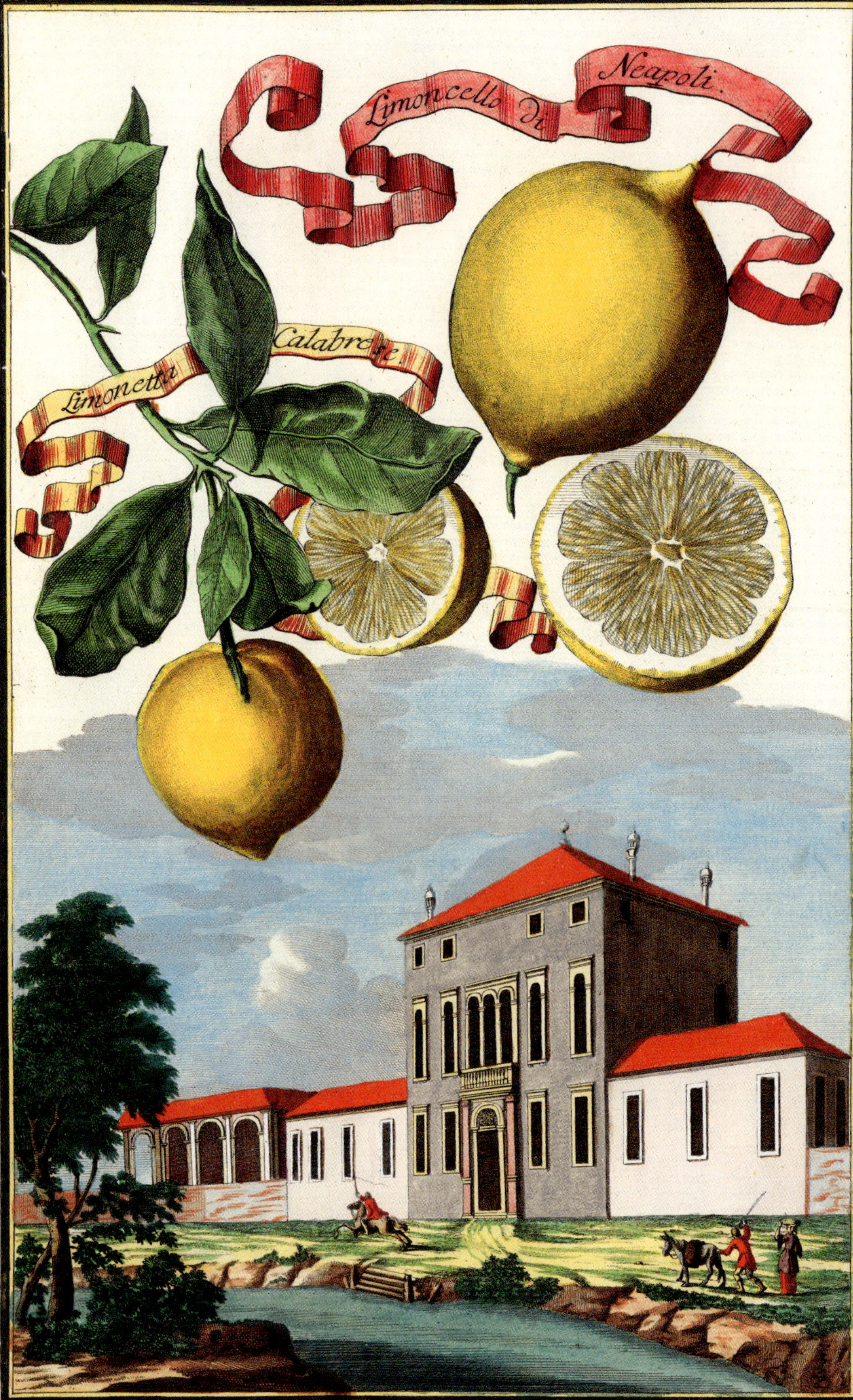

Limoncello di Neapoli
& Limonetta Calabrese

Stra (Venice) – Villa Venier

Limonzin da Portugal
& Limon peretto di fior doppio

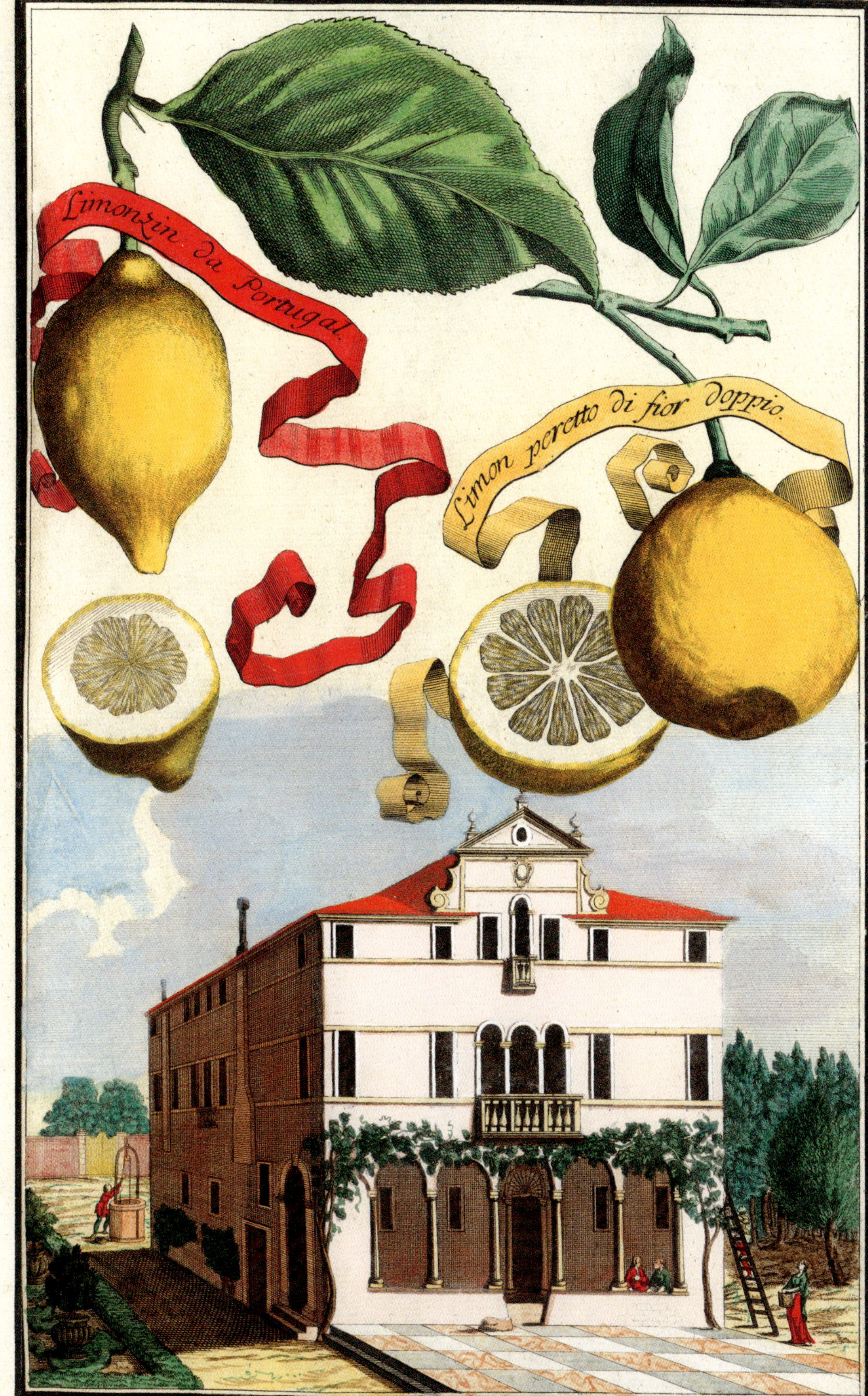

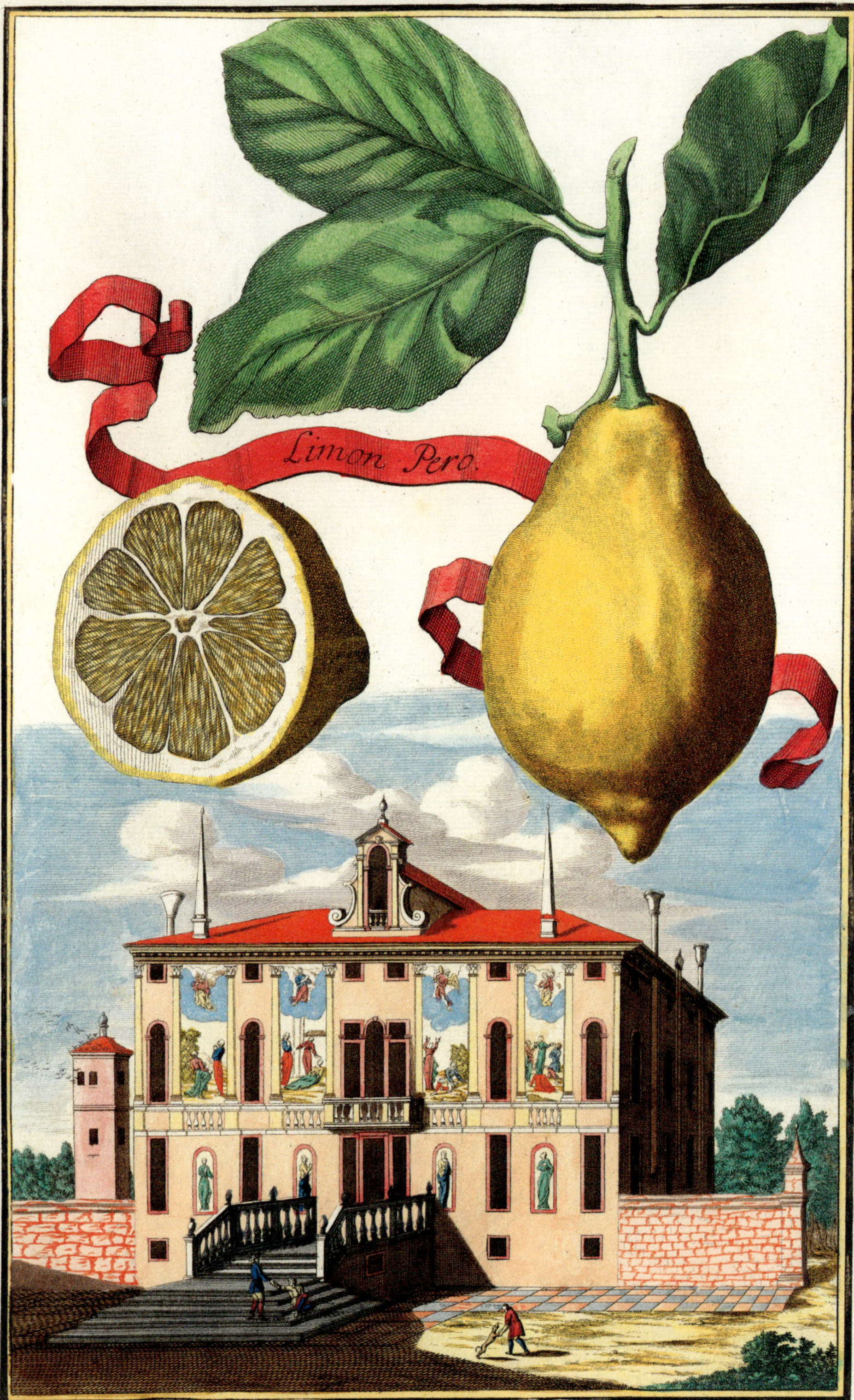

Palazzo del N. H. Soranzo à fiesso.

Ios: à Montalegre sc:

Limon Pero

Fiesso d'Artico (Venice) – Villa Soranzo

Limon Bizantino

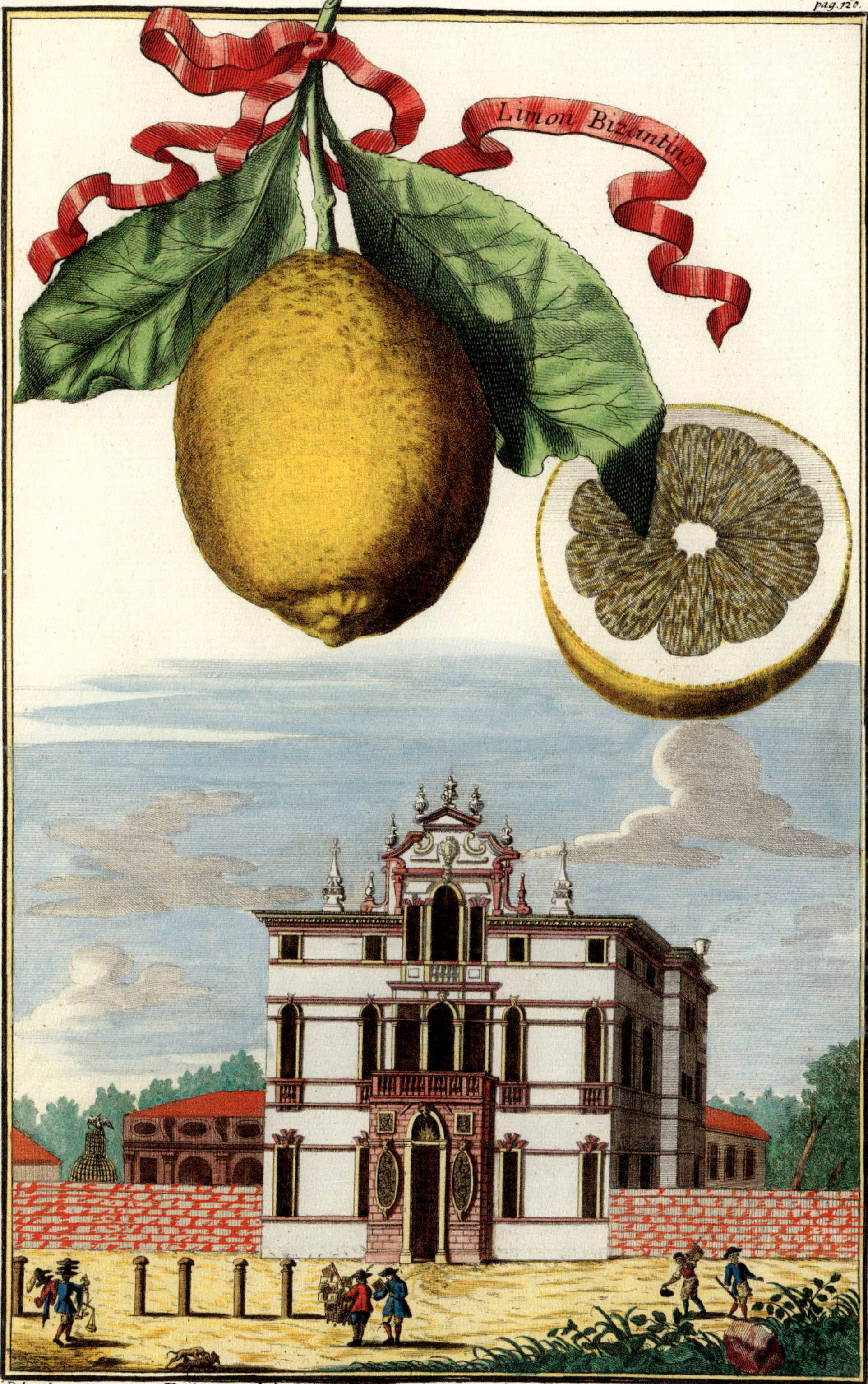

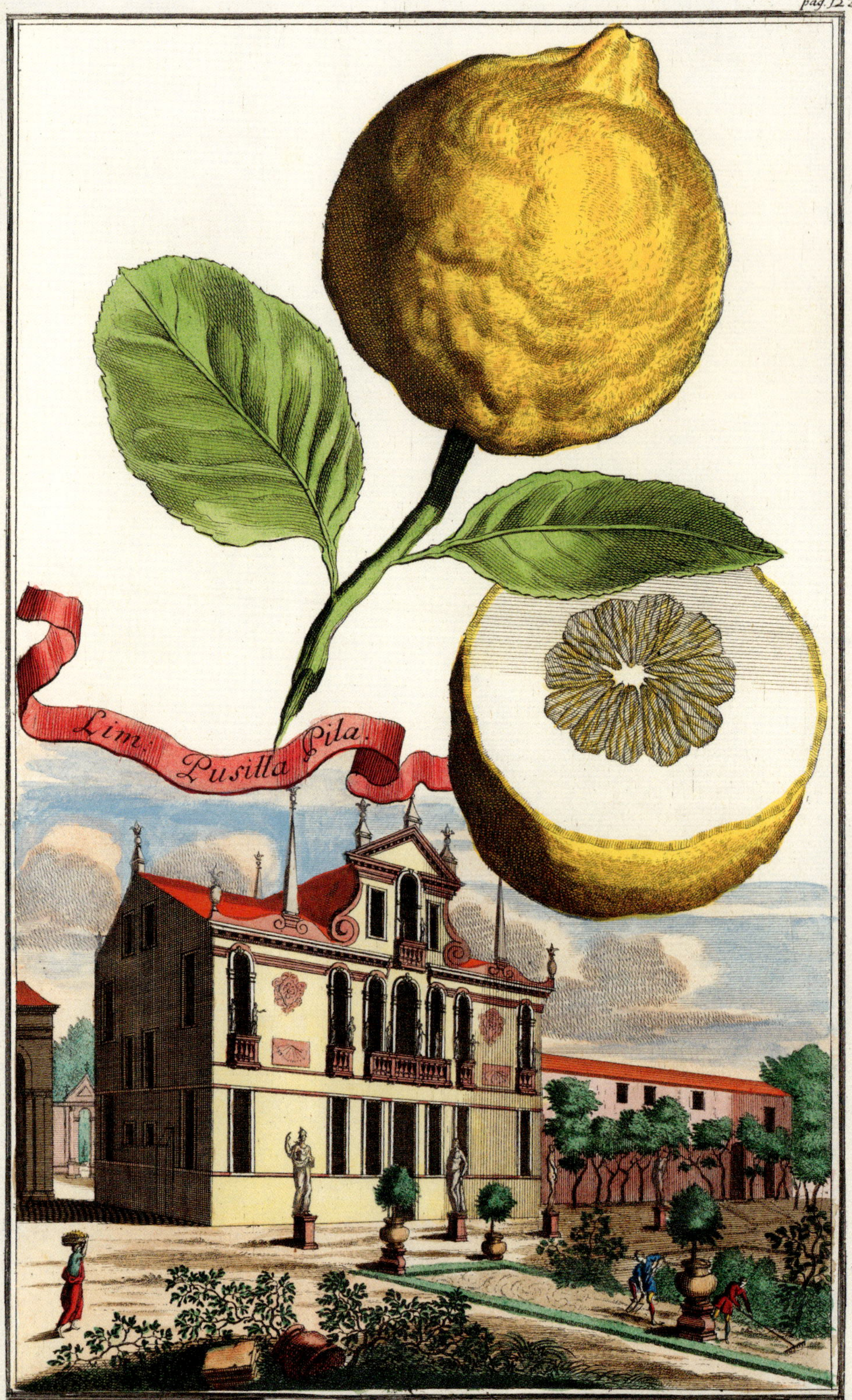

Lim[on] Pusilla Pila

Fiesso d'Artico (Venice) – Villa Mocenigo

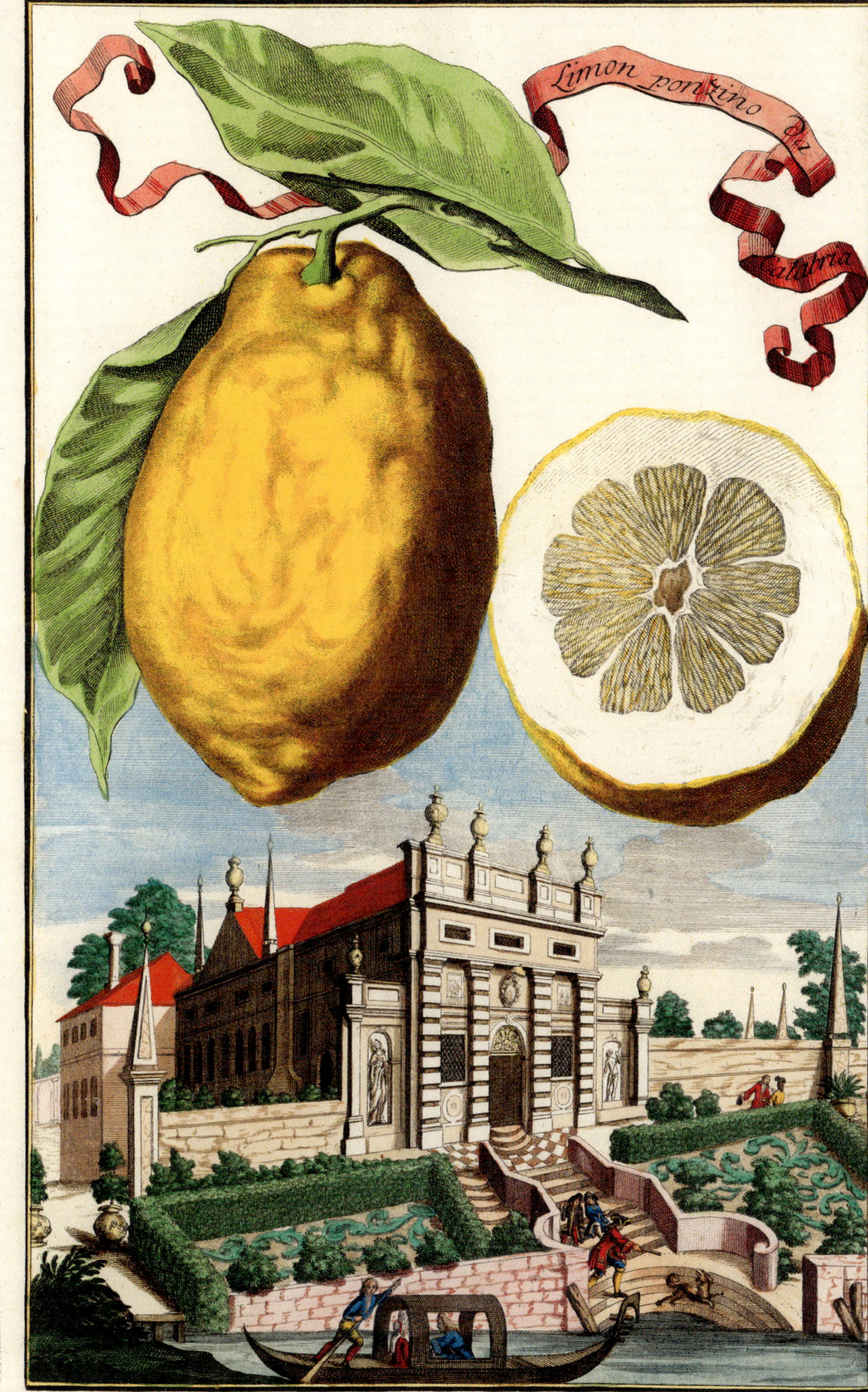

Limon Ponzino da Calabria

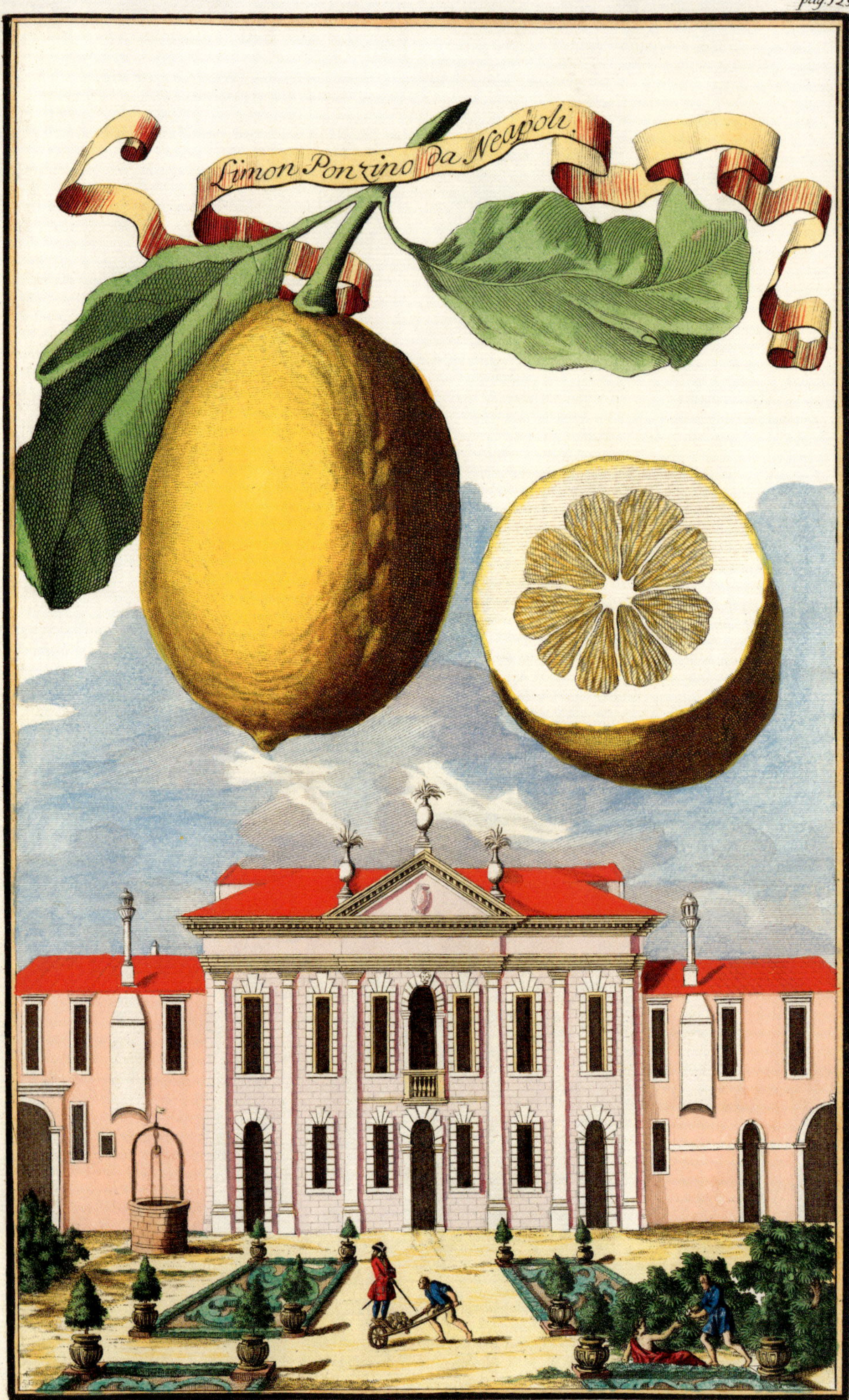

Limon Ponzino da Neapoli

Fiesso d'Artico (Venice) – Villa Corner

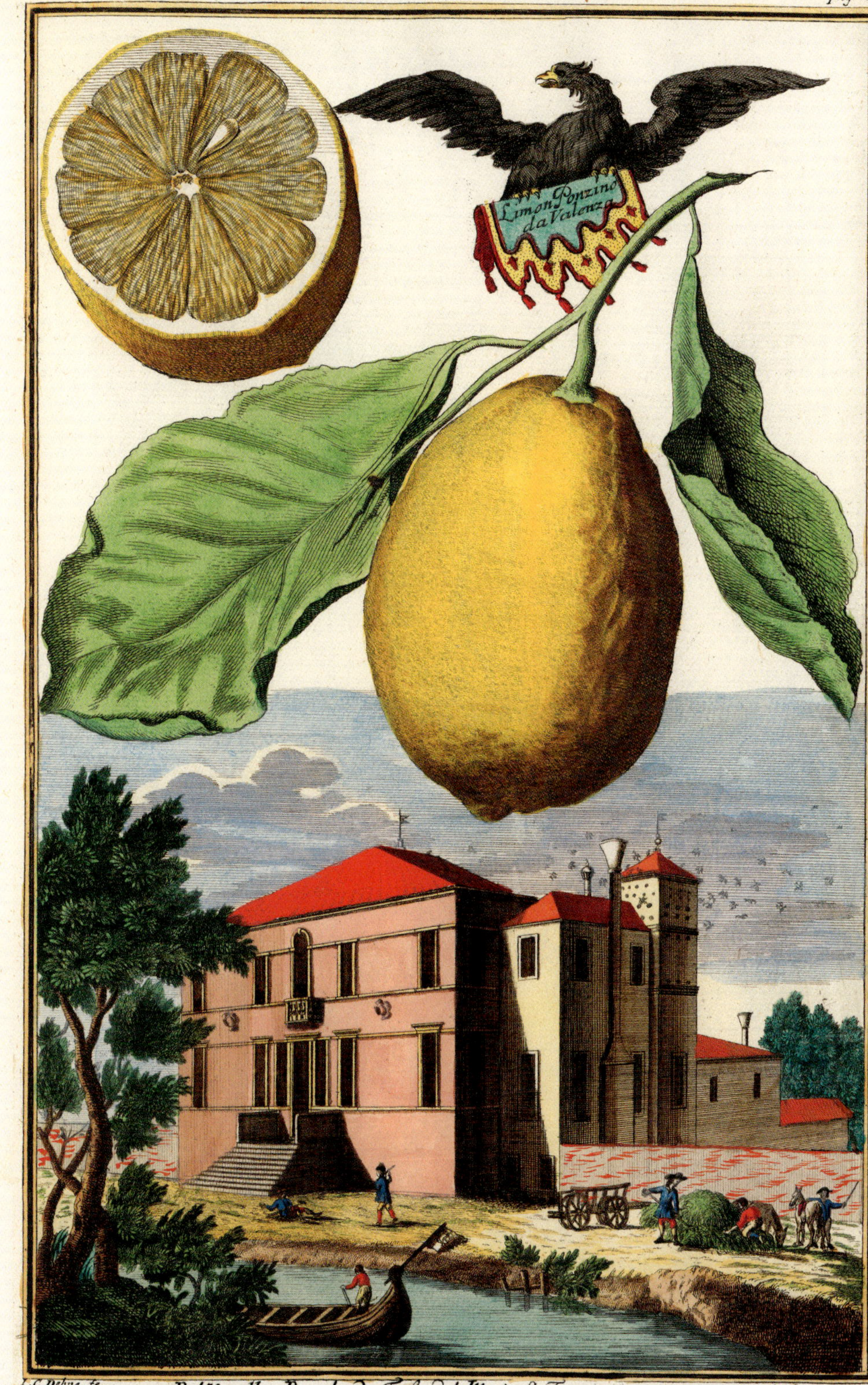

Stra (Venice) – Villa Tornielli

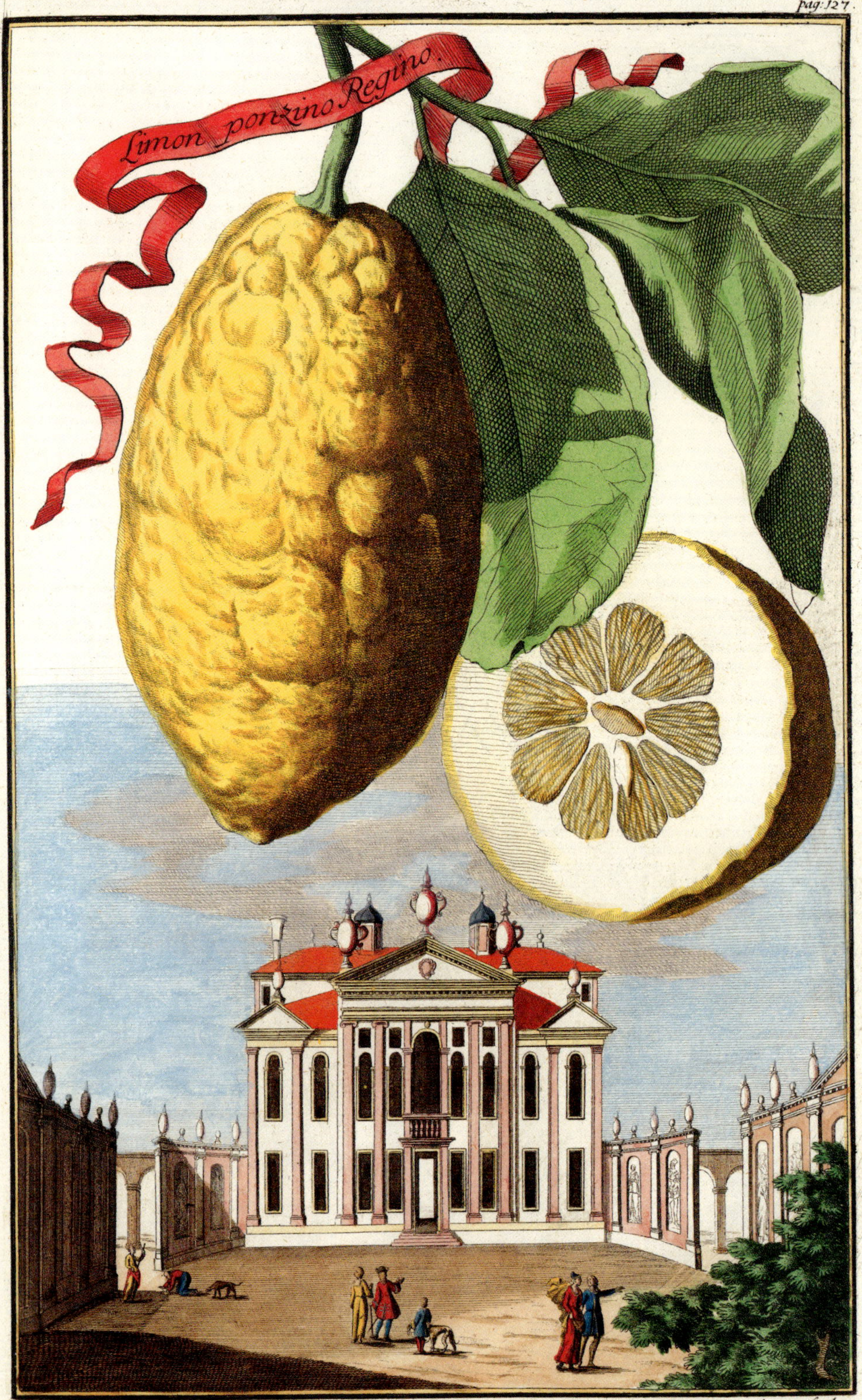

Limon Ponzino Regino

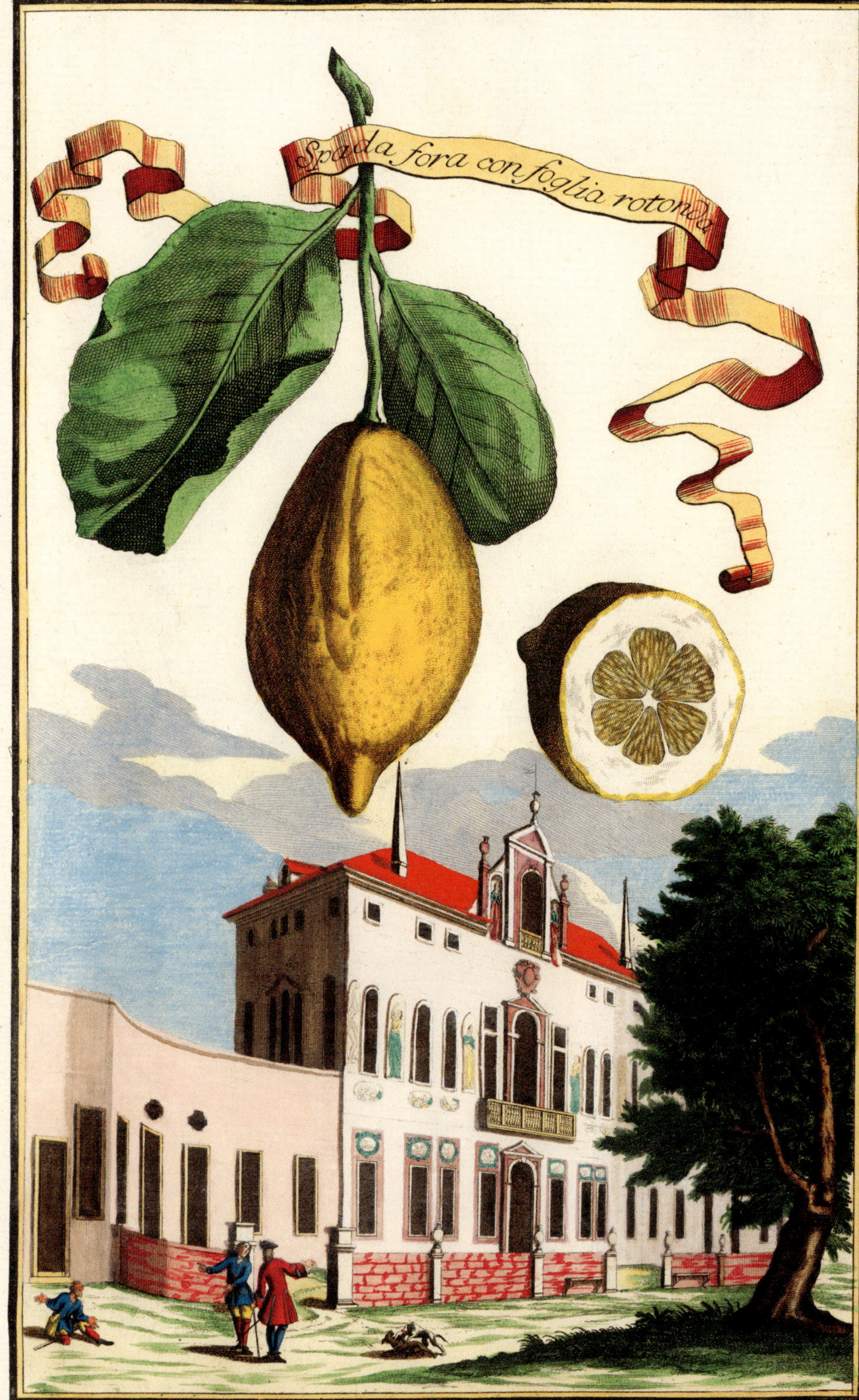
pag. 129
Spada fora con foglia rotonda
Palazzo del N. H. Grimani al' Albero d'Oro à Fiesso
Ios: à Montalegre fc.

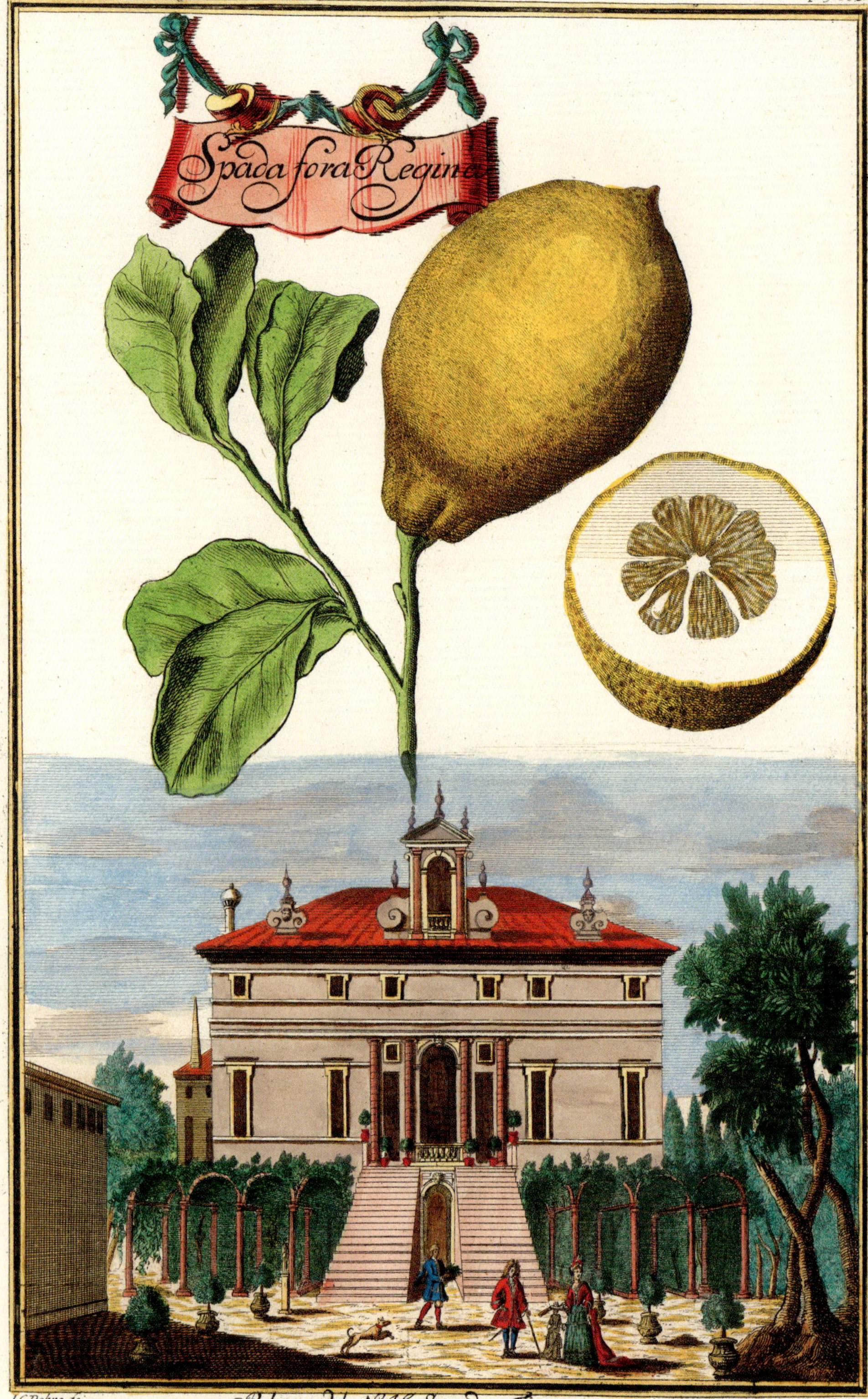

Fiesso d'Artico (Venice) – Villa Sagredo

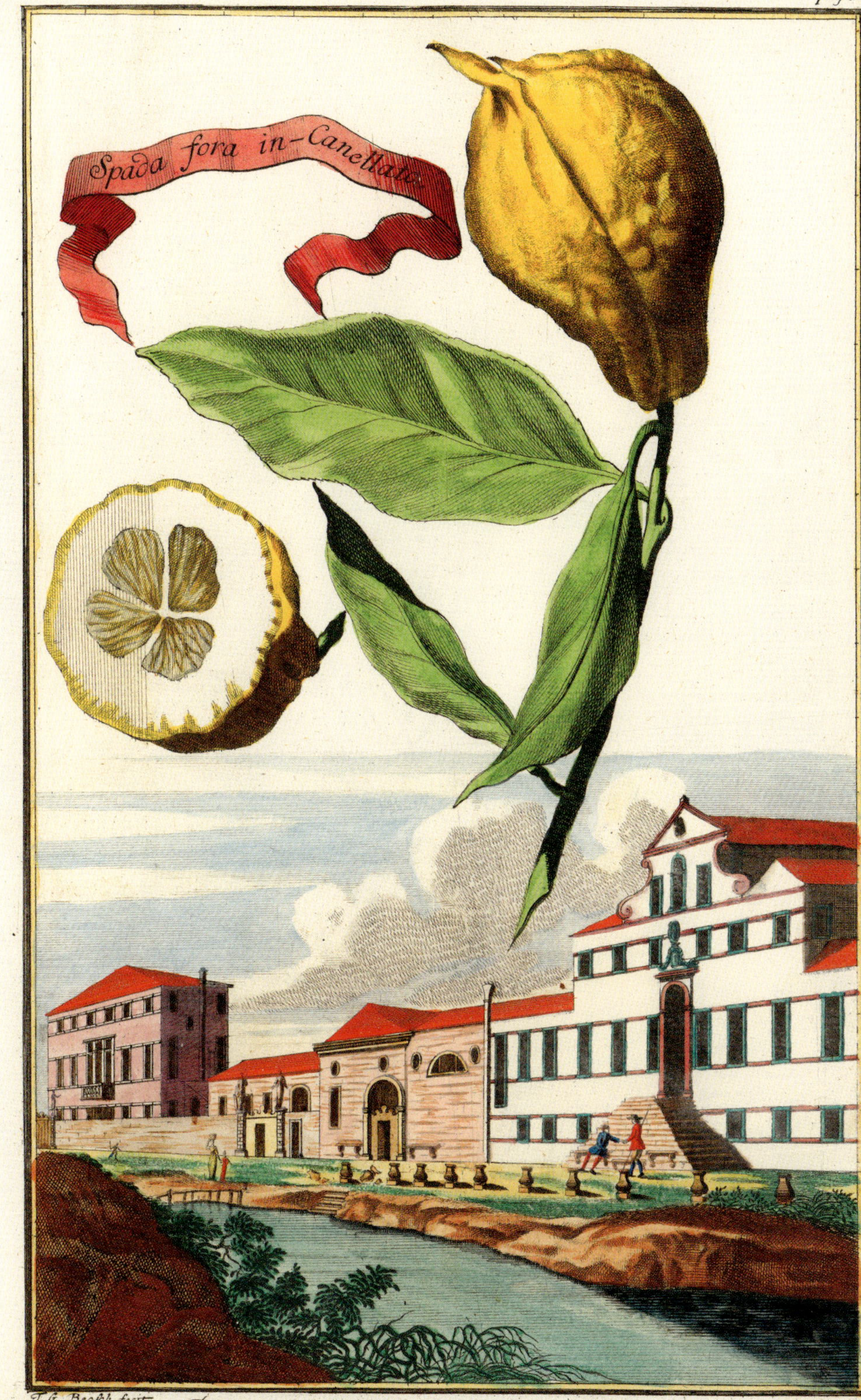
pag. 131.
Spada fora in-Canellata
J. G. Becsch fecit
Pal. del N: H: Farseti al Dolo.

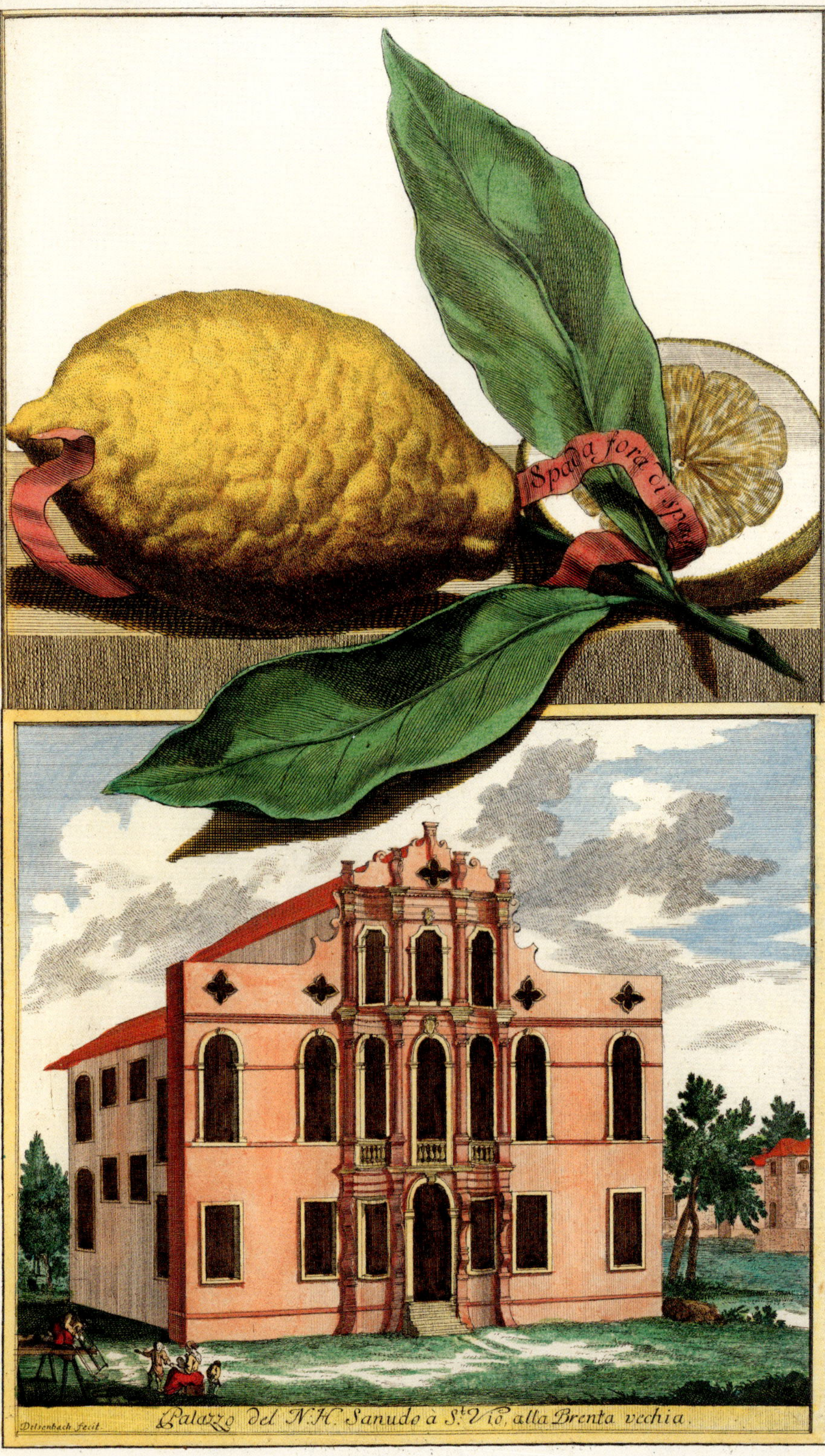
pag: 152.
Spada fora di
Delsenbach fecit.
Palazzo del N.H. Sanudo à S.t Vio, alla Brenta vechia.

Cucumer Limon

Tagliaferro (Verona)

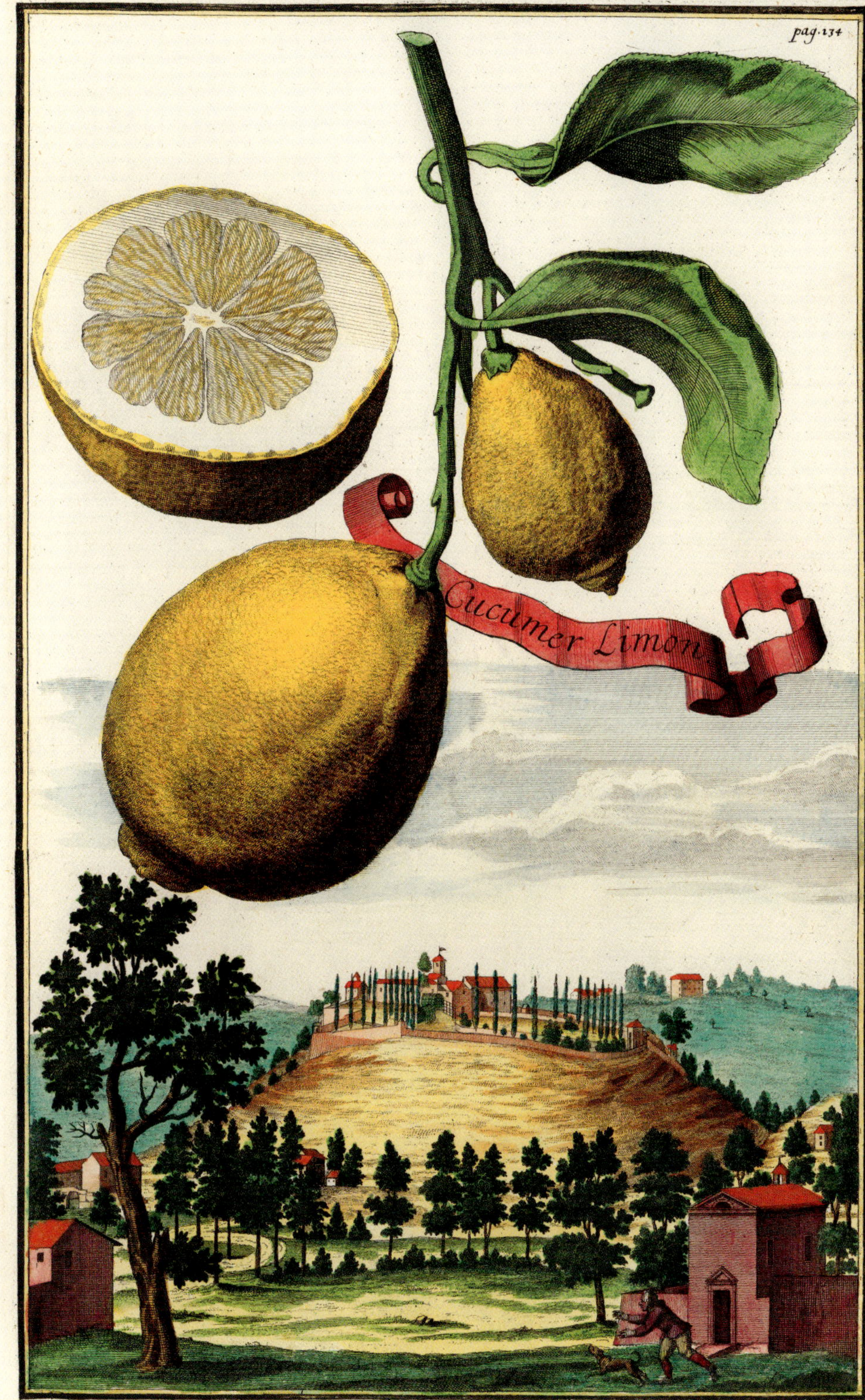

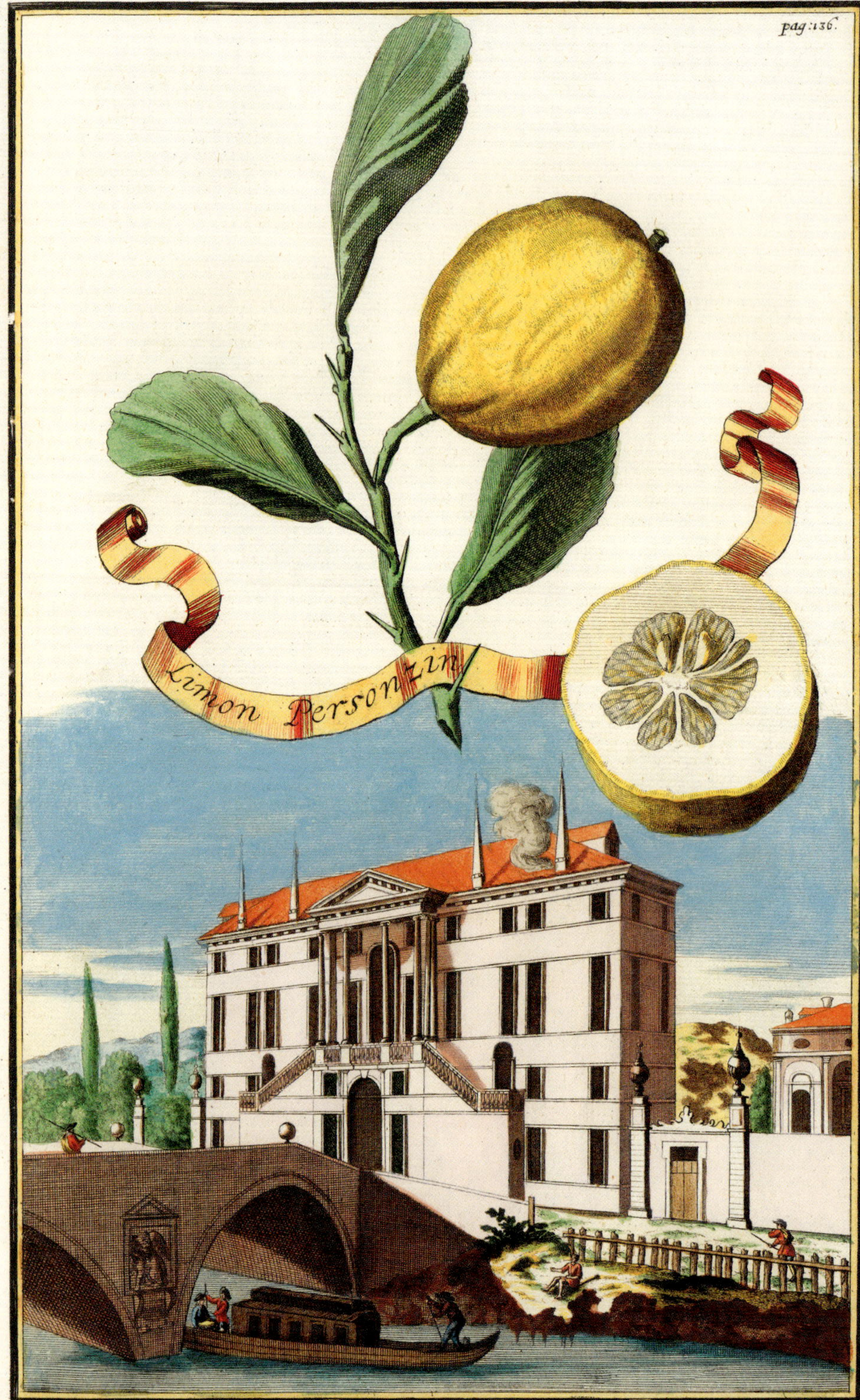

Pal: del N.H. Foscarini à Stra.

Ios: à Montalegre sc.

Limon Personzin

Stra (Venice) – Villa Foscarini

Pomo d'Adamo monstroso

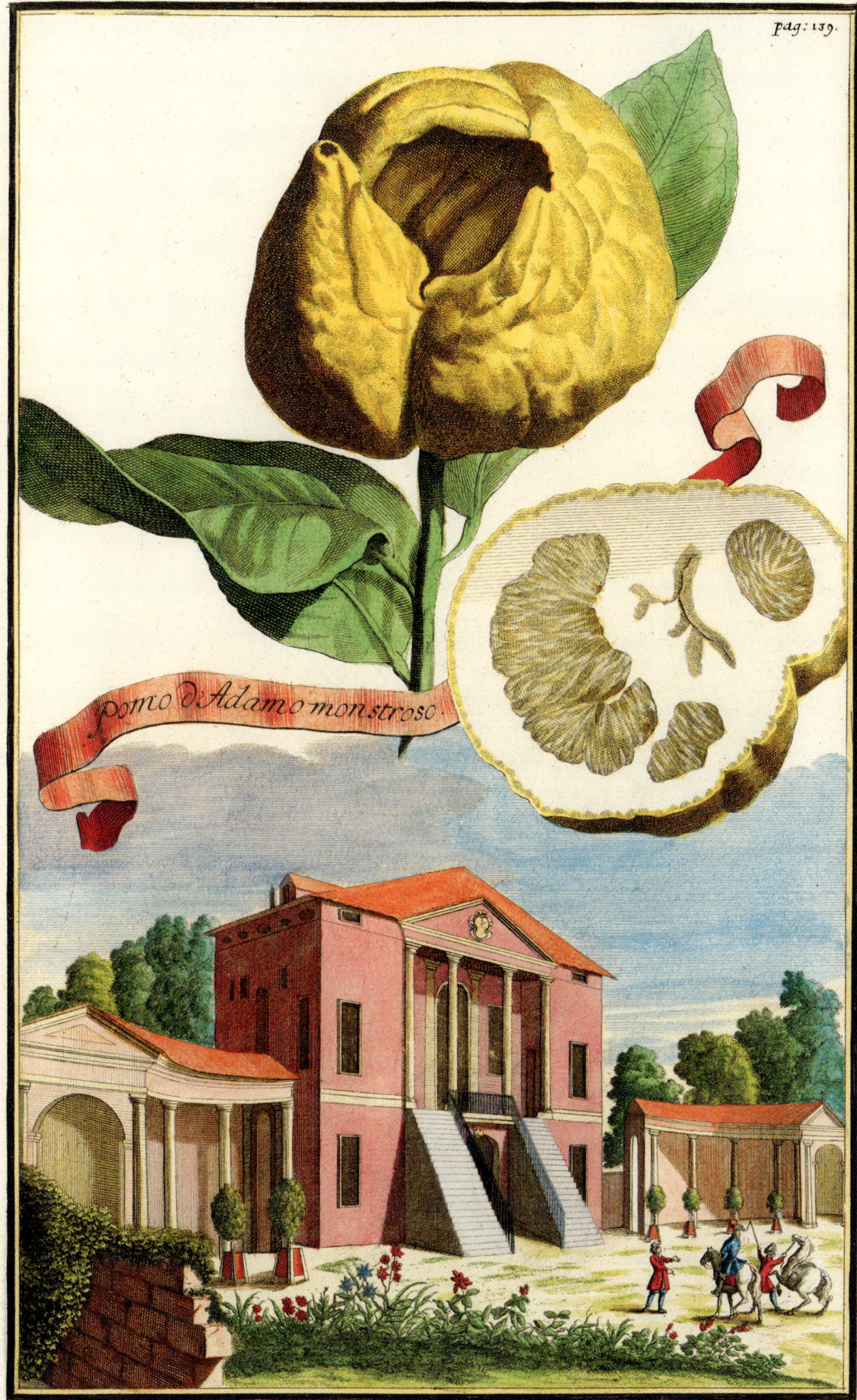

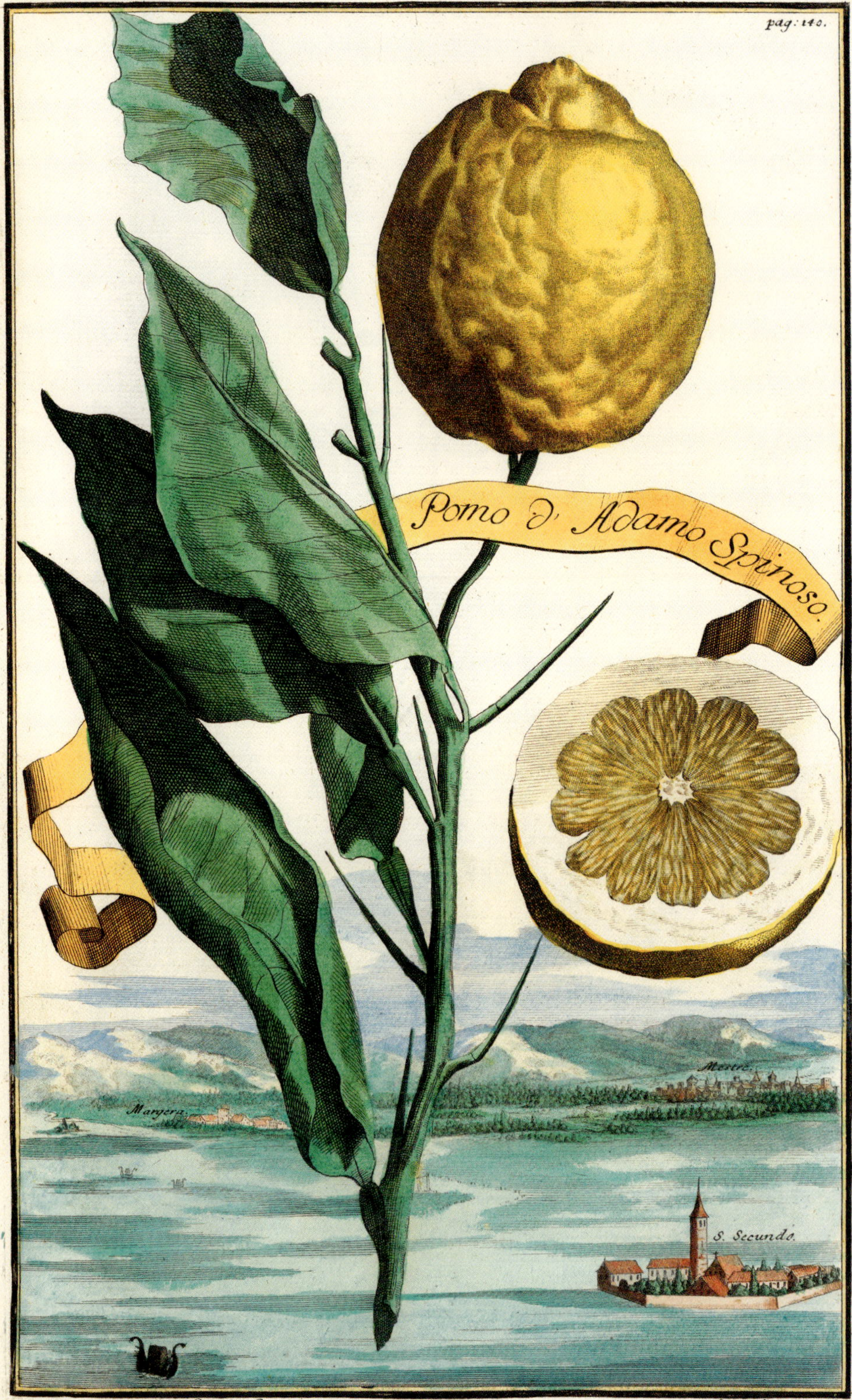

Pomo d'Adamo Spinoso

Pomo d'Adamo foetifero

Noventa Padovana (Padua) – Villa Giovanelli

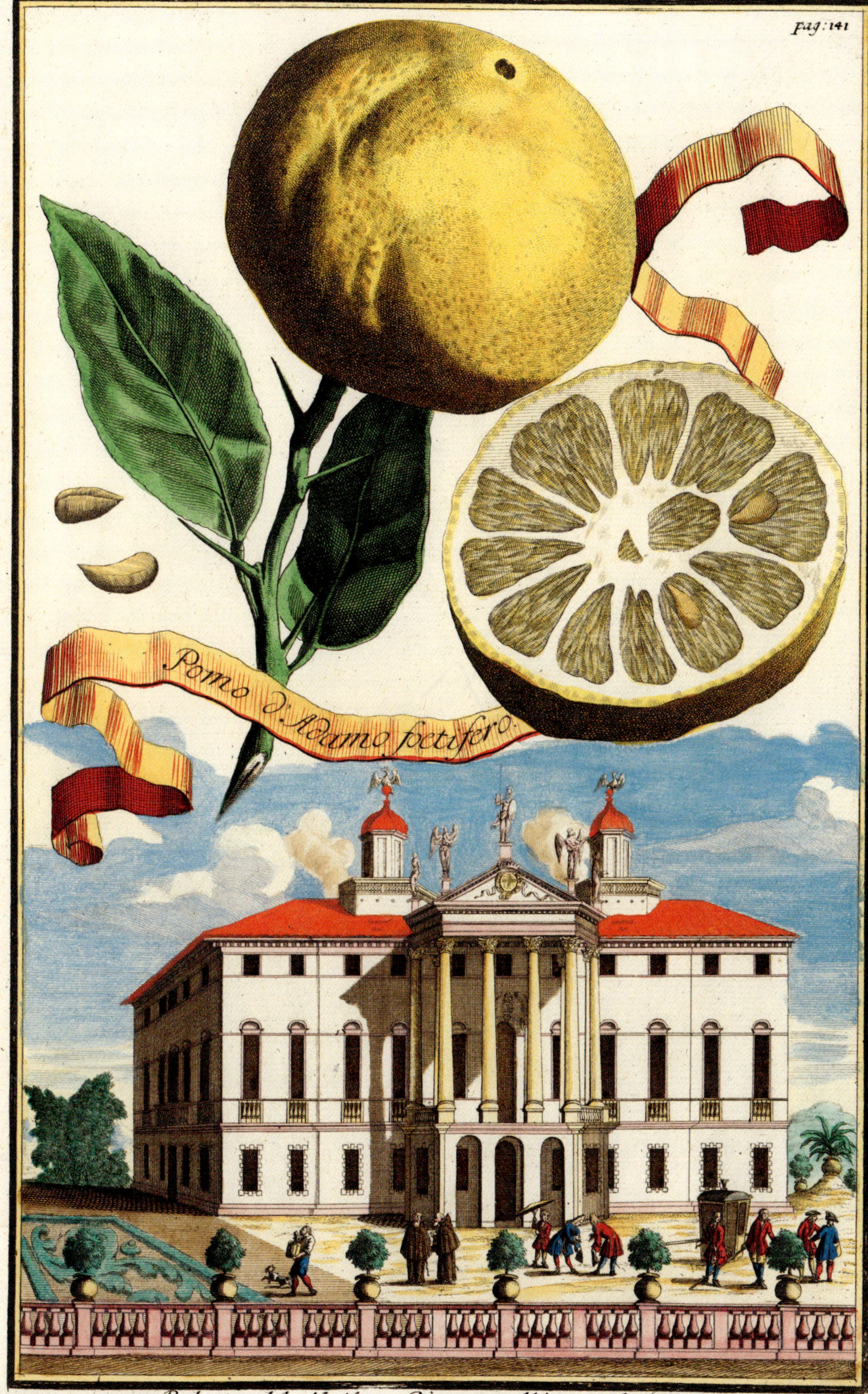

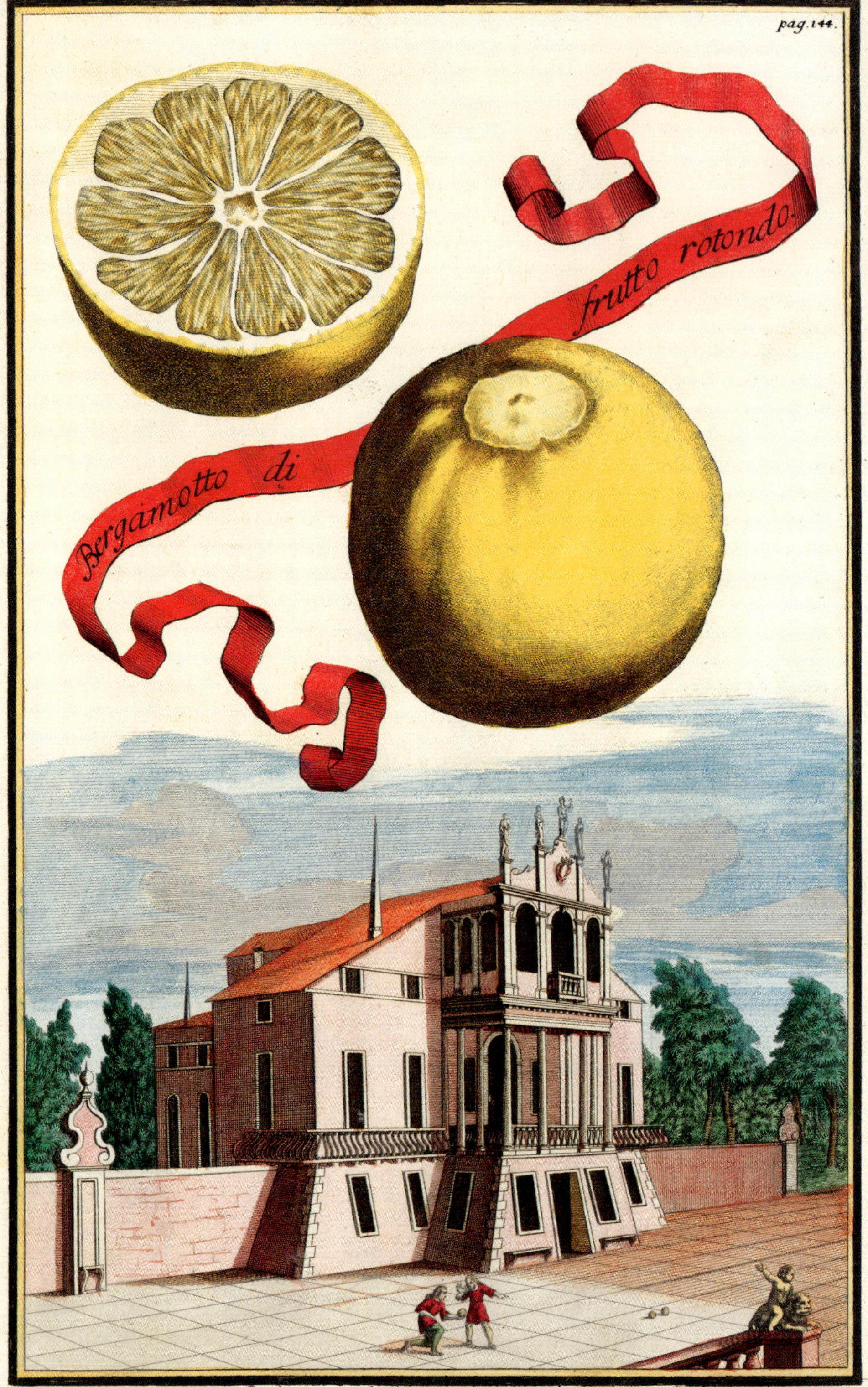

Bergamotto di frutto rotondo

Stra (Venice) – Villa Pisani

Bergamotto foetifero da Padova

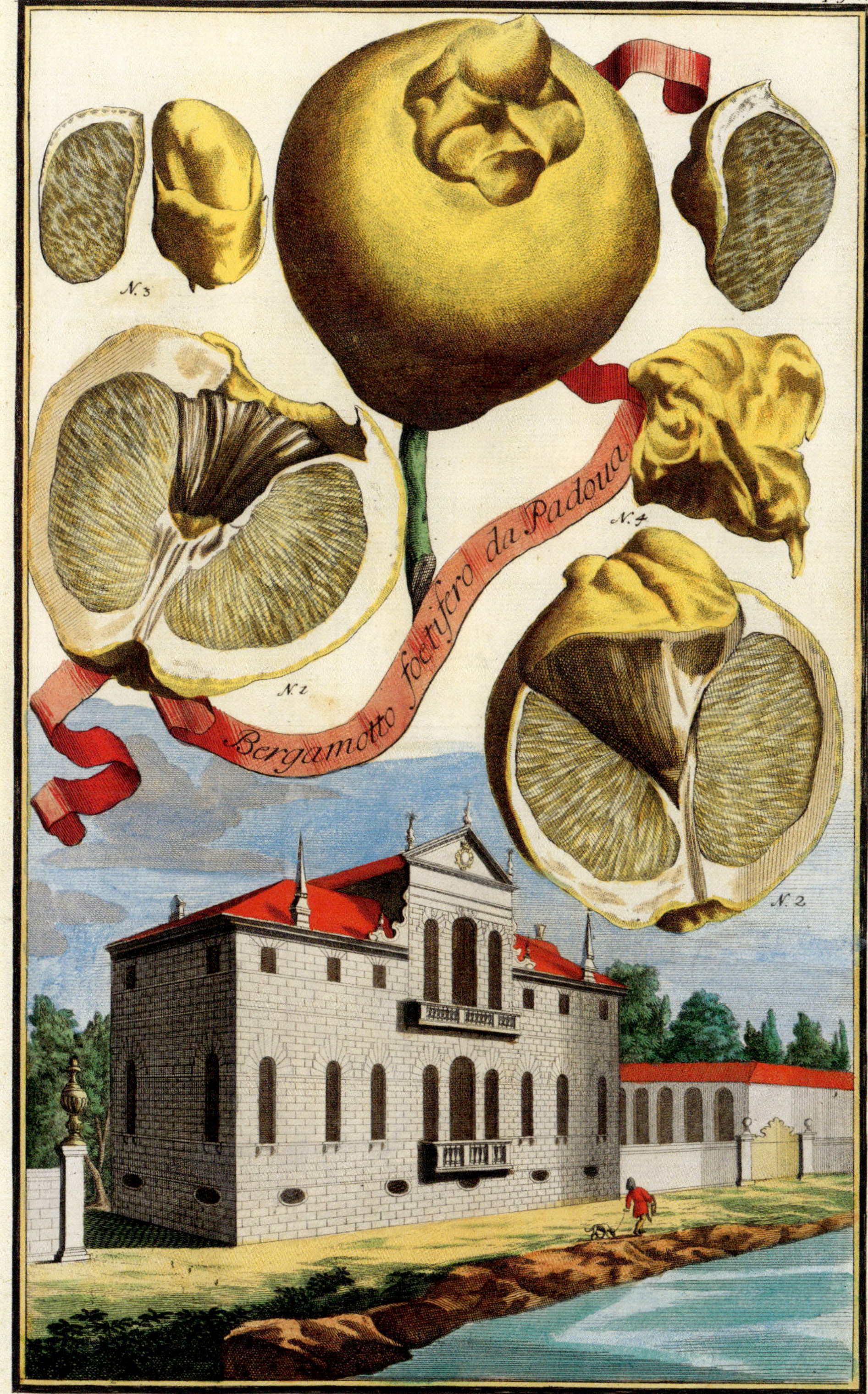

Stra (Venice) – Villa Capello

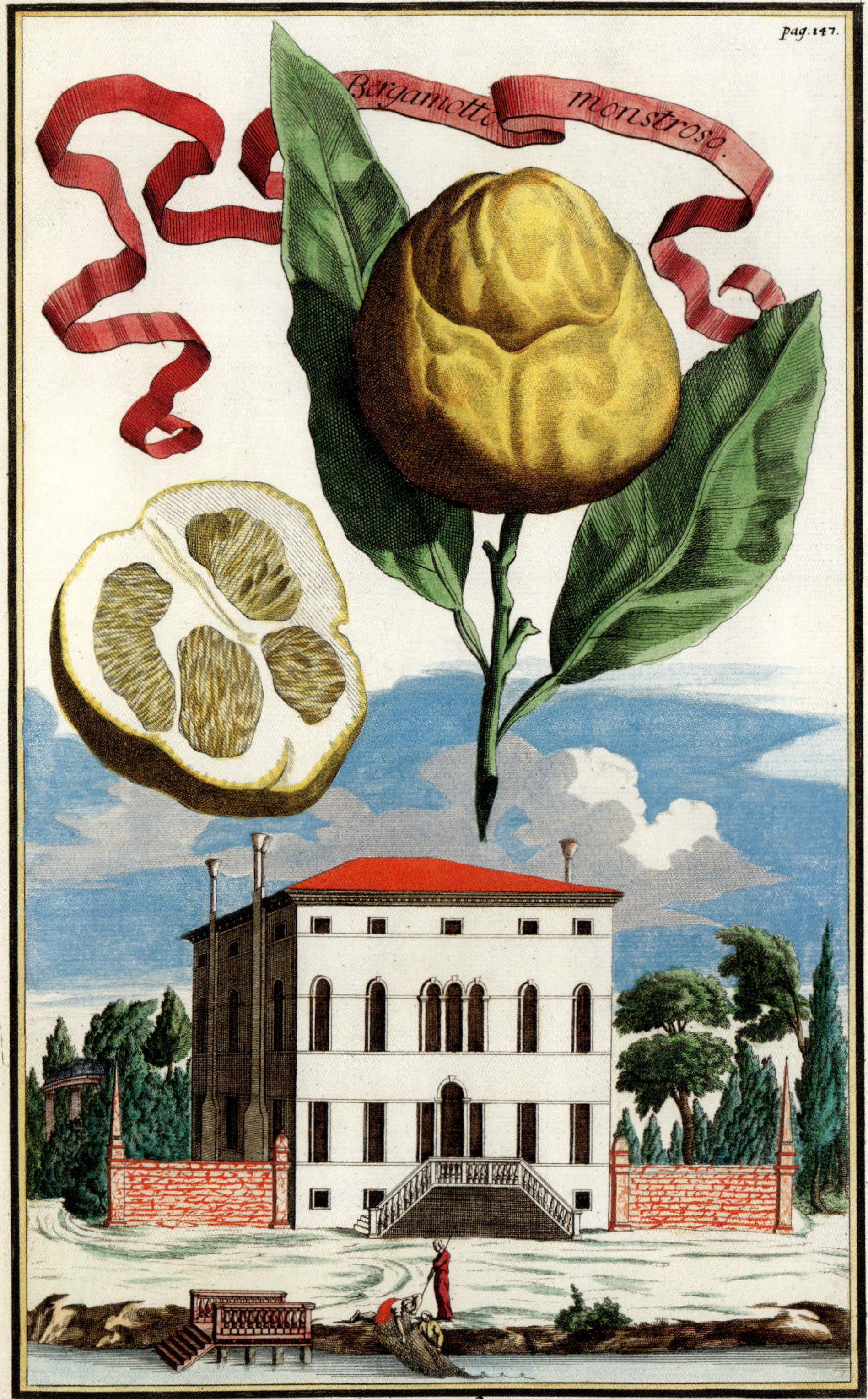

Bergamotto monstroso

Stra (Venice) – Villa Sagredo

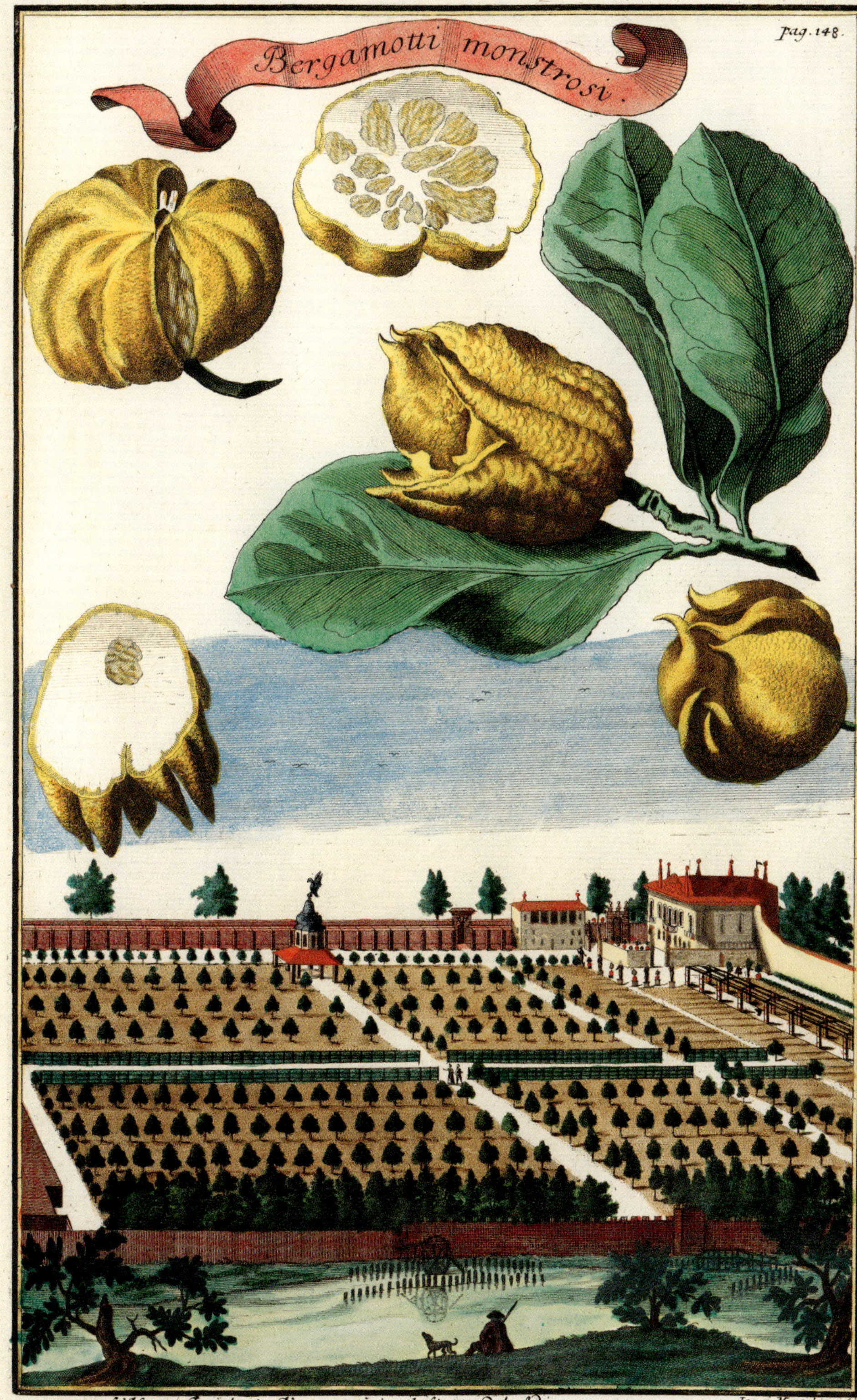
Pag. 148.
Bergamotti monstrosi.
L'Horto Gazola in Verona vicino l. fiume del Adice.
Ios: à Montalegre fec.

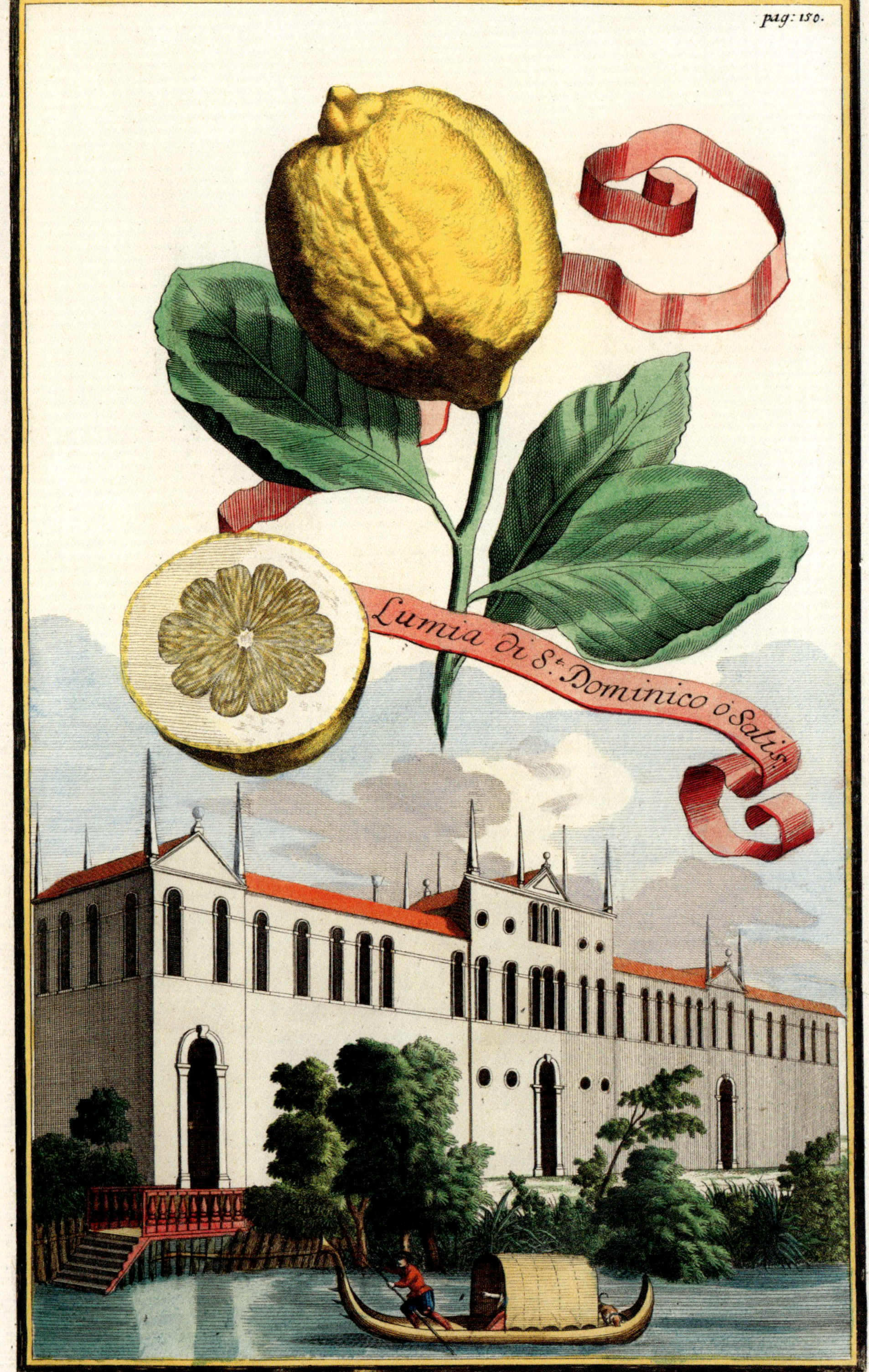

Lumia di S. Dominico o Salis

Lumia tonda ordinaria

Battaglia Terme (Padua) – Villa Grimani

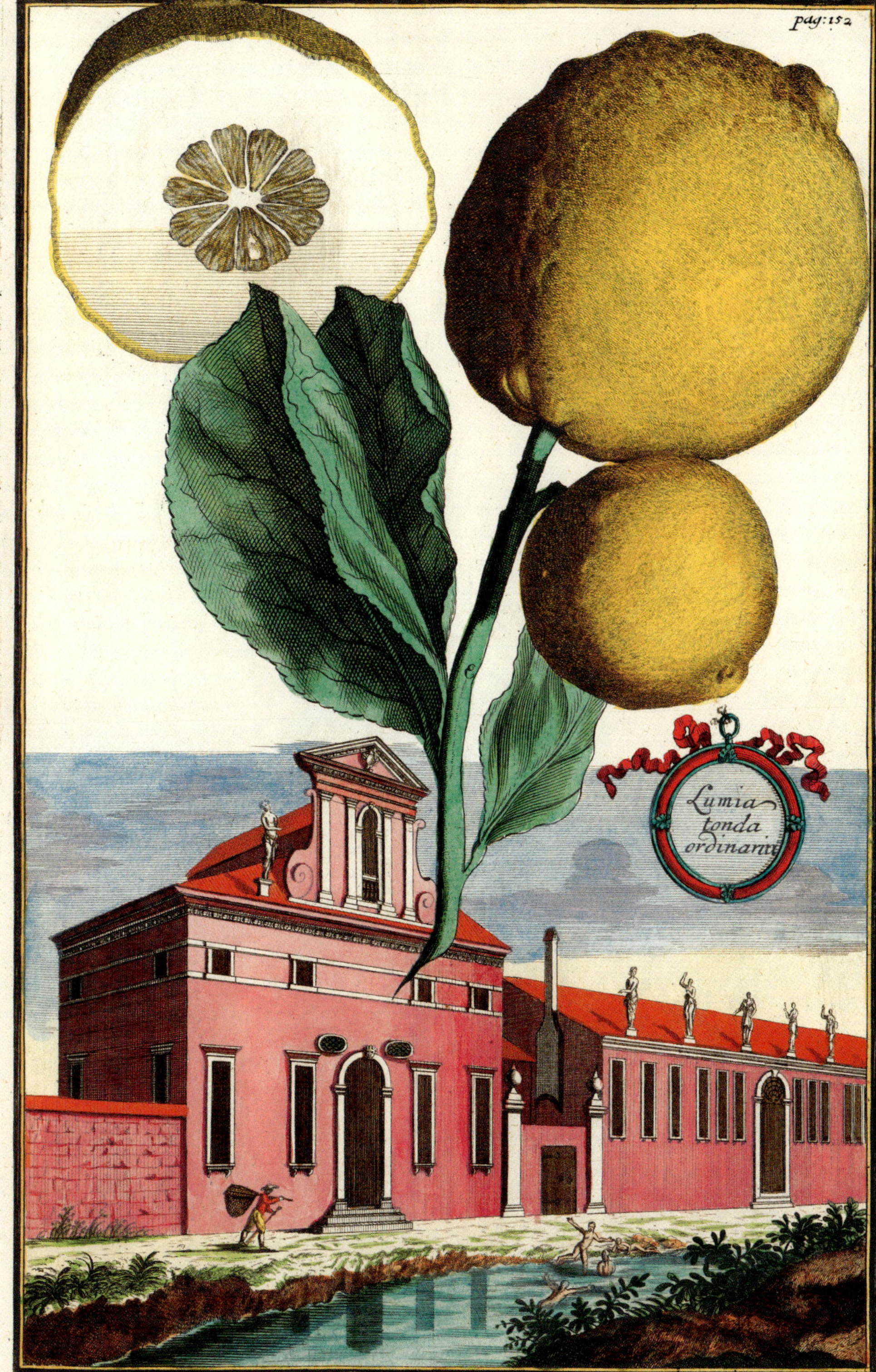

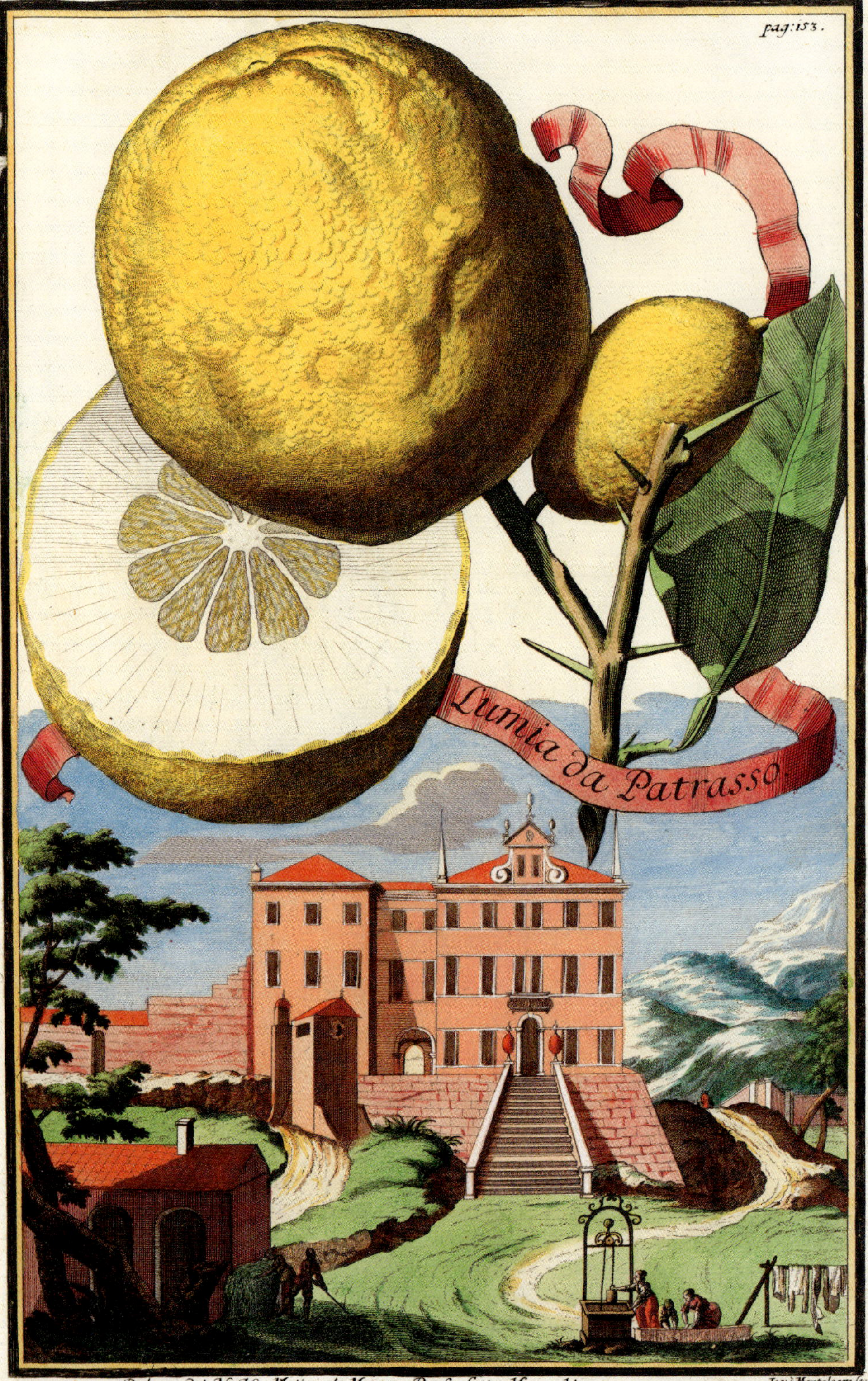

Lumia da Patrasso

Monselice (Padua) – Villa Molin a Monte Buso

Lumia Coronata

Battaglia Terme (Padua) – Villa Selvatico

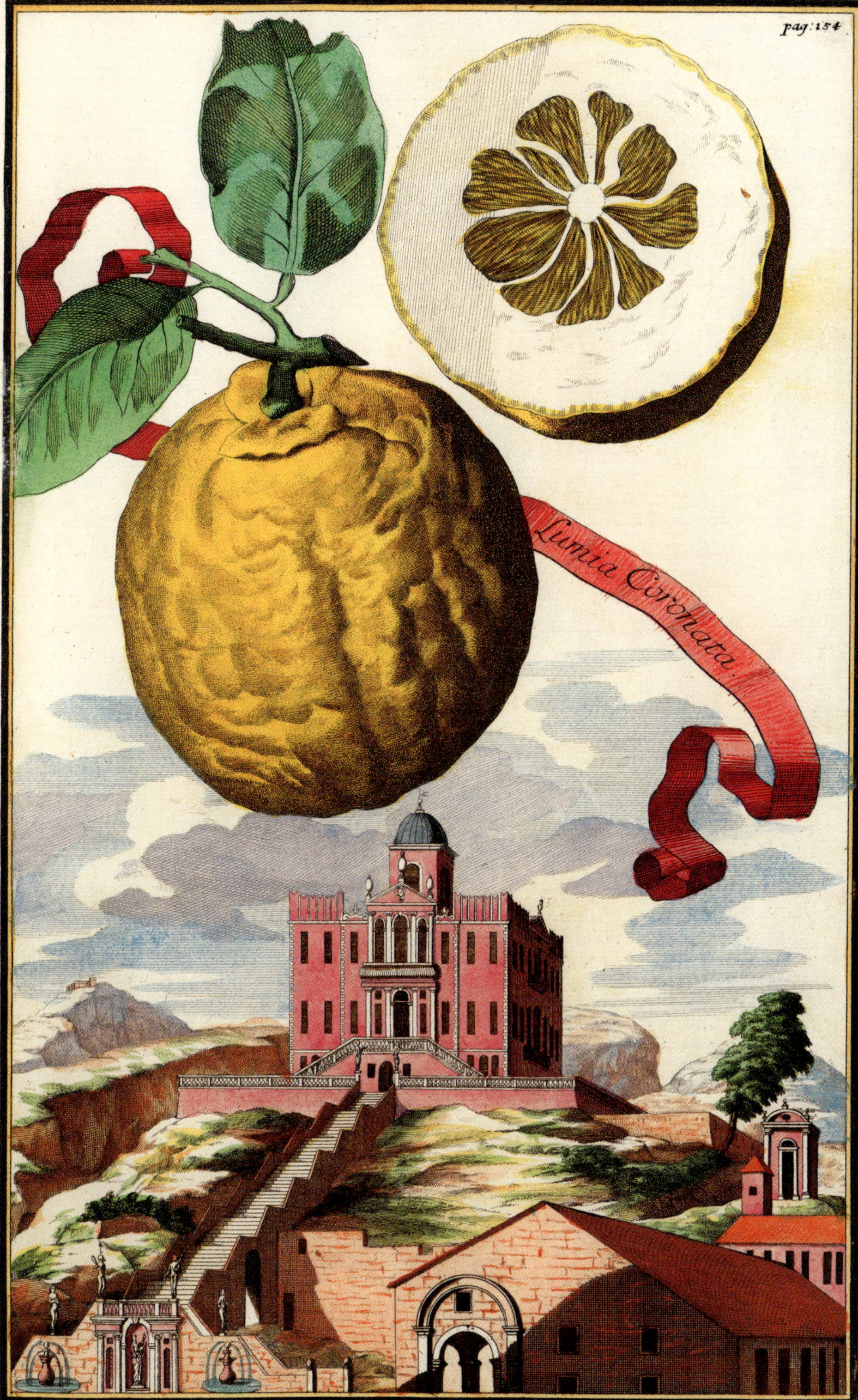

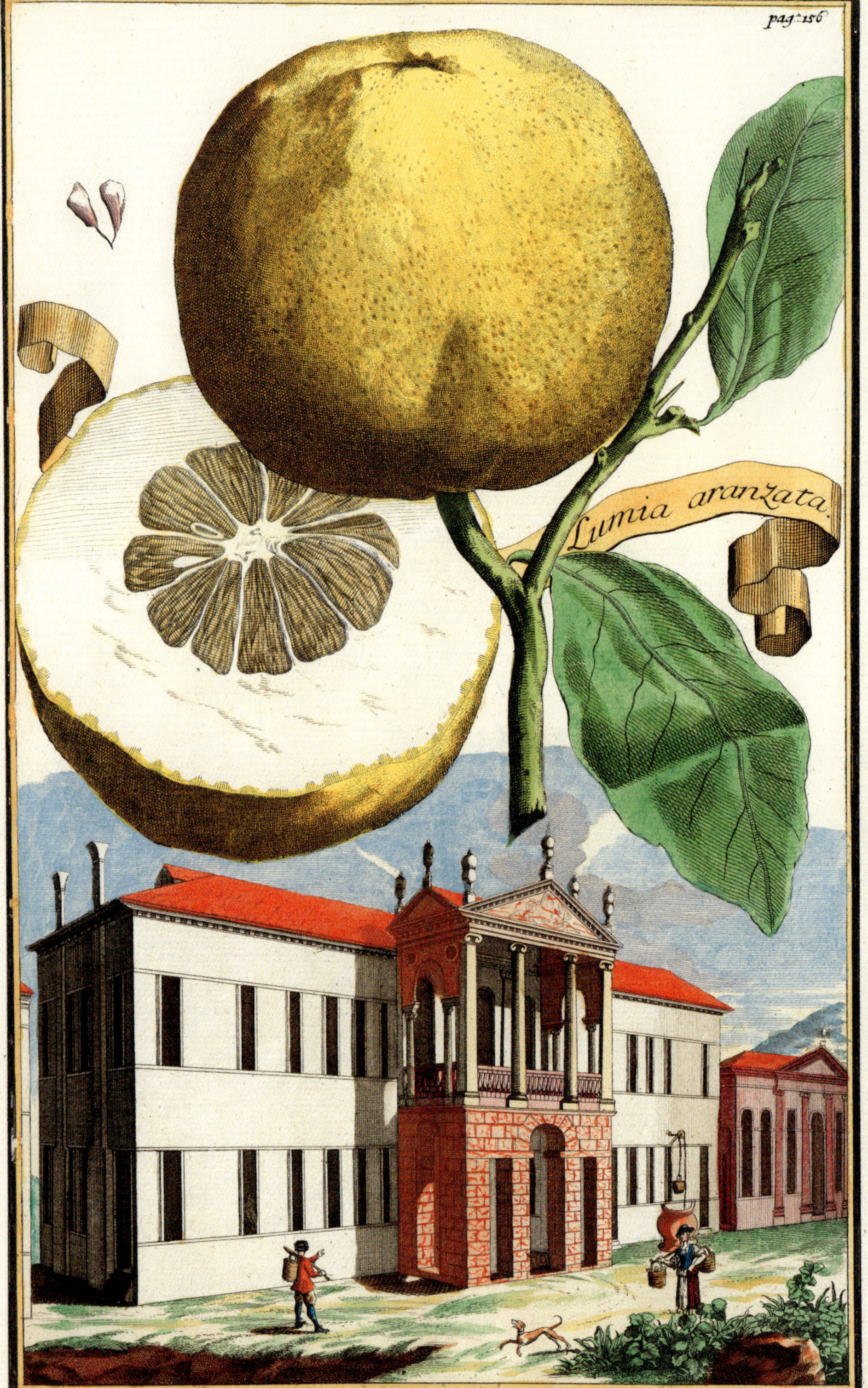

Lumia aranzata

Battaglia Terme (Padua) – Villa Dolfin

Lumia da Gallicia

River Brenta Vecchia – Villa Contarini al Ponte

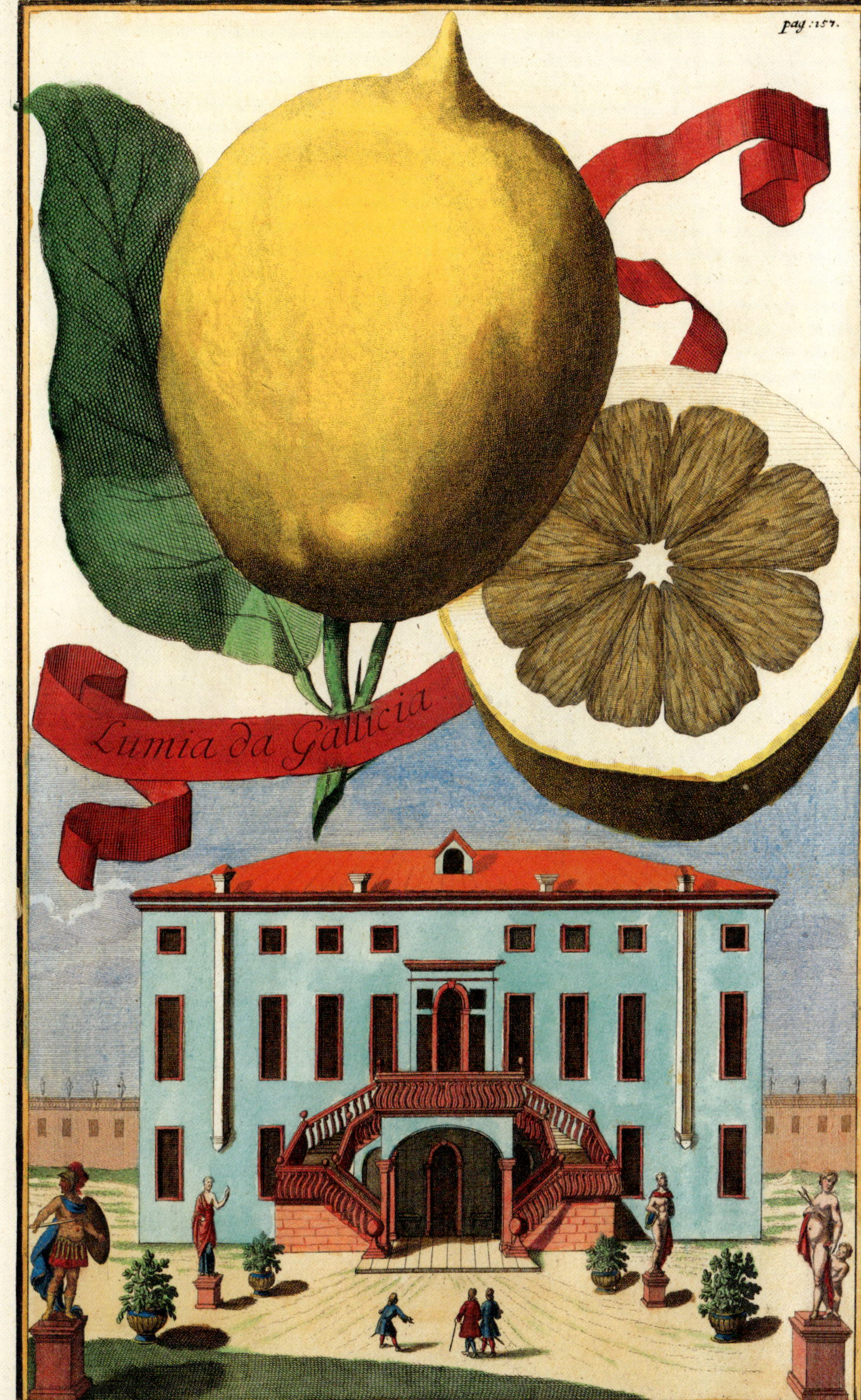

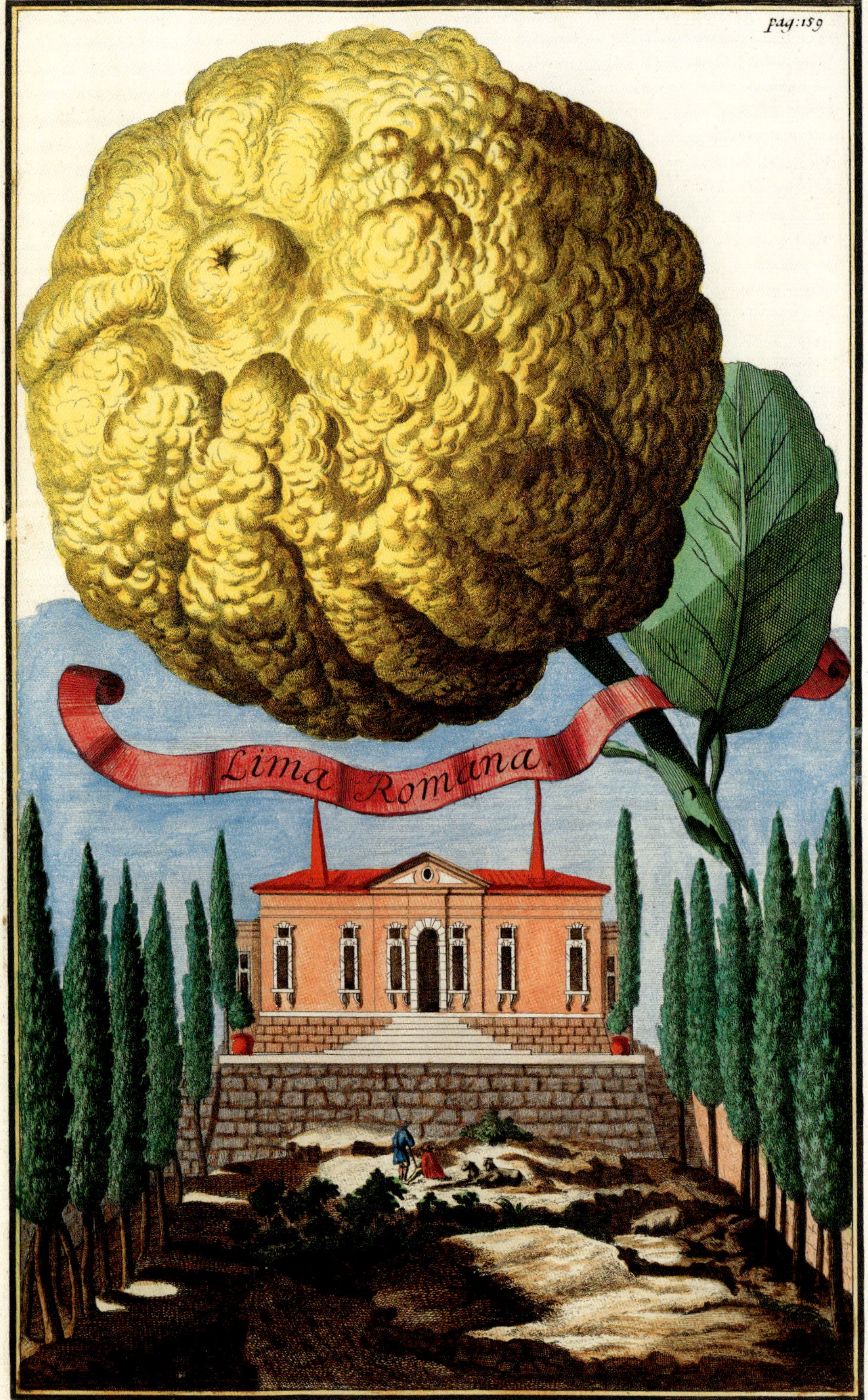

Lima Romana

Este, Caldevigo (Padua) – Villa Contarini (Palazzo del Principe)

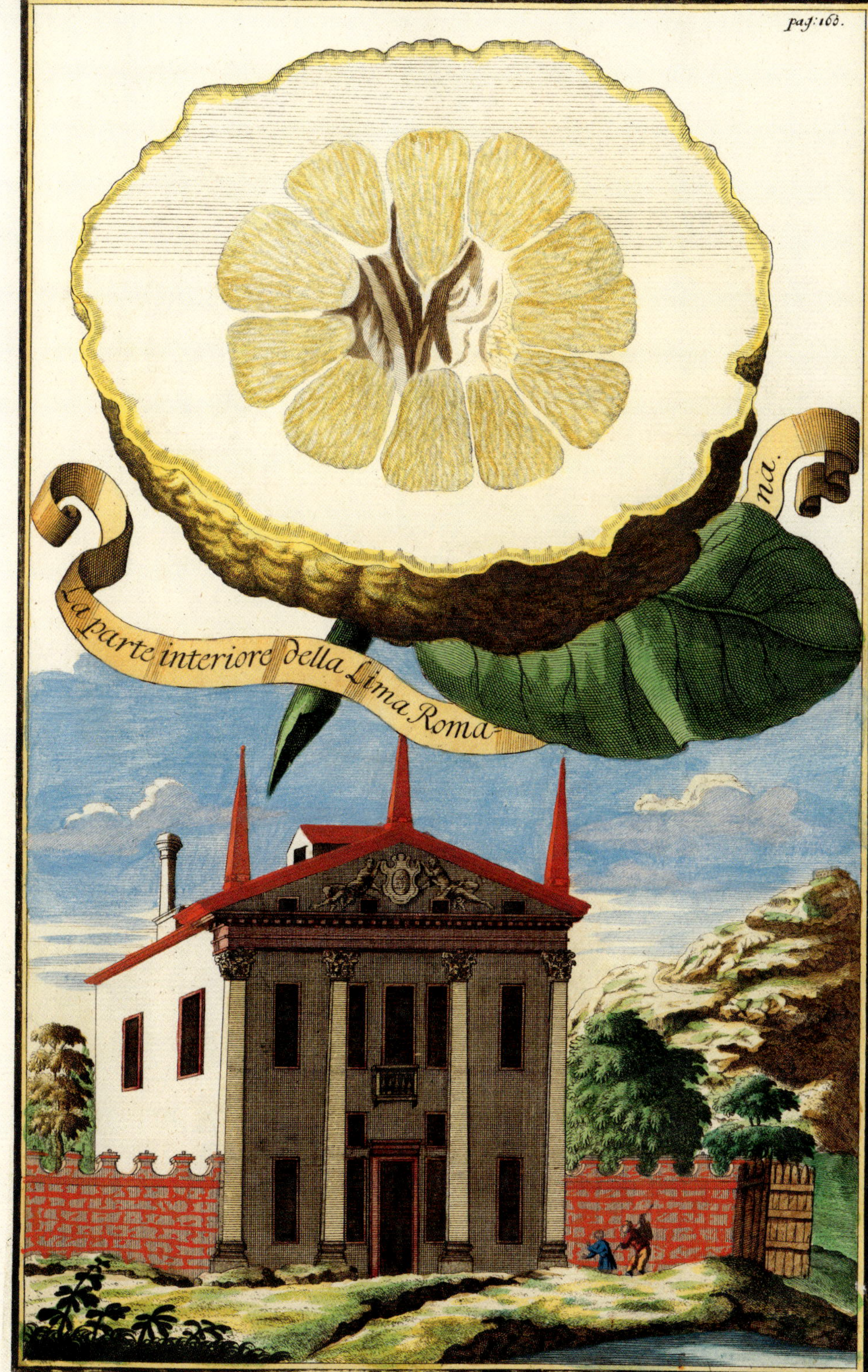

Palazzo del N.H. Corner à Moncelice. Ios; à Montalegre sc.

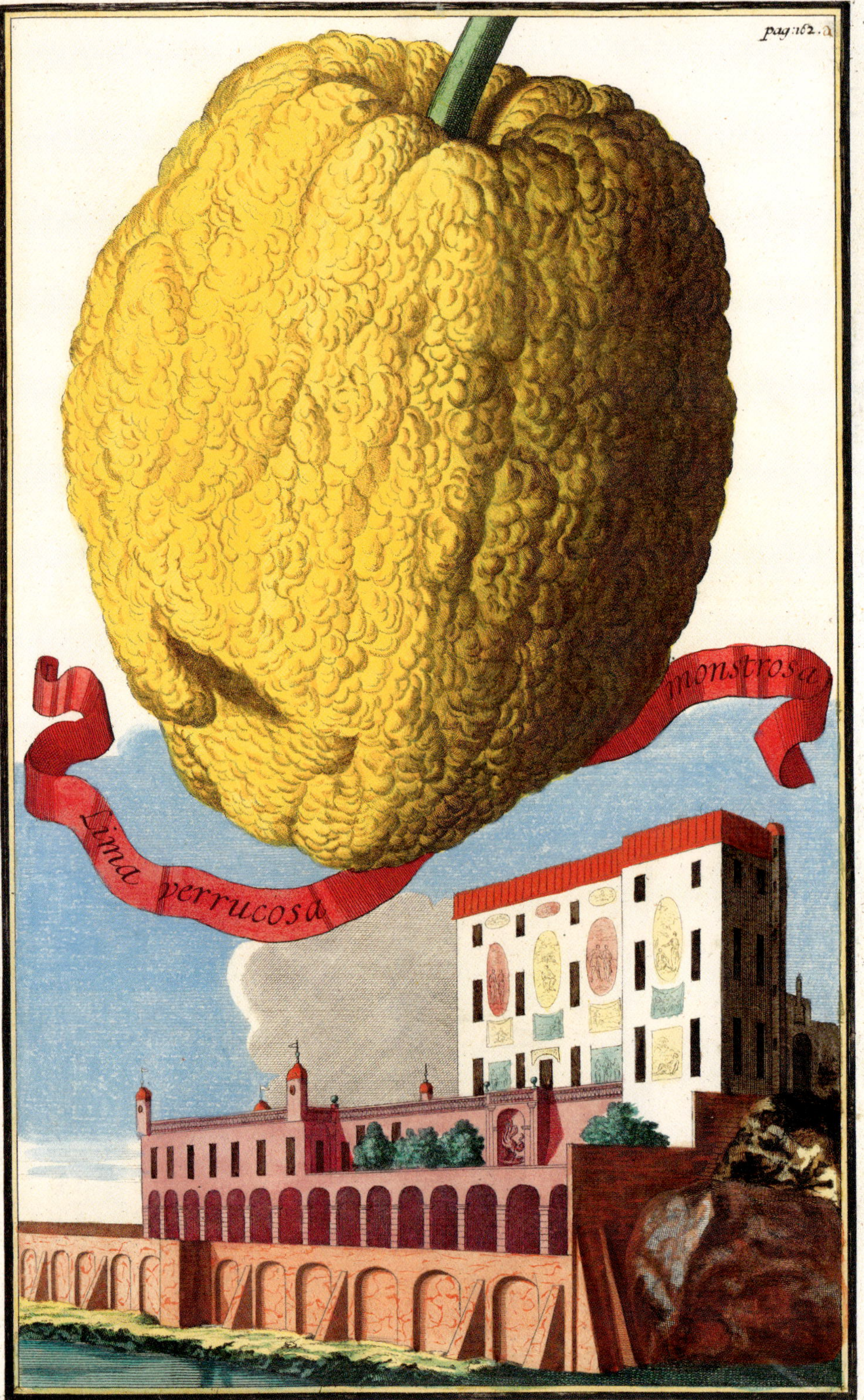

Lima verrucosa monstrosa

Battaglia Terme (Padua) – Villa Obizzi (Castello di Catajo)

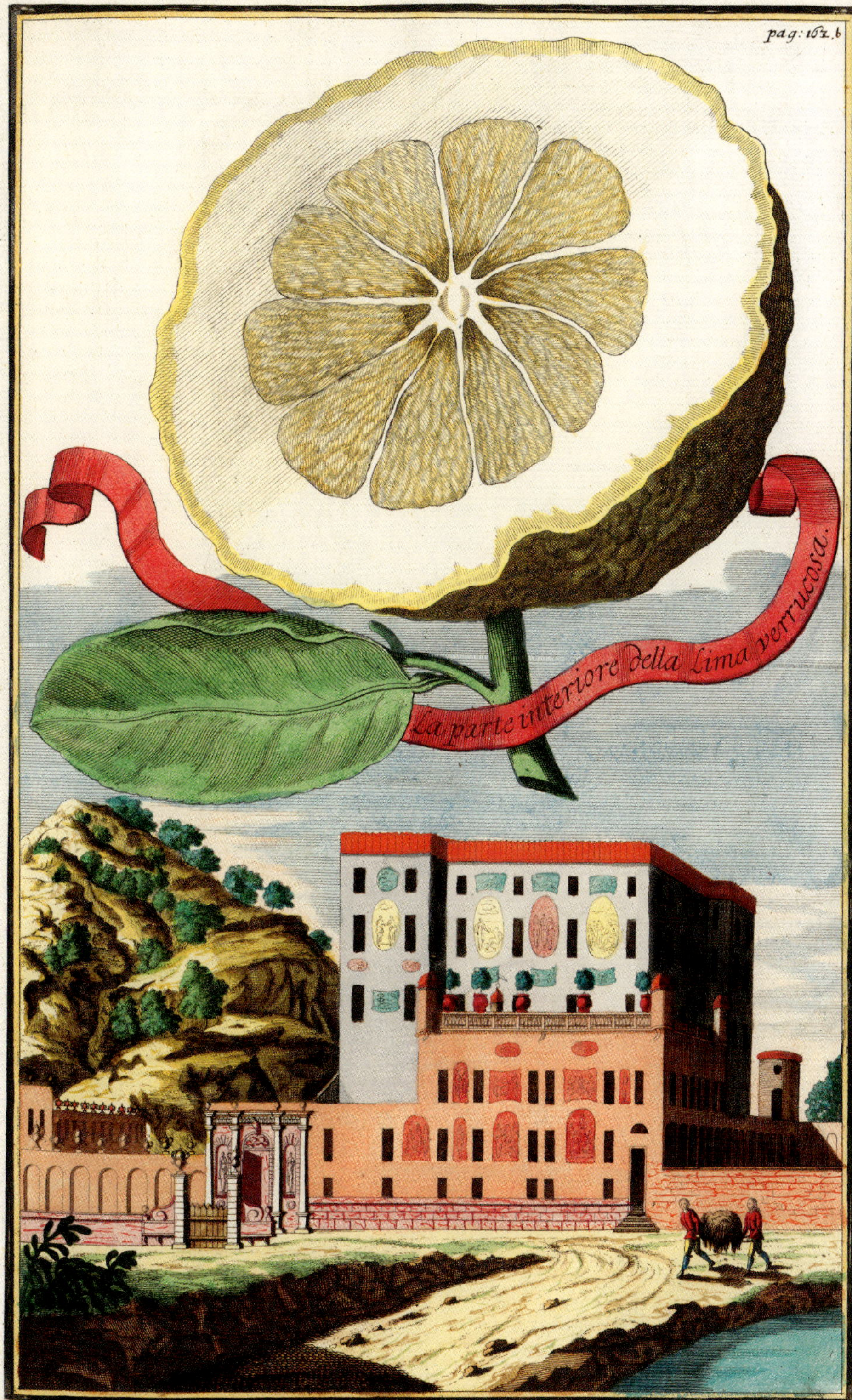

Battaglia Terme (Padua) – Villa Obizzi (Castello di Catajo)

Lima verrucosa [monstrosa]

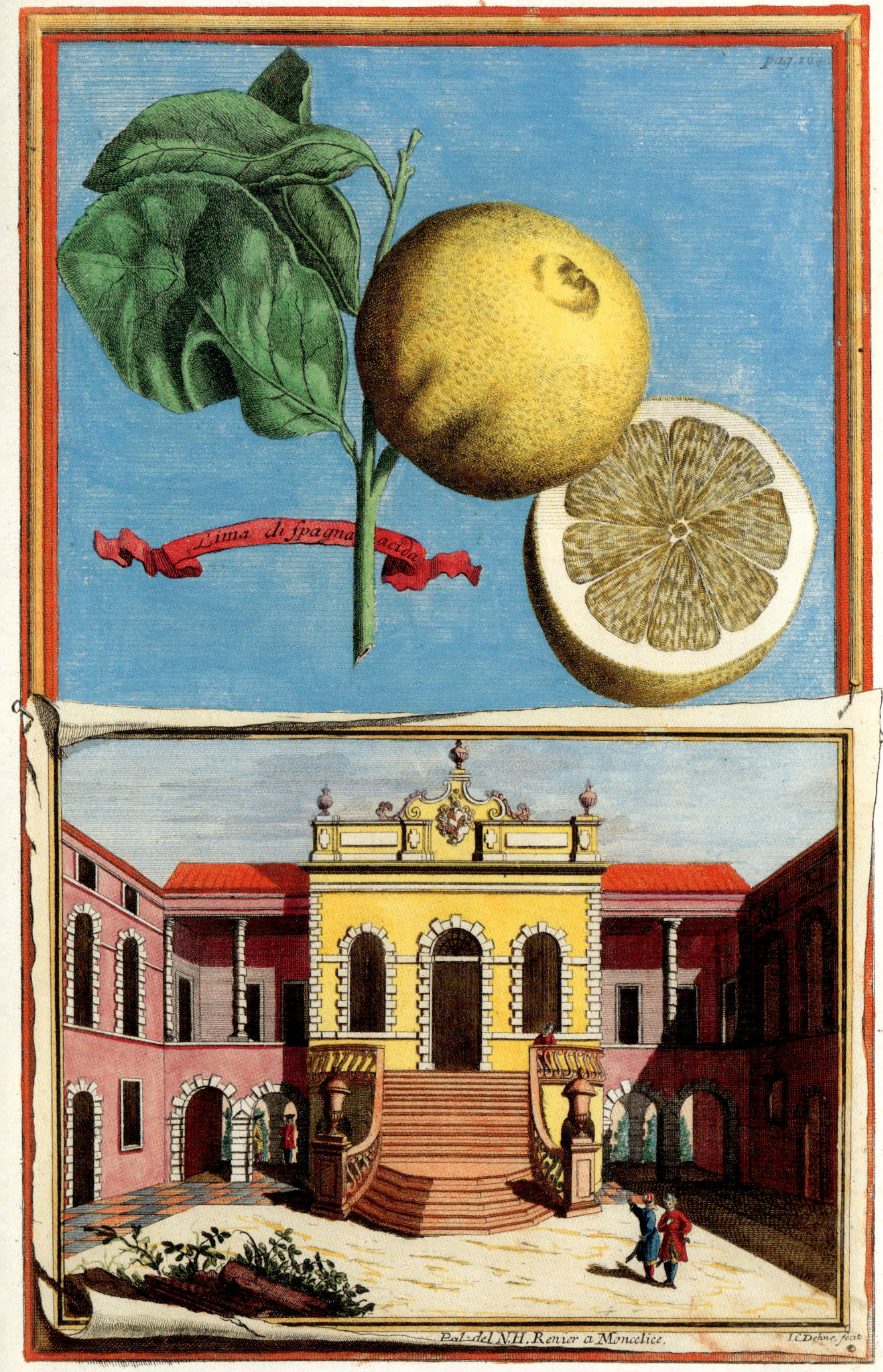

Lima di Spagna acida

Monselice (Padua) – Villa Renier

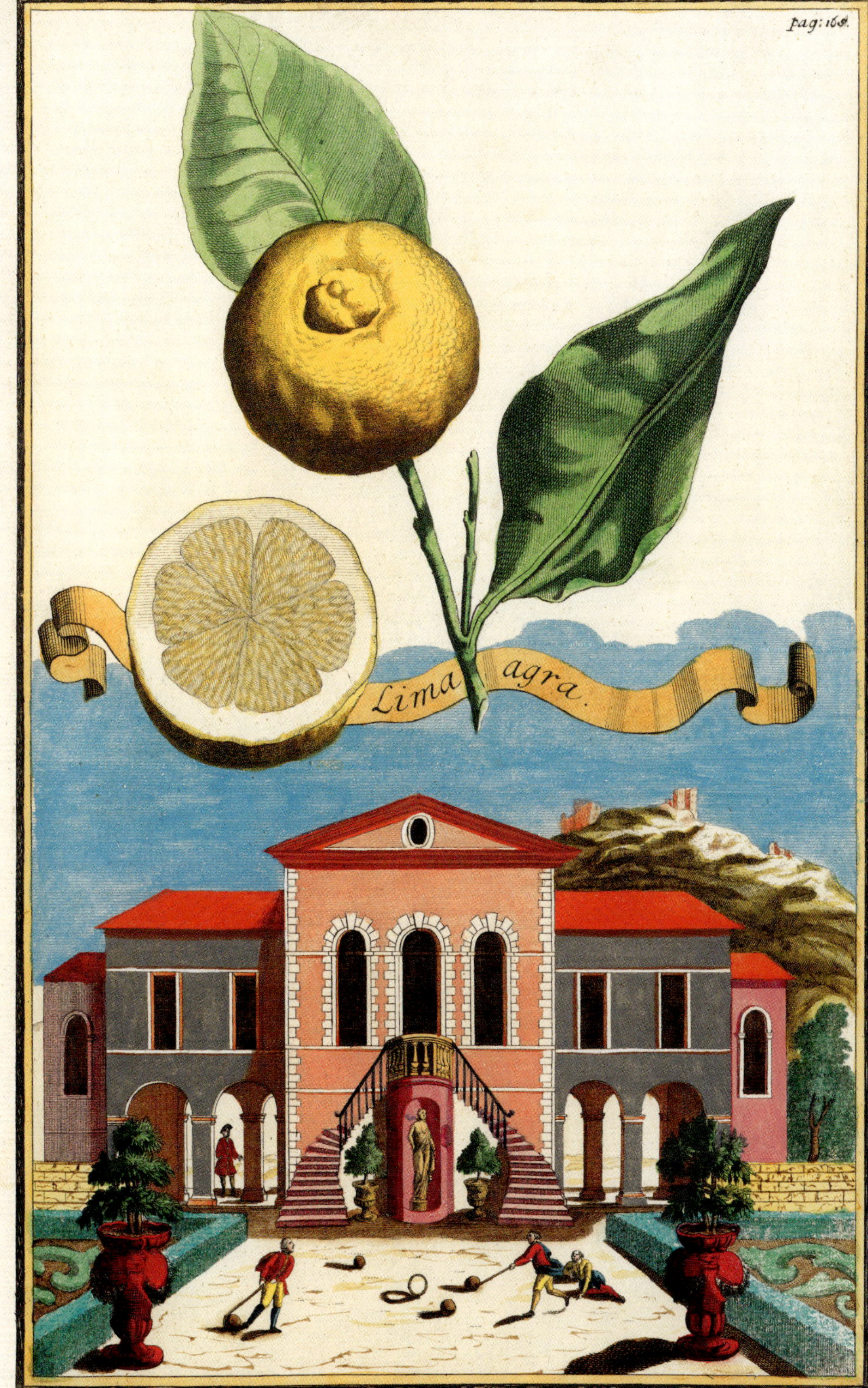
pag: 169.
Lima agra.
Pal: del N.H. Renier alla parte del Giardino.
Ios: a Montalegre sc.

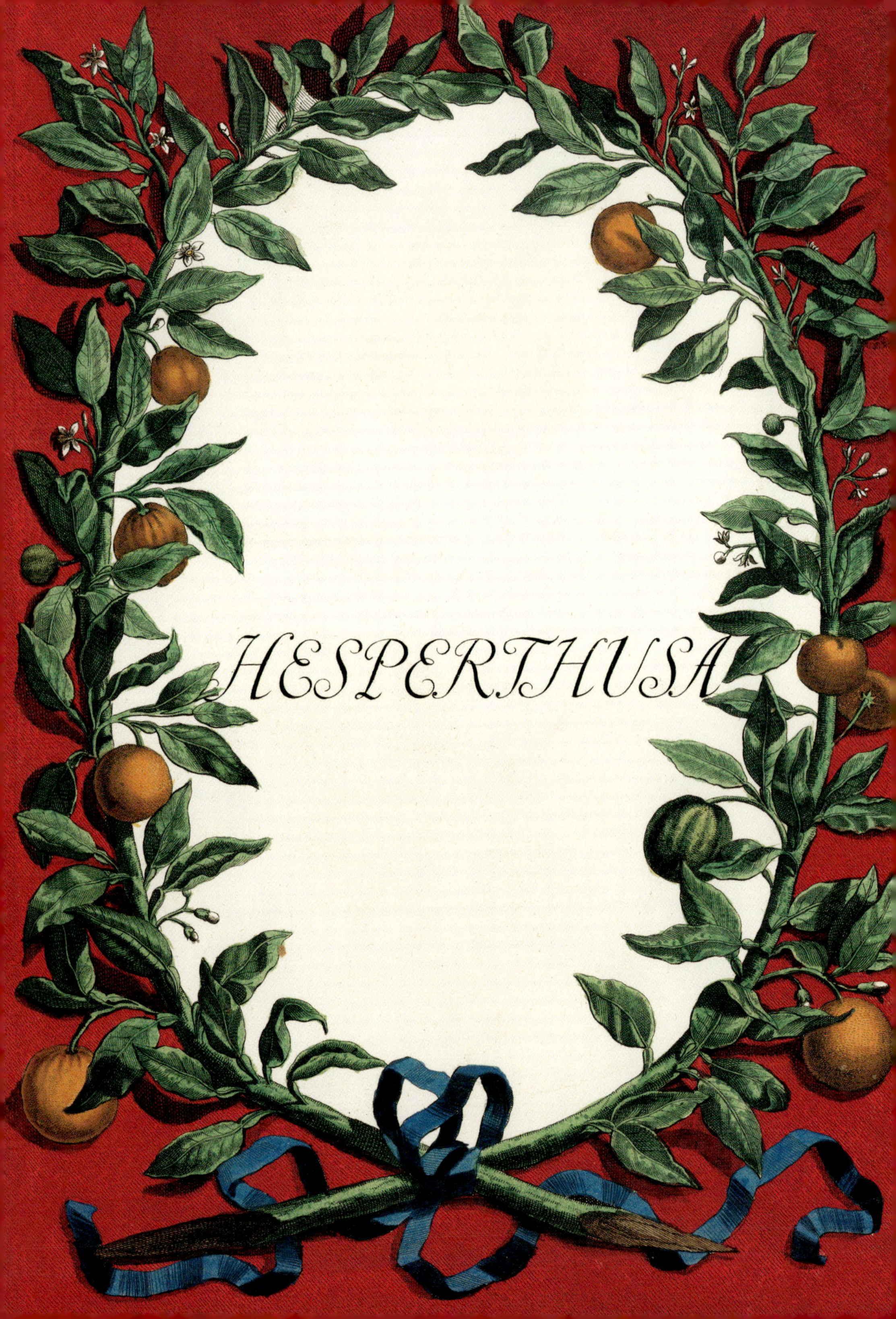
HESPERTHUSA

Der Nürnbergischen HESPERIDUM CONTINUATION, Vierdter Theil.

HESPERTHUSA.

✿ ✿ ✿

Das erste Capitel.

Haben wir / von der Ægle und Arethusa, eine ungemeine Freundlichkeit gespühret / als sie ihre Citronaten- und Citronen-Gärten uns eröffnet / und mit grosser Willfährigkeit / die darinnen befindliche guldene Früchte / uns vorgestellet; so hat deren dritte Schwester / die Hesperthusa, nicht ermangelt / mit aller Liebe und einer sonderbahren Gütigkeit / uns gleichfalls aufzunehmen / und ihren beedes wol angelegten / und überaus herrlichen Pomeranzen-Garten / uns durchzuführen / darinnen uns abermal zeigende / verschiedene rare und schöne Gewächse / welche wir ehedem nicht gesehen hatten / weil sie dazumal theils noch nicht im Flor waren / theils weil sie der Garten / erst neulich noch / zu seiner Zierde überkommen und eingesetzet.

Insgemein ist es gewiß / daß es so vielerlei Arten der Pomeranzen nicht gebe / als man von den Citronen hat; jedoch fehlt es auch hier nicht an besondern und recht schönen Sorten. Das Holz an einem Pomeranzen-Stamm / ist härter und dauerhaffter / als an den Citronat- und Citronen-Bäumen / dahero / und dieweil sie die frische und freie Lufft noch gar wol und bequemer / weder die übrigen Agrumi, vertragen können / so hat man die gemeinere Art der Pomeranzen / in Italien frei in denen Feldern und Gärten stehend. In dem Genuesischen Gebiet / zu St. Remo / ist im freien offenem Feld / unter dem lichten Himmel / eine solche Menge befindlich / daß man sie wol mit einem Wald vergleichen kan. Es gibt daran ein Baum jährlich 2. bis 3000. Stücke ab / doch so / daß es mit dieser rei-

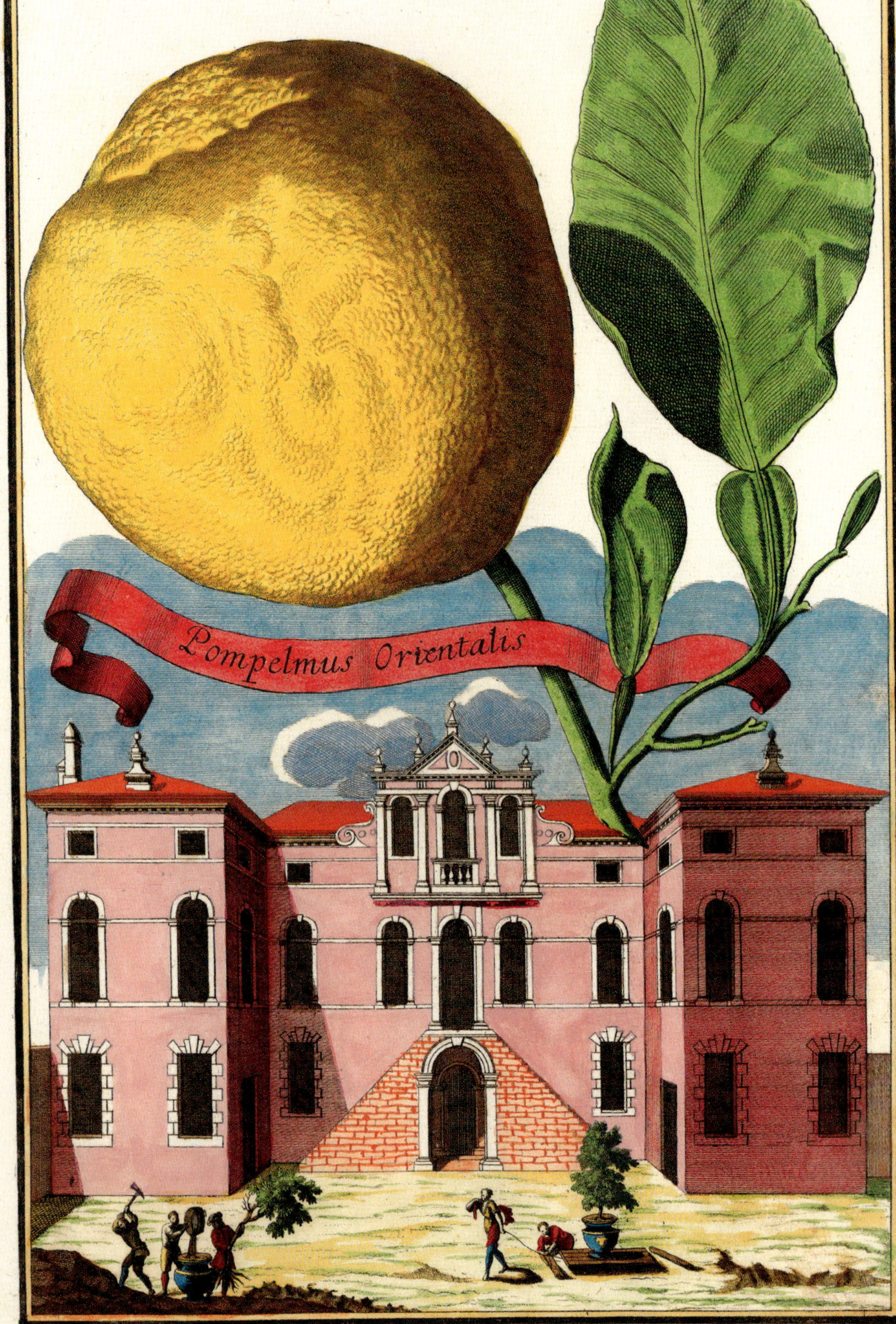

Pompelmus Orientalis

Monselice (Padua) – Villa Venier. *Pages 362/363*
Cartouche and beginning of the fourth section of vol. II

Pompelmus Occident[alis]

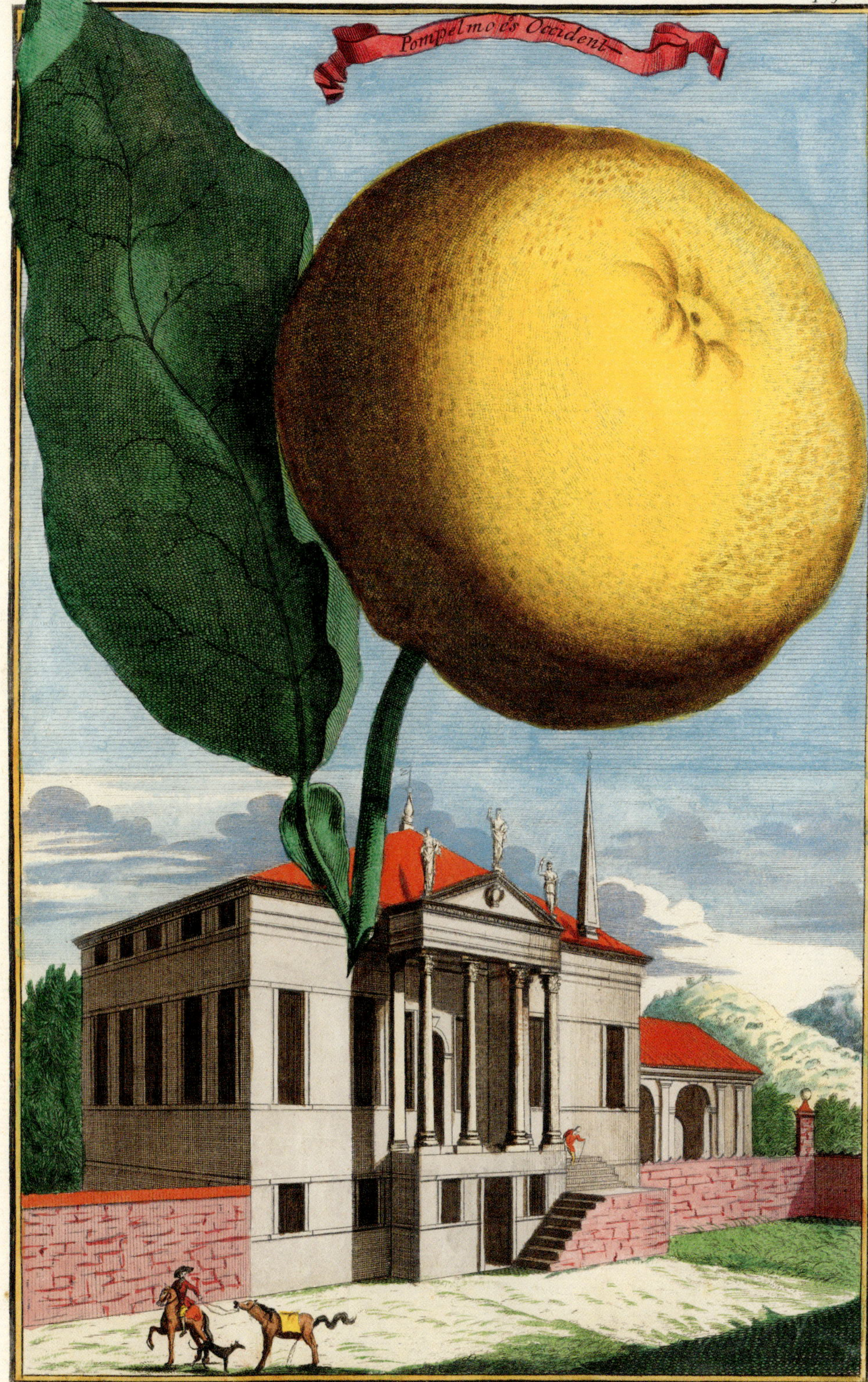

Malcesine (Verona) – Villa Cortusi

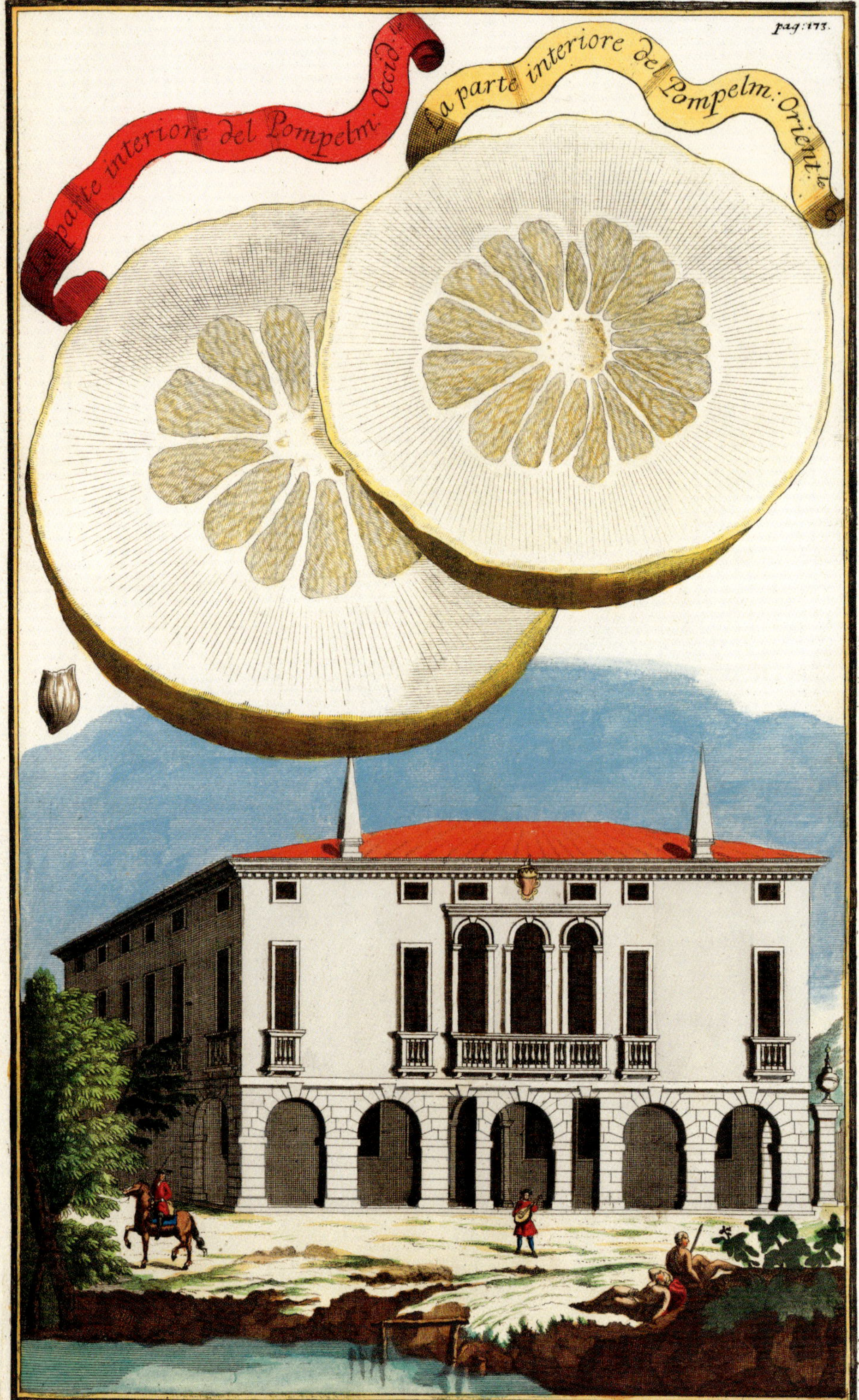

Pompelm[us] Occid[entalis] & Orient[alis]

Este (Padua) – Villa Contarini

Aranzo di mez[z]o sapore

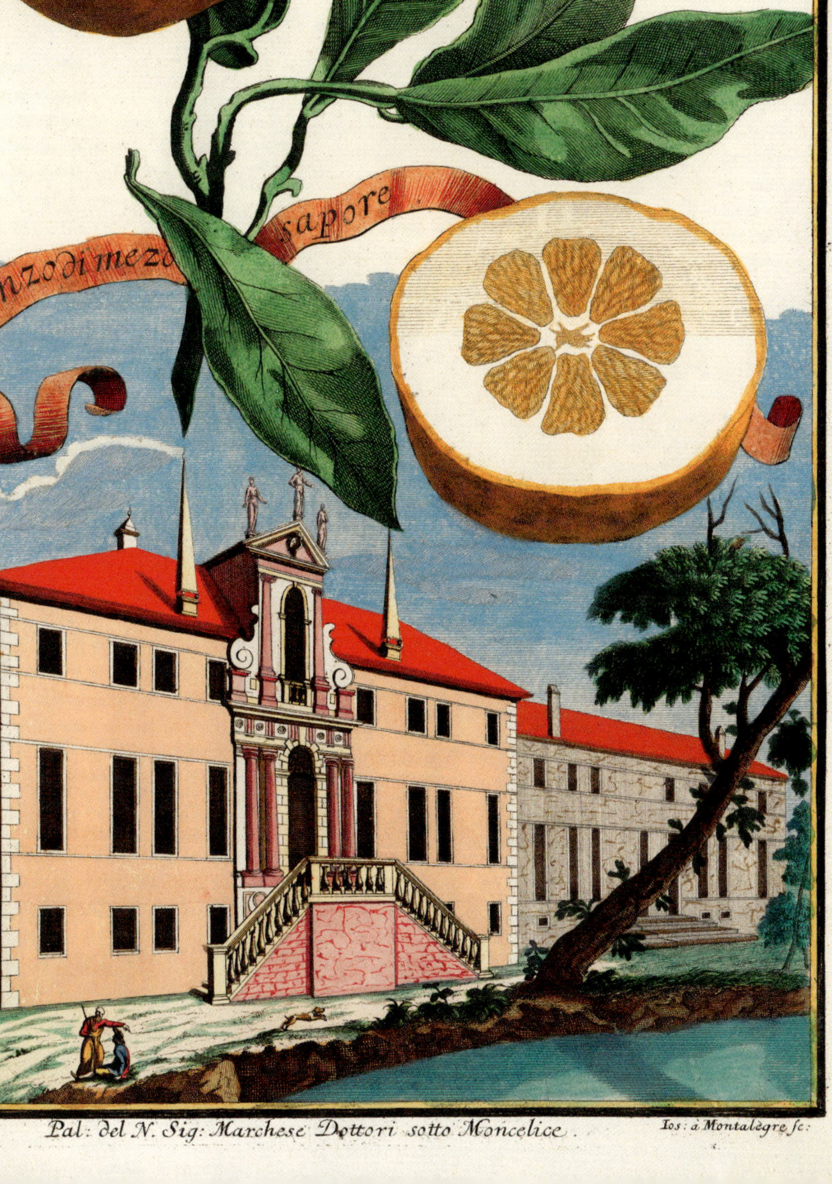

Monselice (Padua) – Villa Dottori

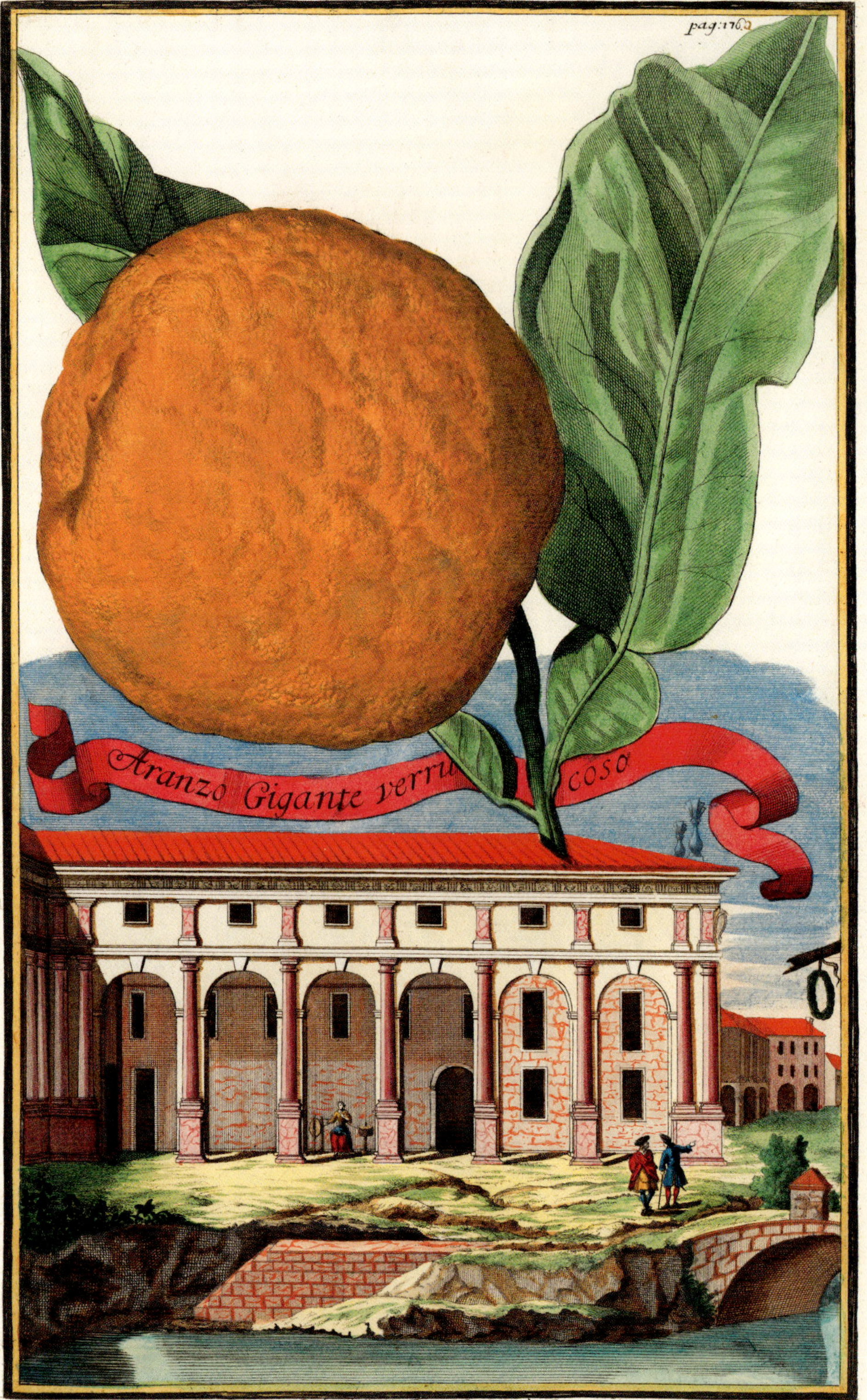

Aranzo Gigante verrucoso

Este (Padua) – Villa Basadonna

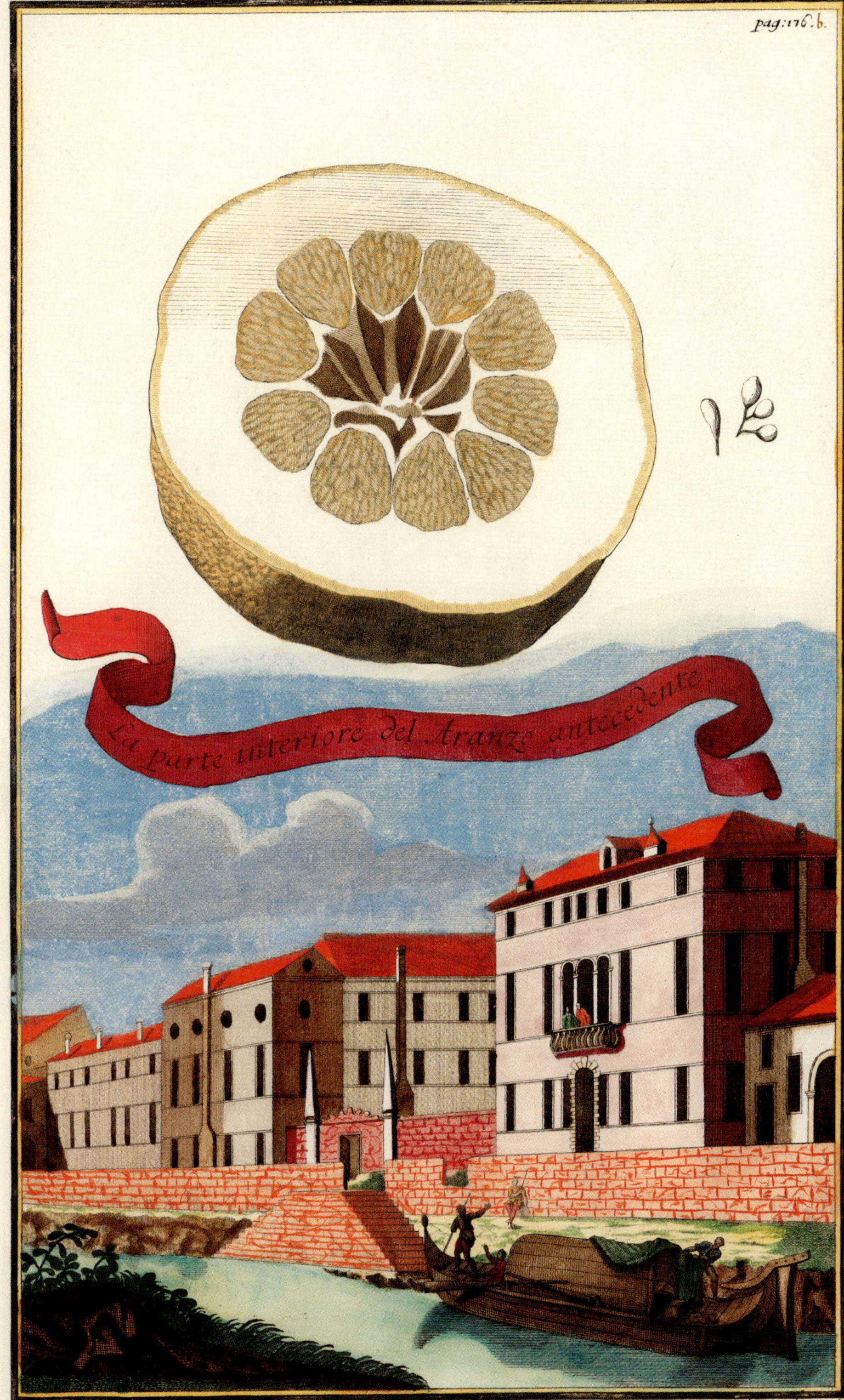
pag: 176. b.
La parte interiore del Aranzo antecedente
Palazzo del N.H. Barberigo à Este.
Ios: à Montalegre sc:

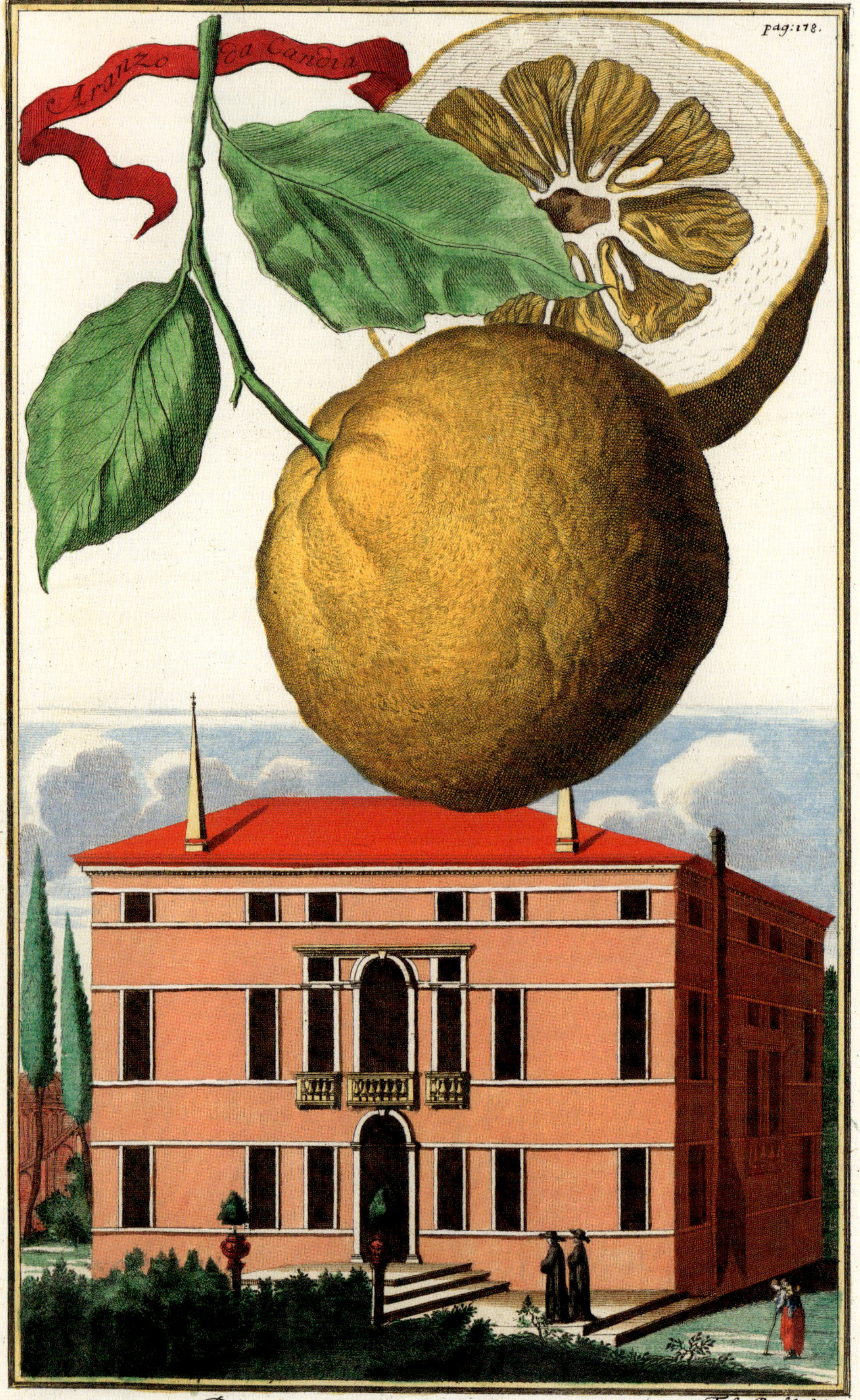

Aranzo da Candia

Este (Padua) – Villa Basadonna

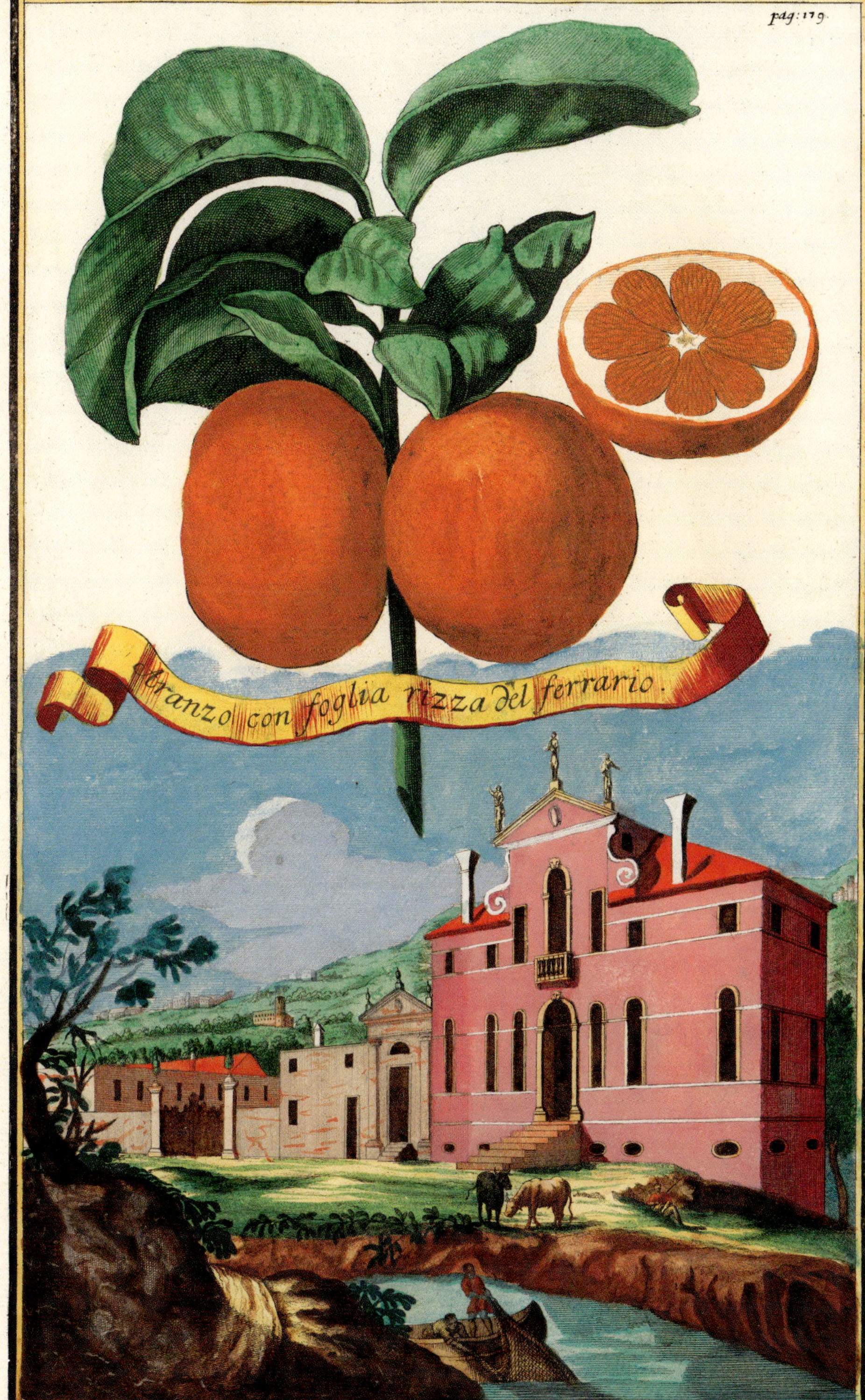

Aranzo con foglia rizza del ferrario

Este (Padua) – Villa Minotto. *Pages 372/373*
Verona – Giusti Gardens, detail (see p. 374)

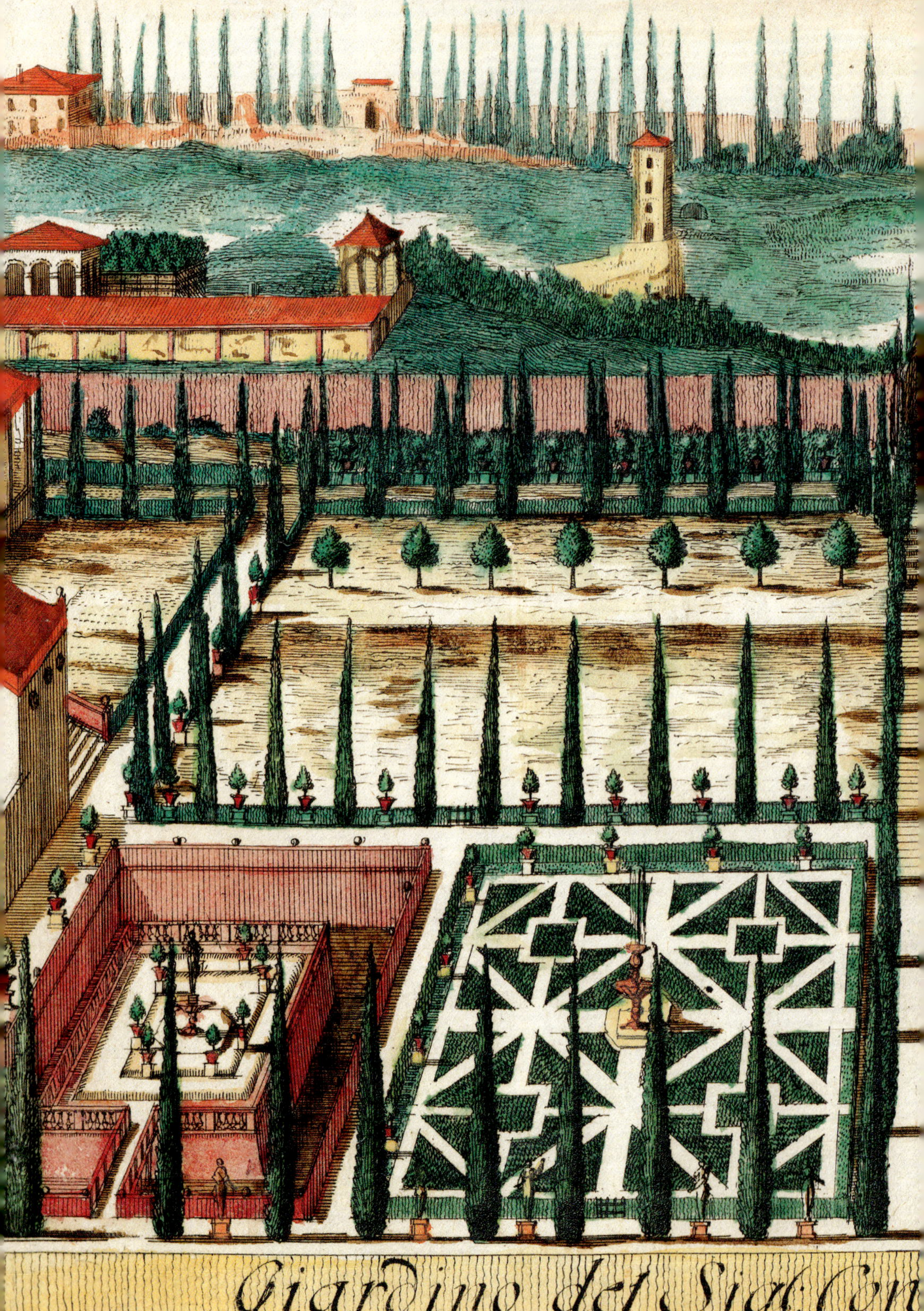
Giardino del Sig.r Con

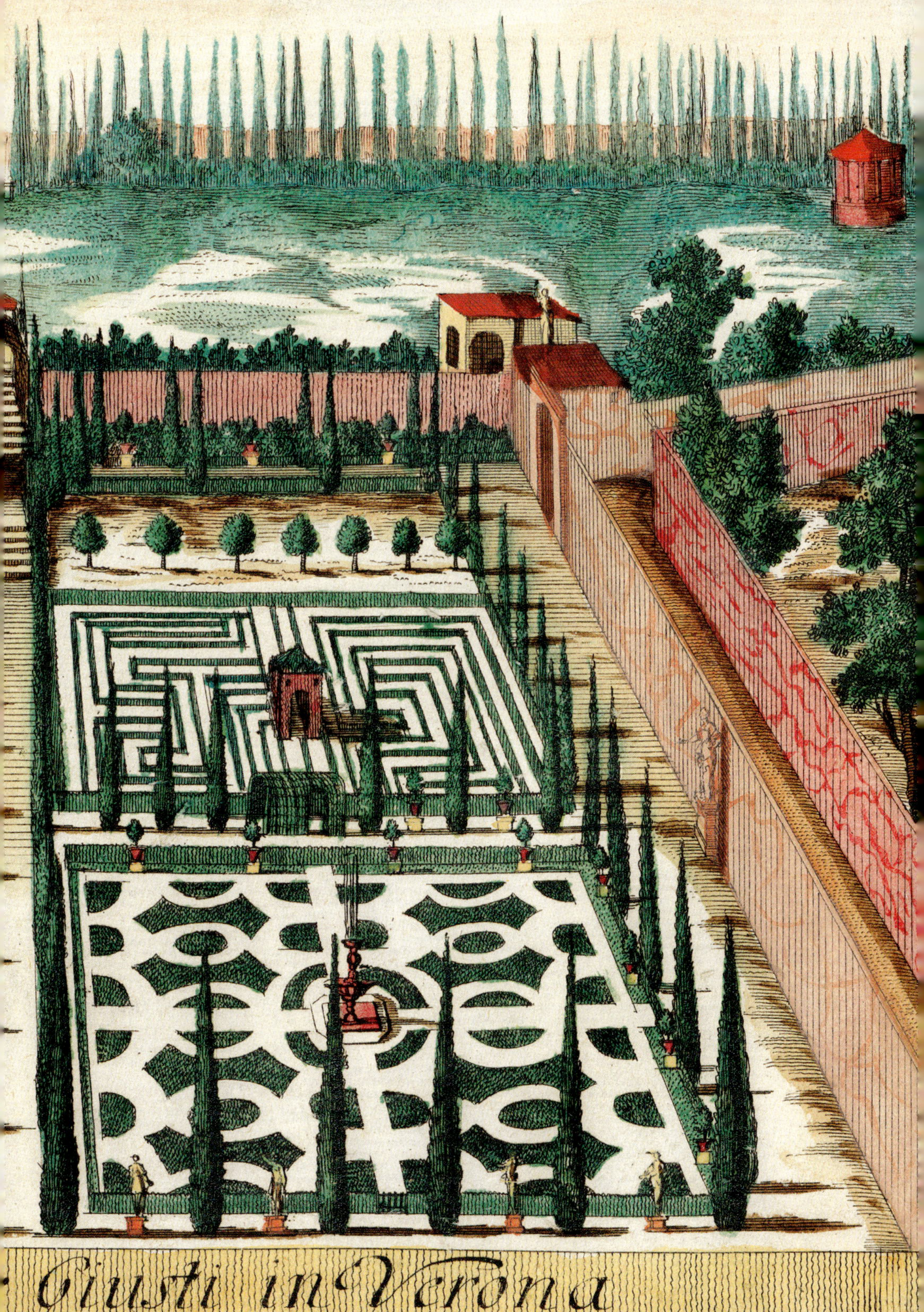
Giusti in Verona

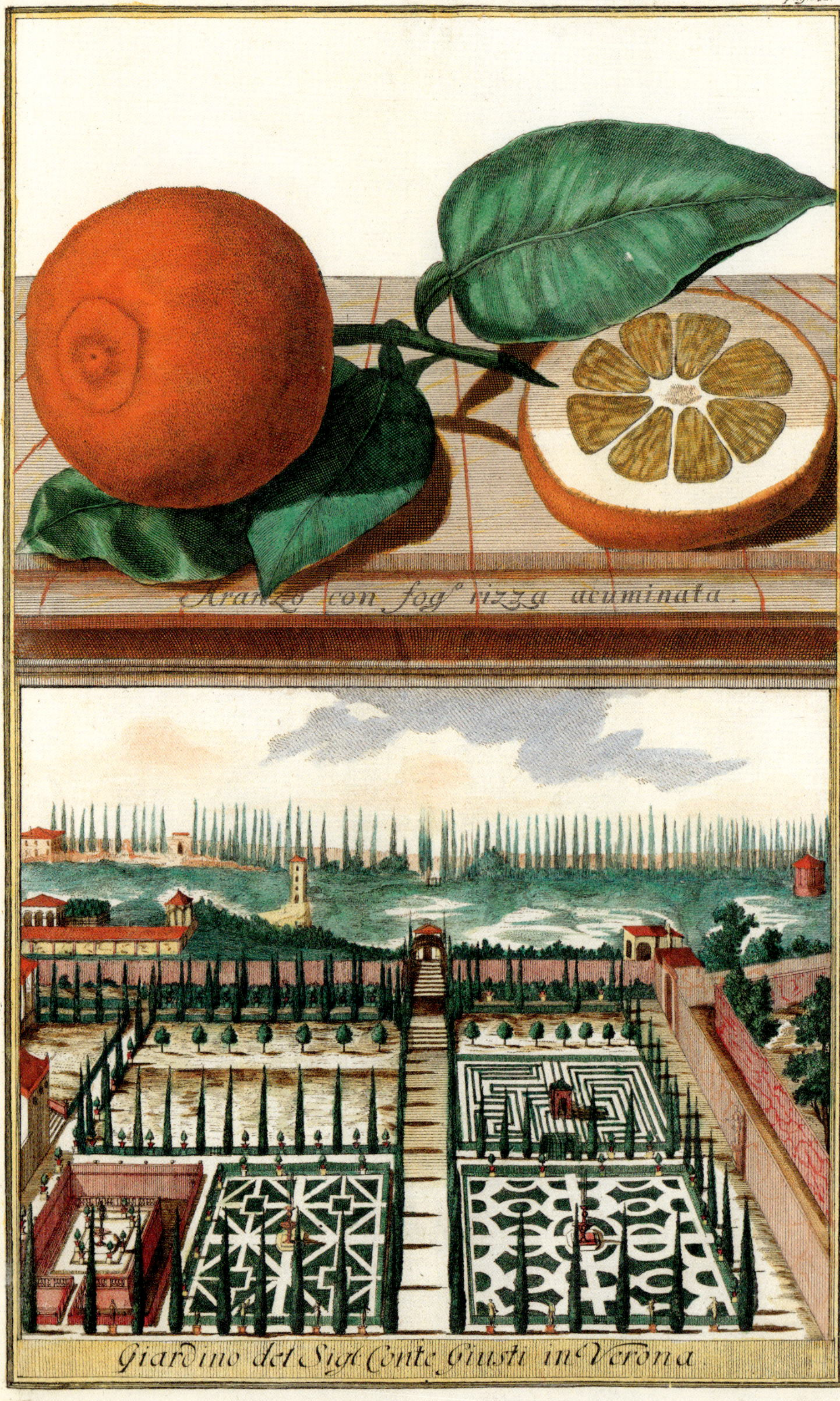

Aranzo con foglia rizza acuminata

Verona – Giusti Gardens

Aranzo con foglia rizza tondetta

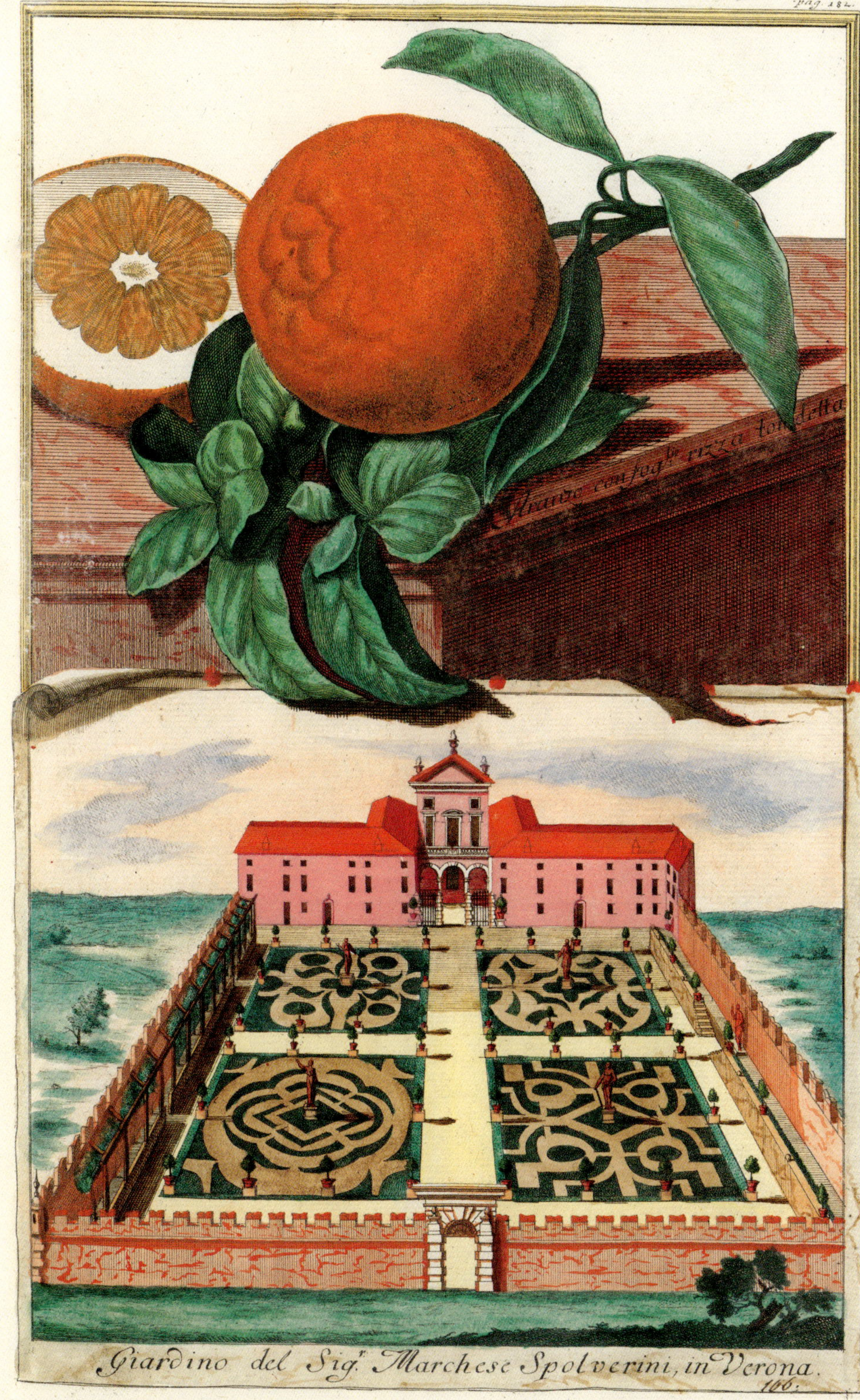

Verona – Spolverini Garden

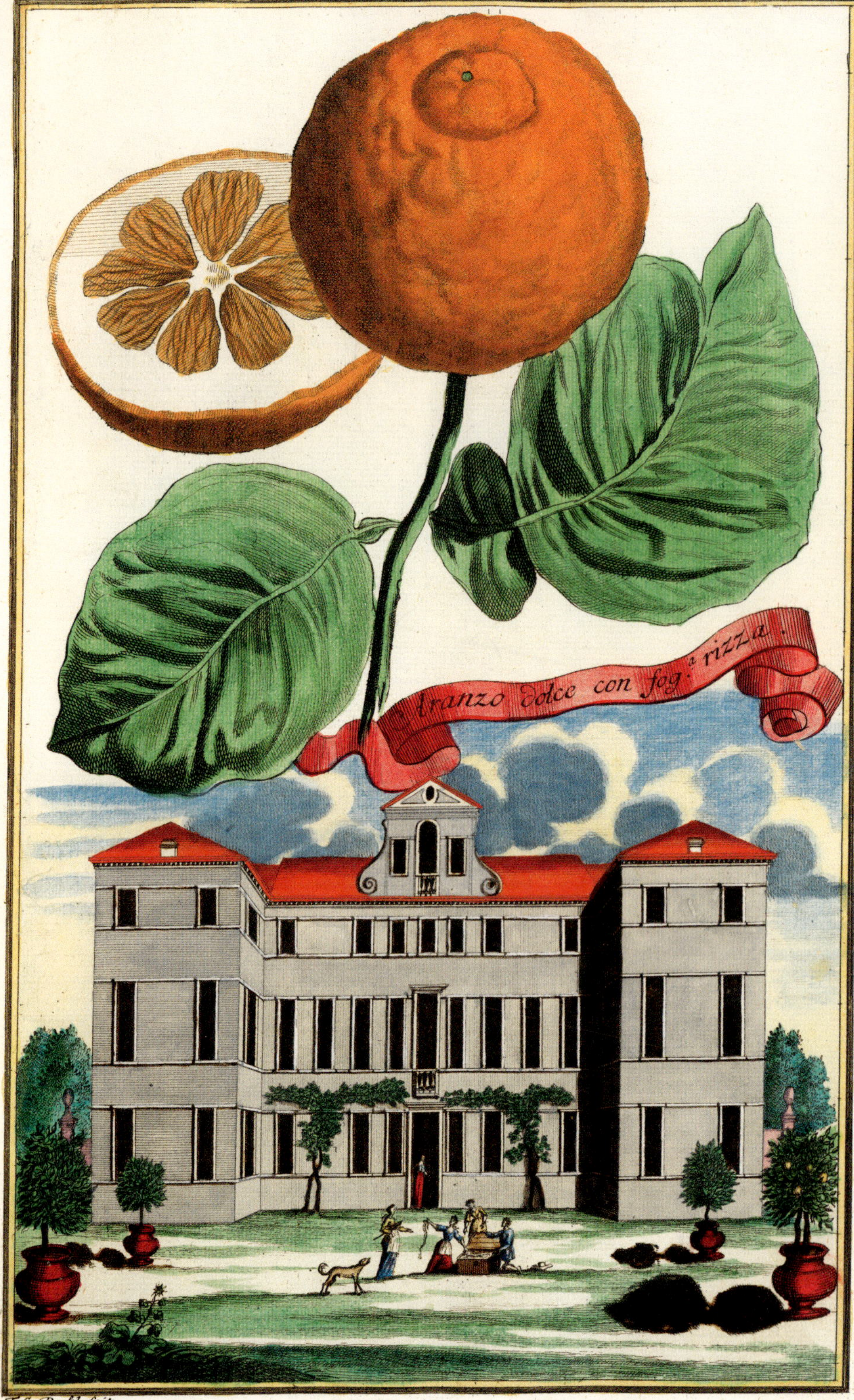

Aranzo dolce con foglia rizza

Noventa Padovana (Padua) – Villa Grimani

Aranzo striato dolce

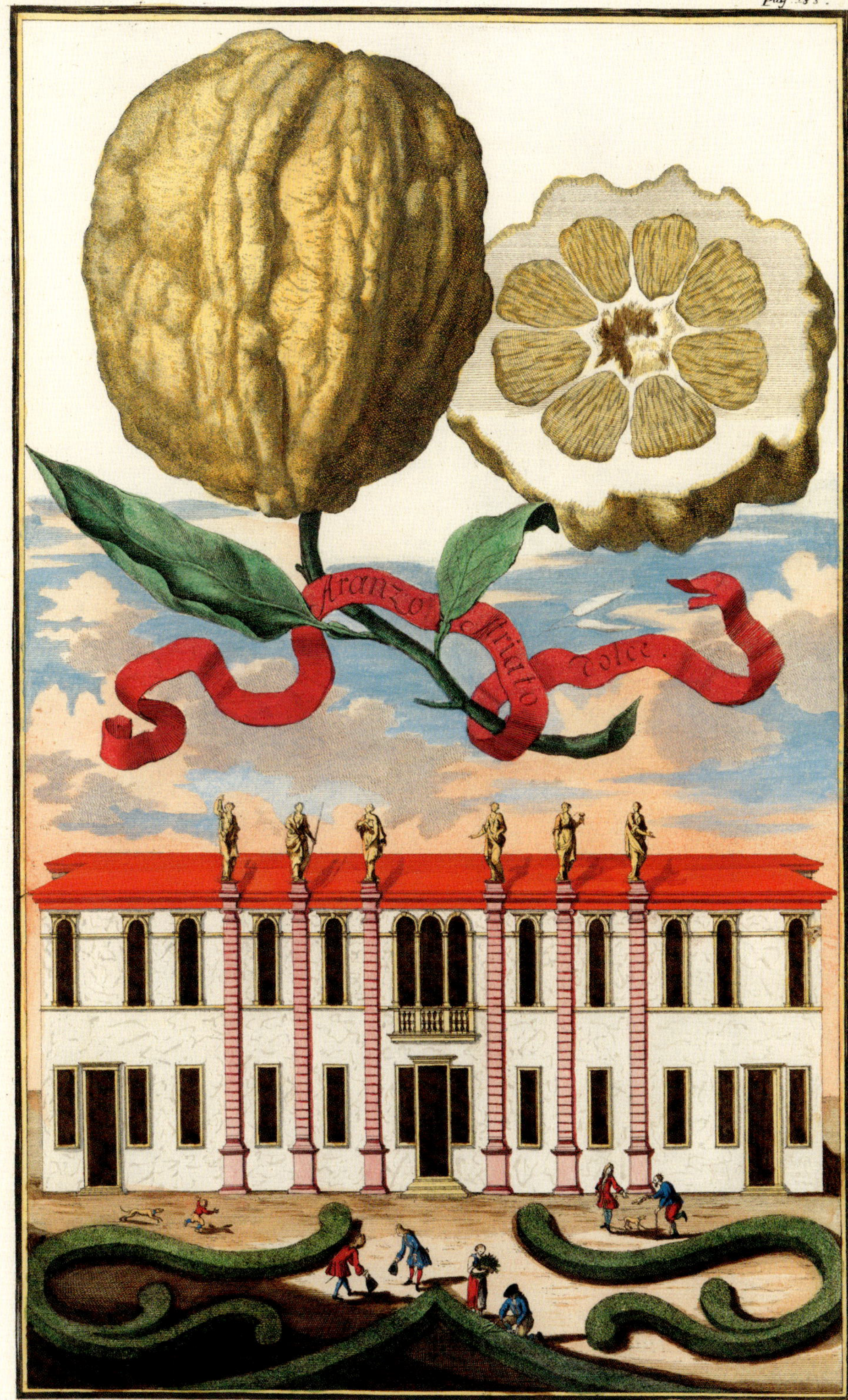

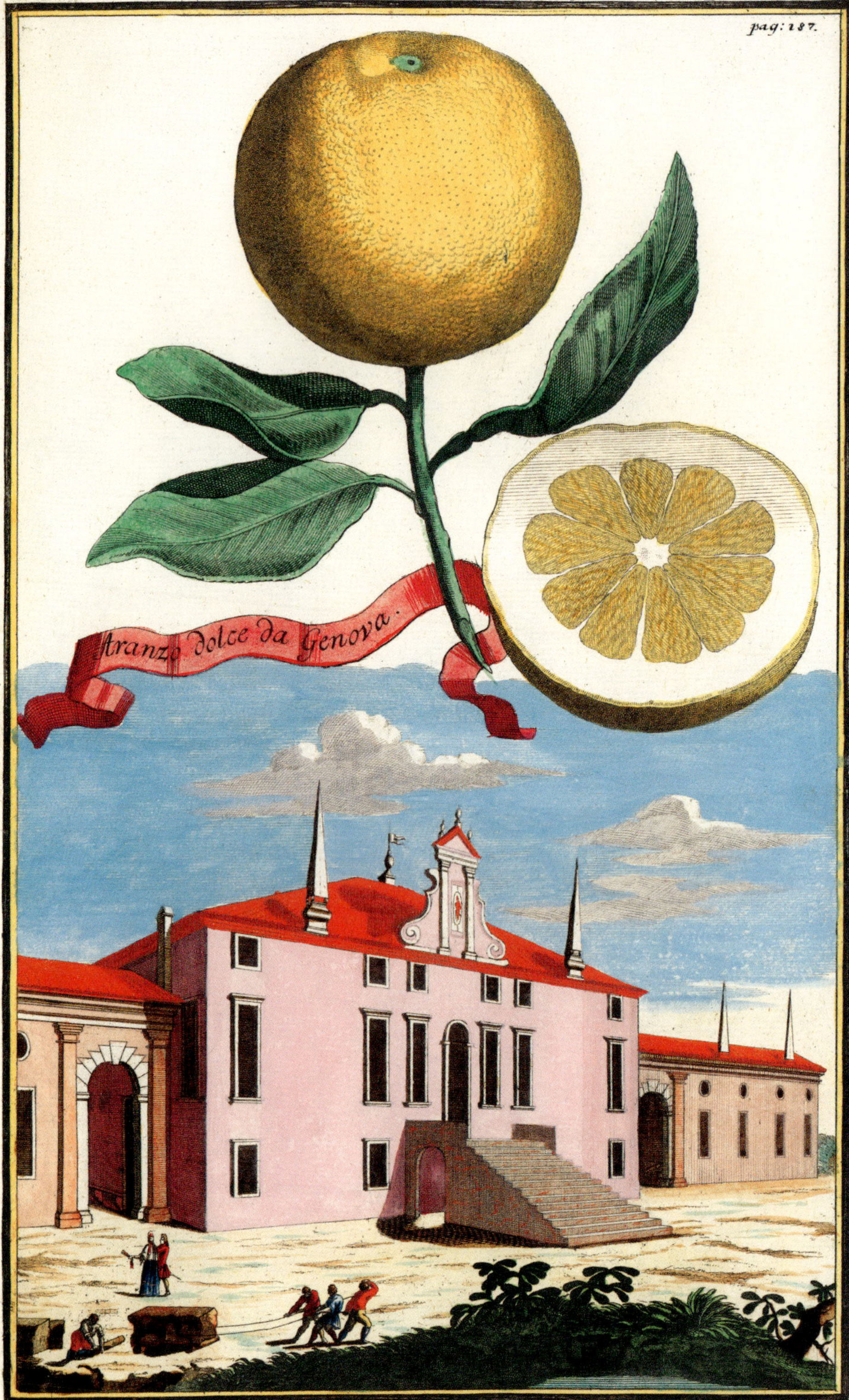

Palazzo del N. H. Morosini a Noventa.

Ios: à Montalegre sc:

Aranzo dolce da Genova

Noventa Padovana (Padua) – Villa Morosini

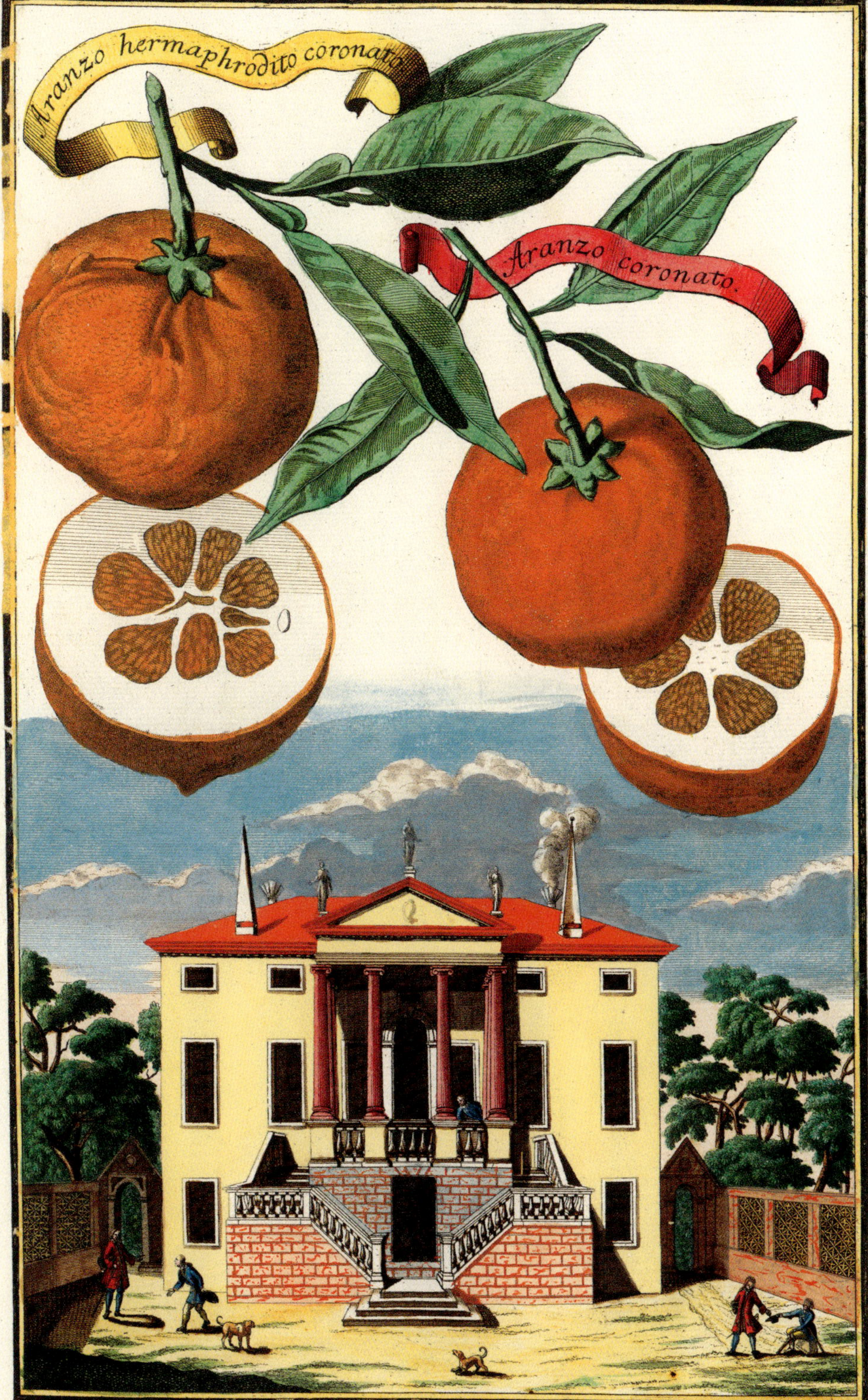
pag. 189.
Aranzo hermaphrodito coronato
Aranzo coronato.
Palazzo del N. Sig: Rota in Este.
Ios: à Montalegro fe.

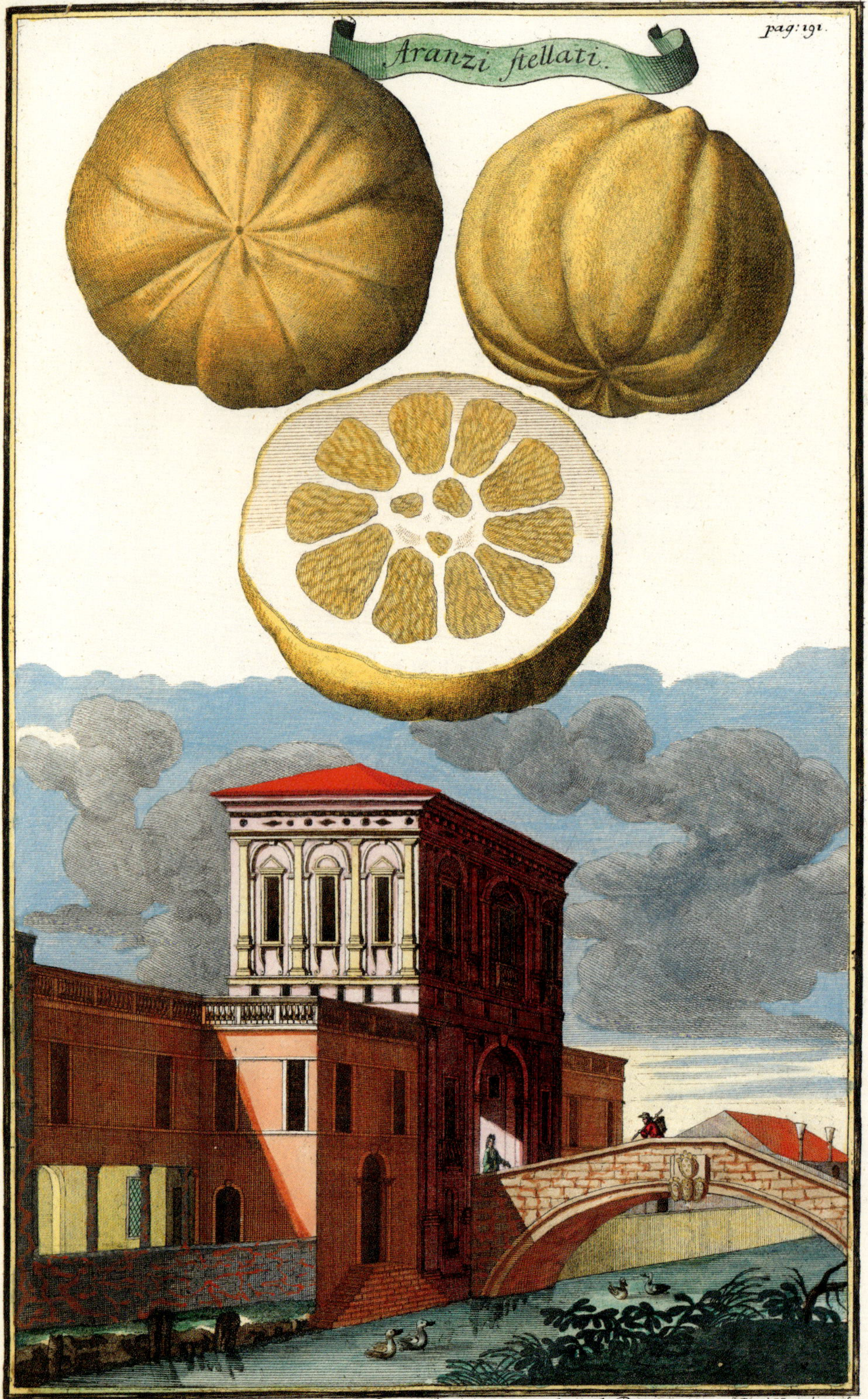
Aranzi stellati.
pag:191.
Pal: del N. H. Avogadro a meza via sop: il Ponte.
Ios: à Montalegre fc:

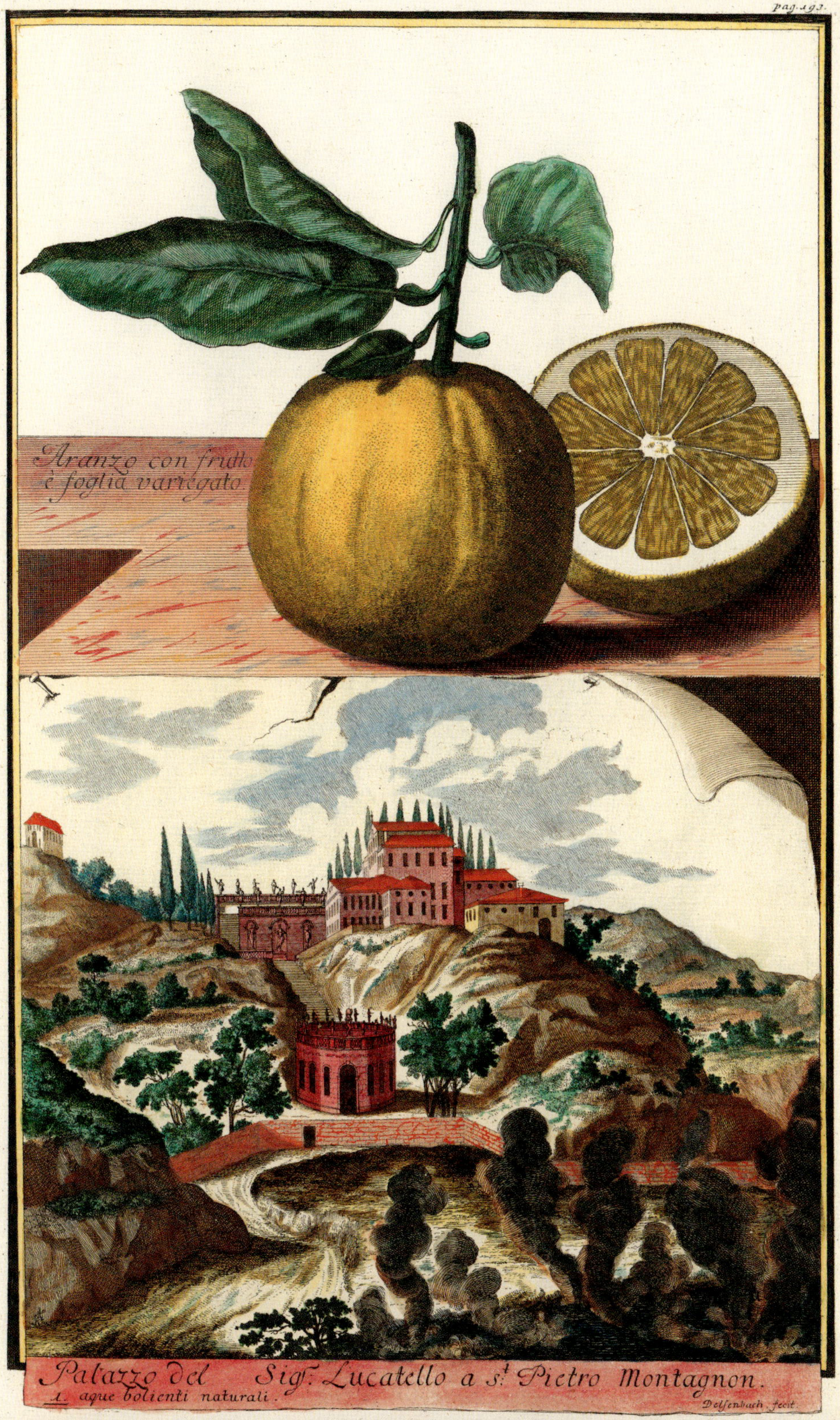

Aranzo con frutto e foglia variegato

Montegrotto Terme (Padua) – Villa Lucatello, later Draghi

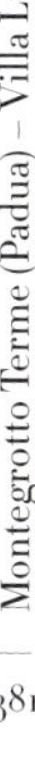

pag. 193.

Aranzo con frutto è foglia variegato.

Palazzo del Sig.r Lucatello a S.t Pietro Montagnon.

1. aque bolienti naturali.

Delsenbach fecit.

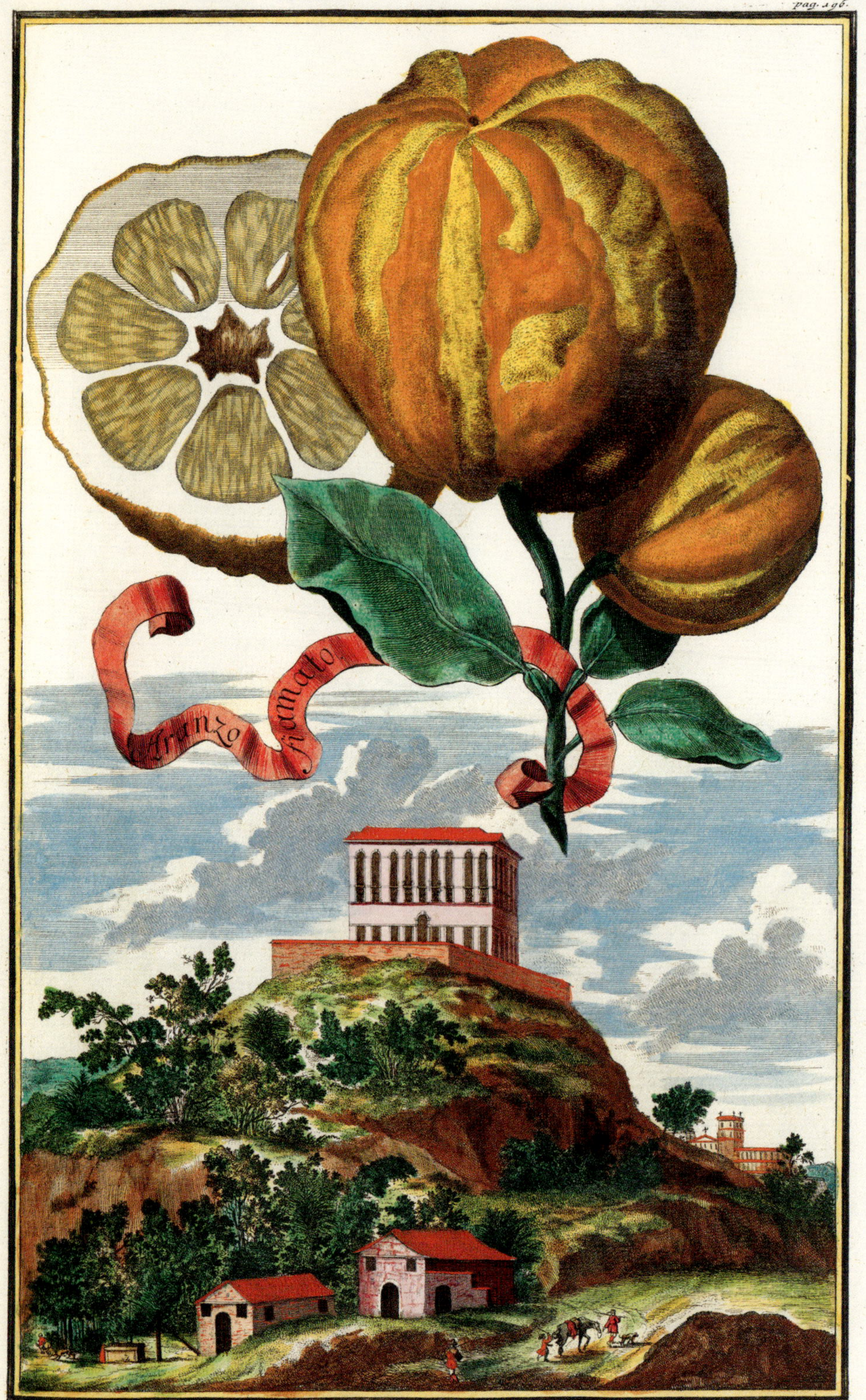
pag. 196.
Aranzo fiamato
Delsenbach. fecit.
Altro Prospetto è Palazzo sopra l monte del Sr. Lucatello a St. Pietro.

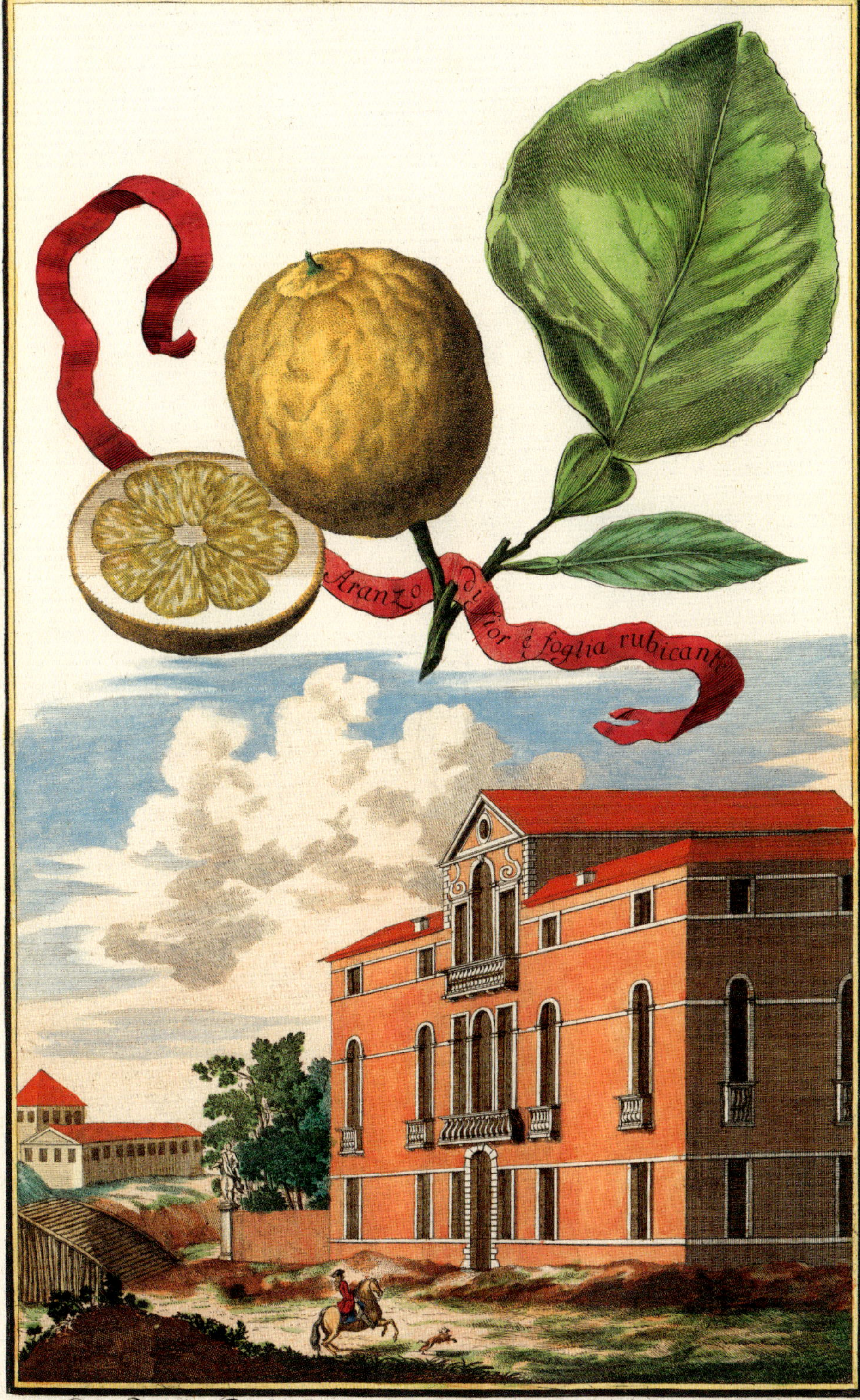

Aranzo di fior e foglia rubicante

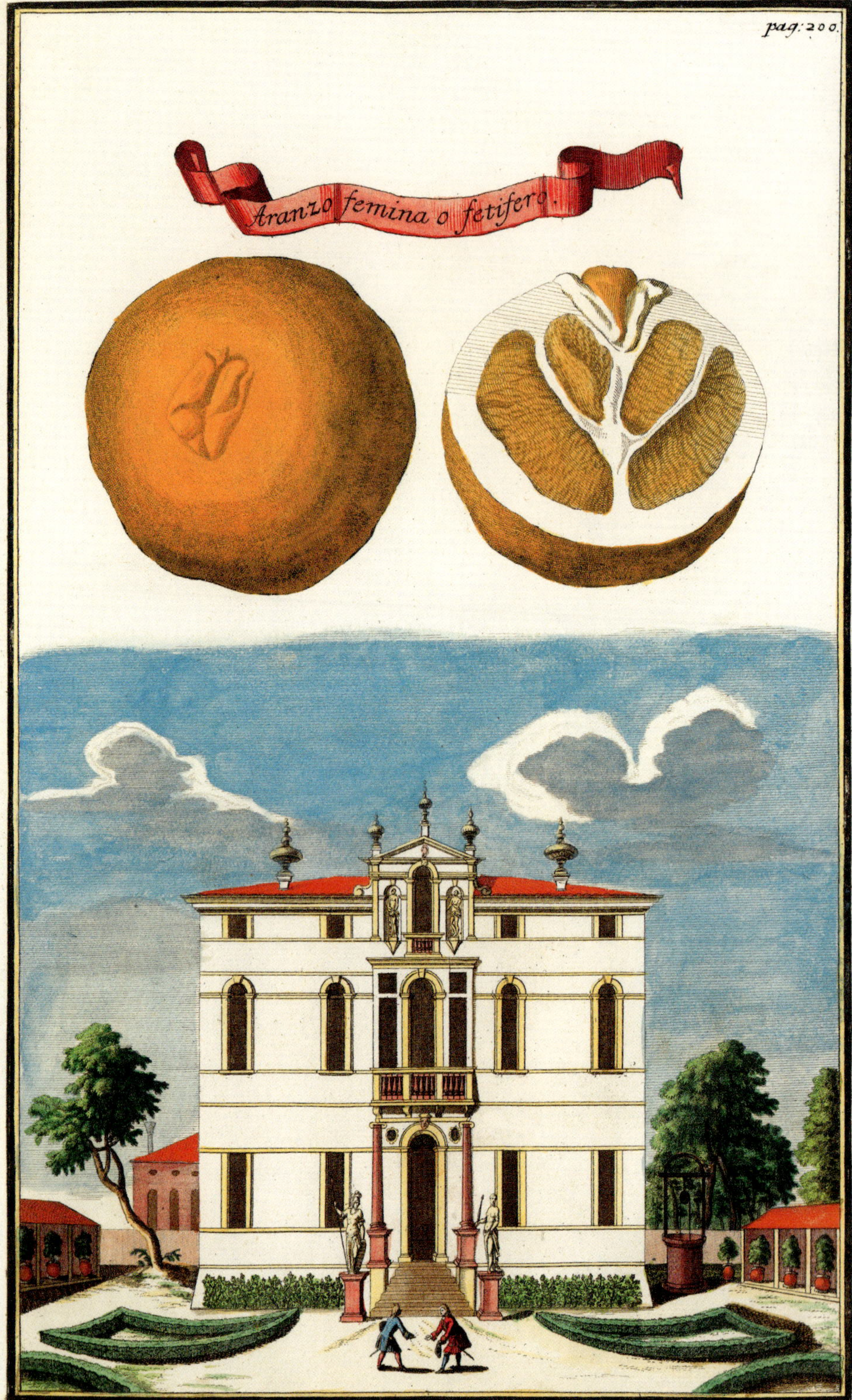

Aranzo femina o fetifero

Noventa Padovana (Padua) – Villa Vendramin

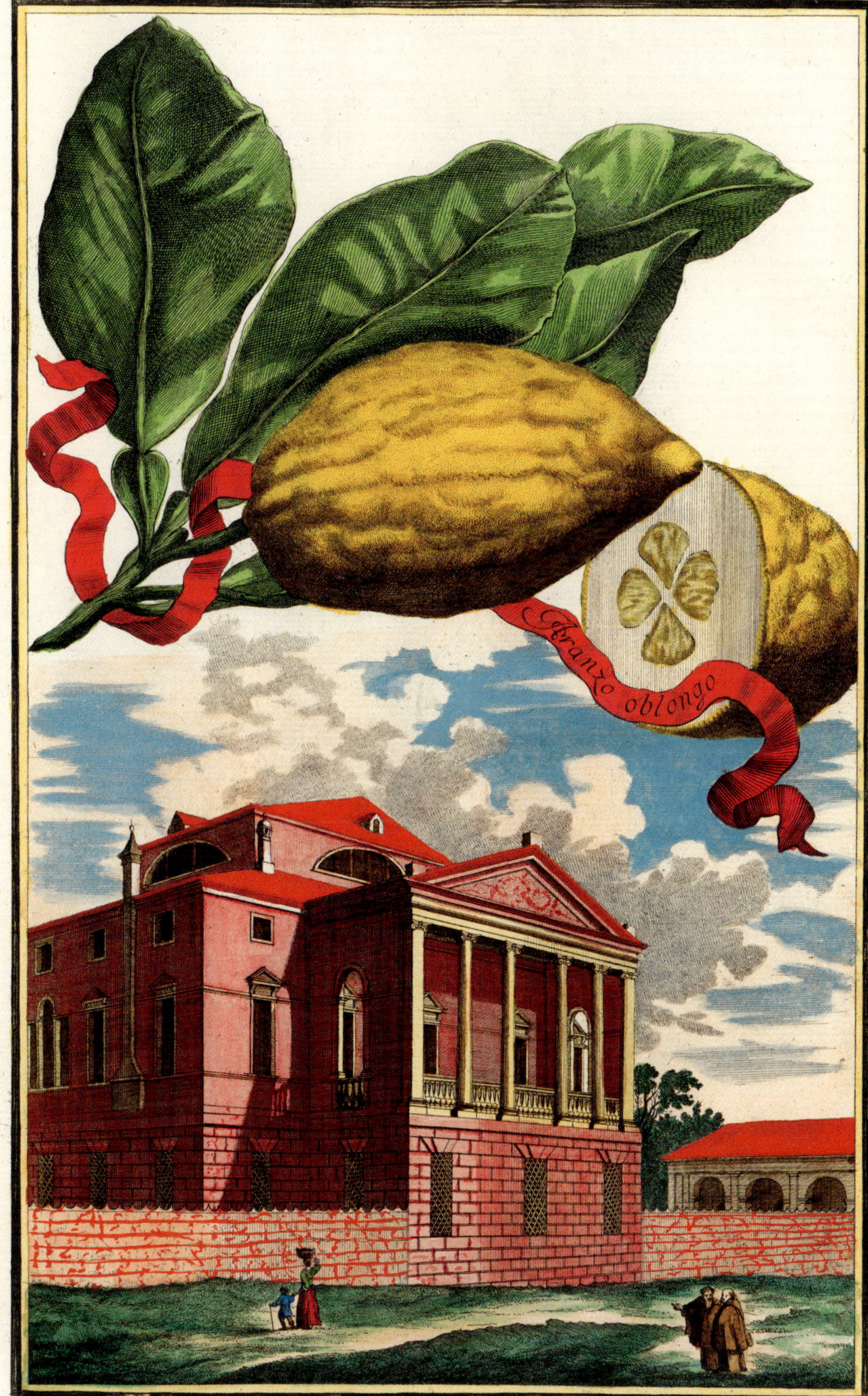
pag: 202
Aranzo oblongo
Palazzo del N: H: Conte Pio sop.a Padoua.
Delsenbach. fec.

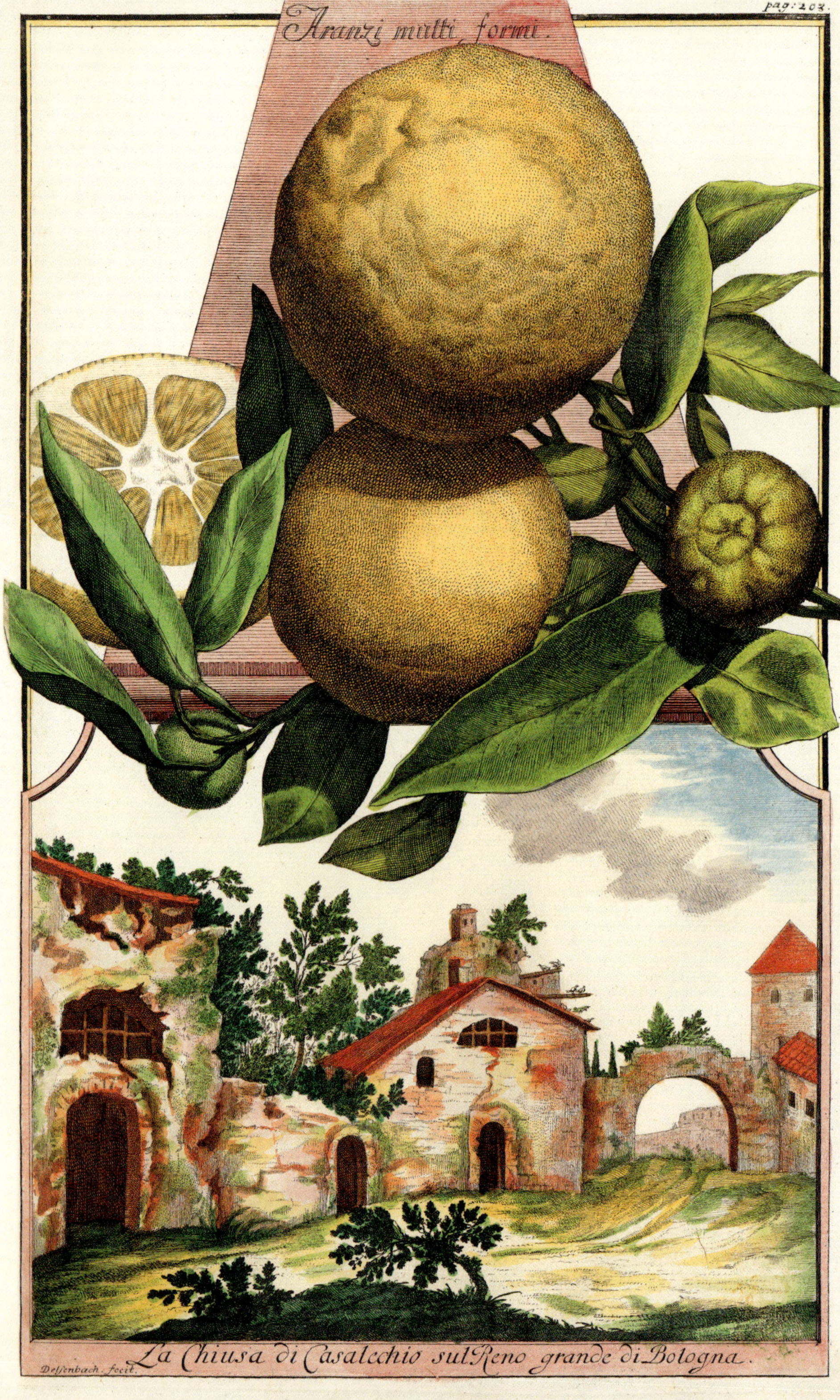

Aranzi multiformi

Casalecchio di Reno (Bologna) – Courtyard

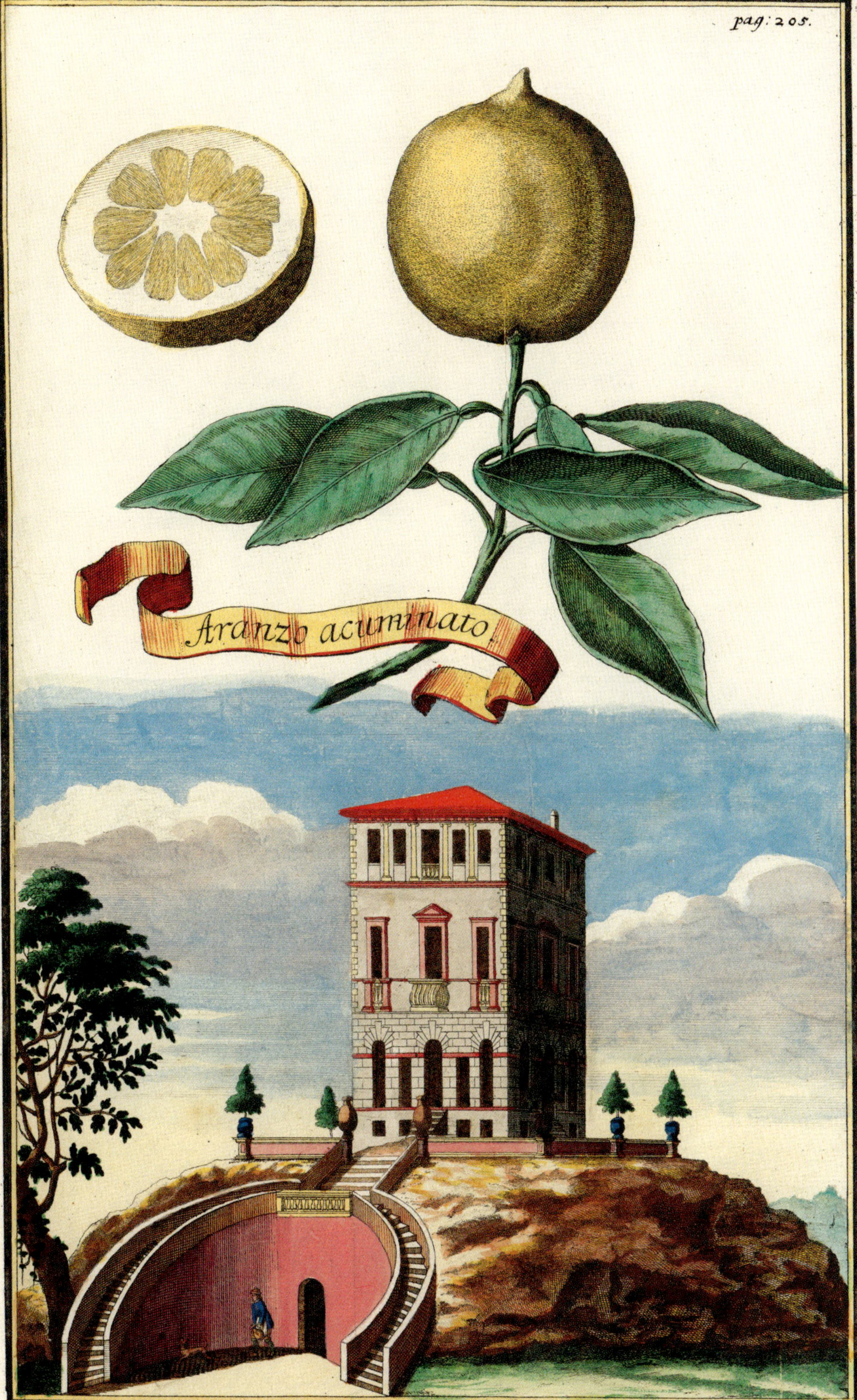
pag: 205.
Aranzo acuminato
Palazzo del N. Sig.r Franc.co Benzi a Montagnola.
Ios: à Montalegre sc:

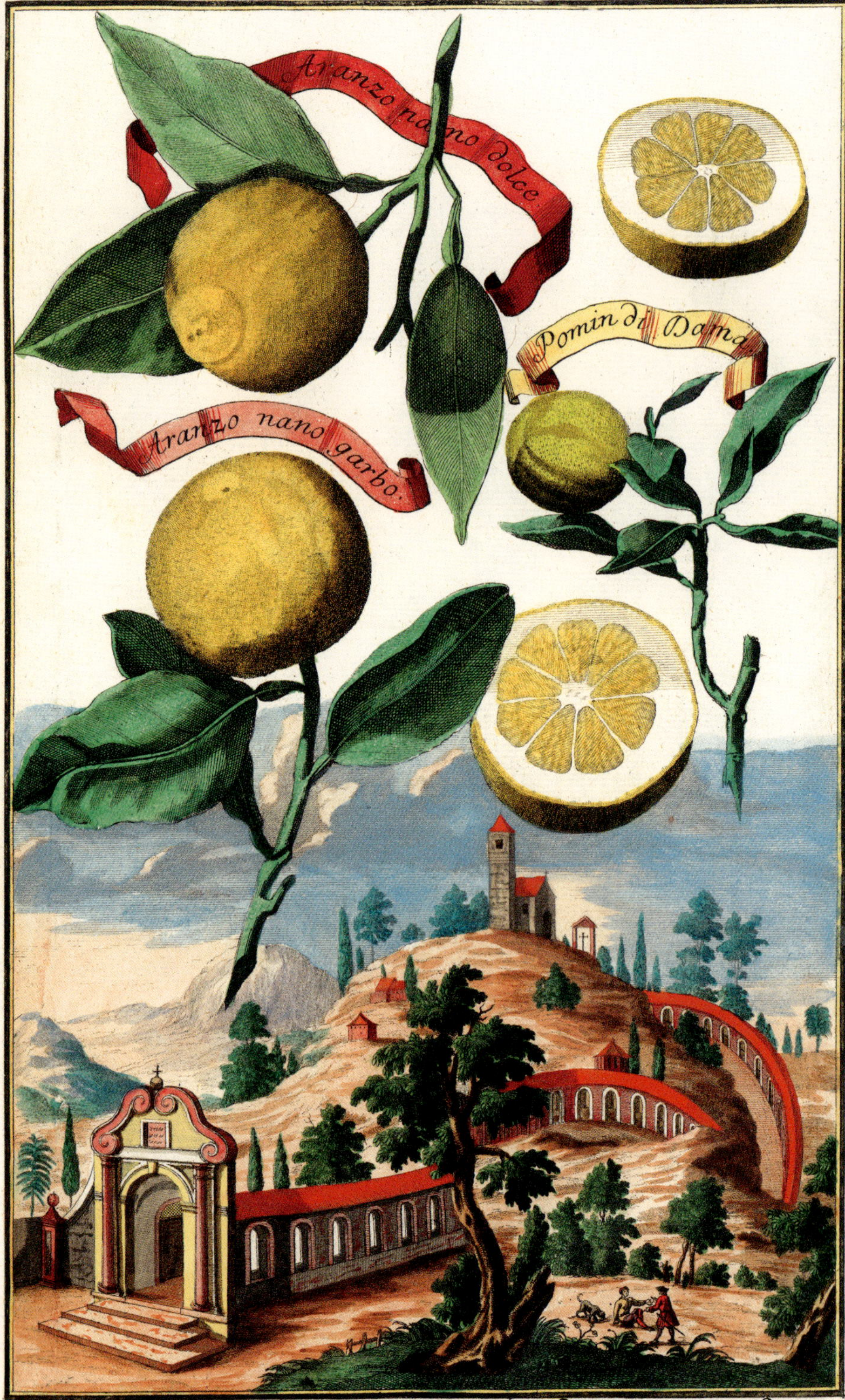

Aranzo nano dolce & Aranzo nano garbo & Pomin di Dama

Bologna – Madonna di San Luca

Citrus aurantium

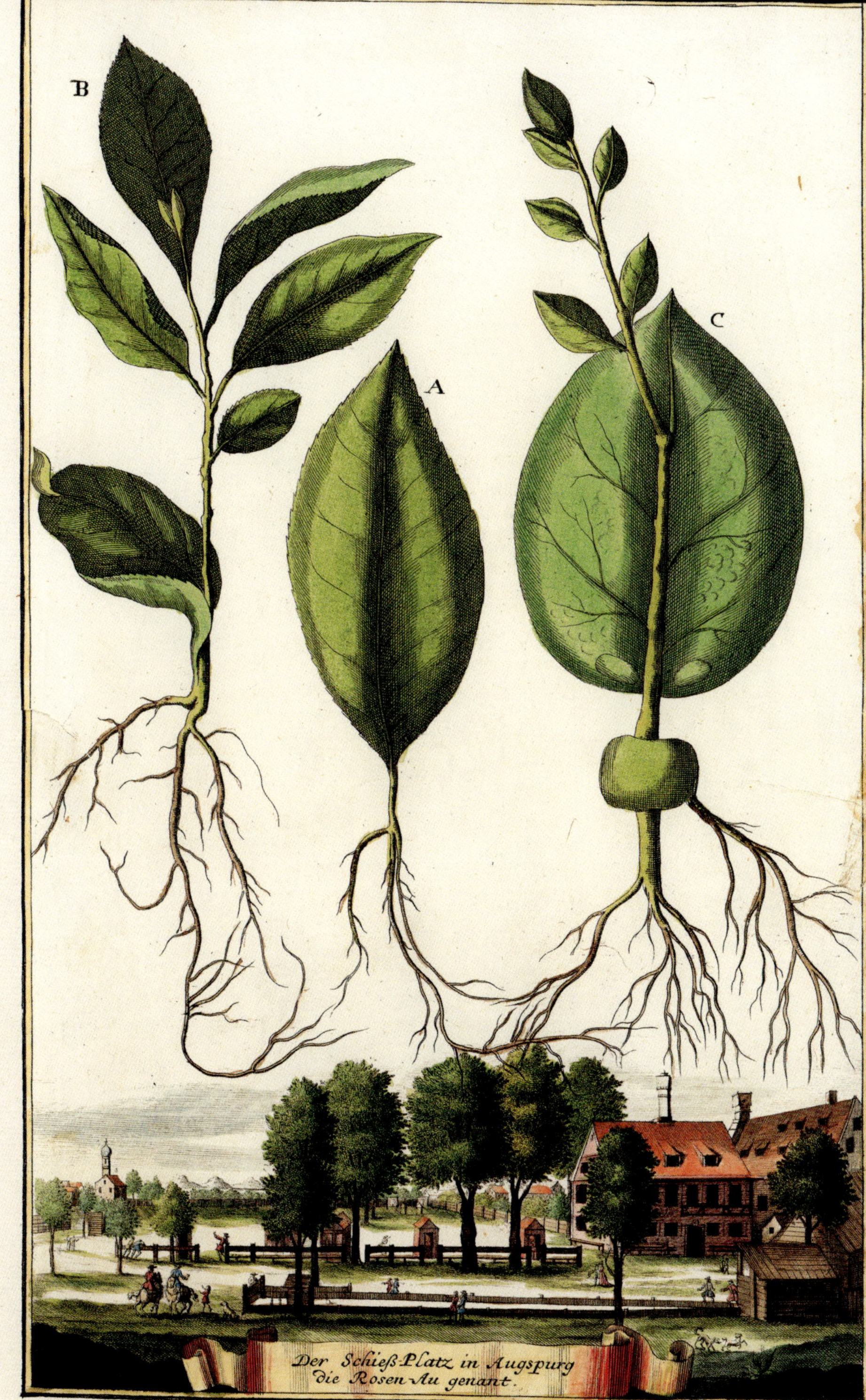

Augsburg – The Castle. *Pages 390/391*
Montagnola – Villa Benzi, detail (see p. 387)

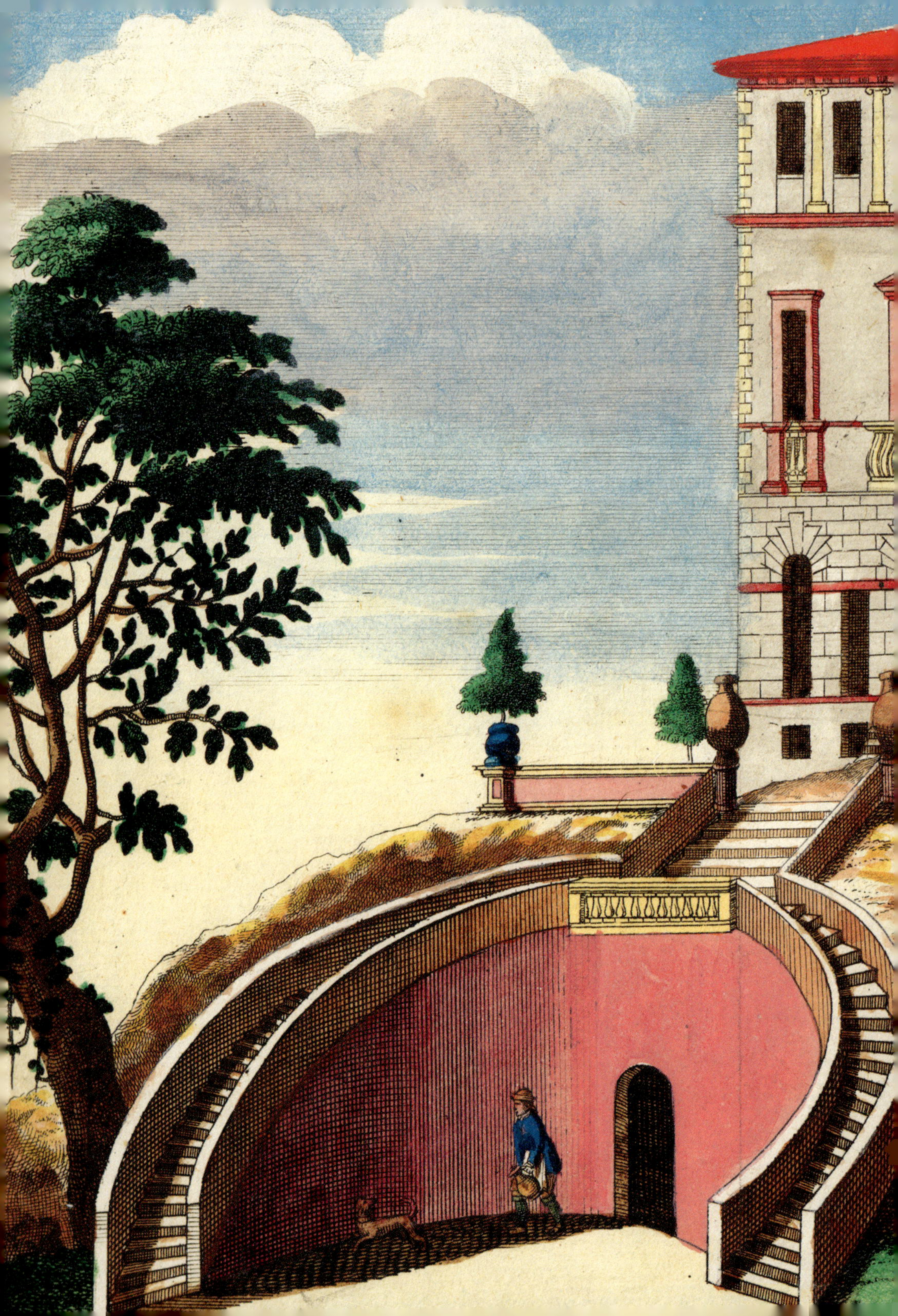

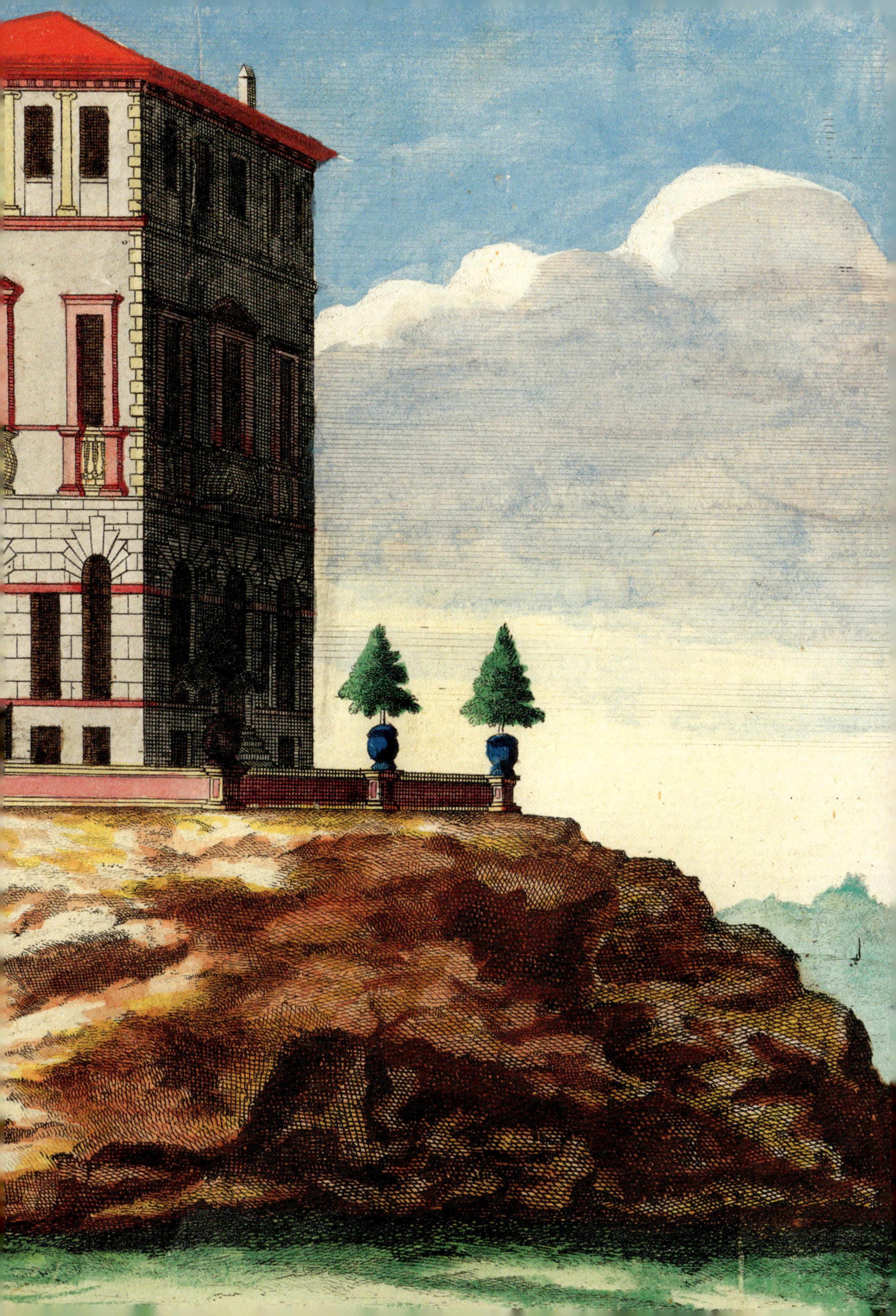

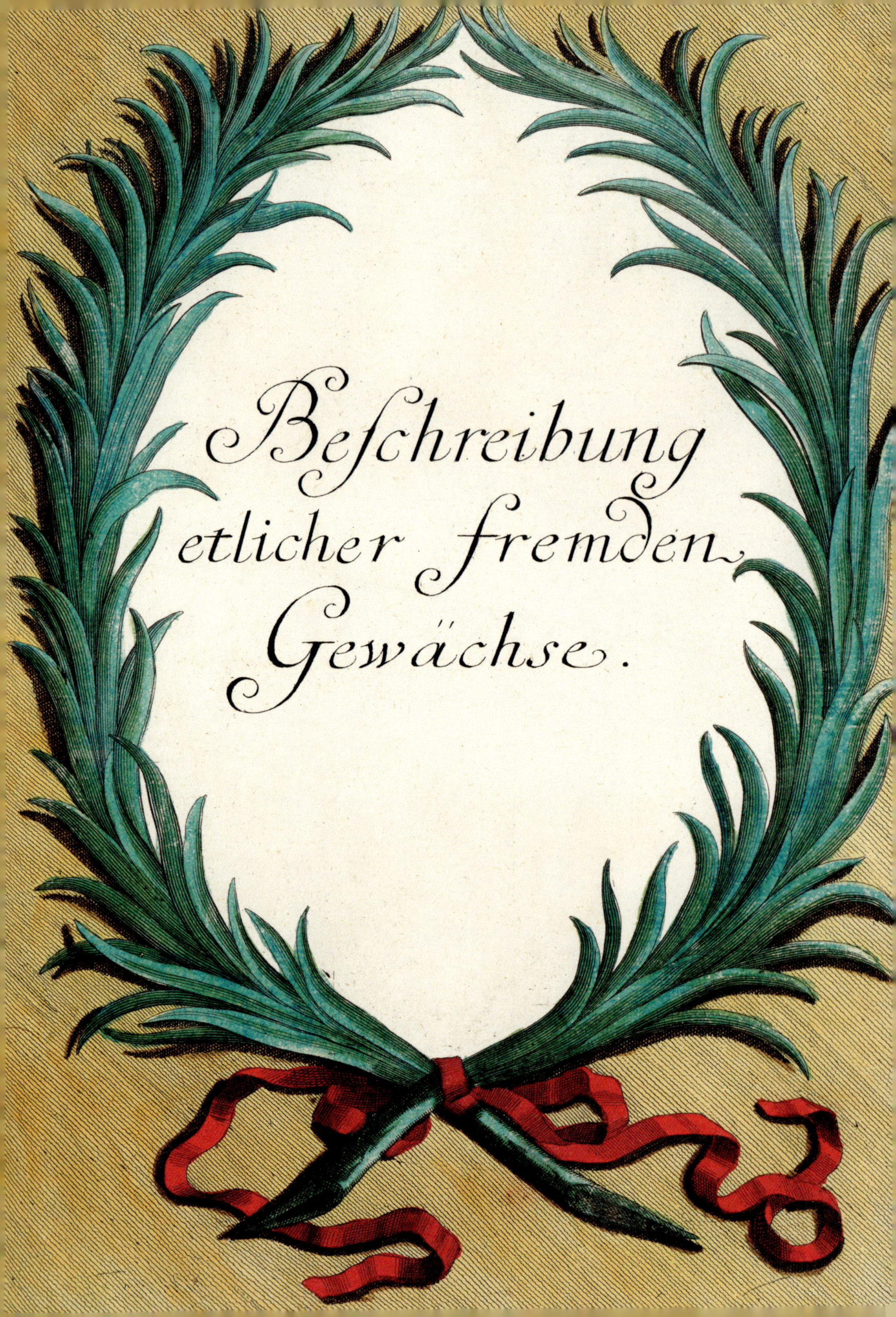
Beschreibung
etlicher fremden
Gewächse.

Beschreibung unterschiedlicher fremder Gewächse.

Das I. Capitel.

Die Americanische Ananas.

Wann einige Frucht vorhanden/ deren man/ wegen ihres herrlichen Geschmacks und leckerhafften Annehmlichkeit/ einen besondern Lob-Ruhm beylegen mag/ so ist es wahrhafftig die denen Augen des geneigten Lesers fürstellig-gemachte Ananas. Ein Ausbund aller Gewächse/deren in denen vier Welt-Theilen fast keines an Niedlichkeit vergleichlich/ daher sie auch billich eine Königin der Früchte zu nennen/in welche alle Lust-Reitzungen des Geschmacks versenket/ und von der All-Mutter/ der Natur/ mit einer Krone von Blättern auf dem Haubt geschmücket/ um dadurch ihren Vorrang vor allen andern auszudrücken. In dieser grünen Krone liegen schon die erste Beginnselen des künfftigen Stamm- und Kron-Erbens verborgen/ woraus/ bey Absterben der bisherigen Zeug-Mutter/ durch den frucht-bringenden Trieb der Natur/ eine neue Frucht herfür stammen muß.

Dieses Geschmack-ergötzende Wunder der Natur/ hat uns/ nebst andern unaussprechlichen Schätzen/ das wunder-reiche America am ersten zu erkennen gegeben. Brasilien/ welches sonst wegen seiner wilden Einwohner/ die ihre Unmenschlichkeit/ durch einen unnatürlichen Hunger nach Menschen-Fleisch/an den Tag legen/ übelberüchtiget/ wird insgemein vor die Nährerin dieser delicatessen Frucht angegeben; aus welcher sie in andere Welt-Theile verpflanzet worden. Doch hat auch das Mexicanische Königreich den Ruhm/daß es diese Gewächse häufig herfürbringe/ und sollen die in der Provinz Heytan wachsende allen bevorgehen. Die von denen Engelländern und Franzosen beherrschte Antillen-Inseln haben auch hieran einen reichen Vorrath/ aus welchen es die Engelländer

Ananas

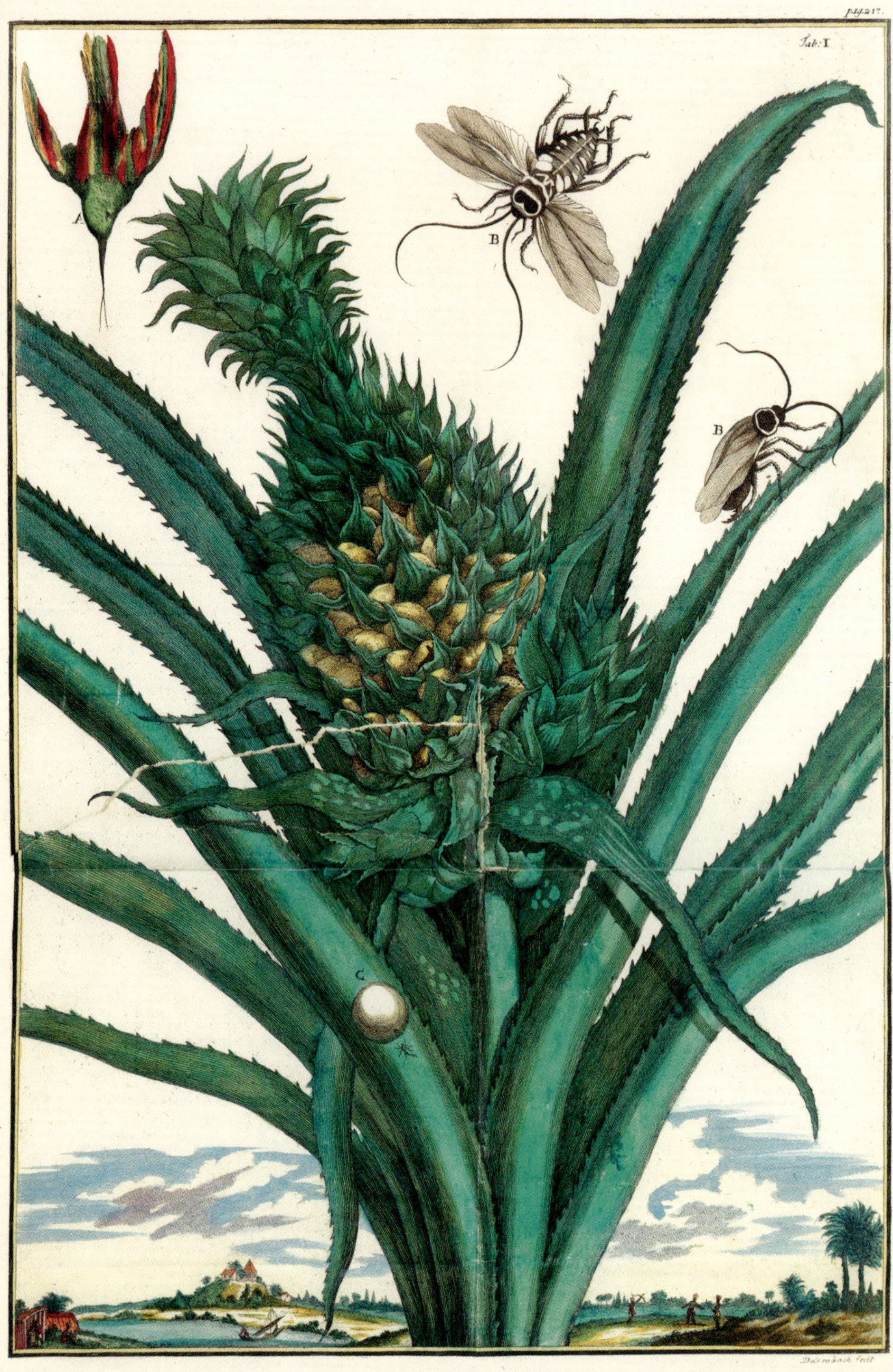

Landscape in Central or South America. *Pages 392/393*
Cartouche and beginning of the "Description of Exotic Plants"

Ananas

Coastal Town in Central or South America

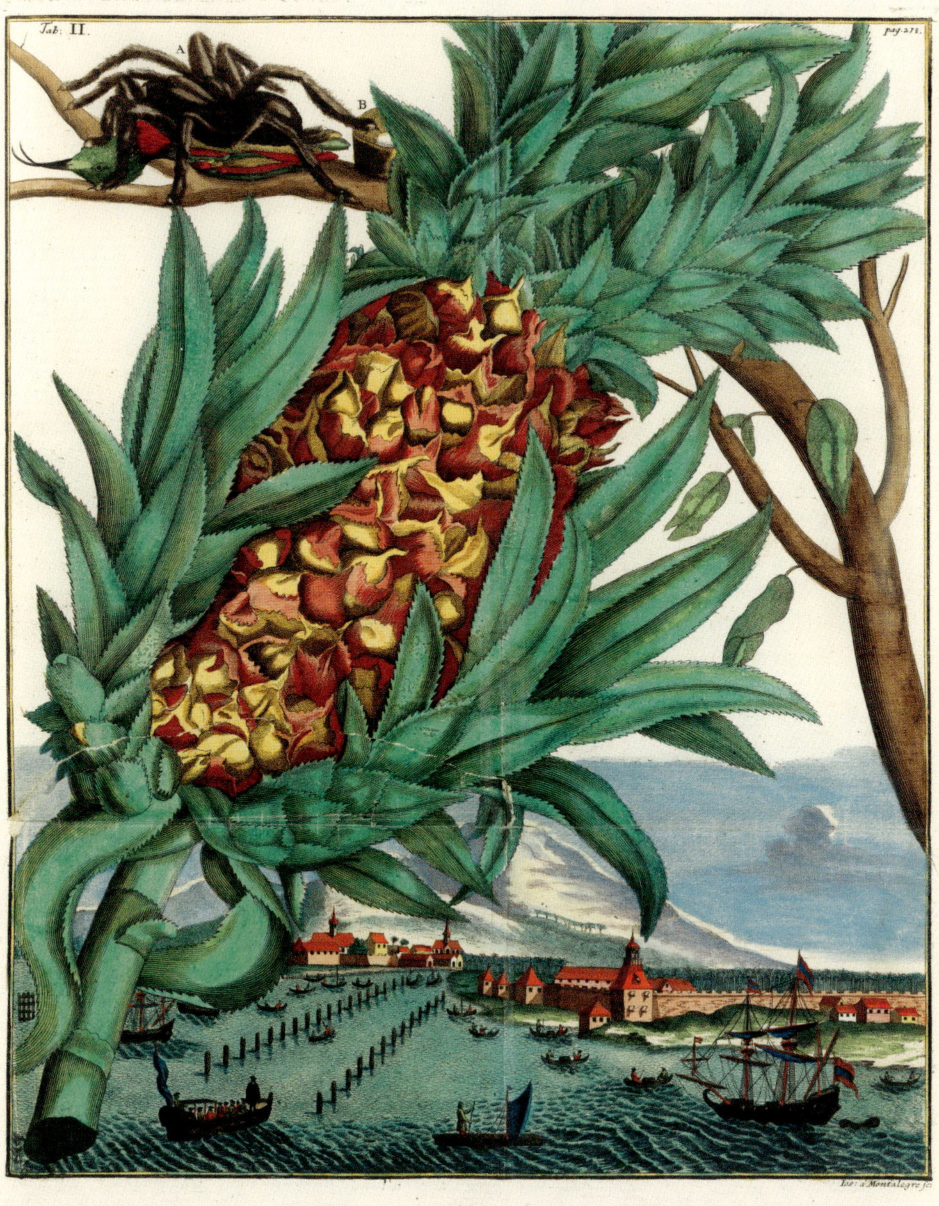

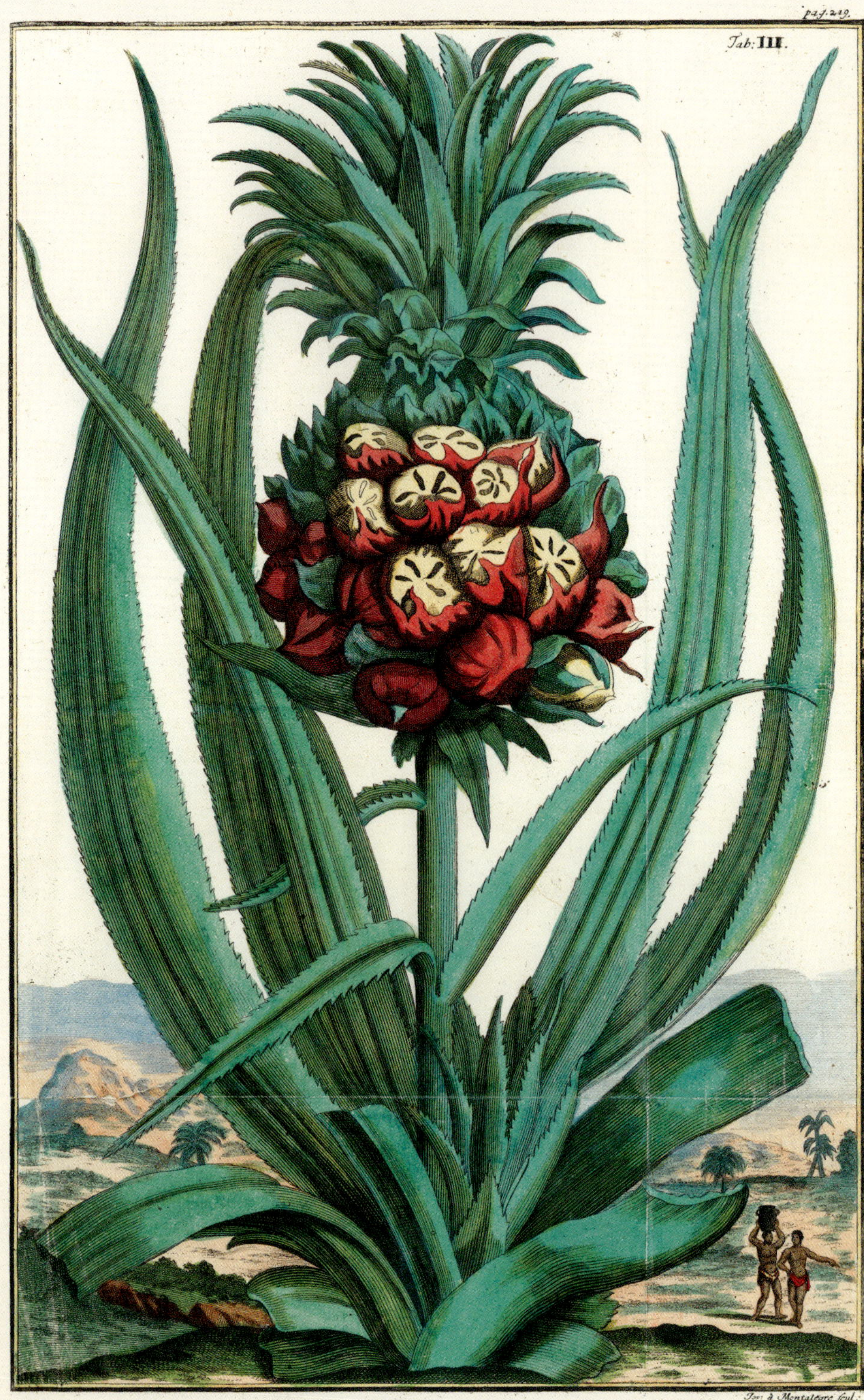

Ananas

Landscape in Central or South America

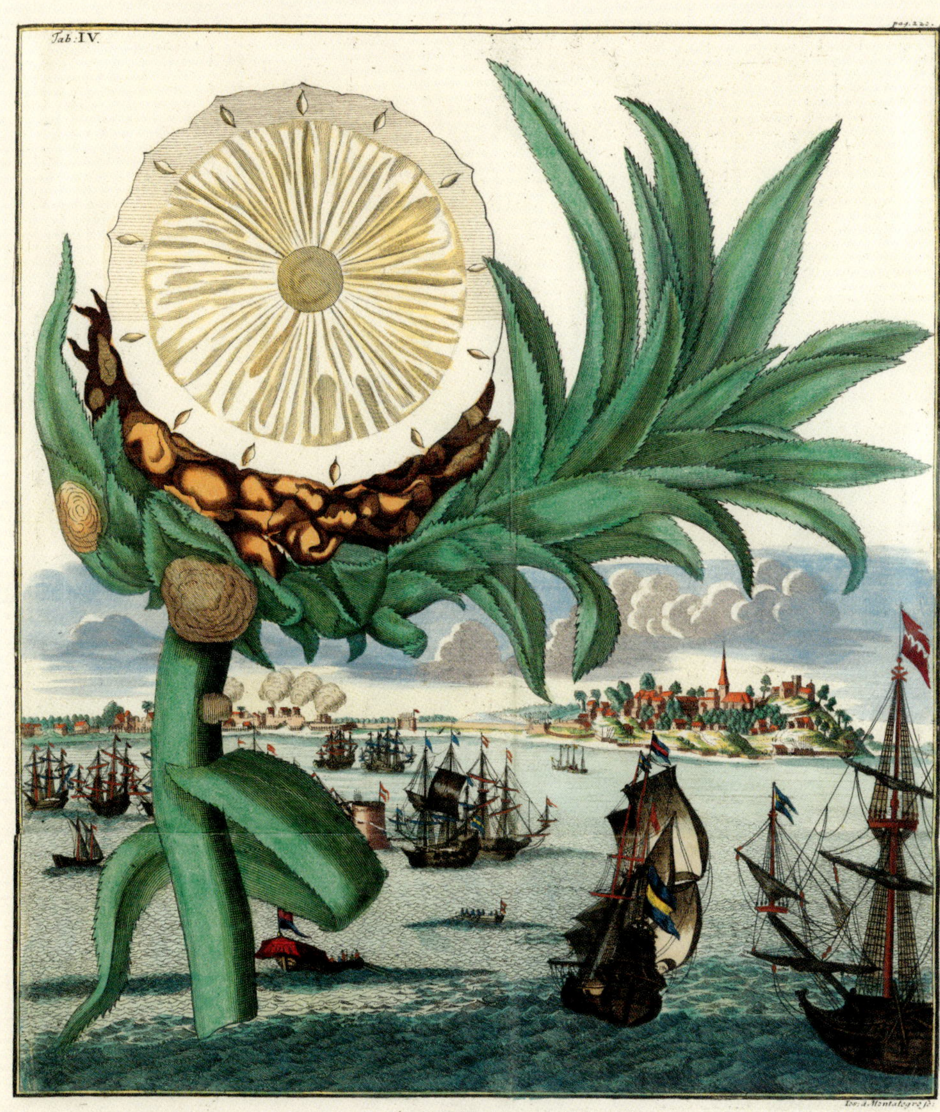

Tab: IV.
pag. 222.
Ios: à Montalegre fe:

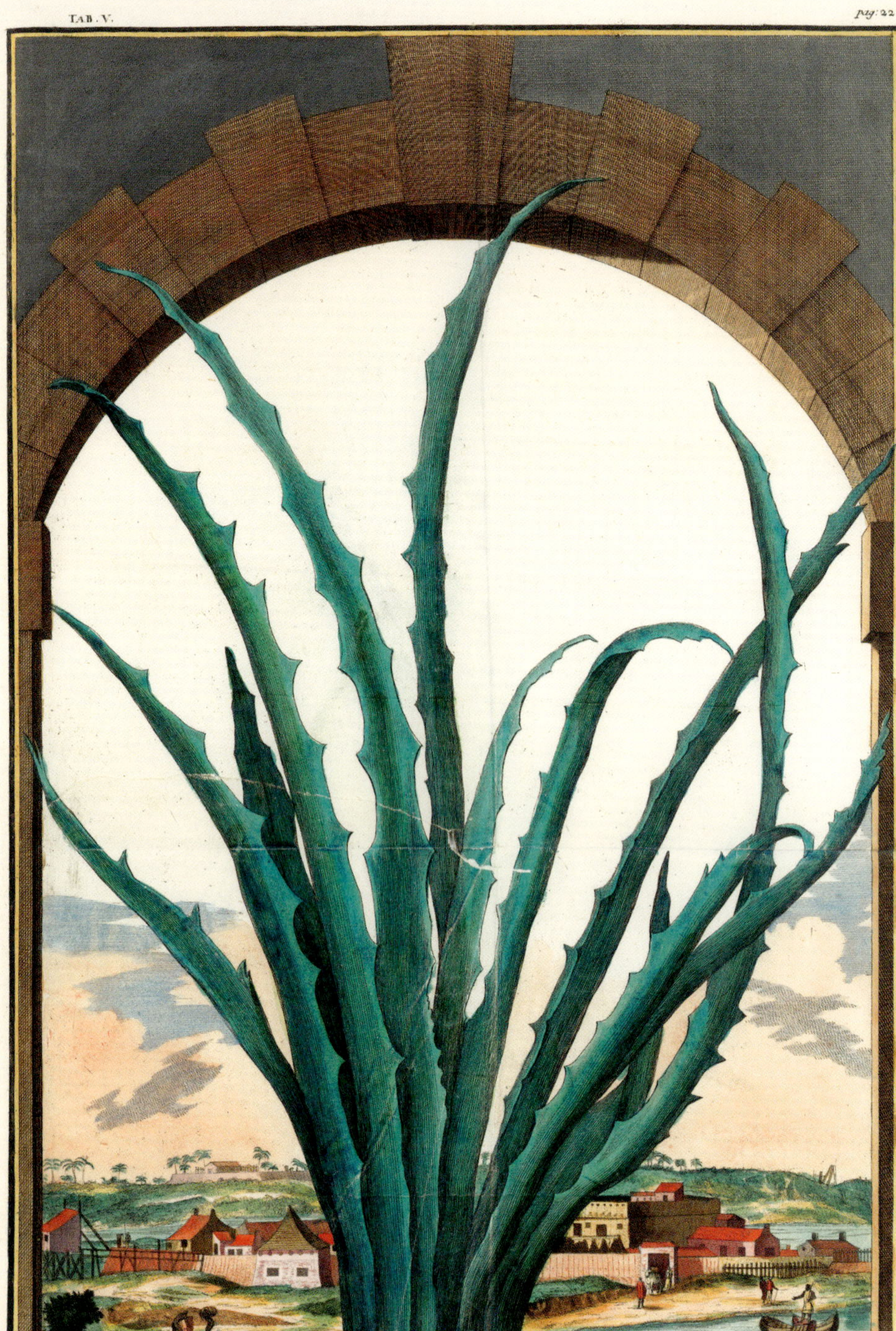

Coastal Town in Central or South America

Dragon tree / Drachenbaum / Dragonnier commun

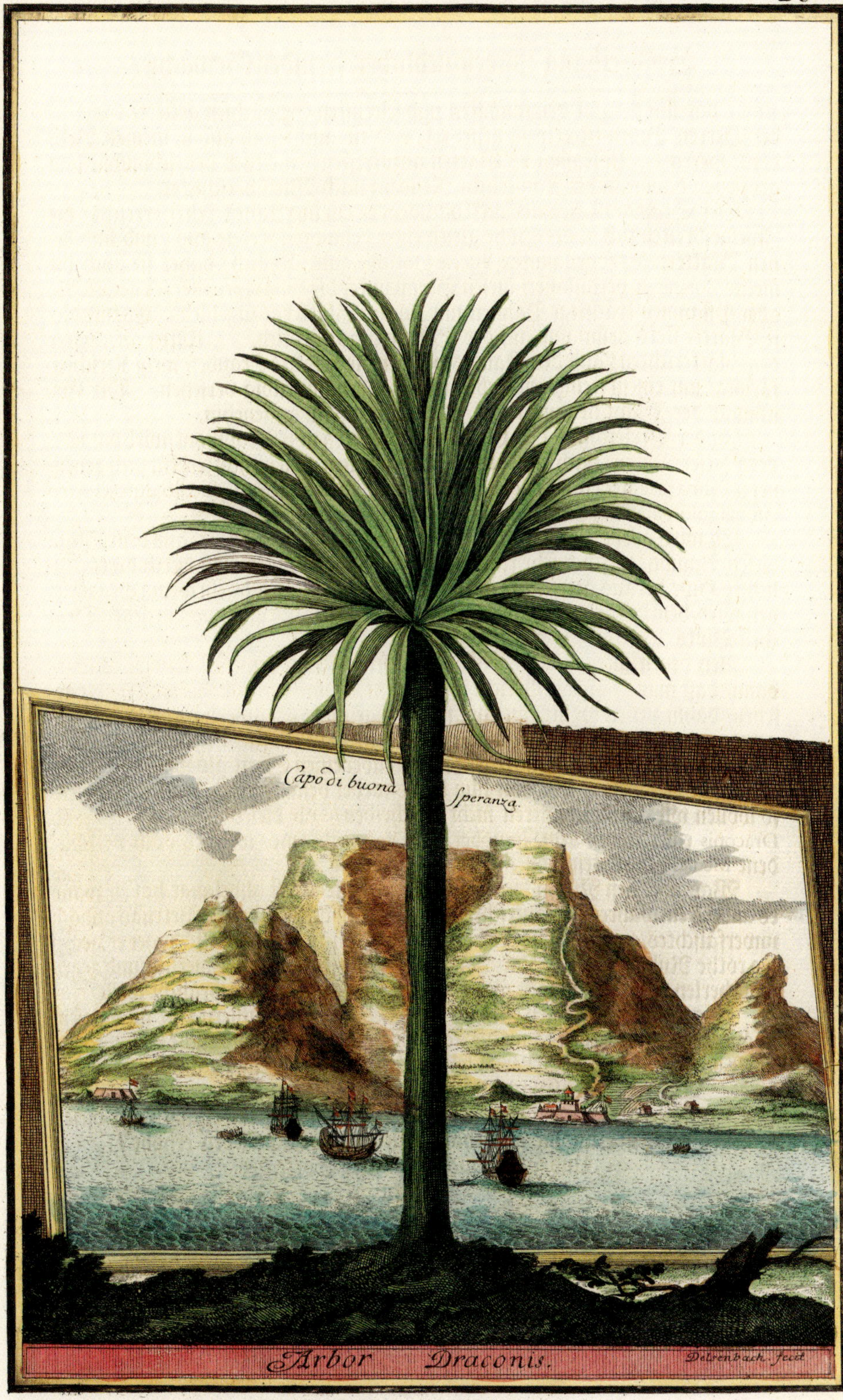

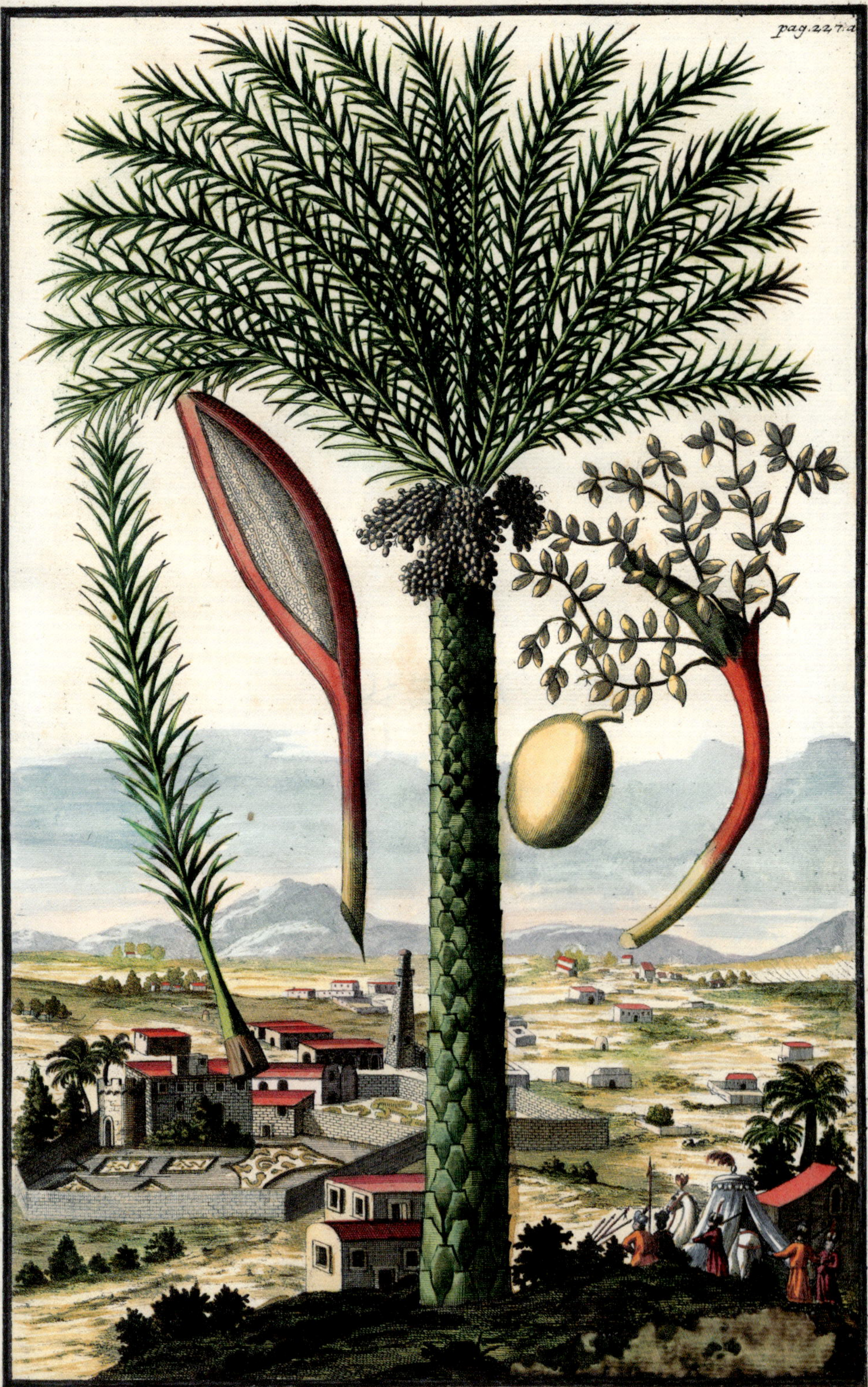

Palma Dactilifera major.

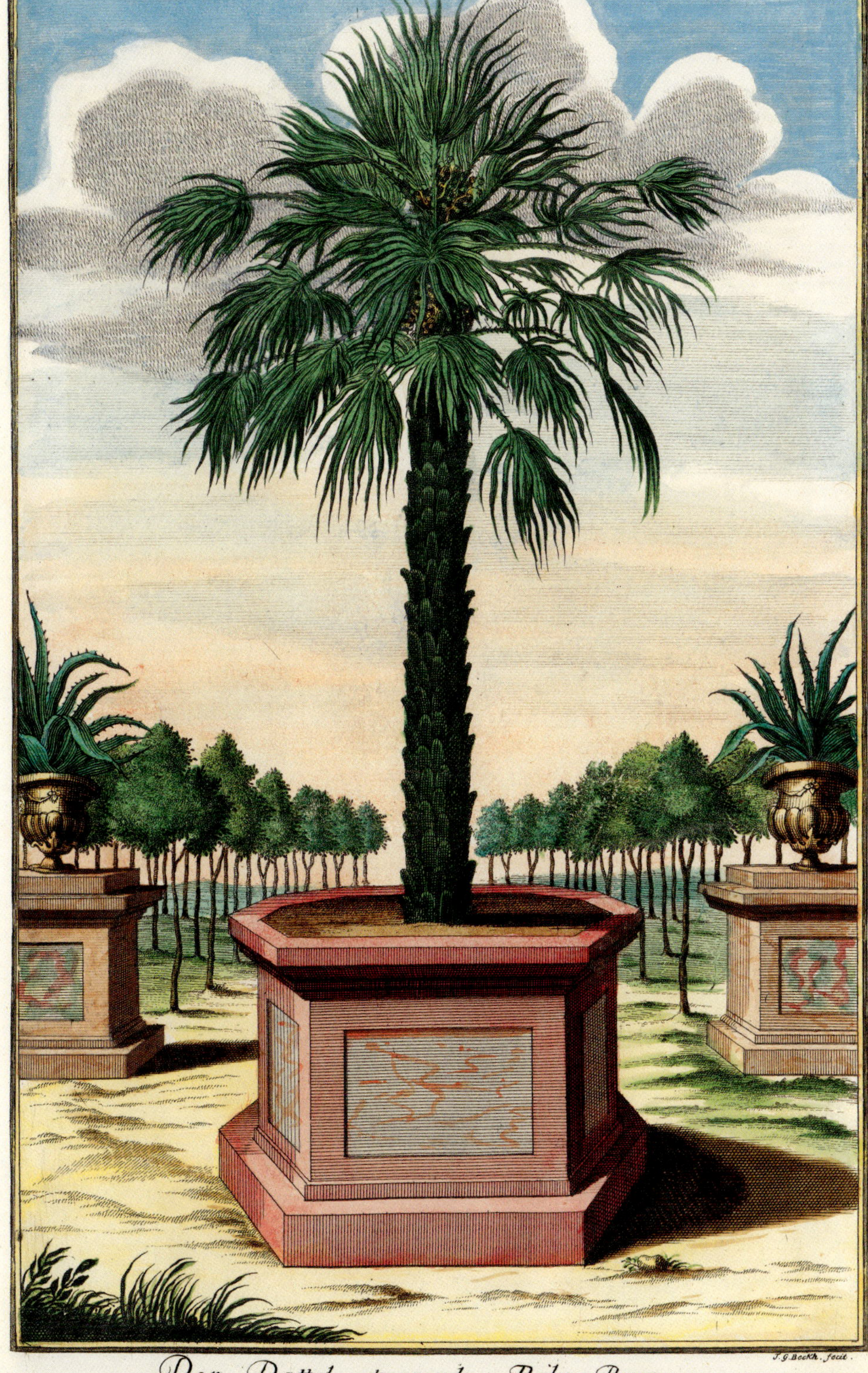
pag. 227.
J. G. Beckh. fecit.
Der Dattel tragende Palm=Baum

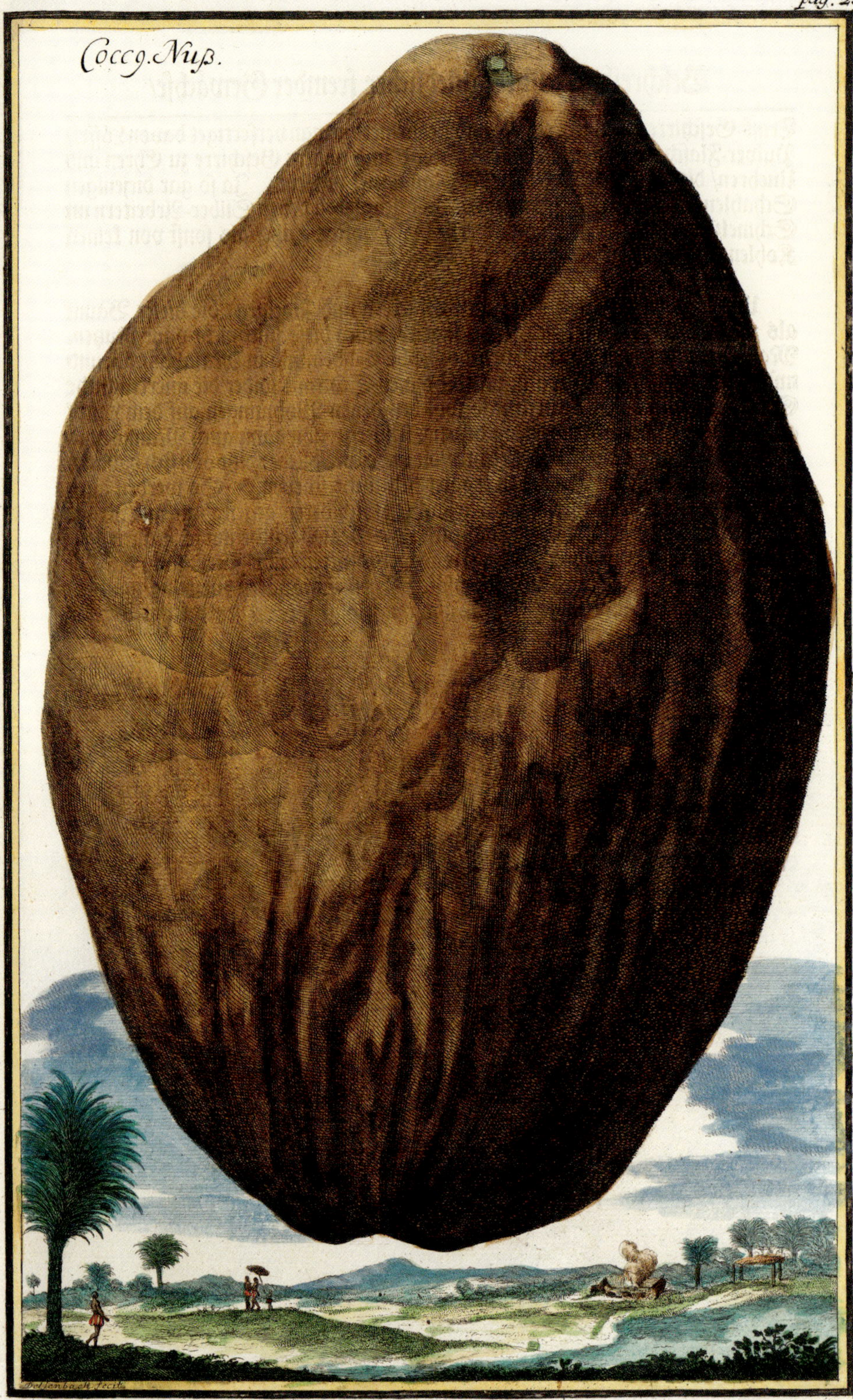

Coconut / Kokosnuss / Noix de coco

Landscape in Central or South America

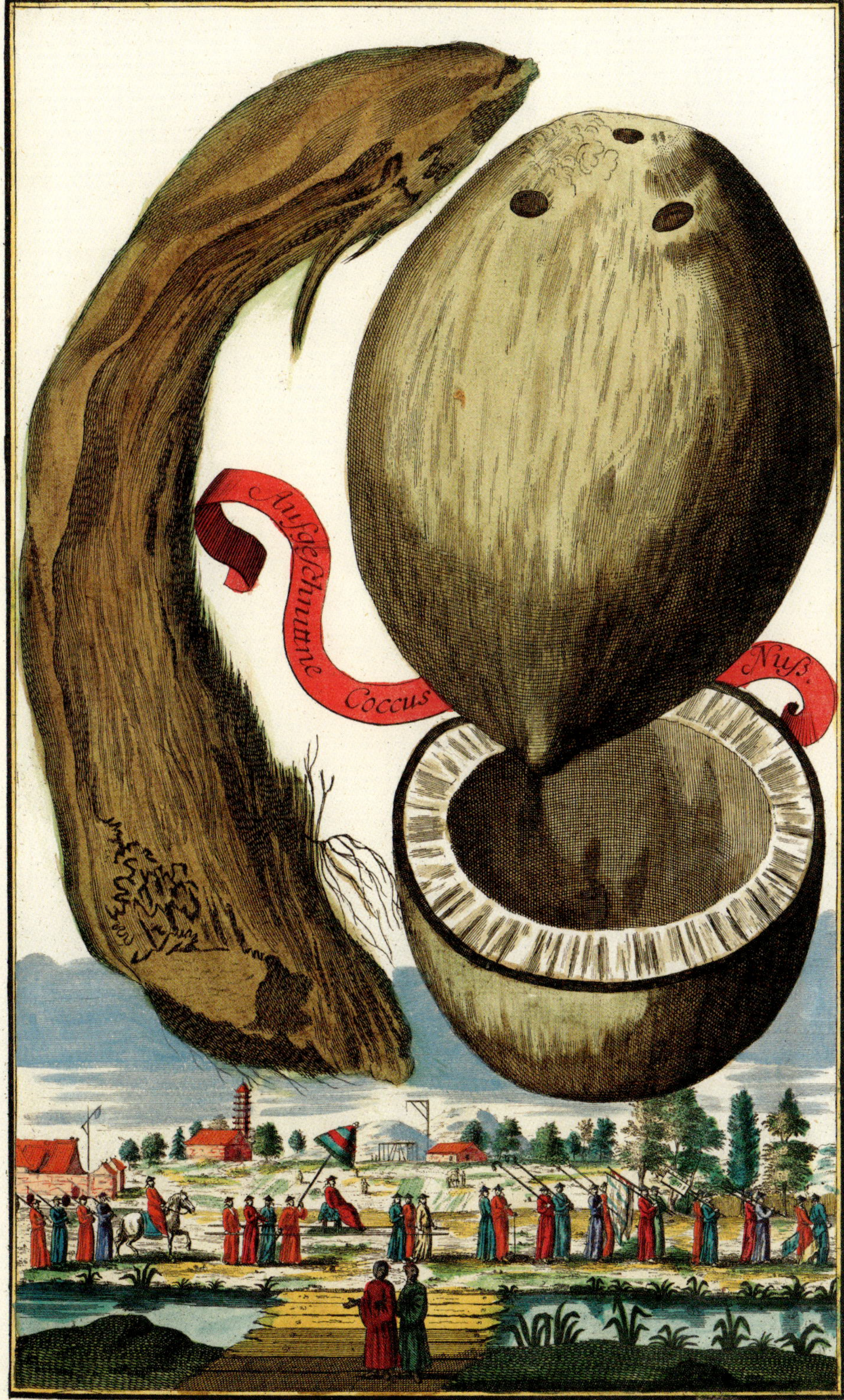
pag: 232.
Außgeschnittne Coccus Nuß.
Vornehmer Herrn Trag=Seſsel zu Pecking in Sina.
Ios: à Montalegre sc.

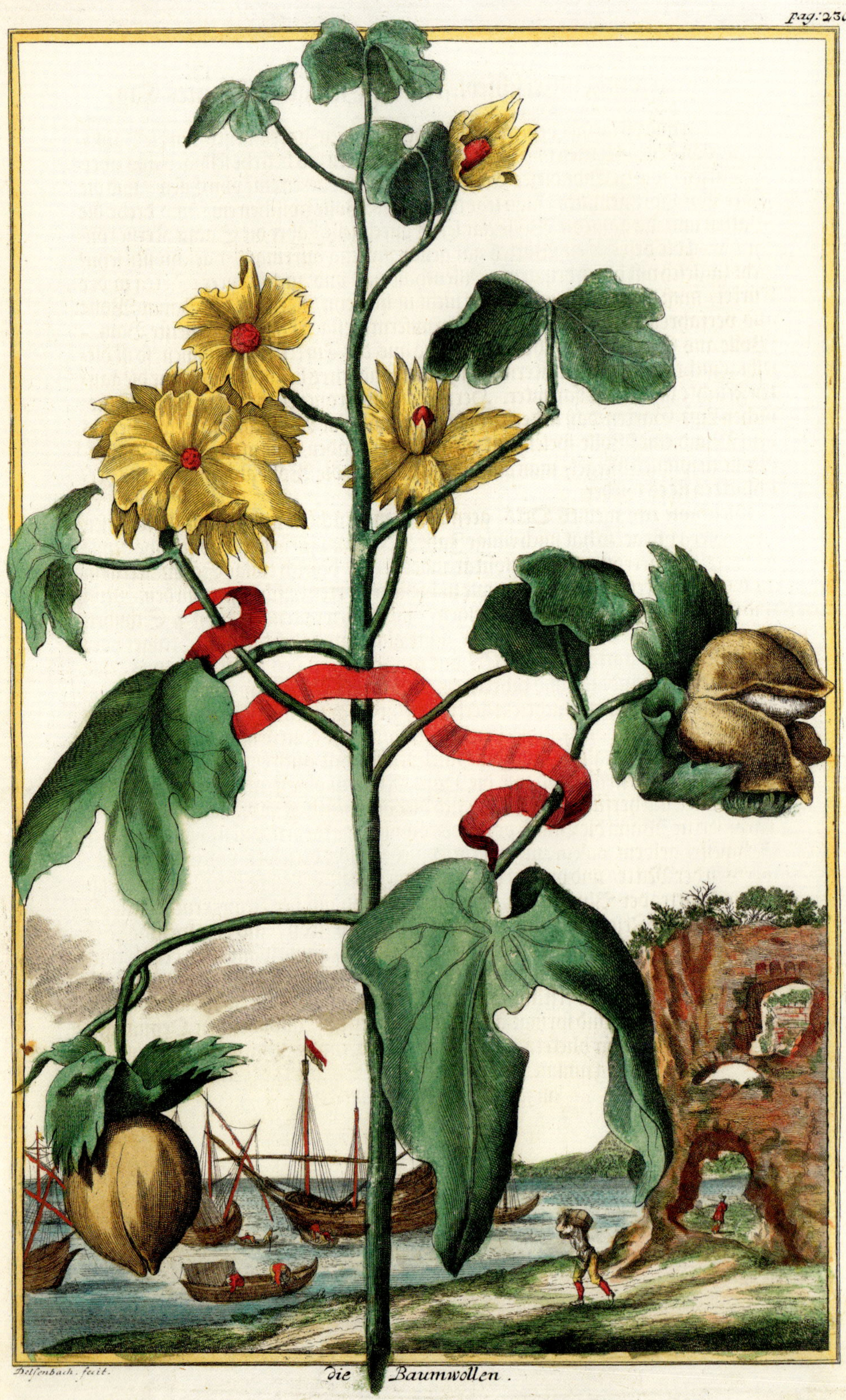

die Baumwollen.

Cotton / Baumwolle / Coton

Coastal Landscape in Asia or in Central or South America

sorgfältigern Fleiß auf jenes Blat gewendet/ und es letzlich dahin gebracht/ daß es vollends aufgebrochen/ und ein sehr zartes Zweiglein daraus entsprossen seye. Als er mir diese Nachricht schrifftlich ertheilet/ so war das Zweiglein/ allbereit einer Spannen lang/ in die Höhe gewachsen. Es ist aber das Blat dabei so dick und hart worden/ als die Rinde eines jungen Pomeranzen-Baums seyn mag/ und hat noch immer seine grüne Farbe beibehalten. In der Mitte mehr-erwehnten Blats/ fahren weiter etliche holzigte Knöpfflein auf/ und zu unterst zeigen sich zwei Warzen/ daß also die Vermuthung ist/ es dörfften auch daraus noch einige Aestlein hervorbrechen. Anbei ist der Stiel des eingesteckten Blats/ und die ganze Rippe in dem Blat/ zimlich dick und aufgeschwollen worden/ woraus nach und nach das junge Zweiglein entstanden ist/ und gleichet es allerdings einem Stämmlein/ welches aus der Erden von einem eingesteckten Kern entsprossen ist. Es ist auch so gar unter der Erden/ ein zimlicher runder Knollen gewachsen/ der einer kleinen Zwiebel ähnlich kommt/ aus welchem dann die Wurzel des zarten Stämmleins worden ist.

Viele/ welche die Beschaffenheit dieser Sache zumal nicht wissen/ werden sich dieses nicht einzubilden vermögen/ sondern auf die Gedanken kommen/ der kleine Stiel/ zusamt den mittlern Adern/ seye eine weiche und safftige Materie/ etwan wie andere Stiele an den Blumen/ an welchen keine Wurzeln anschlagen noch sich ergeben können. Jedoch/ bei genäuerm Einsehen und mehrerm Durchsuchen/ habe ich es anderst gesehen und befunden. Dann ich habe ein starkes Citronen-Blat abgebrochen und genommen/ und die äussere grüne Schelffe daran/ mit einem scharffen Messer abgeschabet/ da hat es sich dann ergeben/ daß das Inwendige wie Holz ist/ und ganz dinn und subtil/ wie ein zarter Drat/ durch die ganze mittlere Rippe hinaufgehet. Nemlich/ gleichwie man das Holz siehet/ so man die äusserste Rinde an einem Aestlein abschabet/ also ists auch mit den gedachten Blättern inwendig beschaffen. Es lässet sich zwar ferner dieses inwendige holzigte Wesen der Blätter gar leicht beugen/ und krümmen/ wie man will; aber so gleich/ und ohne einige Gewalt und Stärke/ lässt es sich nicht abbrechen noch abreissen. Dieweilen nun in den Stielen der Blätter sich was holzigtes herfür thut/ so vermuthe ich nicht ohne Grund/ es werden die Wurzeln daran sich gründen und wachsen/ fast auf die Art und Weise/ als wie man zarte Steck-Reiser in die Erde einstecket/ und sie anschlagen läßt. Man gebe sich nur die Mühe/ und schlage fol. 32. dieser meiner Continuation auf/ so wird/ nebst andern gewurzelten Blättern/ auch ein Citronen-Blat sich vorstellen/ und mit Lit. C. bezeichnet seyn.

Ende des ganzen Werks.

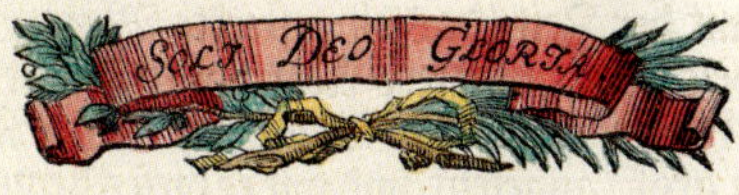

Gg 2 Haupt-

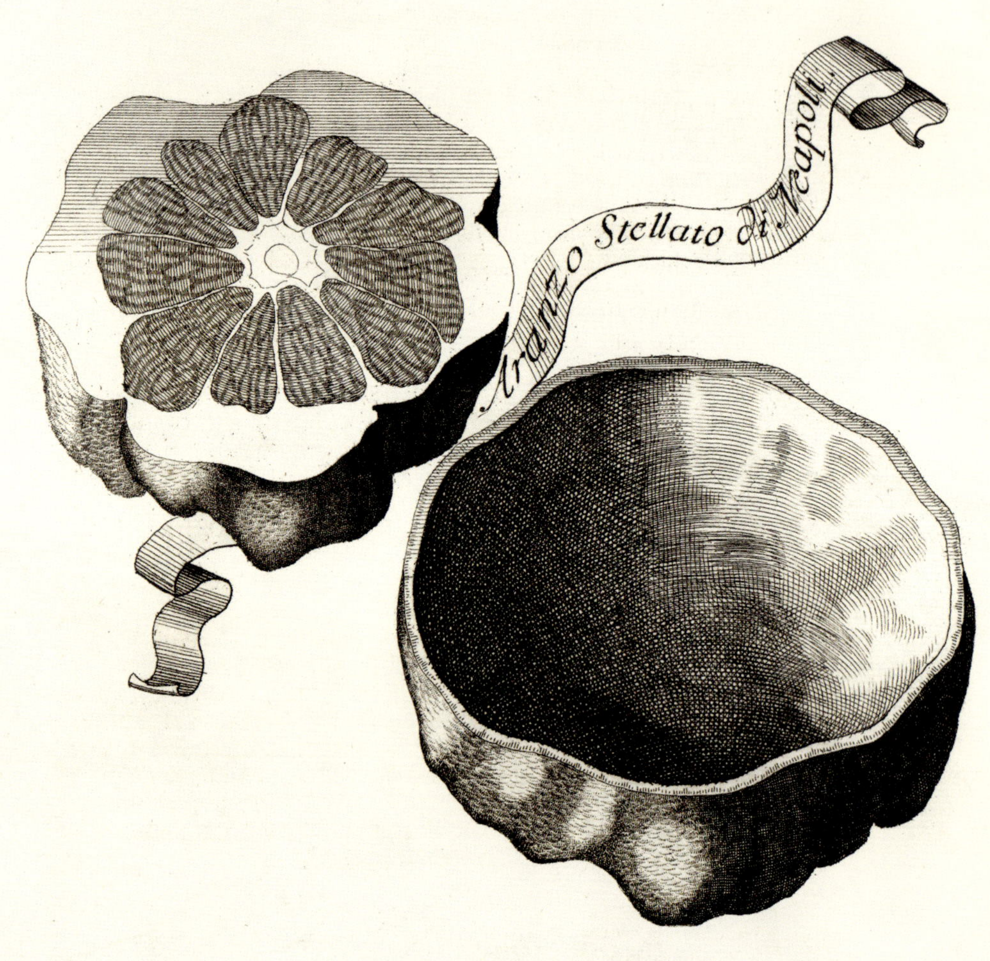
Aranzo Stellato di Napoli.

Volume III

The Universitätsbibliothek Erlangen-Nürnberg houses a set of 62 proofs for the planned third volume of the Hesperides, which was never actually published. The set includes 58 plates together with a title-page engraving and three vignettes. The order of the plates presented here follows a list drawn up by Volkamer held in the Department of Prints and Drawings in the Germanisches Nationalmuseum in Nuremberg: "Specification for the illustrations drawn from life and engraved in copper in the second Continuation, being the third part of the Nuremberg Hesperides" (Sign. ZR 6562 Kaps 1077). Eight proofs, which are not listed in Volkamer's "Specification", have been assigned to the corresponding citrus species.

In der Universitätsbibliothek Erlangen-Nürnberg ist ein Konvolut von 62 Andrucken für den geplanten dritten Band des Hesperidenwerks erhalten, der allerdings nicht veröffentlicht wurde. Er umfasst 58 Tafeln plus Titelkupfer und drei Vignetten. Die Anordnung der Tafeln in der vorliegenden Publikation folgt einer von Volkamer verfassten Liste mit dem Titel „Specification derer nach dem Leben gezeichneten und in das Kupfer gebrachte Figuren, zu der zweiten Continuation, als den III. Theil der Nürnbergischen Hesperidum", die sich in der Graphischen Sammlung des Germanischen Nationalmuseum Nürnberg befindet (Sign. ZR 6562 Kaps 1077). Acht Andrucke, die nicht in Volkamers „Specification" aufgelistetet sind, wurden der jeweiligen Zitrussorte zugeordnet.

L'Universitätsbibliothek Erlangen-Nürnberg abrite une liasse de 62 épreuves, conservée pour le troisième volume du Livre des Hespérides qui n'a toutefois pas été publié. Il comprend 58 planches avec une page de titre et trois vignettes. L'agencement des planches dans la présente publication se réfère à une liste dressée par Volkamer qui se trouve dans la Graphische Sammlung du Germanisches Nationalmuseum de Nuremberg : « Spécification pour les illustrations dessinées d'après nature et gravées dans le cuivre, dans la deuxième continuation, constituant la troisième partie des Hespérides de Nuremberg » (cote ZR 6562 Kaps 1077). Huit épreuves qui ne sont pas répertoriées dans la « Spécification » de Volkamer ont été attribuées à l'espèce d'agrume correspondante.

Aranzo Stellato da Neapoli, detail (see p. 458)

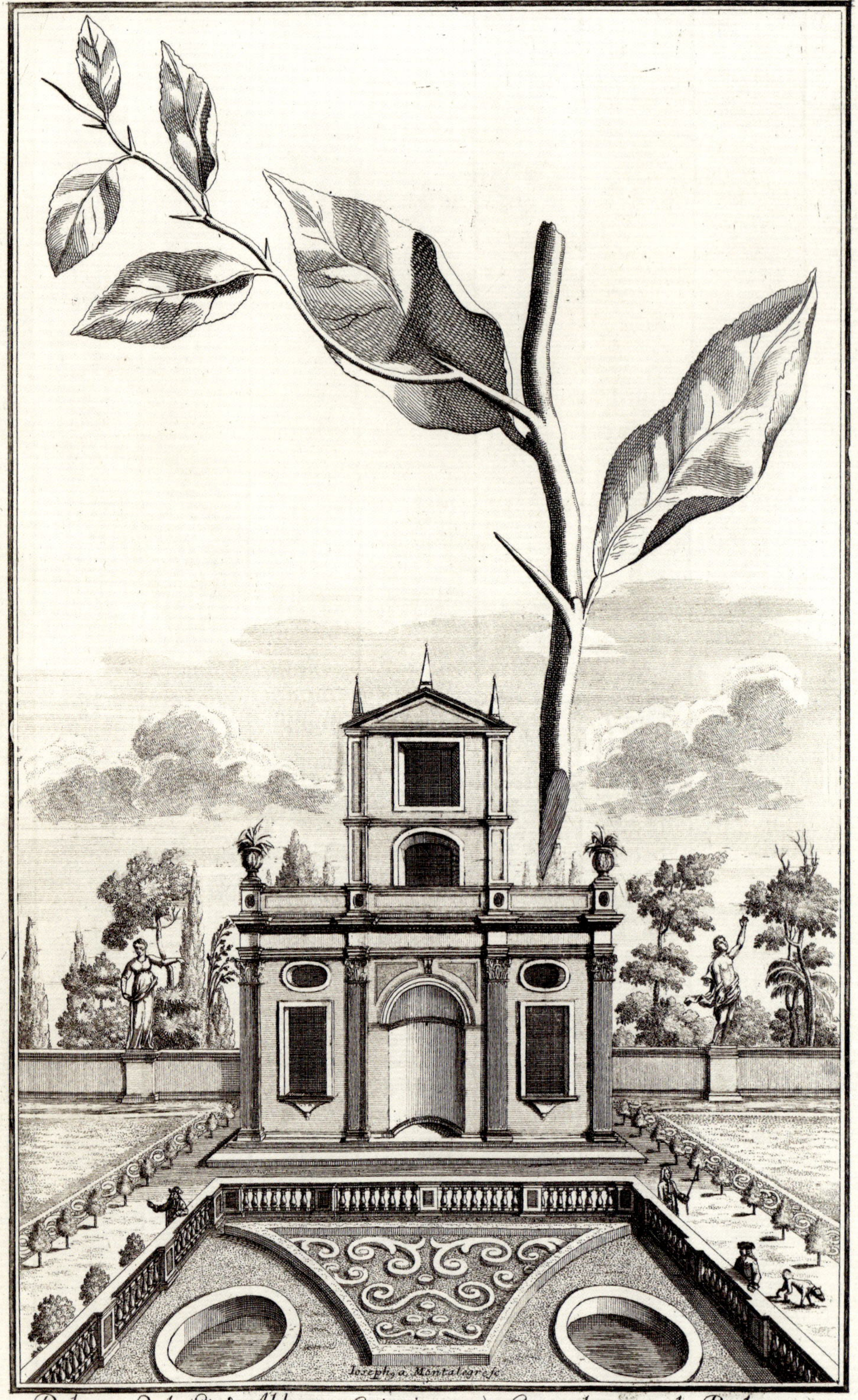

Palazzo del Sig.r Abbate Cristiano à Cuspolano nel Bolognese.

Bologna, Cuspolano – Villa Abbate Cristiano

Cedro con frutto in frutto

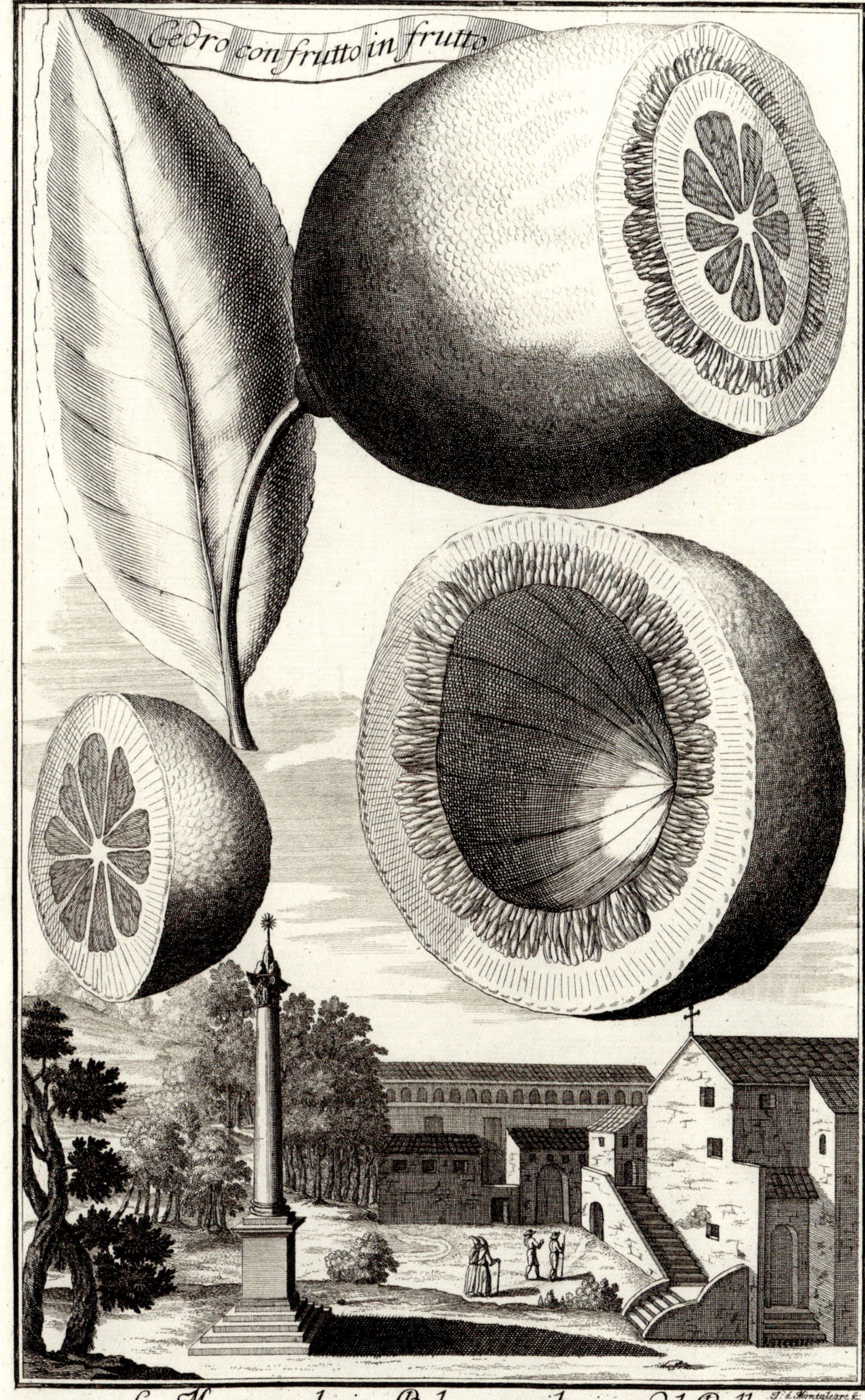

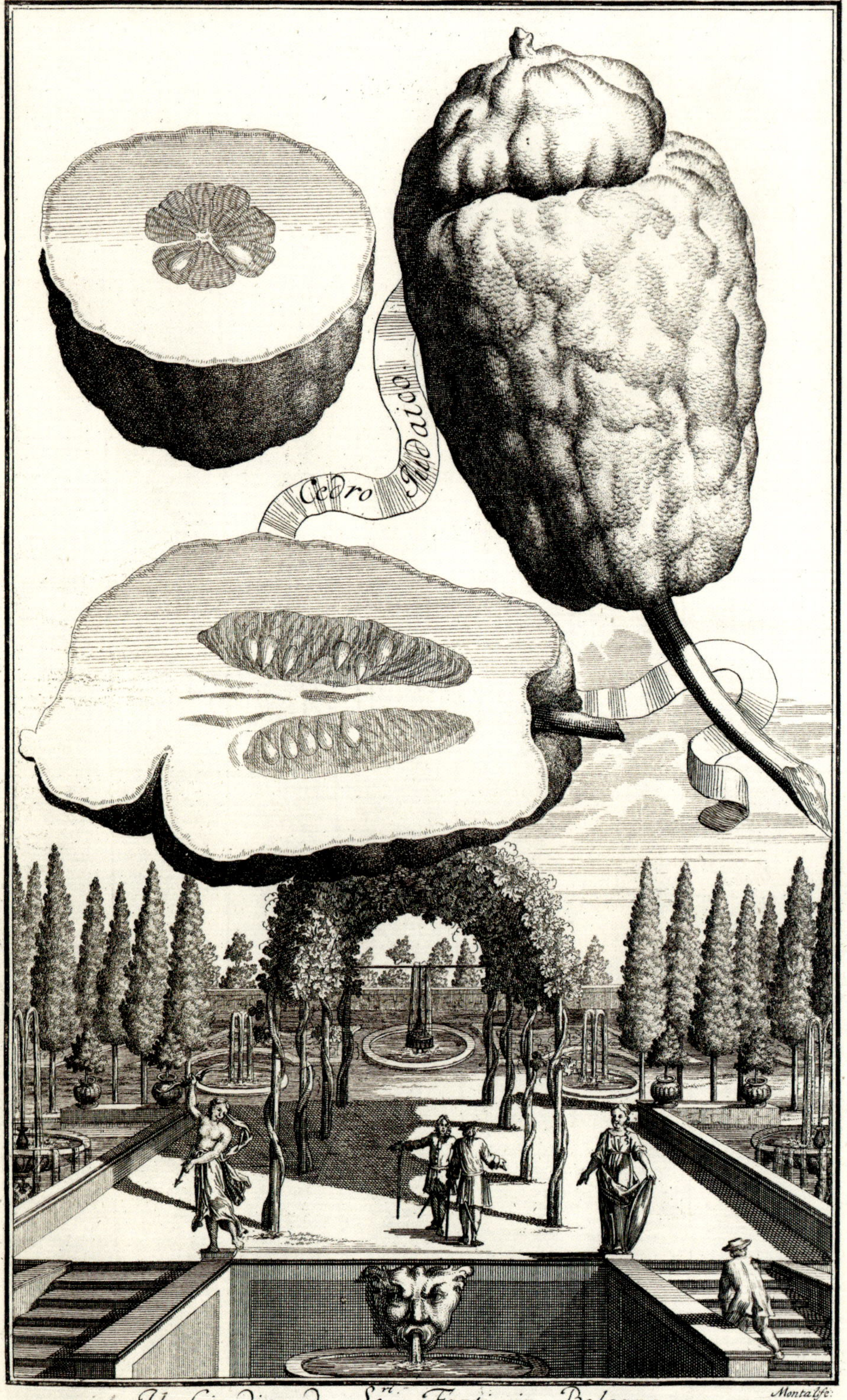
Cedro Iudaico
Il Giardino de Sr. Forti in Bologna.
Montalfe.

Cedro dolce

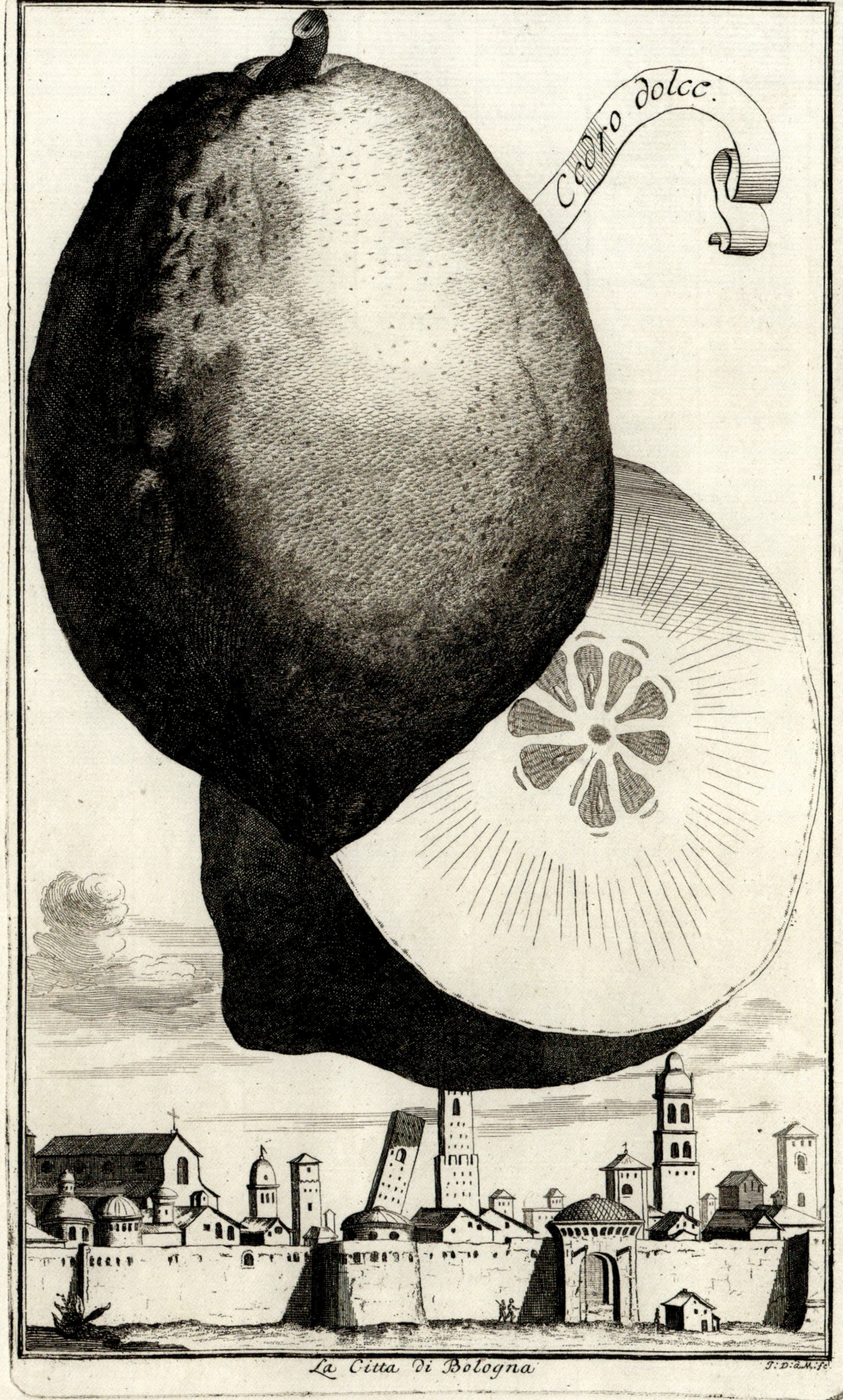

Cedro Bisanzone

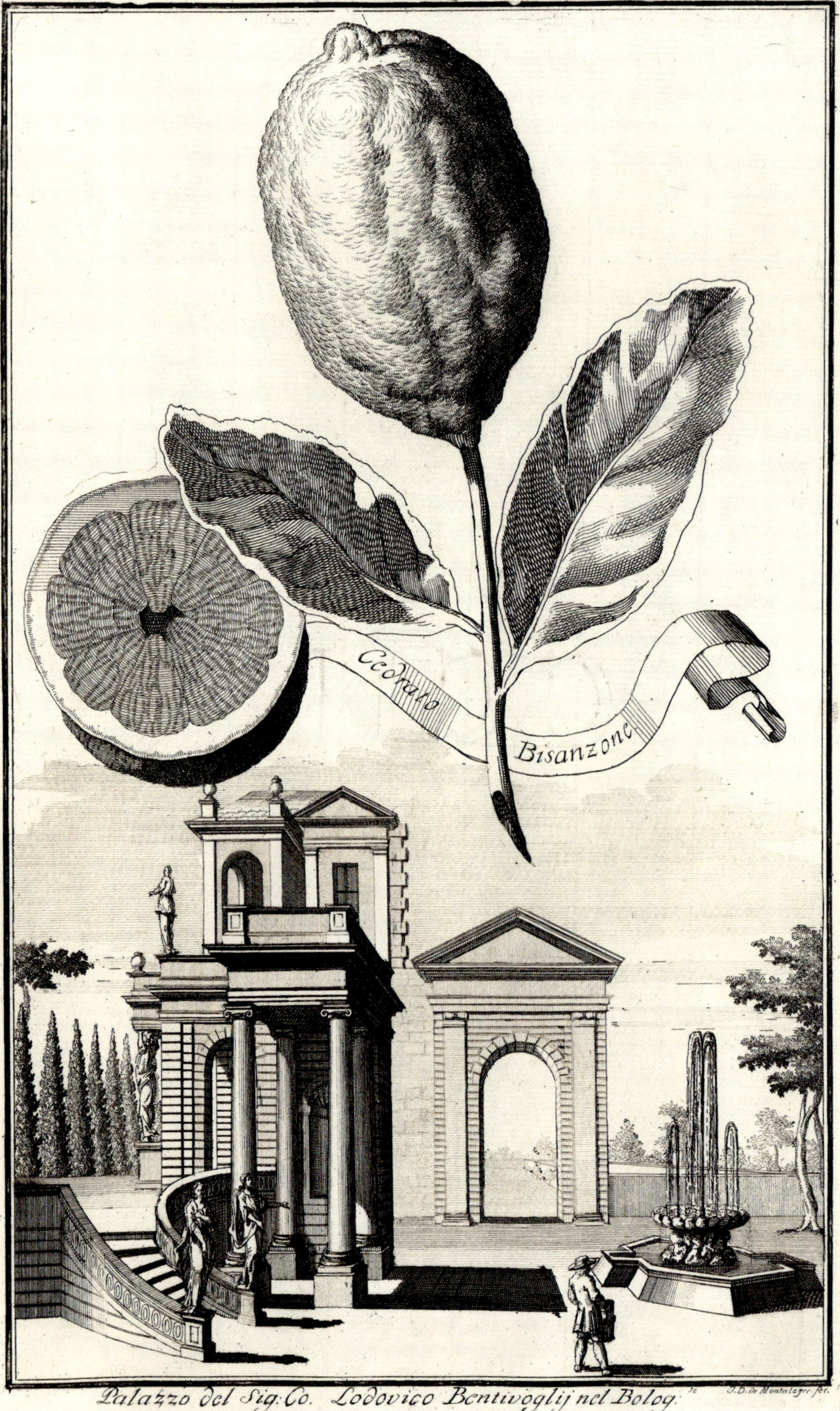

Cedrilia

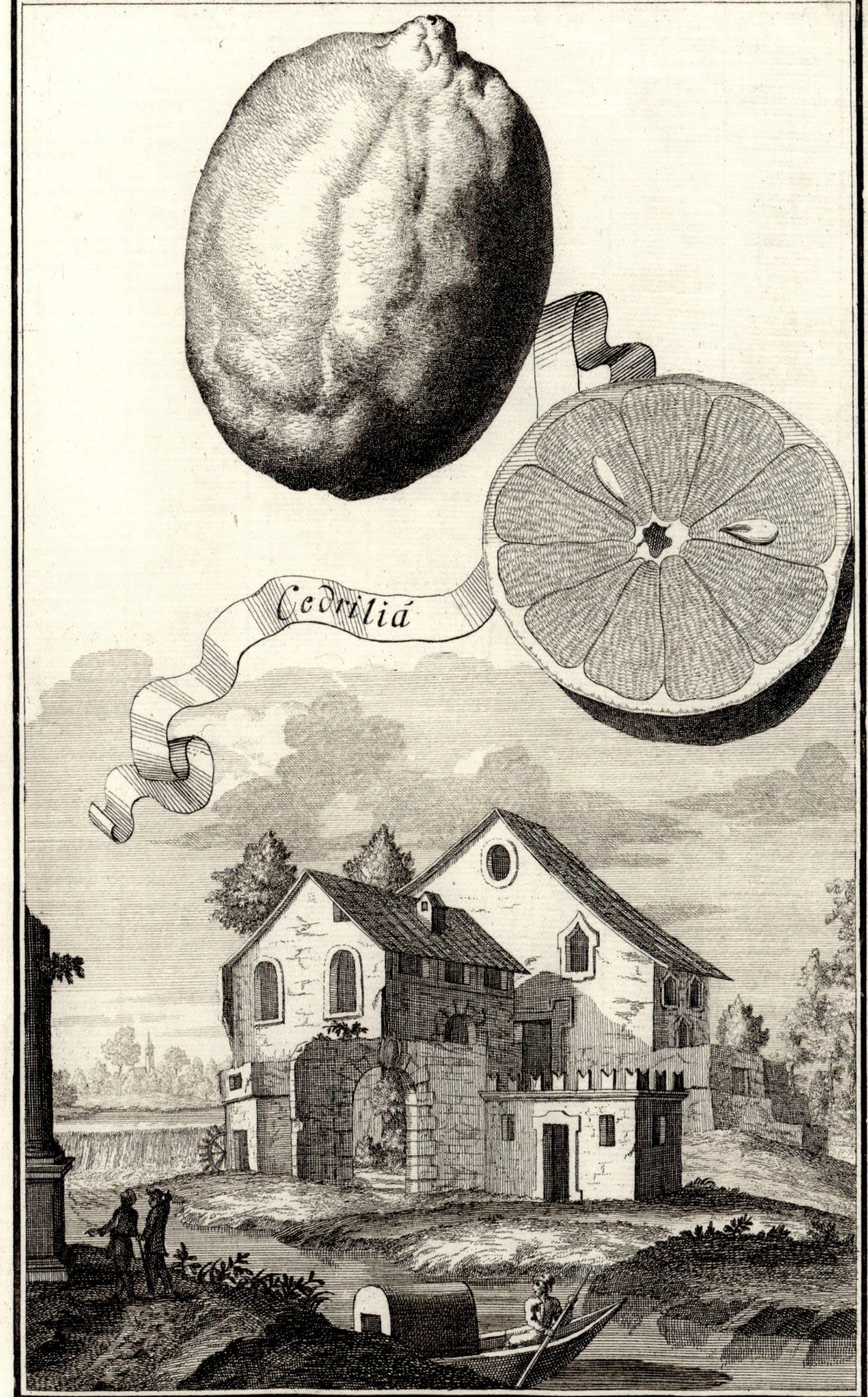

Bologna, Battiferro

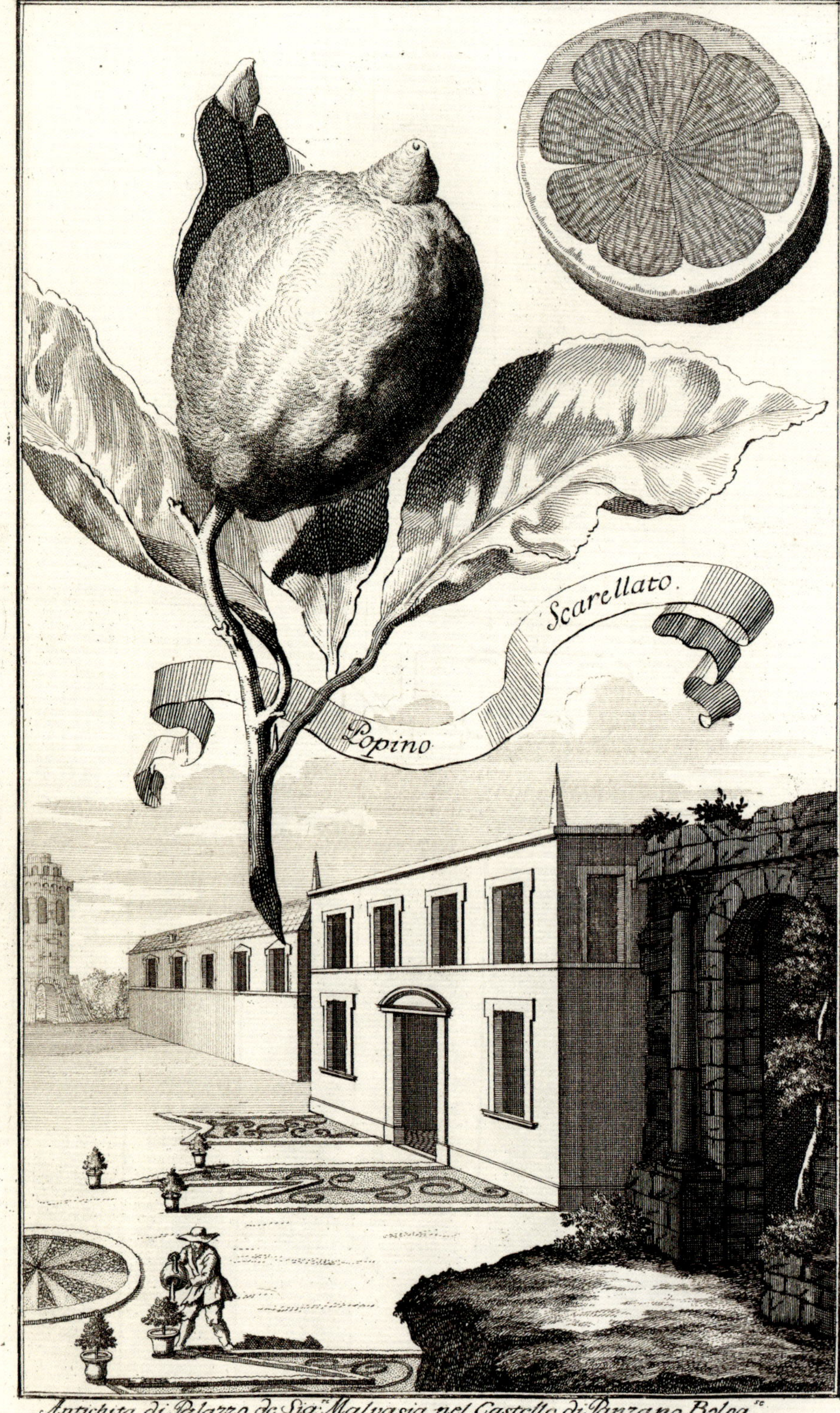

Popino Scarellato

Panzano di Castelfranco Emilia (Modena) – Palazzo Malvasia

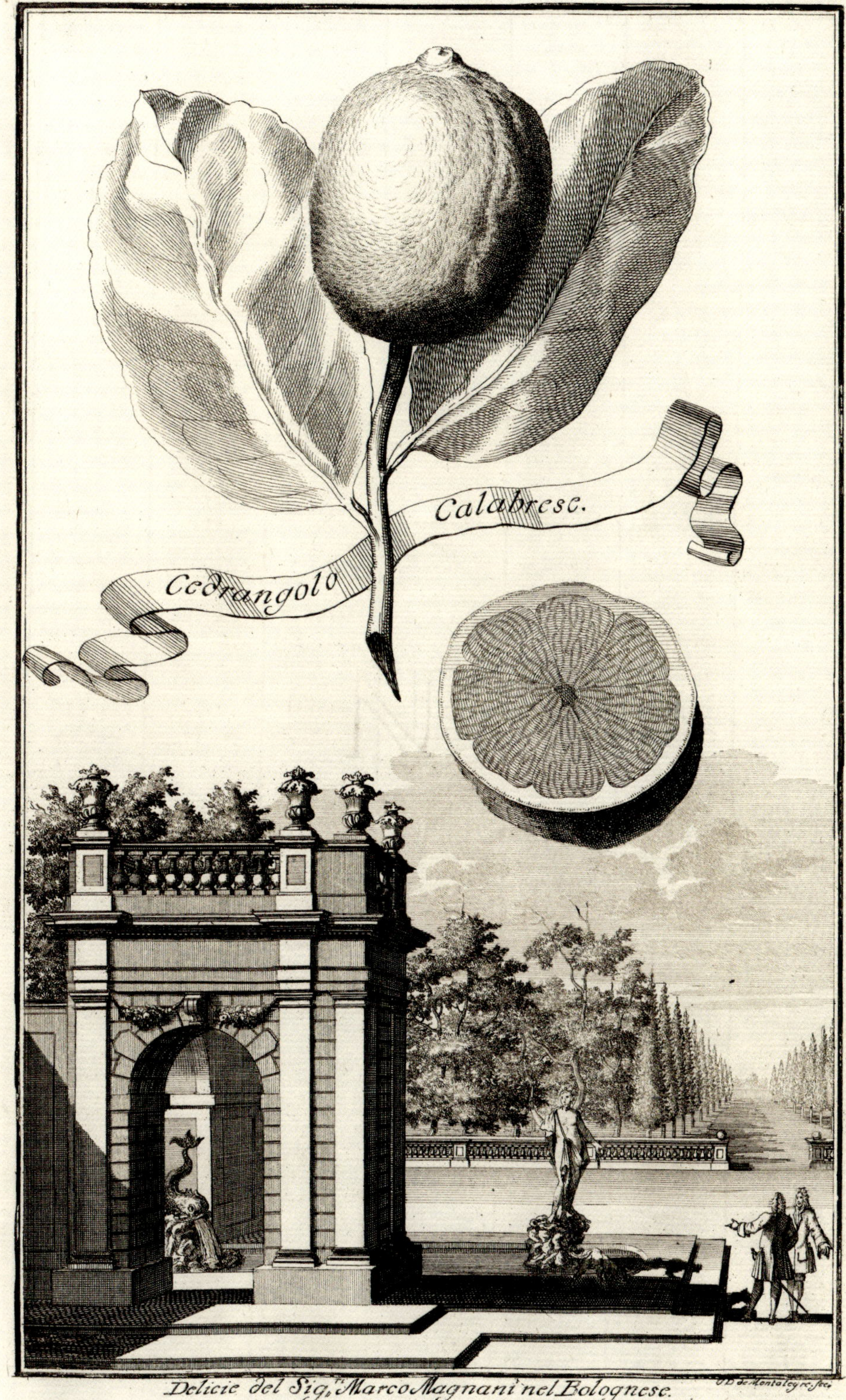
Cedrangolo Calabrese.
Delicie del Sig.r Marco Magnani nel Bolognese.

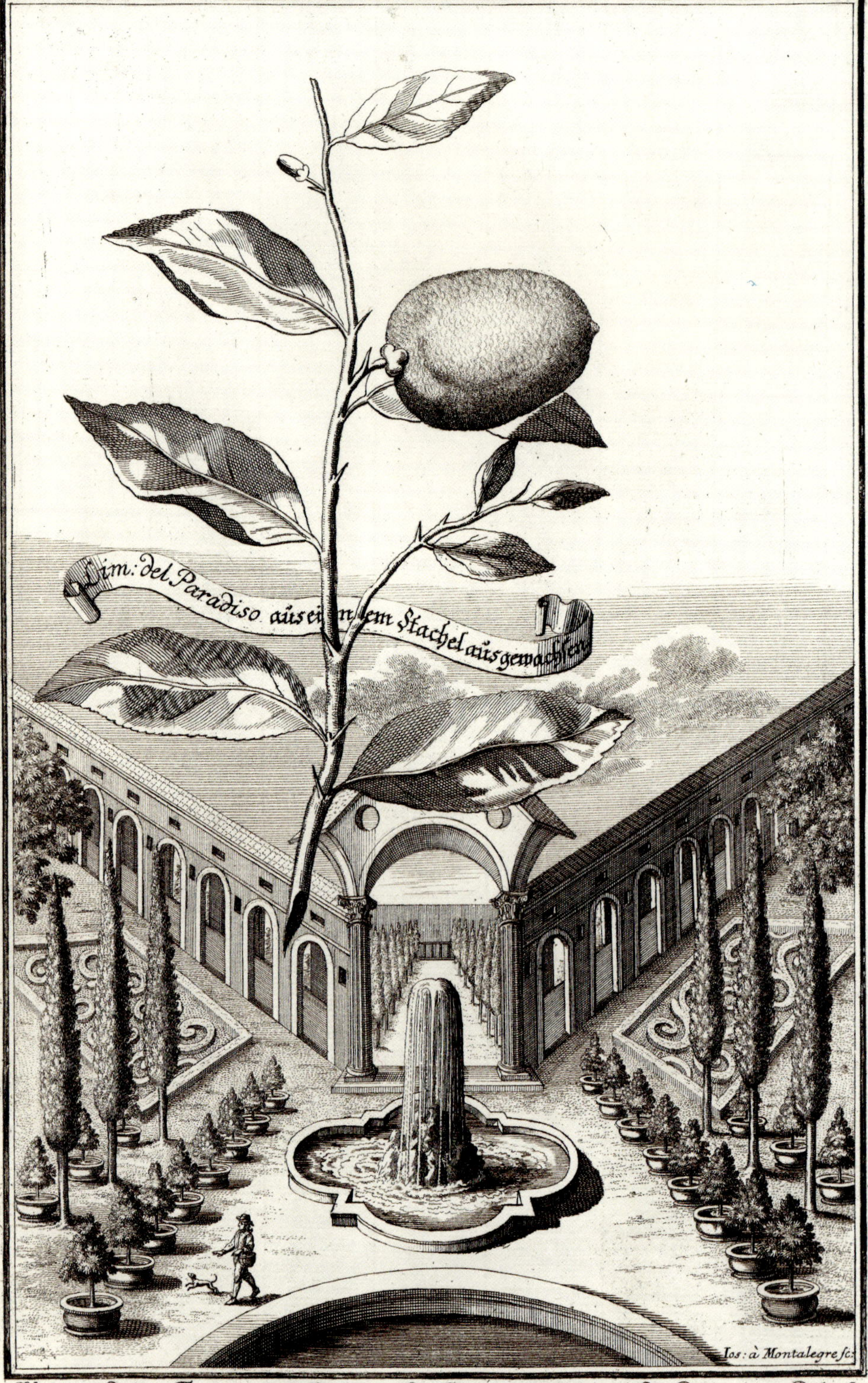

Veduta della Fontana del Ill: Sig: Co: Pepoli nel comune di Rigosa in Bolog:ª

Citrus limon

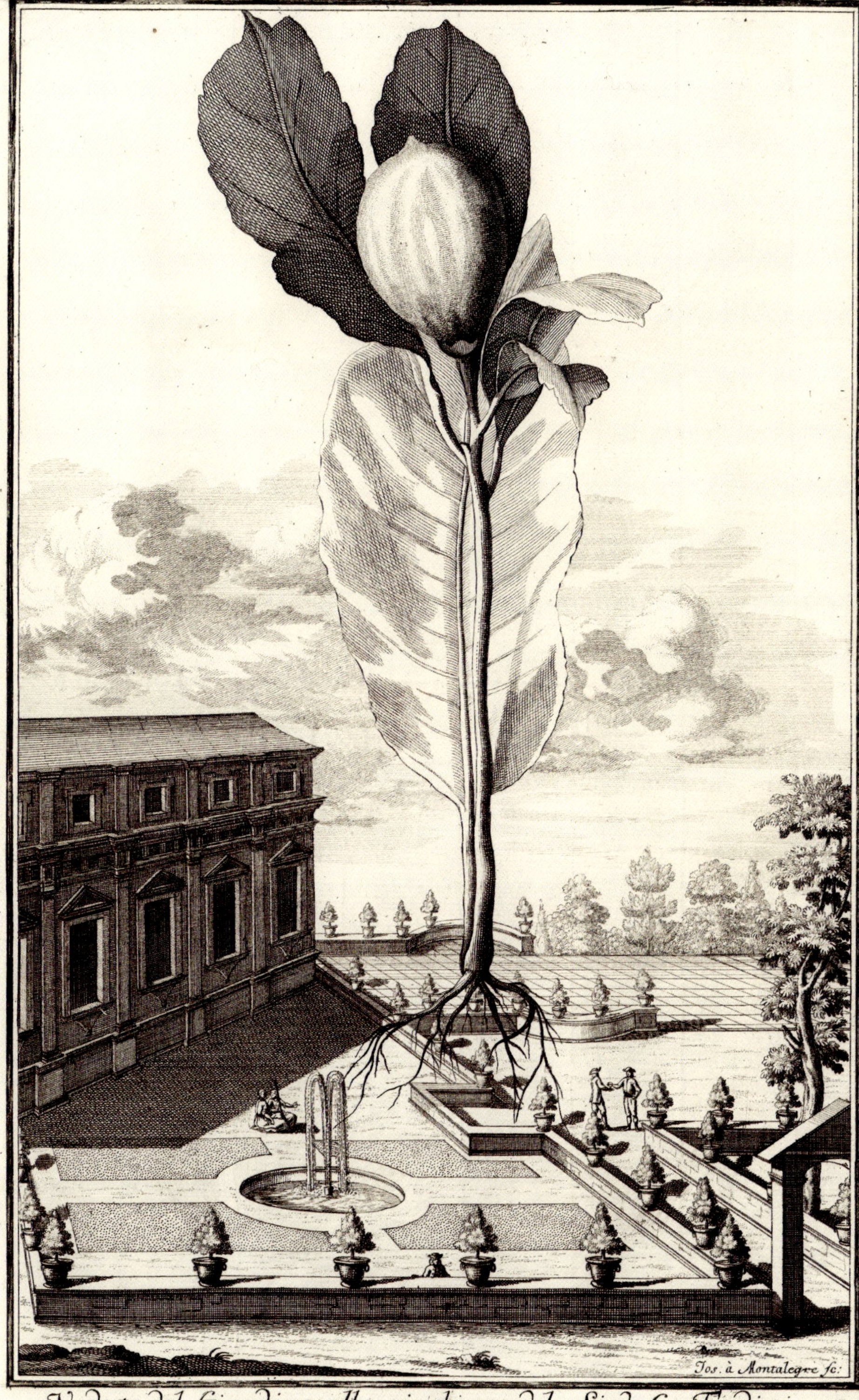

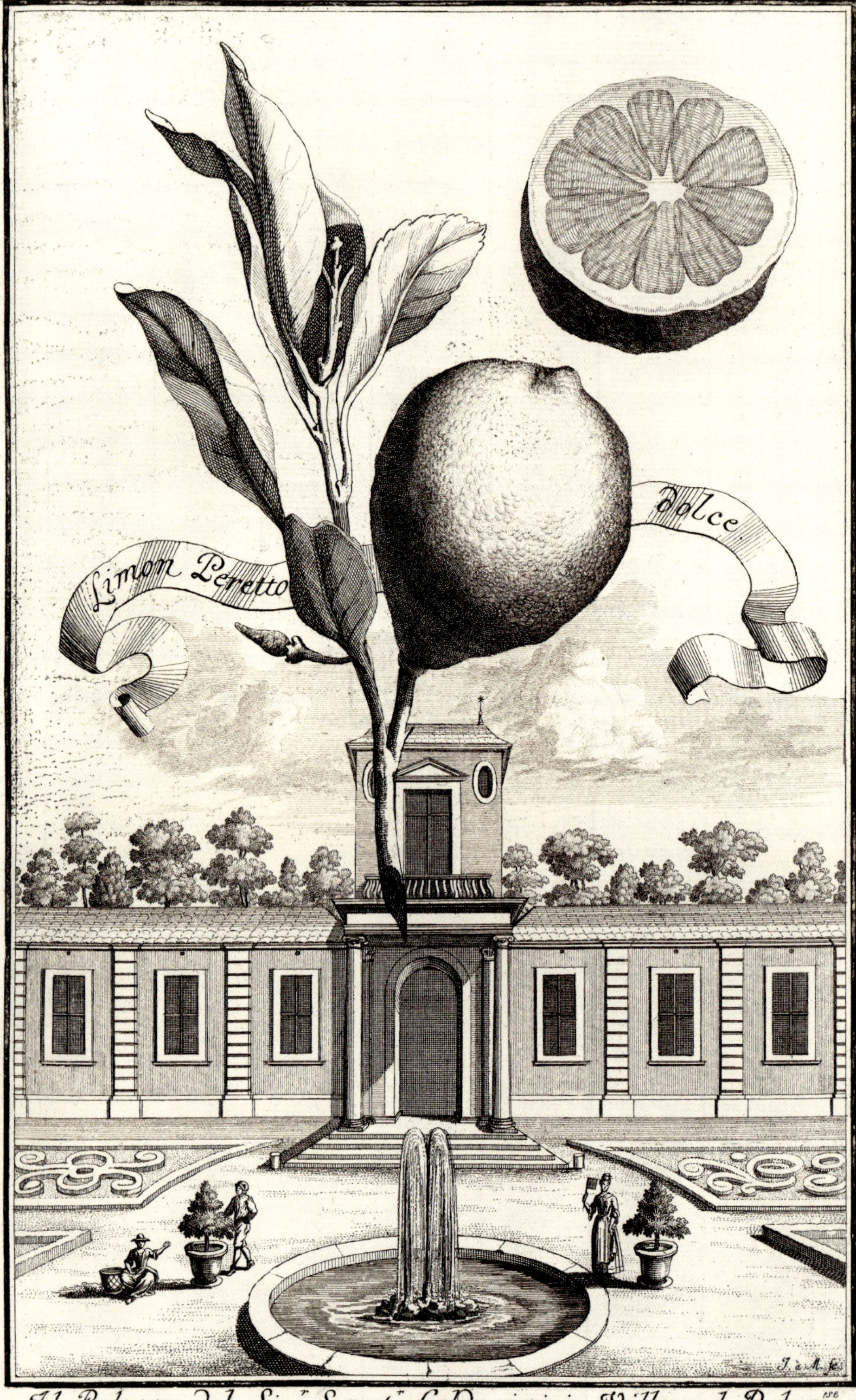

Limon Peretto dolce

Bologna – Villa Calderini

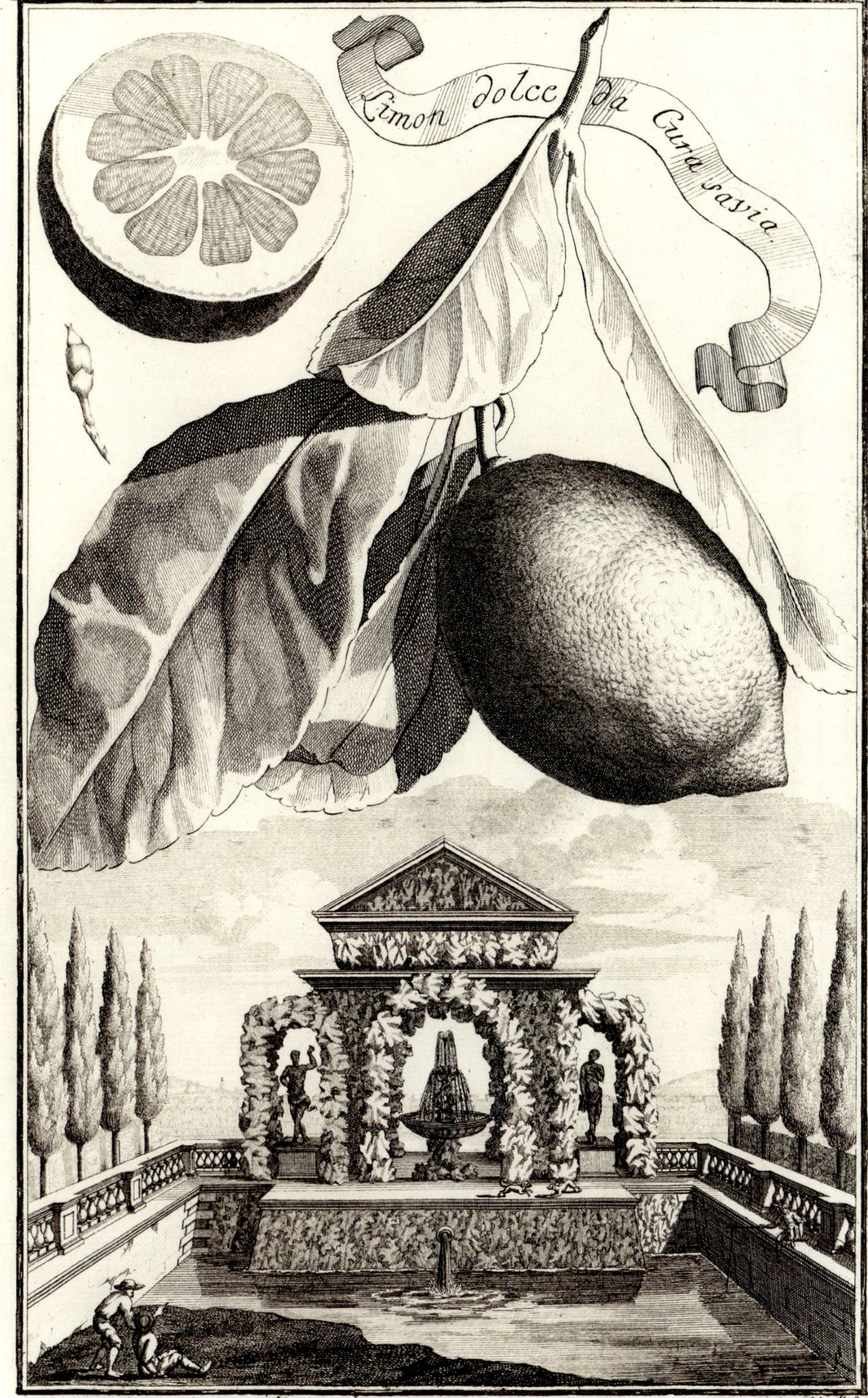

Limon dolce da Cura savia

Mirabello (Ferrara) – Ranuzzi Grotto

Limon dolce con foglia vari[e]gata

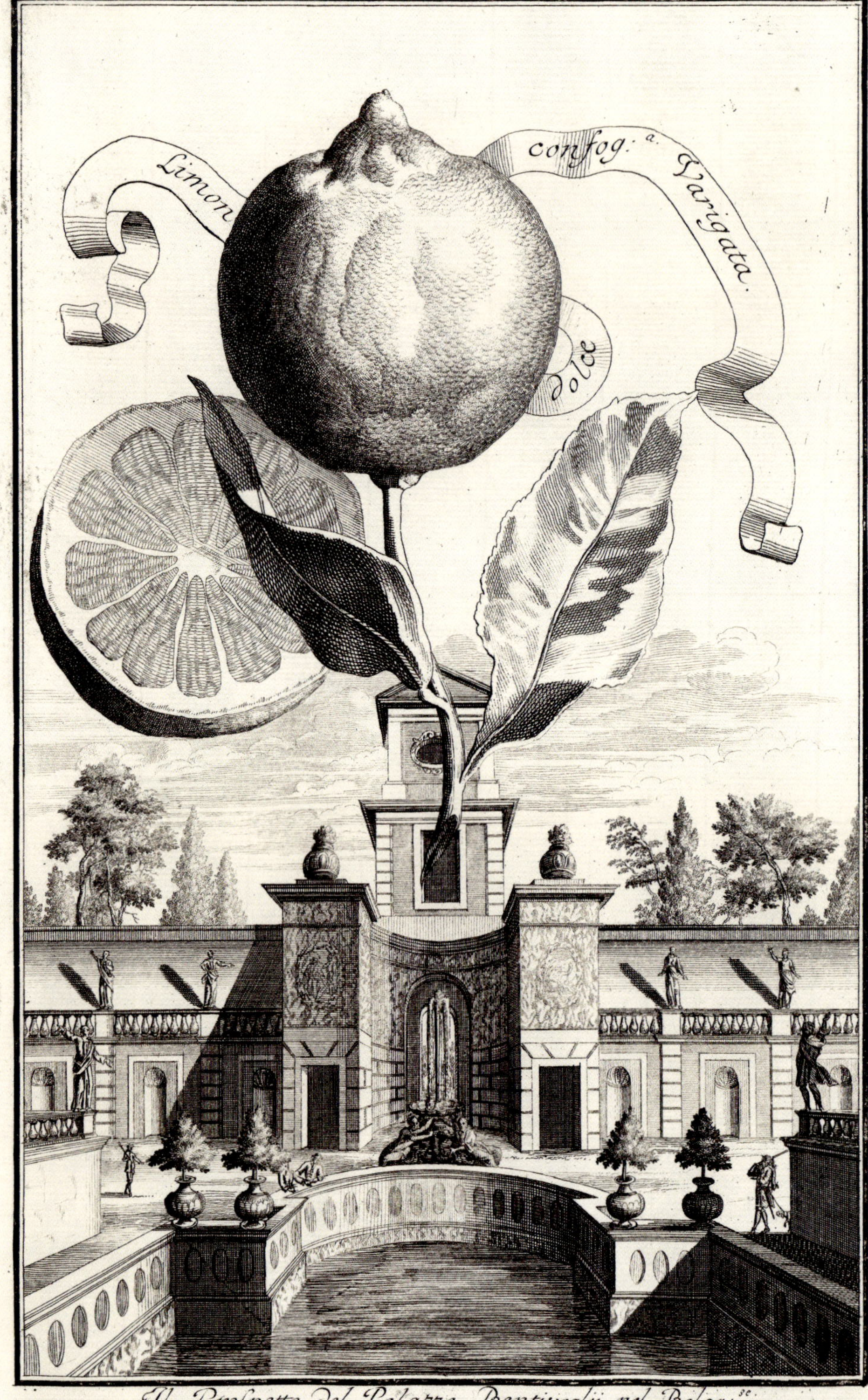

Bologna – Villa Bentivoglio

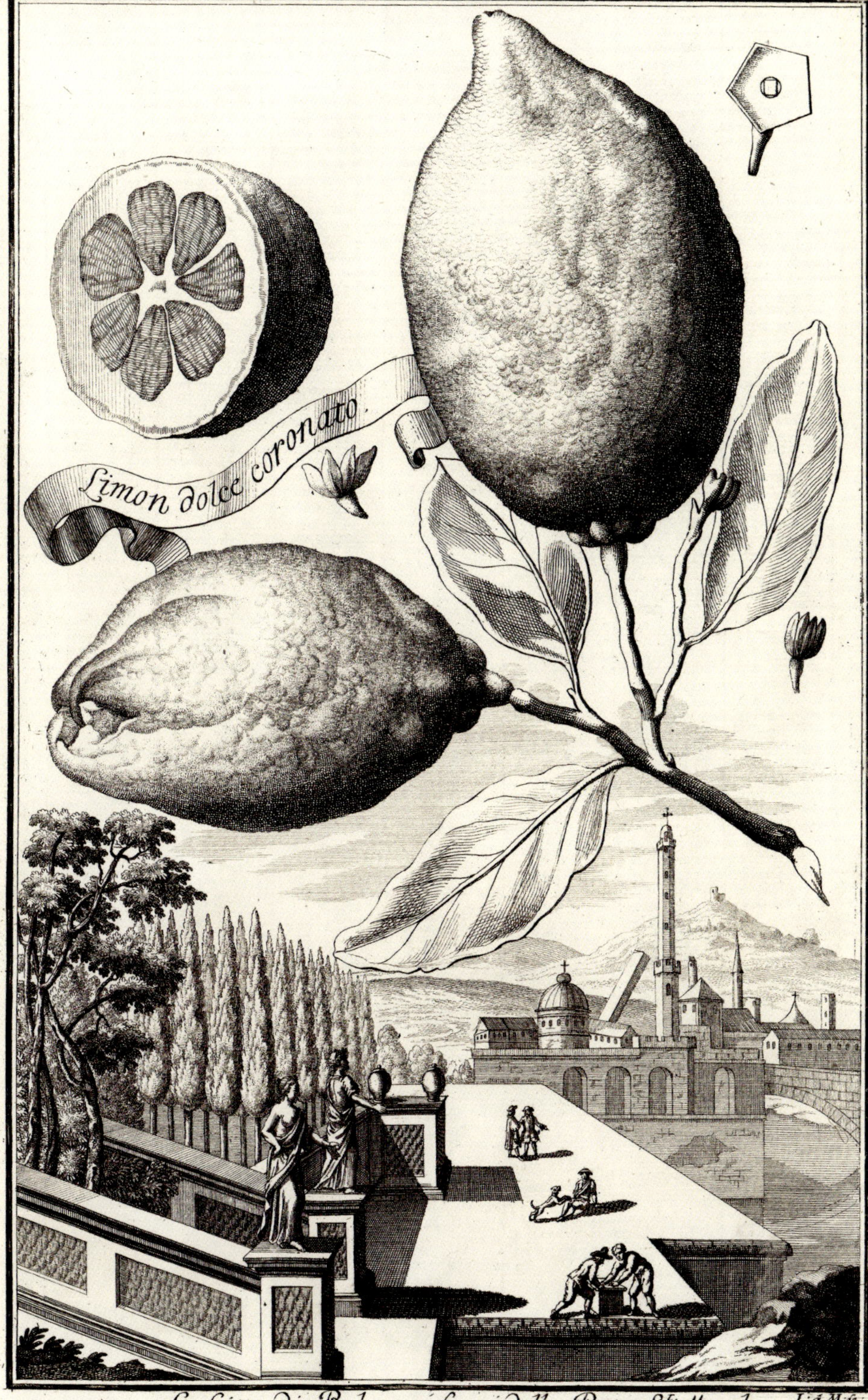
Limon dolce coronato
La Citta di Bologna fuori della Porta St. Mamolo.
I. á M. sc.

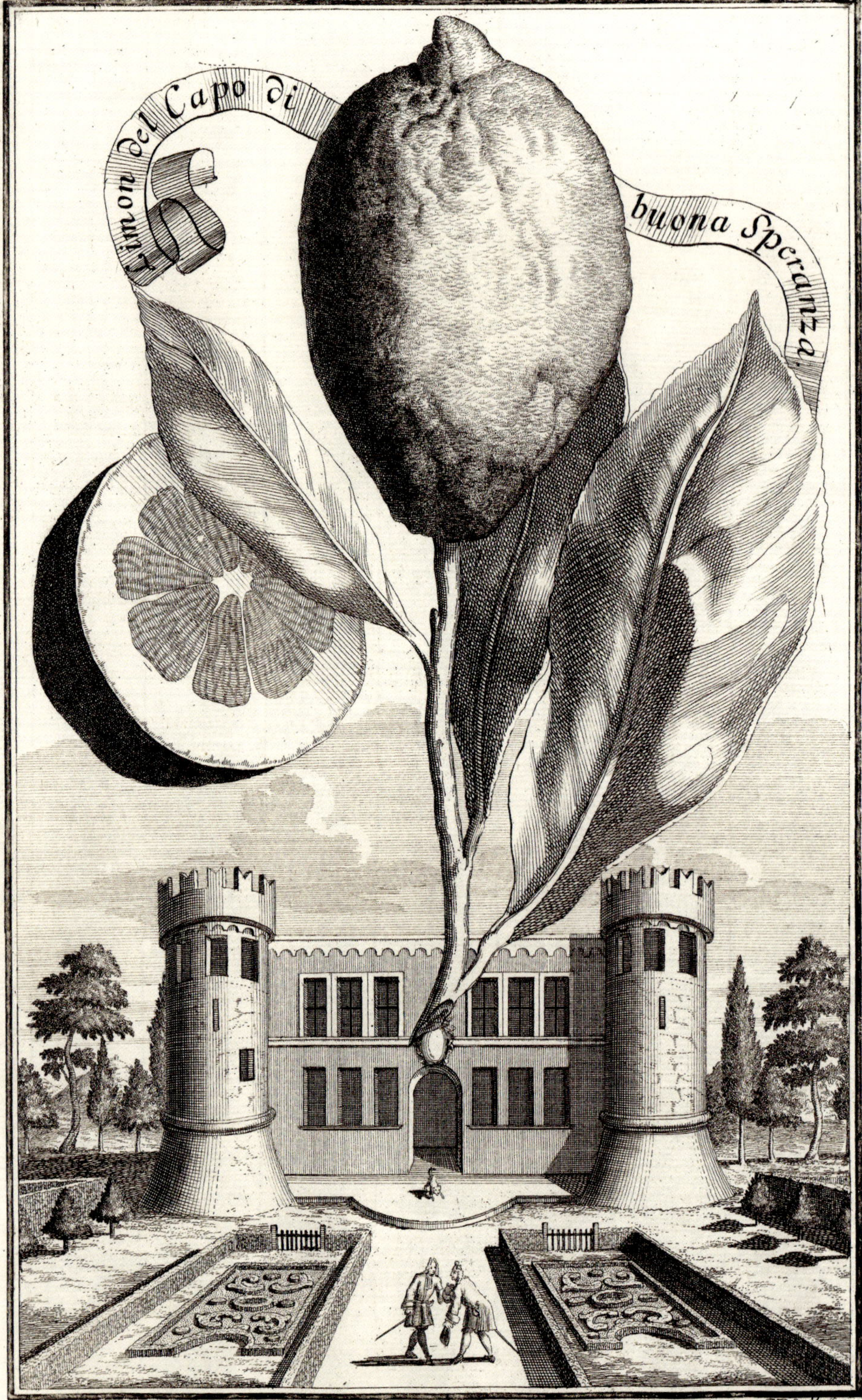

Limon del Capo di buona Speranza

Bologna – Villa Malvezzi

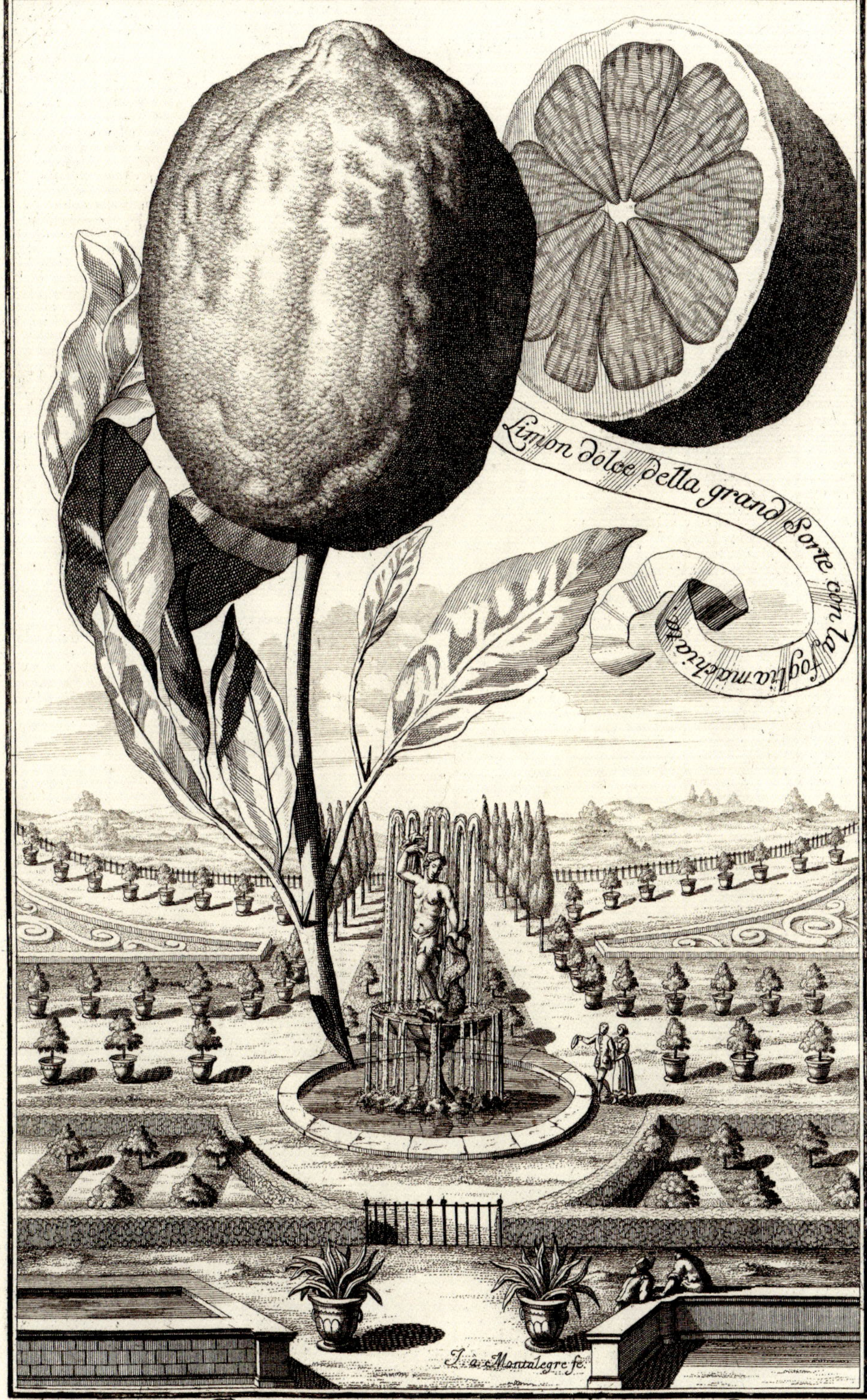

Limon dolce della grand Sorte con la foglia machiata

Bologna, Arcoveggio – Benacci Garden

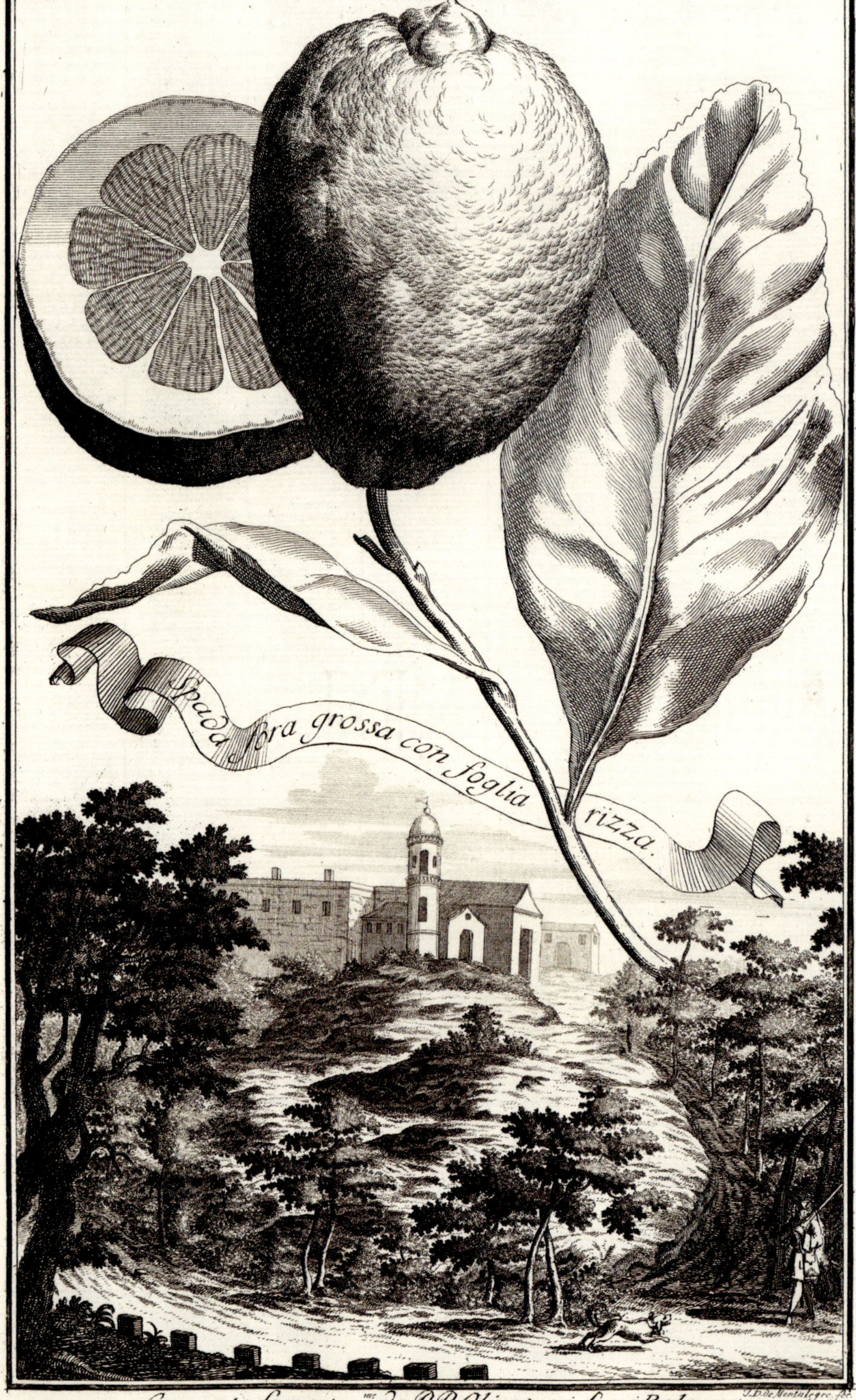

[Limon] Spada fora grossa con foglia rizza

Bologna – San Michele in Bosco (Olivetan Monastery)

[Limon] Spada fora con foglia stretta da Persico

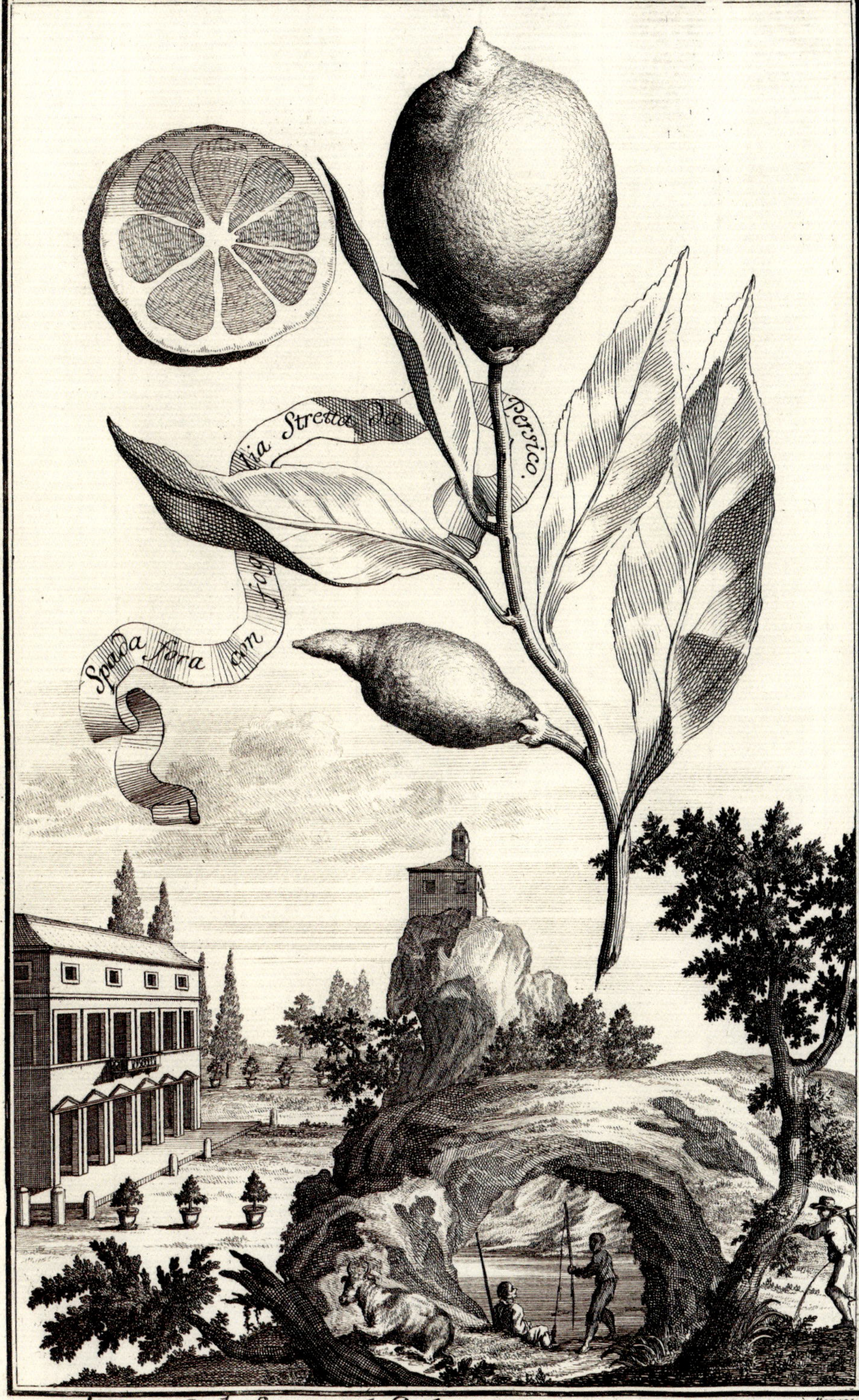

Veduta del Sasso nel Bolognese con sopra una Chiesa

Sasso Marconi (Bologna)

Limon di frutto doppio

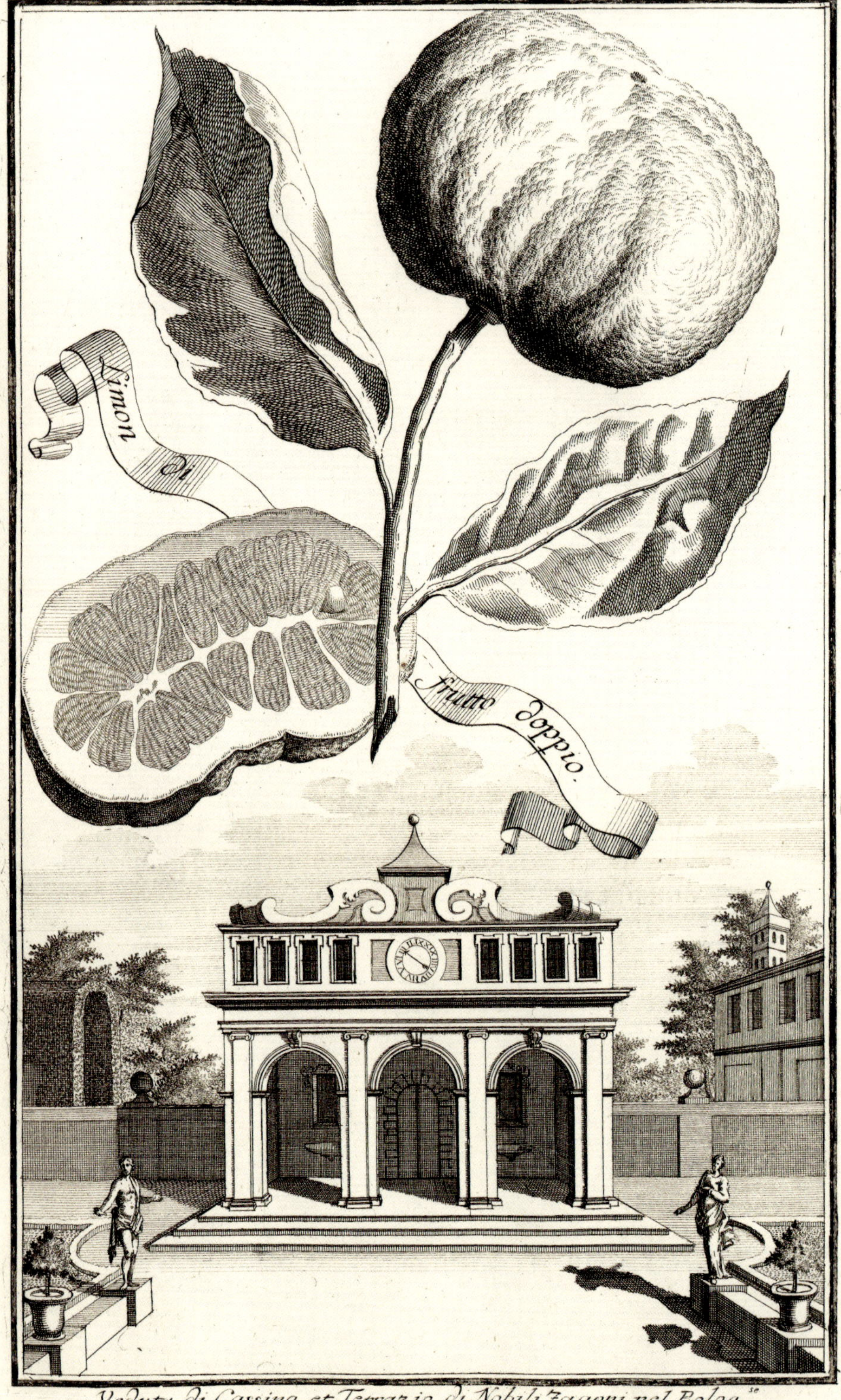

[Limon] Spada fora regina

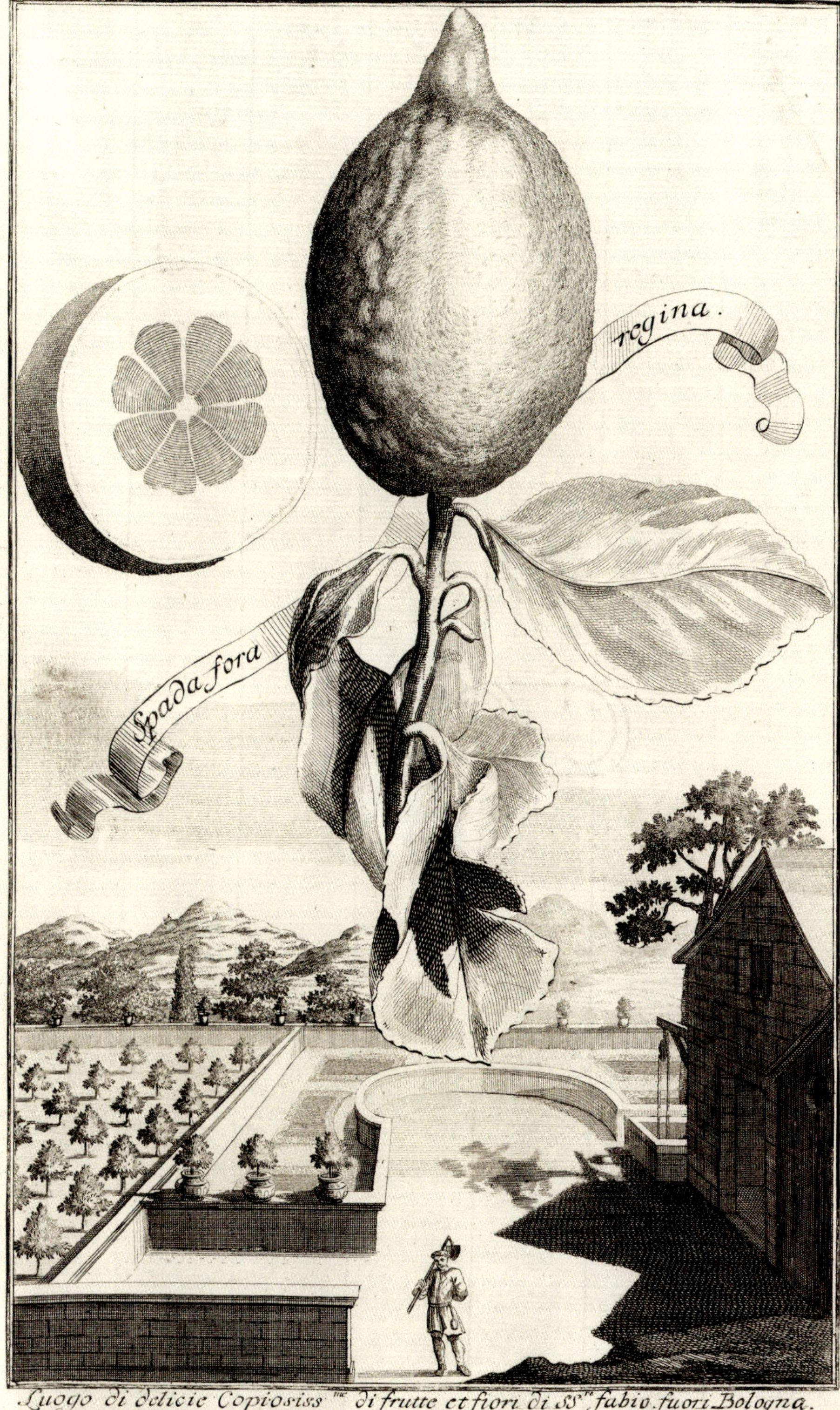

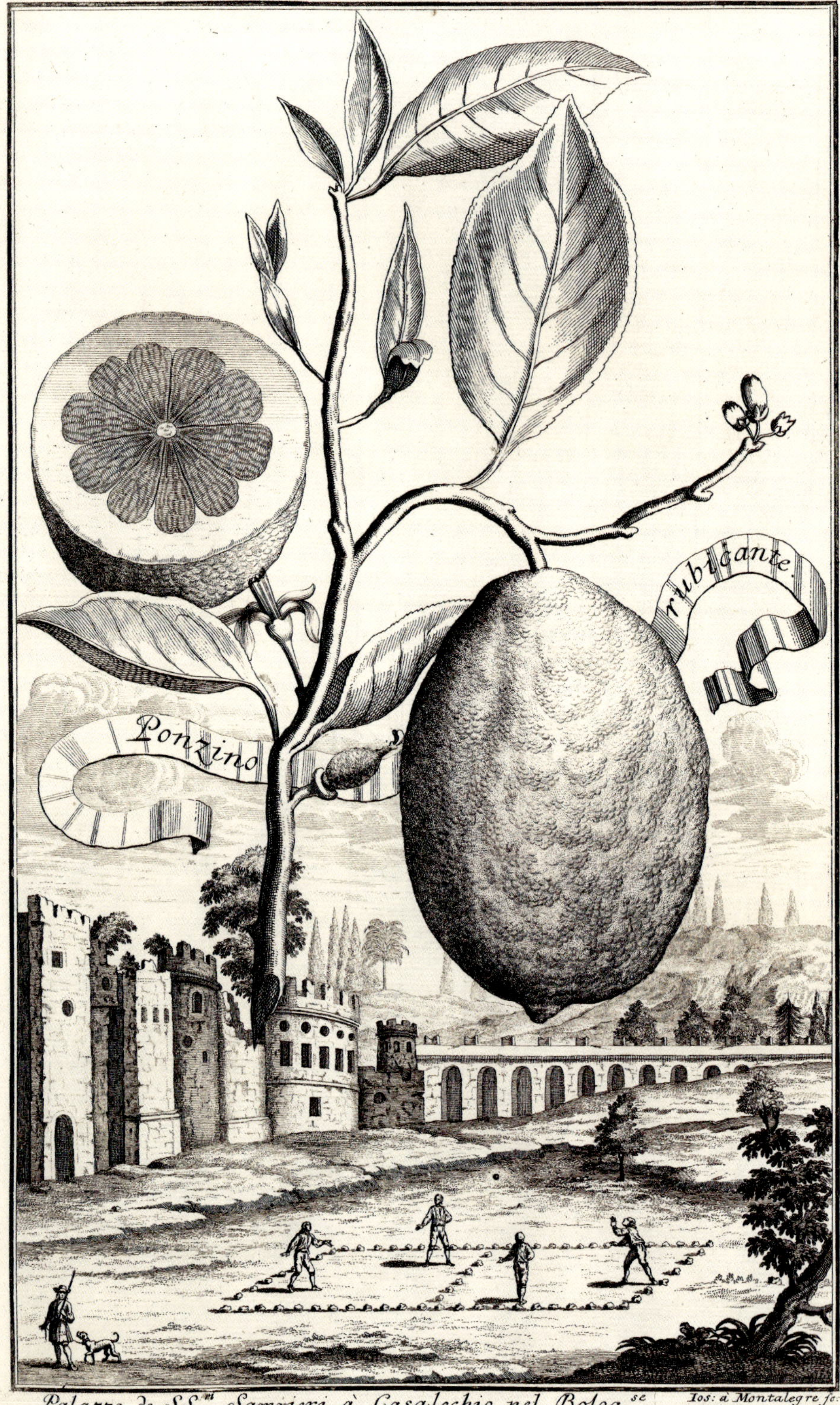

[Limon] Ponzino rubicante

Casalecchio di Reno (Bologna) – Villa Sampieri

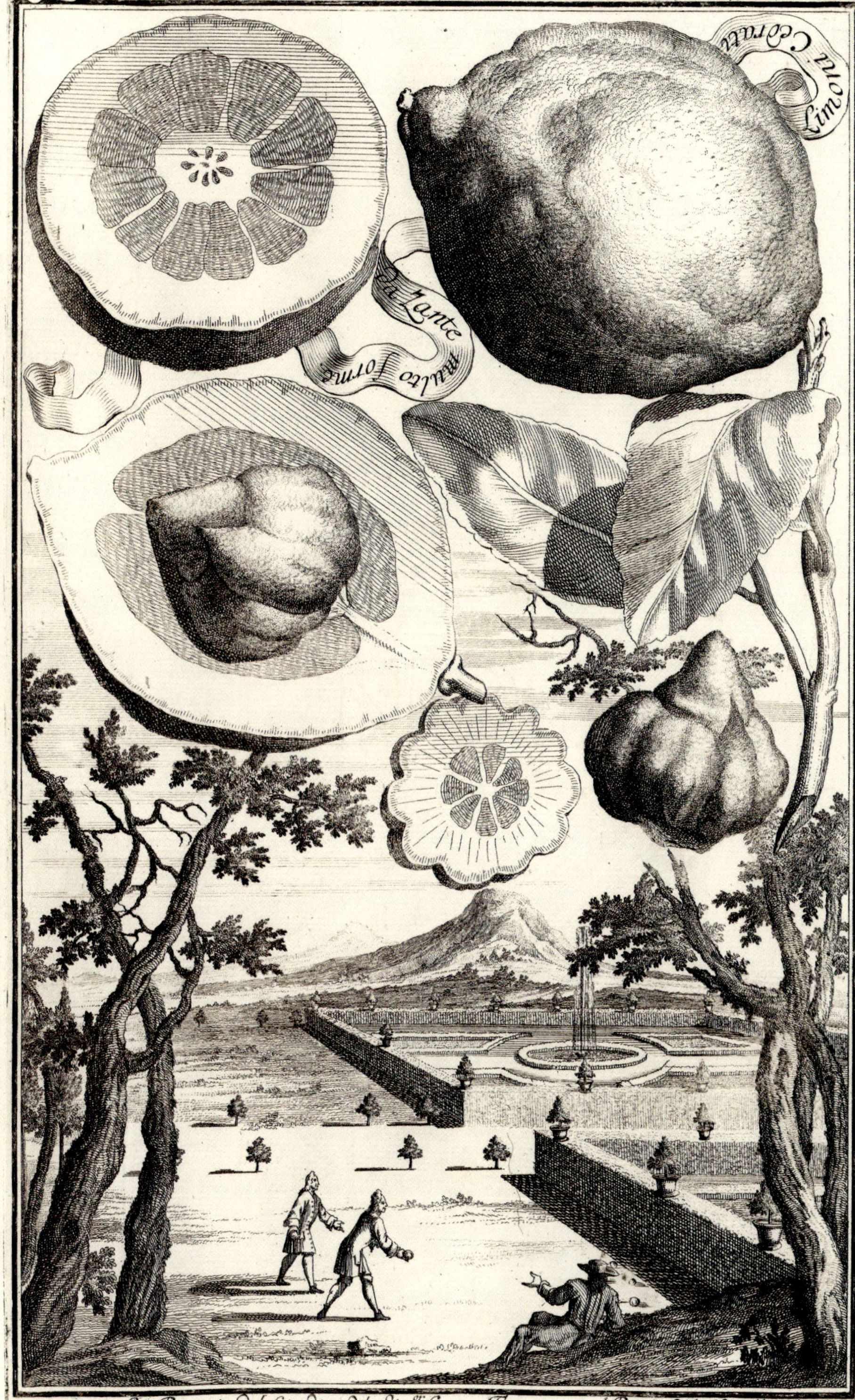
Limoni Cedrati
da Zante
multo forme
La Prateria del Giardino del Sig.r Conte Fontana et il Ponte del Chiselli
Montalegre fe.

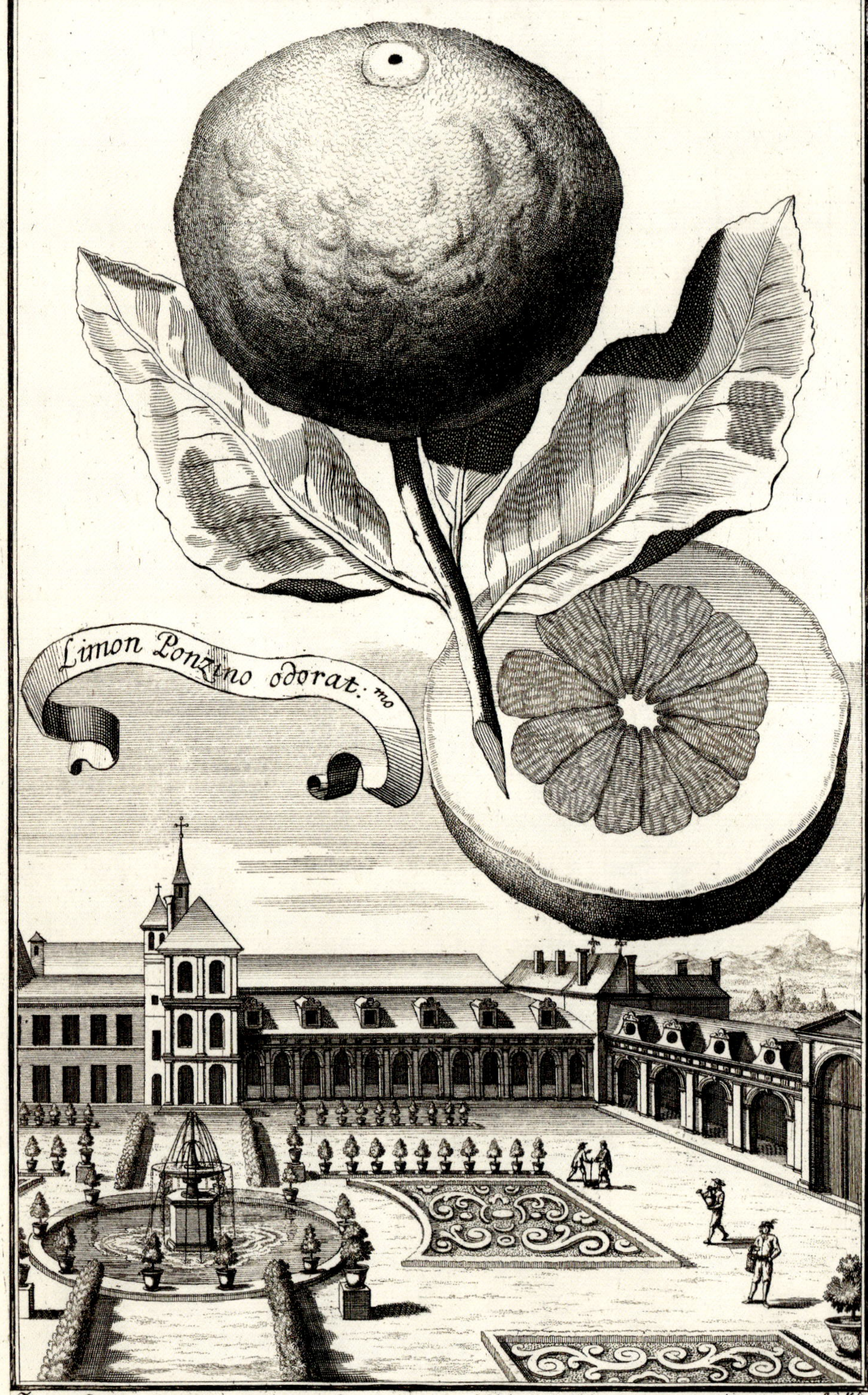

Limon Ponzino odorat[issi]mo

Monteveglio (Bologna) – Monastery of the Canons Regular of the Lateran

Limon Spinoso con foglia variegata

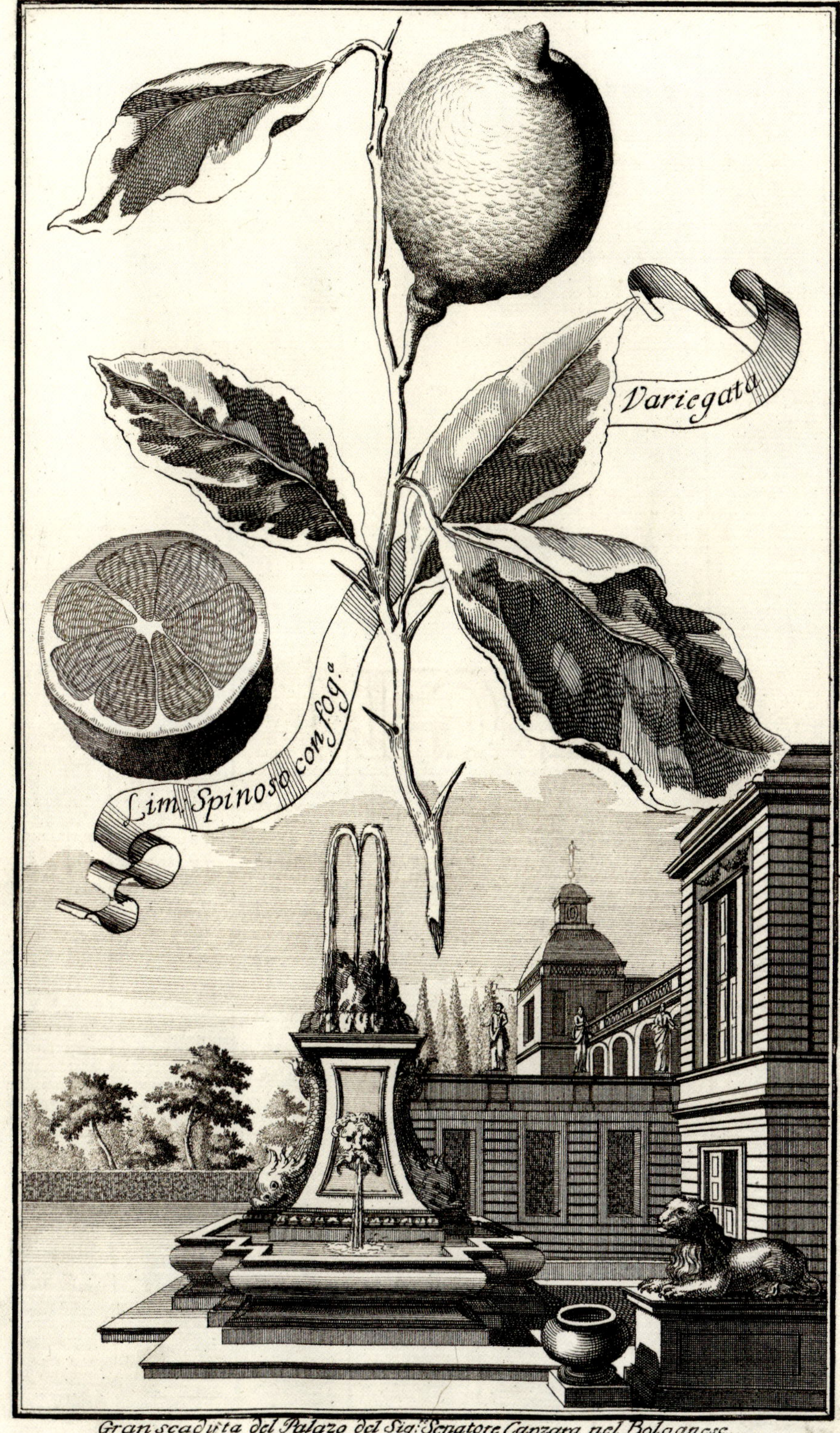

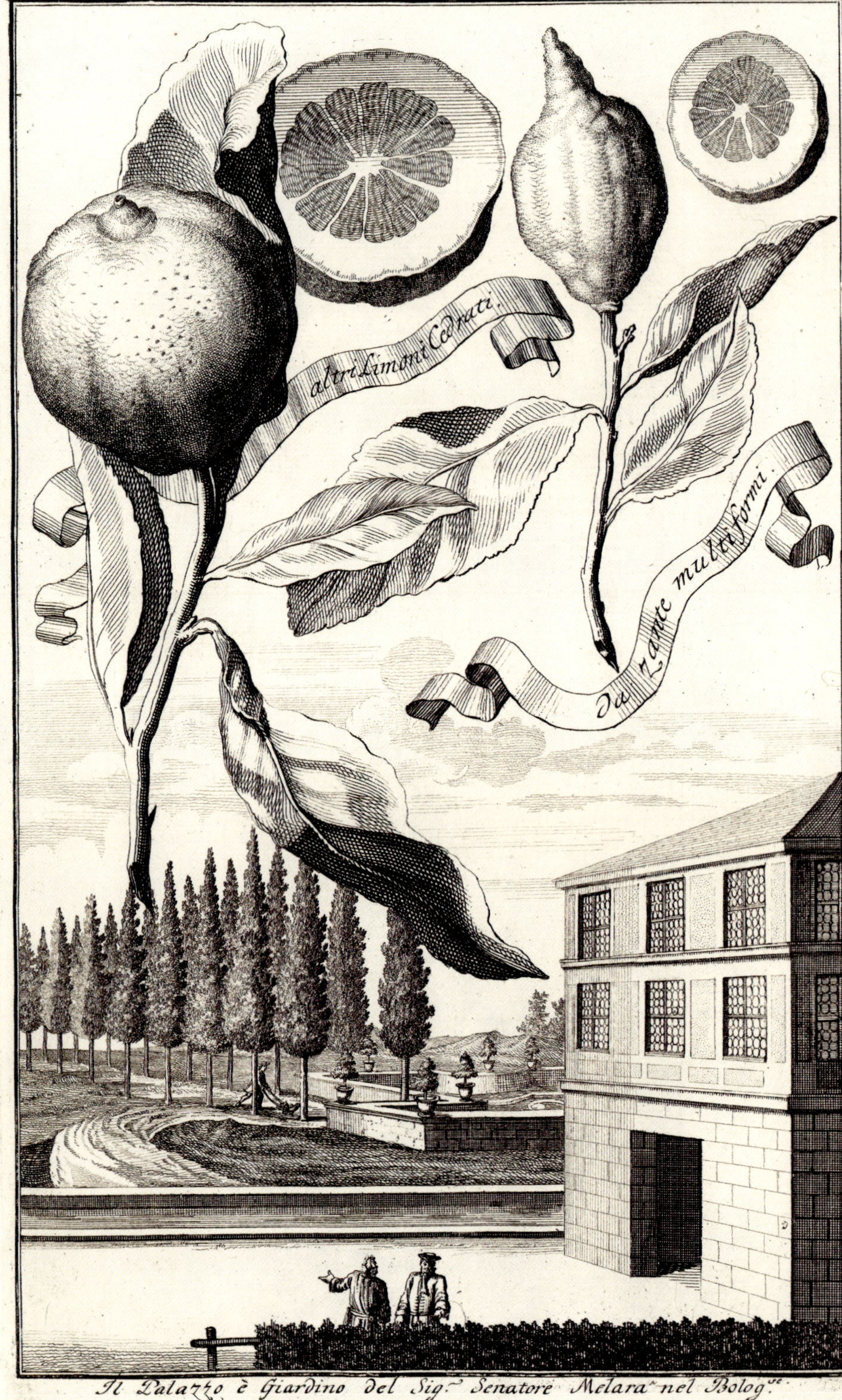

Limoni Cedrati da Zante multiformi

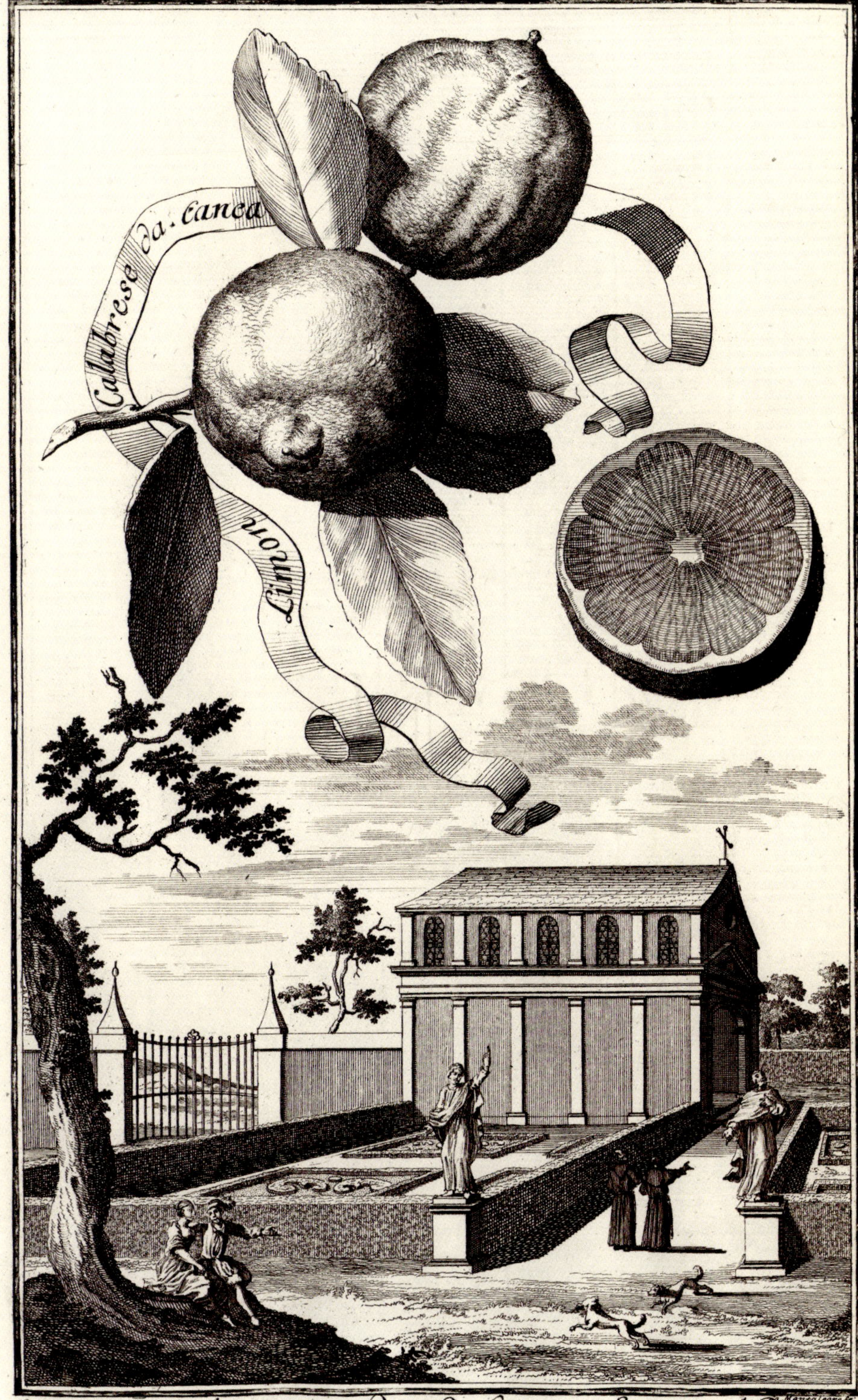
Calabrese da. canea
Limon
a Montalegre fe.
Convento posto nel ampiissima veduta de Canonici Lattrani nel Bolognese.

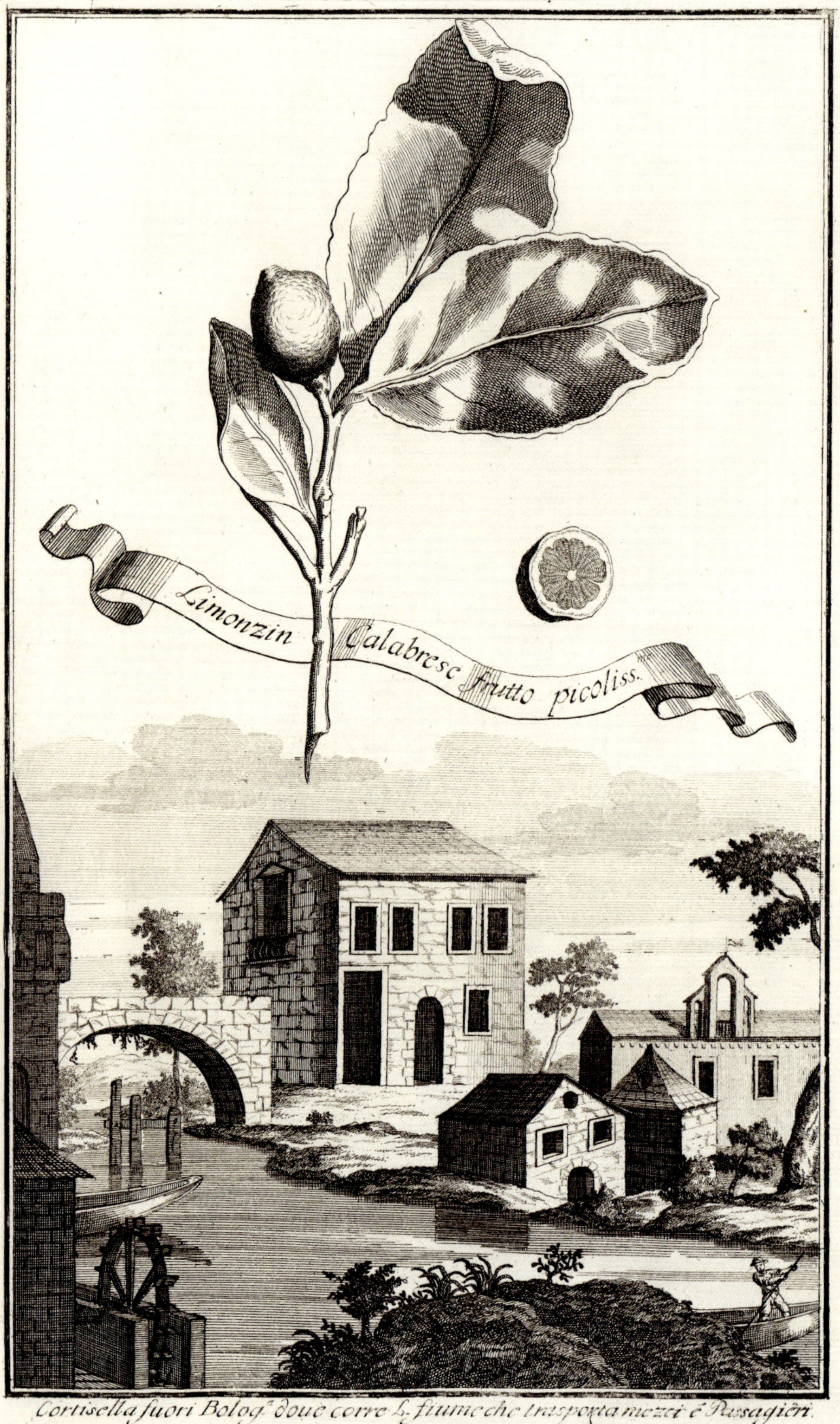

Limonzin Calabresc frutto picoliss.

Cortisella fuori Bolog.a doue corre L. fiume che trasporta mezzi é Passagieri.

Limonzin Calabrese frutto piccoliss[imo]

Bologna, Corticella

Limonzin Personzin con foglia crispa et fior Doppio

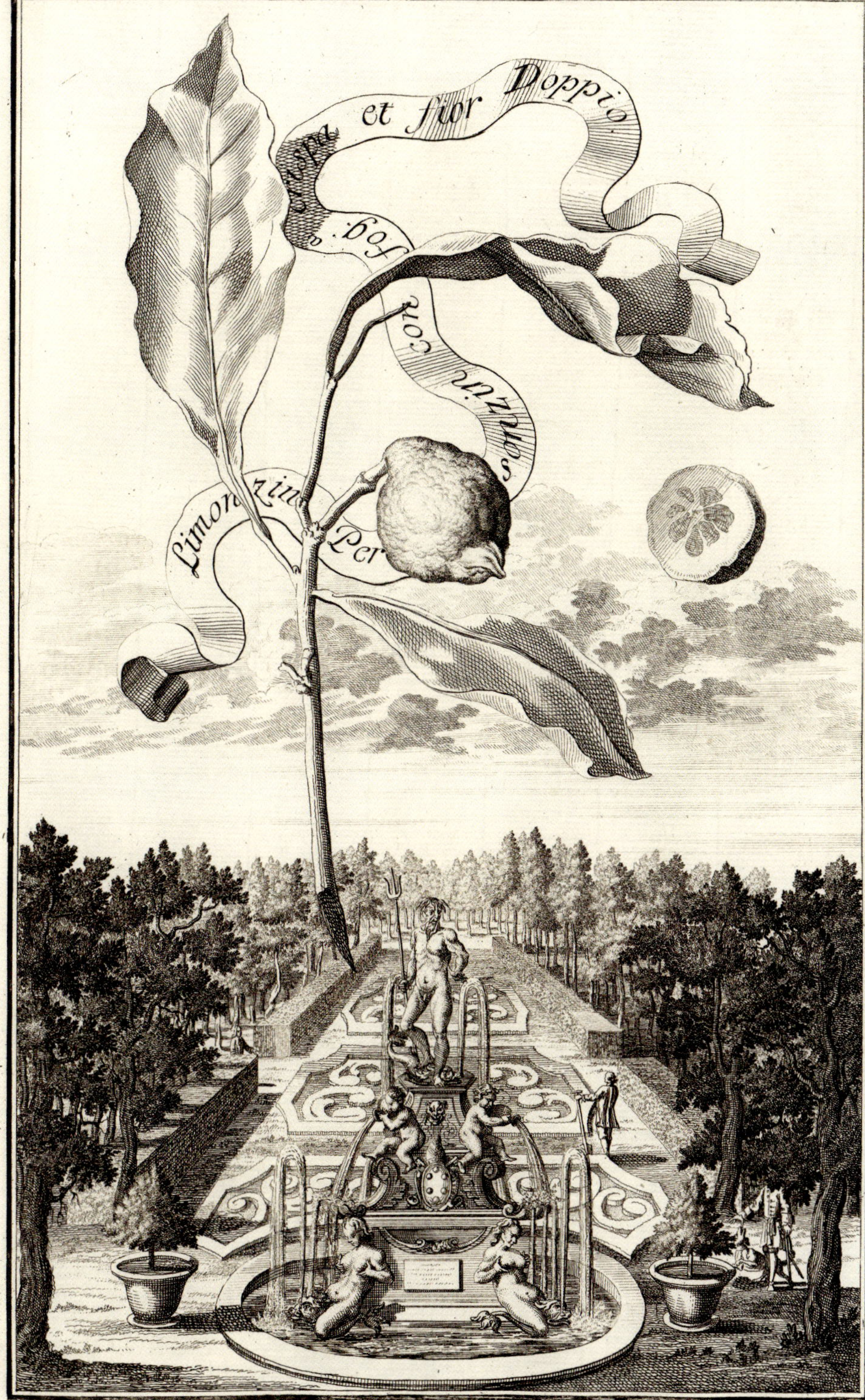

Il Fonte tutta di Bronzo nella Piazza magiore in Bologna. Montalegre.

Bologna – Neptune Fountain

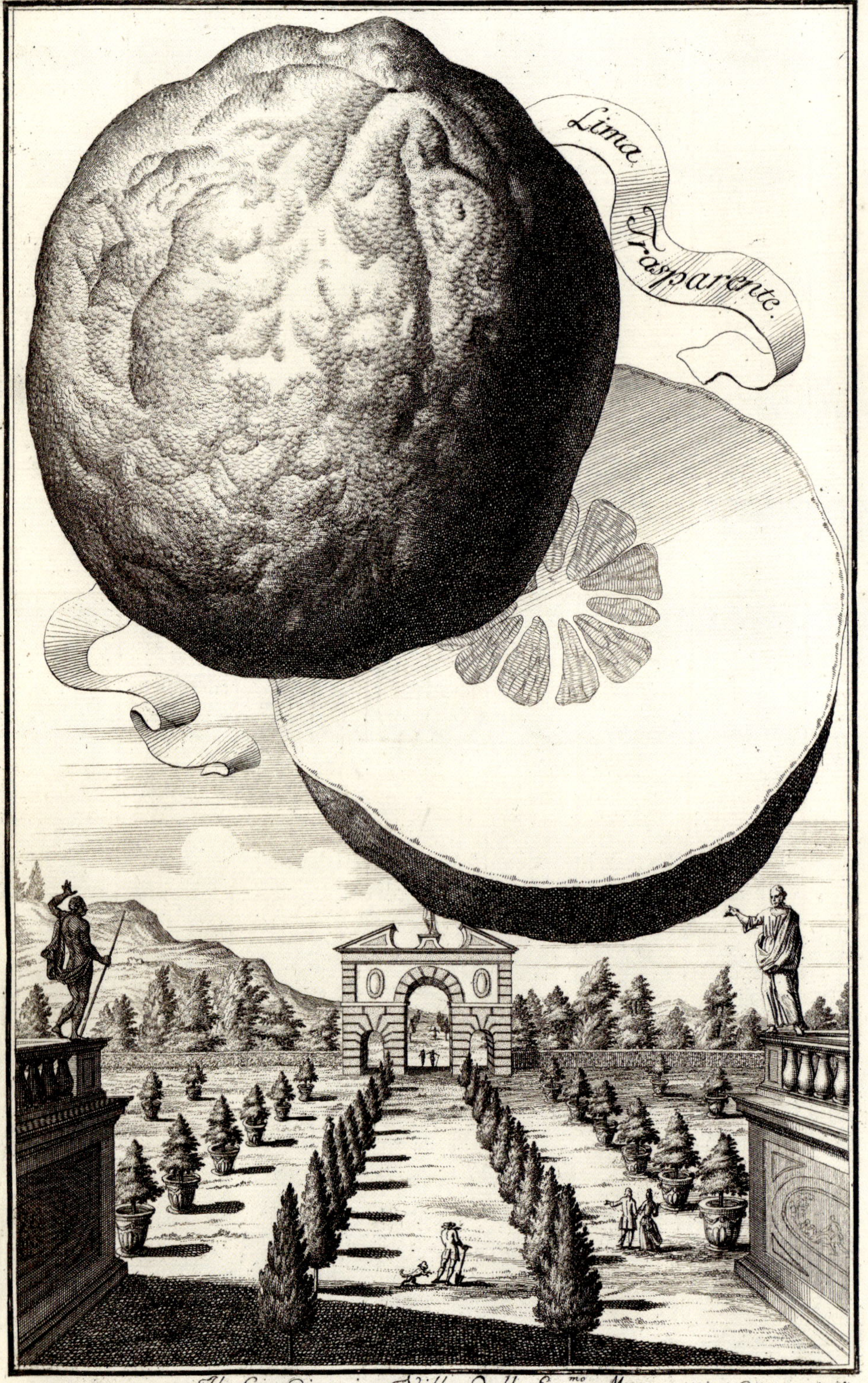
Lima
Trasparente.
Il Giardino in Villa dell Ecc.mo Marescotti. nel Bolog.se
J. D. da Montalegre fe.

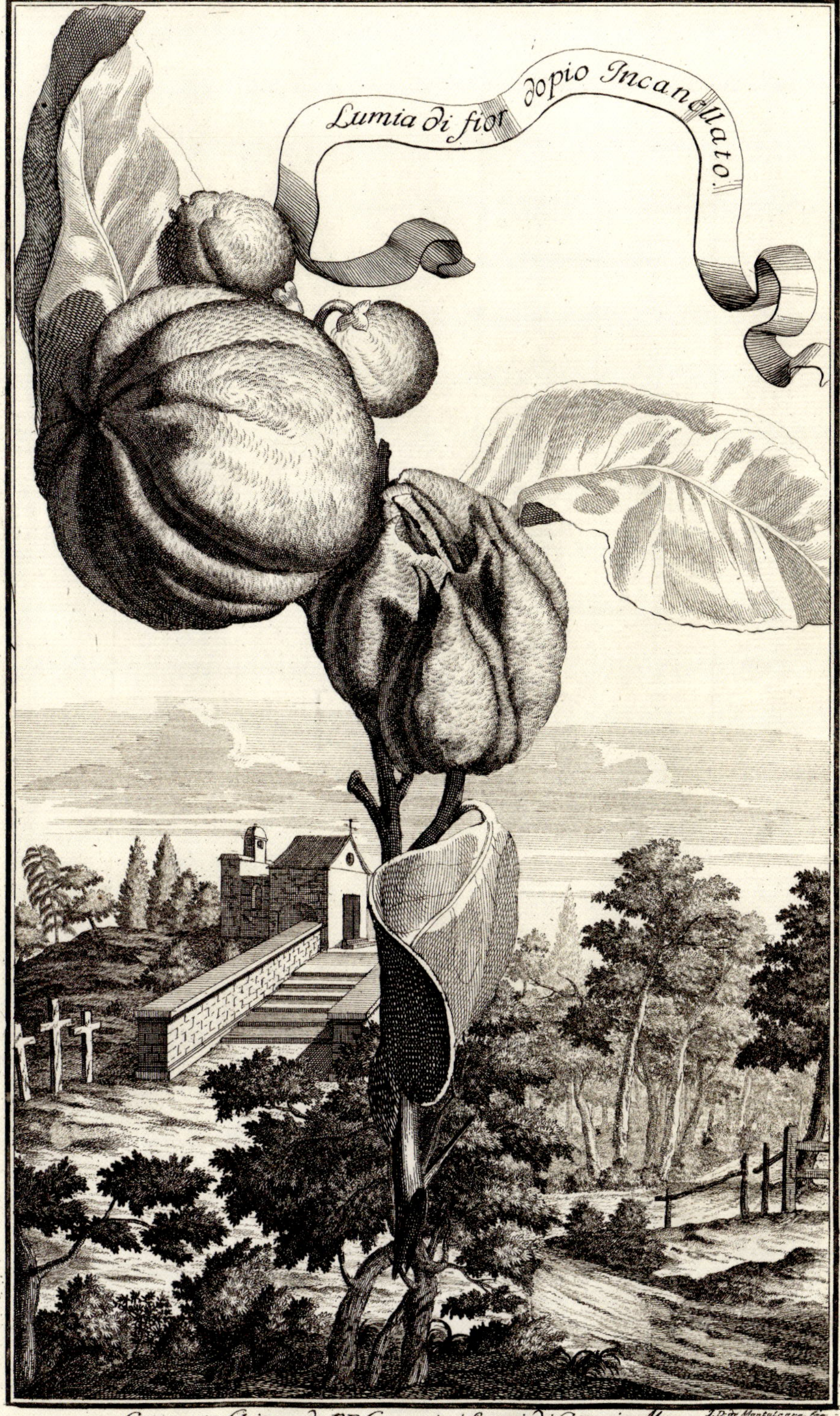
Lumia di fior dopio Incanellato
Convento e Chiesa de P.P. Capucini fuori di Citta in Monte.
I.D. de Monte Legre fec.

Lima agra
Delizzie di Varii Sorte di frutti del Sig.re Senatore Biancheti Gambalonga nel Stato di Bolog.a

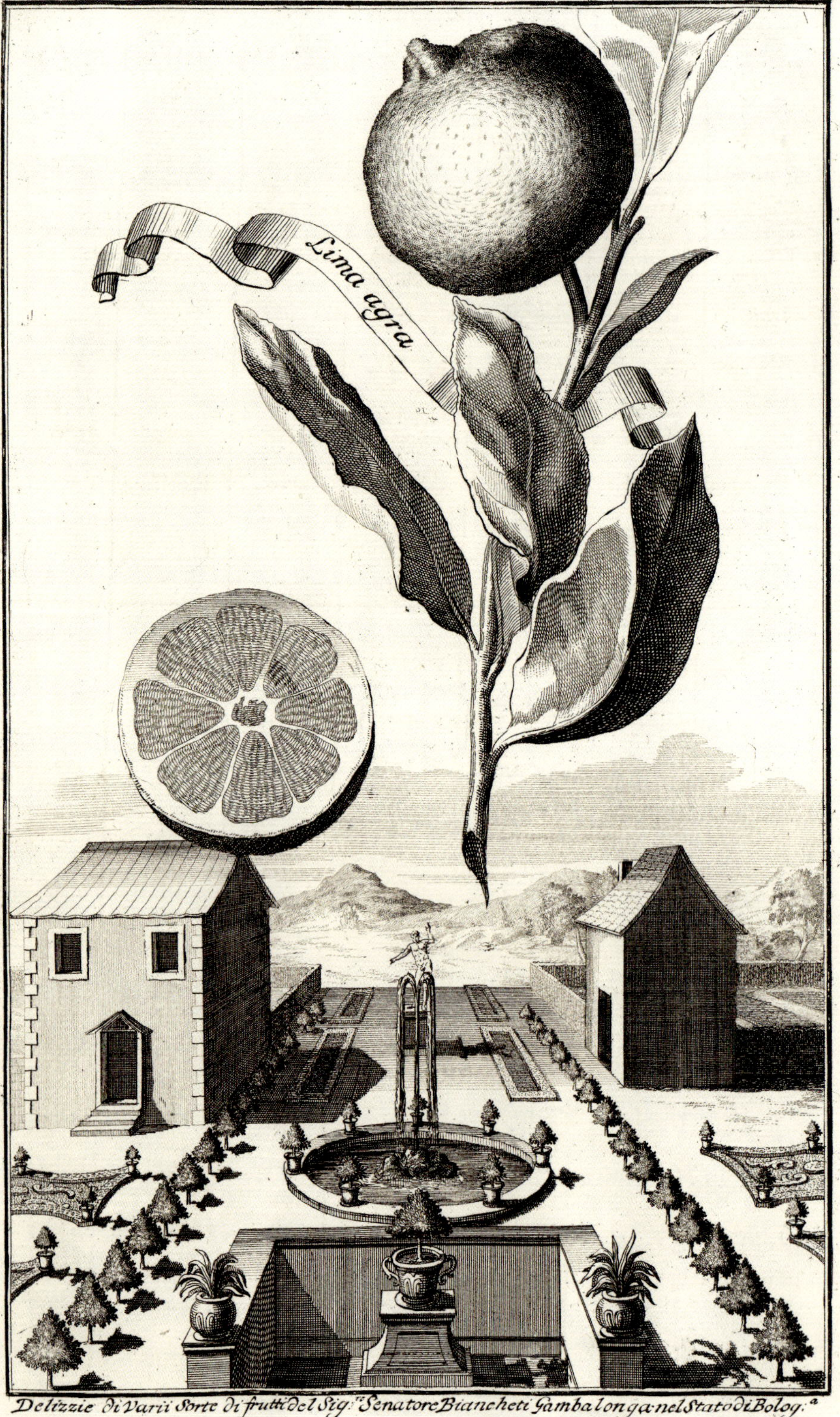

Lima agra

Lima dolce con Foglia tonda rizza

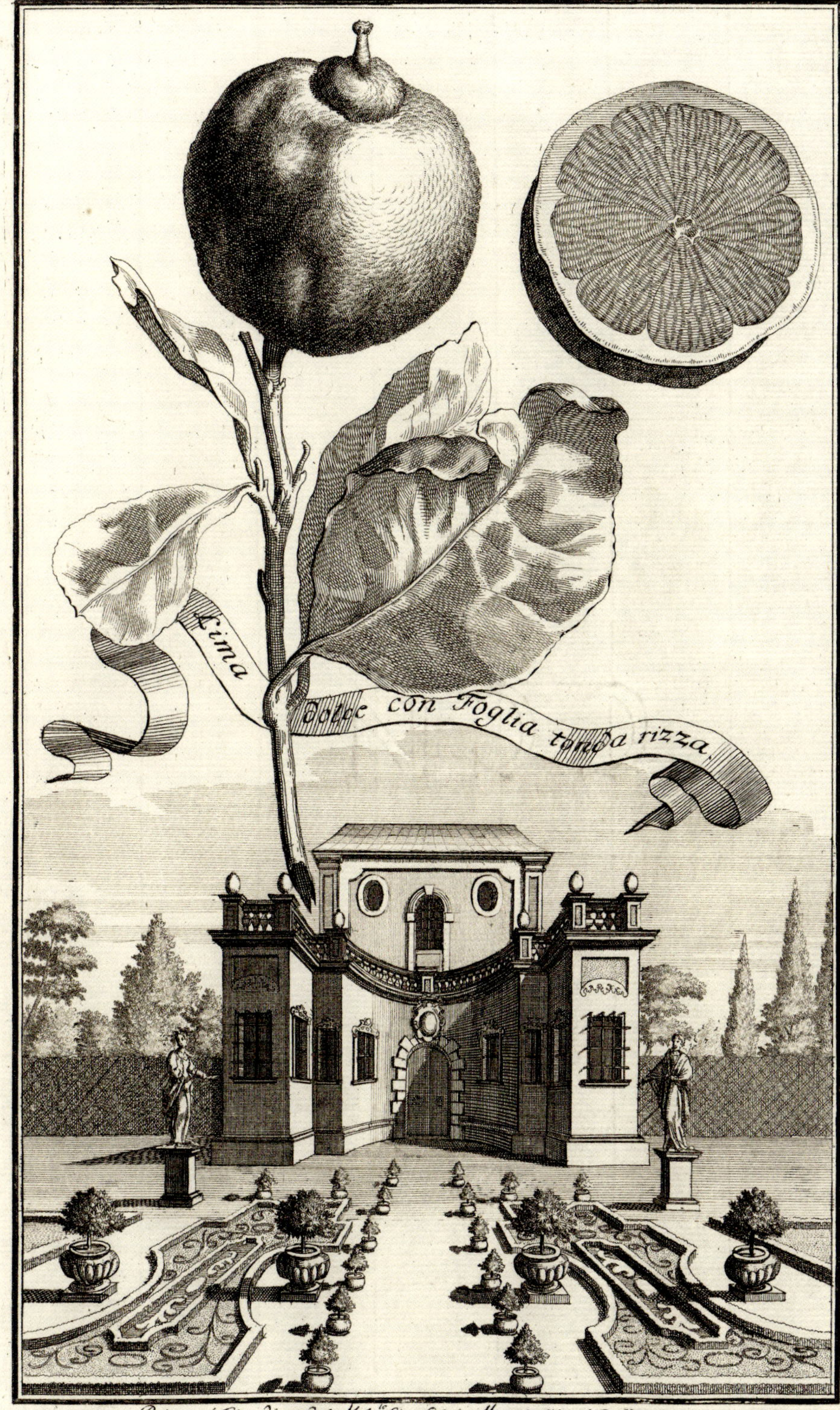

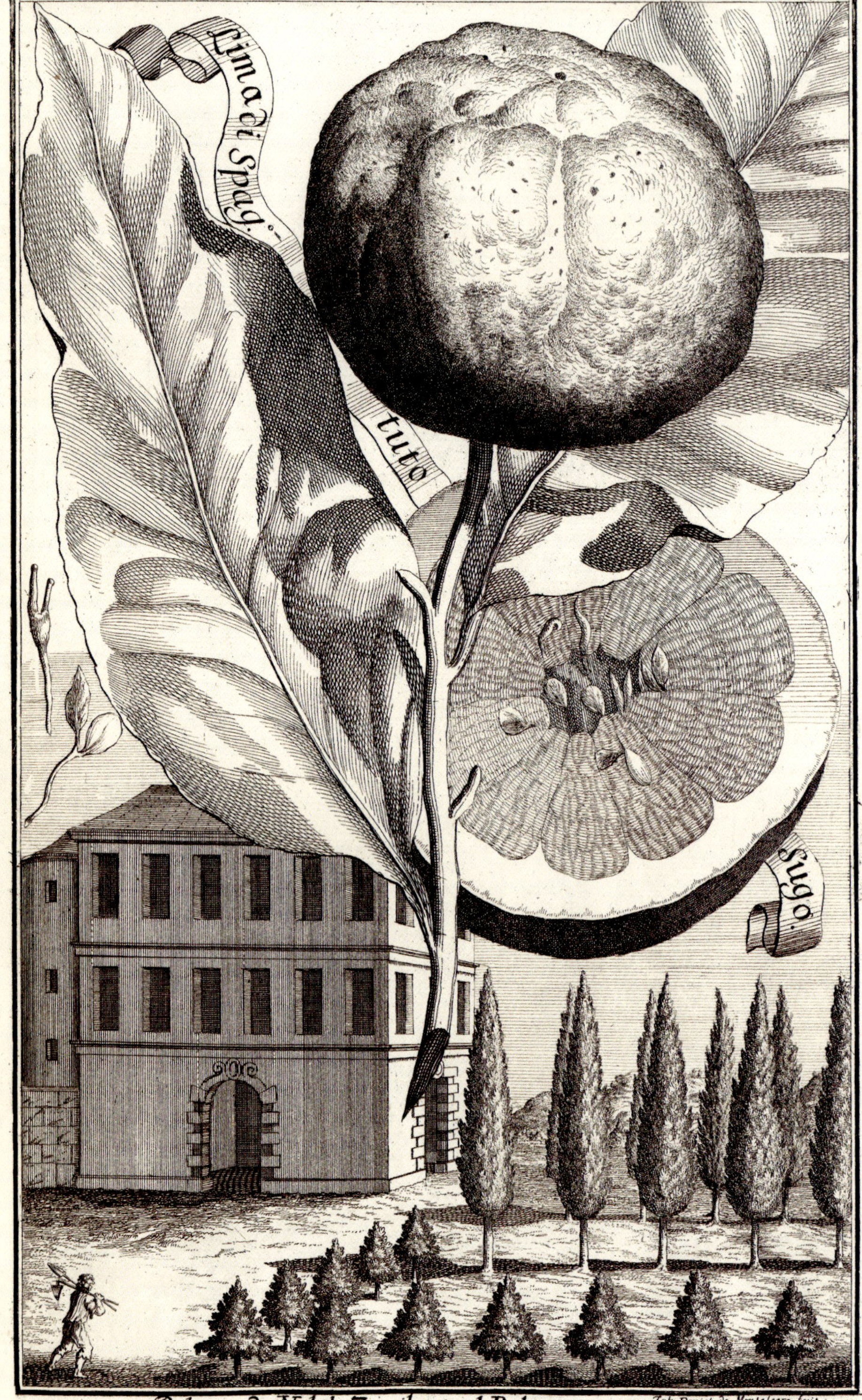

Lima di Spag[na] tut[t]o sugo

Limon racemoso

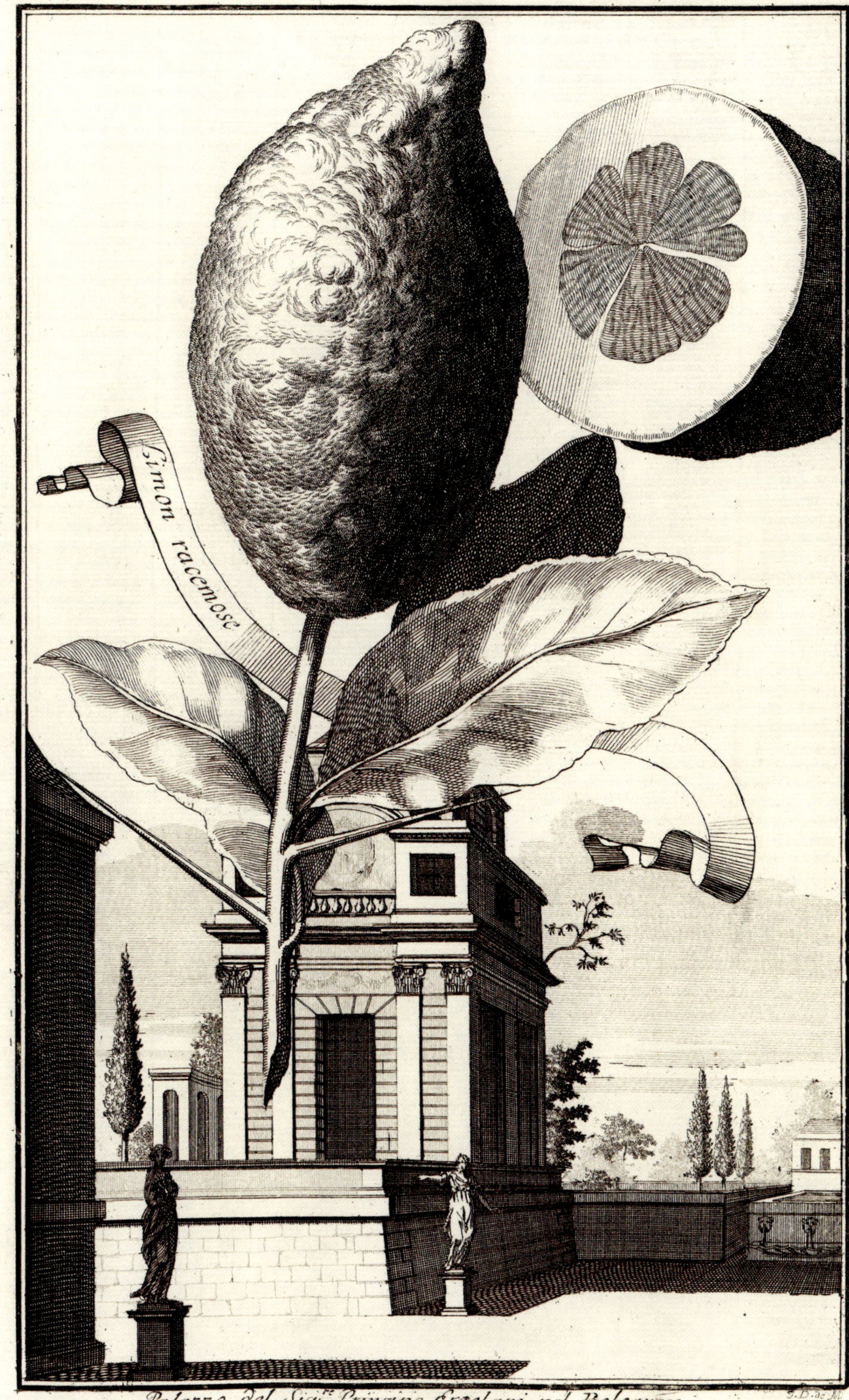

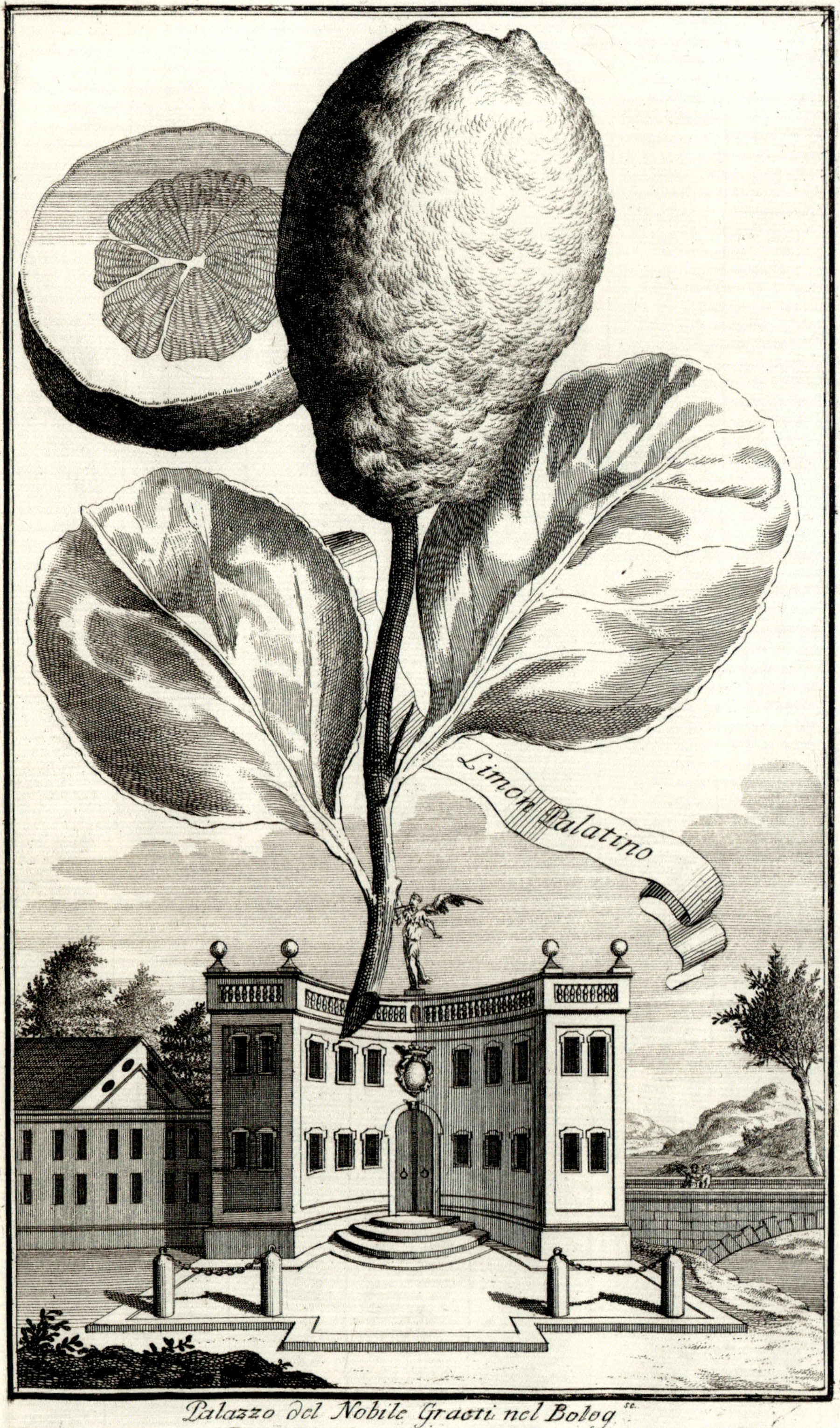

Limon Palatino

[Limon] Spada fora Regina

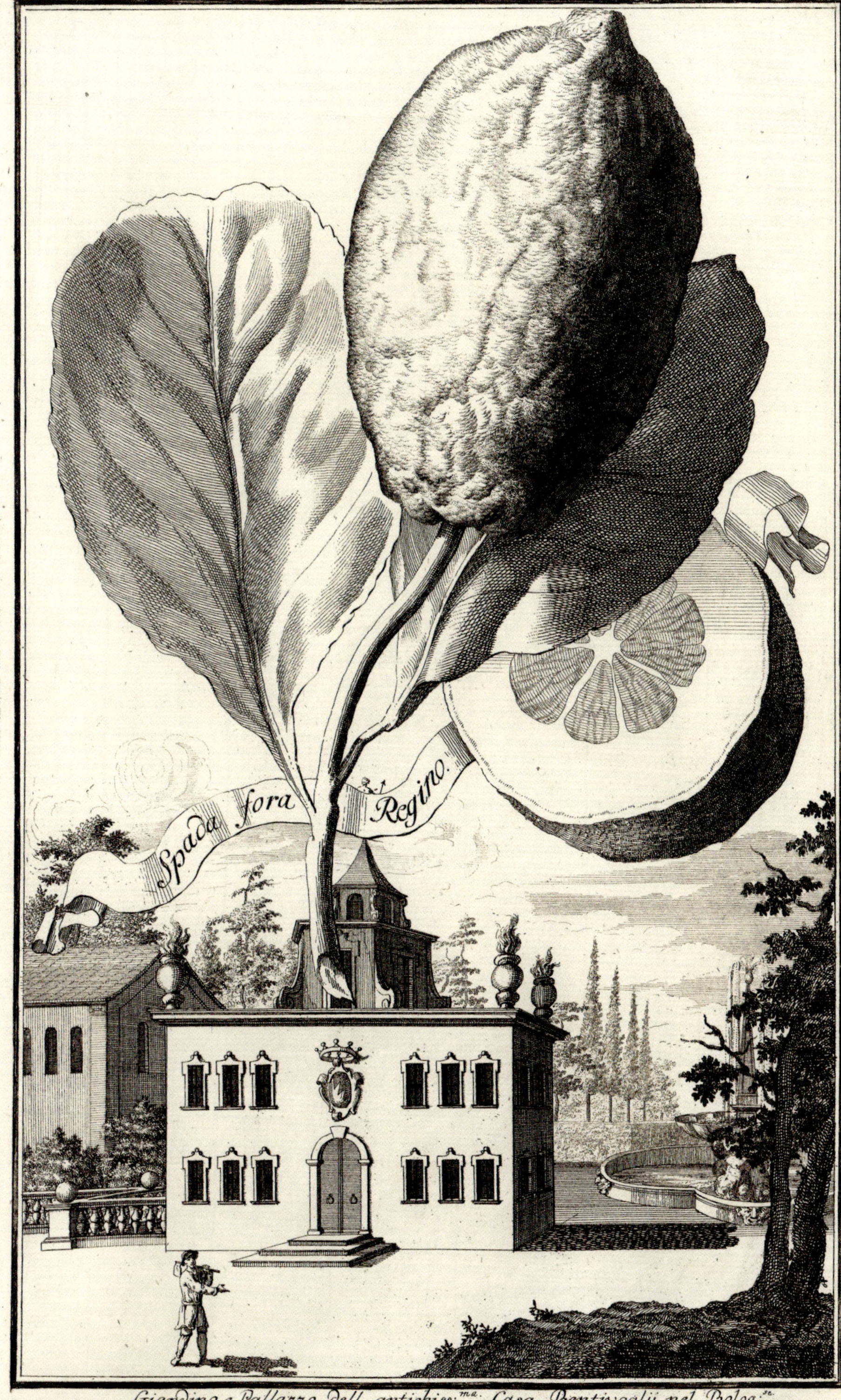

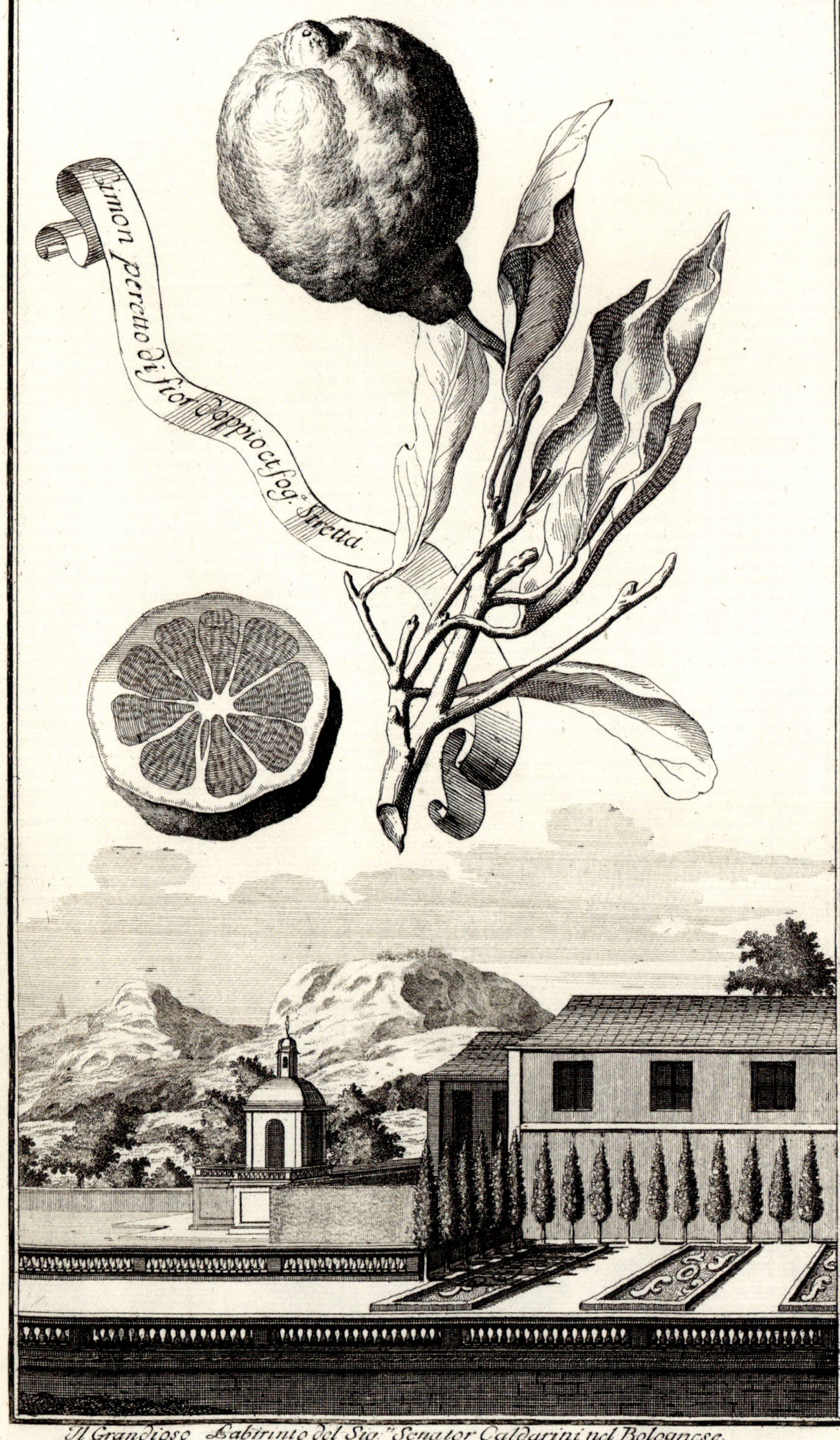

Limon peretto di fior doppio et foglia Stretta

Bologna – Villa Calderini

Limoncello da Napoli

Vedrana di Budrio (Bologna) – Villa Angelo Bellona

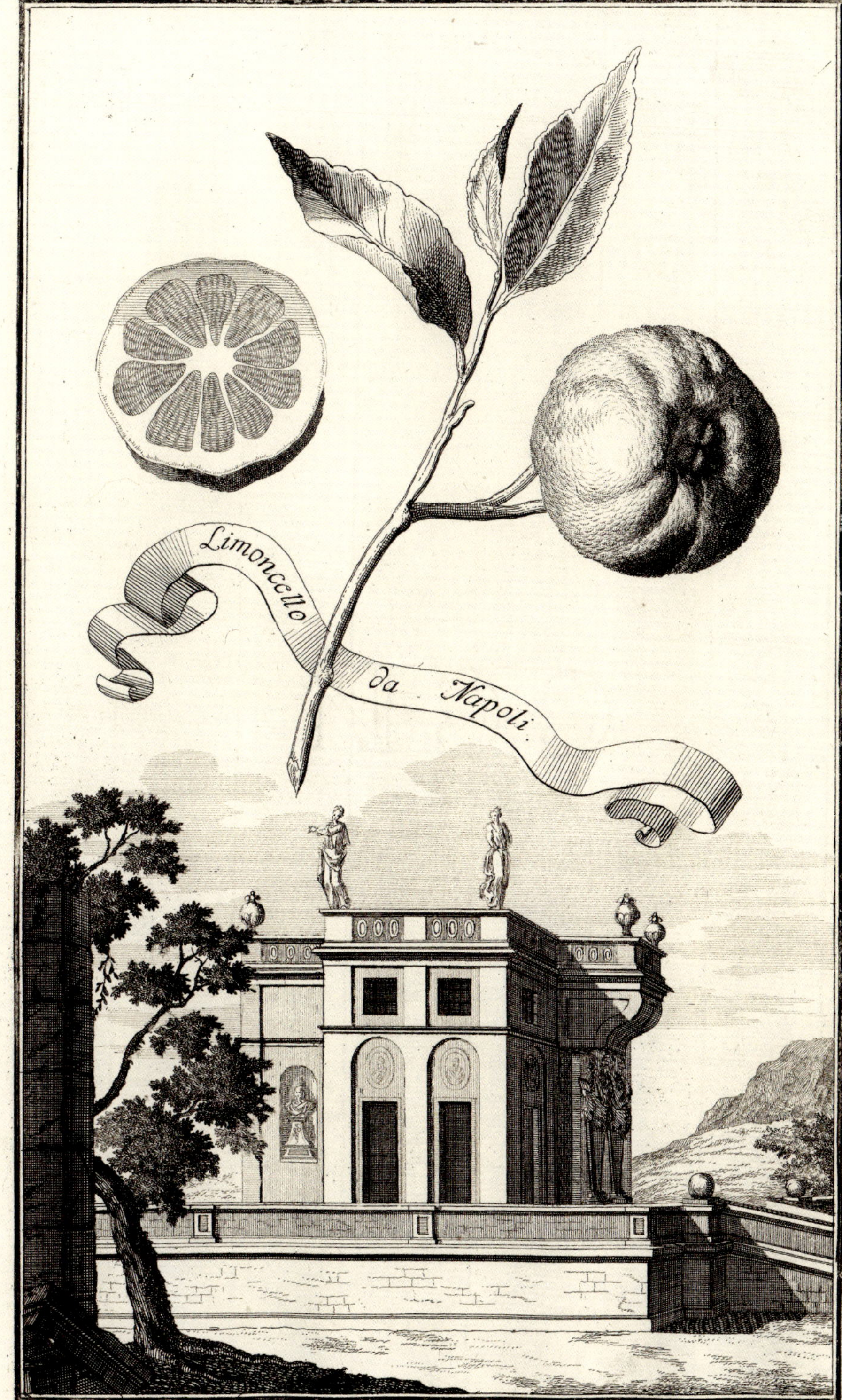

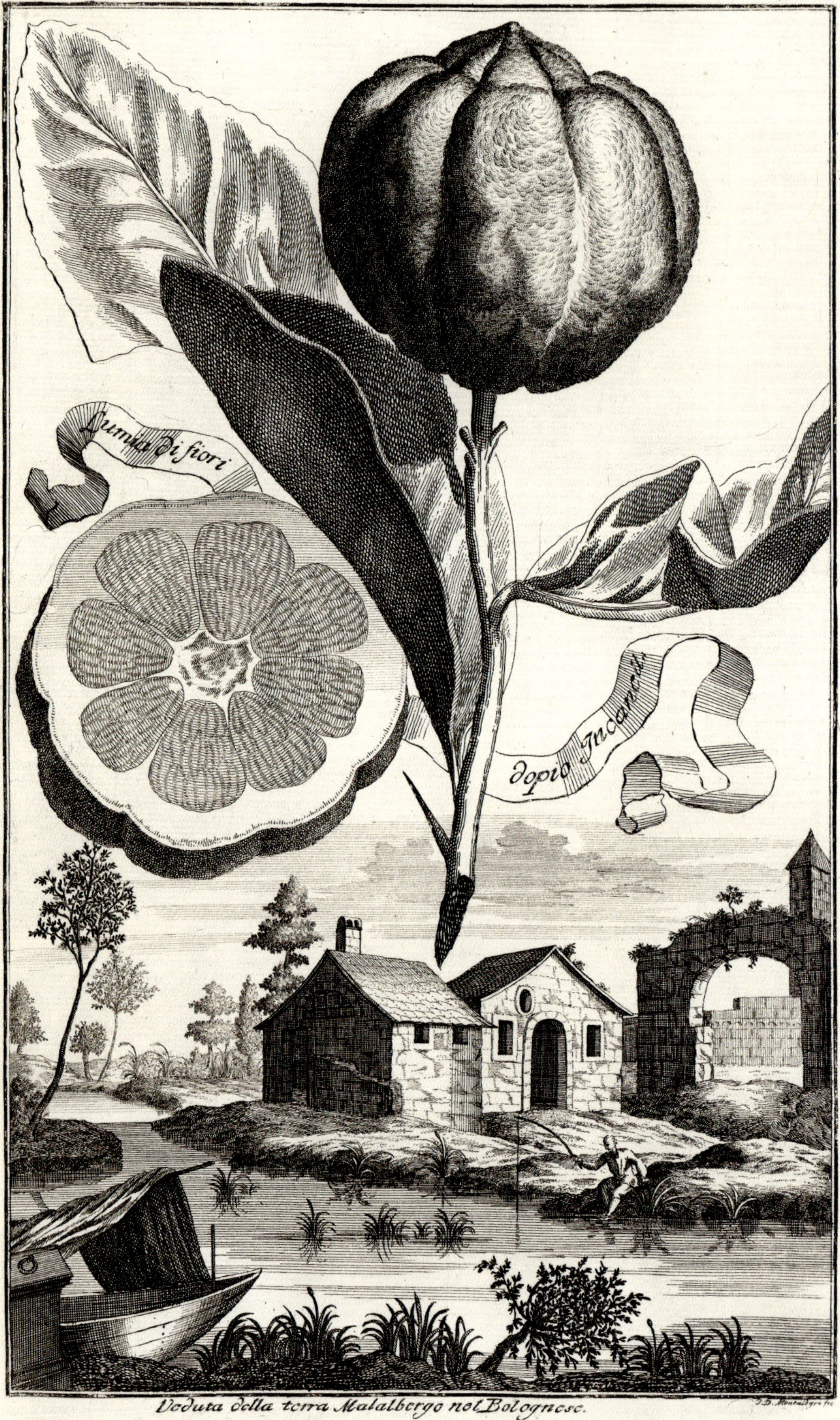

Lumia di fiori dopio Incanellato

Malalbergo (Bologna)

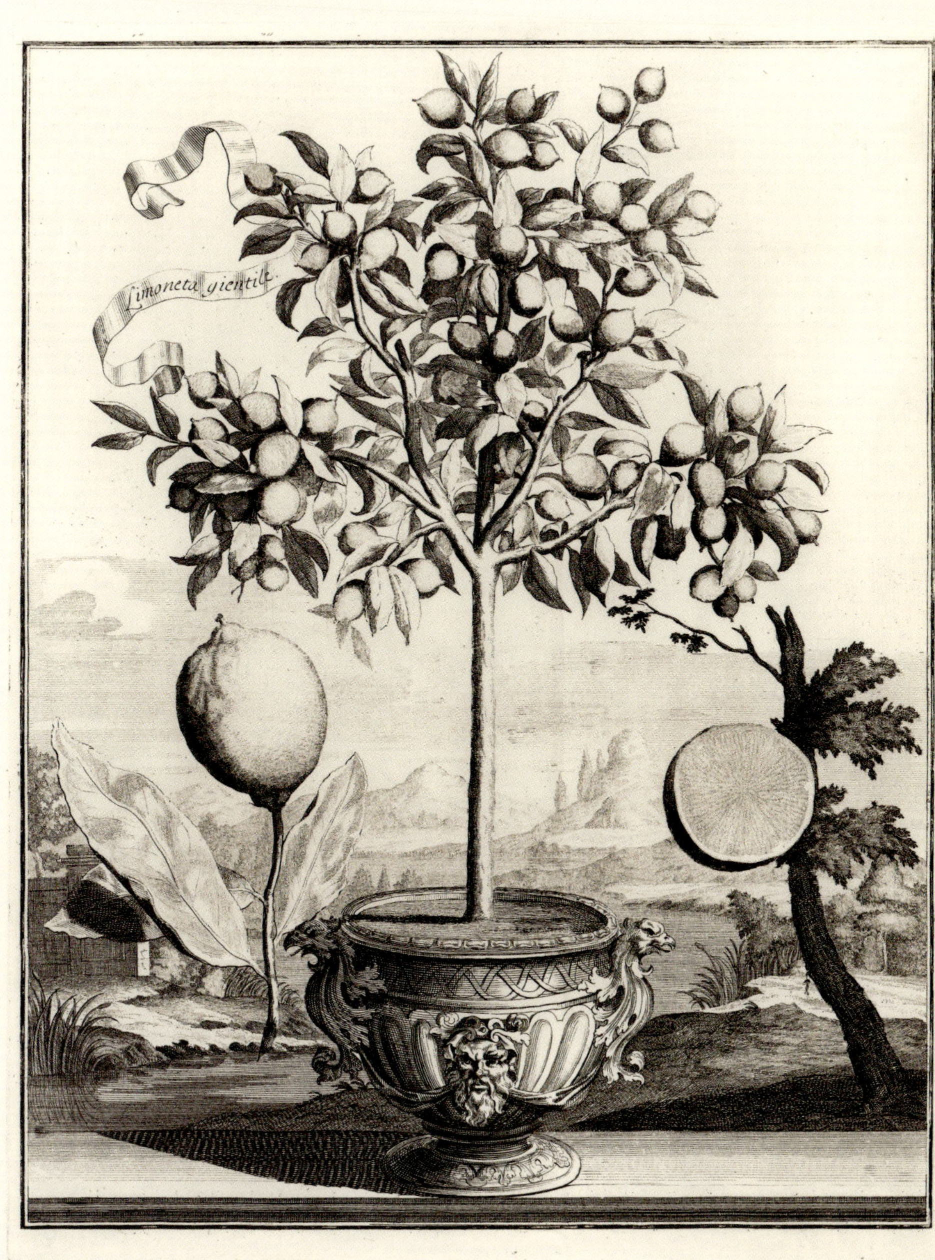

Limonet[t]a gientile

Unknown landscape

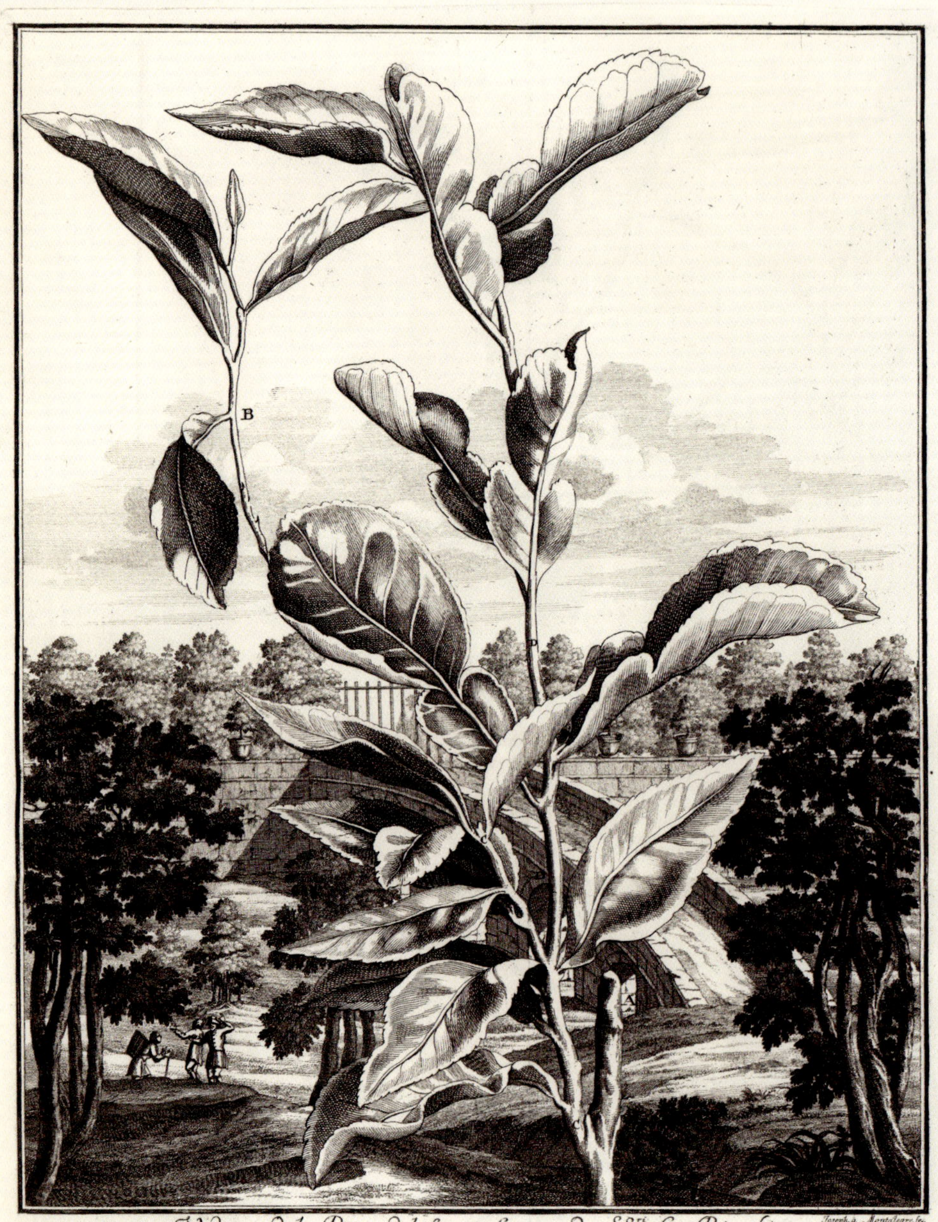

Veduta del Ponte del fiume Lauino de SS.ri Co: Bianchini. Joseph. a. Montalegre fe.

Bologna – Bridge over the Lavino River

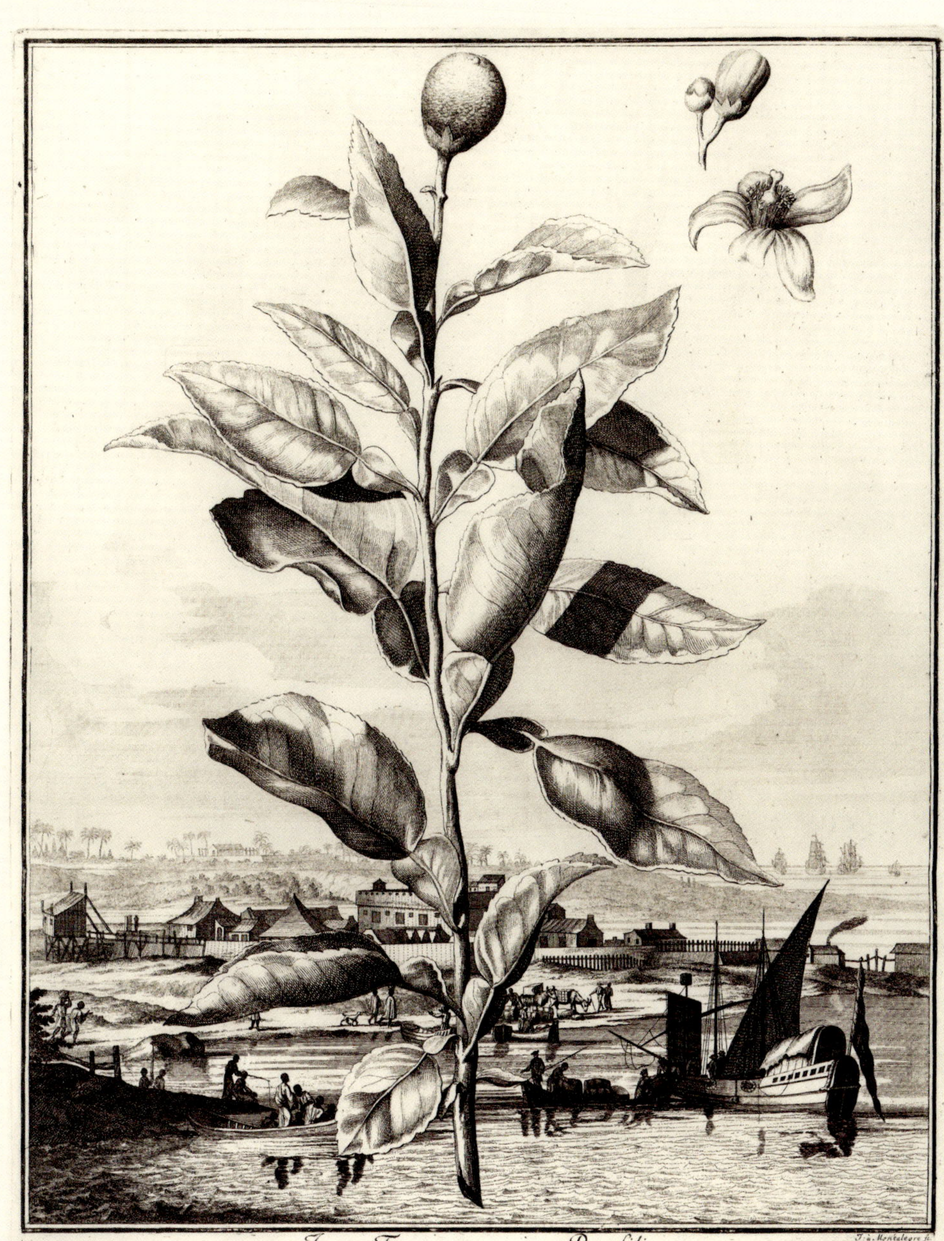
Ins: Tamaracca in Brasilia.

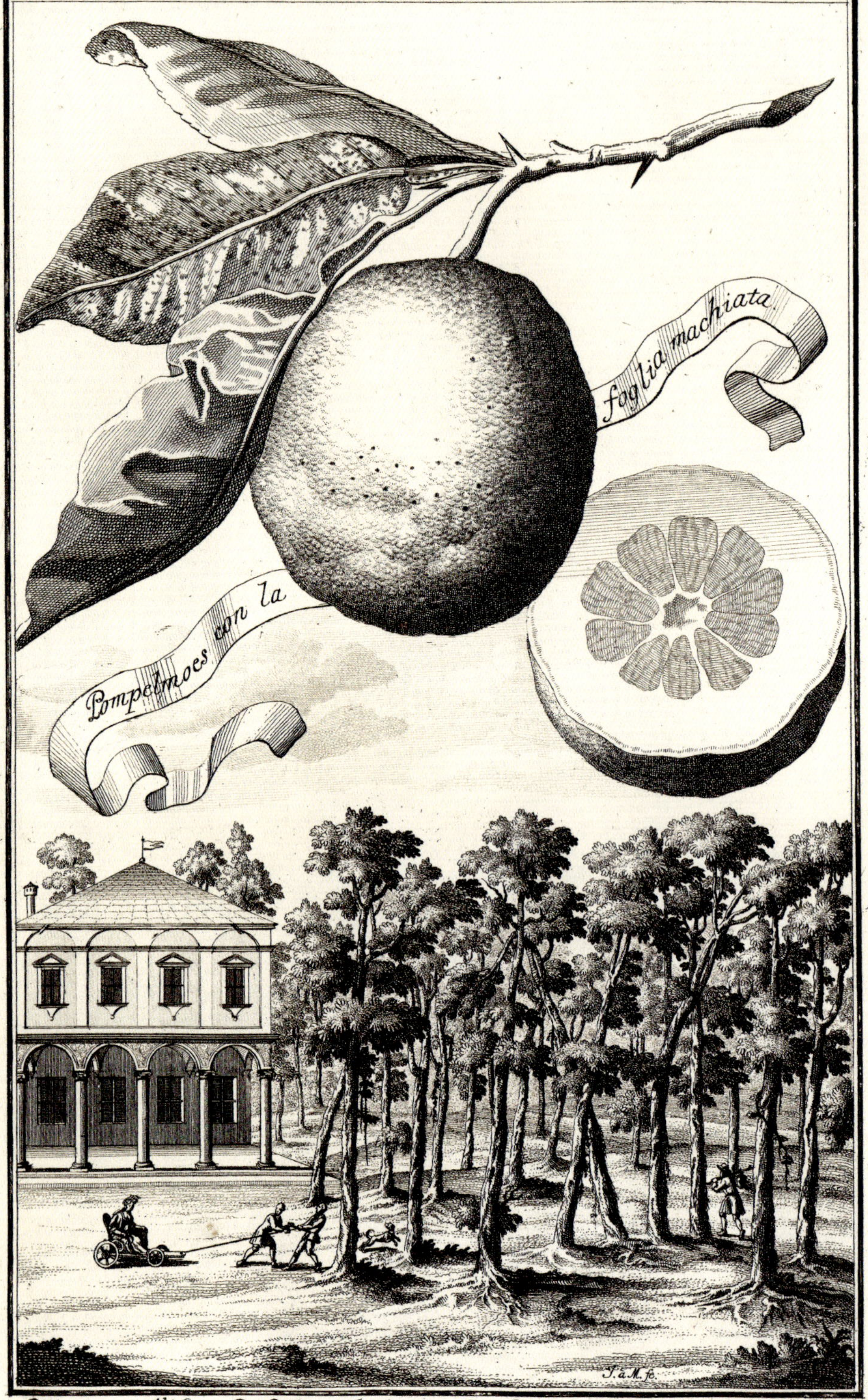

Collegio con l'Horto di delitia habitante da Studiosi detti della Viola nel Bolog:se

Pompelmus con la foglia machiata

Bologna – Palazzina della Viola

Aranzo di fior frutto e foglia rubicante

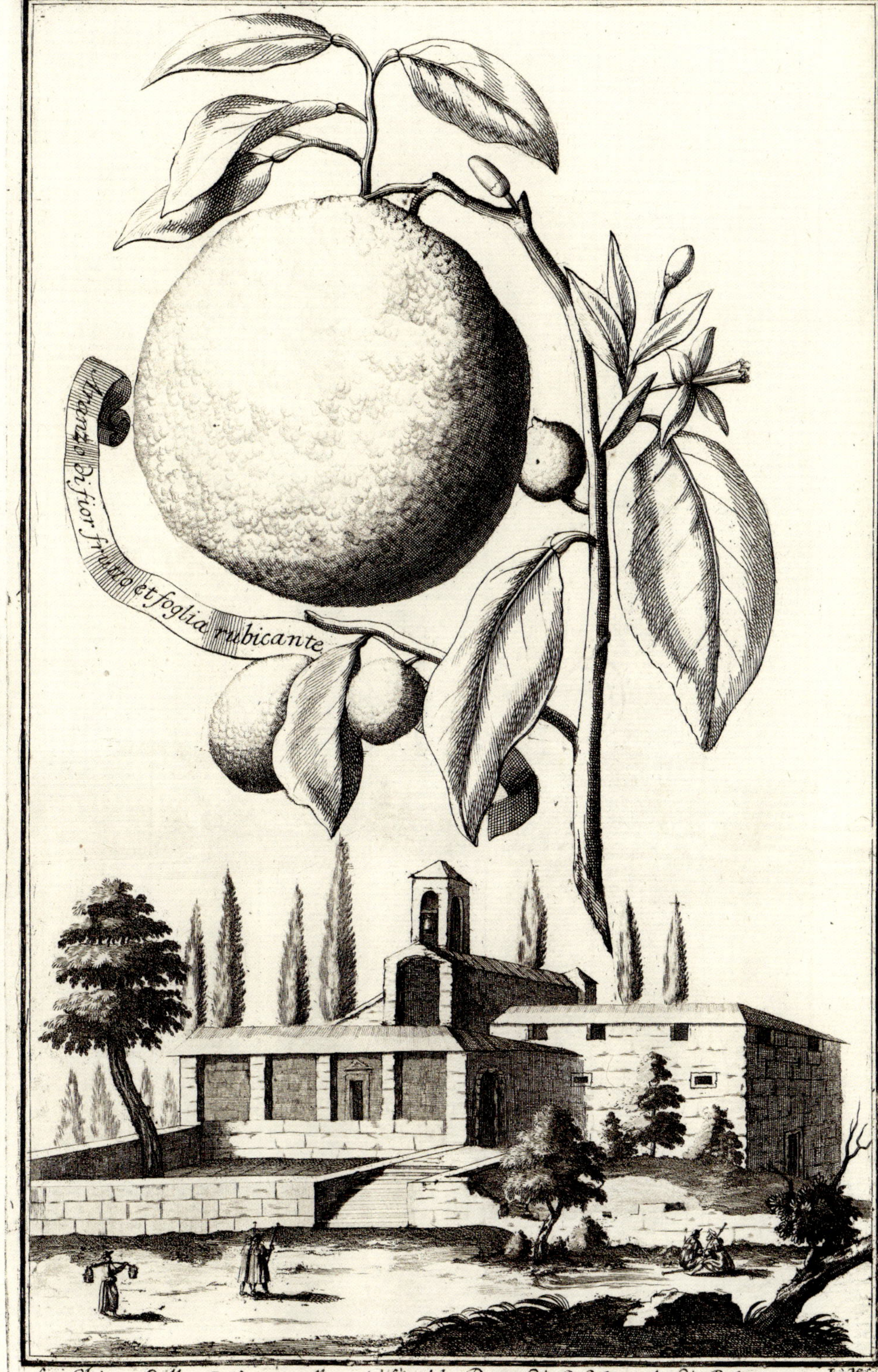

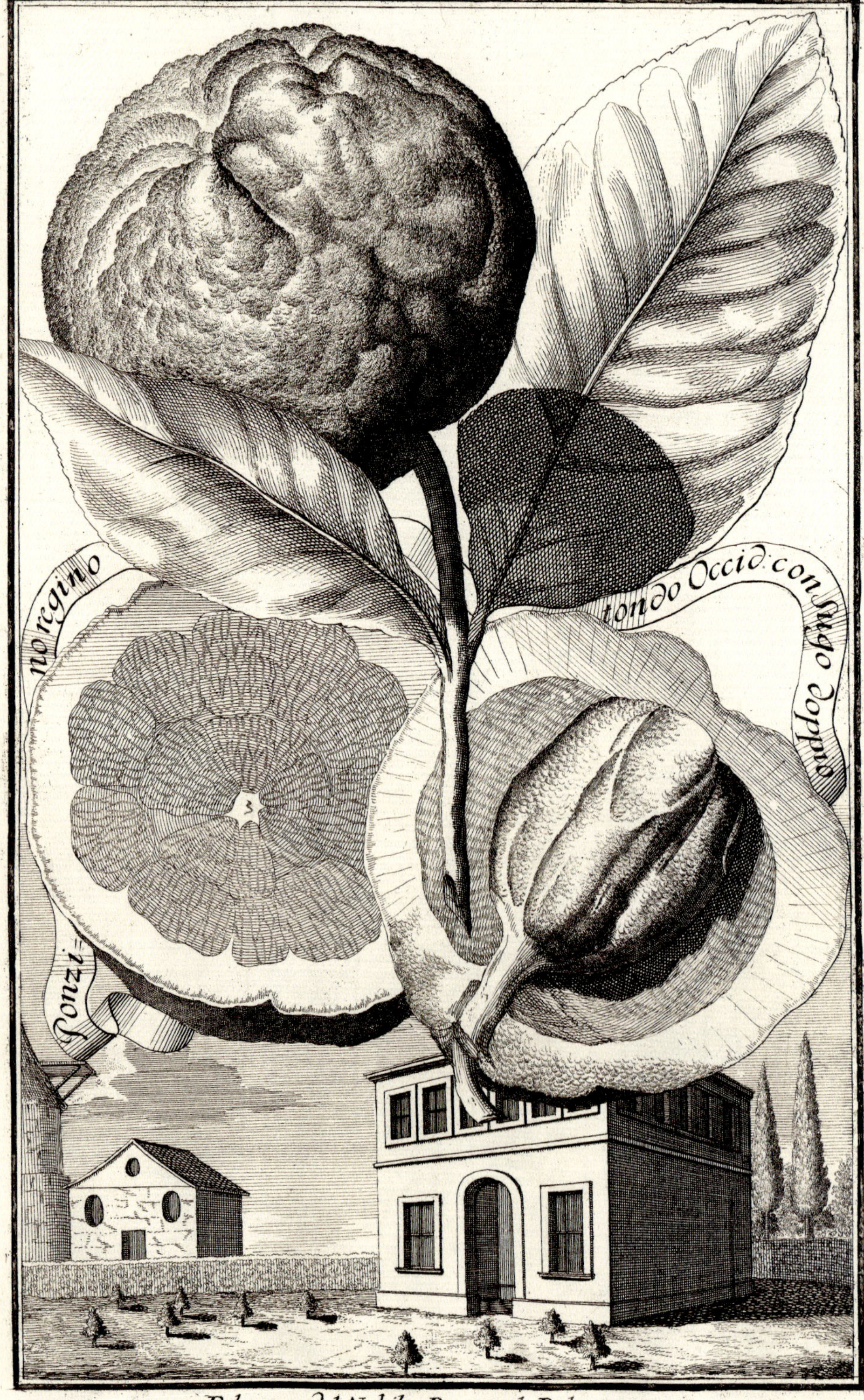

Ponzino regino tondo Occid[entale] con sugo doppio

Aranzo con la foglia strettiss[ima]

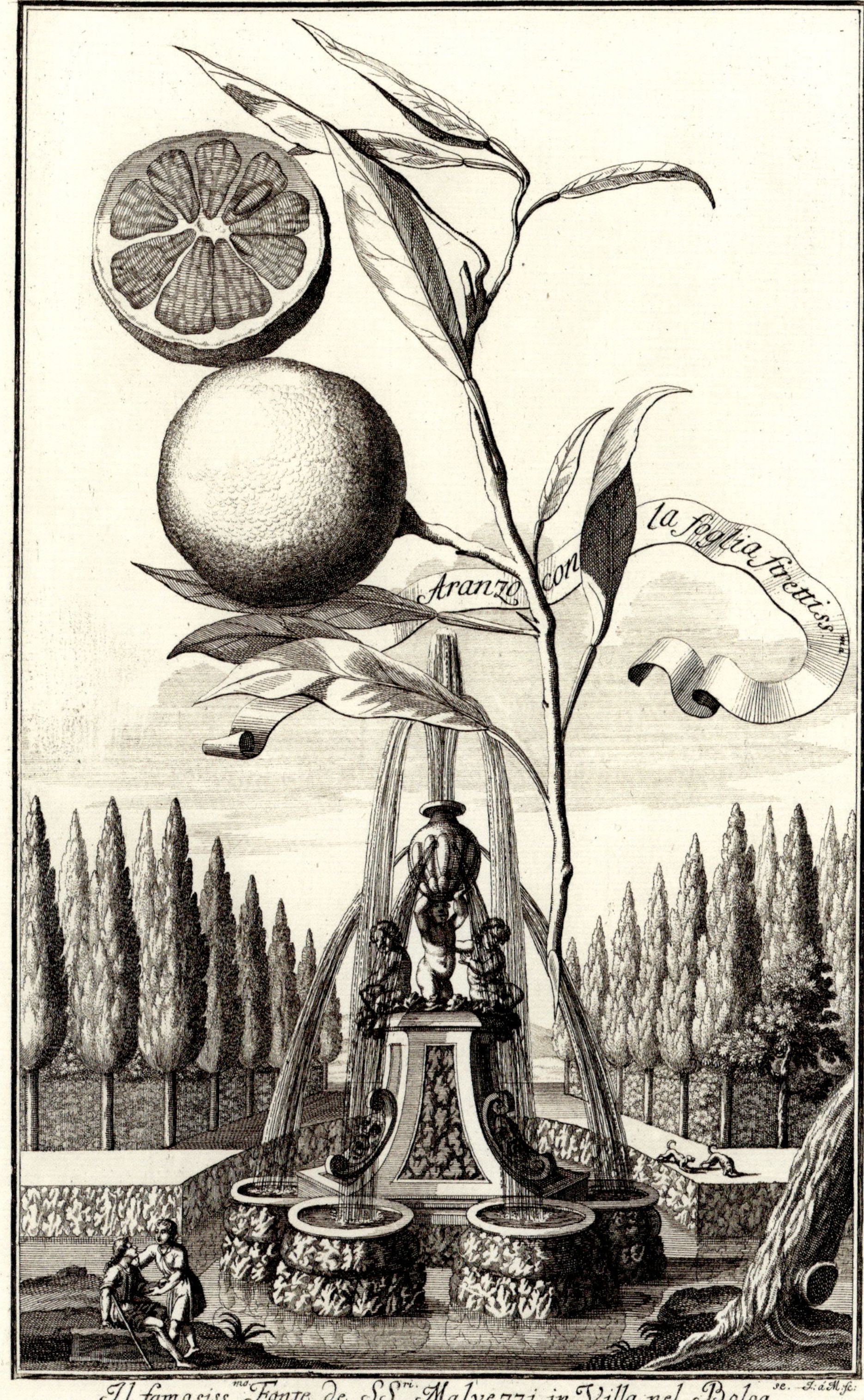

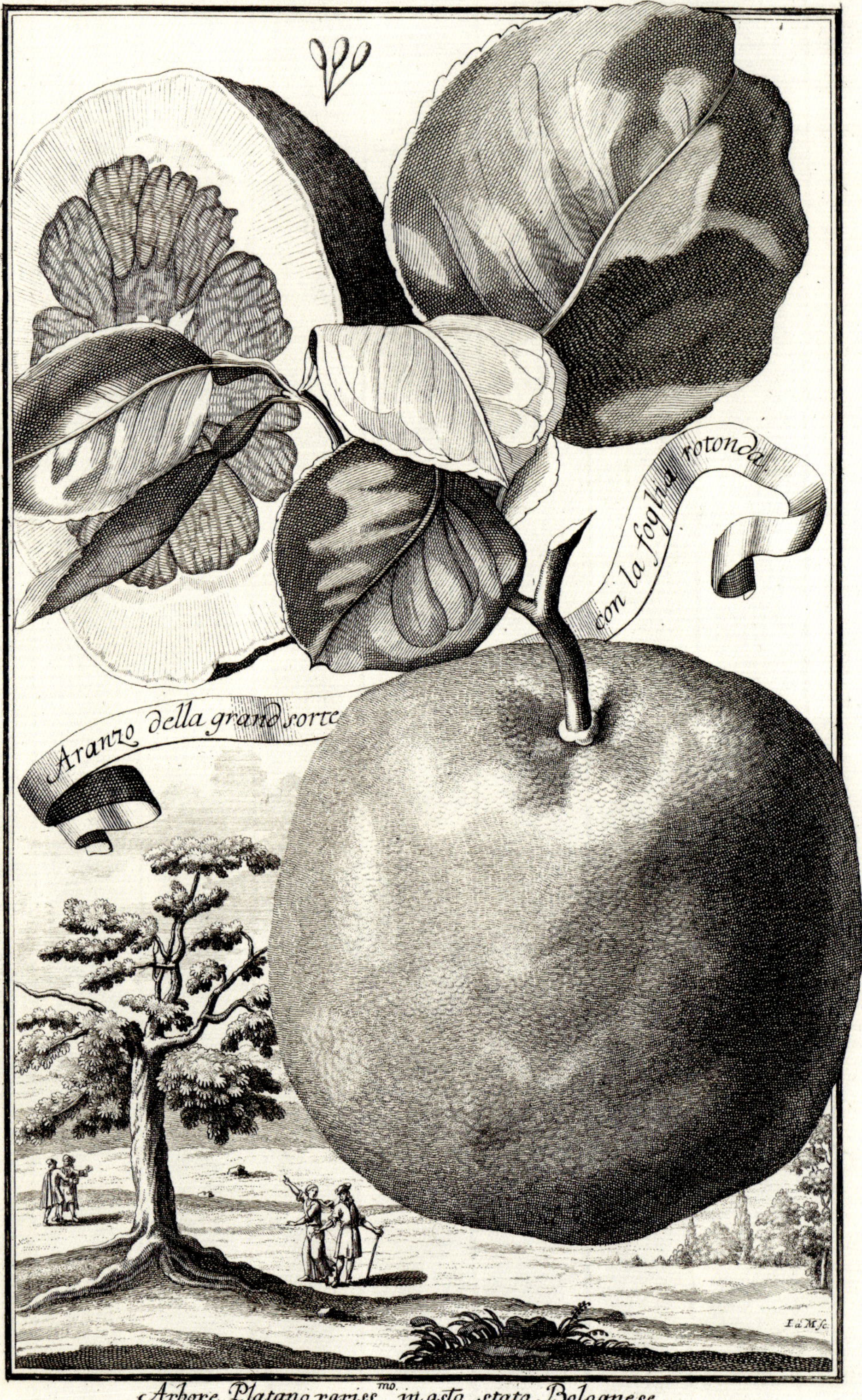

Bitter oranges / Pomeranzen / Bigarades

Aranzo della grand sorte con la foglia rotonda

Landscape in Bologna with a plane tree

Aranzo nano di Color Limonato

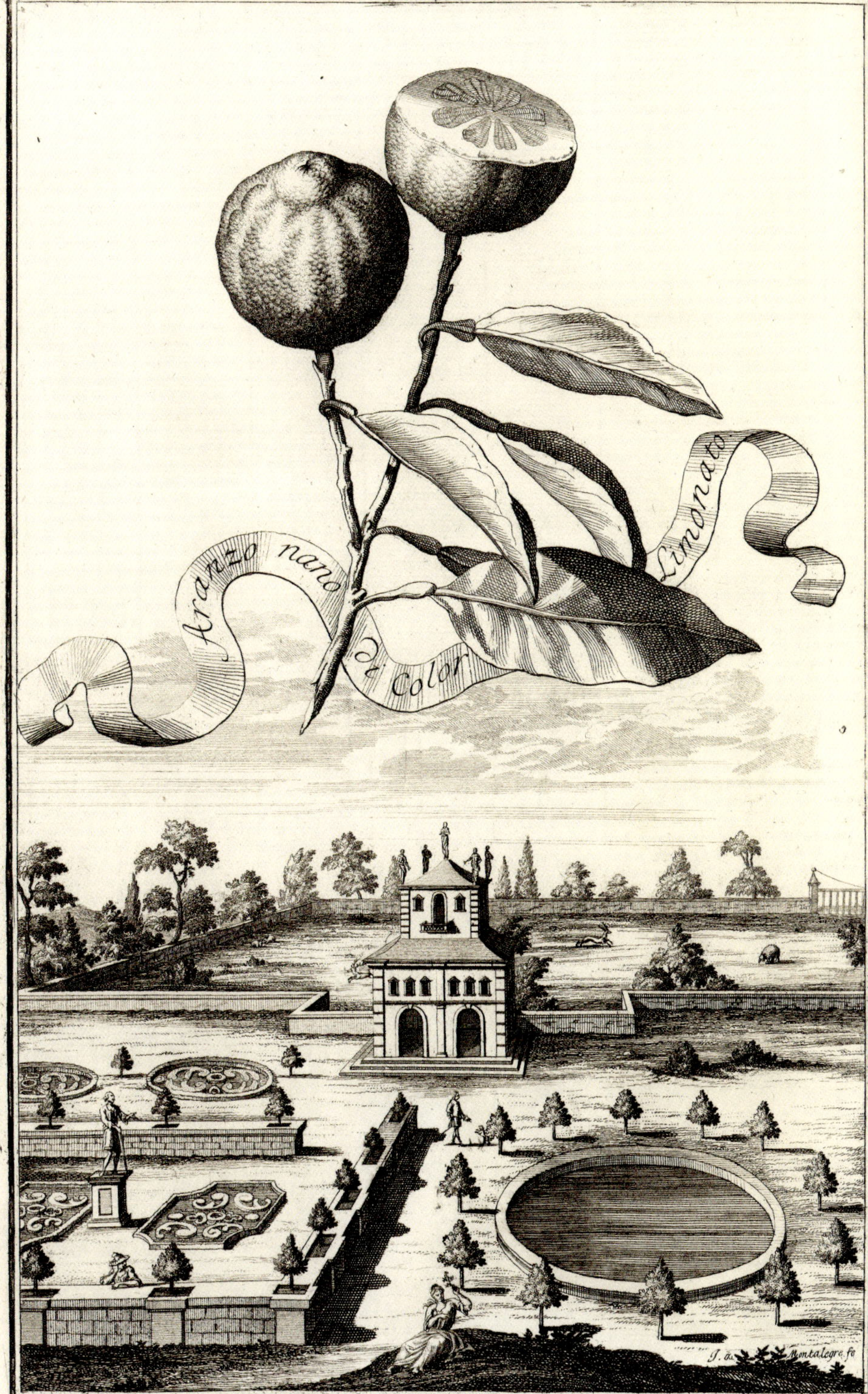

Aranzo Stellato da Neapoli

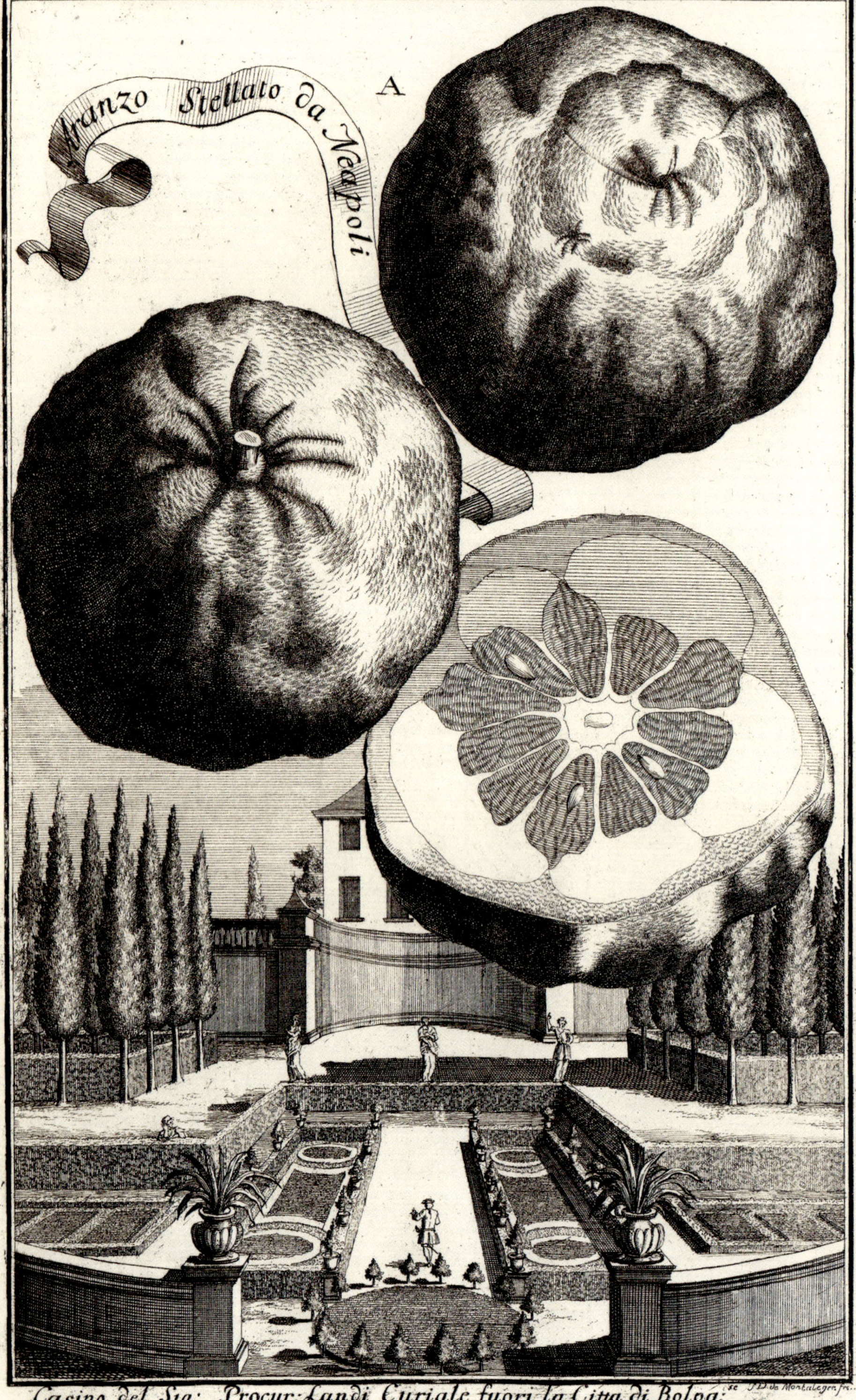

Bologna – Villa Landi

Aranzo Bergamotto

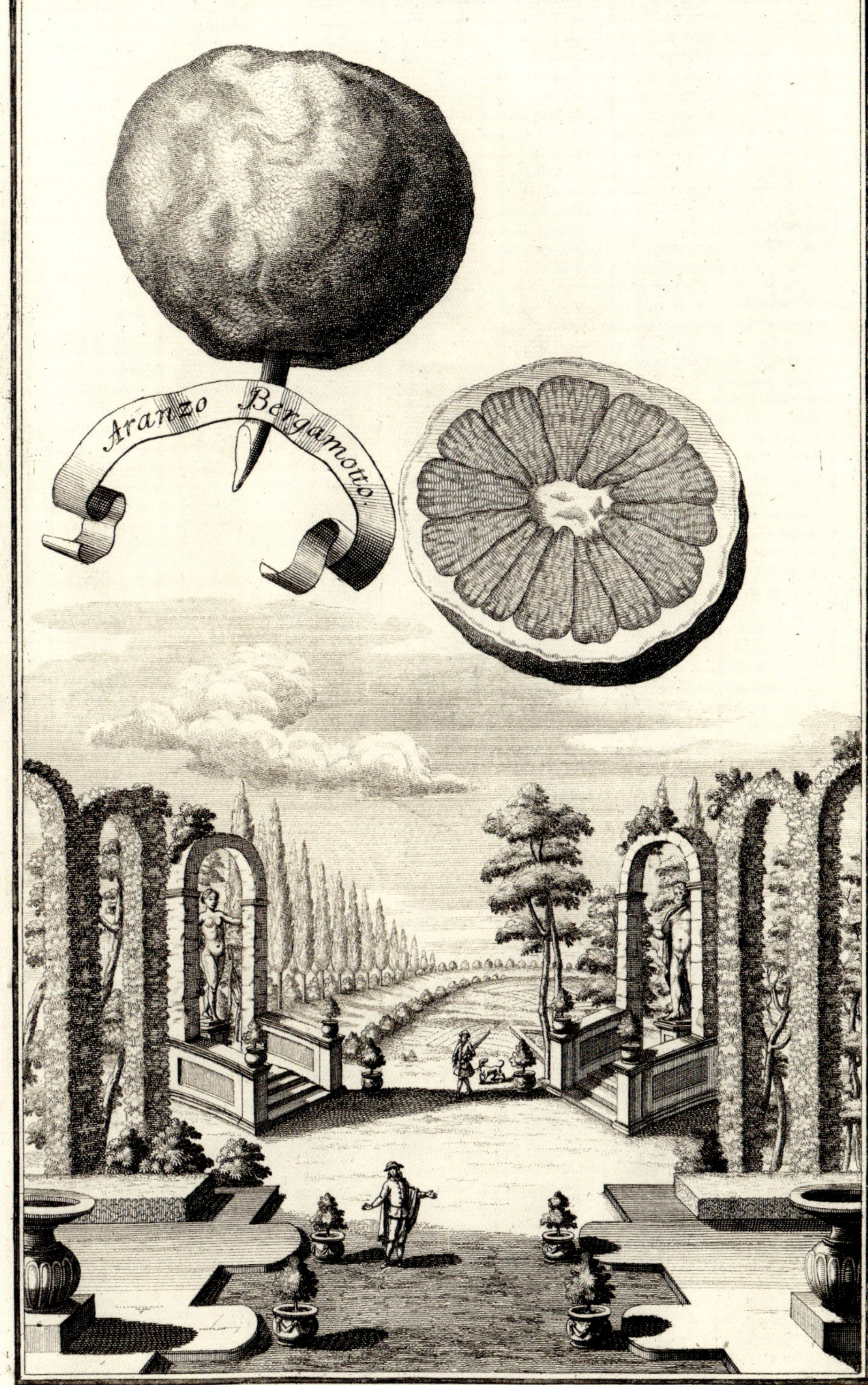

Bologna – Villa and Garden of the Bavarian Ambassador

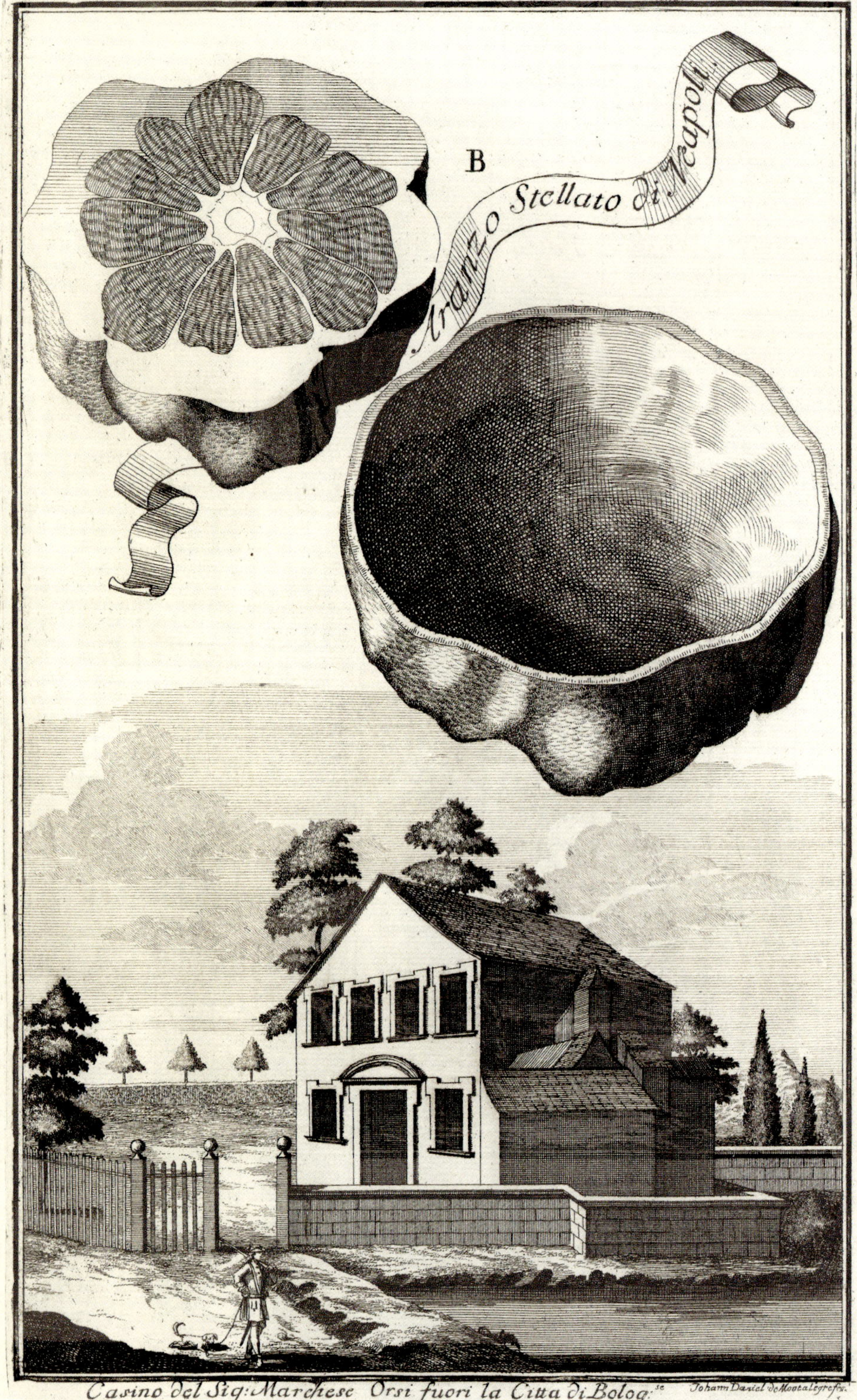
B
Aranzo Stellato di Neapoli.
Casino del Sig: Marchese Orsi fuori la Citta di Bolog:se
Johann Daniel de Montalegre fec.

Aranzo nano dolce con foglia tonda

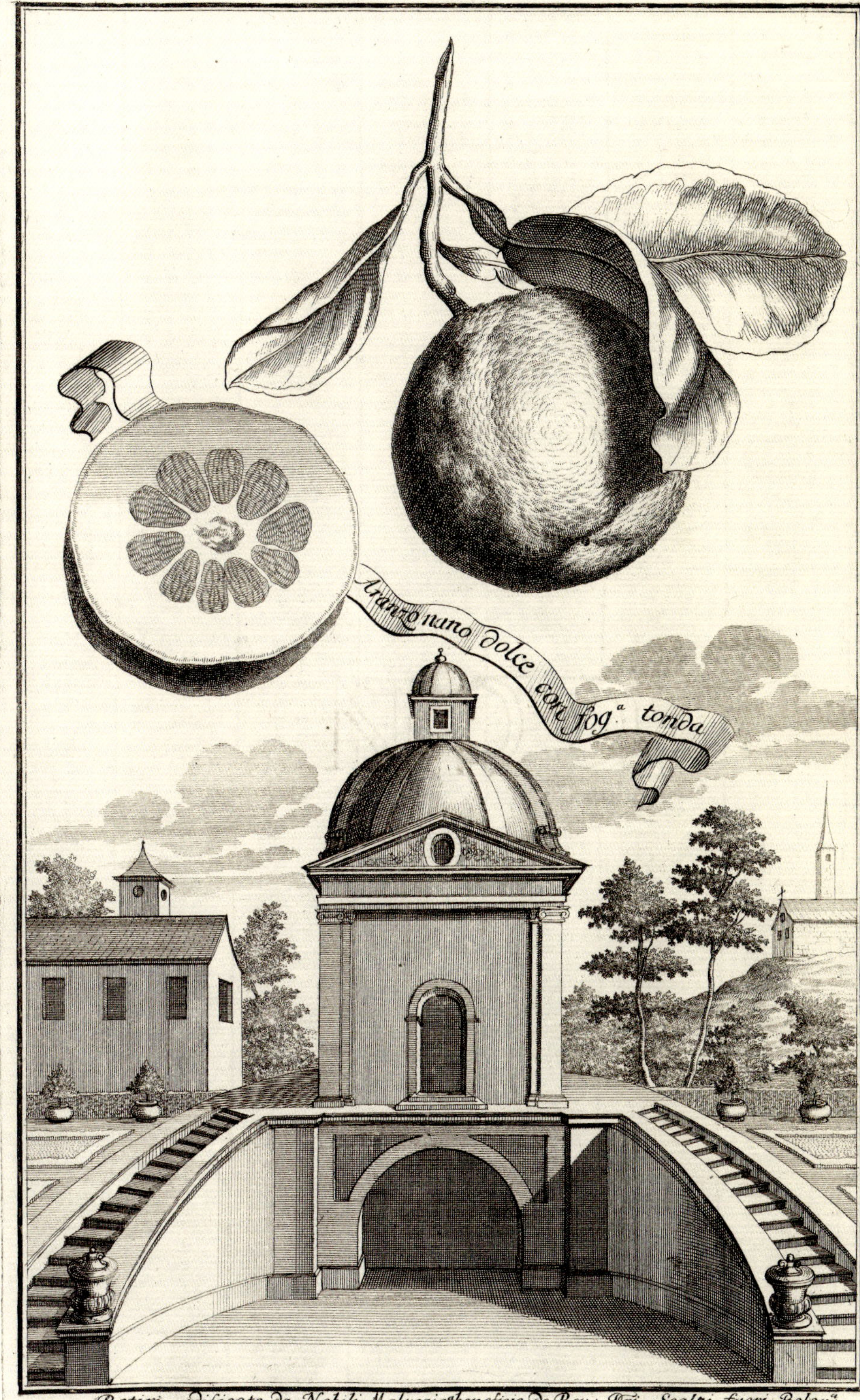

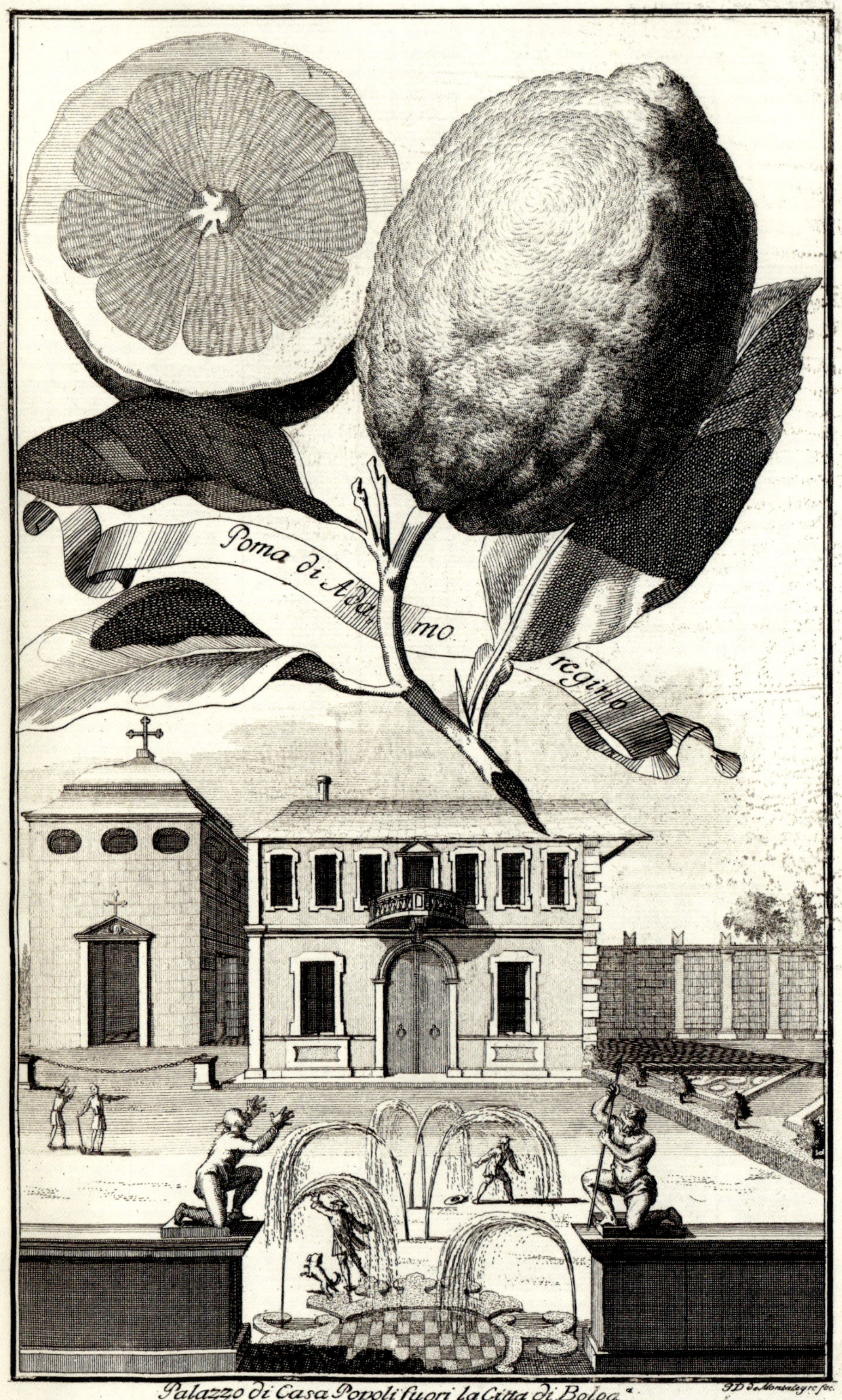

Pomo d'Adamo regino

Pomo d'Adamo fetifero Ferrarij

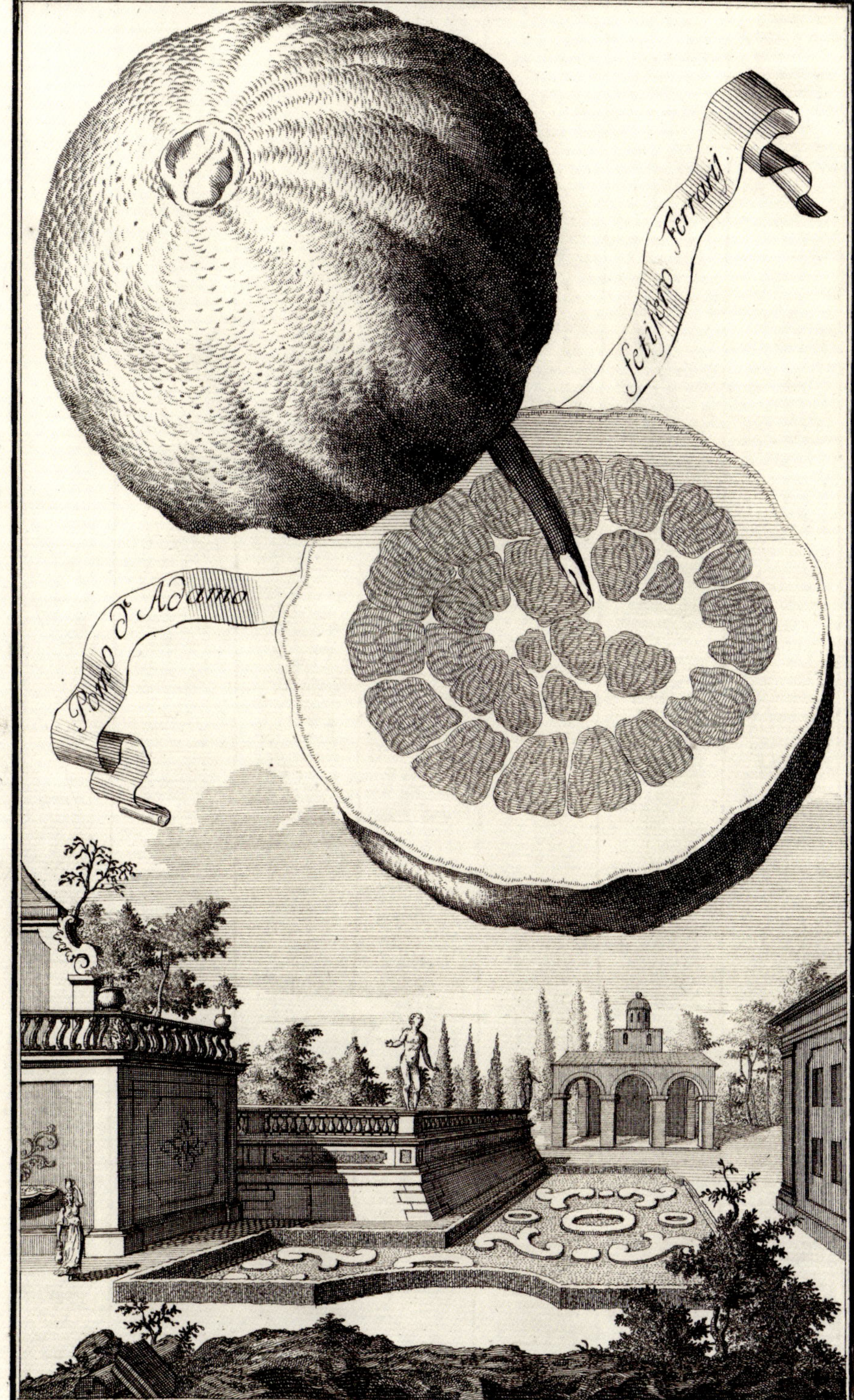

Terrazo di grand veduta del Nobil.mo Senatore Aldrovandi nel Bolognese.

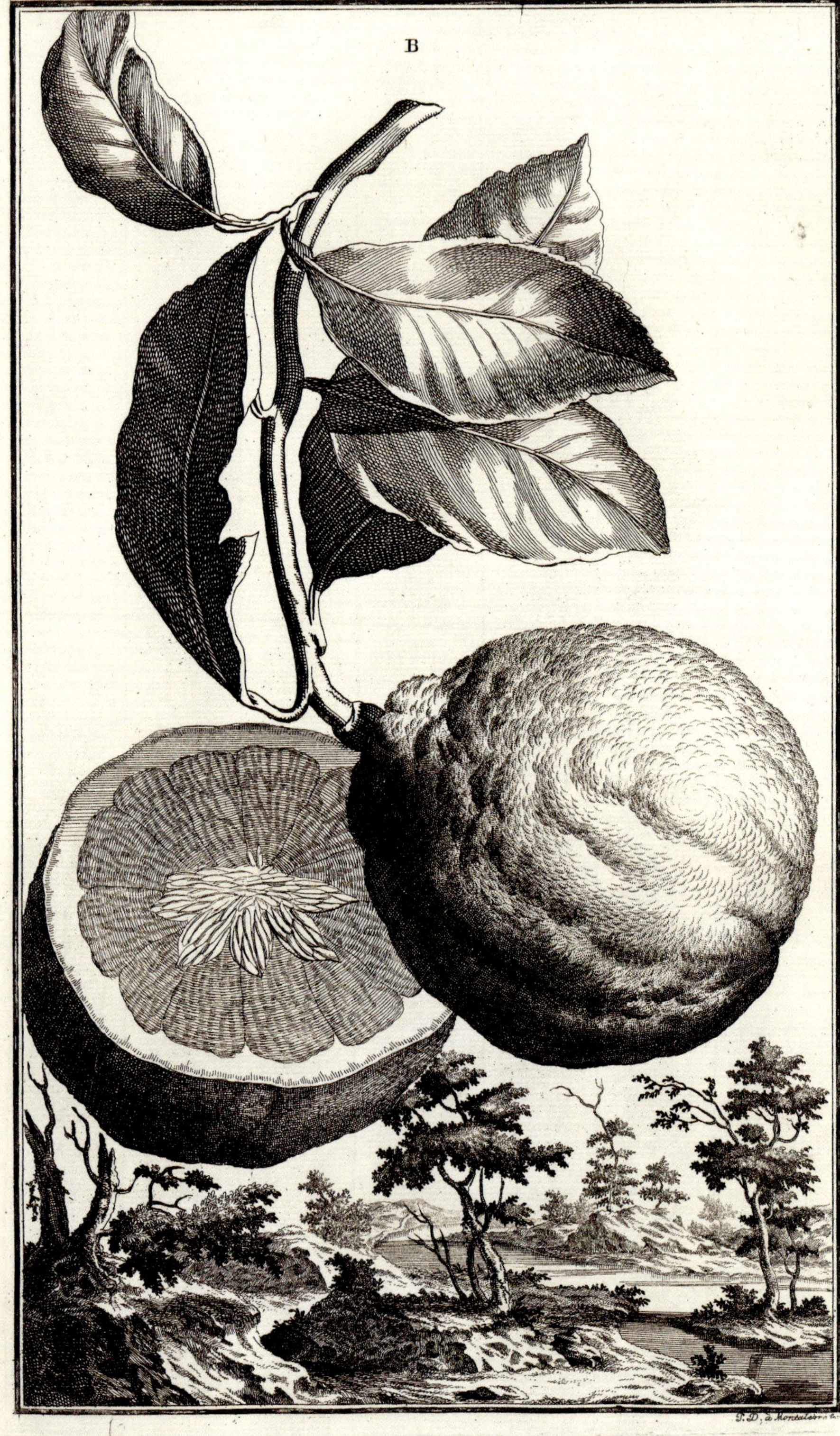

Citrus aurantium

Unknown landscape

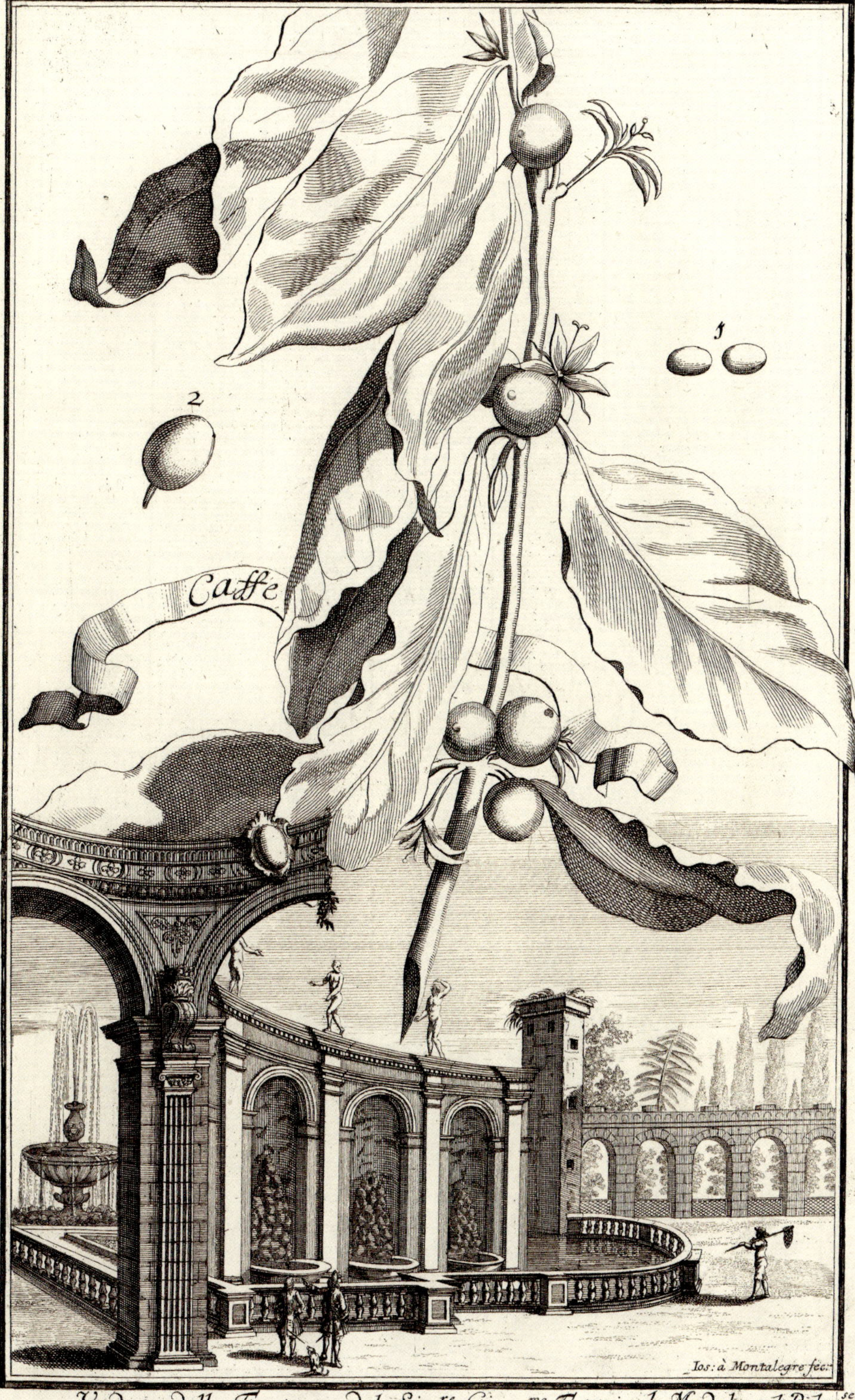
Caffe
2
1
Ios: à Montalegre fec:
Veduta delle Fontane del Sig.re Giac.mo Tazzi al Medola nel Bolog.se

EXTRACT
aus dem
von Ihro Käyserlichen Majestät
allergnädigst-erhaltenen
PRIVILEGIO.

WIr JOSEPH von GOttes Gnaden erwehlter Römischer Käyser / zu allen Zeiten Mehrer des Reichs / in Germanien / zu Hungarn / Böheim / Dalmatien / Croatien / und Sclavonien / König / Ertz-Hertzog zu Oesterreich / Hertzog zu Burgund / Steyer / Kärnten / Crain / und Würtenberg / Graff zu Tyrol / rc. Gebieten allen und jeden / Unsern und des Reichs / auch Unserer Erb-Königreichen / Fürstenthum und Landen / Unterthanen und Getreuen / insonderheit aber allen Buchdruckern / Kupfferstechern / Buchführern und Buchverkauffern / bey Vermeidung fünff Marck Lötigen Goldes / und befehlen ernstlich / und wollen / daß ihr / noch einiger aus Euch selbst / oder jemand von Eurentwegen dieses Buch / die Nürnbergische Hesperides genannt / ohne sein / des Authoris, und seiner Erben Wissen / innerhalb zehen Jahren / von dato an / in keinerley Sprach / auch weder in grossem noch kleinem Format / vermindert / oder vermehret / auch mit oder ohne Kupffer / nachdrucken / oder fremden Druck ins Reich / oder Unsere Käyserliche Erb-Lande bringen / selbige verkauffen / oder auf einigerley Weiß damit handlen solle / wie aus dem Käyserlichen Diplomate mit mehrern zu ersehen / welches gegeben / in Wien / den 16. Martii / Anno 1706.

Josephus.

V: G. v. Schönborn.

L. S.

Ad Mandatum Sac. Cæs. Maj. proprium

Frantz Niclaß Menßhengen.

Editorial Note

Editorische Anmerkung / Note éditoriale

The plates in volumes I and II of Volkamer's *Hesperides* are not numbered consecutively, and have either page numbers using Arabic numerals in the same way as the text pages, or else a reference to the text page that precedes them. In most cases the plates are marked "pag.", followed by the page number in Arabic numerals. The large-format plates are numbered with Roman numerals.

The third volume has survived as an unpaginated set of 62 proofs in the Universitätsbibliothek Erlangen-Nürnberg. It includes 58 plates together with a title-page engraving and three vignettes.

The botanical names in the captions of the plates section and the botanical classification of the fruits follow the forms of those names used by Volkamer and his own classification of the different types of citrus as citrons (*Citrus medica* L., *Citrus limonimedica* L.), lemons and limes (*Citrus limon* L., *Citrus aurantiifolia* (Christm.) Swingle) and bitter oranges, sweet oranges and grapefruits (*Citrus aurantium* L., *Citrus sinensis* L., *Citrus grandis* L.).

Die Tafeln in den Bänden I und II von Volkamers Hesperidenwerk sind nicht fortlaufend nummeriert, sondern wurden gemeinsam mit den Textseiten arabisch paginiert oder tragen den Verweis auf die Textseite, hinter der sie eingebunden wurden. Die Tafeln tragen überwiegend die Bezeichnung „pag.", gefolgt von der arabischen Seitenzahl. Großformatige Tafeln sind römisch nummeriert.

Der dritte Band ist als unpaginiertes Konvolut von 62 Andrucken in der Universitätsbibliothek Erlangen-Nürnberg erhalten. Er umfasst 58 Tafeln plus Titelkupfer und drei Vignetten.

Die botanischen Bezeichnungen in den Bildlegenden des Tafelteils und die botanische Klassifikation der dargestellten Früchte folgen den Angaben Volkamers und seiner Unterscheidung der Zitrussorten in Zedratzitronen (*Citrus medica* L., *Citrus limonimedica* L.), Zitronen und Limonen (*Citrus limon* L., *Citrus aurantiifolia* (Christm.) Swingle) sowie die bitteren Pomeranzen, süßen Orangen und Pampelmusen (*Citrus aurantium* L., *Citrus sinensis* L., *Citrus grandis* L.).

Les planches des volumes I et II du Livre des *Hespérides* ne sont pas numérotées en continu : soit elles ont été paginées comme les pages de textes en chiffres arabes, soit elles renvoient à la page de texte derrière laquelle elles ont été placées. Le plus souvent, les planches portent la mention « pag. », suivie du chiffre arabe de la page. Les planches grand format sont numérotées en chiffres romains.

Le troisième volume est conservé sous forme d'une liasse de 62 épreuves à l'Universitätsbibliothek Erlangen-Nürnberg. Il comprend 58 planches avec un frontispice et trois vignettes.

Les termes botaniques mentionnés dans les légendes du chapitre des planches et la classification botanique des fruits représentés correspondent aux indications de Volkamer et à sa différenciation des sortes d'agrumes en cédrats (*Citrus medica* L., *Citrus limonimedica* L.), citrons et limons (*Citrus limon* L., *Citrus aurantiifolia* (Christm.) Swingle) oranges amères ou bigarades, oranges douces et pamplemousses (*Citrus aurantium* L., *Citrus sinensis* L., *Citrus grandis* L.).

Nürnbergische Hesperides, 1708, vol. I, imperial patent of 1706, permitting publication

Bibliographical Details of the Original Volumes
Bibliografische Angaben zu den Originalbänden
Références bibliographiques des volumes originaux

Volume I
Johann Christoph Volkamer:
Nürnbergische Hesperides, Nuremberg: Johann Andreas Endter (Sohn und Erben), 1708
Stadtarchiv Fürth, inv. Stadtbibliothek Fürth, 2091.2°

Volume II
Johann Christoph Volkamer:
Continuation der Nürnbergischen Hesperidum, Frankfurt and Leipzig: Johann Andreas Endter (Sohn und Erben), 1714
Stadtarchiv Fürth, inv. Stadtbibliothek Fürth, 2092.2°

Volume III
Johann Christoph Volkamer:
Nürnbergische Hesperides, plates before 1718
Erlangen, Universitätsbibliothek Erlangen-Nürnberg, H61/2 RARA.A 35 [2

The Universitätsbibliothek Erlangen-Nürnberg houses a set of 62 proofs for the planned third volume of the *Hesperides*, which was never actually published.

In der Universitätsbibliothek Erlangen-Nürnberg ist ein Konvolut von 62 Andrucken für den geplanten dritten Band des Hesperidenwerks erhalten, der allerdings nicht veröffentlicht wurde.

L'Universitätsbibliothek Erlangen-Nürnberg abrite une liasse de 62 épreuves, conservée pour le troisième volume du Livre des *Hespérides* qui n'a toutefois pas été publié.

Draughtsmen and Engravers
The plates in the first volume presented here are taken from the first edition of 1708. Some of these plates were only signed by the engravers when the volume went into its second edition. All the fruits depicted were engraved after preliminary drawings by Johann Christoph Volkamer.

Zeichner und Kupferstecher
Die Tafeln des ersten Bandes der vorliegenden Publikation stammen aus der ersten Auflage von 1708. Einige Tafeln von Band 1 erhielten jedoch erst in der zweiten Auflage die Signaturen der Kupferstecher. Alle Fruchtdarstellungen wurden nach Vorzeichnungen von Johann Christoph Volkamer gestochen.

Dessinateurs et graveurs
Les planches du premier volume de la présente publication proviennent de la première édition de 1708. Toutefois, plusieurs planches du volume 1 ne présentèrent que dans la seconde édition les signatures des chalcographes. Toutes les représentations de fruits ont été gravées d'après des esquisses de Johann Christoph Volkamer.

Beck(h), Tobias Gabriel (1685–1755)
Böl(l)mann, Hieronymus († 1735/36)
Decker, Paul, the Elder (1677–1713)
Decker, Paul, the Younger (1685–1742)
Dehne, Johann Christoph († 1742)
Delsenbach, Johann Adam (1687–1765)
Glotsch, Ludwig Christoph (1665–1719)
Kenkel, Benjamin (*1705)
Krieger, Christoph Friedrich (1681–1725)
Lindner, Friedrich Paul (1691–1770)
Montalegre, Joseph a (1672–1718)
Montalegre, Johann Daniel de (1697–1768)
Pfann, Wilhelm (1644–after 1703)
Steinberger, Johann Christoph (1680–1721)
Volkamer, Johann Christoph (1644–1720)

Nürnbergische Hesperides, 1708, vol. 1, p. 23 with vignette of Torbole, Lake Garda

Baum vor der Faulung verwahret seye. Wann aber die Bäume blühen / und die Früchte anzusetzen und zu wachsen beginnen / wollen sie etwas mehrers begossen / und dahero desto feuchter gehalten seyn: Nicht weniger auch die Pomerantzen- und Citronen-Bäume fast durchgehend / wann sie im Pomerantzen-Hauß in erhöheten Kästen stehen / (wie ich in dem ersten Capitel gemeldet habe) nicht minder wol begossen werden müssen / ob es schon geregnet hat / weil die Cronen und Blätter derselben den Regen sehr aufhalten / und nur die Tropfen hinab fallen lassen / daß das wenigste in die Kästen / sondern vielmehr beyseits fället / daher / ob sie schon obenher feucht anzusehen / solches doch von schlechter Krafft / weil es nicht tieff in das Erdreich eindringet.

In dem Winter darf man denen in der Winterung stehenden Bäumen (1) nicht so viel Wasser auf einmal geben / als im Sommer / sondern es ist genug / wann die Wurtzeln nur eine wenige Feuchte haben / dahero man dann (2) um den Stamm herum die Erde ein wenig zu erhöhen / und wie ein kleines Gräbenlein zu machen pfleget / worein man das Wasser giesset / und dadurch verhütet / daß der Stamm davon nicht benetzet werde; auch soll (3) solches Wasser ja nicht kalt / sondern überschlagen und (4) in keinem kupfernen Geschirr aufgewärmet werden / (5) wann man die Bäume zu begiessen gesonnen / muß man sehen / ob man auch wegen des kalten Wetters ihnen jedes mal ein klein wenig Lufft geben könne / damit dieser / so wenig er auch ist / solche desto ehender wieder in etwas austrocknen / und die vom Begiessen entstandene Feuchte sich um so viel leichter aus dem Gemach ziehen möge: Einige legen aus einer besonders vermeinten Witz im Winter in denen Winterungen und Kellern Schnee um die Bäume und Gewächse / aber gewiß aus einer sehr grossen Unwissenheit / weil es / wie die Erfahrung mit Schaden lehren wird / bevorab denen Pomerantzen- und Citronen-Bäumen über aus nachtheilich fället / und daher billig zu unterlassen.

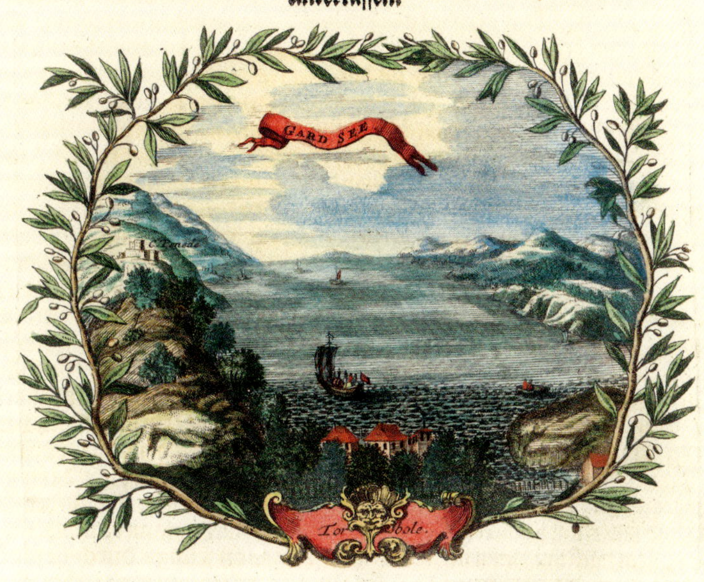

Das

Index of Plants

Register der Pflanzen / Index des plantes

The index of plants lists the botanical names as used by Volkamer on the plates. Citrus species tend to change considerably over time and in Volkamer's day were subject to intensive cultivation, giving rise to a great variety of forms. Volkamer lists a number of citrus types which were not previously known and which did not appear in books subsequently. In consequence, the botanical names and classification of these examples follow the information provided by Volkamer. The range of different ways in which the historical names appear reflects the historical situation. For non-citrus plants the index lists the modern botanical name in addition to the name used by Volkamer. We should like to take this opportunity of thanking Clemens Alexander Wimmer for identifying the botanical names.

Das Register der Pflanzen verzeichnet die auf den Tafeln wiedergegebenen botanischen Bezeichnungen Volkamers. Die Zitrus neigt zu starken Veränderungen und wurde zur Zeit Volkamers intensiv kultiviert, wodurch eine große Formenvielfalt entstand. Volkamer führt manche Zitrussorten auf, die vor ihm nicht bekannt waren und die auch später nicht wieder publiziert wurden. Die botanischen Bezeichnungen und die Klassifikation folgen daher Volkamers Angaben. Der Reichtum und die Differenzierung der historischen Bezeichnungen geben einen historischen Stand wieder. Für Nicht-Zitruspflanzen gibt der Index zusätzlich zu der Bezeichnung Volkamers den modernen botanischen Namen an. Für die Bestimmung sei an dieser Stelle Clemens Alexander Wimmer gedankt.

L'index des plantes répertorie les termes botaniques de Volkamer mentionnés sur les planches. Sujets à de fortes altérations, les agrumes furent cultivés de manière intensive à l'époque de Volkamer, ce qui engendra une grande variété de formes. Volkamer énumère certaines espèces d'agrumes qui étaient jusqu'alors inconnues et qui, même plus tard, ne furent pas rééditées. Pour cette raison, les termes botaniques et leur classification sont conformes aux indications de Volkamer. La profusion et la différenciation des appellations historiques reproduisent un état historique. Les plantes ne faisant pas partie des agrumes sont indiquées sous leur nom botanique moderne en plus de l'appellation de Volkamer. Nous tenons à remercier ici Clemens Alexander Wimmer pour ses travaux de détermination des espèces.

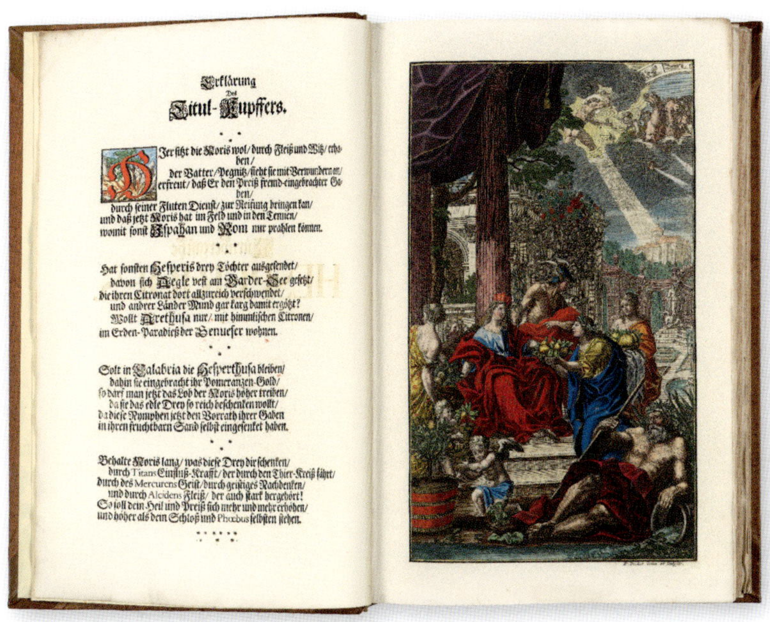

Erklärung
Des
Titul-Kupffers.

Hier sitzt die Moris wol/ durch Fleiß und Witz/ erhoben/
der Vatter/ Pegnitz/ sieht sie mit Verwundern an/
erfreut/ daß Er den Preiß fremd-eingebrachter Gaben/
durch seiner Fluten Dienst/ zur Reifung bringen kan/
und daß jetzt Moris hat im Feld und in den Tennen/
womit sonst Ispahan und Rom nur prahlen können.

Hat sonsten Hesperis drey Töchter ausgesendet/
davon sich Aegle vest am Garder-See gesetzt/
die ihren Citronat dort allzureich verschwendet/
und andrer Länder Mund gar karg damit ergötzt?
Wollt Arethusa nur/ mit himmlischen Citronen/
im Erden-Paradieß der Genueser wohnen.

Solt in Calabria die Hesperthusa bleiben/
dahin sie eingebracht ihr Pomeranzen-Gold/
so darf man jetzt das Lob der Moris höher treiben/
da sie das edle Drey so reich beschenken wollt/
da diese Nymphen jetzt den Vorrath ihrer Gaben
in ihren fruchtbarn Sand selbst eingesenket haben.

Behalte Moris lang/ was diese Drey dir schenken/
durch Titans Einfluß-Krafft/ der durch den Thier-Kreiß fährt/
durch des Mercurens Geist/ durch geistiges Nachdenken/
und durch Alcidens Fleiß/ der auch stark hergehört!
So soll dein Heil und Preiß sich mehr und mehr erhöhen/
und höher als dein Schloß und Phoebus selbsten stehen.

Nürnbergische Hesperides, 1708, vol. 1, frontispiece text and frontispiece (see p. 2)

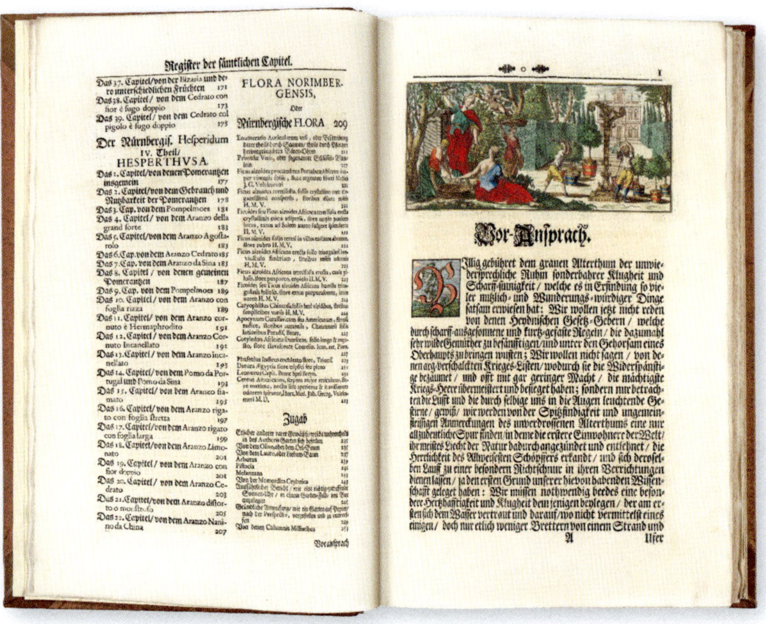
Register der sämtlichen Capitel.

FLORA NORIMBERGENSIS,

Oder

Nürnbergische FLORA 209

Der Nürnbergis. Hesperidum IV. Theil/ HESPERTHVSA.

Zugab

Vor-Ansprach.

Nürnbergische Hesperides, 1708, vol. 1, contents and preamble

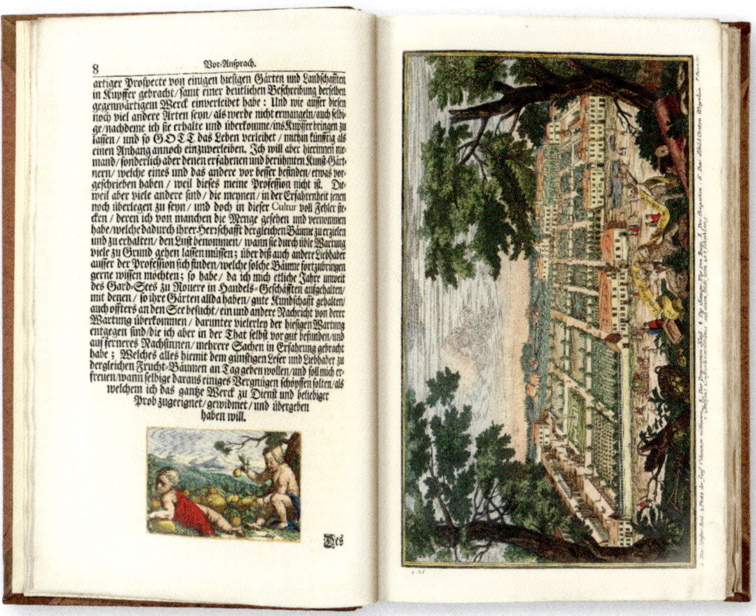

8 Vor-Ansprach.

artiger Prospecte von einigen hiesigen Gärten und Landschafften in Kupffer gebracht/samt einer deutlichen Beschreibung derselben gegenwärtigem Werck einverleibet habe: Und wie ausser diesen noch viel andere Arten seyn/als werde nicht ermangeln/auch selbige/nachdeme ich sie erhalte und überkomme/ins Kupffer bringen zu lassen/ und so GOTT das Leben verleihet/mithin künfftig als einen Anhang annoch einzuverleiben. Ich will aber hierinnen niemand/sonderlich aber denen erfahrnen und berühmten Kunst-Gärtnern/welche eines und das andere vor besser befinden/etwas vorgeschrieben haben/weil dieses meine Profession nicht ist. Dieweil aber viele andere sind/die meynen/in der Erfahrenheit jenen noch überlegen zu seyn/und doch in dieser Cultur voll Fehler stecken/deren ich von manchen die Menge gesehen und vernommen habe/welche dadurch ihrer Herrschafft dergleichen Bäume zu erzielen und zu erhalten/den Lust benommen/wann sie durch üble Wartung viele zu Grund gehen lassen müssen; über diß auch andere Liebhaber ausser der Profession sich finden/welche solche Bäume fortzubringen gerne wissen möchten; so habe/da ich mich etliche Jahre unweit des Gard-Sees zu Rovere in Handels-Geschäfften aufgehalten/mit denen/so ihre Gärten allda haben/gute Kundschafft gehalten/auch öffters an den See besucht/ein und andere Nachricht von derer Wartung überkommen/darunter vielerley der hiesigen Wartung entgegen sind/die ich aber in der That selbst vor gut befunden/und auf ferneres Nachsinnen/mehrere Sachen in Erfahrung gebracht habe; Welches alles hiemit dem günstigen Leser und Liebhaber zu dergleichen Frucht-Bäumen an Tag geben wollen/und soll mich erfreuen/wann selbige daraus einiges Vergnügen schöpffen solten/als welchem ich das gantze Werck zu Dienst und beliebiger Prob zugeeignet/gewidmet/und übergeben haben will.

Des

Nürnbergische Hesperides, 1708, vol. 1, end of preamble and plate after p. 8 (see pp. 26/27)

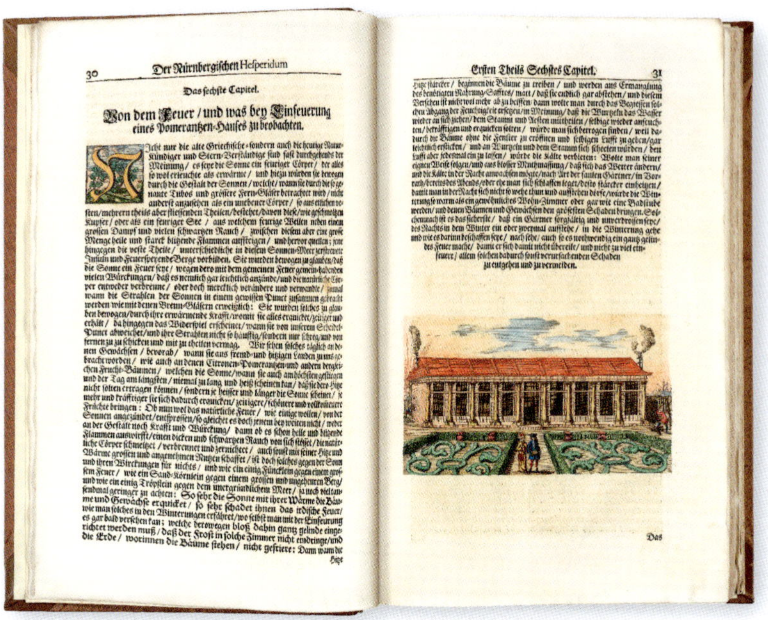
30 Der Nürnbergischen Hesperidum

Das sechste Capitel.

Von dem Feuer / und was bey Einfeuerung eines Pomerantzen-Hauses zu beobachten.

Ersten Theils Sechstes Capitel. 31

Nürnbergische Hesperides, 1708, vol. 1, pp. 30/31 with vignette of an orangery

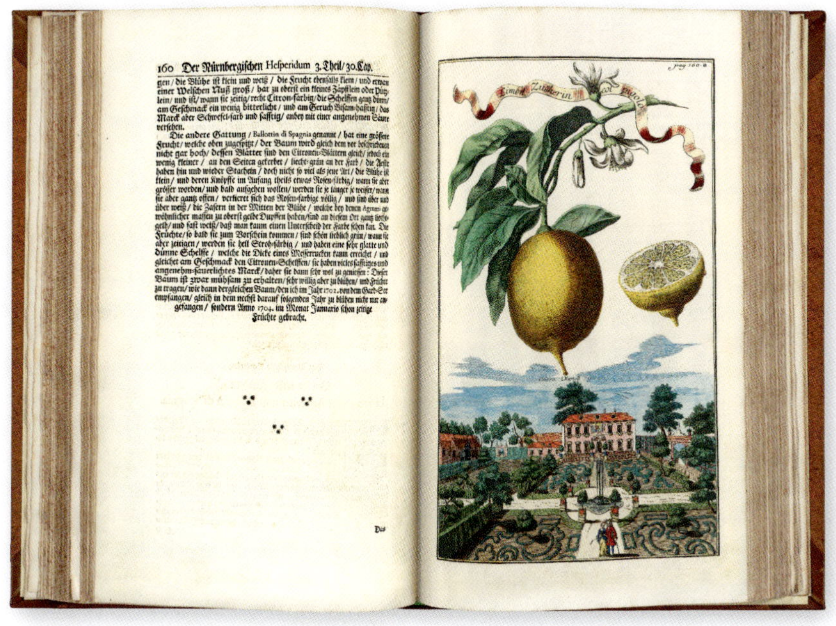

160 Der Nürnbergischen Hesperidum 3.Theil/30.Cap.

gen/ die Blühe ist klein und weiß / die Frucht ebenfalls klein / und etwan einer Welschen Nuß groß / hat zu oberst ein kleines Zäpflein oder Pützlein/ und ist/ wann sie zeitig/ recht Citron-färbig/ die Schelffen gantz dünn/ am Geschmack ein wenig bitterlicht / und am Geruch Bisam-hafftig / das Marck aber Schwefel-farb und safftig/ anbey mit einer angenehmen Säure versehen.

Die andere Gattung / Ballottin di Spagnia genannt / hat eine grössere Frucht/ welche oben zugespitzt / der Baum wird gleich dem vor beschriebenen nicht gar hoch/ dessen Blätter sind den Citronen-Blättern gleich/ jedoch ein wenig kleiner / an den Seiten gekerbet / liecht-grün an der Farb / die Aeste haben hin und wieder Stacheln / doch nicht so viel als jene Art / die Blühe ist klein/ und deren Knöpffe im Anfang theils etwas Rosen-färbig/ wann sie aber grösser worden/ und bald aufgehen wollen/ werden sie je länger je weisser/ wann sie aber gantz offen/ verlieret sich das Rosen-farbige völlig / und sind über und über weiß / die Zasern in der Mitten der Blühe / welche bey denen Agrumi gewöhnlicher massen zu oberst gelbe Dupffen haben/ sind an diesem Ort gantz liecht-gelb/ und fast weiß/ daß man kaum einen Unterscheid der Farbe sehen kan. Die Früchte/ so bald sie zum Vorschein kommen / sind schön lieblich grün/ wann sie aber zeitigen/ werden sie hell Stroh-färbig / und haben eine sehr glatte und dünne Schelffe / welche die Dicke eines Messerrucken kaum erreichet / und gleichet am Geschmack den Citronen-Schelffen/ sie haben vieles safftiges und angenehm-säuerlichtes Marck/ daher sie dann sehr wol zu geniessen: Dieser Baum ist zwar mühsam zu erhalten/ sehr willig aber zu blühen/ und Früchte zu tragen/ wie dann dergleichen Baum/ den ich im Jahr 1702. von dem Gard-Ett empfangen/ gleich in dem nechst darauf folgenden Jahr zu blühen nicht nur angefangen/ sondern Anno 1704. im Monat Januario schon zeitige Früchte gebracht.

Das

Nürnbergische Hesperides, 1708, vol. 1, p. 160 and plate p. 160 (see p. 126)

Index of Places

Ortsregister / Index des lieux

The index of places lists the various different locations that feature on Volkamer's plates using their modern spelling and naming the regions where they are found today. The urban districts of Nuremberg are listed in the captions after a comma following the name of the city, while in the case of the smaller places in Italy the province is also indicated in brackets.

However, it is not always possible in every case to identify an exact location, since these villas, gardens and other sites have been built over and changed in the intervening years. In some cases the view that appears on Volkamer's plate is the only pictorial representation known today for a given location. This applies in particular to the plates in the third volume with their views of villas and gardens in Bologna.

Volkamer's captions for the Italian views tend to name the building shown as a "Palazzo" (palace), or else as a "Casino" (main building, country house), "Fabrica" (building) or "Retiro" (retreat). The gardens are listed as "Giardino" (garden), "Delizia" or "Luogo di delizie" (pleasure garden). Since the terms Volkamer used are not always precise and because the majority of the villas and gardens he chose to depict are situated outside the city, in the plate captions and in the index the general term "Villa" has been used.

Das Ortsregister listet die auf Volkamers Tafeln dargestellten Orte und Anlagen nach ihrer heutigen regionalen Zugehörigkeit und in der heute üblichen Schreibweise auf. Die Stadtteile von Nürnberg werden in den Tafellegenden durch Komma abgetrennt hinter dem Ortsnamen Nürnberg angegeben. Bei eigenständigen kleineren italienischen Orten wird in Klammern die Provinz angegeben.

Eine eindeutige Lokalisierung ist allerdings nicht in jedem Fall möglich, da Villen, Gärten und Orte seither überbaut und verändert wurden. In einigen Fällen ist Volkamers Tafel das einzige heute bekannte Bilddokument einer Anlage. Dies gilt besonders für die Tafeln des dritten Bandes mit ihren Ansichten Bologneser Villen und Parkanlagen.

Die italienischen Bildunterschriften Volkamers nennen die gezeigten Profangebäude in den meisten Fällen „Palazzo" (Palast), in einigen Fällen „Casino" (Hauptgebäude, Landhaus), „Fabrica" (Gebäude) oder „Retiro" (Rückzugsort). Die Gartenanlagen werden als „Giardino" (Garten), „Delizia" oder „Luogo di delizie" (Lustort) bezeichnet. Da Volkamers Bezeichnung der dargestellten Anlagen nicht immer präzise ist und es sich meistens um außerhalb der Stadt gelegene Villenanlagen handelt, wird in den Tafellegenden und im Register der übergreifende Terminus „Villa" verwendet.

L'index des lieux répertorie les lieux et plantations représentés sur les planches de Volkamer d'après leur affiliation régionale actuelle et selon l'orthographe courante de nos jours. Dans les légendes des planches les quartiers de Nuremberg apparaissent, séparés par une virgule, derrière le nom de lieu Nuremberg. Dans le cas de petites communes italiennes, la province correspondante est mentionnée entre parenthèses.

Toutefois, une localisation exacte n'est pas toujours possible car, depuis, on a construit à l'emplacement des villas, jardins et lieux, ou ceux-ci ont subi des transformations. Dans certains cas, la planche de Volkamer constitue l'unique document aujourd'hui connu d'une plantation. Cela vaut en particulier pour les planches du troisième volume avec ses représentations des villas et jardins de Bologne.

Les légendes italiennes de Volkamer désignent les édifices représentés, le plus souvent, sous les noms de « palazzo » (palais), quelquefois, « casino » (bâtiment principal, maison de campagne), « fabrica » (bâtiment) ou « retiro » (retraite). Les jardins portent le nom de « giardino » (jardin), « delizia » ou encore « luogo di delizie » (lieu de délices). Comme l'appellation des jardins représentés n'est pas toujours précise et qu'il s'agit le plus souvent de propriétés situées en dehors de la ville, le terme global de « Villa » est utilisé dans les légendes se rapportant aux planches et dans l'index.

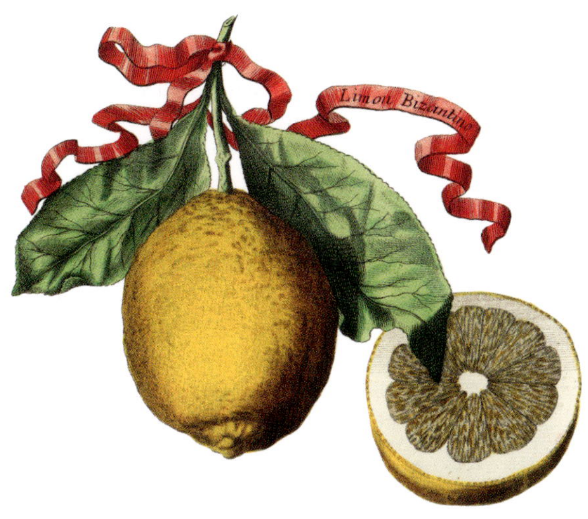

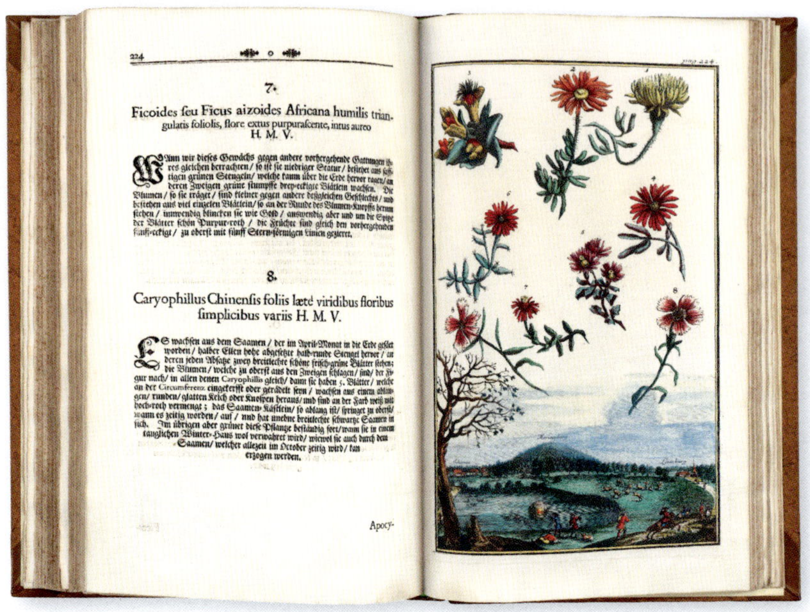
224

7.

Ficoides ſeu Ficus aizoides Africana humilis triangulatis foliolis, flore extus purpuraſcente, intus aureo H. M. V.

Wann wir dieſes Gewächs gegen andere vorhergehende Gattungen ihres gleichen betrachten / ſo iſt ſie niedriger Statur / beſtehet aus ſafftigen grünen Stengeln / welche kaum über die Erde hervor ragen / an deren Zweigen grüne ſtumpffe drey-eckigte Blätlein wachſen. Die Blumen / ſo ſie träget / ſind kleiner gegen andere deßgleichen Geſchlechts / und beſtehen aus viel einzelen Blättlein / ſo an der Runde des Blumen-Knopffs herum ſtehen / inwendig blincken ſie wie Gold / auswendig aber und um die Spitze der Blätter ſchön Purpur-roth / die Früchte ſind gleich den vorhergehenden fünff-eckigt / zu oberſt mit fünff Stern-förmigen Linien gezieret.

8.

Caryophillus Chinenſis foliis læté viridibus floribus ſimplicibus variis H. M. V.

Es wachſen aus dem Saamen / der im April-Monat in die Erde geſäet worden / halber Ellen hohe abgeſetzte halb-runde Stengel hervor / an deren jeden Abſatze zwey breitlechte ſchöne friſch-grüne Blätter ſtehen; die Blumen / welche zu oberſt aus den Zweigen ſchlagen / ſind / der Figur nach / in allen denen Caryophillis gleich / dann ſie haben 5. Blätter / welche an der Circumferenz eingekerfft oder gerädelt ſeyn / wachſen aus einem ablangen / runden / glatten Kelch oder Knoſpen heraus / und ſind an der Farb weiß mit hoch-roth vermengt; das Saamen-Käſtlein / ſo ablang iſt / ſpringet zu oberſt / wann es zeitig worden / auf / und hat unebne breitlechte ſchwartze Saamen in ſich. Im übrigen aber grünet dieſe Pflantze beſtändig fort / wann ſie in einem tauglichen Winter-Haus wol verwahret wird / wiewol ſie auch durch den Saamen / welcher allezeit im October zeitig wird / kan erzogen werden.

Apocy-

Nürnbergische Hesperides, 1708, vol. 1, p. 224 and plate p. 224 (see p. 244)

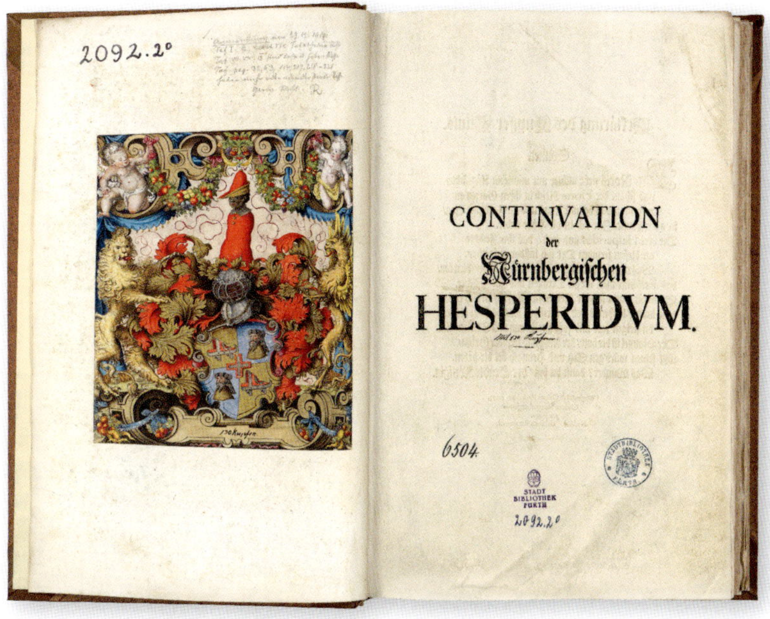

Continuation der Nürnbergischen Hesperidum, 1714, vol. II, Holzschuher family ex-libris and title-page

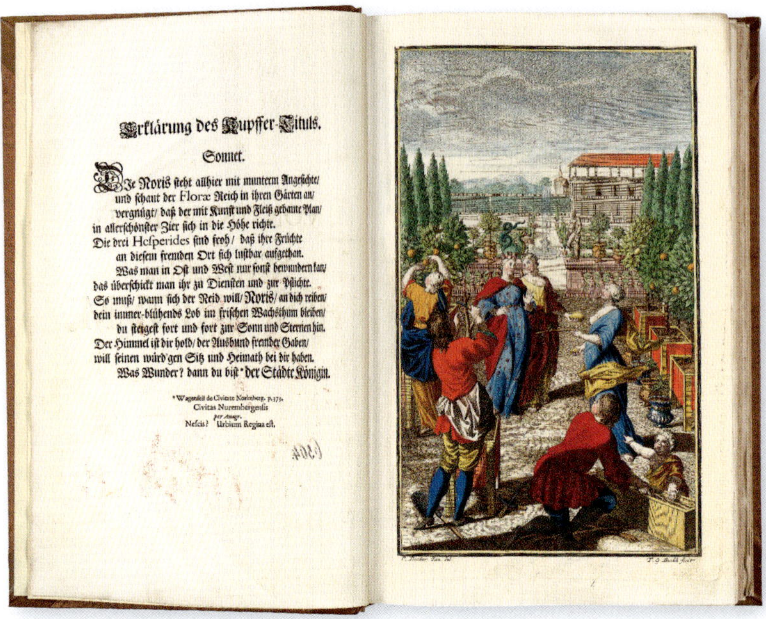

Erklärung des Kupffer-Tituls.

Sonnet.

DJe Noris steht allhier mit munterem Angesichte/
und schaut der Floræ Reich in ihren Gärten an/
vergnügt/ daß der mit Kunst und Fleiß gebaute Plan/
in allerschönster Zier sich in die Höhe richte.
Die drei Hesperides sind froh/ daß ihre Früchte
an diesem fremden Ort sich lustbar aufgethan.
Was man in Ost und West nur sonst bewundern kan/
das überschickt man ihr zu Diensten und zur Pflichte.
So muß/ wann sich der Neid will/ Noris/ an dich reiben/
dein immer-blühends Lob im frischen Wachsthum bleiben/
du steigest fort und fort zur Sonn und Sternen hin.
Der Himmel ist dir hold/ der Ausbund fremder Gaben/
will seinen würd'gen Sitz und Heimath bei dir haben.
Was Wunder? dann du bist * der Städte Königin.

* Wagenseil de Civitate Norimberg. p. 173.
Civitas Norembergensis
per Anagr.
Nescis? Urbium Regina est.

Continuation der Nürnbergischen Hesperidum, 1714, vol. II,
frontispiece text and frontispiece (see p. 48)

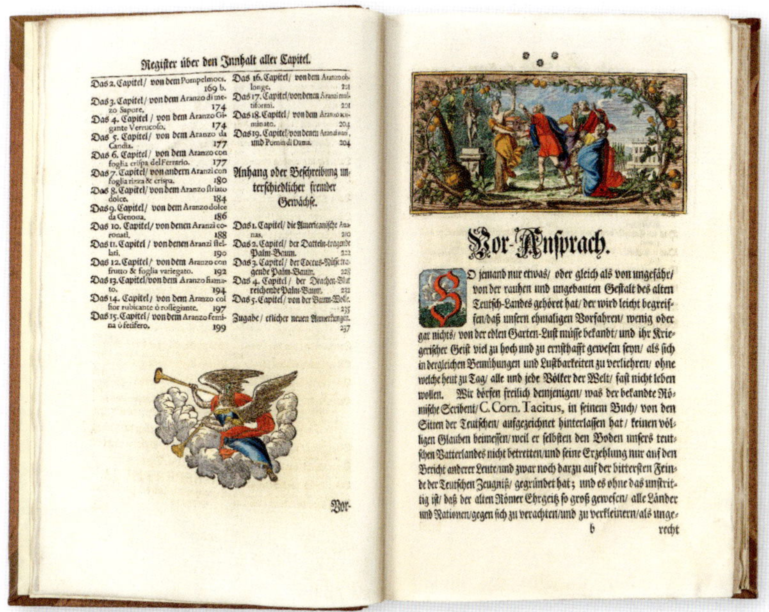

Register über den Innhalt aller Capitel.

Das 2. Capitel / von dem Pompelmoes. 169 b.
Das 3. Capitel / von dem Aranzo di mezo Sapore. 174
Das 4. Capitel / von dem Aranzo Gigante Verrucoso. 174
Das 5. Capitel / von dem Aranzo da Candia. 177
Das 6. Capitel / von dem Aranzo con foglia crispa del Ferrario. 177
Das 7. Capitel / von andern Aranzi con foglia rizza & crispa. 180
Das 8. Capitel / von dem Aranzo striato dolce. 184
Das 9. Capitel / von dem Aranzo dolce da Genoua. 186
Das 10. Capitel / von denen Aranzi coronati. 188
Das 11. Capitel / von denen Aranzi stellati. 190
Das 12. Capitel / von dem Aranzo con frutto & foglia variegato. 192
Das 13. Capitel / von dem Aranzo fiamato. 194
Das 14. Capitel / von dem Aranzo col fior rubicante ò roslegiante. 197
Das 15. Capitel / von dem Aranzo femina ò fetifero. 199
Das 16. Capitel / von dem Aranzo oblonge. 201
Das 17. Capitel / von denen Aranzi multiformi. 201
Das 18. Capitel / von dem Aranzo acuminato. 204
Das 19. Capitel / von denen Aranzi nani, und Pomi di Dama. 204

Anhang oder Beschreibung unterschiedlicher fremder Gewächse.

Das 1. Capitel / die Americanische Ananas. 210
Das 2. Capitel / der Datteln-tragende Palm-Baum. 222
Das 3. Capitel / der Cocus-Nüsse tragende Palm-Baum. 228
Das 4. Capitel / der Drachen-Blut reichende Palm-Baum. 232
Das 5. Capitel / von der Baum-Wolle. 235
Zugabe / etlicher neuen Anmerkungen. 237

Vor-

Vor-Ansprach.

SO jemand nur etwas / oder gleich als von ungefähr / von der rauhen und ungebauten Gestalt des alten Teutsch-Landes gehöret hat / der wird leicht begreiffen / daß unsern ehmaligen Vorfahren / wenig oder gar nichts / von der edlen Garten-Lust müsse bekandt / und ihr Kriegerischer Geist viel zu hoch und zu ernsthafft gewesen seyn / als sich in dergleichen Bemühungen und Lustbarkeiten zu verliehren / ohne welche heut zu Tag / alle und jede Völker der Welt / fast nicht leben wollen. Wir dörfen freilich demjenigen / was der bekandte Römische Scribent / C. Corn. Tacitus, in seinem Buch / von den Sitten der Teutschen / aufgezeichnet hinterlassen hat / keinen völligen Glauben beimessen / weil er selbsten den Boden unsers teutschen Vatterlandes nicht betretten / und seine Erzehlung nur auf den Bericht anderer Leute / und zwar noch darzu auf der bittersten Feinde der Teutschen Zeugniß / gegründet hat; und es ohne das unstrittig ist / daß der alten Römer Ehrgeitz so groß gewesen / alle Länder und Nationen / gegen sich zu verachten / und zu verkleinern / als unge-

b recht

Continuation der Nürnbergischen Hesperidum, 1714, vol. II, fol. 5r and 6v, contents and preamble with vignette of the Hesperides standing in front of the Mausoleum of Augustus in Rome

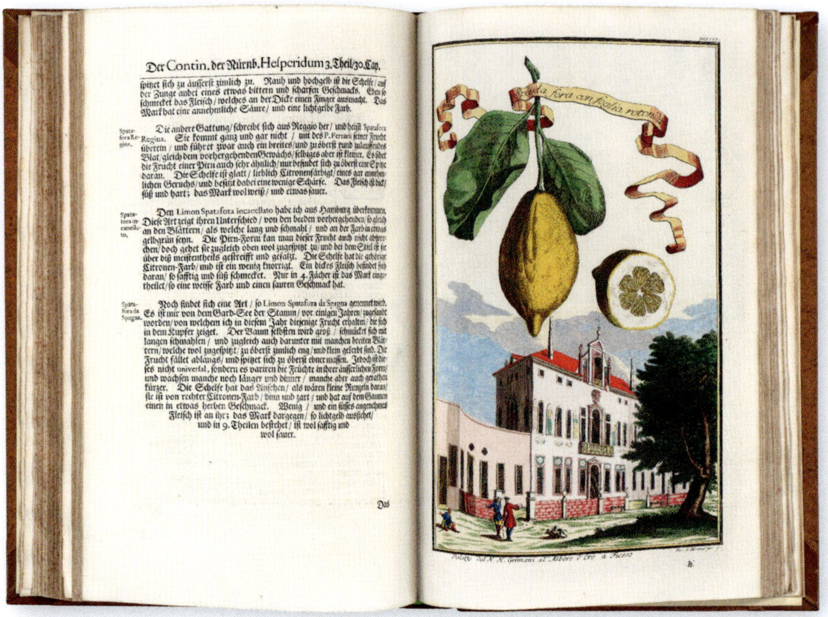

Der Contin. der Nürnb. Hesperidum 3. Theil/30. Cap.

spitzet sich zu äusserst zimlich zu. Rauh und hochgelb ist die Schelfe/ auf der Zunge anbei eines etwas bittern und scharfen Geschmacks. Eben so schmecket das Fleisch/ welches an der Dicke einen Finger ausmacht. Das Mark hat eine annehmliche Säure/ und eine lichtgelbe Farb.

Spatafora Regina. Die andere Gattung/ schreibt sich aus Reggio her/ und heist Spatafora Regina. Sie kommt ganz und gar nicht / mit des P. Ferrari seiner Frucht überein / und führet zwar auch ein breites/ und zu öberst rund zulauffendes Blat/ gleich dem vorhergehenden Gewächs/ selbiges aber ist kleiner. Es sihet die Frucht einer Pirn auch sehr ähnlich/ nur befindet sich zu öberst eine Spitze daran. Die Schelfe ist glatt / lieblich Citronenfärbigt/ eines gar annehmlichen Geruchs/ und besitzt dabei eine wenige Schärfe. Das Fleisch ist dick/ süß und hart; das Mark wol weiß / und etwas sauer.

Spatafora incanellato. Den Limon Spatafora incanellato habe ich aus Hamburg überkommen. Diese Art zeigt ihren Unterschied / von den beeden vorhergehenden/ so gleich an den Blättern/ als welche lang und schmahl / und an der Farb in etwas gelbgrün seyn. Die Pirn-Form kan man dieser Frucht auch nicht absprechen/ doch gehet sie zugleich oben wol zugespitzt zu/ und bei dem Stiel ist sie über diß meistentheils gestreifft und gefalzt. Die Schelfe hat die gehörige Citronen-Farb/ und ist ein wenig knorrigt. Ein dickes Fleisch befindet sich daran/ so safftig und süß schmecket. Nur in 4. Fächer ist das Mark eingetheilet/ so eine weisse Farb und einen sauren Geschmack hat.

Spatafora da Spagna. Noch findet sich eine Art / so Limon Spatafora da Spagna genennet wird. Es ist mir von dem Gard-See der Stamm/ vor einigen Jahren/ zugesandt worden/ von welchem ich in diesem Jahr diejenige Frucht erhalten/ die sich in dem Kupfer zeiget. Der Baum selbsten wird groß / schmücket sich mit langen schmahlen / und zugleich auch darunter mit manchen breiten Blättern/ welche wol zugespitzt/ zu öberst zimlich eng / und klein gekerbt sind. Die Frucht fället ablangs/ und spitzet sich zu öberst ebner massen. Jedoch ist dieses nicht universal, sondern es variren die Früchte in ihrer äusserlichen Form/ und wachsen manche noch länger und dünner / manche aber auch gerathen kürzer. Die Schelfe hat das Ansehen/ als wären kleine Runzeln daran/ sie ist von rechter Citronen-Farb / dünn und zart / und hat auf dem Gaumen einen in etwas herben Geschmack. Wenig / und ein süsses angenehmes Fleisch ist an ihr; das Mark dargegen/ so lichtgelb aussiehet/ und in 9. Theilen bestehet/ ist wol safftig und wol sauer.

Das

Continuation der Nürnbergischen Hesperidum, 1714, vol. II, p. 128r and plate p. 129 (see p. 337)

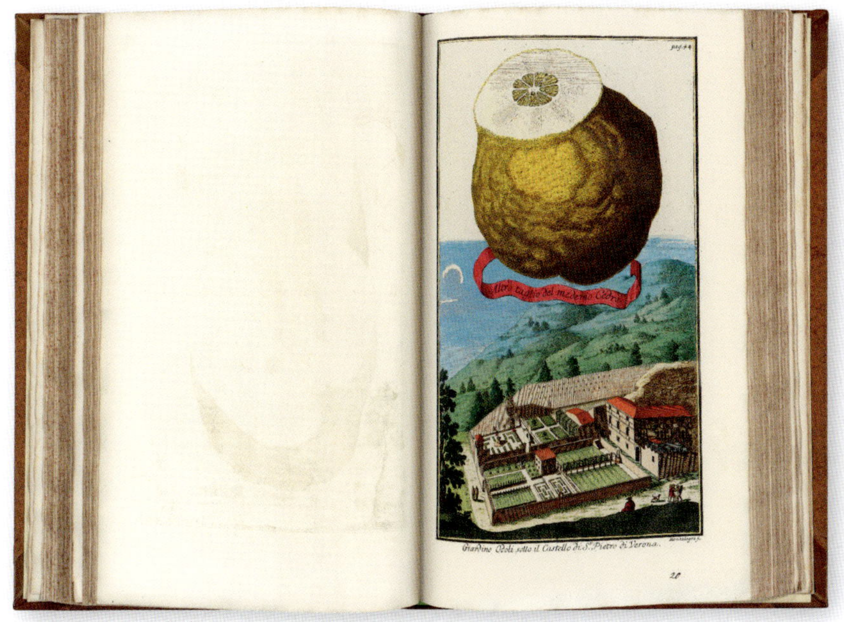

Continuation der Nürnbergischen Hesperidum, 1714, vol. II, plate p. 44 (see p. 282)

Districts of Nuremberg and Municipalities in the Surrounding Region / Stadtteile und umliegende Gemeinden / Les Quartiers de Nuremberg et les communes de la région

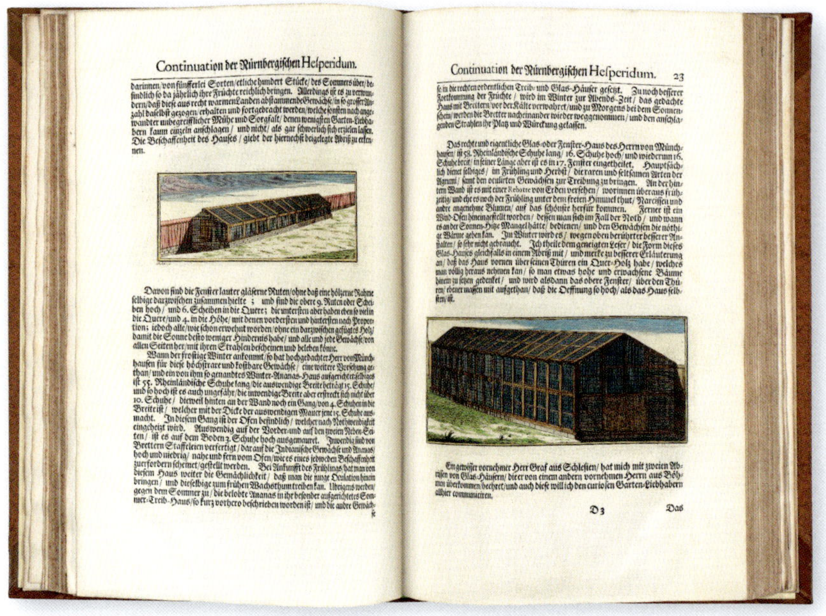

Continuation der Nürnbergischen Hesperidum.

darinnen/ von fünfferlei Sorten/ etliche hundert Stücke/ des Sommers über/ befindlich/ so da jährlich ihre Früchte reichlich bringen. Allerdings ist es zu verwundern/ daß diese aus recht warmen Landen abstammende Gewächse/ in so grosser Anzahl daselbst gezogen/ erhalten und fortgebracht werden/ welche sonsten nach angewandter unbegreifflicher Mühe und Sorgfalt/ denen wenigsten Garten-Liebhabern kaum einzeln anschlagen/ und nicht/ als gar schwerlich/ sich erzielen lassen. Die Beschaffenheit des Hauses/ giebt der hiernechst beigelegte Abriß zu erkennen.

Davon sind die Fenster lauter gläserne Ruten/ ohne daß eine hölzerne Rahme selbige darzwischen zusammen hielte; und sind die obere 9. Ruten oder Scheiben hoch/ und 6. Scheiben in die Quere; die untersten aber haben eben so viel in die Quere/ und 4. in die Höhe/ mit denen vordersten und hintersten nach Proportion; iedoch alle/ wie schon erwehnt worden/ ohne ein darzwischen gefügtes Holz/ damit die Sonne desto weniger Hindernis habe/ und alle und jede Gewächse/ von allen Seiten her/ mit ihren Strahlen bescheinen und beleben könne.

Wann der frostige Winter ankommt/ so hat hochgedachter Herr von Münchhausen für diese höchstrare und kostbare Gewächse/ eine weitere Versehung gethan/ und ein von ihm so genandtes Winter-Ananas-Haus aufgerichtet: selbiges ist 55. Rheinländische Schuhe lang/ die auswendige Breite beträgt 15. Schuhe/ und so hoch ist es auch ungefähr/ die inwendige Breite aber erstreckt sich nicht über 10. Schuhe/ dieweil hinten an der Wand noch ein Gang/ von 4. Schuhen in die Breite ist/ welcher mit der Dicke der auswendigen Mauer jene 15. Schuhe ausmacht. In diesem Gang ist der Ofen befindlich/ welcher nach Nothwendigkeit eingeheizt wird. Auswendig auf der Vorder- und auf den zweien Neben-Seiten/ ist es auf dem Boden 3. Schuhe hoch ausgemauret. Inwendig sind von Brettern Staffeleien verfertigt/ dar auf die Indianische Gewächse und Ananas/ hoch und niedrig/ nahe und fern vom Ofen/ wie es eines jedweden Beschaffenheit zuerfordern scheinet/ gestellt werden. Bei Ankunfft des Frühlings/ hat man von diesem Haus weiter die Gemächlichkeit/ daß man die junge Oculation hinein bringen/ und dieselbige zum frühen Wachsthum treiben kan. Ubrigens werden/ gegen dem Sommer zu/ die belobte Ananas in ihr besonder aufgerichtetes Sommer-Treib-Haus/ so kurz vorhero beschrieben worden ist/ und die andre Gewäch-

se

Continuation der Nürnbergischen Hesperidum. 23

se in die rechten ordentlichen Treib- und Glas-Häuser gesetzt. Zu noch besserer Fortkommung der Früchte/ wird im Winter zur Abends-Zeit/ das gedachte Haus mit Brettern/ vor der Kälte verwahret/ und zu Morgens bei dem Sonnenschein/ werden die Bretter nacheinander wieder weggenommen/ und den anschlagenden Strahlen ihr Platz und Würckung gelassen.

Das rechte und eigentliche Glas- oder Fenster-Haus des Herrn von Münchhausen/ ist 58. Rheinländische Schuhe lang/ 16. Schuhe hoch/ und wiederum 16. Schuhe breit/ in seiner Länge aber ist es in 17. Fenster eingetheilet. Hauptsächlich dienet selbiges/ im Frühling und Herbst/ die raren und seltsamen Arten der Agrumi/ samt den oculirten Gewächsen zur Treibung zu bringen. An der hintern Wand ist es mit einer Rebatte von Erden versehen/ worinnen überaus frühzeitig/ und ehe es noch der Frühling unter dem freien Himmel thut/ Narcissen und andre angenehme Blumen/ auf das schönste herfür kommen. Ferner ist ein Wind-Ofen hineingestellt worden/ dessen man sich im Fall der Noth/ und wann es an der Sonnen-Hitze Mangel hätte/ bedienen/ und den Gewächsen die nöthige Wärme geben kan. Im Winter wird es/ wegen oben berührter besserer Anstalten/ so sehr nicht gebraucht. Ich theile dem geneigten Leser/ die Form dieses Glas-Hauses gleichfalls in einem Abriß mit/ und merke zu besserer Erläuterung an/ daß das Haus vornen über seinen Thüren ein Quer-Holz habe/ welches man völlig heraus nehmen kan/ so man etwas hohe und erwachsene Bäume hinein zu setzen gedenket/ und wird alsdann das obere Fenster/ über den Thüren/ ebener massen mit aufgethan/ daß die Oeffnung so hoch/ als das Haus selbsten/ ist.

Ein gewisser vornehmer Herr Graf aus Schlesien/ hat mich mit zweien Abrissen von Glas-Häusern/ die er von einem andern vornehmen Herrn aus Böhmen überkommen/ beehret/ und auch diese will ich den curiosen Garten-Liebhabern allhier communiciren.

D 3 Das

Continuation der Nürnbergischen Hesperidum, 1714, vol. II, pp. 22r and 23v with illustrations of glasshouses

Families Owning Properties and Gardens in or near Nuremberg / Anwesen und Gärten folgender Familien in und bei Nürnberg / Propriétés et jardins des familles suivantes à Nuremberg et dans ses alentours

kommen ist/ welche in das Kupffer hat müssen gebracht werden/ so habe ich/ damit das Werk nicht allzulang aufgehalten würde/ so gleich unter die Frucht einen gewissen Pallast müssen zeichnen und stechen lassen/ den ich damals auch schon bei Handen gehabt habe. Also sind die zusamm-gehörige und nah-gelegene Gebäude/ um dieser Ursach willen/ zwar nicht stets im Kupffer hier beisammen anzutreffen/ gleichwol aber auch nicht allezeit von einander zertrennet und zerstreuet/ sondern/ so viel es sich thun lassen/ sind sie zusamm gehalten worden.

Dieses ist es/ was ich Vorreds-weise/ den Hochgeneigten Leser freundlichst erinnern/ mich aber und mein Werk/ zu dessen Gunst und Wolneigung/ bester massen empfehlen wollen.

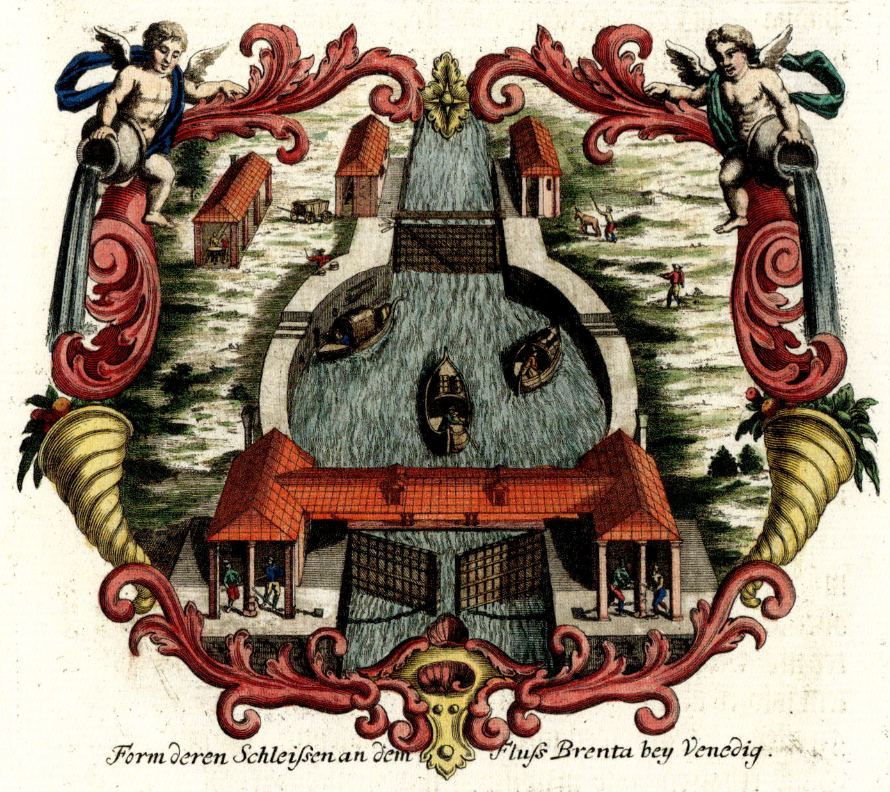

Form deren Schleissen an dem Fluss Brenta bey Venedig.

Bibliography
Bibliografie / Bibliographie

Ammann, Paul, *Hortus Bosianus*, Leipzig, 1686.

Armao, Ermanno, *Vincenzo Coronelli*, Florence, 1944.

Azzi Visentini, Margherita (ed.), *Il giardino veneto: Storia e conservazione*, Milan, 1988.

Azzi Visentini, Margherita, "Johann Christoph Volkamers Abhandlung über Zitrusgewächse und die Geschichte norditalienischer und deutscher Barockgärten", in: *Preußische Gärten in Europa. 300 Jahre Gartengeschichte*, issued by the Stiftung Preußische Schlösser und Gärten Berlin-Brandenburg, concept: Michael Rohde, Leipzig, 2007, pp. 26–29.

Bach-Damaskinos, Ruth, "Gartenlust und Augenschmaus – Vor 300 Jahren verfasste Johann Christoph Volkamer sein Hesperidenbuch", in: *Norica: Berichte und Themen aus dem Stadtarchiv Nürnberg*, vol. 4 (2008), pp. 24–31.

Bibliographie der vor 1750 erschienenen deutschen Gartenbücher, compiled by Clemens Alexander Wimmer and Iris Lauterbach, issued by the Bücherei des Deutschen Gartenbaues e.V. Berlin, Nördlingen, 2003.

Christ, Barbara and Michael, "*Citrus* 'Bizzarria'", in: *Orangeriekultur in Weimar und im östlichen Thüringen. Von den Bauten zur Praxis der Pflanzenkultivierung* (Orangeriekultur – Schriftenreihe des Arbeitskreises Orangerien in Deutschland e.V., vol. 14), Berlin, 2017, pp. 150–165.

Coronelli, Vincenzo, *Viaggio d'Italia in Inghilterra*, Venice, 1697.

Coronelli, Vincenzo, *Singolarità di Venezia*, vol. III: *La Brenta quasi borgo della città di Venezia*, Venice, s.a. [1709].

Cuveland, Helga de, *Flora Exotica: Ein botanisches Prachtwerk von 1720*, ed. Adrian von Buttlar and Marie-Louise von Plessen, Ostfildern-Ruit, 1999.

Dezallier d'Argenville, Antoine-Joseph, *La théorie et la pratique du jardinage où l'on traite à fond des beaux jardins appellés communément les jardins de plaisance et de propreté*, Paris, 1709. German edition: *Die Gärtnerey, so wohl in ihrer Theorie oder Betrachtung, als Praxis oder Übung*, Augsburg, 1731 (reprinted Leipzig, 1986, ed. Harri Günther).

Englmaier, Alois, "Die Schönheit der Zitrus und deren Kultur: Ein paar Worte zur Botanik der Zitruspflanzen", in: *Ein Hauch von Gold: Pomeranzen und Gartenkunst im Passauer Land*, issued by the Landkreis Passau, Regensburg, 2005, pp. 87–98.

Frankfurt am Main / Ostfildern-Ruit, 1997, *Maria Sibylla Merian 1647–1717: Künstlerin und Naturforscherin*, ed. Kurt Wettengl, exh. cat., Frankfurt am Main / Ostfildern-Ruit, 1997, pp. 20–22.

Freedberg, David, "Gli agrumi di Giovanni Battista Ferrari", in: *Miti, arte e scienza nella pomologia italiana*, ed. Enrico Baldini, Rome, 2008, pp. 125–155.

Freedberg, David and Enrico Baldini, *Citrus Fruit*, in: *The Paper Museum of Cassiano dal Pozzo*, Series B, *Natural History*, part I, ed. Francis Haskell and Jennifer Montagu, London, 1997.

Continuation der Nürnbergischen Hesperidum, 1714, vol. II, end of the preamble with vignette of the Brenta sluice near Venice

Giersch, Robert, Andreas Schlunk and Bertold Haller von Hallerstein, *Burgen und Herrensitze in der Nürnberger Landschaft*, Lauf an der Pegnitz, 2006.

Grieb, Manfred, *Nürnberger Künstlerlexikon*, 4 vols., Munich, 2007.

Hamann, Heinrich, "Einführung", in: Johann Christoph Volkamer, *Nürnbergische Hesperides*, reprint of the 1708 Nuremberg edition (Bibliotheca hortensis, vol. 3), Leipzig, 1986.

Hamann, Heinrich, "Johann Christoph Volkamers 'Nürnbergische Hesperides'", in: *Nürnbergische Hesperiden und Orangeriekultur in Franken*, Petersberg, 2011, pp. 9–14.

Heffels, Monika, *Die Handzeichnungen des 18. Jahrhunderts*, vol. IV: *Die deutschen Handzeichnungen*, catalogue of the Germanisches Nationalmuseum Nürnberg, Nuremberg, 1969.

Heilmeyer, Marina, *Die Goldenen Äpfel in Nürnbergs Hesperidengärten*, exh. booklet, issued by the City of Nuremberg – Gartenbauamt, Nuremberg, 2001.

Heilmeyer, Marina, *Ein Blumengarten des Barock: Hortus Anckelmannianus*, Munich / Berlin / London / New York, 2003.

Hesse, Heinrich, *Neue Gartenlust*, Leipzig, 1706.

Kutscher, Barbara, *Paul Deckers "Fürstlicher Baumeister" (1711/1716). Untersuchungen zu Bedingungen und Quellen eines Stichwerks, mit einem Werkverzeichnis*, Frankfurt am Main etc., 1995, pp. 268–270.

Lauterbach, Iris, "Johann Christoph Volkamers Hesperiden-werk", in: *Die Frucht der Verheißung: Zitrusfrüchte in Kunst und Kultur*, Nuremberg, 2011, pp. 237–263.

Lauterbach, Iris, "Mundus in litteris: Der Kaufmann als Gelehrter; Johann Christoph Volkamers Hesperidenwerk", in: *Orangeriekultur im Bodenseeraum* (Orangeriekultur – Schriftenreihe des Arbeitskreises Orangerien in Deutschland e.V., vol. 9), Berlin, 2013, pp. 130–159.

Lauterbach, Iris, "Commerce and Erudition: Civic Self-Representation Through Botany and Horticulture in Germany, Sixteenth to Eighteenth Centuries", in: *Gardens, Knowledge and the Sciences in the Early Modern Period*, ed. Hubertus Fischer, Volker Remmert and Joachim Wolschke-Bulmahn, Basel, 2016, pp. 319–341.

Ludwig, Heidrun, *Nürnberger naturgeschichtliche Malerei im 17. und 18. Jahrhundert*, Marburg, 1998.

Martz, Jochen, "Johann Christoph Volkamer und die Entwicklung der Zitruskultur in Nürnbergs Gärten", in: *Lust und Lieb hat mich beweget. Nürnberger Gartenkultur,* exh. cat., Nuremberg, 2008, pp. 35–39.

Martz, Jochen, "'Agrumen [...] zu einem dritten Theile von seinen Hesperidibus' – Zur unbekannten Kupferstichserie für einen dritten Band der *Nürnbergischen Hesperides*", in: *Die Gartenkunst*, vol. 23 (2011), no. 2, pp. 151–194.

Martz, Jochen, "Zur Entwicklung der Zitruskultur in Nürnbergs Gärten – Von den Anfängen bis in das 19. Jahrhundert", in: *Nürnbergische Hesperiden und Orangeriekultur in Franken*, Petersberg, 2011, pp. 94–105.

Merian, Matthäus, *Florilegium renovatum et auctum*, Frankfurt am Main, 1641.

Müller, Christian Gottlieb, *Verzeichnis von Nürnbergischen topographisch-historischen Kupferstichen und Holzschnitten*, Nuremberg, 1791.

Nehring, Dorothee, "Die 'Hesperidengärten' in Nürnbergs Stadtteil St. Johannis", in: *Mitteilungen des Vereins für Geschichte der Stadt Nürnberg* 71 (1984), pp. 212–241.

Nissen, Claus, *Die botanische Buchillustration. Ihre Geschichte und Bibliographie*, vol. 1, Stuttgart, 1951, pp. 162–164.

Nuremberg, 2008, *Lust und Lieb hat mich beweget. Nürnberger Gartenkultur*, ed. Jutta Tschoeke, exh. cat., Nuremberg, 2008.

Nuremberg, 2011, *Die Frucht der Verheißung. Zitrusfrüchte in Kunst und Kultur*, exh. cat. compiled by Yasmin Doosry, Christiane Lauterbach and Johannes Pommeranz, Nuremberg, 2011.

Nürnbergische Hesperiden und Orangeriekultur in Franken (Orangeriekultur – Schriftenreihe des Arbeitskreises Orangerien in Deutschland e.V., vol. 7), Petersberg, 2011.

Orangerien in Europa: Von fürstlichem Vermögen und gärtnerischer Kunst, booklet published on the occasion of the international conference held by the Deutsches Nationalkomitee of ICOMOS in cooperation with the Arbeitskreis Orangerien in Deutschland e.V., the Bayerische Verwaltung der staatlichen Schlösser, Gärten und Seen and the Arbeitskreis Historische Gärten der DGGL, Schloss Seehof, 29 September – 1 October 2005 (ICOMOS – Hefte des Deutschen Nationalkomitees XLIII), s. l. [Munich], 2007.

Oranien – Orangen – Oranienbaum, issued by the Vorstand der Kulturstiftung Dessau-Wörlitz, concept and scholarly direction of the symposium: Ludwig Trauzettel (Kataloge und Schriften der Kulturstiftung Dessau-Wörlitz, vol. 9), Munich etc., 1999.

Piovene, Guido and Licisco Magagnato (eds.), *Ville del Brenta nelle vedute di Vincenzo Coronelli e Gianfrancesco Costa*, Milan, 1960.

Pirson, Julius, "Die Beziehungen des Pariser Arztes Charles Patin zu Nürnberger Freunden und Gönnern 1633–1693", in: *Mitteilungen des Vereins für Geschichte der Stadt Nürnberg* 49 (1959), pp. 274–338.

Potsdam, 2001, *Wo die Zitronen blühen: Orangerien – historische Arbeitsgeräte, Kunst und Kunsthandwerk*, issued by the Generaldirektion der Stiftung Preußische Schlösser und Gärten Berlin-Brandenburg, exh. cat., Potsdam, 2001.

Puppi, Lionello, "Introduzione", in: *Ville, giardini e paesaggi del Veneto nelle incisione dell'opera di Johann Christoph Volkamer con la descrizione del lago di Garda e del monte Baldo*, ed. Ennio Concina, Milan, 1979.

Puppi, Lionello, "Johann Christoph Volkamer e le Esperidi di Norimberga", in: *Immagini della Brenta: Ville venete e scene di vita sulla Riviera nel '700 veneziano*, exh. cat., Mira, 1996, pp. 39–52.

Risso, Antoine and Alexandre Poiteau, *Histoire naturelle des Orangers*, 2 vols., Paris, 1818–1819.

Roth, Dietrich (ed.), *Die Blumenbücher des Hans Simon Holtzbecker und Hamburgs Lustgärten* (Abhandlungen des Naturwissenschaftlichen Vereins in Hamburg, N.F., 36), Keltern, 2003.

Roth, Dietrich (ed.), *Das Moller-Florilegium: Hans Simon Holtzbeckers Blumenalbum für den Bürgermeister Barthold Moller*, with contributions by Dietrich Roth and Thea Vignau-Wilberg, Munich, 2007.

Schirarend, Carsten and Marina Heilmeyer, *Die Goldenen Äpfel: Wissenswertes rund um die Zitrusfrüchte*, issued by the Fördererkreis der naturwissenschaftlichen Museen Berlins e.V. für den Botanischen Garten and the Botanisches Museum Berlin-Dahlem with the support of the Istituto Italiano di Cultura Berlin, Berlin, 1996.

Schmidt-Herrling, Eleonore, *Die Briefsammlung des Nürnberger Arztes Christoph Jacob Trew (1695–1769) in der Universitätsbibliothek Erlangen*, Erlangen, 1940. Siehe auch: https://ub.fau.de/2019/05/07/briefsammlung-trew-online/ [14. 9. 2020].

Schwemmer, Wilhelm, *So war's einmal: Nürnberg im 17. Jahrhundert; Kupferstiche von Johann Alexander Boener (1647–1720)*, Nuremberg, 1968.

Der Süden im Norden: Orangerien – Ein fürstliches Vergnügen, issued by the Oberfinanzdirektion Karlsruhe, the Staatliche

Schlösser und Gärten and the Arbeitskreis Orangerien in Deutschland e.V., Regensburg, 1999.

Tagliolini, Alessandro and Margherita Azzi Visentini (eds.), *Il giardino delle esperidi: Gli agrumi nella storia, nella letteratura e nell'arte*, Florence, 1996.

Volkamer, Johann Christoph, *Hesperidvm norimbergensivm sive de malorum citreorvm, limonvm, aurantiorvmque cvltvra et vsv libri IIII, bene mvltis iconibus in aes elegantissime incisis ornati*, Nuremberg, s.a. [1713].

Volkamer, Johann Christoph, *Obeliscus Constantinopolitanus oder Kurtze Erklärung des zu Constantinopel auf der Renn-Bahn stehenden nun aber auch in der Nürnbergischen Vorstadt Gostenhof nachgehauenen und aufgerichteten Obelisci*, Nuremberg, 1713 (reprinted Nuremberg, 1985, with an afterword by Klaus Dornisch).

Vollständiges Nürnbergisches Koch-Buch, Nuremberg, 1691.

Weingärtner, Helge, *Nürnbergische Veduten in J. C. Volkamers Hesperidenwerk*, master's thesis, Erlangen, 1990 (this unpublished typescript can be consulted in the Stadtarchiv Nürnberg and in the library of the Germanisches National-museum Nürnberg).

Will, Georg Andreas, *Nürnbergisches Gelehrten-Lexicon*, vol. 4, Nuremberg / Altdorf, 1758, pp. 120–131.

Wimmer, Clemens Alexander, "Bemerkenswerte Zitrus-Literatur vom 16. bis 19. Jahrhundert", in: *Oranien – Orangen – Oranienbaum*, Munich etc., 1999, pp. 49–58.

Wimmer, Clemens Alexander, "'Von denen Lust- und *Blumen*-Bäumen': Das Kübelpflanzensortiment in Renaissance und Barock", in: *Allerley Sorten Orangerie* (Schriftenreihe des Arbeitskreises Orangerien in Deutschland e.V., vol. 3), Dresden, 2001, pp. 72–87.

Wimmer, Clemens Alexander, "Funktion und Bedeutung von Volkamers Zitrusbuch", in: *Nürnbergische Hesperiden und Orangeriekultur in Franken*, Petersberg, 2011, pp. 34–45.

Wimmer, Clemens Alexander, "Volkamers Rezeption in Schlesien: Ein Breslauer Zitruskatalog von 1731", in: *Nürnbergische Hesperiden und Orangeriekultur in Franken*, Petersberg, 2011, pp. 86–93.

Wimmer, Clemens Alexander and Bernhard Böhm, "Von Wartung der Pommerantzen-Bäume", in: *Oranien – Orangen – Oranienbaum*, Munich etc., 1999, pp. 59–81.

Continuation der Nürnbergischen Hesperidum, 1714, vol. II, p. 6v with vignette of the Mausoleum of Augustus in Rome

sers Bildniß/ von Glocken-Speiß künstlich gegossen/ aufgestellet. Die breiten Gänge an denen Auffätzen/ waren ringst herum mit Bäumen dick besetzet.

Unter diesem Gebäu wurde Kaiser Augustus begraben; Hernach sollen mehr Kaisere/ auch einige seiner Anverwandten/ in besondern darein gebauten Kammern/ beigesetzet worden seyn. Es waren nemlich ringst herum viele Zimmer oder Kammern/ mit kleinen Fenstern/ darinnen eines jeden seine Aschen besonders verwahrlich aufbehalten wurden. An jeder Seiten stunde vornen ein Obeliscus, oder viereckigte Thurn-Säule; auch waren des Kaisers Thaten/ wie er in seinem Testament befohlen hatte/ daselbst in eherne Tafeln eingeätzet/ zu lesen.

Ob nun zwar die Stadt Rom siebenmal zerstöret und verwüstet/ auch der oberste Theil von diesem Werk meistens abgeworfen worden; so ist sich doch an denen übergebliebenen Vestigiis sehr zu verwundern/ und zeugen solche genugsam von der Grösse und Herrlichkeit dieses Gebäudes; Wie dann zum öfftern schöne Stücke Marmor ausgegraben werden. Dahero werden denen Fremden/ welche dahin reisen/ unter andern alten Raritäten/ auch diese Vestigia Mausolei gezeiget/ welche sich darob desto mehr ergötzen/ weil aus den verfallenen Hauffen nunmehr ein zierlicher Garten angeleget/ welcher wol unter denen hortis pensilibus passiren kan; wie er dann auch zu Rom davor gehalten wird. Woselbsten auser diesem/ nach unterschiedlicher Scribenten Zeugniß/ heute zu Tage noch mehrere gefunden werden/ von welchen sie aber keinen sattsamen Bericht erstatten.

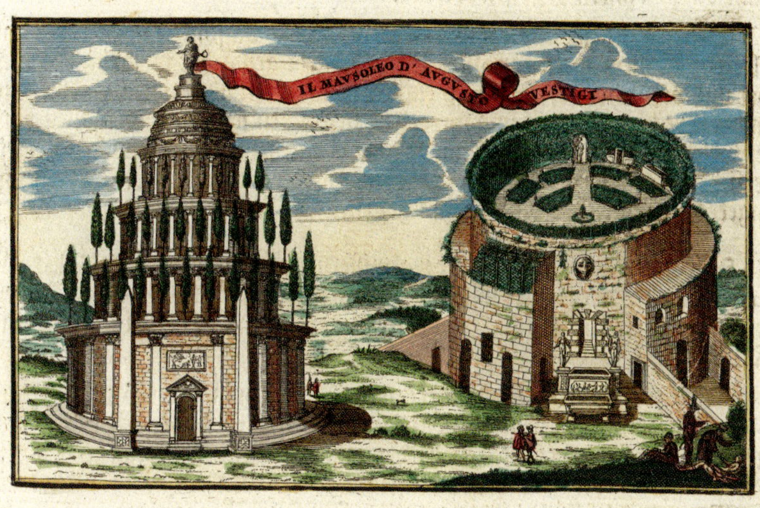

Wolten

Acknowledgements
Danksagung / Remerciements

This reprint was produced using the original publications by Johann Christoph Volkamer now in the possession of the Stadtarchiv und Stadtmuseum – Schloss Burgfarrnbach in Fürth, which kindly provided all the works for reprinting with the exception of the plates of volume III, which was planned but not published and is now in the collection of the Universitätsbibliothek Erlangen-Nürnberg. Our special thanks go to Dr Martin Schramm from the Stadtarchiv und Stadtmuseum – Schloss Burgfarrnbach in Fürth and Dr Christina Hofmann-Randall from the Universitätsbibliothek Erlangen-Nürnberg, who gave their support to the project from the outset. The digital reproduction of the originals was carried out by the Centre for Retrospective Digitisation (GDZ) at the Göttingen State and University Library. We would like to thank Martin Liebetruth from the GDZ for his kind co-operation, help and support. Finally, we would like above all to acknowledge the contribution of our author Prof Dr Iris Lauterbach in bringing these unique hand-coloured volumes as well as the unpublished plates to our attention.

Der vorliegende Nachdruck erfolgte auf Grundlage der Originalpublikationen von Johann Christoph Volkamer aus dem Besitz des Stadtarchivs und Stadtmuseums – Schloss Burgfarrnbach in Fürth, das uns freundlicherweise alle Tafeln für den Reprint zur Verfügung stellte, mit Ausnahme der Tafeln für den geplanten, aber nicht publizierten Band III, der sich im Besitz der Universitätsbibliothek Erlangen-Nürnberg befindet. Unser besonderer Dank gilt Dr. Martin Schramm vom Stadtarchiv und Stadtmuseum – Schloss Burgfarrnbach in Fürth und Dr. Christina Hofmann-Randall von der Universitätsbibliothek Erlangen-Nürnberg, die das Projekt von Anfang an unterstützt haben. Die digitale Reproduktion der Originale führte das Göttinger Digitalisierungszentrum (GDZ) der Niedersächsischen Staats- und Universitätsbibliothek Göttingen durch. Für die gute Zusammenarbeit danken wir Herrn Martin Liebetruth vom GDZ. Unser besonderer Dank gilt der Autorin Prof. Dr. Iris Lauterbach, die uns auf die einzigartigen handkolorierten Bände sowie die nicht veröffentlichten Tafeln aufmerksam machte.

Cette réimpression a été réalisée sur la base des publications originales de Johann Christoph Volkamer, propriété du Stadtarchiv und Stadtmuseum – Schloss Burgfarrnbach in Fürth qui a eu l'amabilité de mettre à notre disposition toutes les planches, à l'exception des planches pour le volume III, en projet mais non publié, propriété de l'Universitätsbibliothek Erlangen-Nürnberg. Nous remercions tout particulièrement le Dr Martin Schramm du Stadtarchiv und Stadtmuseum – Schloss Burgfarrnbach in Fürth ainsi que le Dr Christina Hofmann-Randall de l'Universitätsbibliothek Erlangen-Nürnberg qui ont soutenu notre projet dès le début. La reproduction numérique des originaux a été effectuée par le centre de numérisation (GDZ) de la Niedersächsische Staats- und Universitätsbibliothek de Göttingen. Nous remercions Martin Liebetruth du GDZ pour son excellente collaboration. Nous adressons nos chaleureux remerciements à l'auteure, Madame le Prof. Dr Iris Lauterbach, qui nous a fait découvrir les exceptionnels volumes coloriés à la main ainsi que les planches inédites.

Photo Credits

Bildnachweis / Crédits photographiques

We are much indebted to the museums, libraries and all other institutions cited for their kind assistance in the publication of this volume.

The illustrations from volume I and II of the *Nuremberg Hesperides* are taken from the original copies kept in the Stadtarchiv und Stadtmuseum – Schloss Burgfarrnbach in Fürth. The only exceptions are six plates which are missing from the copies in Fürth. In these instances, plates have been used from the copies in the following libraries: Sächsische Landesbibliothek – Staats- und Universitätsbibliothek Dresden (SLUB): pp. 158, 302; Österreichische Nationalbibliothek, Vienna: pp. 24, 119, 276, 277.

All the images from the unpublished volume III are from the plates held in the Universität Erlangen-Nuremberg.

Bayerische Staatsbibliothek, Munich: pp. 12, 28, 31, 82
Biblioteca Comunale dell'Archiginnasio, Bologna: p. 127
Bibliothèque du Conservatoire et Jardin Botaniques de la Ville de Genève, Geneva: pp. 15, 81, 89
bpk / Kupferstich-kabinett, SMB / Jörg P. Anders: p. 54
Su concessione del Comune di Padova – Assessorato alla Cultura, Padua: p. 120
Germanisches Nationalmuseum, Graphische Sammlung, Nuremberg: pp. 19, 32, 123
Museen der Stadt Nürnberg, Graphische Sammlung, Nuremberg: p. 133
Photo © Nationalmuseum Stockholm: p. 57
Niedersächsische Staats- und Universitätsbibliothek, Göttingen: pp. 8, 60, 68, 71 left and right, 116
© Österreichische Nationalbibliothek, Vienna: pp. 24, 119, 276, 277
Royal Collection Trust / © His Majesty King Charles III: p. 75 left and right
Sächsische Landesbibliothek – Staats- und Universitätsbibliothek Dresden (SLUB): p. 158, 302
© 2020. Photo Scala, Florence – courtesy of the Ministero Beni e Att. Culturali: p. 11
Staatliche Kunstsammlungen Dresden, Kupferstich-Kabinett, photo: Herbert Boswick: p. 100
Staats- und Universitätsbibliothek Carl von Ossietzky, Hamburg: p. 53
Stadtbibliothek Nürnberg, Nuremberg: p. 111
© The Trustees of the British Museum, London: p. 124 left
© Alma Mater Studiorum Università di Bologna – Biblioteca Universitaria di Bologna: p. 72
Universitätbibliothek Basel: pp. 104, 105, 107
Universitätsbibliothek Eichstätt, Bischöfliches Seminar: p. 59
Universitätsbibliothek Erlangen-Nürnberg: pp. 16, 20, 34, 50, 77 left and right, 78, 94, 124 right

Imprint

Cover
Limea da Valenza / Nuremberg, Erlenstegen, detail (see p. 182)

Back cover
Lumia da Gallicia / River Brenta Vecchia – Villa Contarini al Ponte, detail (see p. 355)

Page 1
Limea da Gallitia, detail (see p. 183)

Page 2
Tobias Gabriel Beck(h), after Paul Decker the Elder
The Hesperides presenting Noris with gifts of citrus fruits (detail) / **Die Hesperiden bieten Noris Zitrusfrüchte dar / Les Hespérides offrent des agrumes à Noris**
Frontispiece from *Nürnbergische Hesperides*, 1708, vol. 1

Page 3
Vignette with landscape, vol. 1, p. 47

Pages 4/5
Nuremberg, St Johannis – Garden of Mr Leinckert, detail (see p. 231)

EACH AND EVERY TASCHEN BOOK PLANTS A SEED!
Each year, we offset our annual carbon emissions with carbon credits at the Instituto Terra, a reforestation program in Minas Gerais, Brazil, founded by Lélia and Sebastião Salgado.
To find out more about this ecological partnership, please check: www.taschen.com/institutoterra.
Inspiration: unlimited.
Carbon footprint: (almost) zero.

Want to see more? Visit taschen.com to view our current publications, browse our latest magazine, and subscribe to our newsletter.

English translation: Joan Clough, Penzance
French translation: Jeanne Etoré-Lortholary, Montolieu

Hohenzollernring 53, D–50672 Köln
www.taschen.com

Printed in Bosnia-Herzegovina
ISBN 978-3-8365-9478-3